THE WORKS OF
DAVID CLARKSON

The Works of
DAVID CLARKSON

Volume II

THE BANNER OF TRUTH TRUST

THE BANNER OF TRUTH TRUST
3 Murrayfield Road, Edinburgh EH12 6EL
P.O. Box 621, Carlisle, Pennsylvania 17013, U.S.A.

*

Reprinted from
The Works of David Clarkson, published by James Nichol in 1864

*

First Banner of Truth Trust edition 1988
ISBN 0 85151 529 0 for set of three volumes
Volume 2 0 85151 531 2

*

Printed and bound in Great Britain at
The Camelot Press Ltd, Southampton

CONTENTS.

SERMONS, &c.

		PAGE
THE NEW CREATURE.	GAL. VI. 15.	3
CHRIST'S GRACIOUS INVITATION TO SINNERS.	REV. III. 20.	34
MAN'S INSUFFICIENCY TO DO ANYTHING OF HIMSELF.	JOHN XV. 5.	101
AGAINST ANXIOUS CAREFULNESS.	PHILIP. IV. 6.	137
PRAY FOR EVERYTHING.	PHILIP. IV. 6.	172
GOD'S END IN SENDING CALAMITIES AND AFFLICTIONS ON HIS PEOPLE.	ISA. XXVII. 9.	185
THE CONVICTION OF HYPOCRITES.	MAT. VII. 22, 23.	241
SOUL IDOLATRY EXCLUDES MEN OUT OF HEAVEN.	EPH. V. 5.	299
THE CHILDREN OF GOD SHOULD NOT BE PARTAKERS WITH OTHERS IN THEIR SINS.	EPH. V. 7.	334
UNCONVERTED SINNERS ARE DARKNESS.	EPH. V. 8.	355
OF CHRIST SEEKING FRUIT, AND FINDING NONE.	LUKE XIII. 6.	385
THE LORD RULES OVER ALL.	PS. CIII. 19.	454
SINNERS UNDER THE CURSE.	GAL. III. 10.	517

SERMONS, &c.

THE NEW CREATURE.

For in Christ Jesus neither circumcision availeth anything, nor uncircumcision, but a new creature.—GALATIANS VI. 15.

THE apostle does, in this epistle, dispute against the false doctrine wherewith the Galatians were in danger to be bewitched. In the conclusion of it, he gives some characters of those false teachers who broached that doctrine; that the doctrine itself being discovered to be an imposture, and the teachers impostors, the Galatians might be undeceived, and so return to the truth, to this apostle, the preacher and witness of it; both which they were tempted to reject.

The description of these erroneous teachers begins, ver. 12; and he gives such characters of them as will be useful to us for discovering such deluders as they were.

He describes them, 1, by their hypocrisy. They desired to make a fair show, εὐπροσωπῆσαι, to put a fair face upon their foul opinions and practices. Error is of an ugly shape, and if a handsome vizard be not found to cover its deformities, it will fright any whose eyes are opened from embracing it. Εὐπρόσωπα are plausible arguments; such they used, arguments plausible to the flesh, such as were suitable to carnal hearts, inclinations, humours, interests. And this was the paint which they used to make the face of their errors more comely and taking; and, indeed, the Galatians, though an eminent church of Christ, were even bewitched with it. The simplicity of the doctrine of a crucified Christ, of justification by faith alone in him, which Paul, without paint or varnish, nakedly published, seemed not so lovely; they questioned both Paul's doctrine and his calling. Thus they prevailed, and this was their act.*

2. By their carnal policy, ver. 12. They would urge the ceremonial law with the doctrine of Christ, that they might seem Christians, and yet avoid the fury of the Jews, who, being zealous of the law, persecuted to the death those who cried down the observance of it. Though they pretended conscience, yet it was carnal policy that moved them; though they urged circumcision, as though without it there was no salvation, yet the true reason was their desire to avoid persecution.

3. By their partiality, ver. 13. Though they pressed circumcision, as an engagement to observe Moses's law, yet they would not observe the law

u. 'art'?—ED.

themselves, preposterously urged the means, and neglected the end. They were frequeut and violent in their disputes and endeavours for circumcision, which was but a rite, a circumstantial, a positive ordinance, and now out of use, while they neglected the great things of the law, the keeping of Christ's commandments, the great things of the gospel, faith, love, holiness, mortification; whereas that which they drove at was nothing in comparison of these, as the apostle tells, chap. v. 6, 1 Cor. vii. 19. And oh how sadly does this humour prevail amongst us, to the neglect of holiness and mortification! Some cry up a form of government, some an ordinance, that which they fancy; some an opinion, as the fifth monarchy. But, alas, what are those but the mint, anise, and cummin of the Pharisees, in comparison of those βαρύτερα του νόμου, those weightier duties, studies, employments, which the gospel calls Christians to? Oh the power of Satan, who can prevail the same way now as he prevailed formerly with the Pharisees, and here with the false apostles, that the same snare should take in all ages!

4. *By their vainglory.* They affected multitudes of followers, strove to draw many to their opinion and practice, to submit to their supposed ordinance of circumcision, that they might glory in their flesh; that multitudes having received that sign in their flesh, by their persuasion, they might therein glory.

But this was fleshly glorying, such as becomes such carnal teachers. The apostle was of another spirit; he had another object for his glorying, ver. 14. Express a true gospel temper, a right frame of spirit, according to the mind of Christ, which we should drive on as our greatest design, and aim at as our highest attainment. CROSS OF CHRIST, not the material cross, as some blind papists fancy, but the sufferings of Christ crucified, the love of Christ expressed in those sufferings, the precious benefits purchased by those sufferings. Such excellency he saw in Christ crucified, as cast a shadow upon all the glory of the world, rendered it contemptible in his eye. He gloried in Christ crucified; here was his treasure, his joy, his glory, yea, his life too, for he was dead to the world, and the world unto him. 'By whom,' &c. He was as a dead, a crucified man, to the world, and the world was a dead thing to him. He was a dead man to the world; he did no more regard the pomp and glory, the plenty and power, the pleasures and honours of the world, than a dead man. A dead man he esteems not, he admires not these things; they are not his study, his projects, his designs. He is not affected with them; he neither loves nor desires them, neither delights nor rejoices in them, neither discontent when he wants them, nor grieved when he loses them; they are neither his hope nor confidence. A dead man he sees no worth, tastes no sweetness, feels no weight, no substance, in worldly enjoyments. So was the apostle disposed to the world, and so should we be to it, and the things of it, when compared with Christ.

'World is crucified,' &c. As he was dead to it, so it was but a dead thing to him; saw no more excellency in it than in a dead thing, took no more pleasure in it, &c. That which is most delightful when alive must be removed out of our sight, buried, when dead. He looked for no more profit and advantage by it than a lifeless thing can afford. So did he look upon the world, and so should we rely on it for no pleasure, no advantage; see no worth, no excellency in it, in comparison of Christ crucified; and further, than we may make use of the world to be serviceable to him.

This is that high attainment which should be our study, endeavour, design, and leave those to dispute and contend about trifles and circumstances, and doat upon groundless opinions, who have no experimental knowledge of Christ crucified. Thus we should learn Christ, so as to look upon him, and conformity to him as that one thing needful; that one thing above all in the world, glorious, excellent, delightful.

But how did the apostle arrive at this high attainment? And how must we attain it? Why, by him, by Christ. So we see, 'By whom,' &c. By him these five ways.

1. *Efficienter.* By his efficacy, the mighty working of Christ within us. Nothing but the power of Christ can work this great effect. Naturally, as we are dead towards God, so we are alive to the world. As he only can raise us to spiritual life, so he can only dead our hearts to the world; we must look up to him for it; he purchased this.

2. *Exemplariter.* By looking upon him as our effectual, engaging example. Thus lived Christ for our sakes, as one dead to the world while he lived in it; despising not only the shame, but the glory, of the world; lived contemned, not regarding the world's honours; poor, as not esteeming riches; low, as not affecting power and authority. He regarded none of those things which worldlings prize and admire, and this for our sakes; and therefore so should we much more for his sake. There is a force, a constraint, in his example, to work our hearts to this.

3. *Objective.* By looking on him as an object in whom we may find infinitely more, better things, than the world can afford. In him there is richer treasures than the treasures of the world, sweeter delights than the pleasures of the world, greater honours than worldly preferments, more excellent glory than the pomp of the world; choicer, more satisfying, abiding, enhappying enjoyments than the world can afford. In Christ crucified spring such joys, from him flow such excellencies, as overflow all worldly things; they lie under it, as weeds unseen, unregarded. Now, what need is there to live on a broken cistern, when the fountain of living waters is set open in Christ crucified? What need we feed on husks, when the pleasures of a Father's house are offered in Christ? What need they covet treasures on earth, who have all the treasures in heaven tendered to them in Christ? Paul desired to know nothing, to enjoy nothing, but Christ, to be found in him; counted all that the world counts gain to be loss, all that men count excellent to be dung, all that we think precious to be dross, compared with Christ. And those who have such a sight of Christ as he had, will be of his mind; he that knows what it is to live so upon Christ, will easily be dead to the world.

4. *Impulsive.* The beholding of Christ crucified is a strong motive to get our hearts crucified to the world; for why, it was our sinful living to and upon the world for which Christ was crucified: 'The lust of the flesh, the lust of the eyes, and the pride of life,' is all that is in the world, 1 John ii. 16. For these was Christ crucified, and shall not we be crucified to that which crucified him? Shall we live to that which was his death?

5. *Representative.* Christ, representing his people on the cross, undertook this; engaged himself to his Father, that those whom he represented, those in whose stead he was crucified, should be crucified to the world; and in this sense he says, Gal. ii. 20, 'I am crucified.' As Christ, as our Surety, suffered in our stead, so, as our Surety, he engaged in our name, in our behalf, that we should die to the world. And if he engaged for us, then are we deeply engaged; and if he undertook this in our behalf, then will he (if we seek to him, depend on him) enable us to answer his engagement.

This was the apostle's blessed temper, in opposition to the false apostles, and he gives a reason in the text; as if he had said, These false teachers, they lay out the main of their strength, time, thoughts, endeavours, about a rite, a thing of less moment. All their disputations are about circumcision, all their conferences, discourse is taken up with this; but I have not so learned Christ, I mind that which is more weighty, of greater concernment, and that which Christ more regards and better accepts. If Christ may be admitted umpire betwixt us, he will judge that I have chosen the better part; that it is incomparably more available to mind the new creation, than circumcision, 'for in Christ Jesus,' &c.

Before I describe to you the nature of this new creature, let me, from the pre-eminence the apostle giveth it before those other privileges and duties, propound to you this

Observation. Except a man be a new creature, no privilege or religious duty will avail him anything, as to acceptation with God, or salvation. Uncircumcision was now a duty and privilege to the Gentiles, and circumcision was formerly both a duty and privilege to the Jews; for thereby they were solemnly admitted members of the church, thereby the covenant of grace was sealed to them. This was a badge whereby the Lord owned them, and separated them to himself above all people in the world. By virtue of this, 'to them belonged the adoption, and the glory, and the covenants, and the service of God, and the promises,' Rom. ix. In these respects, circumcision did profit them much every way. As to this, it was available; but as to acceptation and salvation, it availed nothing to any one whose heart was not circumcised, *i.e.* who was not a new creature.

So baptism, and hearing the word, and prayer, they are privileges and duties commanded by God, and necessary to be observed, yea, and many ways profitable; but as to acceptation with God, and salvation of the observer, they avail nothing, except he be a new creature. Dost thou hear? It is well; God requires it; it is necessary, profitable. But this is not enough to evidence that the Lord accepts thee, or that he will save thee, unless thou be a new creature. Dost thou pray? art thou baptized? art thou of this or that form of church government? Why, this is nothing as to the great concernments of acceptation, &c.

Reason 1. Because he that is not a new creature, he wants faith; and he that wants faith cannot be saved, he cannot please God. The apostle tells us it is impossible: Heb. xi. 6, he cannot be saved; for 'he that believes not, shall not see life,' John iii. Now, he that is not a new creature, he wants faith, for faith is a principal part of this new creation; and therefore the apostle speaks in the same language of faith, as here of the new creature, Gal. v. 6.

Reason 2. Because he that is not a new creature, he is not in Christ; and he that is not in Christ, can neither be saved nor accepted. No man whatsoever is accepted but in his beloved, Eph. i. 6; and for salvation, 'there is no name under heaven,' &c, no coming to God but in Christ; as Joseph said to his brethren, Unless you bring Benjamin, come not in my presence. Now, he that is not a new creature is not in Christ, 2 Cor. v. 17.

Reason 3. Till then ye can do nothing that is good; and that which is not good cannot be accepted. Nothing can be done by him that is not a new creature that is spiritually good; for, till the heart be good, nothing that is good can proceed from it: 'A good man, out of the good treasure,' &c., Mat. xii. 35; we cannot gather grapes of thorns, Luke vi. 43–45; 'How can you, being evil,' &c. Now, the heart is not good till it be renewed, till it be new created. Till this, there is no goodness in the heart, for creation is the making of something out of nothing, *productio rei ex nihilo*. The heart is not good till it be new, and so no good can proceed from it, and therefore nothing done till this can be accepted.

Use. Information. See the misery of those that are not new creatures. Whatever ye do, whatever ye enjoy, till then ye cannot be accepted, ye cannot be saved. If it were possible for an unconverted man to steal into heaven, as he without the wedding garment to the marriage chamber, yet would he be cast forth into outer darkness. Profession, and outward performances, if you rest here, will make you no better than foolish virgins. If you want renewing grace, new natures, you want oil in your lamps, you will be shut out of Christ's presence, and left in darkness. Every one that is not a new creature must hear that dreadful word from Christ's mouth, 'Depart from me, I never knew you.' You hear, you pray, read, it is well; you would sin more grievously, your condemnation would be heavier, if ye neglected, omitted these duties. Ay, but this is not enough to save you, or to evidence your title to heaven. He builds upon the sand that raises his hopes of heaven upon outward performances. And if he be not a new creature, woeful will be the ruin of his hopes in the day of trial. These duties must be done, but more than these must be done; one thing more is needful, a new nature, a sanctified heart, else no acceptance, no salvation.

Obs. Unless a man be a new creature, nothing will avail him to salvation: 'Except a man be born again,' &c., he cannot be saved. This is a truth which will hardly be digested, not easily believed; therefore hear how the Lord bears witness to it in other scriptures, John iii. 3. He that is truth itself affirms it, and affirms it with an asseveration; and to put it out of all doubt, he doubles the asseveration. Now, to be born again, and to be a new creature, is the same thing in diverse expressions. It is all one as if he had said, Verily except a man be a new creature, &c., 2 Cor. v. 17. In Christ, if any man be united to him, justified by him, partake of the benefits purchased by him, saved by him, Rom. viii. 30. Now, whom God calls, thereby he makes them new creatures.

Now, because this is a truth of great concernment, and far above the reach of nature, which natural men are more apt to deride as a fancy than receive as truth;—

Man is made a new creature when the Lord creates new and gracious qualities in his whole soul. I shall prove each part by Scripture.

1. Cause efficient. It is God; he alone is able for this work. All the creatures in heaven and earth cannot work the least gracious quality in man's soul. It is above the power of nature, of men, of angels, to make such a new creature; it is God's prerogative, ascribed only to him, Eph. ii. 10; his workmanship, and therefore he that is made a new creature, is said to be born of God, 1 John iii.

2. The act, creation. The act that makes a creature is creation; and this is called a new creature, 2 Cor. v. 17. A new heart cannot be had till it be created: 'Create in me,' &c., Ps. li., Eph. ii. 10.

3. The effect, new and gracious qualities. New qualities; hence, when this work is done, all things become new, 2 Cor. iv. 17. And a new creation is called a new man, Col. iii. 10.; and he that is regenerated is said to be renewed, Eph. iv. 23, 24. Gracious: not natural endowments nor moral qualifications, but divine. Hence these qualities are called the divine nature, holy, sanctifying qualities. The new man is created after God in holiness, Eph. iv. 24. It is a conformity to the image of God, and therefore must be holy qualities, Col. iii. 10.

4. The subject, the whole soul; not any one part or faculty, but the whole, all, and every one. Hence it is called the new birth when every member is formed and so brought forth. And this new creature is called a new man; not a new mind only, or will, but a new man; not one part, but the

whole. These qualities are at first infused, and after increase in every part, 1 Thes. v. 23.

This in general. Now, from hence we may give you a more exact and particular account of the nature of this new creature.

1. Negatively, what it is not, that we may not deceive ourselves with counterfeits.

(1.) It is not a common work, but a creation. It consists not in those gifts and parts which the Lord bestows by a common dispensation, nor those motions and workings which are often begot by a common providence; many have these who are no new creatures. It is not a gift of prayer, or utterance, or tongues, or a gift of unfolding or apprehending difficulties in Scripture or religion, nor assistance, enlargement, dexterity in the exercise of these. Judas had all or most of these, yea, and some gifts extraordinary too, yet was not a new creature, was not born of God, but the son of perdition.

It is not common motions: some sense of sin, some grief for it, some wishes of amendment; a personal affliction, or a national judgment, or some unusual strange occurrence, may raise these and such like motions, and more frequent will such motions be in those who live under a powerful ministry. Herod had some like workings in his heart when he 'heard John gladly;' and 'Felix trembled' when Paul 'reasoned of righteousness, temperance, and judgment to come,' Acts xxiv. 25, and Agrippa was 'almost persuaded,' Acts xxvi. 28; and yet these were no new creatures.

(2.) It is no innovating humour. When ye hear of a new creature, you must not imagine him to be such a one as will reject all old things, those which God has prescribed and Scripture delivers, such as will have a new faith, religion, worship, ordinances; such as is weary of old Scripture light, and will be always changing his judgment into new-fashioned opinions. This is a new creature after the image of Satan, not of God's workmanship. The newness which is of God, will comply with the ancient rule, and walk in the good old way as to doctrine and worship and conversation. Indeed, the old ways of profaneness and ungodliness, the old ways of false worship, and of man's invention, the new creature cannot digest. When a church is corrupted, and God's worship adulterated with man's traditions, a new creature will endeavour (according to the apostle's direction, 1 Cor. iii.), to 'purge out the old leaven.' It will not plead for anything in God's worship merely because it is old, but because it is prescribed by God. Forefathers and former generations (when their error is discovered by the world*), will not mislead a new creature if their ways and worship be not according to the law and testimonies. With the king's daughter, Psa. xlv., it must forget its father's house. But when the worship and ways of God are received and established according to Scripture purity and simplicity, then to affect new things is no property, no part of this new creation, for this is of God; but that is of Satan, who changes himself into new forms every day to deceive.

(3.) It is not only a restraint of the old man, but something new. There may be restraining grace where there is not renewing grace. A man may leave his former gross sins, put off much of his former old corrupt conversation, and yet not be a new creature. The apostle speaks of some who had escaped, &c., 2 Pet. ii. 20. They had left their idolatrous and wicked practices, and yet they were not new creatures, for they were again therein entangled and returned, ver. 22. Now, if they had been new creatures born of God, they had not sinned as formerly, 1 John iii. Fear, or shame, or the light of nature, or moral precepts, or other inferior causes and by-respects, may restrain from gross sins, which are all far below the new creature. The

* Qu. 'word'?—ED.

Lord restrains many from sin whom he does not renew. He restrained Abimelech, Gen. xx. 6, yet a heathen. It is true, he that lives in gross sins can be no new creature. But yet this is true also, he that is no new creature may avoid gross sins. Though ye cannot conclude that ye are new creatures because ye have left, or because you never committed such and such sins, yet ye may certainly conclude that those who live in such sins are no new creatures. If a man may escape these pollutions, avoid these gross evils, and not be renewed, then certainly they are in their old condition who make a practice of these evils.

(4.) It is not moral virtues, or that which we call good nature. The very names shew this. That of which the new creature consists is gracious qualities, such as are divine, supernatural, sanctifying, far above nature and morality. The new creature is not only a sweet, courteous, candid, meek, patient disposition; this some have by nature. But none are new creatures by nature. Though the flesh make a fairer show in some than others, yet, as Christ tells us, 'that which is of the flesh is flesh,' John iii. And till it be spiritualised, renewed, the best nature is but an old creature. 'Flesh and blood,' though of the best temper that nature can frame it, 'shall not inherit,' &c. This seemed a wonder to Nicodemus, yet Christ affirms it with an asseveration, John iii. 3.

Nor is it moral virtues. Temperance, justice, chastity, liberality, prudence, truth, modesty, may be found where there is nothing of the new creature, else Scipio, and Socrates, and other heathens must pass for new creatures, those that were strangers to Christ, the gospel, and the regenerating power of the Spirit. These may be acquired by human industry, but the new creature is the workmanship of the divine power.

It is true, where such virtues are not, there is no new creation; but these virtues may be without it, and *ergo*, it does not consist in them.

(5.) It is not an outward conformity to the law of God, for this is something inward: the workmanship of God within the soul. There may be outward obedience to the first and second table. A man may hear, and pray, and read, and, as to his outward man, observe the Sabbath. He may be faithful in his word, just in his dealings, careful to do no wrong, and yet no new creature. Such were the pharisees as to outward obedience, else they had never been so generally applauded and admired for their appearing piety and righteousness. Such was Paul before he was a new creature, even while he was a pharisee: Phil. iii. 6, 'Touching the,' &c. He that is a new creature will be strict in outward observance of the whole law, and yet a man may outwardly observe and be no new creature.

(6.) It is not a partial change of the inward man. As it is not an outward conformity, so it is not every inward alteration, but a total change of the whole soul as to its qualities, and of every faculty in it; not only of the understanding, affections, but mind, will, conscience, heart, memory.

There may be a partial change in some one or more parts of the soul, and yet no new creature. There may be much knowledge of the things of God, clear apprehensions of gospel truths, and assent to, with persuasions of the truth of revealed doctrine, and yet no new creature, 1 Cor. xiii. 2.

There may be some inclinations in the will towards heaven, and yet no new creature, as in Balaam; some purposes, some resolution to amend, as in Saul. There may be some terrors of conscience for sin, as in Cain; some grief for sin, as in Judas, Mat. xxvii. 3, Ahab, 1 Kings xxi.; some delight in the ordinances, Mat. xiii. 20, Job v. 35; some zeal for God, and yet no new creature, as in Jehu; some faith, Acts. viii. 13, as in Simon Magus; some repenting, as in Judas, Mat. xxvii. 3.

In these instances there was an alteration in some one faculty, but no thorough change in the whole soul. A partial change will not make a new creature.

Use. For conviction. If there may be all these things where there is no new creation, then how few new creatures are there in the world! How many are there who go not so far as these, who yet are far from being new creatures!

May there be a common work where there is no new creation? Then how far are they from being new creatures who have no such work upon their souls! Who will not hear the word gladly, as Herod; who do not tremble when the Lord threatens, as Felix; who are not almost persuaded, as Agrippa, to become Christians, according to the rule of the gospel? Herod and Felix, &c., have more to prove themselves new creatures than these, and shall enter into heaven before them.

Does not the avoiding of gross sins make a man a new creature? Then, how far are they from being new creatures who wallow in uncleanness, drunkenness, and such gross evils! Abimelech, a heathen, may rise up in judgment against these, and bear witness that they have nothing of the new creation, nor ought to enter into the new Jerusalem.

Does not moral virtues, good nature, make a new creature? How far are they from being new creatures who are so fierce, proud, contentious, malicious, revengeful, who are so unjust, intemperate, unchaste and covetous! Scipio and Socrates may better use this plea for salvation than such immoral Christians.

Does not outward conformity to the law of God make new creatures? Then how far are they from being new creatures who neglect the worship of God, call not on his name, in public, private, families; will not hear his word so often as he speaks, pollute his Sabbaths, profane his name by oaths and irreverent use thereof! The Pharisees, whose condition Christ makes so woeful, will pass for new creatures, and enter into heaven sooner than these.

Is not a change in some part of the soul sufficient to make a new creature? Then how far are they from being new creatures who are ignorant, wholly inclined to the world; without sense of sin, or grief for it, or purposes against it; without delight in the ordinances, or zeal for the worship of God! Balaam, and Cain, and Ahab, and Jehu, and Judas, are herein more like new creatures than these. Oh that those would lay this to heart who may hence be convinced, that they have not so much as that which is not enough to make a new creature. If none must be saved but new creatures, then what shall become of them, who are so far from being new creatures, as they are not so much as like them?

Use. 2. If these be not sufficient to make a new creature, then rest not in any, in all of these; rest not in gifts, or parts, or common motions; rest not in your avoiding of gross sins; rest not in your moral virtues, or good natures, &c. If you rest here, you rest short of salvation, for these are not sufficient to make a new creature; and except ye be new creatures, ye cannot be saved.

2. Positively. What is a new creature? He is a new creature whose soul is made new in all its faculties; whose whole soul is renewed according to the image of God, in knowledge, holiness, righteousness; in whose mind and heart the Lord creates new and gracious qualities. The Scripture comprises all parts of the soul in these two, spirit and heart: the spirit containing mind and conscience; the heart comprising will and affections. He is a new creature whose spirit and heart is new. This is the tenor of the new

covenant, Ezek. xxxvi. 26. The mind, will, conscience, affections, are new in every new creature. Let me give you a fuller account of this new creation in these several faculties. A new creature has,

(1.) A new mind, understanding. Putting on the new man is thus expressed, Eph. iv. 23, 24. It is renewed in all its several powers, which we may reduce to six heads.

[1.] New apprehensions. There is a new light shines into the mind, which occasions new apprehensions of what is offered to it, far differing from those of the old man. Before he was darkness, now he is light in the Lord; his apprehensions are more true, more clear; that darkness which blinded his eye is now scattered. Light was the first thing produced in the creation of the world, Gen. i. 3, and spiritual light is the first thing in this new creation. The Lord said then, 'Let there be light,' &c. And amongst the effects of the word of Christ, the gospel, this is the first, Acts xxvi. Knowledge is one of the beauties of this new creature, Col. iii. 10. This renewed knowledge leads the mind to new apprehensions. He had heard much of Christ by the hearing of the ear before, but now his eyes see him, clearly apprehends a transcendant excellency in him, an extreme necessity of him, a complete sufficiency in him; his present apprehensions of Christ differ as much from his former, as a man's apprehensions of what he sees himself differ from those which only are related to him by others.

He apprehended some pleasure, advantage, safety, in sin formerly; but now he sees it extreme evil, loathsome, dangerous, damnable.

His former conceits of the world, and its enjoyments, he now sees to be erroneous, and apprehends no happiness, no contentment, in any, in all; sees they are vain, uncertain, deceitful, ensnaring, unsatisfying.

That holiness of heart and strictness of life which he before slighted, condemned, derided, as a needless or hypocritical preciseness, he apprehends now, not only as necessary, but as most beautiful and lovely.

That good nature, as it is called, which he once relied on, excused and thought so well of, he now sees to be wholly corrupted, deformed, and swarming with as many base lusts as there are motes in the sun: the light discovers them.

That state of nature in which he continued till his new birth, which he apprehended safe and capable enough of heaven, he now sees to be a cursed and damnable condition, in which he had certainly perished if mercy had not changed it by renewing him.

His former good deeds and good meanings, for which he thought the Lord would spare him and reward him, he now apprehends to be worthy of damnation, and all his own righteousness as a menstruous cloth.

His apprehensions in these and other things being erroneous, formed in darkness, all vanish when light appears.

[2.] New judgment and assent. The new creature having truly apprehended these things, he firmly assents to the truth of them: his assent is both firm, convictive, and lively. He rests not in slight, superficial apprehensions, but comes up to full persuasions, that which the apostle calls $\pi\lambda\eta\varrho o\varphi o\varrho ία$ $τῆς\ συνέσεως$. His judgment is carried with full sails into the truth discovered, and that with particular application, in a lively, sensible manner; he sticks not at, doubts not of, what this renewed light discovers, but concludes they are certain, as things that he sees and feels. He is not *almost*, as Agrippa, but *altogether* persuaded, that these gospel mysteries are as true as God is truth.

He is persuaded of such a necessity of Christ, as he whose neck is on the block is persuaded of the necessity of a pardon to save his life. Though formerly, upon hearing the love-sick inquiries of distressed souls after Christ, he was apt to say in himself, as they to the spouse, 'What is thy beloved more than another beloved'? Cant. v. 9; yet now he concludes Christ the chiefest of ten thousand, the peerless beauty of heaven and earth, as certainly, as sensibly, as he judges the sun to be light when it shines at noonday; now he wonders at his former blindness, though then he would not be persuaded of it; now he is astonished at the stupidness of the blind world, that is not ravished with the love and beauty of Christ shining in his soul and the gospel. Formerly, discoveries of Christ's all-sufficiency and unsearchable riches were no more to him than the riches of the Indies viewed in a map, or related in a story; but now he passeth such a judgment on it as he does of his own, where he walks, and feeds, and rests, when it is best furnished and provided; it is no foreign thing to him, but that which he sees, tastes, and lives on, and his judgment of it is answerable.

When the ugliness and destructiveness of sin was formerly declared in the ministry of the word, he looked upon it as a monster painted or wrought in a suit of hangings; but now he judges of the mortal danger of sin, as a man judges of poison when he feels it working in his bowels.

It was a paradox to him that a man cannot be happy in this life if he had all worldly enjoyments that heart can desire; but now he certainly concludes, things of the world can no more satisfy an enlivened soul than stones can satisfy an hungry man, or wind nourish a consuming body; he has found what miserable comforters these are to a wounded conscience.

He was apt to judge, that the new birth, regeneration, the new creature, were conceits and fancies; and whilst he felt no such supernatural work upon his soul, he judged there was no such things. But the Lord having brought him through the pangs of the new birth, and by an almighty power drawn the lineaments of a new creature in his soul, there is nothing that he hears, or sees, or feels, that he is more certainly persuaded of, than this truth, that without regeneration there is no salvation. He has changed his mind; he is quite of another, of a new judgment, in this and other things, than he was formerly.

[3.] New valuations. The estimative power of his mind is renewed; the value of things is quite altered in his judgment; the scales are quite turned; that which was highest is lowest; that which was weightiest in his account, is now lighter than vanity; worldly and carnal things, which were gain before, are now counted loss; spiritual and heavenly things, not before regarded, are now of highest value.

Formerly, the treasures of the world were most precious in his account; but now the reproach of Christ, the very worst condition with Christ, is of greater value than the treasures of the world. Hereby Moses evidenced a new creation in his soul, Heb. xi. 26.

Formerly, interest in Christ he took upon trust, upon common, uncertain grounds, as though it were not worth the looking after; but now that it is assured to him upon gospel terms, he will not part with it for all the kingdoms of the earth; or, if he be kept in a doubting condition, if he walk in darkness, and see no light to evidence his title to Christ, which is the condition of many a new creature, many a child of God, after their new birth, so highly does he value it, as he would be content to live poor, afflicted all his days, upon condition he might obtain it. If Christ would but lift up the light of his countenance, he would be far from envying those whose corn, and wine, and oil increase, Psalm iv. 7, 8.

Formerly, he counted them happy who have the world at will, a confluence of pleasures, honours, riches, to their heart's desire; but now he pities those who have no greater happiness, no sweeter comforts, than these can yield.

Formerly, he could have heard and read the promises in the Scripture, without much regarding them; yet, if a friend had assured him of a rich estate, he would have accounted that a precious promise: but now he would not part with the riches he spies in some one gospel-promise, for all the mines in the Indies, Ps. cxix. 127, Ps. ix. 10, Prov. viii. 19.

Formerly, he had rather have spent his time in merry company, than in seeking God, or hearing a sermon, or conference about his soul's estate; but now one day, one hour in these holy employments, is better in his account than a thousand elsewhere; rather be a door-keeper in the house of God, than a commander, a prince in the tents of wickedness, Ps. lxxxiv. 10.

Formerly, he most esteemed such gifts, parts, as would get most applause and credit, quick wit, profound judgment, free expression, a nimble invention to find out, or set off some taking opinions or notions above the ordinary road. Ay, but now these are vanities in his account, compared with the power of godliness; now he values holiness above the choicest accomplishments in the world. This is the most excellent way in his esteem, as Paul in like case, 1 Cor. xii. 31.

Formerly, his church-privileges or religious performances, his alms-deeds, or outward observance of the law, self or sense, seemed something worth to make his way to heaven. But now he counts all these loss, compared with Christ's righteousness; even those that he counted gain, they are loss, yea, dung, that he may gain Christ, and be found in him, Phil. iii. 7, 8. He has a new esteem of things.

[4.] New designs. The designing power of his mind is renewed, he has new plots, new devices, such as troubled not his head before; and those that he formerly pursued, are laid aside. His designs are cast in a new mould, and run in a new method, such as the old man is a stranger to, the unrenewed mind is not acquainted with.

Formerly, his designs were driven towards sin, himself, or the world; now they are for God, for heaven, for his soul.

Formerly, his design was to ingratiate himself with those that might do him good, make him great or safe in the world; now it is to continue in the favour of God, to walk in the light of his countenance, and enjoy sweet fellowship with the Father and Son.

Formerly, his design was to live plentifully and creditably in the world; now it is to get his heart crucified to the world, and the world unto him, to live soberly, righteously, godly in this present world, and walk in it as one redeemed from it.

Formerly, his plot was to make provision for the flesh, to fulfil the lusts thereof; now it is to mortify his members that are on the earth, to put the old man to death, and in this respect to die daily, to starve his lusts, and crush the interest of the flesh, that though it continue, yet it may not prevail and rule in him.

Formerly, his design was to grow rich, to lay up store for the time to come, to provide plentifully for posterity; now it is to be rich unto God, to partake more and more of the unsearchable riches of Christ, to grow in grace, and abound in the fruits of the Spirit; to lay up treasures in heaven, even that good foundation, for the time to come; to provide for eternity; to get his personal wants supplied, and to bring up posterity in the fear and nurture of the Lord; to bring them up to the terms of the covenant, that they may have a title to the treasures, and may be heirs of the kingdom that cannot be shaken.

Formerly, it was his design to make sure what he enjoys on earth, and to secure it from the claims, injustice, or violence of men; now it is to 'make his calling and election sure,' to make clear his evidence for heaven; to get those spiritual distempers removed, which are as moth and rust to his soul's treasure; to keep his heart with all diligence, that sin, and Satan, and the world may not break through and steal.

Formerly, it was his design, either to be famous in his generation, eminent amongst the sons of men, or at least to have a name amongst, or praise from men, for parts, or performances; but now it is, that God above all, and in all things, may be glorified; that the sceptre of Christ may be advanced, and his crown flourish; that his name may be precious and glorious in the world, and all nations, tongues, languages, may acknowledge his glory, and speak his praises; and that all in heaven and earth may lay their crowns at his feet, and give unto him the glory due to his name, due to his love, for he is worthy. These are the designs of a new creature.

[5.] New inventions. Invention is another power of the mind, which is renewed when a man is made a new creature; his mind is busied about far other inventions and devices, than formerly. Not how to find out new opinions or notions, that he may be cried up as a rare man, as $τίς μέγας$, the humour of Simon Magus; nor how to blast their reputation, who stand in his light and obscure him; nor how to satisfy his lusts in a way of safety and credit; nor how to gratify an ambitious, or covetous, or revengeful, or unclean humour: no, these are the devices and contrivances of the old man, which is corrupt and unrenewed. The inventions of the new creature are quite of another strain, such as the old man, the unrenewed mind, is utterly unacquainted with. I might instance in more than twenty, I will but name them. The new mind employs his invention,—

To find out what are his spiritual wants, where the defects of his graces and affections lie, wherein faith, and zeal, and love, and self-denial, are defective; that he may not languish for want of supplies, that his soul may be kept on the wing of desire after Christ; that, living in the sense of many wants, he may not be puffed up with self-conceit, as having attained.

What hinders his soul's prosperity. Why he does not grow answerable to means, light, engagements; whether remissness in duty, or some unmortified lust within, or too eager pursuit of something without.

His secret corruptions: those skulking traitors, that lie hid in the dark and secret corners of his soul, which in others are not seen nor regarded; stirrings of spiritual pride, secret motions of self-refined stains of hypocrisy.

The decays of his soul at their first rise and appearance; decay of love, zeal, spiritualness of mind, tenderness of heart or conscience; to find out these at first, before they run his soul on into a consumption, which neglected, they are apt to do.

The best ways of improving Christ crucified, of drawing powerful and quickening influences from him, knowing that upon this depends the life, strength, comfort, and welfare of his soul.

What arguments may most prevail with God in prayer. Not that the Lord needs these, but that they are needful for himself, to encourage faith, and quicken the soul to fervency and importunity in seeking God.

What thoughts, what objects, do most affect him, make deepest impressions on his heart. What most powerful to quicken, inflame, put his soul upon motion towards God, and effectual to restrain from sin.

What duty every condition he is cast into, and every alteration in that condition, does especially call for.

The exercise of what grace is most proper and suitable to every juncture of time, to every occurrence he meets with; that he may be always ready, his loins girded, his lamp burning.

What parts of the word of God, whether promises, or threatenings, or examples are more suitable to his soul's estate, that he may take special notice of them in hearing or reading.

Where the new man is weakest, where he lies most open to assaults of spiritual enemies, where Satan gets most advantage, where sin makes its breaches, that he may fortify that especially, set a strong guard.

What the cause of every cross and affliction is, inward or outward. Why the Lord at any time withdraws from him, denies his presence, assistance in ordinances, in his endeavours after holy walking, that if it be sin, he may subdue it.

To find out what Satan's snares are, what his devices, whereby he most prevails in the times and places where he lives, that he may not be ignorant of his devices, nor entangled unawares.

What the deceits of his heart, and the fallacies of sin, these being deceitful above all things, and so intimate with him; that he may not be circumvented, cheated, deluded.

Where the strength of sin lies, what are its strongest holds, what carnal reasonings, what promises or expectations, that he may bend all his force against it here, this being the surest way to victory.

What is the beloved sin, *peccatum in deliciis*, the commander, supporter, encourager of the rest; that this may be chiefly mortified, subdued. He knows if the general fall, the troops will be easily scattered, routed.

The root of every sin by the fruits. When he perceives sin breaking forth, he sets his invention a-work, inquires, whence comes this? *E. g.*, wanderings in holy duties, whence are these? Is it not from carnalness, want of delight in holy employments? is it not from some lust within, worldliness or uncleanness? Having found out the root, he strikes at that, thinks it surest to stay the stream by stopping up the spring.

Where are corruptions, encouragements, abettors, incentives; where it feeds and gets provision, whether in his constitution, or employment, or company, or diet, or accommodations, that he may cut off these.

How to be most serviceable in his generation; how he may improve his talents most for Christ's advantage; which are the ways, which are the services in which his times, parts, gifts, enjoyments, may be best employed; that he may not bury them, nor use them only for himself, nor spend them in ways less necessary, profitable, advantageous for Christ and his people.

How he may win others to come in to Christ, to renounce sin. What carriage, what acts, what words may be most effectual, according to the several tempers of those amongst whom he lives.

What the design of every special providence is towards himself, or the place he lives in, that he may neither disregard nor oppose it, that he may concur with God, and be subservient to him in his promoting them;

What are the provocations of the times and place he lives in, that he may endeavour to reform, mourn in secret for them, seek pardon;

These and such like are the things about which the invention of a renewed mind is employed. And when his studies succeed herein, he has more reason to cry εὕρηκα than Archimedes; these being inventions that find more approbation in heaven than any on earth.

[6.] New reasonings. The discursive power of the soul is renewed; carnal reasonings are opposed, disclaimed as weak, fallacious; his arguings now are of a new mode.

His former inward reasonings were for the flesh against the spirit, now they are for the spirit against the flesh; they were formerly for the world against Christ, now for Christ against the world; for sin and looseness against holiness and strictness, but now the contrary; from the letter of the word against the sense of Scripture, now they are according to the mind of Christ. He draws quite contrary conclusions from formerly abused principles; *e. g.* God is merciful, long-suffering, and patient, *Ergo*, there is no such danger in sinning, no such necessity of a precise reformation; so the old man. But the new creature argues from hence, *Ergo*, this should lead me to repentance, Rom. ii. 4. Therefore I should be ashamed, afraid to sin hereafter, and heartily grieved that I have sinned so much before.

Christ is full of love and compassion to sinners, and therefore we need not be so nice and precise in forbearing, renouncing every sin; so the old man. But the new creature thus: Christ loves me, and therefore how can I do that which his soul hates? He 'loved me, and washed me,' &c.; how shall I do that which shed his blood? The grace of God appearing to all in Christ crucified; *Ergo*, I must deny all ungodliness and worldly lusts, &c., Titus ii. 11, 12.

Christ came to save sinners; *Ergo*, there is hopes of salvation, though I continue in this or that sin; so the old man. But the new creature argues thus: *Ergo*, I must get into and continue in the way wherein Christ has declared he will save sinners; I must believe, break off my sins by repentance, and submit to his laws and government, else his death will nothing avail me.

But the strict and constant observance of all Christ's laws will be hard, and sometimes dangerous. I may lose my estate, liberty, or life by it; *Ergo*, it is better to hope well, and go on as I do; it is folly to launch so far into the deep as we can see no shore; it is good sleeping in a whole skin; so the old man. But the new creature thus: If the observance of Christ in all his holy ways and truths may cost me so much, *Ergo*, it is more proper for me, whom Christ so infinitely engaged. Shall I offer unto him only that which costs me nothing? If Christ had dealt so with me, my soul had dwelt in everlasting flames. Whom should I suffer for, if not for him who suffered all for me? And if I suffer with him, I shall also reign with him; so the apostle.

But there are many ways of religion, abundance of errors, divisions, diversities of opinion; *Ergo*, it is better to keep the old track wherein I was born, bred, and have thus long lived, than to wander and change my old course in such uncertainties; so the old man. But the new creature thus: There are many divisions, wanderings, &c., *Ergo*, I have more need to keep in the strait way, the way of holiness, which is certainly the way of Christ if there be any truth or certainty in Scripture, and leave those to doat upon questions, less material opinions, positions and circumstantials not clearly revealed, who think they have more time than enough to mind that one thing needful.

But some that pretend to holiness and strictness are hypocrites, make a fair show outwardly, when there is no inward reality; *Ergo*, it is better to be as I am than counterfeit what I am not; so the old man. But the new creature thus: There will be hypocrites amongst those that profess godliness, there was a hypocrite amongst Christ's disciples; *Ergo*, I have more need to look to my own security, more reason to give all diligence to make my own calling and election sure.

This way of strictness and preciseness is everywhere spoken against and reviled; *Ergo*, no wisdom to enter into it, to meddle with it; so the old man. But the new creature thus: *Ergo*, it is more like to be the way of Christ, for he himself suffered the contradiction of sinners. The world hates him and his ways, no wonder if they speak evil of them.

The Lord accounts the will for the deed. I mean well though I do ill sometimes, *Ergo*, the Lord will accept me; so the old man. But the new creature thus: *Ergo*, in the strength of Christ I will put forth myself to the utmost in every duty, in all the ways of Christ, and when I fail through weakness, there is hopes of pardon and acceptance.

The time is short, we cannot live long; *Ergo*, let us live merrily, take our pleasures, follow our profits, while we have time; so the old man. But the new creature thus: *Ergo*, I must use all diligence to get the work done, for which he allows me this time, for which he sent me into the world; *Ergo*, I must use the world as though I used it not, rejoice as though I rejoiced not, buy as though I possessed not, use recreations as though I used them not, 'For the fashion of the world passeth,' &c., 1 Cor. vii. 29.

But there are many promises to sinners; *Ergo*, no reason to despair of salvation though I live in sin; so the old man. But the new creature thus: I have many great and precious promises, therefore I should 'cleanse myself from all filthiness of flesh and spirit,' &c. It is the apostle's arguing, 2 Cor. vii. 1.

The thief repented at death, and was admitted into paradise; *Ergo*, why may not I defer my repentance and reformation till the hour of death? so the old man. But the new creature thus: I read but of one amongst many thousands that found place for repentance at his death; *Ergo*, I will not leave my salvation, my soul, at such a desperate hazard, as, ten thousand to one, it will be lost.

But death is uncertain, it may be far off, the Lord delays his coming; *Ergo*, I may eat, and drink, and take my pleasure; thus the old man, with that wretched servant in the parable, Mat. xxiv. But the new creature thus: *Ergo*, I must be continually watchful; I must be always employed in the Lord's work, lest the Lord come in an hour when I look not for him, lest he find me in an evil way, and I fall into the condemnation of that unprofitable servant, Mat. xxiv. 48.

But there is no condemnation to those that are in Christ, and who can tax me as one that is not in Christ? *Ergo*, though I sin I shall not be condemned: so the old man. But the new creature thus: 'No condemnation to those who walk not after the flesh.' If I walk after the flesh, continue in my old carnal condition, stick to my old, superstitious, ungodly customs and practices, if I be not a new creature, I am not in Christ; to such there is nothing but condemnation. The new mind has new reasonings, as appears in these, and might be shewed in more instances.

[7.] New thoughts. The cogitative power of the mind is renewed, old thoughts are passed away. His atheistical thoughts;—God sees not, he regards not, he will not punish; I may sin securely. Revengeful; he does not meditate mischief upon his bed. Lustful; his heart is not a place for speculative uncleanness. Proud; he is not puffed up with self-conceit; the high, lofty, towering imaginations are pulled down. Worldly; he gives not way to immoderate thoughtfulness about what he shall eat, &c. These engross not his mind; he knows a small share of his thoughts is but due to the world, solicitous, anxious thoughts, distempering his mind with fear and distrust, so much carefulness what to eat, &c. When Christ works this new creation in the mind, these are driven out, as buyers out of the temple; it is a part of this great renewing work to bring every such thought into subjection. So wandering thoughts in holy services, which passed before without restraint, he drives these away, as Abraham did the fowls from his sacrifice, Gen. xv. 11. Vain, unprofitable, foolish, impertinent, incoherent thoughts, though they may steal into the mind, they lodge not; he entertains them not as formerly.

The thoughts that are now welcome into his mind are holy, spiritual, heavenly; thoughts of Christ, his love, the sweet expressions, the many precious experiments of it; thoughts of his soul's condition, of the great and precious promises. These are his meditation, these are sweet to his taste. Thoughts of his glorious relations to Christ, of those privileges of a new creature, and of those future enjoyments in glory, these are most frequent, pleasing, abiding.

Such thoughts as quicken him to holy motions, stir him up to heavenly inclinations and affections. His former thoughts were as thorns and weeds to choke these, but his present thoughts are as bellows, to kindle and inflame his heart with love to, and zeal for, and ardent desires after, Christ and spiritual enjoyments; quicken him to faith, fervency, heavenliness; engage him to humility, self-denial.

These are the thoughts of a new mind, which the old man will not believe to be in any, because he never found them.

[8.] New consultations. The advising power, that which the philosophers call βουλευτική, is renewed. He has now new objects to consult about, new counsellors to consult with. He consults not now whether the Lord shall be his chief good, his last end, nor whether his great idol the flesh shall be thrown down, or pleasures, profits, credit, the unrenewed man's trinity, shall give place to God, and be made the footstool of Christ; no, *in re tam sancta non est deliberandum*. This is out of question, he is fully resolved upon it, though the greatest part of Christians (whatever they imagine to the contrary) never came up to such a resolution.

It is not the end, but the means, that he consults about, βουλευόμεσθα οὐ περὶ τῶν τελῶν;* not whether Christ shall have the highest place in his soul, but by what means he may be most advanced; not whether the interest of the flesh and the world shall be cast down, but by what means this may be most effectually done; how he may disengage his soul from carnal interests (that have so fully possessed him) so as he may give up himself wholly unto the Lord. And the business being weighty, needs counsel, συμβούλους δὲ παραλαμβάνομεν εἰς τὰ μεγάλα. The new creature has new counsellors. We see it in Paul; as soon as the Lord had made him a new creature, he chooses a new counsel, rejects the old, Gal. i. 16. So here he consults not with the world, not with the flesh, not with carnal friends, about the things of God. The world and the flesh are enemies and carnal friends, in spiritual things are fools; and who seeks counsel of foes or fools? If carnal friends be consulted with, then in trouble of conscience they will advise you to get into merry, jovial company, to sing, or drink, or cast away those melancholy thoughts, or to follow worldly business with more eagerness, that the noise of the world may drown the voice of conscience. Oh miserable comforters, oh wretched counsellors! When the world or flesh are consulted with, they will advise with much show of wisdom. If sin must be left, if something must be done for Christ, why then engage for Christ against sin with a proviso, with caution and reservation? Take heed, if you be wise, that no sin be left, no duty be undertaken, to the prejudice of ease, credit, or worldly advantage. And so profitable and delightful sins must still be retained; duties of religion that are chargeable, difficult, dangerous, or reproached by a wicked generation, must be baulked, declined. When

* Aristot.

persecution arises for any way of Christ or holiness, then wheel about, excuse yourselves here; in this the Lord be merciful to me, I can, I dare follow Christ no further. Here is the counsel of the wisdom of the flesh, which is enmity to God. 'This wisdom descendeth not from above; it is earthly, sensual, devilish,' James iii. 15. And so the new creature rejects it. It is the wisdom from above which guides him in his consultation, that which is not only peaceable, but pure, fruitful, and without partiality, &c., verse 16. He consults with the oracles of God, David's counsellors are the men of his counsel, Ps. cxix. 24. He goes for advice to the law and the testimony, he inquires impartially; and that which is there delivered sways his judgment, and carries it in all debates, though it be never so cross to carnal interests, though it be to the prejudice of his dearest lusts, though it be to the ruin of his ease, credit, worldly advantages. One glimpse of Scripture light will carry it.

Thus you see explained what a new creature is in respect of his mind, how the mind is renewed in its several acts and powers. Proceed now to the next faculty,

(2). *A new will.* A new creature has a renewed will. As this new creation make a new spirit, *i.e.* a new mind, so it makes a new heart, *i.e.* a new will. This new creature is a new man, Eph. iv. 24, Col. iii. 10. Now there cannot be a new man without a new will, for this is the principal part of a man.

The will is the ruling faculty, it commands the whole man; therefore, such as the will is, such is the man, old or new. The most powerful and distinguishing work of renewing grace is in the will, and therefore, that we may understand what the new creature is, we must apprehend how the will is made new, and wherein its renewedness consists. Now this will appear most clearly in the immediate acts of the will, its inclinations, intentions, fruition, election, consent, application, and resolutions. Where there is a new creature, a new will, there are

[1.] *New inclinations.* That act of the will, which Aristotle calls $\beta o\acute{u}\lambda \eta \sigma \iota \varsigma$, and the schoolmen *simplex volitio*, has a new object. The heart, which was formerly carried after sin, the world and self, has now a new bias, which carries it towards God in Christ as his chief good, towards him as the height of all his glory, the spring of all his pleasures, the treasury of all his riches. Every unrenewed man is an idolater, he makes himself or the creature his idol. And though God usually have the name, yet he moves towards these as his chief good. This is the sad effect of the fall in every son of Adam, an averseness to God, a propenseness to the creature; and this continues in every man from his first birth till he be born again. And when this new creation begins, it finds him in this posture, with the face of his heart towards the creature, and his back towards God. Now it is the effect of this great work to turn the heart from idols unto God, from the creature unto the Creator. Hence it is called conversion; his heart now runs towards a new mark, he has a new centre. Formerly himself or the world was his centre; to these he moved, after these his soul was carried, even as the sparks fly upwards. But now God in Christ is his centre: his heart tends towards God, even as heavy bodies move downwards; his motions towards God are free, powerful, and restless. He has a new nature, and his motions towards God are in these respects natural.

First, He is freely inclined towards God. He is not only forced by terrors, or apprehensions of death, or some great danger; for these may occasion some weak motions towards God in an unrenewed heart; but when there are no such enforcements, yet then his heart is in motion towards

God. There is an attractive virtue in Christ, and the discoveries of his love and excellency in the gospel, which draws a new heart to him; a virtue both secret and powerful, such as we see in the loadstone to draw iron. 'When I am lifted up, I will draw,' &c. The heart is put upon this motion by an inward principle, not by outward enforcements. When the will is thoroughly touched with renewing grace, it inclines towards Christ; as you see a needle, touched with the loadstone, move and tend toward the north pole. This heart-inclination is better felt than expressed, and it will be a mystery to those who have not experience of it, as this new creature is to all unrenewed men.

Secondly, It is a powerful and prevalent inclination, such as does overpower the inclinations of the flesh to sin in the world. Set the world, in all its pomp and glory, all its delights and treasure, before the soul, on one side, and God, as manifested in Christ, on the other, and a renewed heart will turn its back upon the world, and bend itself towards God. Nor is this,

Thirdly, By fits and starts, now and then, in some good mood; but his inclinations are habitual and constant. His motions may be slackened, and in part diverted, by some violent temptations, even as you may force the needle in the compass towards the south; but then it quivers, and shakes, and is restless, till it point north again. So the heart, when by some lust or temptation it is drawn aside from God, this motion is not free, it is against the settled bent; the heart shakes and shivers, till that be removed which stops its course, and hinders its motion towards God. The constant bent and tendency of the renewed will is after God, as its happiness, its joy and delight, its treasure and glory. David was a man after God's own heart, and therefore his heart was formed according to the image of God, *i. e.* it was renewed; and you may feel the pulse, perceive the motions of a renewed heart, in his expressions, Ps. xlii. 1, 2. Paul expresses the temper of a new will under temptations, Rom. vii. He does that which he allows not, that which he hates, that which he would not do, ver. 15, 16. When his soul is hurried to sin, his heart would have it otherwise; when he is carried down with temptation, he moves as he would not move; his heart, his will inclines to God, while he is carried another way: he is carried as a captive, carried as by rebels; so he looks upon himself and upon them, ver. 23. A captive, dragged by rebels, moves not freely: if the force were removed, he would change his motion, alter his course. A new creature has not a heart for sin and for the world; the fixed, usual, constant bent of his will is towards God, as his chief good, only happiness. It is contrary in an unrenewed man.

[2.] New intentions. The renewed will intends God, aims at him in all, and above all things. Christ is to him *Alpha* and *Omega*, the first and the last, the spring of his happiness and the end of his actings. That which is a man's chief good, is his last end. God is both to a renewed heart: he inclines to him as his chief good, he intends him as his last end.

He has new ends and aims, far differing from his former. Heretofore he aimed at pleasure, to live merrily; riches, not to stand in need of others; greatness, that he might not be an underling in the world; honours, that he might not live obscure or contemned. But now, apprehending his sweetest delights, best riches, greatest honours, are to be found in God, he aims at God instead of these, and intends not these but in reference to God, that by these he may be enabled to do him better and more cheerful service.

God is now his end; and that which he intends above all is, 1, to glorify God; 2, please him; and, 3, enjoy him. God is his aim in these three notions.

First, To glorify him. Every action is raised and carried on for his end, and with this intention, virtually if not actually, that God by it may be glorified; and this universally, not only in religious actions. He hears, and prays, and reads, and meditates; not to stop the mouth of conscience, or to be accounted a good Christian, or to make amends for some sin, whose guilt troubles him, but that God may be hereby honoured.

Nor this only in civil actions. The works of his calling, ploughing, or digging, or studying, &c., these he follows for this end; not as formerly, to get his living only, or to provide for his family: his intentions rise higher; that which he principally aims at, is that hereby God may be glorified.

Yea, but even in natural acts. He eats, he drinks, he sleeps, not only for continuance of health and life: he aims at something of greater moment, viz., the advancing of God's glory. This is the law of the new creature, for to such the apostle prescribes it, 1 Cor. x. 31.

And as he intends this universally, by dedicating all and every action to this end, so he aims at it singly, *i. e.* he acts not that which may glorify God, in relation to himself only, or his own ends. The old man may do this; so did the unrenewed Jews; they had a zeal for God, as Paul testifies, Rom. x. 2. They were zealous in doing that which might honour him, as they thought, but it was in reference to themselves, lest the apostle's doctrine (of justification by faith, both to Jews and Gentiles) prevailing, their law, and dignity, and privilege above the rest of the world, should be overthrown. A new creature may, must seek his own good; but this in subordination to God's glory as supreme, and in a way of subserviency to it as principal. He seeks other things, but he intends this in and above all. And this is a special property of the new creature, which the highest improvers of nature could never reach, nor ever will, till renewed.

Secondly, His aim is to please God. Formerly his aim was to please his flesh, or his senses, or his corrupt humours, or such persons and friends on whom he had dependence; but now that which he intends above all is to please God. He will strive to please others, if thereby he may the better please God, as Paul became all things, &c.; but if any thing come in competition with God, if he must either displease his friends, his flesh, his senses, or displease God, in this case he will displease all, rather than displease God; for to please God is his highest end, and the highest end is best; and so the apostles determine in this case, Acts v. 29. In this case, to displease God, we should not yield a finger's breath, *Neque omnibus angelis in cœlo, neque Petro nec Paulo, neque decem Cæsaribus, neque mille papis, neque toti mundo latum digitum cesserim,* [Luther] Comment. in Gal. ii.

Thirdly, To enjoy God. He aims at this in all actions and undertakings whatever; and intending this, nothing short of it will satisfy him.

Formerly, in religious duties he could have rested in the work done, or been satisfied with common enlargements and assistances; or content if others esteemed and applauded him, though his heart was at a great distance from God in the duty. But now no duty will please or satisfy him, except he enjoy God in it; except God draw near to him, and witness his presence by the power, efficacy, or delights of it in his heart. So in civil and natural acts; it is the aim, the intent of the new creature, to enjoy God in all. But this leads me to the

[3.] New fruitions. That in which the new creature rests, that which satisfies, contents him, is quite different from what it was formerly. His life was formerly a vexatious wandering from vanity to vanity; all the contentment he had was in sin or worldly accommodations, or at least in outward performances; but now these are as husks to him. That which gives his heart quiet and content, is the enjoyment of God, communion with Christ, fellowship with the Holy Spirit. *Nihil potest quietare hominis voluntatem, nisi solus Deus,* says Aquinas. It is true, here, nothing quiets a renewed heart but the enjoyment of God; or, as he, *irrequietum est cor nostrum,* &c. Thou madest us for thee, and our heart will not rest but in thee.

The world (as one well compares it) is like a king's court. Unrenewed men are like children, who are taken with the pictures, and please themselves in viewing the hangings and ornaments of several rooms; but a new creature is like a man that has earnest business with the king; he stays not in the out rooms; he takes little notice of the ornaments and rich furniture; his business is with the king, and so he rests not till he come into his presence. Those that rest in outward performances, or worldly enjoyments, they stay in the out rooms. A new heart, like the king's daughter, is then only brought with gladness and rejoicing, when she enters into the king's presence, Ps. xlv. 15; then only satisfied, when Christ leads her into his banqueting house, when he fills the tabernacle of her heart with the glory and power of his presence. Even as a hungry infant will not be content; though ye give it chains of gold or bracelets of pearl, nothing will satisfy it but the breast; so a renewed heart, in the absence of Christ, all that the world can afford will not quiet or satisfy it, none but Christ, none but Christ.

Formerly, he could rest in a religious duty performed, or at least in the plausible performance of it; but nothing now contents him, except he there find him whom his soul loves; nothing satisfies him, except the presence of God go along with him in these duties; except he find the Spirit of God moving in them, affecting his heart, and working upon his soul in the use of ordinances. His heart raises itself in the ordinances, as Zaccheus, Luke xix. 4, got up into a sycamore tree, that he might see Jesus passing by. It will not satisfy him, no more than Absalom, to return to his house, except he may see the king's face, 2 Sam. xiv. 32. It is that which he seeks, as the angel told the woman: Mat. xxviii., ' I know that ye seek Jesus that was crucified.' Ay, this is it which a renewed heart seeks; nor will it ever rest till it find Jesus that was crucified.

Formerly, if by labour and industry in worldly employments he could gain well, and increase his estate, and thrive in the world, he was herewith content (so far as such things can give contentment); but now, whatever he gains, whatever he gets, he is not satisfied, except, while his outward man is busied in the world, his soul enjoy communion with Christ, except his labour and travail in these outward things be a walking with God.

Formerly, he was apt to say, as that rich man, Luke xii. 19, ' Soul, thou hast much goods, &c., take thine ease,' &c. But now he will rather say, with that famous Marquis of Vico, ' Let his money perish with him, who prefers all the gold of the world before one day's communion with Jesus Christ.'

Formerly, he was apt to fancy some contentment, if he might have riches and friends answerable to his desire, meats and drinks suitable to his appetite, habit and accommodation suitable to his fancy; but now all fulness is empty, if Christ make it not up; the sweetest accommodation is distasteful, if the presence of God sweeten it not; no enjoyments satisfy him, but those in which he enjoys Christ. And when he has found him, he can let out his heart's contentment in David's expression, ' The Lord is my portion, I have enough; return to thy rest, O my soul, for the Lord has dealt bountifully with thee; my lines are fallen in a pleasant place,' &c., Ps. iv. 6, 7, Ps. lxiii.

[4.] New elections. The will shews its renewedness, in its choice of means for promoting of the ends on which it hath pitched: προαίρεσις ἐστὶ τῶν πρὸς τὸ τέλος. Election of means, the former acts were about the end. His choice is different from what it was heretofore. He brings not down that which should be his end, to serve his turn as a mean, as those do, who make religion a stirrup to advance them in the world.

Nor does he choose unlawful means to promote his ends. Formerly, so he might compass his intentions, he stood not much upon the quality of the means, whether good or bad, allowed or disallowed of God. How visible is this in men of the world! But now he pitches upon none but such as Scripture has sealed to be acceptable unto God. He will not set up calves, false worship, to gain or secure a kingdom, nor make priests of the meanest of the people to strengthen a faction, as Jeroboam did, who made Israel to sin, and is so branded. He will lose his ends, rather than accomplish them by deceit, falsehood, injustice, or what reflects on his profession.

His choice is regulated by the word, and what it prescribes he will pitch on, though it seem to his own prejudice. He will choose to cross his own humour or offend his dearest relations, rather than offend God. He chooses afflictions for Christ, rather than the pleasures of sin. It was Moses's choice, Heb. xi.

He chooses those for his companions that fear God, Ps. cxix. 63, and those above all that are most conscientious, most eminent for holiness, strictness, watchfulness over themselves and others. Those that he did formerly hate, jeer, abuse for strictness, holiness, they are now his delight, as David, herein a type of Christ, Ps. xvi. Spiritual conference of godly persons, which was formerly a burden, he now prefers before vain worldly discourse; and the company of profane men are his burden, as it was to David, Ps. cxx. 5, 6. He had rather have a friend that will reprove him for sin, than a companion that will soothe him in an evil way, Ps. cxli. 5.

In choice of a minister, he will not incline to one who will sew pillows under his elbows, cry peace to him while he lives in sin, or encourage him by doctrine or practice in any evil course; nor to him who will please his fancy with quaintness, notions or niceties; but he prefers him that will search his conscience, deal faithfully with his soul, not suffer him to live at peace in any wickedness, that delivers sound, searching, quickening truths, and teaches Christ, as the truth is in Jesus.

If he find ordinary means not sufficient to subdue his lusts, remove soul distempers, keep his heart in a spiritual heavenly temper, or to prevail for public mercies and deliverances, he then makes choice of extraordinary. If his usual praying every day be not effectual, he will set apart whole days for prayer and fasting to obtain those blessed ends.

He chooses not only those means, duties which are most plausible, but those also that are most spiritual; not only public exercises of religion, but secret duties; such wherein common gifts are not so much exercised, such as have nothing of outward form or pomp wherewith an unrenewed heart may be taken; for example;—

Secret prayer, in his closet, where no eye is witness. I mean not an heartless repeating of words got by rote, without fervency or affection; but the strivings, wrestlings of the heart with God in secret, in a humble, reverent, importunate, affectionate manner. This he chooses, and it is his practice.

Secret meditation of spiritual things. Not for increase of knowledge only, or to enable him to discourse or dispute; this an unrenewed heart may choose; but to quicken his soul to spiritual motions, holy inclinations, heavenly affections; to find out the state and temper of his soul, communing with his heart, Ps. iv., that he may judge or encourage himself, according as the condition of his soul requires.

He chooses not only such duties as are easy, but those that seem difficult; rather forego his own ease, than leave his soul in a remiss, lukewarm, unthriving temper.

Nay, he will not refuse those duties that are chargeable, reproachful, or dangerous, when the Lord requires them. Daniel would pray to the God of heaven, though the penalty was casting into the den of lions. The primitive Christians would sell their estates rather than the poor should want, to the dishonour of the gospel. The apostles would preach Christ crucified, though therefore they were accounted the outcasts and offscouring of all things; rather expose his credit, break with friends, or make a breach in his estate, than break his peace with God by neglecting his duty.

[5.] New consents. This is another act of the will, which when it is renewed, has a new object. I might give many instances, but I shall only instance in that one which is the vital act of a new creature.

He now consents to enter into covenant with God upon the terms propounded in the gospel. Formerly, he consented to sin and the world, yielded to their terms, upon condition he might enjoy them; his heart, though hardened against God, yet was as wax to receive the impressions of sin; and he was a voluntary fugitive to Satan and his lusts, led captive by him at his will. But now his heart is hardened, his will is obstinate against sin and the world, yet it runs freely into the mould of the gospel, and consents to take Christ upon gospel terms, to take him as Lord, for holiness, power against sin, &c. He is so sensibly convinced of his misery without Christ, of that happiness which is to be enjoyed in Christ, he so clearly apprehends the infinite worth of Christ, his extreme necessity of him, that he will yield to anything the Lord propounds, if he will but give him Christ.

The Lord tells him in the gospel, if he will have Christ, he must part with all, with every sin: 2 Tim. ii. 19, 'Let every one that nameth the name,' &c.; those sins wherein thou hast so much delighted, whereby thou hast got, or expectest so much gain or advantage. He that is Christ's must crucify the flesh, &c. The renewed heart answers, Yea, Lord, and happy were I if I might be quite freed from all sin. Oh, happy exchange, to part with sin to gain Christ! What have I to do any more with idols? How much better is it to part with those sometimes dearest lusts, than, by retaining any one member of that body of death, to have both soul and body cast into hell! The will freely yields to this proposal.

The Lord tells him further in the gospel, he that will have Christ must deny himself. 'If any man will be my disciple,' &c., Mat. xvi. 24. He that will be Christ's must deny his ease, his humours, his credit, his gifts, his own righteousness, his own interests, inclinations, accommodations, for Christ's sake. The heart answers, all these are nothing compared with Christ; yea, verily, and I count them all loss that I may gain Christ, as Phil. iii. Yea, and let him take all, if my Lord Christ will return to my soul.

The Lord tells him in the Gospel, he that will have Christ must take up the cross, must be willing to endure reproaches, afflictions, and persecutions; must be willing to suffer in his relations, in his estate, in his liberty, and in his life too; to lose all these, if the glory, and ways, and truth of Christ call for it, Luke xiv. 26, Mat. x. 37, 38. He that will have Christ must make account to have the cross. The soul answers, Welcome the cross if

Christ come with it: I can never suffer anything so grievous for Christ as he has suffered for my soul. There is enough in Christ to make up all losses, to sweeten all sufferings. *Mallem ruere cum Christo, quam regnare cum Cæsare*, as the father. None ever was a loser by Christ, whatever he seemed to lose. The greatest sufferers now in heaven could rather wish they had endured more, than repent that they suffered so much for their dear Redeemer. Nothing more true in all experience than Christ's promise, Mark x. 29, 30.

Thus the renewed will comes off freely, and consents to take Christ upon any terms, whatsoever the gospel offers, πῦρ καὶ σταυρὸς, θηρίων τε συστάσεις, &c., ἵνα Χριστοῦ ἐπιτύχω.

[6.] New applications. The renewed will applies the rest of the faculties to prosecute what it has pitched on. The will is the commander of the whole man; the *primum mobile*, that which sets all the rest on motion. It is ruler in the soul; the rational, sensitive, and moving faculties are subject to it; and part of them with some freedom as to their sovereign, the rest more absolutely as to a master. Now, when it is renewed, having pitched on the chief good for its end, and chosen the best means for the attainment thereof, it sets the rest of the faculties to work to prosecute these, and diverts it from what might hinder the soul in the pursuit thereof; being moved by the Spirit of Christ, and fortified with renewing grace, it diverts the mind from carnal reasonings, vain thoughts, wicked plots and devices. Formerly, the mind could employ itself in these without control; but now, when these appear, the will gives a check to them, commands the mind to better employment, turns the current of the understanding into a new channel. It applies the mind to spiritual designs and inquiries; and when holy thoughts are offered, it commands their entertainment; they are not checked, discountenanced, thrust out, as formerly they were.

The fancy is now restrained, the folly and vanity of it receives check from the will, it has not such license to bring in provision for lust, or to bring fuel into the soul for corruption to feed on.

The sensitive appetite is now curbed. That which too often ruled the soul is now overruled; that which hurried the rest of the faculties to a blind correspondence with its motions towards objects of sense is now controlled, and is put to obey instead of commanding. Sensual proposals are spiritualised, made subservient to holiness, or occasions of it.

It exercises authority over the outward senses. They are employed in a way of serviceableness to Christ, and set to work for that end. These, which formerly were as windows to let in temptation, as doors to let in sin, are now closed at the renewed will's command,—it sets a guard upon them. A covenant is made with the eyes, as we see in Job; the tongue is bridled, and the door of the lips kept warily. Not only wicked, but idle words are restrained; if they get passage, it is by surprisal.

[7.] New purposes and determinations, new resolves. A new creature is resolved against every way of sin, and for every way of Christ; being by renewing grace become Christ's disciple, he resolves not only to deny himself and take up his cross, but also to follow him. And he that follows Christ must resolve to walk in every way of Christ, and to abandon every evil way; for he that resolves upon any way of sin, resolves to leave Christ, not to follow him. Christ cannot be followed but in his own ways, those wherein he went, or which he prescribes. He is not only willing, content, but resolute, fully determined; and his resolutions are impartial and permanent.

Impartial, to leave all, every sin. Not only open sins but secret, sins of mind and heart; not only gross sins, but those that are more excusable, refined;

not only chargeable, expensive, but advantageous; not only those that are disgraceful, reproached, but countenanced, in credit; not only burdensome, troublesome, but pleasing, delightful; not only dangerous, such as are punishable by law, but safe. Resolves to strive against every known sin, and to entertain any light that may discover what is sinful; and to endeavour not only to reform his conversation, but to get his heart cleansed; not only to crucify the members, but the body of death; not only avoid actual sin, but subdue natural corruption. This is to put off the old man; this is to act like a new creature; this is to become a new lump.

Resolve to walk in every way of Christ, even in those that seem difficult and painful, require diligence and trouble, and crossing the flesh; that are hazardous, by which ye may lose friends, credit, or accommodations; that are reproached, disgraceful, make you censured, reviled, jeered; that are chargeable, make a breach in your estates, may cost your liberty, expose to indignation of great ones, or endanger life; as Paul, Acts xx. 24.

Permanent and fixed, too. This resolution is not some fit to which his will is forced by some rousing sermon, or some awakening providence, or some sharp affliction, or some apprehensions of approaching death. Even unrenewed men will resolve much upon such occasions; but when the enforcement is removed, the fit is over, the will returns to his former posture, as a broken bow. When the affliction is removed, or the sermon forgotten, the fear of hell or death vanished, these purposes vanish, too; no more resolvings then against sin. Such unconstant resolutions, though they pass for goodness, yet they are but like that of Ephraim, of which the Lord complains, Hos. vi. 4.

But when the will is renewed indeed, these resolutions are constant, habitual, durable; not to-day resolved for Christ against sin, and the next day unresolved, as the Jews in that particular, Jer. xxxiv. 15, 16: 'Ye were turned to-day, and had done right; but ye turned again, and polluted my name.' Or as Pharaoh resolved to let Israel go while he lay under the plagues, but when they were removed he was again unresolved. This inconstancy argues there is no new creation, but only some common superficial work. This is essential to a new creature; though there may be some declinings in respect of degrees, yet this is the constant bent of his will, he is resolved against every way of sin, and for every way of Christ.

Use 1. *Conviction.* If none can be saved but new creatures, and so much be required to the constitution of a new creature, then how few shall be saved! If the gate be so strait that leads into the New Jerusalem that none but a new creature can enter into it, then few there be shall enter, few in the world, few amongst Christians.

Few shall enter, because there are few new creatures; for it appears from what has been delivered, that they are no new creatures,

1. Who are ignorant. When God begins this new creation, he says, 'Let there be light, and there is light;' therefore, where the darkness of ignorance, covers the face of the mind, there is no new creation. Those that sit in this darkness, they sit in the shadow of death, of eternal death; the way of life they have not known, they are far from it. This darkness, this ignorance, is the suburbs of hell; this is inner, and hell is but outer darkness. When Christ comes to give the children of light possession of their inheritance with the saints in light, he will come with flaming fire, 2 Thes. i. Yet how few are there that know Christ, his excellency, all-sufficiency, savingly, effectually! How few are there that know this new creation, the new birth, experimentally; who know what a new creature is, by what they find of it in their own souls!

2. Who are not convinced of what they know, who, though they apprehend something of Christ, and of sin, and of the new birth, yet not so apprehend as to bring their minds under a sensible, effectual conviction.

Those who think this new creature a mere conceit, a fancy of some singular men, or else that it is needless, a man may be saved without so much ado, think they may safely continue in the condition wherein they were born and have lived, without any such almighty work as this new creation, without any such universal change, such a mighty alteration. These make it plain enough that they have neither lot nor portion in this matter; those who never were convinced that themselves were unrenewed, or not effectually convinced of the danger in so continuing.

They that tremble not at the threatenings denounced against sin, and can rest quietly when the Lord tells them of so many curses hanging over the heads of unregenerate men, though they have no good grounds to believe but that they are the men, like the horse, in Job xxxix. 22.

3. Those that value the world more than Christ, and outward things more than holiness. How evident is this amongst us! Yet who will confess their guilt in this particular? You use not to jeer men for being rich or noble, wise or learned; yet ye can deride some for their strictness and holiness, and brand the image of God with the odious names of puritanism and preciseness. Is it not clear, then, that holiness is vile in your eyes, while the things of the world are too precious? Or suppose ye be not come to that height of wickedness as to jeer and deride holiness, yet do ye not neglect it? Do ye not think much to bestow half of that diligence and seriousness for obtaining or increasing of holiness, which you lay out for getting or keeping things of the world? You will have the best assurance, the best evidence that can be, to shew for your estates; and yet be content to take your interest in Christ upon trust, upon common, weak, unevidencing grounds. And is it not clear that Christ is of less value to such than their estate?

4. Those who have no higher designs than nature can reach, than sense or carnal reason can propose; whose chief design it is to live in ease, credit, plenty, safety in the world; who mind but God, heaven, and their souls upon the by; spare but little, even of their spare time, to mind these; and then look to this, not so carefully, not so seriously, not with such earnestness, intenseness, as they look to things that concern the outward man; mind spiritual things as though they minded them not; those that seek outward things in the first place, and the kingdom of God, with the righteousness thereof, in the second.

5. They that are strangers to spiritual inquiries, the voice of whose souls is that of the worldlings, Ps. iv., 'Who will shew us any good?' not that of the converts, 'What shall we do to be saved?' think it strange that any should busy themselves in inquiring, &c.

6. They whose minds are captivated to carnal reasonings; that will secretly argue for continuance in sin, from the mercy and long-suffering of God; argue for the salvation of unreformed sinners, from the love and sufferings of Christ; against strictness and holiness, from the miscarriage of some professors, or the reproaches of the world; against a gospel profession, from the divisions and diversities of opinions that are amongst us; for voluptuousness and indulgence to the flesh, from the shortness of our lives.

7. They whose minds are closed against holy, spiritual, heavenly thoughts, who know not what it is to commune with their hearts about spiritual things, who are strangers to heart-searching, self-judging, soul-quickening thoughts.

8. They that consult rather how to make provision for the flesh than how to crucify it; how to enjoy both Christ and his sins, his sins here, Christ

hereafter, rather than how Christ alone may be advanced in his soul; consults with flesh and blood in spiritual matters, makes choice of the world and the flesh as his counsellors; and if his conscience will not serve him wholly to neglect the service of God, advises how he may serve both God and mammon.

9. They, the inclination of whose heart is not towards God and spiritual communion with him.

10. Who make it not their chief aim to glorify God, to please him and enjoy him.

11. Who can quiet, satisfy his heart in any performance, or any enjoyment wherein he does not enjoy Christ.

12. Who make choice of such means only for promoting spiritual ends, as suit with their own ease and interests.

13. Who are not willing to take Christ, upon any terms, whatsoever the gospel propounds.

14. They whose reason, fancy, appetite, senses, are not taught subjection to Christ.

15. They who resolve not to practise every known duty, and renounce every known sin.

Use 2. *Exhortation.* 1. To those that are not yet new creatures. Since without this new creation there is no salvation, therefore, as you desire to be saved, if you would not perish eternally, rest not in anything for salvation till ye be new creatures; till then, ye are out of the way, ye are without hopes of heaven.

Every man fancies hopes of heaven; but upon what do ye raise them? It concerns ye eternally to be careful ye be not deluded. If your hopes should prove delusions at the day of judgment, how woeful will your condition be! And delusions they are if they rise not from this ground. Till ye be new creatures, ye build your hopes without a foundation, for nothing will avail ye to salvation, except ye be new creatures; neither circumcision nor uncircumcision, neither duty nor privilege, neither opinion nor practice, will be available to salvation, unless ye be new creatures. You that daily hear of gospel salvation, and, withal, know that by nature ye are out of the way to salvation; if ye be not desperately careless, should seriously inquire, what shall we do to be saved? Now if your souls be serious in asking this question, ye will seriously mind what the text answers; if ye will be saved, ye must be new creatures. And this being so, he that is not an infidel as to this truth, or wretchedly careless of his salvation, will be apt to ask,—

Quest. What means shall I use, that I may become a new creature?

Ans. In answer to this, let me premise one thing, to prevent mistakes. It is not in the power of man to make himself a new creature; for creation requires an infinite, an almighty power. No man, no angel can effect it; no, nor be the instrument of it, as the more judicious divines conclude. It is ὑπερβάλλον μέγεθος, an exceeding great power, such as was necessary to raise Christ from the dead, that is required to create faith and holiness in the soul, Eph. i. 19; it is God's workmanship only, Eph. ii. 10.

Yet, because the Lord is not pleased to effect this work immediately, but has prescribed means as the way wherein he will work it, and without which ordinarily he will not work it, therefore the means that the Lord has prescribed must be used by those that desire to attain the end. And though there be no necessary connection betwixt those means and this end, no sufficient inherent virtue in them, necessarily and infallibly, to create holiness, God having reserved this in himself as his own prerogative, yet there is a probability that the Lord will concur with the means of his own prescribing. And this probability affords hopes to every sinner, encouragement to be diligent in the use of them; whereas there are no hopes, no probabilities in an ordinary way for those who enjoy not the means, or wilfully neglect them.

The poor impotent man that lay at the pool of Bethesda, John v., though he could not go into the pool, nor convey a healing virtue into the waters, yet he was in more hopeful way to be cured than those who, being insensible of the like infirmity, never endeavoured to come near those waters.

Christ compares the regenerating power of the Spirit unto the wind, John iii. 8. The mariner cannot sail without wind, nor can he procure a wind at his pleasure, for it bloweth when and where it listeth; but he may thrust his vessel off a shore, and spread his sails, to take advantage of a gale when it bloweth. Those that wait upon the Lord in the use of means and ordinances, they hereby spread their sails, are ready for the Spirit's motions, which bloweth where it listeth; there is more hopes of these than of such who lie a-ground, neglecting the means of grace, which are both as sail and tackling.

The two blind men of whom we read, Mat. xx. 30, they could not open their own eyes; that was beyond their power; but they could get into the way where Jesus passed by, and they could cry to him for sight who only could recover it. Those that are diligent in the use of means and ordinances, they sit in the way where Jesus passes by, who uses not to reject those that cry unto him.

So, then, it is clear, though this new creation be the work of God alone, yet having prescribed means wherein he is pleased to work it, notwithstanding the unrenewed man's woeful impotency, there are no small hopes, there are great encouragements for him to wait upon God in the use of those means and ordinances wherein he puts forth his almighty power in making new creatures: 2 Cor. v. 17, Let him be. This denotes not man's ability but his duty, not that he is able to make himself a new creature, but that he is bound to use those means wherein or whereby the Lord renews sinners, makes them new creatures.

But what are those means and ordinances wherein I must wait upon God, that I may be made a new creature? I will instance in some few:

1. Attend the word preached; attend it carefully, constantly. As we should preach it, so ye should hear it, in season and out of season. Neglect no opportunity that God offers; ye know not what ye lose by losing a sermon. This is the way whereby Jesus passes; Oh be not out of the way when he passes by! The Spirit that blows where it listeth ordinarily blows in this quarter. This is the pool where there is a healing, a quickening, a creating virtue, when the angel of his presence descends into it. Oh, miss no opportunity of getting into the pool, lest your souls languish in their unrenewed state, and perish for ever. It is this by which the Lord begets his children, makes them new creatures, James i. 18. This is the incorruptible seed by which ye must be begotten, or else die in your sins, 1 Pet. i. 23, 25. Those that contemn the ministry of the gospel contemn the means of life, that which the Lord makes use of in this new creation.

Those that neglect the word to hear it, shew that they are no new creatures, shew that they have no mind to be so, shew they are either atheists, not regarding God in his word, or desperate, not regarding salvation or their souls.

Nor is it enough barely to hear; but you must hear so as to remember, remember so as to meditate, meditate so as to apply it to your souls, and mix it with faith, and act according to it.

2. Persuade not yourselves that ye are new creatures, when ye are not. Look upon this as a delusion of Satan, of dangerous consequence. There

are two devices of Satan whereby he usually deludes poor sinners about this weighty business. First, he endeavours to persuade them that there is no necessity of this new creation, that this is but a conceit of some preciser men, and that, indeed, there needs not so much ado to get to heaven. This is his first attempt. But if the clearness of Scripture evidence discover this to be a false suggestion, then he endeavours to persuade men that they are new creatures when they are not, and uses false grounds to make them believe it. Their good meanings, their harmlessness, their avoiding of gross sins, their moral virtues, outward performance of some religious duties, some change in their lives, sorrow for some sin, and zeal for some way of worship; all which, and more, may be in those that were never renewed.

Now, if upon these or such like grounds he can persuade them that they are new creatures, while this persuasion continues he will keep them from ever being new creatures. For hereupon he will draw them to neglect the means wherein God works this new creation, or else, if they use the means, hereby they are rendered ineffectual. The conscience is hereby armed against the dint of the word. Threatenings and exhortations, proper to their condition, are neglected, put off as not concerning them, and the mind is shut up against conviction, which is usually the first step to conversion. Therefore if ye would not fall into, or not be kept entangled in, this snare of the devil, conclude not that ye are new creatures unless ye have clear Scripture grounds for it, except ye have found those lineaments of a new creature drawn upon your souls which I offered to your view in the explication of the doctrine. If upon serious examination ye find no such real universal change in your minds and hearts as I there described, then do not gratify Satan, do not delude your souls, by keeping off the application of it to yourselves. Take it home to thy heart, and say, I am the man: I never had experience of any such almighty work, of any such new creation in my soul; for anything yet appears, I am no new creature. And then, if the Lord please to bring you to this conviction, you are in a hopeful way to this new creation. But then you must

3. Consider seriously and frequently the misery of your present unrenewed state. It may seem harsh counsel to persuade yourselves that you are miserable, and Satan may tell you this is the way to despair; but he was a liar from the beginning. And, though it seem harsh, yet it is necessary, and through the Lord's concurrence it may be saving. Christ came to seek and save those that are lost: lost, miserable, undone, as in themselves, so in their own apprehension. You are never the further from happiness by being sensible of your misery; no, sense of misery is the highway out of it. Meditate, then, seriously of the misery of your unrenewed state; that it is a state of wrath, of damnation, of enmity with God; a cursed state, a hopeless state, against which are darted all the curses and threatenings that are written in the book of the law; that ye can never come to heaven till ye come out of it; and that there is but a step between you and hell while you are in it. And in sense hereof—

4. Cry mightily unto God for renewing grace. Lie at his footstool, and cry, 'Help, Lord, or else I perish!' 'Create in me a new heart, and renew a right spirit within me!' Renew me in the spirit of my mind, renew me in the inwards of my soul! Take away this old mind that is so blind, so vain, so carnal! Take away this old will that is so obstinate, so perverse, so rebellious! Take away this old conscience that is so partial, so seared, so senseless! Take away this old heart that will never delight in, comply with, submit to thee! Let old things pass away, let all things become new! Thou, Lord, who broughtest this world out of nothing with a word,

canst with a word work in me this new creation! Oh suffer me not to perish when thou canst so easily make me happy! Speak but the word, and it shall be done! Speak but the word, and this soul, now a dark, a woeful chaos, a lump of corruption and confusion, shall become a new creature! Thus follow the Lord with strong cries, and give him no rest till he hear, till he answer. And, to encourage you, urge the covenant, Ezek. xxxvi. 26. Here is an absolute promise, no express condition to exclude, to discourage. And though ye are not (while unrenewed) in covenant by participation, yet ye are by proposal. Though ye yet partake not of it, yet it is propounded to ye. Plead it then: Lord, give me this new heart, put this new spirit into me. Though I be a dog (as was objected to the Canaanitish woman), yet it is this old heart, this corrupt nature, that makes me so. And this is it I complain of, this is it I would be rid of: Lord, take away this, &c. Oh, if ye were come thus far as that your hearts could put up such petitions frequently, unweariedly, then we might conclude ye are not far from the kingdom of God.

Obj. But while men are renewed, they are wicked, and the prayer of the wicked is sin; God will not accept it, answer it; it is unlawful, they must not pray.

Ans. Unrenewed men are bound to pray. Prayer is so far from being an unlawful practice, that it is their necessary duty. 1. The light of nature discovers it to be a duty. It is an act, not of instituted, but of natural, worship, by which every man had been bound to have acknowledged his dependence upon God, if the Lord had never revealed his will in Scripture. 2. If such must not pray because they sin in praying, by the same reason they must not eat, they must not work, for they sin in eating, in working. 'The ploughing of the wicked is sin, Prov. xxi. 4. 3. Prayer is nothing but the desire of the soul expressed; therefore, if they must not pray for renewing grace, they must not desire renewing grace. And who dare say to such a man, Desire not to be a new creature. The apostle Peter puts it out of question (if no other Scripture did bear witness to it). He commands an unrenewed man, one whom he certainly knew to have no part nor lot in this matter, one whose heart was not right in the sight of God, one who was in the gall of bitterness, &c. He commanded Simon Magus the sorcerer to pray, Acts viii. 22.

2. It is not prayer itself, for that is a duty; but the wickedness of their prayers, that is sinful, that is an abomination. When they make prayers a cloak for their wickedness, or pray that they may prosper in wicked practices, or pray for pardon of sin when they do not intend to leave sin, or pray with their lips, speak the words of a prayer but desire not in their hearts what they pray for, this, though ordinary, is a mocking of God; no wonder if it be abominable in his account.

3. Though an unrenewed man's person be not accepted, though the Lord take no special delight in his performance, though he have not promised to hear their prayers, yet sometimes he hears them; we have examples for it in Scripture. Ahab, though an unparalleled wicked man, yet when he humbled himself, the Lord made some return to his prayer, 1 Kings xxi. 29. The Ninevites, though heathens, cried mightily to God upon the preaching of Jonah, and the Lord repented him of the evil he had said, and as they desired, turned away from his fierce anger, so as they perished not, Jonah iii. 9, 10.

4. When the Lord gives a heart to pray constantly, importunately, affectionately, it is a sign he intends to answer. The experience of those that observe the returns of their prayers sufficiently confirm this; no reason then for us to forbear the urging of this means to unrenewed men; no rea-

son for them to be discouraged from the use of it. If ye would be new creatures, seek it of God by earnest prayer.

Second branch of the exhortation, to those who are renewed, who are already made new creatures, who can truly say, the Lord has given them a new heart and a new spirit, that old things are passed away and all things become new. This engages you to several duties.

1. To thankfulness. You ought to praise the Lord for this while you have any being; your hearts should rejoice in him, your lips should praise him, your lives should express all thankfulness to him; you should be thankful according to the greatness of the mercy, so far as your weakness can reach. Now, this is a transcendant mercy, of everlasting consequence, because it avails to salvation, as other things which you are much taken with do not.

If you had riches, and honours, and pleasing accommodations, even to your heart's desire; if you had success in all your outward undertakings, and all the prosperity you could wish; if you had a kingdom, or as many kingdoms as Ahasuerus had provinces; if you had assurance to live healthfully, delightfully, prosperously, in the enjoyment of these, an hundred years, yea, or a thousand, you would think all this a favour that calls for exceeding thankfulness. Oh, but all this is nothing in comparison of what the Lord has done for you if he have made you new creatures, for all this would not avail you to salvation; if you were not renewed, you would be for all this children of wrath, under the curse of God, the objects of his hatred and indignation, condemned already by him, and reserved for execution unto the judgment of the great day. And after those days of outward prosperity were expired, and though they were a thousand years they would have an end, they are little or nothing to eternity; they are but to everlastingness, as a day or an hour is to a lifetime; and being ended, and this shadow of happiness vanished, you must go down to hell and dwell with everlasting burnings. Then, then, what would all those kingdoms, and the riches and splendour of them, avail you? Then you would say, It had been infinitely better for me to have had a new heart than to have had all these, though it had been ten thousand years longer. Better I had lived poor, and despised, and afflicted all my days, than to have fallen short of renewing grace.

Oh, if the Lord have vouchsafed thee this, how low, or mean, or necessitous, or distressed soever thine outward condition be, he has done incomparably more for thee than if he had given thee all that this world can afford, all that is desirable to a carnal heart on earth; he has given thee that which requires unspeakable more than thankfulness. Let thy soul then bless the Lord, and all that is within thee; let thy tongue, let thy life give him the honour his grace calls for.

2. Labour to partake more and more of this renewing grace, to be renewed more in the spirit of your minds, to be daily putting off the old man, Eph. iv. If you be born again, see that you grow up; it will be monstrous to continue still infants or dwarfs. Whatever your outward condition be, be sure you may be able to say with the apostle, 2 Cor. iv. 16, 'Though our outward man perish, the inward man is renewed day by day.' The more ye are renewed, the more will ye have of salvation, the more 'abundant entrance,' 2 Pet. i. 11. The more assurance you will have of salvation for the future, yea, the more of salvation you will have at present. For what is salvation but freedom from that which makes us miserable, and possession of that which makes us happy?

That which makes us miserable is sin, and the effects of sin; and the more you are renewed, the more you will be freed both from sin and the woeful issues of it; the more you put on the new man, the more will the old be put off with its affections and lusts; and as the cause is removed the effects will cease.

That which makes us happy is joy, glory, perfection. The more renewing grace, the more joy. Light is sown for the righteous; as this grace grows, joy will grow up with it; the more [grace, the more] glory, for grace in Scripture phrase is glory.

3. Pity those who are not new creatures. Children, relations, whatever you leave, friends, credit, estate, a settled, hopeful condition, you leave them miserable unless they be made new creatures. Travail in birth with them till Christ be formed in them.

CHRIST'S GRACIOUS INVITATION TO SINNERS.

Behold, I stand at the door, and knock: if any man hear my voice, and open the door, I will come in to him, and will sup with him, and he with me.—
Rev. III. 20.

These words are part of an epistle which Christ sent by the apostle John to the church of Laodicea. In it there is matter of conviction, direction, encouragement, admonition.

1. By way of conviction, he shews her sin, her misery, lukewarmness, ver. 15, 16; self-conceitedness and carnal confidence, ver. 17; none so apt to conceive themselves rich, &c.

2. By way of direction, he shews her the means to escape this misery; from whom, and how redress may be had, ver. 18.

3. By way of admonition, ver. 19; these distempers must be corrected; do not promise thyself security from my love and indulgence, rather expect the contrary.

4. By way of encouragement, to use the means prescribed, improve the providences offered for recovery, and this, ver. 20. Wherein two propositions, 1, simple, categorical; 2, compounded, hypothetical.

In the first, 1, The matter of it; wherein considerable; (1.) The agent, *Jesus Christ*, described, chap. i. 13, &c.; 2, his posture, *stand*; 3, act, *knock*; 4, the place, *the door.*

2. The momentousness of it, of which he gives us notice by the particle *Behold*. The Holy Ghost uses the word ἴδου frequently to stir up, to attend to something wonderful, worthy of admiration; so Mat i. 23 and ii. 9, Luke xiii. 16. It has the same use here. By fixing an *ecce* in front of this verse, he gives us notice we should attend to that which follows, as worthy of admiration and full of wonder. Hence

Observe, that Christ should thus offer himself to sinners in a way of mercy, is a matter of admiration. It is like himself, whose name is Wonderful. As he is wonderful in himself, his person, his nature, offices, so in his administrations; and amongst the rest, this is wonderful, that he should condescend to offer himself.

This is worthy to be considered, and the consideration of it should raise our minds to admiration: Ps. viii. 'Lord, what is man'? so Isa. ix. 5. You will see great reason to wonder at this, if you consider, 1, who it is; 2, To whom it is; 3, in what manner it is; 4, what it is he offers.

1. *Who.* Consider (1.) his majesty; he who is the mighty God; he who is Lord of lords, and King of kings, and Prince of the kings of the earth, Rev. i. 5; who has the keys of hell and death, ver. 18; all power in heaven and earth, who is *Alpha* and *Omega*, &c., ver. 6; who is higher than the heavens; who is exalted far above, &c.; in comparison of whom the sun is but a lump of darkness, the heavens are but a span, the vastest regions of the world are but as small dust, and all the inhabitants of the earth as grasshoppers, and the glorious angels little better than vanity; the glory of whose majesty is so far from being expressed, as the apprehensions of the highest angels come infinitely short of it. That this glorious majesty should stoop so low, should condescend thus far, is wonderful, worthy of all admiration.

(2.) His all-sufficiency. He, who has all things within the compass of his own being, whereby he is infinitely happy and glorious; whose glory, whose happiness, had been nothing less than it is, if man had never been created, and would be nothing less, if all mankind should sink into nothing. He who stands in no more need of us, to add to his glory and happiness, than the angels stand in need of men, which is just nothing; nay, he stands in no more need of the angels. He was infinitely glorious and happy before any creature had a being, and had continued infinitely so, if the creatures had for ever continued in the state of nonentity, of nothing. *Et infinito nihil addi potest.* Our goodness extends not unto him, no, not that of the angels. He is infinitely above both, Job xxii. 2. All that can be expected from either is to acknowledge him glorious. But an acknowledgment makes no addition, adds nothing to what it sees, only takes notice of what is in him, and would be no less in him, if it were not at all taken notice of. The sun would have no less lustre, would be no less glorious, if no eye ever saw it. So here, the Lord declares how little need he has of man, Ps. l. 9–12. He stands in no more need of man to make him happy and glorious, than the heavens stand in need of a gnat to move them, or the earth of a grasshopper to support it, or the sun of a glow-worm to add to its light and lustre, or Solomon in all his glory of a nest of ants to make it more illustrious.

If the Lord Christ could not be happy or glorious without man, then the wonder would be less in that he condescends thus far unto him; but since he is infinitely happy and glorious without him, since he can gain, can expect nothing at all by him, stands not in the least need of him, it is wonderful he should stoop so low as to offer himself in such a way unto him.

(3.) His independency. He is so free, so absolute, in his being and actings, as nothing can necessitate him, nothing lay any engagement on him. If man could oblige Christ, if he could deserve anything from him, if he could present any motive effectual to persuade him to offer, &c., the wonder would be less; but there is not, there cannot be, the least merit, the least motive from without, to engage the Lord to any such thing; nay, there is exceeding much to disoblige him, to engage him against any such gracious condescension.

But here is the wonder: Christ does this when man is so far from deserving it, so far from engaging him, so far from moving him to it, as he does not so much as request it, not so much as desire it, not so much as think of it. He is 'found of those that sought him not.' He condescends thus far, stoops so low when there is no necessity laid on him, no desert, no motive, no desire, no thought of it, in or from the sons of men.

(4.) His sovereignty. This makes this condescension a wonder. Christ might, before he had otherwise determined, without any prejudice, annihilate all mankind, if it had continued innocent, and might have justified the act, upon the mere account of his sovereignty. 'Shall I not do what I will with my own?' Mat. xx. 15; but after sin, he might have executed the sentence of death upon the sons of men in the very moment when they receive life; and, as he threatens Ephraim, Hos. ix. 11, might have made the glory of man to fly away as a bird from the birth, womb, conception. He might have crushed this cockatrice in the egg, &c.; and this, too, with advantage to his glory, and thereby much prevented that dishonour which the continuance of our lives occasions. 'It is the Lord's mercy that we,' to whom he is now offering himself, ' were not consumed' in our infancy; a wonder of mercy that we not only live, but live to hear Christ offering life, &c.

What a wonder, when Christ might, with so much glory to his justice, power, wisdom, sovereignty, have destroyed us, he should rather choose to offer salvation!

When there was, as it were, a contest betwixt justice and mercy, and when there was so much reason for the execution of justice, so little or none from us for the tenders of mercy, that the Lord should here interpose his sovereignty to prevent man's ruin, and when there was no other reason to offer him mercy, because he would offer it. As Exod. xxxiii. 19, as if the Lord should say; There is no reason in man, why I should thus condescend to him. I see many weighty reasons why I should utterly, entirely, destroy him; my severity will be justified before all the world, and my justice much glorified thereby. Yet for all this, though there be much reason from my own glory, and all the reason in the world from man himself, why he should perish without the least tender of mercy, yet will I spare, yet will I stoop so low as to offer myself unto him. Oh how full of wonder is this condescension of Christ! How ought we to admire it! How may we be astonished at it, if we consider but who it is that stoops so low; that is the first. More wonderful it will appear, if we consider,

2. *To whom* it is he thus offers, he thus condescends. If the sovereign Majesty of heaven, so all-sufficient, so infinitely glorious, will vouchsafe to stoop to any, we may think in reason he must be some person of worth and honour; no, it is to men, it is to sinners, it is to his enemies. Here is the wonder, this is it that calls for the *Ecce*, the *Behold* in the text. The great God stoops thus low to man. The sovereign Majesty of the world vouchsafes this to a slave. The absolute commander of heaven and earth condescends thus far to an enemy. Behold and wonder, consider this and be astonished, and let your admiration rise by these three steps.

(1.) It is to man, it is not to the angels, it is not to the seraphims of glory; no, it is to man, contemptible man; it is to him who is but dust and ashes; it is to ' man who is a worm, and to the son of man who is but as a worm' compared with Christ, Job. xxv.; it is to man that Christ thus condescends, in comparison of whom man is not so much as a worm: ' He is but as a moth,' Job. xxvii. 18. Nay, compare him with Christ, he is inferior to this small contemptible creature, Job. iv. 19. 'He is crushed before the moth.' And will Christ wait upon dust and ashes? Will he come to the habitation of a moth, and stand and knock at the door of a worm? Oh what a wonder is this, that the brightness of infinite glory, the mighty God of hosts, should stoop so low! Nay,

(2.) It is to sinners; it is to man by sin made worse than those creeping things, worse than the beasts that perish. Man by creation was but dust, and in this contemptible enough; but by sin he is become polluted dust, and so not only vile, but odious, loathsome, so loathsome, as the Lord is of purer eyes than to behold, cannot endure to see him. A wonder then he will endure to come so near him, that he will stand and knock at the door of such a leper, so deformed, so loathsome, so infectious! See how he describes those to whom he offers love, ver. 17, Wretched and miserable, twice miserable, extremely miserable, and (which makes the gracious offer wonderful), wilfully miserable. Misery, when it is not voluntary, may move pity; but when it is wilful, when a man throws himself into it, is obstinate against freedom from it, rejects the means offered, contemns the offer, slights him that offers it, boasts of his own happiness, when he is admonished of his misery, will not know it, will not seek redress, will not desire it, will not accept it; who will relieve such misery? Such is the misery of a wretched sinner. He has wilfully brought it upon himself, and wilfully continues in it. Christ in the gospel tells him of his misery: he will not believe him; he says, 'I am rich,' &c. Christ shews the way out of it, he obstinately refuses to walk in it; Christ shews the means, he rejects them; Christ offers happiness, he contemns the offer, and despises Christ himself that offers it. Oh woful misery! And yet Christ will come and knock, and stand waiting, to shew mercy to such wilful wretches; and continues thus, notwithstanding their obstinacy, their contempt of those gracious offers, and of Christ himself that makes them. Oh how wonderful is this!

Add to this; Christ offers it to those that are poor, blind, and naked; so poor, as they have nothing to cover their soul's deformity and nakedness, and yet so blind, as they will not see that which has nothing to cover it. And will Christ offer himself to such poor, blind, loathsome, obstinate, miserable wretches? Oh how wonderful is this! See the woful condition of sinners described by the Lord himself, when Christ offers himself to them; behold it and wonder, Ezek. xvi. 4, 5, 6, 8. Will he condescend so far to such wretches, when they lie in their blood and are covered with loathsome pollution? Will he pity those whom no eye pities, who will not pity themselves? Will he spread his garment over such defilement? Shall the time of loathing be the time of his love? Oh how full is every word with wonder! It is to sinners that Christ stoops, to sinners; and that is the worst, the most odious, the most loathsome thing that earth, nay, that hell, can afford; and will he condescend so far to these?

(3.) It is to enemies. Not only to those that are hateful to Christ, but those to whom Christ is hateful; to those that are his utter enemies, enemies in their minds, in their hearts, in their lives; to those that hate Christ, and all his; hate him without a cause, hate him with a mortal hatred, even to the death; hate him implacably, so as they will never cease to hate him till their old hateful hearts be plucked out of their flesh, Ezek. xi. 19; those that join with his deadly enemies, shew themselves enemies to his crown, nay, to his life. Such an enemy is every unregenerate sinner unto Christ; and yet to such enemies does Christ come, and stand, and knock, that he may shew them mercy. To such does he offer himself, communion with himself; and waits till they will open, waits till he may enter, to feast them with his own joys and comforts, and to entertain them as his dearest friends. Oh the wonder of this condescension! If men will not, heaven and earth will, be astonished at it, to consider to whom. It will appear more wonderful if we consider,

3. *How* it is he offers himself. He comes, knocks, stands, entreats, importunately, compassionately, again and again.

(1.) He comes. It is the great concernment of sinners, and their duty too, to come unto Christ, to seek him, and not to look that he should come to them. It is thus with men; they stand upon terms, and will have their inferiors to know their duty, or else suffer for it. How much more might the great God stand upon it, and let men perish if they will not come and seek to him for happiness? Are they not more concerned than he? Does he lose anything if we perish? Must he condescend to careless, undutiful wretches, as though he were beholden to us for making us happy? Must he condescend further to man than one of us will stoop to another? Will he come to those who will not come to him, though they die for it? Oh how wonderful is this! yet thus it is. While men mind not their greatest concernment, while they neglect their duty, while they take no notice of their distance, yet Christ stands not upon terms; while they refuse or delay to come to him, he vouchsafes to come to them. Oh wonderful condescension!

If we consider the infinite distance betwixt Christ and sinners, we cannot but count it a wonder that he should suffer such vile, loathsome, hateful wretches to come near him, though they were willing to do it. How much then is it to be admired, that he will stoop so low as to come to them, who are unwilling, as they are most unworthy, to come to him! Will Christ come to make them happy, that will not so much as come to him for happiness? Will he come to save them from death, who will not so much as come to him for life? Will he come to seek and save those that are lost, when they will rather lose their souls for ever than come to him for salvation? This is the condition of every unregenerate sinner: 'No man comes to me,' says Christ, 'except the Father draw him,' John vi. 44; and so he complains, 'Ye will not come to me,' &c., John v. 40. Oh if Christ should stand upon terms here, as most justly he might, and the very custom of the world would justify him in it; if he should say, If I be not worth the coming to, if life and happiness be not worth the coming for, why, then, stay where you are, and be without it. Oh if Christ should say thus, why, then, no flesh would be saved. Oh but when careless wretches, forgetful of their souls, unmindful of their duty, regardless of Christ's honour, will not come to him, rather than they shall perish, he condescends, he humbles himself, to come to them. Here is that we may for ever wonder at: the King of glory comes to a slave to make him happy, to a slave who refuses to come to him. The sovereign Lord of the world comes to offer peace to his mortal enemy, whom he could crush into nothing; seeks peace with a sinner that refuses peace with God. The glorious Majesty of heaven vouchsafes to come to dust and ashes, which refuse to move towards him. The holy God, of purer eyes than to behold iniquity, comes to deformity and pollution, though it be loathsome to him; comes and offers heaven to that which provokes him to spurn it at the greatest distance from him, even into the lower hell. Would you see this wonder? Look into the text, and behold Christ, the King of kings, the Lord of lords, the Holy One of Israel, coming unto men, to sinners, to enemies; coming with life, and peace, and happiness, to wretched, condemned, deformed slaves, while they refuse to come to Christ for them. But, which adds to the wonder, behold,

(2.) He knocks. That implies the door is shut (as you shall hear hereafter); but though he finds the door shut, though the heart of the sinner be closed against him, though he finds none ready, since none willing to open to him, yet he knocks. Though he sees the sinner sometimes bolting the door faster against him, sometimes taking no notice of him, sometimes stopping his ears that he should not hear, sometimes withdrawing himself, as counting the gracious importunity of Christ troublesome; always admitting his deadly enemies at their first approach when himself is shut out, yet he knocks.

Oh what a wonder is it, that Christ does not depart in indignation, and swear in his wrath that he will never enter under the roof of such a wretch!

If Christ expected any great advantage by being admitted, then it would be less wonder that he should knock, and continue knocking. But he desires to enter, that he might make that wretch happy that shuts him out. He expects no costly entertainment; he will put the house neither to cost nor trouble; he brings his entertainment with him, and gives the sinner notice of it: Rev. xxii. 12, 'Behold, I come shortly, and my reward is with me.' He comes not empty-handed: 'Length of days is in his right hand, and in his left hand riches and honour,' Prov. iii. 16. He would have entrance, that he might pour out his treasures into the bosom of the sinner; and yet he is shut out, and glad to knock, that he may have admission. He knocks in the ministry of the word; knocks by the law, by the gospel; knocks by the motions of the Spirit, knocks by afflictions, knocks by checks of conscience, knocks by reproofs and admonitions of his people, knocks by variety of providences; and yet seldom, and, if ever, hardly gets admission.

Oh the wonder of Christ's patience! Would any prince on earth do as the Prince of the kings of the earth here does? Coming to the cottage of some peasant to make his condition rich and honourable, would he stay to knock when he sees himself shut out, and none regard to open to him? Yet will the King of kings digest this affront from dust and ashes, and knock for admission though it be denied; whenas he might fire the house about the ears of sinners, and with the breath of his nostrils tumble them into destruction: 'The Lord's ways are not as our ways,' &c.

(3.) He stands. Continues in a posture not easy to us, not becoming the majesty of men in honour. He waits on vile sinners; he is not weary of waiting, he stands. Though the sinner sometimes plainly refuse to admit him, sometimes puts him off with excuses; though he tell him he is not at leisure, he has something else to do than to run to the door; though he bid him come another time, when he is not busy; though he tells him he has other guests, and those that he likes better; though he see him entertaining sin and the world, so taken up with them as himself is not regarded: yet he stands. Oh the wonder of Christ's patience! And what heart will not be filled with admiration that considers who it is that thus stands, and at whose door? 'Behold, I stand;' I, says Christ, I stand, whose seat is the throne of glory at the right hand of the Majesty on high. I, 'at whose name every knee should bow, both of things in heaven, and things on earth,' Philip. ii. 10; I stand, before whom all the glorious angels of God bow down and worship, Heb. i. 6; I stand, at whose feet the glorified, triumphant saints do cast their crowns, Rev. iv. 10; I stand, before whom the glorious host of heaven do fall. I stand waiting upon dust and ashes, waiting upon sinners, the very worst of all my creatures, waiting upon my enemies. I stand while they sit in the seat of scorners, while they lie wallowing in lusts and pleasures, while they sleep securely in ways of sin, not regarding me. I stand without, while base lusts are freely entertained, and the worst of my enemies heartily welcomed within. I stand at the door while Satan has the throne; I am shut out while every vanity is let in. And will Christ stand upon such terms, after so many refusals, affronts, after so much disrespect and contempt cast on him? Yes, he stands, and so continues, till his locks be wet with the dew, and his head with the drops of the night! Oh, who would not stand amazed to see Christ thus stand at the doors, at the hearts of sinners!

(4.) He entreats. Here is a wonderful condescension indeed, that the great God, speaking to the vilest of his creatures (so man is by sin) should use the language of entreaty; that he who commands winds and seas, he who has heaven and earth, angels and all creatures at his command, should humble himself so to entreat, to beseech his creature! And entreat what? To do him some favour, to help him to some advantage? Then indeed the wonder were less. No; but the Lord is infinitely above any such thing. That which he entreats is, that they would admit him, admit him whose presence is the glory, the happiness of heaven. That they would be reconciled to him, reconciled to him whose favour is life to them, but no advantage at all to himself, but what he can otherwise procure though they perish. He can as easily get himself glory in destroying the proudest of his enemies, the greatest of sinners, as in pardoning any; and yet he beseeches, he stoops so low as to entreat condemned sinners to accept of a pardon, 2 Cor. v. 20. If a prince should do this, if he should come to one of his meanest subjects, by whom he had been highly offended, from whose displeasure he fears no loss, and from whose friendship he expects no advantage, and should entreat him to be reconciled and accept of his favour, would not this be the wonder of all that hear of it? Yet thus does the glorious God to those that have shewed themselves traitors, enemies to his crown and dignity; he comes to them, offers them his favour, his pardon, stands waiting for their acceptance. And when they are slow to accept it (who are most concerned to sue for it), he beseeches, he entreats them to accept of his favour, not to refuse a pardon, whenas without it they perish, soul and body, eternally. Oh how wonderful is this condescension!

(5.) He bewails their unkindness to him, their cruelty to their own souls. When other means are not effectual, he takes up a lamentation. Here is a wonder indeed! He stoops so low as to take the weakest of our infirmities that can without sin be expressed. When sinners regard him not, his knocking, his entreating; when they continue obstinate against him, and resolute to continue in sin, notwithstanding all the means used to reclaim them, he lifts up his voice and weeps over them.

When he prevails not by coming, by standing, by knocking, by waiting, by beseeching, why this is his grief, his sorrow, and he vents his sorrow in tears. Behold the compassions of the Lord to obstinate sinners, as he expresses it over Jerusalem. Behold it, and wonder! He represents himself as clothed with the weakest of man's infirmities; he falls a-weeping, Luke xix. 41, 42. Behold the wonderful compassions of a dear Saviour. Now if one should ask him, as he did the woman, John xx. 15, Blessed Lord, 'what seekest thou? why weepest thou?' we may suppose this would be returned: Why, I seek not myself, I weep not for myself, there is no need of that; I shall be infinitely, eternally glorious; though sinners be not gathered, I am infinitely happy, whatever become of them. But this is the grief of my soul, that sinners will rather cast their souls into hell than give me admission into their hearts; that they will rather force me to forsake them than forsake their sins; that they will rather part with me, who am their life and hope of glory, than part with the world, than part with their lusts, which will certainly ruin them. When I come, they do not admit me; when I knock, they open not to me; when I stand, they do not regard me; when I entreat, and beseech, and promise, they do not believe me. I know what this will cost them, it will be bitterness in the end; and if my compassions move them not, nothing remains for them but weeping and gnashing of teeth for ever. This he foresaw in Jerusalem, and this he foresaw in others disobeying the gospel as they did. And hereupon his bowels were turned within him, his compassions vented themselves in tears. And O, did the Lord weep for them who will not weep for themselves? Oh how wonderful is this compassion! how full of wonder this condescension!

(6.) He does this frequently, again and again. He comes, and though sinners provoke him to depart, he comes again; he knocks, and though they will not open, he knocks again; he stands, and though they force him to remove, he returns and stands again; he entreats, and when he is not regarded, he doubles his entreaties, he enforces them, by presenting his tears, his blood, to the view of sinners in the gospel. The preaching hereof, in season and out of season, is his appointment, that therein sinners may see him daily set forth as crucified before their eyes, that they may behold him stretching out his hands all the day long unto them, that they may hear him, as though he were now, as in the days of his flesh, mourning, complaining, and weeping over them, Luke xiii. 34. How often would the Lord have gathered you! how often has he come, knocked, stood, waited, entreated, lamented! If it be a wonder that he will condescend to any of these for once, how wonderful is it that he should condescend to these so often!

This will be yet more wonderful if ye consider,

4'. *What* it is that he offers. Behold what it is the great God offers to men, to sinners, to enemies, with such condescension, affection, compassion, importunity, and you will see matter of highest admiration. He offers (1.) his love; (2.) himself; (3.) his blood, and all that he purchased by it; (4.) his comforts; (5.) his glory; and (6.) his kingdom. He comes, to give these; he stands, to offer these; he knocks, that these may be admitted; he entreats, that these may be accepted; he laments, when sinners regard not these offers. And this day by day, year after year; and that to those that have made themselves the vilest of his creatures. Let all these things meet together in your thoughts, and you will apprehend Christ wonderful. You will get some acquaintance with the employment of heaven, admiration of Christ in his tenders of mercy to sinners. You will see there was reason to begin this verse with a note of admiration, *Behold!*

(1.) His love. Such a love as it is a wonder any creature should be the object of it; more wonderful that Christ should offer love to the vilest of creatures. Consider what love it is that Christ offers.

[1.] An ardent love. Many waters could not quench this love. Not the floods of reproaches, injuries, sufferings from men; not the waves and billows of God's wrath and indignation. All these went over him, yet did this love flame forth in the midst thereof; nor was it ever more ardent than in the height of sufferings.

[2.] A transcendent love. No love found in the breast of any creature is worthy to be compared with it. We may say of it with more reason than David of Jonathan's, 2 Sam. i. 26, 'His love was wonderful, passing the love of women.' Greater love than this was never visible in the world, John xv. 13. His love, like his ways and thoughts, is far above the creature's, John xv. 9. There is not an equality, but there is resemblance. No love comes so near the love of the Father to the Son as the love of Christ to his people; greater love than a man bears to himself, more love than Christ shews to heaven or earth. He left heaven to manifest, to offer this love. He refused all the kingdoms of the earth, offered to stop the current of this love, Mat. iv. 8–10. If [thou wilt] desist from this great work, render thyself incapable of redeeming man, and so lay aside the thoughts of loving him.

[3.] An **everlasting** love, John xiii. 1; Isa. liv. 10. Such a love it is that Christ offers to such creatures. He stays not till they sue for it, but offers it; and that to worms, sinners, enemies; those who have no love in them to Christ when he makes this offer, no, nor anything lovely. From the crown of the head to the sole of the foot, nothing but bruises, &c.; the face of his soul covered with a filthy leprosy; as full of noisome sores as Lazarus's body, whose sores the dogs licked; full of more loathsome boils than Job's body, when he sat in the ashes and scraped himself. A soul polluted with sin is far more loathsome in the eye of the holy God than that which is most loathsome to us in the world. And will Christ offer love to that which is so loathsome? such a love to such a deformed wretch as man is become by sin, especially seeing the soul is as full of hatred as it is of deformity? Will the glorious Majesty of the world, the brightness of infinite glory, the beauty of heaven, the wonder of angels, love such deformity, love that so much which is so much an enemy to him? Will he come and stand, and knock, and sue, and entreat that this love may be accepted? Oh how wonderful! How may we break forth into admiration with the Psalmist, Ps. viii. 4, 'Lord, what is man?' What is he but a lump of pollution, a mass of deformity, as full of hatred to Christ as a toad of poison? And is this a thing to be loved, to be loved of Christ, to be loved with such a love? Would it not be a wonder if such a creature should prevail for any love from Christ if he should sue for it to eternity? Oh what wonder is it then that Christ should of his own accord make the offer!

(2.) Himself. It is not some lesser expression of love, but it is the highest, the greatest that heaven can afford. It is himself, it is no less than himself, which is more than ten thousand worlds, that he offers. He offers himself to be theirs by covenant, by marriage covenant, and that for ever; to be thine assuredly, intimately, eternally; to be thy God, thy friend, thy husband, thy Jesus, thy Saviour, thy Christ, thy king, thy priest and prophet, thy advocate, thy intercessor. Oh what infinite riches is there in this little pronoun *thine!* Canst thou say, Christ is *mine?* Why, this is more than if thou couldst say, All the treasures of the world are mine, all the kingdoms of the earth and the glory of them are mine. Why, this is it that Christ offers, no less than himself, to be thine for ever. This is it which he offers when he stands and knocks at thy heart: Open to me; I will be thy God, the Lord thy Redeemer. Though thou hast rebelled against me, and followed after strange gods, yet now renounce those idols, open to me, I will be thy God, and that by covenant more durable than heaven and earth.

Open to me, thy Redeemer will be thy husband. Though thou hast played the harlot with many lovers, thy unkindness, disrespects, disobedience, ingratitude, disloyalty shall not part us. I will marry thee to myself in an everlasting covenant that shall never be broken; I will rejoice over thee as a bridegroom over his bride.

Open to me, I will make over no less than myself unto thee. Thou shalt have that which it is the glory and happiness of heaven to have, myself, communion with me; I will come and sup with thee, and thou with me. Art thou poor? Open to me; the commander of heaven and earth will be thine to enrich thee. Art thou vile and contemptible? The King of glory will be thine to honour thee. Art thou deformed? The Sun of righteousness will be thine to beautify thee. Art thou distressed? The great Redeemer will be thine to relieve thee. Art thou weak? The Lord of hosts will be thine to strengthen thee. Art thou dejected? The God of all consolations will be thine to comfort thee. Art thou in darkness? The bright Morning Star will be thine to enlighten thee. Art thou wretched and miserable? The Fountain of bliss and happiness will be thine to enhappy thee. Thus Christ offers himself; and oh how wonderful is it, that he should come to vile worms, and knock, and wait, and entreat that himself may be accepted!

(3.) His blood. He offers not himself in a common, easy, cheap way, but himself as dying for those that will open to him, Eph. v. 2. He offers that which the sons of men will least part with, skin for skin, &c. He offers his life, his blood, Rev. i. It is not silver, or gold, or wealth, or honours only that he offers; it is something of more value than sceptres, or crowns, or earthly kingdoms: it is 'his precious blood,' 1 Pet. i. 18. Take those things which the sons of men do most value, and they are but corruption compared with what Christ offers: it is his blood. So transcendently precious is the blood of Christ, as all the treasures of the earth are so vile compared with it, as that which the Scripture counts vilest, as corruption itself. Christ comes, and stands, and knocks, to offer his blood, when he comes to the hearts of sinners. He comes, as he is described, coming from Bozrah: Isa. lxiii. i. 2, 'with dyed garments, red in his apparel; with garments like him that treadeth in the wine-fat, dyed with his own blood.' This he offers, and all those infinitely precious things which are the purchase of his blood. If thou wilt open, all shall be thine. Is the wrath of God kindled against thee? My blood shall pacify him. Is the justice of God incensed against thee? My blood shall satisfy it. Is heaven shut against thee? Open to me, my blood shall open it. Is thy conscience a terror to thee? My blood shall speak peace to it. Fearest thou any thing? My blood shall secure thee. Wantest thou, desirest thou any thing? My blood shall purchase it, procure it for thee. This Christ offers. He will not think his blood too dear for sinners that will open to him. Oh what wonder is it that Christ will offer his blood for vile worms; nay, his blood for his enemies; that he will come, and knock, and stand, and wait, and entreat, that his precious blood may be applied, may be accepted! If a physician, having a patient desperately sick, and knowing no other remedy for him but his own blood, should come, and knock, and entreat, and after affronts and repulses, and many expressions of hatred and contempt from the patient, should yet continue importunate that he would accept of his own blood for his cure, would not this astonish all that should hear of it? Much more wonderful is this, that the King of glory, though despised and hated by sinners, should offer his own blood to save them from death; and when the offer is slighted and neglected, should yet knock, and call, and cry, and beseech, that it may be accepted. Oh, if any thing affect us, this must needs be wonderful in our eyes.

(4.) *His comforts.* Those comforts which flow from his presence, in whose presence is fulness of joy. Those joys which spring from communion with himself. 'I will come in, and sup with him,' &c. The wellspring of heavenly joys, the fountain itself will flow in, if the sinner will but open. And this is it that Christ intends, when he comes, knocks, and stands, and waits, that joys unspeakable and glorious may fill those souls who have been a grief, an affliction, a dishonour to him. You have made him a man of sorrows, he offers you everlasting joys. You have given him gall and wormwood, he brings you the foretastes of heaven, the first-fruits of the land of promise. He stands, and calls, and entreats, that this may be accepted. Oh how wonderful is this!

(5.) *His glory and kingdom,* John xvii. 22. He offers glory to dust and ashes; his own glory to despised worms. Such glory as himself enjoys, not equal to it, yet much resembling it. When David promised Mephibosheth the honour to sit at his table, how is he transported! How does he express his sense thereof! 2 Sam. ix. 8. Oh how much better does this admiration, this expression become those to whom Christ offers his glory! What is thy servant, that thou shouldst take notice of him? What is dust and ashes? What are poor worms, that they should sit at thy table as one of the King's sons? That the great God should offer this great glory to vile creatures, and that by way of entreaty, oh how wonderful is it! Not only to sit at his table (which Mephibosheth, though a king's son, thought so great an honour from a king), but to sit on his throne, ver. 2; and now we are so high, as admiration should be raised to the highest. The King of glory stands, that vile sinners may sit; stands knocking at their doors, hearts, that they may sit on his throne, on his own throne; entreats those who are enemies to accept of his kingdom, his own kingdom.

Use 1. *Information.* This shews the reason why sinners are so much, so exceedingly affected at their first conversion. No wonder if they be astonished, transported with admiration; for herein they have a clear discovery of these wonders; a deep sense of their own vileness, misery, enmity against Christ; a clearer view of his transcendent excellencies; a more tender resentment of his condescensions in coming, standing. They are as one born blind; when he recovers his sight, every thing almost is a wonder to him, much more the sun. When men's eyes are opened, all the carriage of this business is wonderful, especially Christ. Why do they see so much to astonish, transport them, whenas others see little or nothing, or are little or nothing affected with what they discover in Christ, in themselves? Why, till converted, they are in darkness; but upon conversion are 'translated into marvellous light,' 1 Pet. ii. 9.

Use 2. *Reproof.* Those that slight, neglect, despise these condescensions of Christ in offering these things. Are things so wonderful thus to be undervalued? Do ye neglect to hear? Regard ye not, when Christ comes, knocks, stands, entreats? Can you withstand all his importunity, and resolve for sin, put him off with excuses, delays? Oh take heed! You take the course to provoke the Lord to make your plagues wonderful, Deut. xxviii. 59.

Use 3. *Exhortation.* Since it is a wonder in itself, let it be so in our eyes. Be much in meditating on those things that represent Christ wonderful. Consider him, how glorious, all-sufficient, &c. Consider thy own vileness, sinfulness, how wretched. Let these things lie on thy thoughts till they affect thy heart, till they raise thy mind to admire, adore, as the queen of Sheba, 1 Kings x. 5. Consider how often Christ has come, how long stood, how much entreated, how many motions, providences, convictions. Consider what he offers, as Elizabeth, Luke i. 43; and then break forth in praises, rise up into admiration, fall down astonished at the wonders of Christ's condescension. This is the employment of heaven; hereby you will do the will of God as it is done in heaven. This is it which Christ calls for by the first word, *Behold.*

Pass we from the consequence of this proposition, *Behold*, to the matter of it; wherein, 1, the person; 2, his posture; 3, the place; 4, his action. The person is Christ; his posture, standing; the place, man's heart; that is the door, and there he knocks. These, put together, afford two observations, one implied, the other expressed. That implied is this:

Obs. The hearts of sinners are shut against Christ; every soul by nature is closed against Christ. If it were not, there would be no need for Christ to stand and knock, there would be no ground to represent him in such a posture.

That the strength and evidence of this truth may appear, we will take it in pieces, and so explain and confirm it by opening and proving two propositions contained in it. 1. Christ is *extra*; 2. *exclusus*. 1. Christ is without, there he stands, there he knocks; 2. The sinner is unwilling to let him in. He is not only without, but shut out; therefore he stands, he knocks.

1. Christ is *without*, he is not in the soul of a sinner naturally. While a sinner is in the state of nature, he is without Christ, so described, Eph. ii.

12. We are born without Christ, live without him, nor has he place in us, till an almighty power, which the Lord usually puts forth in the ministry of the gospel, make way for him in our hearts. Till conversion, till the Lord open the heart, as he did Lydia's, Christ is not present in the sinner, nor entertained by him; he is not present in respect of his special and gracious presence (so understand it).

He is not in the mind, he is not present there as a prophet, to instruct, to enlighten it; darkness covers the face of it; the Sun of righteousness shines not there with a saving, a spiritual ray; the Day-star does not there arise. Though he may apprehend much by natural light, yet nothing spiritually, savingly, effectually. The things of the Spirit of God are not discerned, 1 Cor. ii. 14

Christ is not in the will, he is not present there as a king; his throne is not there established, his sceptre is not there advanced; the heart submits not to him, complies not with his laws, is not ruled by him, breaks his bonds, casts his cords from him, says, I will not have this man to rule over me.

Christ is not in the conscience; he is not present there as a priest; his blood has not yet been there sprinkled, does not purify it, mollify it; does not free it from guilt, nor make it tender. If it scruple at sin, restrain from it, accuse for it, the love of Christ, the blood of Christ, does not constrain it so to do; it is from some other enforcement, some more foreign consideration.

Christ is not entertained; other things are admitted before him, take place of him. And this leads me to the reason of this point.

Christ is without, because the soul is so taken up with other guests, as there is no place left for him. The like reason why Christ is not admitted into the heart of a natural man, as there was why he was not admitted at his birth into the inn, Luke ii. 7. Christ finds no better entertainment, when he comes spiritually to a sinner's heart, than when he came in the flesh to Bethlehem. He lodges without, because there is no room within. The soul of a sinner is full of other guests; sin, and the world, and Satan have taken up every room in the soul. The mind, the will, the heart, the conscience, they are full of sin, full of corruption, crowded with multitudes of lusts; and *intus existens prohibet alienum*, so much corruption within keeps Christ without. Man brings into the world a soul full of corruption, a nature wholly depraved, a heart abounding with all manner of lusts, full of pride, unbelief, worldliness, uncleanness; full of rebellion, obstinacy, security, self-love: these and many other so take up the heart as there is no room left for Christ; these must be whipped out before the soul can become a fit temple for Christ; it must be emptied of these in some degree before the glory and power of Christ's presence will fill the tabernacle of the soul.

While these strong men armed keep the house, as Luke xi. 21, Christ stays without, these cannot rule together; no serving of two such masters; no entertaining of these so differing guests; one heart cannot hold them, because these lusts of corrupted nature are in possession and rule within, Christ is without. That is the first.

2. Christ is *shut out*. He is not only without, but the sinner is unwilling to let him in. The heart is closed against him, and many means are used to make it fast, many bolts and locks are added to make it sure. Were not the heart closed, the door shut, Christ would not need to knock; were not the sinner unwilling to open, Christ would not be put to stand knocking, the heart would open to him at his first approach, at his first knock. But the Holy Ghost, by these expressions, plainly declares to us the sinner's un-

willingness to open to Christ. The reasons of it are many, I shall but mention three; prejudice against, distrust of, disaffection to, Christ.

(1.) Prejudice against Christ. This shuts Christ out of the mind, makes the sinner unwilling to admit him into the outer room. The mind of every man naturally is full of prejudice against Christ; it is part of that enmity of which the apostle speaks, Rom. viii. 7. Hearing in the gospel upon what terms Christ will be admitted, it forthwith judges his admission dangerous, troublesome, or needless, and so shuts him out. This prejudice shews itself by judging it.

[1.] Dangerous. If I open to Christ upon these terms, I must forego all my unjust gains, all my forbidden pleasures; I must be no more wanton, intemperate, or revengeful, how much pleasure soever I have taken herein; I must not commit the least sin to gain the greatest advantage; I must cut off every dear lust, though it be to me as my right hand, &c.; I must not leave a hoof behind if Christ be admitted; nay, I must not only part with my pleasing and gainful sins, but be ready to sacrifice my estate, credit, liberty, life, when he calls for them. Hereupon the sinner thinks Christ offers him loss when he offers to come in upon these terms, and so shuts him out.

[2.] Troublesome. If I open to Christ, I must bid adieu to my carnal ease, humours, interests; I must be diligent in mortifying duties, which are so irksome to flesh and blood; I must spend so much time in prayer, meditation, self-examination; I must be always watchful over my heart, thoughts, ways, senses; I must beat down my body, bring it into subjection; maintain a continual combat with my own corrupt nature; expose myself to the reproaches and scorn of the world, by strictness, scrupulousness in matters which they judge of small moment; I must live in continual exercise of repentance, self-denial, mortification. These, and such like, Christ requires if he be admitted. And so the sinner looks upon him as a troublesome guest, and shuts him out.

[3.] Needless. Think it not needful to admit Christ further than they have done. They are baptized in his name, submit to his ordinances, profess him openly, have a name to live; sometimes pray, read, and hear his word; order their outward conversation, as they think, inoffensively; so conclude they are Christians good enough, that it is not needful further to admit or entertain Christ, and so close their hearts against him, when he should enter to purpose and take full possession of them. What needs all this stir? Cannot a man be a Christian, &c., except so strict, precise? This is to be hypocrites. Do ye not see what becomes of them that profess and pretend to so much? Christ is not so scrupulous as some men would make him. He may be in my heart as well as theirs, though I make not so great a show. How many content themselves with such thoughts as these, and are ready to express it upon occasion? Prejudice against the holy ways of Christ makes them willing to judge, that an outward profession of Christ is a sufficient admission of him; account more needless, are not willing to open to him further, and so indeed shut him out. This is the first bolt whereby the soul is made fast against Christ.

(2.) Distrust, unbelief. This shuts him out of the will. Man by nature has neither that faith, which is consent to receive Christ as he is offered, nor that faith which is an assent to what Christ has delivered. The first is a belief on Christ, which the Scripture calls πιστεύειν εἰς τὸν Χριστόν. The latter is belief of Christ, which we call πιστεύειν τῷ Χριστῷ. Every man by nature is defective of both. The consent to receive Christ on gospel terms, is either the essence of saving faith, or a property inseparable from it; for to believe on his name, and to receive him, pass for one and the same thing, John i. 12. Now, unbelief in this sense is such a bar to keep out Christ, as nothing but an almighty power can remove, Eph. i. 19.

Now that a natural man consents to receive Christ upon the terms offered, will appear further, in that he assents not to these terms as delivered in the gospel. The terms on which Christ will be admitted, are laid down by Christ himself, Mat. xvi. 24. Let him renounce every sin forbidden, though as dear to him as himself; this is to deny himself. Then let him endure every suffering for my sake inflicted; this is to take up his cross. Let him practise every duty commanded, even as Christ was obedient in all things; this is to follow him. These are the terms. Now, either men will not believe that Christ will not enter but upon these terms, fancy some of their own, more suitable to their corrupt inclinations, humours, interests, or if they yield that they are Christ's terms, yet they will not believe that they are so pleasing, so advantageous as the gospel declares them to be. Whatever he say, if this be his burden, they will not believe it is light; if this be his yoke, they cannot believe it is easy, and upon this account reject these terms; and since he will not enter upon any other terms, they shut him out. Thus does unbelief close the hearts of sinners against Christ. That is the second.

(3.) Disaffection to Christ. Men naturally are so well pleased with the guests that they have already entertained, as they are loath, by admitting Christ, to dispossess them. This shuts Christ out of the heart. They are more in love with the world than with Christ, take more pleasure in fulfilling their lusts than they can expect delight in communion with Christ. They affect not spiritual enjoyments, relish not those pleasures which Christ promises upon his admission, value not Christ's offer to sup with them in comparison of what the world and their lusts afford them. Hence, Mat. x. 37, 'He that loveth father or mother, &c., is not worthy of me.' He hereby refuses Christ, prefers what he enjoys before what Christ offers, shews himself unworthy of Christ's company by excluding him, James iv. 4. He that is so much a friend to the world as he will not cast it out of his heart for Christ, hereby shews himself an enemy to Christ by shutting him out.

Use 1. *Information.* This shews us the misery of every man by nature. Christ is not in him. He shuts him out, in whom is all the hopes and comforts and happiness of sinners. How miserable is he who is without happiness, without hopes of it! He that shuts out Christ excludes all happiness, all hopes of it. Yet this is the condition of every man in the state of nature; he is without Christ, Christ is not in him. Oh, take notice of the misery of this condition, that you that are in it may be affected with it, that you whom mercy has delivered from it may pity those who languish under it! But because *generalia non pungunt*, we are not affected with generals, take a survey of this misery in some particulars. He that is in the state of nature, he that excludes Christ, is—

1. In the possession of Satan. Christ and Satan, they have *divisum imperium*, they divide the world betwixt them. Where Christ rules not, there Satan has his throne. He that shuts out Christ shuts in Satan. The soul that is not in the possession of Christ is possessed by the devil. And oh how large are his possessions! You think a diabolical possession dreadful. Why, this is the dreadful estate of every unrenewed man; Satan has possession of him! That this may be evident, observe the Scripture speaks of a double diabolical possession: one corporal, when Satan enters into the bodies of men, and there immediately exercises his power by or upon them;

of such there is mention, Mat. iv. 24, viii. 28, xv. 22. Another spiritual, when Satan enters into the souls of men, and there exercises his power by and upon them. And this is the possession we speak of. Satan does thus possess the soul of every natural man. So he did Ananias, Acts v. 3, ἐπλή-ρωσεν, he was possessor. So he possessed Judas, Luke xxii. 3. Not that Satan was not in him before, but because he did then more manifest his presence by that devilish act. As Christ is said to be with his people in special (though always in them), because he manifests his presence by some special influence or assistance. Satan is always in the hearts of sinners, though he manifest his possession of them at some time more than other. And lest we should think this diabolical possession of the soul to be peculiar to some notorious sinners, such as Judas was, the apostle speaks it both of himself and of all the Ephesians, before they were regenerate (Eph. ii. 2, 3), and all disobedient sinners. He is in all disobedient sinners, and he works in them. He is in their souls, in like manner as he is in the bodies of those miserable creatures whom he possesses; for the apostle uses the same word. Those that are bodily possessed are called ἐνεργούμενοι, and those souls that are in the possession of that spirit τοῦ νῦν ἐνεργοῦντος. The spirits that possess men are called ἐνεργοῦντες. Satan has as much possession of the souls of sinners as he has of the bodies of those we call demoniacs. Nay, soul possession is more dangerous, makes a man more miserable than bodily possession. This is more sensible indeed, but the misery of soul possession is upon this account also greater, because the sinner is senseless of it. What more miserable spectacle can you see than that man bodily possessed! Mark ix. 18, 20, 22, 26. What more rueful than to see the devil tear and rend that wretched creature, sometimes casting him into the waters and into the fire! to see him foaming, and gnashing of his teeth, and pining away, and brought to the gates of death! This is a woeful sight indeed, and such as may draw tears from and strike compassion into the heart, not only of a father, but of a stranger. It is sad indeed. Ay! but there is one spectacle more woful, if we could see it. A soul possessed by Satan, grievously vexed, wofully rent and torn by him, sometimes cast into the water, sometimes into the fire, into such dangerous evils as are more dreadful than any water or fire. Satan exercises more tyranny, more cruelty, upon the souls of sinners than upon possessed bodies, only we see it not, and therefore are so slow to believe it, so insensible of it, so little affected with it. But the misery is nevertheless for the sinner's senselessness; nay, it is the more, his misery is so deep, sense cannot reach it. And this is the misery of every soul that shuts out Christ; he hereby makes sure Satan's possession. Oh, consider it, ye that are yet in the state of nature! Till Christ be admitted, you are under the power, in the possession of Satan. When the heart opens, then, and not till then, is the soul 'turned from darkness to light,' &c. Till then Satan dwells in him, works in him, uses him as his slave, oppresses him as a tyrant, employs him as his own, has full possession of his soul.

2. Under the curse of the law, without redemption. For it is Christ only that redeems, Gal. iii. 13. And those that are without Christ are under all the curses and threatenings, without redemption. Every sin is attended with many curses, and every curse (if we were sensible of it) more intolerable than the hills and mountains. Therefore, when the Lord comes to execute them, and the soul is awakened out of the lethargy whereinto sin brings it, he shall call to the mountains to fall upon him, and the hills to cover him. The Scripture speaks no peace to such a sinner. What peace to that rebel who shuts the Prince of peace out of his soul? The gospel speaks no comfort to such a sinner. What comfort when

Christ, the God of all comfort, the spring of all consolations, is rejected? There is no promise wherein he can claim interest, for all promises are in Christ yea and amen. No comfort, no peace, no promise of either, while Christ is shut out; nothing but curses and threatenings are the portion of such a sinner, and no redemption from these till Christ be entertained.

3. Under the wrath of God without mercy. The wrath of God abides upon him while Christ is not entertained by him, John iii. 36. The children of disobedience are children of wrath, Eph. ii. This is their portion. And who are children of disobedience but those who will not hearken to Christ when he calls, not open when he knocks, not entertain him when he entreats for admission? Their portion is wrath: it is entailed on them; no cutting it off till Christ come in. As all the ways of God are mercy to those who admit Christ, so all his ways are wrath to those that reject him. Even those things that are given to others in love are sent to them in wrath; all their enjoyments, all his dispensations. Their table is a snare, their prayer an abomination, the word the savour of death. Prosperity hardens their hearts. Afflictions, the first drops of that deluge of wrath, which will one day overwhelm all those that persevere in rejecting, excluding Christ.

4. Under the sentence of condemnation without pardon. He that believes not is condemned, John iii. 18, 19. This is the condemnation, light is come, the gospel is preached, Christ is discovered. You see him standing, waiting; you hear him knocking, entreating for admission; yet are so much in love with the works of darkness as to shut out the light, shut out Christ the light of the world, the glory of heaven. Here is ground enough of condemnation. No wonder if such a man be condemned already, if the sentence of eternal death be past! Does not that man deserve to die without mercy, who shuts him out of doors that brings him a pardon? All men by nature are condemned persons; Christ is sent to some with a pardon; he comes, stands, knocks, entreats condemned sinners to open to him and accept of this pardon, this pardon which cost him so dear, his own life, his dearest blood. Oh, but sinners will not hearken, will not regard, will not believe his report, are not willing to receive him; this is not to believe him; and therefore are condemned already, yea, and will continue so to eternity if they continue to shut out Christ; for what pardon without him?

5. Near the confines of hell, without a Saviour. Upon the brink of that pit which is bottomless destruction. Every one that runs on in sin is posting towards eternal ruin. Every sin is a step towards hell, and every act of wickedness sinks the sinner some degrees lower. And who shall save him from going down into the pit, since Christ, who only can do it, is rejected? It is Jesus only that delivers sinners 'from the wrath to come,' 1 Thess. i. 10. There is wrath coming apace towards sinners, and they are posting towards it; there will be a dreadful meeting, except Christ interpose; and what hopes of that while Christ is shut out and denied admission?

Oh consider this, all you who prefer your sin before Christ; you have long heard the voice of Christ in the preaching of the gospel; who have heard him knock at your hearts in the ministry of the word, and have not yet been persuaded to part with those sins that keep him out. Consider what it is to be in the possession of Satan without a redeemer, under the curse of the law without an intercessor! And if this estate appear miserable, if you have any sense of soul misery, any desire to be freed from it, freed from Satan's power and possession, &c., make haste, delay not, open forthwith unto Christ, who stands and knocks for admission. Turn out those woful intruders that have kept Christ out of possession; abandon those lusts, renounce those sins that have closed your hearts against Christ. Then shall it be well with you, who are now in the midst of woes and miseries; then shall Satan be cast out, and the prince of the world judged; then shall the curse be turned into a blessing; then shall the wrath of God, which now overshadows you, clear up into beams of mercy; then shall the sentence of condemnation give place to a gracious pardon; then shall you be brought from the confines of hell and the shadow of death into the suburbs of heaven and glory. Oh that to-day you would hear his voice, who still calls on you, who still knocks and entreats you would open to him! Oh that you would hear his voice while it is called to-day, lest he ' swear in his wrath you shall not enter into his rest;' lest he swear in his wrath he will never enter into your souls.

Use 2. *Examination.* Try whether you be those who keep Christ out of your hearts, whether your souls be closed against him. Those that thus refuse Christ are in a miserable condition, under the power of Satan, &c., 2 Cor. xiii. 5. Therefore it highly concerns every of us seriously to examine whether this be our state. Oh, but how shall I know? By these two particulars:

1. If Christ be admitted, thou hast had experience of a great alteration. We seldom read of Christ's coming in Scripture, but we find some great alterations attending. When he came to the temple, Mat. xxi. 10, 12, see what follows. Here is work indeed; he seems to turn all upside down; he rectifies disorders to purpose. Indeed, while the strong man armed keeps the house, all is in peace; but when Christ, a stronger than he, comes and disarms him, casts him out, takes possession of the place, then the sinner's peace is broken. This is not done without contest and opposition. The soul will find a great alteration, it will not be so with it as formerly. Malachi prophesies of Christ's coming to his temple; see how he describes it, Mal. iii. 1–3. He makes clean work where he comes; the soul is purified and refined when he comes. He sits in the soul as a refiner. When Christ comes, old things pass away; old lusts, old sinful practices, old hearts, old ways, they are abandoned. The refiner's fire consumes them, all things become new. ' If any man be in Christ, he is a new creature,' 2 Cor. v. 17. It is as true the other way. If Christ be in any man, he is a new creature; for this in-being is mutual. When the soul is in Christ, Christ is in the soul. Are ye new creatures? Are all things become new? New judgments, new apprehensions, new thoughts, new hearts, new motions, new inclinations, new consciences, new affections, new delights, new desires, new designs, new conversations. Such a change there is when Christ comes. If you be the same men as formerly, if you be not thoroughly renewed, you may conclude Christ is yet shut out.

2. If you admit Christ, you admit his word. If the word of Christ take no place in you, then Christ himself has no place in you. Where the word is shut out, Christ is shut out; where that abides, he abides, 1 John ii. 24. These two are joined together by Christ, John xv. 7. Does the word abide in your souls? Is it effectually admitted into every faculty? Does it abide in your minds, to enlighten them; in your thoughts? Is it your meditation? Or are you strangers to meditation? Can other things be carefully ruminated, and what Christ speaks in the ministry of the word easily forgotten?

Does it abide in your consciences, to convince you of sin, and restrain you from sin, and stir you up to the practice of what you hear? If it take not hold on your conscience, but you go on in sin, and neglect the duties urged upon you notwithstanding, how does it then abide?

Does it abide in your wills, to bring them to a conformity with the will of Christ there revealed, to lead them to a compliance with what is well-pleasing in his sight?

Does it abide in your affections, to quicken your affections, to kindle your love, to stir up your zeal, to fill you with delight, to possess you with hatred against sin, to melt you into sorrow for sin, to raise you to high esteem of Christ and spiritual things? If so, it argues the word abides in you, and consequently Christ himself.

But if the word of Christ, which you daily hear preached, pass from you as words of course, pass away as a tale that is told, as an ordinary discourse; if it be no more regarded, no more remembered; if you be no more affected with it, no more ruled by it; if, after sermon is ended, you can lay aside thoughts of it as that which little concerns you; if you can shut out conviction, withstand reproofs, run into those very sins which you hear reproved, neglect exhortations, and neglect those duties to which Christ by his word exhorts you: if it be thus, the word is shut out, Christ himself is shut out. If it be thus with any, I have a sad message for them, but it is a message from the Lord. I must tell them, or be unfaithful. Their hearts are closed against Christ, they are yet in Satan's possession, under the curse of the law, under the wrath of God, under the sentence of condemnation, in the confines of hell, and will be till Christ be admitted.

3. *Observation.* Though Christ find the hearts of sinners closed against him, yet he *stands at the door and knocks.*

For explication, let us inquire, 1, what is meant by the door; 2, what by knocking, and how Christ may be said to knock; 3, what by standing, what this expression signifies. For these are all metaphorical, and something is denoted, intended, that the words do not properly signify. Christ does not stand and knock, as men do at a door when they would be let in. We must not understand any bodily approach, or any corporeal action or posture; for Christ, as to his body and human nature, is in heaven, there circumscribed, and will be there contained till the restitution of all things. Yet though he do not stand and knock properly as we do, yet something he does which much resembles our knocking, our standing. Some likeness there is betwixt what Christ does that he may be admitted into the hearts of sinners, and that which we do when we would be admitted into the house of a friend. There is some ground for these metaphorical expressions, and when we know what this is the words will be clear. And this is it we now inquire after.

1. By *door*, understand the heart of man, as I told you before. The heart comprising two faculties, the will and understanding; the will principally, for the two principal acts of the will, consent and dissent, are as the opening and shutting of the door. When the will consents, it opens; when it dissents, it shuts out that which moves for admission. And therefore opening here is called consent elsewhere, as Isa. i. 19. Here, if you will open, Christ will sup, &c.; there, if you will consent, ye shall eat, &c. So shutting is expressed by dissent or refusing, Isa. i. 20. So that by the door is principally meant the will. When this consents to receive Christ as he offers himself, then Christ is admitted, the soul is opened to him; he comes in, makes the opening soul the place of his abode, he walks in them, dwells in them, feasts them. When this dissents, refuses to receive Christ, &c.,

the soul hereby shuts out Christ, closes itself against him. Thus the will resembles a door, and therefore is so called.

The understanding, that is as a key-hole or a window to the door. Through it light is conveyed into the soul, by which it discerns who it is that stands and knocks, who it is that seeks admission; and according to what it discerns so it moves, opens or shuts. If it like the person, his motion, his business, then it opens, consents, admits him; if it approve not hereof, apprehend it dangerous, troublesome, needless, it refuses, shuts him out. Thus you see what is meant by the door, and why so called.

2. By knocking, understand those means which Christ uses to draw the sinner to come and open. That is the end of knocking with us. When Christ uses means to win the sinner's consent to admit him, to receive him, then he knocks. That this may be clearer, we will shew (1.) how he knocks, what means he uses; (2.) why he knocks, wherefore he uses such means to draw the soul to open.

(1.) For the first, the means are diverse. We will reduce them to these four heads. He knocks, [1.] by checks of conscience; [2.] by acts of providence; [3.] by the ministry of the word; [4.] by the motions of his Spirit. I beseech you, observe them. It much concerns you to know Christ's knock; for what more powerful motive to open than to know that it is Christ that knocks? Christ when he knocks is little regarded, because men consider not, take no notice that it is Christ that knocks. The everlasting gates are not opened when it is not minded that the King of glory knocks thereat. When Samuel knew not the Lord's voice, 1 Sam. iii. 4, he runs to Eli. Thus sinners, not discerning that Christ knocks, run another way, and many times further from him, instead of running to open to him. Durst sinners be so bold as to shut their hearts, if they effectually considered that it is Christ that knocks there? Oh no, they have this for their excuse: We never heard, we never remembered, that Christ came and knocked, and yet was shut out, was not admitted by us. Just like those on Christ's left hand, Mat. xxv., when Christ charges them that when he was hungry they gave him no meat, &c., ver. 42, they have an answer as ready as any obstinate sinner amongst us, 'Lord, when saw we thee an hungered?' &c., ver. 44. Oh no, far be it from us. We never saw thee in such a condition, else we should have been as ready to relieve thee as those righteous ones. We never saw thee; otherwise, if we had not relieved thee, that heavy sentence, 'Go, ye cursed,' had been too light for us.

So when Christ now in the ministry, &c., charges sinners with refusing to open to him, I come, and stand, and knock again and again, and yet ye shut me out, how readily will many answer as they, 'When saw we Christ?' &c.; we never saw Christ in such postures; we never heard him knock, and shut him out; if we had, then were we wretches indeed to shut out Christ. Why, but is it so indeed? Did ye never hear Christ knock? Why, sure, then, ye know not when Christ knocks.

Well, we will leave no room for this excuse, when I have shewed you how Christ knocks. There is not one of you but must acknowledge that Christ has long, has often knocked at your hearts. Whether you have opened to him must be referred to your own consciences. Most certain it is Christ has knocked longer, oftener at your hearts than ever man knocks at your doors; for he knocks,

[1.] By checks of conscience. When the sinner's heart smites him, then does Christ knock. Conscience is Christ's deputy; when he employs it to smite the sinner, he then knocks at the heart. When the weight of sin is felt, and the conscience smarts in the sense of the sinfulness of unlawful practices, Christ is then knocking; the wounds of conscience are as dents in the door, they argue forcible knocks. Hereby Christ would draw the sinner to open; for there is no way to remove guilt, and silence an accusing conscience, but by letting in Christ. If he be not admitted, that which now but pricks will gnaw the soul to eternity as a never-dying worm. These checks of conscience, these knocks of Christ, should move the sinner to make haste to open. This was the effect of it in Peter's hearers. When his sermon had awakened them, and brought them to the sense of sin, it is said they were 'pricked in their hearts,' Acts ii. 37, and forthwith they were willing to open; they cried out, 'Men and brethren, what shall we do?' Now how long, how often has Christ thus knocked at yours? I hope there are none of you in that desperate condition, as to have your conscience seared, and made past feeling, past sense of sin. And if you be not cauterised past feeling, you have often felt the checks of conscience, your hearts smiting you for sin. Why, this is Christ knocking; he hereby seeks admission, and would draw you to open. As often as conscience checks, Christ knocks; and as often as you suppress, neglect those checks of conscience, so often as you disregard Christ, so often you refuse to let him in.

[2.] By acts of providence, whether they be acts of bounty or acts of severity. For the former, all your comforts and enjoyments, all your deliverances and preservations, all the acts of his patience and longsuffering, are as so many knocks at your hearts; Christ hereby would stir you up to open to him. Oh that you would mind them! All the expenses of the riches of his goodness and forbearance, and longsuffering, should draw you to open to Christ. This should be the issue of them, Rom. ii. 4, 'Lead to repentance.' What is that but leading you to open to Christ? For the great sin you are to repent of is your shutting out Christ, refusing to receive him, admit him. When this is repented of, the heart opens to Christ. And this is it that goodness should lead you to; it calls, it knocks for this.

Now, how much, how long, has Christ thus knocked? Can you reckon up the good things you enjoy? Can you give an account of all your deliverances? Are they not more in number than the hairs on your head? are they not past numbering? Why, then, so often, you cannot tell how often, Christ has knocked all your lives. No day, no hour, no minute, but he has been knocking at your hearts. Oh, how does it concern you to look that he be let in!

For the latter, he knocks by afflictions. The knock of mercy makes small impression, hardened sinners little regard it. Therefore Christ knocks in another method,—he lets fly afflictions upon the sinner, and these are as so many stones cast at the door. When the sinner minds not Christ's gentler knockings, he takes his rod (and his rod can make the rocks to open) and beats upon the door, makes the heart of a sinner shake under the weight of his strokes. If ye will hear nothing else, 'hear the rod,' says he, Micah vi. 9. He has variety of rods wherewith he knocks at the hearts of sinners. If no other will prevail, he will take his rod of iron, and knock so as he will make the foundations of the house to shake. This was his method with Manasseh, 2 Chron. xxxiii. 10, 11. 'In their afflictions they will seek me,' Hos. v. 15. Christ knocks and seeks to them before, and they will not regard. Ay, but if he take his rod, he will make them seek to him; make them run trembling, as the gaoler, open and beseech him to enter. Now, has not the Lord often thus knocked at your hearts, with one rod or other—by sickness, losses, wants, disappointments, crosses, or other afflictions? If you open not, take heed of his rod of iron. If you belong to him, he will make you regard his knocks, or you shall smart for it, if you sink not under it.

[3.] By the ministry of the word, preaching of the law and of the gospel. This indeed is the principal means whereby Christ knocks. When he knocks the other ways without this, his meaning is not understood, and so sinners open not. The heathens have both checks of conscience and acts of providence to awaken them; but wanting the word, they know not the meaning of those knockings, and so they prove ineffectual. But though these be not effectual without the word, yet these are good enforcements of the word where it is enjoyed. Secure sinners are apt to slight the word, make nothing of it. But when the Lord awakens them by checks of conscience, and some sharp dispensations, the word, shewing Christ's meaning herein, hereby becomes more regarded; it is brought to remembrance, the dent of it is deeper. These joined fall with more force and weight upon the heart, and the sinner hears Christ's knock to purpose. Hence the word is called a hammer, Jer. xxiii. 29.

Christ knocks by the law. This discovers sin in its colours, and the dreadful wrath of God as the sinner's portion, and eternal torments into which he is sinking. And as the law was at first delivered with thunder and lightning, so now it falls upon the heart as a thunderbolt, a terrible knock indeed. The experience of many thousands who have opened unto Christ bears witness to it, though carnal hearts will either deride it or not believe it.

The knock of the law sounds thus in the ears of a sinner: Wretched creature, the fire of God's wrath is kindled on thy soul, thy sins are a continual fuel to it; if thou open not, that Christ may quench it, it will burn to the bottom of hell.

Thus Christ knocks by the law at the heart of Laodicea: ver. 17, 'Thou sayest, I am rich,' &c. Thou thinkest (and this is the very thought of most unrenewed sinners) thy soul is rich and happy enough, thy condition for eternity is good and safe enough. Thus every natural man before the law knocks at his heart. So Paul says of himself: Rom. vii. 9, 'I was alive without the law.' I had good conceits of my soul's condition, and made no question of life. Ay, but when the law came, when that discovered the sinfulness of his nature and life, and the wrath of God due to him for sin, why then, says he, I died, all my good hopes and high conceits they withered and died,—one knock of the law overthrew them all; and I then looked on myself as a dead man, even at the gates of eternal death. And so must every sinner before he will open to Christ; he must apply to his soul what Christ applies here to Laodicea. Thou knowest it not, thou wilt not believe it; but as sure as Christ is true, this is the truth of thy soul's condition. Thou art wretched and miserable, as blind as the prince of darkness can make thee, as naked as he that has not a rag to cover his nakedness, as wretched and miserable as the curse and wrath of God can make thee. Thus thou art, and thus more and more thou wilt be everlastingly, if thou shut out Christ, and shut up thy soul in this condition. Thus Christ knocks by the law.

He knocks also by the gospel. This discovers Christ, and the riches of his love, and the all-sufficiency of his redemption, and the overflowings of pardoning mercy through his blood. And this bears upon the heart with a sweet and heavenly violence; and if the sinner open not at this knock, his case is desperate. Thus he knocks by the gospel at the heart of Laodicea, ver. 18. The knock of the gospel sounds thus in the ears of a sinner: Thou art naked: open to me, and I will clothe thee with my own robe; thou art blind: open to me, I have eye-salve that will cure those that are born blind; thou art poor: open to me, thou shalt share with me in my unsearchable riches; thou art wretched and miserable: open to me, and then if my love, if myself, if my blood, if my comfort, if my kingdom, can make thee happy, thou shall be happy.

And oh how often, how long, have you in this place heard Christ thus knocking! How long have you enjoyed the gospel! how has he knocked by the law! how has he knocked by the gospel, day after day, year after year! With what patience, with what importunity! Oh take heed that ye be not found in the number of those that shut out Christ, who regard not when he knocks!

[4.] By the motions of his Spirit; when the Spirit of Christ concurs with acts of providence, or with the word preached, so as these make some impression on the heart, bring the soul to some sense of its sinfulness and misery, and beget some inclinations to leave old, sinful practices, and take a new course. How frequent is this in sickness, when death is before his eyes, and apprehensions of eternity seize on him! How then will he resolve! How many promises will he make, that if he may be freed from the present danger, he will then be another man! Those that enjoy the gospel, and live under a powerful ministry, cannot but have experience of Christ's knockings by his Spirit. When sin is discovered, and the conscience in some degree awakened, and the danger of sin, the wrath of God hanging over it, apprehended, then there will be many times some inclinations, some semi-purposes, to abandon sin. These are the issues of Christ's knocking by his Spirit.

So when the necessity, the excellency, the all-sufficiency of Christ is discovered, the happiness, comforts, glory that sinners may receive from him apprehended, there will be some half resolutions to close with him. When you find these, you hear Christ knocking. These inclinations, semi-purposes, they are as it were an opening half way to Christ; but the suppressing of these motions is a shutting the door against Christ when he is entering; as I may say, a thrusting him out when he is half way in, a throwing the door upon his face. A most high affront, a grievous provocation; and yet what more ordinary? Have ye never, while ye have been hearing, praying, found such motions, inclinations? Sure they have hardened their hearts as the adamant that have no such experience. I will not suppose any here given up to such a reprobate sense, or rather the senselessness of reprobates. Well, then, when you find such motions, &c., Christ is knocking; and so powerfully, as you are brought to open in part to him. Oh, but do these motions, &c., vanish? Do the cares, the employments, the pleasures, the thoughts of the world, choke them? Why, then, when Christ is as it were coming in, you shut the door against him; when his foot is within the threshold, you thrust him out. This ye do by suppressing these motions of the Spirit, and suffering them to come to nothing. This is resisting the Holy Ghost, when he is striving to get possession for Christ. Oh how dangerous is this provocation! Verily there is but a step betwixt you and that dreadful sentence, ' My Spirit shall no longer strive,' &c. Oh take heed, this is Christ's knock!

Thus you see how many ways Christ knocks. And now I dare appeal to you, if there be any room for that excuse, I would have opened if I had heard Christ knocking. What sinner is there at whose heart he has not knocked many years? There is none wait so long, so often at his posts, the posts of wisdom, as he waits, as he knocks at your hearts. Oh how does it concern you to look that he be let in!

(2.) Why does Christ knock? what need is there of it? That is the next. And so you will have both the manner how, and the cause why, and thereby a satisfying account of Christ's act. Why, what needs this? There is great need every way; if Christ should not knock, we would never open, Christ could never enter. Such is the condition of every man by nature. Unrenewed sinners are not so well affected to Christ, they have no such mind to admit him, as to watch at the door that they may be ready to open at his first approach. No; there is by nature a strong antipathy against him, and wonderful disaffection to him; but of this formerly.

To shew you why Christ knocks, what necessity there is for him so to do if he will enter, let us a little follow the metaphor. It is needful, because,

[1.] Sinners by nature are far off from Christ, far from opening. When we come to a man's house whom we know to lodge in many rooms from the door, we knock, and knock aloud, else we cannot expect he should hear or open. Why, this is thy condition, the state of every sinner by nature; you lodge many rooms from the place where Christ stands. Sin has set every man a great distance from Christ. All are far off, at like distance with the unrenewed Ephesians, ii. 12: οἱ ποτὲ ὄντες μακρὰν. *Sometimes;* when was that? Why, till they opened, &c. It is the privilege peculiar to those who open to Christ; they are a people, as Israel, near unto God. Till sinners open, they are far off, whatever be their accomplishments, privileges, enjoyments. It is true there is a latitude in this distance, some are farther off than others. The heathens that enjoy not the gospel, they are farthest off; those that have apostatised, outrun their holy profession, they are at a woful distance indeed; those that, by refusing Christ and long resisting his Spirit, have caused him to withdraw from them, these are farther off than at first, their latter end in this respect is worse than their beginning. Yet though some be farther off than others, yet all by nature are far off, and so far off as they are out of hearing, would never be drawn to open but that Christ vouchsafes sometimes to knock with an almighty force. Since sinners are at such a distance, Christ must knock, or else not enter; they will not hear him, not open to him.

[2.] Sinners are very busy. Their heads, and hearts, and hands are full of business; such a crowd, as leaves no room for thoughts of Christ. He may stand long enough, if he knock not, before he be admitted. They have something else to do than to wait for Christ's approaches, so as to be ready to admit him, without putting him to the trouble of knocking. They are so taken up with the world or their lusts, as it must be some loud importunity that will draw them to the door.

When we come to a man's house who we know is full of business, we expect not to be admitted till we knock again and again. Sinners are full of business, even those who seem least employed; Satan will be sure to find them employment enough, on purpose to keep them from attending Christ's approaches. One is busy in the world to get and increase an estate; his thoughts, his affections, are all taken up. Another has a design to be great and eminent; his heart is filled with this. Another, making provision for the flesh, &c., plotting, contriving how to satisfy a worldly, unclean, revengeful lust. Here is such a crowd of business, such a noise, as it is a wonder if Christ be regarded when he does knock; he might stand long enough unregarded if he did not. The sinner thinks much to leave his business and run to the door, till the loudness, the frequency, of Christ's knocking, enforced with his mighty power, draw him to it. He is too busy to open to such as will not knock.

[3.] Sinners are at rest; they are asleep; yea, in a dead sleep. This is their condition by nature, which I express by this gradation. The Scripture holds it forth in these expressions, to shew a sinner's carelessness of Christ and of his soul's concernments; his loathness to rise out of it, his impotency to open, till he be roused and awakened by Christ's knocking. He is at rest, stretched upon the bed of security. He is at ease, well contented with his natural condition; takes pleasure and delight therein; fancies his spiritual estate safe, good enough; counts it a needless trouble to rise out of it; thinks it a disturbance to leave his present repose to go and open to Christ. When he in the parable was desired by his friend at midnight to open to him, Luke xi. 5, the man counts it a trouble, ver. 7. It is midnight with every sinner in the state of nature; he is in darkness, sees not his miseries, however they encompass him; he lies down on the bed of security, and is at rest, and now it is a trouble to him to rise and open; it must be no easy knocking, or little importunity, that will draw him to it. If it was thus with the spouse when Christ came to give a special visit, much more is it thus with natural men. But thus it was, Cant. v. 2. Thus Christ came, thus he knocked, thus he entreated, but he is put off with excuses: ver. 3, 'I have put off,' &c.: Oh what trouble is this! 'I have washed:' Oh what disturbance is this! If it were thus with the spouse in a fit of security, oh how much more is it thus with sinners in the state of nature! They are well enough, so they conceive; they have ease, quiet, repose enough in their outward accommodations, worldly enjoyments; it seems unseasonable, it is night, a time of rest and darkness too. Alas! they see not the necessity of Christ; it is a trouble, &c. Things being thus, Christ must knock, and knock to purpose, before they will come and open.

Further, they are not only at rest, lain down, but asleep. No opening, till they be awakened, and no awakening unless Christ knock. The state of nature is a night, a state of darkness, and sinners in that state are answerable thereto, said to be asleep, 1 Thes. v. 5, 6. Though they be busy as to natural employments, and the things of the world, yet to anything that is spiritual they are asleep. The steam, the gross vapours that arise from the corruption of our natures, obstructs all passages, so as there can be no conveyance, no operation of the Spirit, and consequently all the senses are bound up. A sinner in this state can no more, in a spiritual way, hear, see, smell, relish spiritual things, than a man asleep is sensible of outward objects. He must be awakened, else no opening, and nothing can awake him but Christ knocking, therefore he knocks. The sinner is asleep.

Nay, further, he is in a dead sleep; a sleep indeed which is no less than death in a spiritual sense. A dead sleep has seized on every sinner, such a sleep as the Holy Ghost calls death, Eph. v. 14. His sleep is so deep, as he is counted amongst the dead. Stand up from the dead! It must be a loud knock indeed, that will rouse a man out of a dead sleep; a powerful knock, that will raise a man from the dead, a knock from an almighty arm. Why thus must Christ knock, else sinners cannot, will not hear, much less open, John v. 25. Great need to knock, and knock aloud, when those that should open are in a dead sleep. This for the second.

3. What by standing? We must not conceive anything outward or corporeal in this posture of Christ. He speaks to our capacities, and vouchsafes to represent himself after the manner of men. But what are spoken of God, of Christ, who is the mighty God, ἀνθρωποπαθῶς, we must understand θεοπρεπῶς. What he speaks after the manner of men, we must conceive in a way becoming the majesty of God. Thus standing imports some or all of these five things:

(1.) Christ's condescension. He stoops low indeed, when he vouchsafes to stand at our door. It is infinitely more than if the greatest prince in the world should humble himself to stand at the door of a beggar. He is wonderfully gracious, when he will stand, when he will wait to be gracious. But of this in the first.

(2.) His approach. He is come near to a sinner, when he stands at his door, stays at his heart, and knocks. Nor does this disagree from what I said formerly. Those may be absolutely far off who are comparatively near. All are far from Christ by nature; but he is nearer unto those to whom he comes in the ministry of the gospel, than to those whom he leaves to sit in darkness, &c. When the gospel comes to a people, the kingdom of heaven is at hand, and Christ the prince of that kingdom does approach. Yet are sinners far enough from the kingdom, far enough from Christ. While he stands but at your hearts, he is not near indeed absolutely till you let him in. Though he stand at your hearts, and the kingdom of heaven in the gospel come to your doors, yet shall ye never enter into it unless you let Christ enter into your hearts. Christ coming so near, nearer to you than others, if you let him not in, will cast you further from him in hell than others. Outer darkness is for them who shut out greatest light; and the greatest destruction from Christ hereafter for them to whom he came nearest here, and was excluded. For the present, here is a blessed opportunity, Christ is near you, he stands at your hearts, he is at hand. This is the second intimation of this posture.

(3.) His desire; his readiness to enter. He is even at the door, so near he is come, there he stands. If any man will open, he is willing, he is ready to enter. What more can be expected on his part, to shew him willing to come in? If you see one standing at your door and knocking, how can ye interpret this, but that he is willing, desires to enter? Christ is more ready to come in to sinners than they are to open to him. There is no bar, no backwardness on his part; he is at the door, and there he stands and knocks. That which keeps him out is the unkindness, the obstinacy of sinners, who will not open. That Christ is thus ready to enter, is unquestionable, in respect of those whom he has purposed from eternity to take possession of. How it holds in respect of others, we may have occasion to shew hereafter. And what a strong motive, what a great encouragement should this be to open? Christ stands at your hearts, ready to enter, to take possession, if you will but admit him.

(4.) His patience. This posture denotes the exercise of patience. He stands at the door. When he comes to the heart of a sinner, though he find it shut against him, he does not presently depart in a fume, as he might justly, to see himself thus slighted, and all the happiness that attends his presence disregarded; he does not instantly for all this leave the heart, but he stands. Though those who resolve to open are slow in coming, though others put him off with delays and excuses, nay, though some give him plain denials, yet he stands. Though this be the voice of sinners generally, yet a little more sleep, &c. He stands notwithstanding, and that long. Sometimes whole days, yea, day and night; sometimes whole years, yea, sometimes many years: 'All the day long do I stretch out my hand,' &c.; 'These three years have I come, seeking fruit;' 'Forty years long was I grieved with this generation.'

(5.) His readiness to depart if he be not admitted. Though he stand long, he will not stand always. As his standing shews he is ready to enter, if the sinner will open, so it shews, if the heart be obstinately shut against him, he is as ready to be gone. He sits not, as though he would make a continued abode before the hearts of rebellious sinners; he stands, and that implies a readiness to depart, if admission be denied. Though the patience of Christ be wonderful, and his condescension to sinners exceeding great, yet he is more tender of his honour than to endure it should be always slighted. If ye will not open to him, he will be gone. When he had stood some hours knocking at the door of the spouse, Cant. v., and she put him off with excuses, he stands no longer, but departs; though she opened, she found him not, he was gone, as she sadly complains, ver. 6. And if Christ deal thus with his spouse, the people of his love, engaged to him by marriage covenant, what may they expect who have no interest in him, no such affection to him?

It was a day he waited on Jerusalem, a long day indeed. But when they would not make use of the light of it to discover their concernment to entertain Christ, away he goes and leaves them in darkness. That happy sight should be for ever hid from their eyes, they should never see him standing more; instead of Christ's visits, they should be encompassed with devouring enemies. Utter desolation should succeed the day of their despised visitation, Luke xix. 41, 42, &c. Christ came often, and stood long, to gather Jerusalem, to take possession of them, but they would not be gathered, Mat. xxiii. 37. But what follows? That house that will not entertain Christ shall be left desolate. Desolate must that place be that Christ forsakes. Those that will not see Christ standing shall find him departing, and so departing as they shall see him no more, ver. 39. When he had come unto the fig-tree three years, and found it still barren, what follows? Luke xiii. 7, 'Cut it down.' When he had stood forty years waiting on the Israelites, and they still grieved him with hardening their hearts against him, what is the issue? 'They err in their hearts,' and a fatal error it is to shut Christ out of the heart, while Satan and base lusts are shut in. 'They have not known my ways,' they consider not effectually that Christ was come to them. They considered not, so as to open to him, to hear his voice. 'Wherefore he sware,' &c.

Oh consider this. Christ now stands, but if you open not, he is ready to be gone. Has he not stood many hours, even till his head be filled with dew? &c. He will not stand always, the spouse herself cannot expect it; he will be gone, and then, though ye seek him, ye shall not find him, and whither he goes shall ye not come.

Has he not long sought to gather you? &c. Well, if ye will not be gathered, your souls that will not entertain him shall be laid desolate; shall become cages for unclean birds, dens for the devouring lion. Ye shall no more see him till he appear in the clouds to render vengeance for this disobedience.

Has he not long stood, discovering to ye in the gospel the things that concern your peace, of which this is the sum in short, to admit Christ? If ye will not know, if ye will not obey, the day will come when desolation and misery shall seize upon those hearts that would not give Christ possession. This day of Christ's visitation, wherein he stands at your hearts, will be turned into a dismal night, wherein Christ shall be hid from your eyes.

Has not Christ come to you these three years, yea, many threes, seeking fruit? If he find not this the fruit of his coming, of his standing, if the issue of it be not your opening to Christ, that dreadful sentence will follow, 'Cut them down.'

If you will still harden your hearts, if this error still prevail, Christ is admitted far enough, more of him in your hearts and lives is needless. If you will not know his ways; his ways of conversion and regeneration, wherein Christ is admitted; his ways of holiness and gospel obedience, wherein Christ is entertained and honoured, his patience will end in wrath. He will swear, those sinners that will not let Christ enter into their hearts, shall never enter into his rest.

Now he stands, this is the day wherein Christ draws near your hearts; if ye will not know, &c. Christ the light of life, of hope, of glory, of happiness will be gone, you shall see him no more. He stands now for your answer, and his posture tells you, if he be denied, he is ready to depart.

Use 1. *Information.* This observation acquaints us with several other truths, which, as so many corollaries, follow from it:

1. The riches of the goodness and compassion of Christ to sinners. Does he, though he find the hearts of sinners shut against him, yet stand and knock for admittance? Oh what riches of mercy are here! It may justly seem much that the Lord, after such an affront, should vouchsafe but a look to such sinners; how much more to come, &c. It is more than such wretches could expect, that the Lord should send to us, how much more that he should come himself, &c. For what can the Lord expect from us, or what advantage can he gain by us? That he should come, draw near to us so full of provocations; that he should stand, shew himself willing to come under our roof; that he should wait to be gracious when grace is contemned; that he should knock, use all means to gain admission, knock so long, so loud, so often!—Oh the riches of his goodness, the wonders of his condescension, the greatness of his mercy, the infiniteness of his patience! What like proceedings do we find amongst the sons of men? The Lord's ways are not as our ways. The Lord leaves not himself without a witness; gives clear testimony that he is abundant in longsuffering, not willing that sinners should perish, but that they should come to repentance; that they should be as happy as that which is the happiness of heaven, as the presence of Christ can make them.

2. This shews the heinousness of their sin who do not open unto Christ. Oh that ye would consider it and be affected with it! The light of this observation discovers it to be loaded with those aggravations that make sin exceeding sinful, exceeding grievous. Since Christ stands and knocks, if you do not open, you sin against means, against mercy, against knowledge, and that wilfully and inexcusably.

(1.) Against means. Christ comes and knocks; what means is there that he uses not to gain admission? He knocks by checks of conscience, by acts of providence, by mercies and afflictions, by the ministry of the word, by the law and by the gospel, by the motions of his Spirit. Here is a burden of aggravations in one bundle, able to oppress any soul that has but any competent sense of sin. When you open not to Christ thus knocking, you sin against conscience, against providence, against mercies, against judgments, against law, against gospel, against resolutions and purposes raised in you by the Spirit of grace, and against that Holy Spirit itself, grieving, opposing, resisting it. What could the Lord have done more to you, that he has not done? as he says of his vineyard. See the issue, Isa. v. 5, 6.

(2.) Against mercy; mercy in its choice appearances and manifestations to the world; against not only the mercy of God, but the indulgence of Christ. What more grievous offence than that which is against love, against mercy?

[1.] Condescending mercy: he stoops so low as to stand at a polluted heart. [2.] Preventing mercy: against Christ drawing near you, coming to you, standing at your heart. [3.] Free mercy: against Christ, ready, willing to come in. [4.] Forbearing mercy: Christ waiting to be gracious.

If ever the Lord open your eyes to see sin in its own colours, this will make it appear exceeding sinful. How does the Lord aggravate Solomon's sins from such a consideration! 1 Kings xi. 9. Was he angry because he had appeared to him twice? Oh, how do you provoke him to anger, to whom he has appeared so often, who have so long, so often, both heard and seen him, seen him standing, heard him knocking!

(3.) Against knowledge. You have heard, you have been convinced, that Christ hath both stood and knocked at your hearts. If you would deny it, your own consciences will accuse you. The providence of God in many acts testifies it. The gospel, preached so long amongst you, bears witness of it. The Spirit of Christ, that has so long strived with you, brings in this evidence. It remains as writ with a pen of iron and point of a diamond, writ in great, and large, and lasting characters, in characters of greater, larger guilt. If you open not to Christ, you sin against all this light; and you know how near a sin against knowledge borders upon that sin that leads irrecoverably to outer darkness, John ix. 41.

(4.) Wilfully. Christ comes and stands; he stands and knocks. Why does he not enter? Why, you will not open. He stands, he is ready to take possession; why is he yet without? Why, you will not give it him. If Christ did not stand, did not knock, you might pretend a better reason why ye do not open. But when he stands ready to enter, what can be alleged why he is not admitted, but because you will not open? Oh, methinks any sensible heart should tremble to come so near the brink of that dreadful place, Heb. xii. 26, 27.

(5.) Inexcusably. Christ standing and knocking leaves the sinner that opens not to him without excuse. 'If I had not come to them,' John xv. 22. If Christ had not stood and knocked, your sin had been less; there had been some excuse why you did not admit him. But since he has come so often, stood so long, knocked so loud, and yet is not admitted, now there remains no more cloak. There is no excuse will be sufficient to cover this sin, so great is it. The height and depth is such as you can say nothing, can do nothing, to cloak it.

If a heathen should be asked at the day of judgment, why didst thou not open to Christ? why didst thou not entertain him? Alas, may he say, I never heard of him; he came not, he stood not, he knocked not at my heart; the gospel never discovered him to me in this posture. Ay! the heathen have a fair excuse; the Lord will proceed with them upon some other account. Oh, but when the Lord, the Judge of heaven and earth, shall turn his speech to thee! Thou enjoyedst the gospel, thou sawest me standing, heardest me knocking at thy heart so many Sabbaths, so many years together, why didst thou not open to me? Why didst thou shut me out? What answer canst thou make? Surely, then, thy case will be like his in the parable. Thou must needs be speechless; here is not the least colour of an excuse for thee. If Christ be not admitted now, nothing will be left thee then but a fearful expectation of judgment and fury. Oh consider it before it be too late! You see the grievousness of the sin; though it seem light now, it will lie heavy one day, and every of these considerations will lie upon thy soul as a mountain. Oh make haste to prevent it by making haste to open to Christ!

This shews a reason why the Lord's wrath falls heavier upon those that enjoy the gospel, those at whose hearts Christ stands and knocks, than upon others; why he makes their plagues wonderful; why he appears more terrible, both in his threatenings and executions, against them than the rest of the sons of men. Here is a sufficient plea to justify the Lord's severity.

He does more for them: he stands and knocks to be admitted by them, and they shutting him out, it is a righteous thing with the Lord, upon this account, to pour more vengeance upon them.

Obj. We see those who live in drunkenness, swearing, uncleanness, profaneness, disobedience, contempt of the gospel and its ministers, despising of holiness, aud hereby they shew they shut out Christ; we see them enjoy health, peace, plenty, and prosper in the world as much as any.

Ans. It is true. God may exempt them from temporal judgments a while, for the elect's sake who are amongst them, who have been persuaded to open.

But in the mean time he curses their blessings, Mal. ii. 2, Zech. v. Besides, he sends a plague into their hearts; he gives them up to spiritual judgments, blindness of mind, hardness of heart, searedness of conscience, a reprobate sense. And these are the greatest plagues on this side hell; and however the sinner be senseless of them, they are the portion, and will be of every one that perseveres to shut out Christ.

Moreover, he gives Satan a commission to load their souls with chains of darkness, to make them sure against the judgment of the great day. So they lie fettered, and then the furnace of everlasting burnings will be heated seven times hotter for them. This is, and will be, the doom of all that continue to shut out Christ.

Use 2. *Exhortation.* The light of this observation leads us to several duties; it calls for several things from all of us.

1. Does Christ stand? And will you sit still in your evil ways, not move towards him when he waits at your hearts? Will you lie down on the bed of security, take your rest in carnal enjoyments, wallow in the pleasures of sin and the world, and not stir out of your old posture, your old courses? Is this all the respect Christ must have from you: to sit still when he stands, to lie down when he stays for you, to rest yourselves in the embraces of the world and your lusts? Must these be entertained while Christ stands without? Must Christ stay your leisure if he will be admitted? Must he stay till you have done with the world, till you have your fill of sin? Is this all you care for Christ? Have you dealt thus with Satan, with the world, with your lusts? Did they stand and wait so long before they had entertainment? Oh, well were it with sinners if they were as averse, as disrespectful of sin, yea, of Satan himself, as they are of Christ! But oh, what guilt is here, what a wickedness is here in the mean time! Christ shall stand without when these are let in. Oh, will you continue in this wickedness? Will you increase this guilt? Will you run farther off when Christ comes and stands so near you? Oh he is patient, says the wretched heart, though I neglect him a little, and follow my worldly sinful humours; he will not be gone, he can bear with sinners and wait long. Oh the dreadful abuse of Christ's indulgence! Is this all the use you make of his patience, to encourage you to let him still stand without? Will you thus provoke the Lord? Will you thus turn his grace into wantonness? When mercy and patience abounds in Christ, will you make your sins superabound? How can you do this great wickedness, and sin against Christ? Far be it from you thus to requite the Lord. Since he stands, cast off sin, cast off the world, cast off every weight that so easily besets you, that is so apt to hinder you. Arise, make haste towards him!

2. Does he knock? Take heed, then, you neglect not his knocking. Will you stop your ears that you should not hear him? Will you busy yourselves so in the world, as the noise of your employments shall make you deaf to

Christ's knock? Or, if you hear it, will you turn aside to such cares, thoughts, delights, as shall make you forget it, regardless of it? Beware of this, if either Christ or your souls be dear to you.

Take care you neglect not, when Christ knocks by conscience, of refusing Christ, of going on in sin against checks of conscience. If you do, and persevere so doing, one of these will follow: your conscience will either be wounded or seared. One of these you may expect. The Lord can send a hell into the conscience, and set that soul a-fire that shuts him out. We have sad instances of it, and for what, but going against conscience? Or else the Lord will give thee up to a seared conscience. That conscience that will be senseless, shall be senseless. That will be Christ's sentence, 'He that is unjust, let him be so;' he that is senseless, let him be so: so without sense, as if seared with a hot iron, 1 Tim. iv. 2. As Christ has his seal whereby he marks his people, 2 Tim. ii. 19, so Satan has his; and those that are thus seared, the Lord gives them over to Satan. He hereby brands them, marks them for his own. Beware your disregard of Christ's knocking by conscience; end not thus.

Neglect not Christ's knocking by providence, especially by mercies. These are as sweet-smelling myrrh, which he leaves upon the handles of the lock, as the spouse expresses it, Cant. v. 5. If ye will not regard when Christ knocks by the hand of mercy, you will provoke him to take his rod, his rod of iron: a knock with this may break you to pieces, Ps. ii.

Neglect not Christ knocking by afflictions. If Christ enter not, after promises, resolutions, either you will provoke the Lord to change his rod into one more weighty, more smarting, and to double his strokes, and to punish yet seven times more, as he threatens, and make your plagues wonderful; or else to give you over as desperate, and to say, He will afflict no more, he will knock no more. And though blinded sinners, not acquainted with the Lord's paths, think that a good condition to be freed from affliction, yet is there scarce any dispensation that speaks more wrath than when the Lord says, as Isa. i. 5, ' Why should ye be smitten any more?' It is as if a father, after all means used to reclaim a rebellious son prove ineffectual, should resolve to trouble himself no more with him, should say, He regards not me, &c. Let him take his course, let him run on till he comes to the gallows. How can a man testify more anger than thus? Why thus the Lord, as the extremity of his indignation: Hosea iv. 14, ' I will not punish your daughters,' &c.

Especially, neglect not Christ when he knocks by the word. If the sound of the gospel move you not, there is little hope for you. If you neglect this, expect that one day Christ will as much neglect you, Prov. i. 24, 33.

Neglect not Christ's knockings by his Spirit. These motions are Christ's messengers; they are sent to prepare his way, to try what entertainment the Master may expect. If you resist, suppress, quench, choke these, Christ will look for no better at your hands, if himself were in your power. When men look upon Christ's message by his Spirit, as Elisha did upon the king of Israel, and use these motions as he did the messenger, how, think you, does he resent it? 2 Kings vi. 32. If, when Christ's messengers come, these motions of the Spirit, ye do give order to shut the door, take care to hold them fast at the door, and for this reason, because the sound of his Master's feet, &c.; if you shut out the harbingers, and use them so coarsely, Christ knows what himself may expect, he will not trouble you with his company. Take heed this be not the issue of your quenching motions, suppressing inclinations, suffering resolutions to vanish. If you use his harbingers, those that bespeak his entertainment, he may interpret it thus, it is because the sound of my master's feet, &c. Oh how will this provoke Christ! As you would not be found quenchers of the Spirit, resisters of the Holy Ghost, take heed of neglecting, suppressing these motions of the Spirit.

3. Does he stand and knock? Oh make haste to open to him. I shall urge this more largely when the text leads me directly to it. Now a word of it briefly. Why does he stand and knock, but that he may be admitted? Will you still shut him out? Will you still frustrate the gracious intention of Christ? Will you do your endeavour to make him come short of his end? Shall he stand so long, shall he knock so much in vain? Shall all his patience, all his condescensions be in vain, except it be to render you more miserable, to vindicate the righteousness of his wrath in destroying you, and to leave you without excuse in the great day of account? Christ will secure his glory; he will take care it be not in vain to him, whatever you may render it to your own souls.

If the issue of his patience and longsuffering be not the glory of his mercy, in making you happy with his presence, it must be the glory of his justice in making you miserable, by departing from you. And will you provoke him to depart? Shall sin and the world be dearer to you than Christ? Must Christ be excluded, that these may still have entertainment? Oh what horrible unkindness is this to Christ, what cruelty to your souls! Heaven and earth may be astonished at it, if hardened hearts, if careless sinners will not; and to these the Lord appeals, Jer. ii. 12, 13. You hereby forsake Christ, the fountain of living waters, &c., joy, comfort, peace, glory. You forsake the fountain; and when the spring of all would place itself in your hearts, you shut it out. This is one great evil: and withal you hew cisterns; you prefer the cistern before the fountain, earth before heaven, sin before Christ; broken cisterns before the eternal fountain; cisterns that will hold no water all, before the fountain that flows everlastingly with waters of life. If you will not consider this, if you will not be afraid of such a dreadful evil, if you will not be astonished at it, heaven and earth may be astonished, and greatly afraid, to see their great Creator set at nought by a wretched man. They may be horribly afraid, lest a provocation of this nature should move the Lord not only to destroy man, but the whole creation; and in his just wrath turn heaven and earth, and all wretched man has benefit by, into confusion and nothing. If man will be so senseless as not to consider this, the senseless creatures will rise up in judgment and condemn him. If sinners will make no answer, take no notice of Christ standing, knocking at their hearts, the dumb creatures will find a mouth to justify God, when he sends him to eternal ruin, when he casts him into everlasting burnings.

Oh consider this! Let the wonderful patience of Christ in standing, let the gracious importunity of Christ in knocking, lead you to repent, lead you to the door, persuade you to open. The Lord makes use of the wonderful strangeness of his condescension as a motive, and oh that it might prove a powerful motive to open to him, Jer. xxxi. See how his bowels yearn to wretched sinners; and suppose him, while he stands at thy heart, to express himself as he does to Ephraim, ver. 20; and then hear him expostulating, wondering at thy delay to open to him, ver. 22; and then consider what a motive he adds to enforce thee to open. 'For the Lord hath,' &c. That Christ should stand and knock, that Christ should seek to thee, it is a new thing, a thing so strange and wonderful, as the like is seldom seen on the earth. It is as if a woman should offer love to a man. תסובב *ambit*, does solicit, does woo, does seek love, when she should be sought to; forgets herself, her sex, her condition, against all custom, against all nations on earth. Thus far does the Lord stoop, thus strangely does Christ condescend, when he comes and offers love to sinners. It is as if a woman should compass, &c.; it is he that should be sought to, yet he seeks to thee. It is his love that men and angels should desire above life; yet he offers love when it is not desired. He seems to forget himself (if we may so say) when he so strangely condescends to seek to sinners, to stand and knock at their hearts. This is a new thing, a wonderful thing; and since his love herein is so strange, so admirable, it should be a strong motive to sinners to entertain it. Oh how long wilt thou go about, O backsliding sinner? How long shall Christ stand and knock, before he be regarded? When wilt thou open to him, who has stooped below himself to come to thee? Remember, as his condescension is strange and wonderful in seeking admission, so his indignation will be strange and wonderful if thou dost not open. Since Christ comes and stands, make haste to open.

So we pass from the positive proposition, the first part, to the conditional promise, the second part of the text. Herein consider both its form and matter.

1. The form. It is propounded conditionally. Christ's presence and communion with him is offered upon condition.

2. As to the matter of it. It consists, as do all hypothetical propositions, of two parts; the antecedent and the consequent. In

(1.) The consequent, we have the things promised. These are two; [1.] Christ's entrance, ' I will come in;' [2.] His entertainment, and that is mutual. He will entertain the soul, and will accept of the entertainment which he enables the soul to provide for him : ' and will sup with him, and he with me.'

(2.) In the antecedent, we have the conditions upon which these things are promised, and these are two: [1.] Hearing, ' If any man hear my voice;' [2.] Opening, ' and open the door.' Of these in order.

1. From the form of the proposal, in that these things are promised conditionally, take this

Obs. Some gospel promises are conditional. Not only promises of outward blessings, common mercies, but promises of spiritual, special, and distinguishing mercies. Not only promises of the law, which belong to the covenant of works, but promises of the gospel, special branches and articles of the covenant of grace. Such is this in the text, a promise of Christ, of the gospel, of spiritual and special mercies, of the presence of Christ and communion with him. These are offered conditionally; and the premise is plainly, expressly, and *in terminis* conditional. ' If,' &c. I shall not insist long on this, nor enter into the controversy started in this age, but rather explain it in such a way as may prevent mistakes, and leave no room for any controversy; for those who would walk with a right foot in the way of the gospel, and prefer truth and peace before contention, must be careful to avoid controversy.

Those things that are annexed to gospel promises in the form of conditions, they are not conditions in these five respects; remove but those ingredients from them, which indeed the Lord never mixed with them, and there need be no scruple at all in granting the promises to be conditional. They are not conditions in respect

(1.) Of merit. When the condition is performed, we do not thereby deserve the Lord should bestow the mercy promised. ' When we have done all, we are unprofitable servants.' Such conditions are a popish imagination, they never entered into the Lord's thoughts, they are a high disparagement to the freeness of grace, and stain the glory of it.

(2.) Of dependence. It is not in the will, in the power of man, to perform by his own strength what is annexed to any gospel promise. If he that does promise and require did not give strength to perform, neither promise nor condition would be performed for ever. He requires we should hear his voice and open to him, but we can do neither without him; it is he that worketh in us both to will and to do. Conditions depending upon man's will and power are the proud inventions of Pelagians; there is no place, no ground for them in the gospel.

(3.) Of inducement. When that which is annexed to the promise, in form of a condition, is performed through the strength of Christ, the Lord is not hereby moved, induced hereby, as we are, to accomplish the promise. It is inconsistent with his divine perfections to be moved by any thing *ab extra*, without. Those expressions which seem to intimate our moving of God are after the manner of men; and when we speak properly, they must be explained in a way becoming the perfections, the majesty of God.

(4.) Of uncertainty. Man, when he propounds a condition, is uncertain whether or no it will be performed. But there is no such uncertainty with God; he knows from eternity who will hear his voice, who will open to him. The accomplishment of the promises is not suspended for the uncertainty of the condition, as it is amongst men, but for the incapacity of the subject, because, till they perform what he requires, they are not capable of what he promises.

(5.) Of obligement. When we perform that which is required in the promise, God is not thereby obliged to accomplish the promise, without the interposal of pardoning mercy, *e. g.* when we hear, when we open, this lays no engagement upon Christ to enter. Our slowness to open does more disengage him, more provoke him to depart, than our opening, accompanied with such provocation, obliges him to enter. These things I might easily open and prove at large, if I thought it seasonable; but let this suffice at present. If you take not conditions in such a sense as is made up of one or all these respects, it casts not the least shadow upon the glory of free grace to grant some promises to be conditional.

By a condition, understand no more than a necessary antecedent, or a duty to which the Lord will enable his people before the performance of his promise; and there need be no scruple, no controversy about the terms, the promises may be counted, with safety enough, to be conditional.

2. And so we pass from the form to the matter of this proposition, and in it first take notice of the antecedent, containing the conditions of this promise; the first whereof is hearing Christ's voice, 'If any man hear.' Here we might observe, that opening depends on hearing, and that men are backward to hear Christ's voice; hence he makes an *if* of it, ' If any man ;' as also that Christ not only stands and knocks, but calls at the heart, makes use of his voice to procure admission. But to waive a particular discourse of each of these, we shall comprise the sense and meaning of these words in this, and a little insist on it.

Obs. Those that will have Christ to come into them, must hear his voice. It is the means to this end, it is the condition of this blessed privilege, and so proposed in the text.

' Hear, and your souls shall live.' Christ's entering into the soul, is as the soul's entering into the body. As that is life to the body, so Christ is life to the soul, when he enters, unites himself to it, and becomes its life, the fountain, the principle of spiritual life. Now the way for Christ to enter is by hearing: 'Hear, and your souls shall live.' So Christ comes not in till the heart be open, and it opens not till it hear the voice of Christ; so that those who will have Christ to come in, must hear his voice.

Two things explained will make this truth clear. (1.) What is the voice of Christ? (2.) What is it to hear his voice? For the

(1.) Christ's voice is that which you hear principally in the gospel. He gives some intimation of his will by conscience, by providence; but in the gospel he speaks out, there his voice is heard clearly, distinctly, there he speaks aloud; particularly, there you hear

[1.] His voice of command. He exercises his authority as King and Lord of the world, sends out his royal edicts, his commands. And this is the sense of them, that sinners would open to him, Isa. lv. 1; come and open that the waters of life may flow into your souls, that the spring of life, and joy, and happiness may seat itself in your hearts.

Oh, but these waters are precious, they cost dear, &c.

He has left his commands on record in the word, in the Scriptures, and he sends his messengers daily to publish them. To disobey him, is to affront him in his highest dignity, in his royal office, to rebel against the King of kings, &c.

All the commands to believe in Christ, are commands to open to him; for to believe in Christ is to receive him, and to receive him is to open to him. This is the great command of the gospel, to open to him, John xiv. 1, vi. 26. Christ, who might exercise his sovereignty, &c., had rather shew it by commanding. The whole creation is at the command of Christ; there is not one creature in heaven or earth but punctually obeys him, except wretched man only. And wilt thou be one of these rebels, worse than the plants and trees that grow at his command, worse than the beasts and birds that move at his command? Wilt thou be worse than the beasts that perish? Wilt thou be a rebel especially in this point? Wilt thou shut out the King of glory when he commands thee to open to him? It is no great matter he commands; it is but to open. Nor is it any loss to thee that he commands; it is to open to him whose presence will make thee happy. Oh that you would hear Christ's voice commanding. This is his voice of authority.

[2.] The voice of Christ threatening. He sets an edge upon his command, and that it may not be slighted, enforces it with threatenings. If thou wilt not hear him now, and open, he threatens he will not hear thee hereafter. Thou wilt find sooner or later a day of distress, when thou wilt have need of Christ, at least death is not far off, &c., and judgment is approaching. How much soever you neglect it now, you will be glad to call to Christ then. Ay! but if you will not hear him now, he threatens he will not hear you then, Prov. i. 27, 28. If you will not open to him on earth, he will not open to you in heaven; if you will shut him out here, he will shut you out there. Time may come when, with the foolish virgins, you may knock and cry, 'Lord, open to us;' but those that regard him not now shall have their doom then, 'Depart from me, I know ye not.' Christ would now entertain, 'I will come in and sup,' but if ye shut him out, the same thing he denounces to you which he threatened, Luke xiv. 24, 'Not one of them shall taste of my supper.'

If you will not open to Christ, who brings with him unsearchable riches, your debts can never be paid; justice will seize on you and cast you into prison, into outer darkness, till you have paid that which can never be discharged, till you have paid the uttermost farthing. If you will not admit Christ, who would make you happy with his presence, you shall be punished with everlasting destruction from the presence of the Lord. If you will not open to him who brings you life, ye shall die in your sins, John viii. 24. Thus the Lord lifts up his voice and threatens sinners, in case they will not open to him: Oh that you would hearken! If ye will not suffer Christ to enter into your hearts, ye shall never enter into his rest. This is his terrible voice; it can rend the rocks, and cause the mountains to tremble. Oh, be not you senseless of it!

[3.] *The voice of Christ promising.* This is Christ's voice in the latter part of the text. There he promises his presence and fellowship with him to all that will open to him; all the joys, the comforts, the bliss, the glory, that the presence of Christ can afford, or communion with him.

The heaven of heavens cannot contain him, he dwells not in temples made with hands; yet if thou wilt open, he promises thy heart shall be his temple, 'I will come in.'

The presence of Christ is the glory and happiness of all that are happy and glorious; this is it which glorifies the saints, and makes the angels blessed, yet this thou shalt have if thou wilt open.

The presence of Christ is light in darkness, and plenty in want, relief in all distresses, comfort in all sad exigencies, life in death, all in all; yet all this thou shalt have, the presence of Christ, and all its blessed attendants, if thou wilt hearken unto him and open.

Communion with Christ is the very heaven of heaven, and that which can make a dark habitation on earth to be as a corner of heaven; but this thou shalt have, if thou wilt hear his voice and open. But of this more fully when we come to the latter part of the text. This is Christ's still voice, the sweet voice of promise; oh that you would hearken to it!

[4.] *The voice of persuasion.* This is it he counsels, this is it he advises; and he urges it, enforces his counsel with many motives and arguments. This is Christ's voice in the verses before the text, ver. 18.

[5.] *The voice of entreaty.* He beseeches sinners with a loud voice to open. He who commanded heaven and earth to issue out of nothing; he who commands the winds and the seas, and they obey him; he who commanded the apostate angels out of his presence, and shut them up in the bottomless pit; he who commanded the earth to open her mouth, and swallow those rebellious sinners, Korah and his accomplices; he who could command thee immediately into hell, and shut thee up in outer darkness: he vouchsafes to beseech thee; this is his voice, 2 Cor. v. 20. Upon what terms an ambassador treats with another state, if by way of threatening, or, which is more strange and unusual, if by way of entreaty, it is as if his master did it. So it is interpreted by us. Ministers of the gospel are Christ's ambassadors; they are sent, employed, authorised by him. He gives them instructions to pray, to beseech sinners, and they do it ὑπὲρ Χριστοῦ, *i. e.* 'in Christ's stead.' It is as if Christ himself should do it; it is as if he should with his own mouth pray, beseech, entreat you to open to him. When the minister comes and entreats you, beseeches, importunes you to abandon those sins that keep out Christ, it is as if Christ himself should do it in person. So it is in our account in embassies amongst men, so it is in Christ's account. It will be in vain to say at the day of judgment, I never heard Christ use any such language, he never entreated; the ministers that we disregard are but men. Ay, but they are Christ's ambassadors, they speak in Christ's stead; and what they speak according to his instructions, he owns it as though it were spoken by himself, and will accordingly vindicate the contempt of it and disobedience to it. You shall then hear what you will not now regard: 'He that heareth you, heareth me;' 'Inasmuch as you did it to one of these, you did it unto me.' It is Christ's voice you hear when you are entreated to open. If you will have him enter, you must hear. And the wonder of Christ's condescension in stooping so low as to beseech you, should be a strong motive to open, or will be a great aggravation of your wickedness if you open not.

[6.] The voice of reproof. This is Christ's voice too, and that which he frequently makes use of when sinners are so slow, so backward to open to him. It is Christ that speaks, Christ the Wisdom of the Father, and there frequently called Wisdom, Prov. i. And that which he speaks is reproof: ver. 23, 'Turn you at my reproof.' He tells sinners how they offend, what the nature of their offence is, how sinful, how provoking, how heavily aggravated, when they refuse to open, when they retain those sins that keep out Christ. The Spirit of Christ in the Scriptures abounds herein; take but briefly three or four instances.

He shews it is a grievous contempt of Christ, a most unworthy slighting and undervaluing of him. The sinner that shuts out Christ (as every one does that lives in sin) values him no more than he that sold him for thirty pieces of silver. For which of you would not open your door were it but to gain thus much? And yet will not open to Christ! Do ye not clearly manifest you think Christ less worth, value him not so much? A goodly price indeed that Christ is prized at by you! Zech. xi. 12. Hereby you shew you value him no more than that wretch that betrayed him; you value him no more than a slave, Exod. xxi. 32. Oh what ground is here for reproof! Will you thus set Christ at nought, and shew yourselves as bad as Judas? Why, this is the way you contemn him as you would do a slave,—nay, as one would not do a slave,—when you will not open to him.

This is against all your relations, engagements, professions as Christians. You call Christ Lord; but what a servant is that who will let his lord stand and knock, and call at the door, but will not stir to open to him! You call him Father; but what a child is that who shuts his father out of doors! Mal. i. 6. While you do thus, whatever you speak of Christ as related to him, that you love him, would obey him, are his servants, his children, these are but pretences and dissembling words. You shew plainly you are gross hypocrites, whatever you say or think, so long as Christ is shut out. Can any without blushing call Christ his Saviour, while he will not open his heart to him? Do ye really count Christ so? or does it not hereby appear it is a mere pretence? Will any man shut his Saviour out of doors? All your pretences to Christ are but hypocritical till this be done.

Further, this is a preferring the devil and the lusts of your hearts before Christ. These, though the vilest evils in earth or hell, have more respect, more honour, more service, more obedience from you, than Christ. When Satan does but intimate his pleasure by some wicked suggestion, forthwith he finds admission; but though Christ call and cry, lift up his voice like a trumpet, command, promise, threaten, persuade, beseech, reprove, he is shut out. When a lust gives but an inkling, insinuates by some sly motion, this is instantly, daily entertained, while Christ stands without. Here is a great respect shewed to Christ indeed, when his mortal, deadly enemies are admitted, entertained, and himself refused, rejected! What iniquity, may he say, do ye find in me, that the devil, and that which is worse than the devil, your lusts, should be preferred before me?

Finally, the whole creation may rise up in judgment against such as exclude Christ, and may condemn them. Christ doth whatever he will in heaven and earth; he opens, and no man shuts; he shuts, and no man opens; he finds no resistance, no opposition, till he come to the heart of man. There is not the least creature in the world but will cast in something to make the judgment of that sinner heavier who opens not to Christ, to aggravate his condemnation who shuts out Christ.

To this effect doth Christ reprove the generation with whom he conversed, Mat. xii. 42. If she would come from the uttermost parts of the earth to see Solomon, sure if he had come so far to visit her, she would with all joy have admitted him. And yet, lo ! a greater than Solomon is here excluded. Christ comes not from the uttermost parts of the earth, but from the highest heaven; not to visit the court of some glorious king, but to seek entrance into a wretched defiled heart; and yet is excluded, it shuts itself. Here is not the queen of Sheba, but the King of glory, excluded; not king Solomon, but Solomon's King, is affronted, excluded by a wretched sinner, by a sinful heart. For this he reproved the Jews then, for this he reproves you now; he comes to his own, and his own receive him not: to his own, to those who have most need of him, most reason to own him. He comes and owns you, by coming to you when he passes by the rest of the world. He comes to his own, &c.

Oh what ground is here for a sharp, a cutting reproof ! This is another way wherein you may hear Christ's voice. Oh let it not be said, ye would have none of my reproof!

(2.) What by hearing. It includes these six things :

[1.] *Attendance.* When he attends diligently to the word preached. When he is serious and conscientious; not as before, customary and careless. When he listens to it as to the great, the eternal concernment of his soul. When he desists from those things that have hindered him from listening diligently to the word in times past. When Christ's voice puts him to a stand. For example: a man riding, running, or otherwise busied, hears some voice that concerns him; he stops his course, stands, and listens. Thus, when Christ speaks to the heart of a sinner, if he hear his voice to any purpose, it puts him to a stand; it takes him off from his immoderate following the world, from his eager pursuit of his lusts; he hushes those cares, thoughts, delights, and that business which made such a noise before, as Christ's voice was not heard or not regarded.

Thus, when Saul heard Christ's voice from heaven, he fell to the earth, Acts ix. His former designs were nonplussed. It is true that voice was extraordinary; but whenever Christ's voice is heard, it has some like effect. The sinner is stopped in his career; his mind and heart are at least for the present taken off from sin and the world; he stands and listens. And till he be put to such a stand, though he may seem to hear, he hears not indeed; his hearing is to little purpose. He that will open unto Christ must thus hear.

[2.] *Belief.* He that hears so as to open, believes it is the voice of Christ he hears. While he counts the word preached the voice of man, he finds many evasions, so as he keeps it off from his heart and conscience. Till he believe it is the voice of Christ, he hears as though he heard not; it is to little purpose, to no great effect, leaves small or no impression. But when he hears it and hearkens to it, as the voice of Christ speaking to him from heaven, then, and not till then, he hears so as he is in the way to open. The men that were with Saul, they 'heard a voice, but saw no man,' ver. 7. They knew not whence it came, nor who it was that spoke. But Saul knew it to be Christ's voice: the voice satisfied him of that; and hence the different effect in them and him. Saul opens, embraces Christ; we read no such thing of them. 'It is the voice of my beloved, says the spouse, Cant. v. 2. If she had not perceived this, she had lain still and not opened to him. While you are filled with conceits that it is but man that speaks, and that he speaks his own thoughts only, and such as prejudice against you, or ill apprehensions of you lead him to; while Satan thus persuades you, he cares not how much you hear. He knows, till you hear the word preached as the voice of Christ, your hearing is as good as no hearing, you are far enough from opening. Till Samuel knew it was the Lord's voice, he run the wrong way.

[3.] Application. If thou wilt hear so as to open, thou must hear Christ's voice as directed to thee in particular. Thou must not put it off to others, and say the word met with such a one, it fell foul upon such a man's sin, was suitable to his condition; but bring it home to thy own heart and conscience, and hear Christ in the ministry of the word speaking to thee, as if he singled thee out and spoke to thee by name. Apply what is delivered in general as though thou heardest Christ telling thee, as Nathan did David, 'Thou art the man,' 2 Sam. xii. 7. It is I Christ intends, it is myself he speaks to; this is my sin, my guilt. It is I that have shut out Christ; it is I that have been so eager on my lusts, so busy in the world to neglect Christ. He now speaks to me, he now calls upon me to open. Till you hear thus, till you thus apply what you hear, you will never open. The voice of Christ, till thus applied, gives but an uncertain sound (as the apostle in another case) nor will you ever prepare to open.

[4.] Consideration. Hear it so as your thoughts may work upon it, as though ye were always hearing. Christ's voice should have such place in your hearts, should be fixed there by frequent meditation, serious consideration of it, as if it were still sounding in your ears. How many souls has non-consideration cut short of Christ! When you mind but the word while it is preached, it slides away as water falling on a rock; it must stay upon the heart, else it will not open. Remember it when you lie down and when you rise up, whatever ye do, wherever you are; let your thoughts represent Christ as still lifting up his voice and calling on you to open to him, as that ancient said of the voice of Christ at the last day, &c. What you hear must stay in your thoughts as though ye were always hearing, as though the voice of Christ were still in your ears, 'Arise and open!' Thus you must hear if you will open.

[5.] Conviction. If ye will hear so as to open, ye must so hear as to be convinced of an absolute necessity of opening. Be convinced that thou art lost, undone, condemned, till thou open to Christ. So Christ tells Laodicea, ver. 17. And it is the condition of every man till Christ be admitted: 'Thou art poor, and blind, and wretched, and miserable;' if death knock before thou open to Christ, there is nothing but hell to be expected, nothing but the wrath of God to seize on thy soul, nothing but the bottomless pit to open and swallow thee for ever. This conviction, which sinners are so backward to admit, which Satan uses all means to put off, is the first step to the door. Till the sinner thus hear as to be thoroughly convinced of his misery while Christ is excluded, there is no hope of opening.

[6.] Persuasion. Then the sinner admits Christ, when he so hears his voice as to be fully persuaded to open to him. The former are but motions towards it; when it comes to this, the heart is open. A sinner's judgment may be convinced that he is miserable while Christ is excluded, and yet the will not persuaded to admit him. For the will has three powers: to consent, to refuse, to suspend its acts. When the understanding is convinced that he is miserable if Christ be not admitted, the will so far follows the understanding as it cannot consent to exclude him, it cannot refuse to admit him, yet it may hang in suspense. But when it so hears as to be persuaded, it hangs off no longer, but opens unto Christ. This is the hearing that Christ calls for, to hear so as to obey, to listen to Christ's voice so as to comply with it; Heb. iii. 8: 'To-day if ye will hear my voice,' &c. When the sinner hears but does not obey, he hears but so as to harden his heart; his heart is stone against Christ; no passage for him through it, no entrance by it. But when he so hears as to be persuaded, so hears Christ's voice as to obey it, to open to him when he calls, then he hears so as Christ enters. Thus you see how many ways Christ makes his voice audible, and how you may hear so as Christ may enter; by which the observation is clear.

Use. Information. This shews the sad condition of many amongst us who profess Christ. Many there are who bear the name of Christians, who yet shut Christ out of doors, who never opened their hearts unto him. Such are they who care not to hear his voice, such are they who are careless in hearing it. The light of this truth discovers these to be such as shut out Christ. If he enter not but by hearing, then those that will not hear, care not how they hear, how seldom, how carelessly, do hereby shew Christ is yet without, he never yet came into them. They are not yet under the influence of this promise, they are far from the condition of it; and consequently without Christ, without life, without hope, without God in the world. Particularly,

1. Those who neglect to hear when Christ speaks, who will not take the opportunities to hear his voice, so often as they are offered. A small occasion will keep them from hearing the word preached; though Christ speaks here, in the ministry of the word, if his voice be to be heard anywhere in the world. Divers there are who think once a day enough (though they have but this day once a week), nay, so profane are some, they think it too much; yet such will think themselves wronged if they be not counted Christians. Do they deserve the name of Christians who shut Christ out of doors? Let your consciences judge. And do not they shut out Christ who will not so much as hear his voice when he calls upon them to open? How often has Christ, by his unworthy messenger, reproved this sin, this woful contempt of Christ in this place! And yet the thinness of our assembly is a sad testimony the voice of Christ is little regarded, the reproof of Christ is set at nought.

Can you shew more contempt of Christ than to refuse to hear him when he speaks? And does he speak more plainly otherwise to the world than in the ministry of the word? What! not hear a voice from heaven, not hear the voice of Christ speaking from heaven; not hear the voice of Christ speaking to you, not hear the voice of Christ calling on you to open to him! Shall Christ stoop so low as to utter his voice in all kind of expressions? Shall he threaten, promise, reprove, complain, yea, entreat vile worms? And will they not so much as give him the hearing? Do ye not affront Christ enough by shutting him out? Will you not so much as hear him when he beseeches you to let him in? Oh the wonder of Christ's patience, that some remarkable judgment does not cut off such a Christ-contemner! It is a sad complaint he makes, that his report was not believed. More grievous may his complaint be, that his report is not so much as heard.

But it is like many of those whom this concerns are not now in hearing. Well, they will not hear Christ now; but time will come, if reformation prevent it not, when they shall hear Christ speak in another tone. No more 'Open unto me,' no more of that; but 'Depart from me; depart, ye cursed.' In the mean time this is your misery,—you shut out Christ now, and Christ will shut you out hereafter; you will not hear him now, he will not hear you hereafter. Here is misery enough for them, and grief enough for those whom Christ sends to them,—that which was the prophet's of old: 'If ye will not hear,' &c., Jer. xiii. 17.

2. For *conviction* to those who hear indeed, but so as it is evident they do not open, Christ does not enter. It is not every kind of hearing that makes way for Christ's entering, but that described, that intended. Those, therefore, do not open, Christ does not enter,—

(1.) Who hear carelessly, as though they heard not, as though it were not of such concernment as indeed it is; who hear customarily, negligently. When Christ enters, the blessing enters; but there is a curse hangs over those who do the work, &c., Jer. xlviii. 15. If they who are negligent in destroying God's enemies are blameworthy, then sure those who are negligent in saving their own souls are much more so, to which hearing Christ's voice is so necessary.

(2.) Who hear it, but not as the voice of Christ. There is a power, a majesty, in the voice of Christ; and those that hear it as such will hear it so, so as they would attend to what is powerful and majestic. See how it is described Ps. xxix. If you hear it as the voice of the Lord, it will be evident by like effects; it shakes, you will tremble at it. If you never so heard it, Christ never yet entered. It is such a heart which the Lord chooses for his temple, Isa lxvi. Your hearts are not yet Christ's temple, you never had such respect to him as to open to him, if you do not so respect his word as to tremble at it. He never had such respect to you as to enter, as to take possession of you, if his voice have not been so powerful as to make you tremble at it.

(3.) Who hear it, but apply it not. Christ comes not home to your souls till the word be brought home to your hearts. While you put it off, you shut Christ out; while you do not apply the word to yourselves, as directed to you in particular, Christ comes to your ears, he comes not into your hearts. If the word abides not in you, Christ abides not in you, he comes not there. Now it is so far from abiding, as it has no entrance unless it be applied.

(4.) Who hear, but consider not, make it not their meditation. Where Christ is entertained, he is not contemned. But what contempt is this of Christ, to cast his word behind your backs, and mind it no longer than it is sounding in your ears! Are not the words of Christ worthy to be thought of? Those that shut out the thoughts of his word, so as not to make them their meditation, it is plain they shut Christ out of their hearts. Shall he lift up his voice to the unworthy sons of men, and shall not what he speaks be remembered? Shall it not be laid to heart? So far will he be from blessing you with his presence, as he will even 'curse your blessings,' Mal. ii. 2. Not only those who refuse to hear, but those who hear and lay it not to heart, are under this curse. Their blessings, their enjoyments, even the gospel itself, will prove curses to such. That is the bitterest curse, which curses our blessings. A blessing turned into a curse is the most dreadful curse. Yet this is their portion who lay not the word to heart; instead of enjoying Christ, they inherit the curse. It is a cursed heart, &c., a heart that Christ never entered into. Though you will not think of his word, Christ will remember. Though you will not find time to meditate on it, Christ will find time to call you to an account for it; for thus slighting him, not giving entertainment to his word in your thoughts, you shut him out of your hearts.

(5.) Who hear not so as to be convinced of their necessity of opening; will not be convinced of their sin, their misery, which should possess them with apprehensions of a necessity to open; will not believe but they have opened already, though the temper of their hearts and course of their lives testify against them; shut their ears against that voice which tells them of sin and wrath; think this is the way to be miserable, when it is the first step out of it; look upon him who would lead them to the sight of their misery, while they live in sin, and so without Christ, as he did on the prophet, 'Hast thou found me, O mine enemy?' judge him uncharitable, no friend to them, count him their enemy because he tells them this truth, that they are wretched till born again, miserable while they live in sin, because Christ lives not in them.

When thoughts of sin and misery seize on their hearts, they make not use thereof to lead them to Christ, they are not quiet till they have stifled them. While you thus shut out conviction, you shut out Christ, Heb. xii. 13. This is the property of God's word, the efficacy of Christ's voice. And this effect it must have before you enter into his rest; as the connection with the 11th verse shews, before Christ enter into you to give you rest. Till this conviction of sin and misery have emptied the heart of high thoughts, good conceits of its natural estate, it is too full of them to open, there is no room for Christ in such a heart.

(6.) Who hear not so as to be persuaded to open; listen to the voice of Christ, but obey it not, comply not with it. This is no hearing, in Scripture language. He that obeys not, hears not. So inseparable should these be, as one is put for the other.

Then you hear Christ's voice to purpose, when you are persuaded to admit Christ upon his own terms, so as to thrust out every sin, so as to take his yoke, so as to resolve upon all the ways of holiness. Till then you do not hearken unto Christ's voice, for these are joined, Ps. lxxxi. 13. And while you thus hearken not to Christ, you reject him, ver. 11. You declare hereby you will none of Christ, you shut him out. Christ enters not till his voice be thus heard. And if you thus hear it not, it is plain you have not yet opened, Christ has not yet entered.

Pass we from the first condition, hearing, to the second, opening. 'And open the door.' Hence take this

Obs. Those that would have Christ to enter must open to him. It is not Christ's ordinary way to come in to sinners as he came to the disciples, when the door was shut. No; he requires us to open if we will have him to come in; the everlasting gates must be lift up, &c., Ps. xxiv. 7, 9. The Lord there calls upon his people to prepare for the admission of Christ; their hearts are these everlasting gates; not like those of the material temple, which endured but for a season, but these are immortal, must endure to everlasting; these must be lift up; he repeats the command. And this repetition denotes two things, as we learn, Gen. xli. 32; it was doubled for the certainty, the celerity of it. It signifies the like here, certainty on Christ's part; he will surely enter if admission be granted. Celerity on our part, we must speedily open that the King of glory may enter.

Quest. But what is it to open the door? In what manner must we open? These explained, the truth will be clear. For the

1. Take it in these severals.

(1.) He that will open must come to the door; no opening at a distance.

All by nature are far from opening. If ye will lift up these gates, ye must come to them.

They, then, are far from opening, who lie down securely in their natural condition; who are at rest there, and cry Peace, peace to themselves, whatever the word say to the contrary; who are asleep in a sinful state, and there dream with Laodicea, that they are rich, &c. This was her condition when Christ here calls upon her to open; and it is the condition of all men by nature till the voice of Christ awaken them. They say, as those, Jer. ii. 31, 'We are lords,' &c. These are far from coming to the door; this is not the way to open.

Those also that sit in the seat of wickedness, fix themselves in their evil ways, will not be removed out of them; will not leave intemperance, worldliness, profaneness, swearing; neither mercies nor judgments, neither promises nor threatenings, neither commands nor entreaties, neither Christ's rod nor his word will make them rise out of sin; they sit still, they are far from opening.

Those also, who, when they are roused, awakened, and seem to be in a fair way of coming to open, instead of coming forward, go backward, run another way. Such are those, who, having some sense of sin and misery, some trouble of mind, some disquietment of conscience, instead of coming to open to Christ, turn aside to the world, or run to their merry companions, or quiet their hearts with some outward comfort, or build up some unsound peace upon unsafe grounds. So their latter end is worse than the beginning. They ran well at first, what hindered them? What turned them backward? These are further from opening than before: they run further from the door instead of coming to it.

Those that come but half way. Such are those who, having got some knowledge of Christ, of gospel truths, and having taken up a profession of Christ, and performing some outward duties, such as may quiet their consciences, and get the repute of Christians, they set up their rest here. Oh, but you must go further, else you will never come at the door, never open to Christ. This is but, with Agrippa, to be almost persuaded to be a Christian. You are yet a great way from the door; you must come to it if you will open.

(2.) He that will open must take away the bars, remove those bolts which make fast the door. No gate in the world can be so bolted, so blocked up, as a sinner's heart is against Christ. Satan is the porter, the strong man armed, he keeps the door. There is a Cerberus in every man's heart; he must be removed, cast out, else no opening.

Then there is the world, that blocks up the door; it is as a rampart of earth cast up against it to secure it. You must make your way through this, turn it aside, that you may come to open to Christ. The thoughts, cares, delights, desires, love of the world and the things of it, how do they block up the way! These must be digged through, cast off, else no opening, no passage to Christ or for him.

Then there is the flesh and all the lusts of it, every one a strong bolt to make the heart fast against Christ. A worldly lust, or proud, or unclean, or intemperate, or revengeful; any one of these, or those many more than can be numbered, is enough to keep the heart shut. Each of these must be plucked out of the heart if it open, if Christ enter.

Then there is blindness of mind, ignorance, spiritual darkness. This is a great security to the door; the sinner cannot find it, and so he is not like to open. He that walks in darkness knows not whither he goes.

Then there is hardness of heart, a heart of stone, as it is called. This is a stone wall raised against the door to strengthen it. This rock must be divided, this stony temper must be dissolved if Christ enter. The heart of stone that has so long continued in thy flesh, that has so long resisted the word, the Spirit, it must be broken that Christ may enter.

Then, to mention no more, there is self-sufficiency, self-dependence, self-confidence, self-conceitedness, imaginations and conceits of his good name, good meanings, honest dealings, religious performances; the heart is so filled with these, there is no room to open, no room for Christ to enter. The heart must be emptied of these, they must be whipped out, before he make thy heart his temple. This course Christ takes with Laodicea that she may open. Whatever thou thinkest, thou, &c. These imaginations are strongholds which make sure the passage against Christ; these must be battered, cast down, and the heart laid low in his own thoughts. Here is need of ordnance to make a breach, here is need of those weapons which are mighty through God, 2 Cor. x. 4. All these bolts and impediments that block up the way must be removed, &c.

(3.) He that will open, must put to his hand and lift up the latch: there must be the hand of faith; this is the essence of the act we speak of. To open, is to be willing to admit Christ upon his own terms; to consent to receive Christ, &c. What those terms are, I have shewed heretofore.

Obj. But it appears by the premises, that sinners of themselves are not able to open, the heart is too fast shut. There are so many difficulties, so much opposition from within and without, that it exceeds a natural man's power, especially since he is without strength, without spiritual life, not only unable to do this, but to will it. And therefore it seems strange the Lord should make this the condition of a promise, that he should call upon men to do that which they cannot do. Why does the Lord call upon sinners to open, who of themselves cannot open? This seems strange and to no purpose.

Ans. 1. Sinners were once able, but they have disabled themselves; they had power, but have wilfully lost it. The Lord enabled man in his creation to hear his voice and obey it. We all had power in Adam to obey Christ's voice, but in him we sinned that power away. Though we have lost power to obey, no reason to think God should lose his power to command. The proceedings amongst men makes this apparent: if you entrust a man with a sum of money, and he go and spend it in gaming, drinking, and unwarrantable courses; will you not, therefore, think it reasonable to demand it of him? Will you lose power to ask what he owes ye, because he has prodigally spent it? Shall it be thus amongst men, and is not the Lord as righteous in this proceeding? He entrusted us with power to do what he requires, we have sinned it away; no such prodigals as sinners. But shall this hinder the Lord from demanding what is due? No; nothing more reasonable, nothing more righteous; the Lord has many wise and holy ends in thus proceeding.

It may be said, the case is not alike, for he, of whom the debt may be lawfully demanded, did willingly and deliberately spend the money entrusted with him; but the sin whereby our first parents lost the power which we want, was not actually consented to by us, for we were not then in being.

I answer, A loss or penalty may justly and reasonably fall upon those who never actually consented to the fault for which it was incurred, nor were in being when it was committed. For instance, a man has an estate given on these terms, that if he be faithful to the donor, he and his heirs shall enjoy it for ever; but if he prove treacherous, he and his posterity shall lose it in all generations. He proves treacherous, and so is deprived of it, and his posterity in following ages have no benefit by it; yet the proceeding is just and reasonable in the sense of all the world.

Ans. 2. The word of Christ is operative. He many times empowers his word to effect that which he calls for: not only demands this, but conveys a power with his word enabling sinners to perform what he demands. He said, ' Let there be light, and there was light ;' he ' sent forth his word and healed them ;' he ' works all things by the word of his power.' You think it in vain to call upon the dead, but if you could convey a power along with your voice to quicken them, it would not be in vain so to speak. Thus did Christ : he speaks to Lazarus who was dead, and had lain some days in the grave, ' Lazarus, come forth ;' but there was a secret power accompanied the voice which made it effectual ; he spake, and it was done. He says to dry bones, Live; but there is a quickening power in his word, and, therefore, though he speak to the dead, he speaks to purpose ; he speaks so as to make the dead both hear and live. The dead shall hear, &c., John v. 25, therefore you need not wonder that Christ calls upon sinners to do that which of themselves they cannot, because he has a power to send along with the word, when it pleases him, to enable them to do what he calls for, though as to their own power it be impossible. You need not wonder why Christ calls sinners to open, whenas they cannot do it; the word of his power, by which he calls for this, will enable them to open. He does that by such exhortations which he exhorts to ; he puts forth his power with his word, when he pleases, and his word, so accompanied, whoever it be spoken to, never returns in vain.

When the Lord intends to enter into the heart of a sinner, he calls upon him to open in the ministry of the word ; for he deals with us as with reasonable creatures, by way of persuasion, exhortation, and argument. He not only speaks to him, calls on him by the voice of man, but he puts forth therewith the power of God: the voice we hear, the power we see not.

This is the Lord's way, to speak to our ears, but therewith to convey a power to the heart, that he that hears may open. Such calling on us, when it is thus empowered, is to purpose, though sinners that hear it be most impotent.

Ans. 3. The Lord may call upon them to open who are not able, that they may go to him to make them able. Though the Lord do not always accompany the word with a converting power, yet if he thereby convince the sinner of his own weakness, it is not to no purpose; if it make sensible, as he, 'Lord, help my unbelief ;' if he be brought to this, *Da, domine, quod jubes, et jube quid vis.*

It is just with the Lord to condemn men for not doing that which they have lost the power to do, because they will not be persuaded but they are able enough, and yet endeavour not, neglect him who should enable them. Are not these the thoughts of many hearts : Oh we can open to Christ when we please ; and therefore put it off till hereafter, neglect the means, think not of going to Christ for strength ? What more reasonable than to call on a man to do that which, being his duty, he thinks himself able enough to do ?

Now if this be but the issue of those exhortations, to ' hide pride from man,' to bring men to a sense of their own wretched impotency ; if it stir them up but to try what they can do, that so, having experience of their own weakness, they may go to Christ for strength ; if it bring a sinner to know and feel, and say, I am guilty of shutting out Christ, and yet how miserable am I without him ! And though life and death lie on it, I cannot open. Oh if Christ pity me not, if he break not open this stony heart, so fast closed against him, I shall shut him out, and be shut out from him for ever. If they be but thus far effectual, they are not in vain. They tend to lay men low, and shew the freeness of grace, and discover the necessity of it. The promoting of these ends justify such means, such exhortations which tend hereto.

Ans. 4. Sinners may do more than they use to do, than they are willing to do, and therefore there is reason to call upon them. They cannot open; though they can do nothing spiritually that tends thereto, yet in a natural and moral way they may do much more than we see done by any of them. Spiritual good is above the power of nature, without Christ no such thing can be done; but that which is morally good they may do, and that which looks towards opening, though it do not reach it.

They cannot subdue the corruption of nature, nor of themselves crucify the flesh, &c.; but they can avoid the outward acts of gross sins. Mere moral men, we see, can do it, without the power of higher principles.

They cannot free themselves from the miseries into which sin has plunged them; but they can assent to a plain word discovering their misery, and consider and think of it as they do of other things which are of consequence.

They cannot enlighten their own darkened minds, nor mollify their hardened hearts; but they can place themselves in the way where the light shines, and where mollifying influences are wont to fall, and where the Sun of righteousness has appointed to rise.

They cannot meditate, nor read, nor pray, nor hear spiritually; but they can attend the ordinances, as they do any other ordinary business which concerns them.

They cannot convey a healing virtue into the waters of the sanctuary, nor put themselves in when the waters are troubled, no more than the impotent man that lay at the pool of Bethesda could do it; but they can wait at the pool, and there they are in the way where Jesus may meet them and cure their impotency, how long soever they have laboured under it.

They cannot command a gale of wind; but they can put the vessel into the channel, and spread their sails, that they may be ready to take the advantage of a spiritual gale, whenever it shall please the Spirit of Christ to blow.

It seems very hard, and they would make advantage of it, who over-magnify the power of nature to the prejudice of the grace of Christ, that the Lord should condemn men for not doing that which they have no power to do. But I take it for an undoubted truth, that amongst those who are in a capacity to use the means, he never condemns any who really do what they can to be saved; none perish who do their utmost to avoid condemnation. Amongst the most zealous asserters of free grace, I find none that question it. None who shall be found at Christ's left hand at the last day, will be able to say truly, Lord, I used all the power that I had to avoid the misery, and prevent that dreadful sentence. It may seem harsh that any should perish for not opening to Christ when they were not able to open; but there are none perish who do all they can to open to him. Though for the wise and holy ends mentioned, he may require what sinners have disabled themselves to perform, yet he condemns no man but such as neglect what they are able to do.

Obj. But may not the difficulty propounded about Christ's calling on those to open who have no power to open be better satisfied by granting that the Lord vouchsafes sufficient grace to all men, as the patrons of free will do?

Ans. To grant that the Lord vouchsafes sufficient grace for the salvation of all and every man, is both against Scripture and the experience of the world in all ages. For divers parts of the world do not now, nor never did, enjoy the gospel; and what grace can there be sufficient for salvation without the gospel? But we grant that Christ does vouchsafe such sufficient grace, even to many of those who never open to him, as is both sufficient to remove the difficulty, and to shew that we are unjustly charged for too much straitening and contracting the grace of God. For,

(1.) We grant that the Lord vouchsafes all more grace, *i. e.* more common assistance, than ever they make use of. He enables them to do much more towards opening to Christ, and in order to their salvation, than they are wont to use, or willing to improve; and thereby he is justified in condemning those who open not to Christ, because they are able to do more towards it than they will do; and thereby his calling on them to open is justified, because they can do more in order to it than they are willing to do. If a man cannot pay all his debt, yet if he can do something towards it, it is just and reasonable to call upon him for it.

(2.) We grant that the Lord vouchsafes to those who enjoy the gospel, and to many of those who never open to Christ, all that sufficient grace which the patrons of free will contend for, and more than that to many. For all the grace which they are for, is only that which they call suasive; *i. e.* the proposal of such things in the gospel as have the force of arguments and motives, and are apt to persuade those who hear them. For this we acknowledge, and also some illumination of the understanding, convictions of sin and misery, some common motions of the Spirit exciting the will to yield to Christ for freedom from this misery. This is all, if not more, than their suasive grace amounts to; and all this we grant is vouchsafed to many that never open. But we say more is needful, and is vouchsafed to all that open indeed. So that we do not straiten the grace of God, we are not for less of it than they; but we are for all theirs, and more too.

(3.) We grant that the Lord vouchsafes, even to many who perish, grace sufficient to make their salvation probable, and their condition hopeful. And this is all the grace that they pretend to, such as makes the salvation of the best only probable and hopeful; they are for no grace, at least ordinarily, that makes the salvation of any certain.

For when grace is offered to the soul, they say such is the nature of the will, that it may either accept or refuse it, and so it is uncertain whether it may yield or not till the event shew it; for the will (by their principles) has still power to resist when the grace of God has done what it can. And if it yield to the power of grace to-day, yet it may resist it to-morrow; if it should receive it this hour, yet it may expel it or fall from it the next hour. And the Lord, as they hold, never vouchsafes so much grace, in an ordinary way, as will make the perseverance of any certain, and so never enough to make the salvation of any certain.

But we hold that the Lord disposes his grace so as to make both conversion and perseverance certain; and so as to make salvation not only probable or hopeful, but also certain to his chosen, and probable to others. So that still we are not injurious to the grace of God by straitening it, but are for as much and more of it than they. And therefore, if the grace which they are for be sufficient to justify the urging of those exhortations, then will that which we are for as much, or more, justify, and make them appear as evidently reasonable, if not more.

Use 1. *Reproof.* Here is a just reproof for those who open not to Christ, and those that open deceitfully.

1. Those that open not, that keep their hearts shut against him. Oh

that Christ should come, and stand, and knock, and call at the hearts of sinners; that he should condescend to come, and be so patient as to stand, and be so gracious as to knock, and be so importunate as to call; use all language, all importunity; that he should command, threaten, promise, beseech, exhort, complain: and yet be disobeyed, slighted, disregarded, denied, rejected! Oh that sinners should thus sin against Christ, thus sin against their own souls; that their hearts should be thus fast shut against Christ, when they are set wide open for sin and for the world; that the happiness of enjoying Christ, the comforts of communion with him, should be thus set at nought; that Christ's presence, which he here offers, should be refused, when all enjoyments without him tend but to make you more miserable; that fellowship with Christ, which he here promises, should be rejected, when all things else, without this, tend but to bring on that woful fellowship which disobedient, gainsaying sinners shall have with the devil and his angels!

But who are those that open not to Christ? Far be it from me to do this wickedness, will most be ready to say. Something I must answer to this, that the reproof may come home, that I may not speak to the air. I will shew you who they are who open not.

(1.) Those who are not at home when Christ knocks; whose minds and hearts are abroad; their thoughts, affections, inclinations employed about the world and outward affairs; who enter not into their own hearts, to consider seriously, frequently, effectually, what the condition of their souls is, and to provide accordingly for their eternal state; who have no mind, no heart to such thoughts, to such employments as most concern their souls, can put these off till hereafter, or think of them so slightly, as though they were of less concernment than worldly things. A sad thought it is, that men who believe they have souls, and believe that they shall be happy or miserable to eternity, according as they are provided for in this little time, should spend nothing, or so very little of this time in thinking of, in providing for eternity; should let the world, and things of less moment, carry them so far, so much from that which most nearly concerns them; should be such strangers to their soul's condition, and so little acquainted with their own hearts, and so little employed about that which is within them, that their estate, their livelihood, their bodies, what they shall eat, &c., should be more minded than their souls. Sure these men are not come to themselves, they are a great way from home, and so not like to open.

(2.) When Christ's voice is not heard. These you see are joined in the text: 'If any hear my voice.' He that will not hear will not open. Ay, but do we not hear? Truly there are too many that will not do thus much, as give outward attendance to the voice of Christ in the ministry of the word. The practice of such proclaims to the world that they shut out Christ with a high hand. But further, for those who are not so impudently wicked, you must know this, the hearing with the ear only is no evidence that you open. Hearing is no hearing in Christ's account, except the hearing of the ear be joined with a compliance of the heart. *Non esse, et inutiliter esse, pro paribus habentur.* To hear, and hear unprofitably, to hear and not obey, is no hearing in the sense of the text. You may hear so long enough before you open. If you hear Christ reproving, and be not convinced; hear him promising, and be not affected; hear him threaten, and tremble not; hear him command, and obey not; hear him exhort, and are not persuaded: you do not hear so as to open, you will never open till you hear otherwise. If you put off convictions, slight promises, evade threatenings, do what he forbids, neglect what he commands in the ministry of the word; if you continue the same men for all your hearing, do neither more nor less, no more of what is pressed as your duty, no less of what is forbidden as your sin, are no more affected, reformed, no more careful of your souls, no more conscientious in keeping your hearts, ordering your ways, serving the Lord in your families, minding him in your affairs; if thy hearing be to no more effect than this, thou art the man that shuts out Christ.

The word of Christ is his messenger; he sends it to prepare the way of the Lord, to make his paths straight, as it is said of John Baptist, Mat. iii. 1, that he may come into his temple, that he may enter into the heart of a sinner, and make it his temple. Now, if the word prevail not, if Christ's messenger be shut out, he expects no better entertainment; when his voice is not heard, himself is shut out.

(3.) Those who think it an easy matter to open to Christ; either imagine they have already opened, though they never perceived it, though it be not discernible either in their hearts or lives, or else put it off till hereafter, to do it at their leisure, as though it were in their power to open when they list. How ordinary is it for men to think that it is easy to repent and believe! The two great hinges upon which the door moves when it opens to Christ, they make no great matter of them.

As for faith, they think they did believe ever since they can remember, ever since they had any knowledge of Christ.

For repentance. They defer it till old age or sickness. Do they not make it an easy matter to repent, who think they may do it when they please; or think it enough to be a little sorry for sinning, and ask pardon for it?

Alas! those men are far from opening, who do not so much as know what it is to open. They are not acquainted with the desperate wickedness of their own hearts; they take no notice of the stone that is in their hearts, and how they are by nature obstinately hardened against the admission of Christ. They never were convinced of the necessity of Christ, and of an almighty power to make way for his entertainment. They never had experience of the mighty workings of Christ in their hearts, which they are well acquainted with who have opened to him. They hereby declare they never yet did so much as try to open, so far are they from having opened.

(4.) Those who are under the command and the dominion of sin. Where sin reigns, Christ is excluded. While sin commands, Christ will have no admission. Those that are under the power of sin are under the power of Satan, for he 'rules in the children of disobedience,' Eph. ii. There the strong man armed keeps the house, and that is evidence enough a stronger than he is not yet come. Where sin and Satan have possession, so as to reign, they block up the door against Christ. Till the covenant with death and hell be dissolved, there can be no consent to entertain Christ. But those that are under the dominion of sin are in league with hell and death, there is a strong conspiracy against Christ to keep him out.

But where, in whom, does sin reign? Why, where it is not mortified, subdued. Where it is obeyed in the lusts thereof. When it says, Go, and the sinner goes; Come, and he comes; Do this, and he doth it. He is under the dominion of sin, who lives in the practice of sin, drunkenness, uncleanness, worldliness, profaning of the Sabbath, neglect of the word and ordinances, public or private. The Scripture is clear in this. 'He that commits sin is the servant of sin. He that is born of God sinneth not,' 1 John iii. Not that sin is not in him, or that he never is guilty of an act of sin; but it is not his delight, it is not his custom, he follows it not with full consent, he makes not a trade of it. He that thus sins, the seed of God abides not in him; and where this is not, Christ is not. Those that live in known sins do but deceive themselves, when they think they have any part in Christ, and it is a wonder those that pretend to any knowledge of the word of God should think so, Eph. v. 6, 1 Cor. vi. 9. You may as well reconcile light and darkness, or bring heaven and hell together, as entertain Christ while you live in sin.

He that allows himself in the neglect of any known duty, public, private, secret, or in the practice of any known sin, gross or refined, open or secret, small or great, Christ is not in him, Christ is shut out by him. For he that thus lives in sin, is the servant of sin; and he that is the servant of sin, will think he owes not Christ so much service as to open to him. If it be thus with you, you are yet in the gall of bitterness, you are yet in your sins, Christ is not in you, you never opened to him.

(5.) Those that have not felt the effects of Christ's presence have not experience of communion with him. Whoever opens, Christ will enter, and sup with him. He knows what it is to enjoy Christ, has tasted the sweetness of fellowship with him. Now, what are the effects of Christ's presence? Why, principally light and holiness. Christ is the light of the world, the Sun of righteousness, the bright Morning Star. When he arises, darkness is scattered, ignorance vanishes, the works of darkness find no place.

Holiness. Christ is called the holy of holies, Dan. ix. When he comes, holiness comes with him. The heart is sanctified, purity is no more slighted and derided, there appears a singular beauty in holiness. You may as well imagine Christ in hell, as in a heart destitute of purity and holiness. You may as well imagine a day without light, as holiness of heart without holiness of life. By this you may know whether you have opened. Then for communion with Christ, those that open to Christ taste the sweetness of it, an exceeding sweetness, which renders the ways of holiness wherein it is enjoyed exceeding delightful; so that the pleasures of sin and the world, those that have formerly been most delightful, are now rank and unsavoury to him that has opened to Christ. By this you may know whether you have opened.

And since it is thus, since all these, &c. do shut out Christ, how many are there who fall under this reproof! As strait is the way and narrow the gate that leads to heaven, so strait is the way, &c., that lets Christ in to us on earth, and few there are that find it; and it is to be lamented, that so many who enjoy the gospel, hear his voice, should shut themselves out of heaven by shutting out Christ.

2. It reproves those that open deceitfully. Many such there are.

(1.) Those who will let Christ in at the window, but not in at the door; into their understandings, but not into their hearts: such are those of whom we read, Heb. vi., who were once enlightened, admit the light, take some pains for knowledge, yea, and rejoice in the light; but when this light should come to be effectual upon their wills, consciences, affections, conversation, to purify their hearts, expel their lusts, quash the motions of sin, reform their conversations in their families and in the world, as becomes children of the light, here they stop; Christ must not enter here, thus they shut him out of their hearts. Light without influence, notion without efficacy.

(2.) Those who will let him in at the outer door, but not into the closet, will admit so much of Christ, as to bring them to a fair plausible compliance in the profession and outward exercises of religion. They will hear, and pray, and read, and discourse too of religious matters. This is easily done, and they get some credit by it; and it stands not in the way of their humours, lusts, worldly interests; but for the power of godliness, the exercise of holiness, close and strict walking with Christ, in secret as well as openly, this they relish not. They will be Jews, such as the apostle speaks of Rom. ii. 28, ἐν τῷ φανερῷ, make a show of admitting Christ in their profession, discourses, and outward performance, but not ἐν τῷ κρυπτῷ, but not let him into their thoughts to lodge there, their wills to rule, their affections to be embraced there without a rival. They will make a fair show in the flesh; but for serving Christ in the Spirit, rejoicing, submitting the whole rule of their souls unto him, here they shut him out.

(3.) Those who let him but in half-way, stand and parley with Christ; will accept of some of those terms he propounds; cannot digest all; will renounce some of their own righteousness, but not count all loss and dung; will part with some sins, those that are gross and disgraceful, those they can gain nothing by, or take little pleasure in, those that are open and out of credit. Ay! but there is some Delilah, some gainful or delightful lust, they cannot live without it; they say of this, as Lot of Zoar, 'Is it not a little one?' 'Oh let my soul live in it;' 'the Lord be merciful to me in this,' I cannot part with it; if Christ will but dispense with this, he shall be welcome. Ay! but Christ will not have a hoof left behind if he enter.

They will comply with some duties of religion, both in secret, and in their families, and in public. Herod did many things, and heard John gladly; Agrippa was almost persuaded; the foolish virgins had lamps as well as the wise. They did not a little who profess so much, Mat. vii. 22. They will go far in many duties, and so as they cannot be discerned from those that indeed open to him, in respect of external acts. Oh but for such constancy and fervency in secret prayer, such frequency in secret meditation, heart-examination, and self-judging; for such strictness, and watchfulness, and precise circumspection about their hearts and ways; for the exercises of self-denial, repentance, and mortification: these are hard morsels, they cannot down with them. If Christ will compound with them, and abate something of his demands, they will agree to admit him; they will yield far, they will open half-way. Ay, but Christ will not enter upon such terms, either all or none. He will not creep into your hearts, the gate must be lifted up, else the King of glory will not enter.

You see who are to be reproved. Oh that those who are guilty in any of these respects, would not deceive themselves as though they had opened already, but go about to open!

Use 2. *Exhortation.* Since those that will have Christ to enter, must open to him, oh be persuaded to open unto Christ. Let it not be in vain that Christ comes, and stands, and knocks, and calls, and uses all importunity to gain admission. If you shut out Christ, to whom will you open? Will you shut out him who is your life, your happiness, in whom is all our hopes, &c.? Can anything save them who shut out a Saviour? Can they find mercy, who will not open when mercy is offered? Can they expect to live, who will not admit life? Will you prefer sin before Christ, the worst thing in earth or hell, before the King of glory? Shall that dwell in you, rule over you, take up mind and heart, while Christ stands and knocks, and is excluded? Does sin love you? was it crucified for you? or will it save you in the conclusion? Nay, will it not certainly damn you, if it be not cast out, forsaken, crucified? And shall a damning evil find easier entertainment than a Saviour? Is there any love like his love? And can you shew any greater hatred and despite of him, than to keep him out, while his and your deadly enemy is let in, and kept in to keep him out?

Is there any patience like to Christ's, who comes so often, stands so long, knocks so loud, calls so importunately? And can there be any provocation like yours, who turn the deaf ear, who will not mind, will not regard; who tell him you have let him in already, he is admitted far enough, when it is plain he is quite shut out? Sin will not be tolerated where Christ is admitted. You affront Christ, and mock him, when you say your hearts are open to him, while your lives testify there is something else rules in you; while swearing, drunkenness, uncleanness, neglect of the word, ordinances, families, souls, these cry aloud, God is not here. All his knocking, calling, has not yet prevailed. Is this nothing to you, all ye that pass by? See if there be any love like Christ's love, any condescensions like Christ's, any patience, any importunity; and see if there be any hatred, contempt, neglect, unkindness, like yours. Shall Christ come to his own, and his own not receive him? Would you have him still a man of sorrows and sufferings? Shall he have still occasion to complain, ' Who has believed our report?' Who has hearkened when I have called? Who has regarded when I have stretched out my hands? Who has yielded when I have entreated? Who has opened when I have knocked? Shall it be thus still with Christ? Shall he not have a place whereon to lay his head? Ay! so it may be for you, who will give him no place in your hearts.

Where shall Christ have entertainment in the world, if not amongst us? Where shall he be admitted, if shut out where he stands and knocks? He expects no entertainment from the heathens; he knocks not, he calls not there. He expects none as yet from the Jews; they rejected his first offer, and he took them at their word, and never sought to them since. He expects none from Turks and apostate Christians, they have entertained others. Where shall Christ be entertained, if not amongst us? While you shut him out, you do what you can that Christ on earth may have no place to lay his head. Expect you to be entertained by Christ, while you refuse to give him entertainment? Will he open to those who shut him out? Be not deceived, Christ will not be mocked. Open to him now, if ever you expect to see him hereafter. Shut him not out, who has done, who has suffered so much for sinners. Be not thus unkind to Christ, be not thus cruel to your souls. Open to him as King, Prophet, Priest.

Motives. 1. Consider what danger there is in not opening; what equity there is you should open; what advantage you may get by opening.

1. For the danger. Take it in these severals.

(1.) Till you open to Christ, you are shut up in darkness. The state of nature, the condition of a sinner without Christ, is expressed by darkness, Acts xxvi. 18. Till a sinner be turned, converted, *i. e.* till his heart be opened to Christ, he is in darkness. So Col. i. 13; they are ' under the power of darkness, who are not translated,' &c.; and they are not in his kingdom, in whose hearts he rules not as king, and he rules not in them who shut him out.

Now a state of a darkness is a state of misery, a dismal, sad, woful condition. It is frequent in Scripture to express the greatest miseries on earth by darkness. It joins darkness with the valley of the shadow of death. So sad is this condition, as it is even a shadow of death, of that which is most dreadful to men. And well may all miseries on earth be expressed by darkness, since the state of darkness, the condition of a sinner without Christ, is next to hell. There is but this difference: that is outer darkness; this is inner darkness: a hell in the heart, a little hell on earth. No better is your condition, till ye open to Christ, you are even on the confines of hell. It is true sinners are not sensible of this misery, but even this makes them more miserable. Would you not think it a sad condition to be shut up in a dungeon all your |days? Such is your condition while ye open not to Christ; and more miserable, by how much spiritual darkness is more dismal than outward. The misery of it is herein evident, that those that are in it know it not, see not where they are, nor will not believe they are in Satan's dungeon.

(2.) Till you open to Christ, your hearts are possessed by Satan. They are cages, not of unclean birds only, but of unclean, of damned spirits. You are in darkness, till the Sun of righteousness arise in your hearts. Now the devils they are called the 'rulers of the darkness of this world,' Eph. vi. 12; not only of that darkness of the other world, but of this. Satan has two dungeons, hell, and the heart that shuts out Christ; he rules, he tyrannizes in both. You are under the power, in the possession of Satan, Eph. ii. 2. You see how they are; Satan has his throne in that heart that opens not; and this will be your state if you do not open. I told you this soul-possession is worse than bodily.

(3.) Till you open to Christ, the wrath of God is shut in. Children of disobedience are children of wrath, Eph. ii. 2, 3. Wrath is their portion, all that they enjoy, all that they can look to inherit, while they continue so. And who are children of disobedience, but those that open not to Christ? I beseech you, consider that expression which I have often occasion to mention, John iii. 36. It is not anger, displeasure, but wrath; it is not the wrath of a man, or of a multitude, or of a king, but of God; it is not a transient, fading passion, which, though it be high and violent, may soon be over, but it is abiding wrath. And it abides not at a distance, or near unto him only, but upon him; he that believes not, *i.e.* opens not. To shut your hearts against Christ, is as if a man should shut his doors, that nothing should come in or out, when his house is on fire; this is the way to have it consumed without remedy. The wrath of God is kindling in every disobedient heart; it is often compared to fire, and it abides there. When you shut out Christ, you shut out him who only can quench it. What remains, then, but if you so continue, it will burn to the bottom of hell?

(4.) If you open not to Christ now, he will shut you out hereafter. Time is approaching when, as Christ comes to you, so you will be glad to come to him. He knocks now, you will be glad to knock hereafter. Those who will not now open, shall fare then as the foolish virgins. Oh consider it, when all your outward comforts and supports have left you, when you must expect the sentence of life or death from Christ's mouth, will it not be sad to hear nothing from him but these dreadful words, 'Depart from me, I never knew you'? I called, and you would not hear; do ye expect I should hear you, who stopped your ears against me? I knocked, and ye would not open, and do ye expect that I should open to you, whom you shut out of doors? I stood, and ye took no notice of me, and shall I now own you? No; 'Depart from me, I know ye not.' See now whether it be better to entertain sin or Christ. You would not believe it before, now you may feel it. I was a stranger, and ye took me not in; you used me strangely, and shut me out; what follows? 'Depart from me, ye cursed, into everlasting fire.' This will be the doom of all that had rather live in sin than open to Christ. Oh, as you would avoid that sad departure, that everlasting fire, that woful fellowship with the devil, &c., be persuaded now to open.

Means. What means shall we make use of that we may open to Christ?

1. Be convinced that you have not yet opened to him; for those that shut out Christ, the first step to the door is to be satisfied in his judgment that he has not opened. He that dreams the door is open whiles it is shut, will be so far from making haste to open, as he will wonder at, if not deride, those that call upon him to do it. This is one of Satan's devices to secure the heart against opening, to persuade a sinner he has opened already, though indeed Christ never was admitted. While you are fast in this snare, he has you sure enough. If you would escape, examine impartially by the rules before delivered. Are you not abroad? Do ye not disobey Christ's voice? Think you it not an easy matter to open? Are you not under the command of sin? Can you shew the effects of Christ's presence? Search impartially, and judge of your estates, as you expect to be judged. To deceive yourselves herein may be your ruin for ever. Follow the apostle's rule. To know you have not opened, when it is so indeed, is the first step to open.

2. Consider your misery while Christ is without. Let not the world and these outward things take up all your minds. Shew so much respect to Christ, so much respect to your souls, as to spare some serious thoughts for them. Think seriously what it is to be in darkness, in the possession of Satan, under the wrath of God, in danger to be shut out from Christ for ever. While you think yourselves safe and happy enough in your present condition, you are in danger never to open, being not sensible of your danger in not opening.

3. Be apprehensive of your inability, of your unwillingness, to open; of the desperate wickedness of your hearts, and their obstinateness, averseness to Christ. Bewail this frequently, seriously, heartily, as your greatest misery. Let this affect you, that though you be miserable, yet are you utterly unable to free yourselves from this misery. When a sinner is lost in his own apprehension, this is Christ's opportunity to be found of him. He is not valued, he is not esteemed, till the sinner see himself lost without him. He comes to seek and to save that which is lost.

4. In sense of your own inability, go to Christ for strength to open. As he comes to thee, so go thou to him; as he calls to thee, so cry thou to him; and when he knocks, importune him to open. Say, Lord, thou hast the key of David, thou shuttest, and no man opens; thou openest, and no man shuts; Lord, open this heart that has been too long closed against thee; break down these strongholds that keep thee from me; cast out sin, cast out the world, that have so long kept thee out of possession; bind the strong man armed, and cast him out. Other lords have had dominion over the, they have made me miserable by keeping my Lord, my happiness, from me. Oh cast out these intruders, take possession of me, and let me be mine for ever! Thou callest for my heart; Lord, it is thine. Though I have dealt treacherously with thee, and given it to other things, it is thine. It cost thee dear; Lord, enter, take possession of it. Thou knockest at this wretched heart, oh why dost thou stay so long without? Come in, thou blessed of the Lord, and bless this wretched heart with thy presence. Oh it would be still resisting thee! but break it open with an almighty power, and suffer it no longer to shut thee out. Follow the Lord with such cries.

5. Wait upon the Lord in the use of those means which he makes use of to open the hearts of sinners: reading the word, conferring with others whose hearts the Lord has opened, especially hearing, this is the Lord's ordinary way, and that which he is wont to make effectual for the opening of the hearts of sinners. This is the way to open, this is the way for Christ to enter: 'If any man hear my voice, I will come in,' &c.

Pass we from the conditions to the things promised, which offer themselves in two branches: 1, 'I will come in to him.'

Obs. If any will open to Christ, he will come in to him. Those that open to Christ, shall have his presence. When the everlasting gates are left open, the King of glory will come in. Christ will vouchsafe his presence to those that will admit him. To explain this;—

Quest. Some may ask, Is not Christ in every place? Is not this one of his perfections as he is God? If in every place, he is in my heart already. How can he be said to come thither, where he is already? Coming implies he was not there before he comes, it denotes absence; but how can he be absent who is everywhere present?

Ans. There is a twofold presence of Christ: a general presence, as he is governor of the world; and a special presence, as he is a Saviour.

As to the former, since he is God, he is in every place in respect of his essence, his power, his wisdom, and other perfections, with the effects thereof. This presence the psalmist gives an account of, Ps. cxxxix. 7, &c.; hence he is said to know all things; and to uphold all things, Heb. i. 3. This is his presence as he is governor of the world, and so he is present with every creature. And in this respect he is not only with the wicked, but with the damned, as he upholds them, continues them in being, orders and proportions their sufferings to his glory. In this sense he does not here promise to come; for he is there, even in the souls of obstinate sinners already. In this respect he can never be shut out, he can never be excluded. But,

2. There is a special presence, a presence of peculiar love and special favour: when he comes as a saviour, as a redeemer; when he is present as a king, as a prophet, as a priest, to this or that particular soul; when he comes in as a friend, a brother, a father, a husband, and shews himself in a way suitable to these sweet relations. So he promises to come in the text, to vouchsafe a special presence; which I call special in respect,

(1.) Of special manifestations. When he will manifest a peculiar love, a redeeming love, the love of a dying, a crucified saviour; such a love as none taste of but his glorified favourites in heaven, and his excellent ones on earth.

(2.) Of special communications. When he communicates himself as a head to its members, as a prince to his favourites, as a husband to his spouse. When he bestows the precious fruits of his unspeakable love, the invaluable purchase of his precious blood, in light, holiness, comforts, the first fruits of glory, and such as none partake of but those that must enter into the harvest, for whom is reserved the inheritance.

(3.) Of special operations. When he walks, and works, and acts in them, as in those only whom he prepares for eternal rest, those only whom he intends to crown, and for whom he reserves an eternal weight of glory.

This is the presence Christ here promiseth. Thus will he come to those that open. And till sinners open, though they have his general presence, yet they shall never enter into the secret of his peculiar presence. He may be with them as governor of the world here, and as judge of quick and dead hereafter, but not as a Saviour. It is another kind of presence which Christ here promises than ever those had experience of who live in sin, and give up themselves to the world. And that ye may apprehend it more distinctly, and take a clearer view of what Christ offers, when he says he will come in, observe these particulars. He will come in,

(1.) To join himself to the soul; to enter into covenant and league with it, to contract the opening sinner to himself in an everlasting covenant; to unite himself to it, that it may be one with him, that it may be a member of him, 2 Cor. xi. 2. 'The head of every man is Christ.' He comes that he may espouse it to himself, to shew it is as near, as dear to him, as the spouse to her husband. Wherein consists the union betwixt man and wife (which the Scripture so frequently uses to illustrate the union betwixt Christ and a believing soul)? It is expressed, Gen. ii. 24, 'They shall be no more twain,' &c. Such an intimacy does Christ intend, when he comes in, &c. Only it is spiritual: 1 Cor. vi. 16, 'He that is joined to Christ is one spirit.' He comes to give his own Spirit to it. And this gives some light to that expression, whereby is held forth an intimacy almost incredible betwixt Christ and such souls, John xvii. 21, 22. It is Christ's prayer for all believers; and he prays not only that they may be one amongst themselves, but one with him, as it follows, ver. 23, and so one with him, as the Father is one with him. But this must be cautiously understood. Not that they may be of the same essence as the Father and Son are, nor that they may be assumed into a personal union with himself or the Father, as the human nature of Christ is assumed into a personal union with the Godhead; but that they may be of the same Spirit, that the Spirit of the Father and the Spirit of Christ may be in them. Hereby they may become one with Christ, as he is one with the Father. For consider him in his human nature, and how is he one with the Father? Why, besides the union of his own nature in the person of the Son, we can conceive no other union betwixt the Father and Christ incarnate but that which consists in the indwelling of the Spirit in the human nature of Christ. Now this is it he prays for, that they may be one with him by the dwelling of the same Spirit in me and them, whereby I am one with the Father. The return of this prayer Christ brings when he comes into an opening soul, he makes it one with him as he is one with the Father, viz., by making them of one spirit. He joins himself thereto; and he that is joined to Christ is one spirit.

(2.) To express his kindness to it. We use to come to our friends for this end. But no such kindness can be expressed by the sons of men as Christ exercises to an opening soul. Before, while shut up against Christ, the soul was under the wrath of God, under the stroke of justice, under the curses, threatenings, and terrors of the law, without comfort, without God, without hope in the world. But when Christ comes it is a time of love; he expresses this love by coming, even that loving-kindness which is better than life. He tells the soul, justice is satisfied, the law fulfilled, the threatening executed, the curse removed, the Lord reconciled; and that he has effected all this out of love to it. He has satisfied justice, he has borne the wrath of God, the curse was executed upon him, he has slain enmity upon the cross, his blood has quenched the flame, his death has procured life, he has blotted out the handwriting; there is now no curse, no wrath, no condemnation. Oh, how beautiful are the feet of Christ bringing these glad tidings of good things! He was anointed for this end, and to this end he comes. 'The Spirit of the Lord is upon me,' Isa. lxi. 1.

(3.) To shine in the soul. Then may it be said to the soul as to the church, Isa. lx. 1, 2. While Christ is shut out, the heart is a dungeon, a place of darkness, a sad, a dismal place, a shadow of death; but when Christ comes, it becomes like the firmament, when the sun shines in its glory, Mal. iv. 2. Some clouds and mists there will be, but when the sun is once risen, this light will shine more and more unto perfect day. Before, the god of this world did blind its eyes; but now 'the light of the glorious gospel,' &c., he comes to 'give the light of the knowledge of the glory of God in the face of Christ;' the veil is taken away, and now he may, as in a glass, with open face behold the glory of God, &c.

He was 'sometimes darkness, but now light in the Lord.' Oh what an alteration is here! Even as in one that is born blind, on a sudden restored to sight; or as one shut up in a dungeon all his days, brought out to see the sun. Oh how are his apprehensions changed! He sees that in sin that he never saw before, that in himself which he would not believe, that in the world which he would never have been persuaded of, that in holiness which he never imagined. Oh how does he look upon Christ, his sufferings, his love, his intercession, his righteousness! He wonders that he should have heard so many times of these, and yet never see no such thing in them as he now apprehends. The light is come, the day-star is risen, the sun is up, Christ shines in his dark heart, he comes to this end.

(4.) To adorn it. Nothing so loathsome, nothing so deformed, as the soul of a sinner without Christ. *Corruptio optimi est pessima.* The best thing corrupted becomes worst of all; the most beautiful bodies, when putrefied and rotted, are most loathsome. The soul of man, when created, was the most excellent piece of the creation in this world; but corrupted by sin is the most noisome, the most loathsome. The Lord cannot behold it without loathing and detestation. Hence is this corruption by sin expressed by things most offensive: the poison of asps, the stench of an open sepulchre, the vomit of a dog, the mire wherein the sow wallows, the deformity of a leper, the putrefied matter of an ulcer, the corruption of a festered wound. Put all these together, and the soul of sinners is a more loathsome spectacle in God's eye, than such a compound, a filthy medley, would be in ours. Now, is this a place fit to receive Christ? No; but he will make it so; he comes to this end, to cleanse the soul, to purge out its filthiness, to take away its deformity, to clothe it with beauty and glory, that he may delight in it, Eph. v. 25, 26, 27. He does it effectually, makes the soul a fit object of love, so as he can call it his love, his undefiled; so as he can express love to it in such a wonderful strain, 'My sister, my spouse,' Cant. iv. 1, 7, 9, 10, chap. vi. 4, 10, chap. vii. 6; so as he can rejoice in it, according to the tenor of that high expression, Zeph. iii. 17.

(5.) To enrich the soul. Christ comes not empty-handed, he brings those treasures with him that will make thee rich for ever. But what is this? thou wilt say; is it gold, or silver, or pearls, or worldly possessions? Alas! these are trash compared with it, not worthy the account, the name, of riches. It is better than rubies, and all the things that may be desired are not to be compared to it. Hear Christ himself asserting this, Prov. viii. 17, 18, 19, and chap. iii. 13, 14, 16. But what are these riches? What is the sum, the value of them? Do you ask this? Oh, it is far above me to tell you; nay, the great apostle, who was rapt up into the third heaven, cannot herein satisfy; nay, the angels themselves are not sufficient to express. For why, they are unsearchable riches, they are infinite, there is no end of them. Dig in these mines to eternity, you will never make a full discovery; they are unsearchable. Eye has not seen, ear has not heard, &c. The eye of man has seen much, the ear has heard more than his eye has seen, his heart can conceive more than either his eye has seen or ear heard; but eye, and ear, and heart, let them see, and hear, and conceive as much as is possible, can never reach a full discovery.

But though I cannot give you a full account of these riches, yet I may point at them. There are riches of righteousness, of joy, of grace, of glory. I will but add one word more, but there is more in that one word than all the men on earth, or angels in heaven, can fathom. What is that? Why, it is himself. When he comes to thee, he comes to give thee himself, no less than himself. And this is more than all the earth, more than all the kingdoms of the earth, and the glory of them; nay, more than heaven and earth put together. Oh happy soul, if Christ be come into thee! Thou art far from want, thou needest never complain; thou needest never envy the greatest, the richest, under heaven; he is thine, who is more than heaven and earth. Go thy way and break forth into praises; say, I have enough, I have all, he is mine who is more than all; my lines are fallen in a pleasant place, I have a goodly heritage; a goodly heritage indeed, for Christ is my portion. Ahasuerus his hundred seven and twenty provinces are but a small pittance, an inconsiderable nothing, compared with my possessions. Christ is come, and has given me possession of himself. 'Return to thy rest, O my soul, for the Lord has dealt bountifully with thee.' Thus bountifully he deals with every soul that opens to him.

(6.) To reign in it. That heart shall be his throne. It was before one or Satan's dungeons, a cage for unclean lusts; but Christ comes to make it his throne. There was much riches in the former, here is as much honour in this. 'Whence is this to me,' says Elizabeth, Luke i. 43, 'that the mother of my Lord should come unto me?' With how much more admiration may that soul say, What honour is this, that the Lord himself should come to me; that he should choose this unworthy soul to be his throne, this polluted heart to be his temple! Yet thus it is; Christ comes for this end, to erect his throne there, to expel those tyrants that have so long oppressed the soul with cruel bondage, worse than that of Egypt; he comes to make thy lusts (his and thine enemies) his footstool; to whip out those buyers and sellers, that the soul may be his temple; to make thy heart his chamber of presence, to walk there, to act there, to abide there. That is the seventh.

(7.) To abide there. He comes to stay, to make his abode; not as a stranger, but as one that would dwell with thee, John xiv. 23. He will not be as a stranger, or as a wayfaring-man that turns but in for a night, but he will abide with thee for ever: ver. 16, 'I will never leave thee, nor forsake thee.' If thou be unkind, unfaithful, froward, disrespectful of him, this will cloud the glory of his presence, eclipse the comforts of it, he will hide himself, seem to withdraw, but he will never utterly forsake thee, Ps. lxxxix. 30, 31, &c., Isa. liv. 7–9. When he comes to the heart, he says, This is my resting-place, and here will I dwell. Here is a covenant of peace.

Use I. For information. The light of this observation discovers the misery of those that open not to Christ; those that are so much engaged in sin, so much entangled in the world, as Christ hath no admission. If you open not to Christ, he is not yet come in; and if he be not come in, you are without happiness, without hopes of it, extremely miserable. For

1. You are not joined to Christ; and if not joined to him, you are in conjunction with sin and Satan. You are not members of Christ; and he that is not a member of Christ, is a limb of Satan. You are not one spirit with Christ; and he that is not one spirit with Christ, what spirit is he possessed with, but that evil, that unclean spirit, which fills every heart that is not taken up with Christ? You are not in covenant with Christ; and he that is not so, has made a covennat with death and hell, he is in league with Satan. Indeed, every heart that shuts out Christ says to Satan, as Jehoshaphat to Ahab, 1 Kings xxii. 4, 'I am as thou art, my people as thy people,' &c. They have the same projects, carry on the same design, act the same things. 'Ye are of your father,' John viii. 41, 44. Whatever thou workest, it is the devil's work; and all thou doest is but a promoting of his expeditions. What greater misery than this!

Besides, till thou open to Christ, he shines not into thee. Till then, the blackness of darkness covers thee. Whatever saving light shines without, thou seest it not till Christ come and shine within. What says the apostle? 2 Cor. iv. 3. Now the gospel is hid to thee, if the light thereof lead thee not to open to Christ. While it is hid, thou art lost; and it cannot but be hid if Christ be not come in. He adds the reason, ver. 14. This is thy condition, the God of this world has blinded thy eyes. Oh, sad estate, to have thy eyes put out by Satan! How woful was Samson's condition when the Philistines put out his eyes, and made him grind in the prison-house, and bound him with fetters of brass, Judges xvi. 21. This will be thy condition, till Christ come in, and far more miserable. Satan has put out thy eyes, he has bound thee with fetters stronger than brass, and he makes thee grind in the prison-house. Thy own heart is thy prison, thy own lusts are thy fetters, and thy work is worse drudgery than grinding. And it is he that is thy task-master, thou goest when he commands; but thou art blind, alas, thou knowest not whither thou goest, thou seest not he drives thee on in the paths of death. When Israel heard what conditions Nahash offered to Jabesh-Gilead, they all lift up their voice and wept, 1 Sam. xi. 4. Why, what were those lamentable conditions? see ver. 2. Oh, but much more reason hast thou to weep, much more reason have all that know thy condition to weep over thee. Satan has not put out thy right eye only, but both thine eyes; not those of thy body, but that which is far more woful, those of thy soul. He has quite blinded thee; he does not offer this, as Nahash, but he has already done it. Oh that every one that hears this to be his condition, would with Israel lift up his voice and weep! Or if thou seest no reason to bewail it, even this shews Satan has blinded thee, that thou canst not see reason to weep, to bewail so sad a condition. Thou thinkest thy estate good enough, with Laodicea; but even this shews, as Christ tells her, that thou art blind.

Further, till Christ come in, thou shalt never have experience of his loving-kindness, never taste that the Lord is gracious. Some things thou mayest receive from common bounty; but these, embittered with the curse, and mixed with the wrath of God; but the loving-kindness which is better than life, thou shalt never taste of. And if that be better than life, is not thy condition without it worse than death? Make as much as thou canst of thy husks, thou canst not taste of the bread of life.

Till then, thy soul is deformed, leprous, loathsome, in the eye of God. Nothing in it but wounds and bruises, and putrefied sores, full of corruption. He cannot look upon thee without loathing and detestation. The temper of thy heart, and all its actings, both its complexion and motions, are all an abomination in his sight, Prov. xv. 8, 9, 26.

Till then thou hast neither part nor lot in Christ's riches, not the least dram of those treasures belong to thee; nothing to do with his righteousness, no interest in his blood, no share in what he has purchased. Thou canst lay no claim to his person, he is not thy portion. And what then? The curse, the wrath of God, everlasting misery, is thy portion, thou canst expect no portion but with hypocrites. Thou pretendest to Christ, but in thy life deniest him; or if thou seem to open outwardly, thy heart is shut against him. This is the character of hypocrites, and their portion is set out in the place where there is weeping, &c.

Till then thy heart is the place where Satan has his throne; he rules in the children of disobedience. What more dreadful than the condition of Babylon? Rev. xviii. 2, 'It is become the habitation of devils,' &c. This is the condition of thy soul; it is a habitation of devils, and a hold of every foul spirit, and a cage of every unclean and hateful bird; of that which is more unclean and hateful than the hatefullest birds, it is a cage of unclean and hateful lusts. So it is, and so it will be till Christ come; these unclean birds will never be chased away, but prey upon thy dead and putrefied soul; it will never be dispossessed of these foul spirits till Christ have possession; it will be the devil's habitation, till Christ come and make it his temple.

Oh that the Lord would open the eyes of every soul, who will not part with sin to let in Christ, to see his misery without Christ, that thou mayest never give rest to thy soul, till it be a resting-place for Christ!

Use. 2. For examination. By this ye may try, by this ye may know, whether ye have opened unto Christ. If ye have opened, Christ is come in: 'If any man open the door,' &c. But how shall we know whether Christ be come in? If you will be directed by the word, you need not want direction.

1. When Christ comes in, he comes as a friend. This is clear. Now, if you entertain him as a friend, you love him. But how shall this be known? Why, the Lord shews you this by the psalmist, Ps. xcvii. 10. If you love Christ, you hate evil, you hate every evil way, every sin.

Now try by this. Do you hate everything you know to be sin? There is none of you but formerly have loved some sin or other, and lived in the practice of some evil or other. Now, do you hate that which you formerly loved? that which you have been accustomed to? that which you have delighted in? How shall we know we hate it? Why do you not act it? Do you avoid the occasions of it? Do you not nourish it? Do you not think of it but with sorrow and indignation? If you still act it, make provisions for it, run into the occasions of it, count it a matter of nothing, why, then, it is evident you hate it not; and if so, you love not Christ; and if so, you have not admitted him as a friend; and if so, he is not come into you.

I beseech you, deal impartially with your souls herein. It is the greatest madness in the world to deceive yourselves in a business of eternal concernment. Can you, dare you, appeal to God, as David? Search me, try me, if there be any wickedness in my heart, my life, that I act, that I tolerate, that I hate not; I am content this sentence shall be passed on me, I am not one that loves Christ, I am one that shuts him out. Whether you be content or no, the Lord in his word passes this sentence on thee, Christ is not yet come into thee.

2. When Christ comes in, he comes as a husband; if he be admitted as a husband, you give your consent. This makes the match, you consent to take Christ as he is, whole Christ; not only as he comes by blood to pardon you, but as he comes by water to purify you; not only for happiness, but for holiness; not only for justification, but sanctification. You may know if Christ be come in by the temper of your hearts in reference to holiness: where it is derided, slighted, neglected, Christ is far from being admitted; Christ himself suffers therein, for it is his image. When he comes, he plants it; it grows, flourishes, is fruitful more or less; there is a high esteem of it, a dear love to it, strong desires after it, constant endeavours to obtain, increase, promote it in himself and others; sorrow for the weakness, decays, unactiveness of it.

Be not deceived; if you be strangers to holiness, to the being, increase, life, exercise of it, you are strangers to Christ. If enemies to holiness, to deride, scorn it, under the names of purity, preciseness, dissembling, you are enemies to Christ, he is far from coming in.

3. When Christ comes in, he comes as a king; if you admit him, so you will be ruled by him; you will think it treason to run cross to his word, to cast his commands behind your backs. Briefly, are you conscientious to

practise every duty that Christ requires of you in his word? I leave this to your consciences. Is it your design and business to bring yourselves wholly under Christ's government, and more and more under it? Your minds, to judge of things as his laws represent them, that good, best, contemptible, &c., which he declares so? Your wills, to get them subdued to his will, so as when they come in competition his may be preferred; your affections, to have them move and fix as he orders; your lives, to have your conversations ordered by him in spiritual and common affairs?

4. When Christ comes in, he enters as a conqueror. Though sin be in you, though lust have abode in your hearts, they reign not. Are your lusts subdued, mortified, weakened? Do they languish, as having received a deadly wound from the hand of Christ? Are you crucified to the world? Is that as a dead thing to you, which others admire, covet? Christ overcomes the world where he comes. If it overcome you, if you be slaves, drudges to your enjoyments, to your employment; if your hearts be not dead, crucified to these things; Christ has not entered.

5. If Christ be come in to you, you have a high esteem of it, such as becomes him who has the King of glory for his guest. Those that profess themselves Christians must needs say they have a high esteem of Christ. But it is one thing to say it, another to feel it. When he in the parable had found the pearl of great price, how does he express his esteem of it? He went and sold all that he had, and bought it, Mat. xiii. 44–46. Christ is this treasure, this pearl; if you value him, all other things will be vile compared with him. Your own humours, interests, pleasures, profits, you will part with all for Christ; you will say as Mephibosheth, So did he rejoice in David's return, as his estate was nothing to him compared with it: 2 Sam. xix. 30, 'Nay, let him take all, for as much as my lord the king has come in peace,' &c. Not only part with his sins, but renounce his own righteousness, that which he formerly made the ground of his confidence so as to neglect Christ: so the apostle, Philip. iii. 7, 8. By this you may know the truth of your esteem, when Christ and other things which you have formerly valued come in competition, which of these gets the place? If you had rather displease Christ than cross your humours, rather dishonour him than decline your worldly interest, rather offend him than abate of your pleasures, rather hazard the loss of his favour than lose an outward advantage, oh your esteem of Christ is little or nothing; it is not such as will afford you assurance that Christ is come in. If he be in you, your esteem of other things will decrease, your esteem of him will increase, it will overgrow, overshadow all; that which others reject will be head of the corner, elect and precious to you that believe, 1 Pet. ii. 6–8. Those that stumble at the word are disobedient, will not part with sin when Christ commands; to them he is a stone of stumbling, a rock of offence, their base lusts are preferred before him, he has no place in such hearts.

6. If Christ be come in, he has possession of you. For this end he comes to take possession of the soul, and if you admit him you will not disappoint him. Try by this. Have you given Christ possession of your minds, of your consciences, of your hearts and affections? But how shall this be known? Why,

If Christ be in your minds, they will be much taken up with Christ, there will not be so much room for other things; the world will not find such free entertainment in your thoughts. The mind is the eye of the soul; when this glorious guest is come in, your eye will be much upon him, you will be frequent and much in thinking of Christ, how full of love, how full of beauty, how sweet in his promises to thee, how wonderful in his undertakings for thee. Such thoughts will come often, and stay long, longer than formerly; they will be welcome, pleasing, delightful; you will think of him as of your treasure, your glory, your sweetest comfort.

If Christ be in the conscience, it is purged, and you will be fearful to defile it. You will say as the spouse in another case, 'I have put off my coat, how shall I put it on again? I have washed my feet, how shall I defile them?' Christ has taken away my guilt, those filthy garments, how shall I put them on again? He has washed my soul, how shall I defile it? So you will find a greater reluctancy against that which offends Christ; you will be loath to give him distaste; he that regards his guest will not lay his excrements in the place where he lodges. Such is sin in the eye of Christ; and therefore conscience, when Christ possesses it, will say, How can I be so vile, so disloyal, so uncivil? 'How can I do this great wickedness and sin against Christ?'

If Christ possess the will, it will be new moulded. The will of Christ is its mould; into this it is delivered; it runs into it. Before it was hard and stiff; nor threatenings, nor promises, nor commands could move it. If it were fixed on this or that way of sin or the world, whatever was said by Christ in the ministry of the gospel, it would not move from its hold. Ay! but now it offers itself freely to comply with him: 'Behold, I come to do thy will!' 'Thy people shall be willing,' Ps. cx. It yields to what it knows, and it desires to know the whole will of Christ, that it may yield to all. It was hard before, it was a rock, would fly in the face of his messenger then rather than yield to reproofs, exhortations. Ay! but now the presence of Christ, the love of Christ, has melted it; it runs into every part of the mould, fashions itself, conforms to the whole will of Christ, moves so as Christ did. 'I come not to do my own will,' &c.

If Christ be in the affections, they all attend him. There is love to him in all his appearances. There is delight in present enjoyment; there is desire after fuller fruitions; there is fear of losing, there is grief for offending, there is hatred of what is contrary to him; there is anger that he can be no more officious, serviceable, respectful; there is jealousy lest anything should distaste Christ, cause him to withdraw. When Lot had entertained angels, how jealous was he lest the wretched Sodomites should wrong them! He would expose his own daughters rather than they should be injured. The heart that has entertained Christ, the Lord of angels, will be careful to do nothing to offend him.

Come we to the second thing promised. 'I will sup with him. Hence !

Observe. Christ will sup with those that open to him. He will feast every soul that admits. He will vouchsafe not only his presence, but sweet and intimate fellowship and communion with himself. ' I will sup :' it is a pregnant word. Let me open it that you may see what comforts, refreshments, privileges, are wrapt up in it; that those who have opened to Christ may see their happiness; that those who yet shut him out may be hereby stirred up to open. It implies,

1. *Provision.* Christ has made provision for every soul that will open, he has made it ready beforehand. Nothing hinders sinners from these blessed enjoyments but their not opening, Luke xiv. 16, 17. It is Christ has made a great supper, and he stands and knocks, and says, Come, open, all things are now ready. It is Christ the Wisdom of the Father, of whom Solomon speaks, Prov. ix. 1, 2, 3, 5. He sets forth this spiritual provision, these soul refreshments, by such things as we are best acquainted with. He has provided such things as will more refresh the soul than these do our

bodies. They are all ready, Mat. xxii. 4. Do these things nourish? Do they refresh? Do they strengthen? Do they delight us? Do they promote growth? Do they preserve life? Do they continue health? Are they serviceable to the outward man in these respects? Such, and much more, will Christ's provisions be to the soul; they will more nourish, strengthen, refresh, delight it; they tend more effectually to promote and continue spiritual life, health, growth. All that tends thereto are ready, Christ has provided them.

2. Plenty. The Jews used to make their greatest entertainments at supper, and this may be the reason Christ says not I will dine, but I will sup, to denote the plenty of soul-refreshments he will afford those that open. He has spared no cost, no pains; he thinks nothing too good, nothing too much for those that open. If we consider the price, what these refreshments cost Christ, we shall not wonder that they are so many, such abundance of them. They were not bought with silver and gold, but with the precious blood of that Lamb without spot. Where shall we expect, where find bounty, if not in the King of glory? It is for the honour of his majesty that those whom he entertains should have no reason to complain of want. No good thing will he withhold. 'He that cometh unto me,' &c., John vi. 35. He will fulfil the desires. Let the heart be never so empty, never so capacious, he brings enough to fill it, to fulfil it. Let it be stretched out by intense desires to its utmost capacity, he will satisfy it, he will abundantly satisfy it, Ps. xxxvi. 8. The things of the world, get as much of them, as many of them as you can, will never satisfy, the heart is too large for them. But Christ has provided enough to fill, to satisfy, Isa. lv. 1, 2. The whole world cannot fill the heart of man. Christ's provisions are more in this respect than the whole world. Here is plenty indeed, Ps. xxiii. 5; fulness of joy, &c.

3. Variety. There may be plenty where there is not variety. There may be enough, yea, too much of one thing. But it is a feast that Christ promises. He has variety of ordinances, variety of promises, and there are variety of comforts, variety of refreshments in every one. Nay, what is it that Christ offers in these but himself? Now, when he offers himself, he offers all. Here is variety indeed. Can ye have more than all, than he who is all in all? When he comes in, he is yours, and you are his; and what does the apostle infer from this? 1 Cor. iii. 21, 23. Christ only is that object, that can please and satisfy every faculty. To the mind he is the highest truth, to the will he is the chief good, to the conscience he is peace that passes all understanding, to the affections he is the most lovely, the most desirable, the most delightful object. Here is food for the mind, he that is truth itself. Here is a feast for the conscience, he that has slain enmity, he that brings the peace of God. Here is satisfaction to the will, the fountain of goodness. It need not lose itself in searching for drops, and following shallow streams, and digging broken cisterns; here is the spring-head. And here is food for the affections. Love may satisfy itself in embracing the chiefest of ten thousand, fairer than the children of men, the sun of beauty, where all the scattered rays meet and shine in the brightness of their glory. Desire may here satisfy itself in clasping the Desire of all nations. Delight may here bathe itself in rivers of pleasures that are at Christ's right hand. And when Christ sups with thee, thou sittest by him, thou art not far from his right hand. Here is variety.

4. Delicacies. It is a feast, a feast of Christ's providing. You will expect no ordinary fare when the King of glory entertains you. Here is choice rarities, such as the world affords not. 'I have meat to eat that ye

know not of,' John iv. 32 ; 'Not as the world giveth give I unto you,' John xiv. 24. The world are strangers to such refreshments, as Christ affords an opening soul. A stranger does not enter into his joy. Such fare does Christ provide as will not only satisfy but get a stomach, such as will not only continue life where it is, but raise to life where it is not. Such as taste of it shall never see death: hidden manna, angels' food, bread from heaven, the fruit of the tree of life which grows in the midst of the paradise of God. Adam longed to taste it, but then it was forbidden; now Christ brings it into the soul that opens. Himself is the tree of life, Rev. xxii. 2. He comes into thee that thy soul may taste him and live for ever, John vi. 31, 32, 33, 35. The virtue of this provision is everlasting, it far exceeds the manna in the wilderness; that did preserve life for a season, but it could not secure from death. But he that feeds on this can never die, not spiritually, not eternally, ver. 47, 48, &c. It is called water, but it is water of life; he that tastes but a drop shall find it become an everlasting spring in his soul. He that tastes it need not thirst after carnal refreshments; he need not go to the world, to the creatures, to draw, this shall satisfy him for ever. So Christ tells the woman, John iv. 10, 13, 14. He will let thee drink of the pure river of the water of life, clear as crystal, which proceeds out of the throne of God and of the Lamb. What think ye of this manna, of the fountain* of the tree of life, of that water that proceeds out of the throne of God? Is not this worth your opening? Would you taste of those grapes that grow in heaven, those fruits which grow in the land of promise? And now, when you are in this dry and barren wilderness, does thy soul long to taste of those dainties which that city affords, whose maker and builder is God? Why, Christ offers this; he that opens to him shall sup with him He will set before thee some clusters of those grapes which grow in Canaan. He will give thee the first fruits of heaven. Thou shalt have some taste of the pleasures of his father's house. Here are rarities indeed; the world knows them not, and will not believe them. But those that have opened to Christ know what I say. They are hidden enjoyments, Rev. ii. 17; the earnest of the Spirit, the peace of God, the riches of assurance, the joy that is unspeakable and glorious, the hidden manna, the water of life. These are enjoyments that differ but in degree from those in heaven. And those that open to Christ, that sup with him, do taste of some or all these.

5. Familiarity. Christ will deal familiarly with thee as with an intimate friend. We take it as a great argument of intimate friendship when one will say to another, I will come and sup with thee. When David would aggravate the disloyalty of Ahithophel, he does it in these terms, 'It was thou, my familiar.' And how was he his familiar? Why, it was 'he that ate bread with me,' Psa. xli. 9. Thou hast been a stranger to Christ, lived without him in the world, at a great distance from him. Thy hatred of him and rebellions against him have provoked him to shew himself an enemy; but now he is upon terms of kindness and friendship with thee: if thou wilt open, he will come and sup with thee. The mighty God, the Prince of the kings of the earth, will stoop so low as to shew himself kind to thee. When David would express the remembrance of a friend to Jonathan, he thus expresses himself, 2 Sam. ix. 3. It was an exceeding great kindness, the kindness of God, that David would shew. And how does he shew this kindness? see ver. 7. 'Thou shalt eat bread at my table.' This is it, and more than this, that Christ offers; if a sinner will open, he will shew the kindness of God to him, a wonderful, an exceed-

* Qu. 'fruit'?—ED.

ing great kindness. And how? He shall eat bread with me, I will sup with him. Oh what intimacy, what familiarity does this denote, especially when to one far inferior! Mephibosheth, though a prince's son, was astonished that David should offer him such kindness: ver. 8, 'What is thy servant?' &c. Oh, how should sinners run to entertain such kindness from the King of kings! How should those that enjoy it wonder at it! 'What is thy servant, that thou shouldst look upon such a dead dog as I am!' What kindness, what friendship, what honour! What is this to me, that the Lord of glory should come and sup with me?

6. *Complacency.* Christ will shew he much delights in the soul that opens to him. This we learn by their posture at meat, in use amongst the Jews. They, like the Romans, had beds about their tables, on which they lay when they went to eat, so that those which lay on the same bed, the one did rest his head in the other's bosom. So it is said of John, John xiii. 23. So that when Christ promises, I will sup with him, it is as much as if he should say, he shall lay his head in my bosom. He that opens to Christ, he shall have the place of the beloved disciple. So much delight will Christ take in him, as in one whom he will admit to rest in his bosom. Oh blessed posture! Oh happy soul, whom Christ will take so near to himself, whom he will lodge in his bosom! Well may it be said of Christ, that his delights were in the sons of men, when he will shew he takes so much delight in them, as to lay them so near his heart, to take them into his bosom. Well may he say, 'As the Father loved me, even so love I you,' John xv. 9. And yet if he had not said it, what worm amongst us could have presumed, could have believed a love which seemed so incredible? As the Father loves me, &c. There is not an equality, but there is a similitude. And as in other things, so it holds in this. Such is the Father's love to Christ, as he is said to be in the bosom of the Father, 1 John i. 18. And such is Christ's love to thee, such his delight in thee, as if thy heart be opened, thou art in the bosom of Christ. If thy heart be opened, it is Christ's banqueting-house, he will sup there. His banner over thee is love, as Cant. ii. 4. With what delight mayest thou lie down under his shadow! How sweet will the fruits of his delight be to thee, while his right hand does embrace thee, and his left hand is under thy head, thy head rests in his bosom! Oh what sensible soul will not be transported to think of this with believing thoughts! What delights can the world afford like unto these! when, as the spouse expresses it, Cant. i. 13, Christ lies betwixt thy breasts like a bundle of myrrh, and thy head rests in his bosom! Thus will it be when Christ sups with thee; and he will sup with thee when thou openest to him. Then will he shew as much delight in thee as if thou wert admitted to rest in his bosom.

Use. Exhortation. 1. To those to whom Christ is come, whom he feasts, to whom he vouchsafes communion with himself. Be careful to continue in this happy condition. Be afraid of whatever may provoke Christ to withdraw, what may interrupt this communion. Be careful to abide in this blessed fellowship. Use all means to continue this communion with Christ, that he may still feast you, and you may continually sup with him.

Quest. But what means shall we use to this end, to continue? &c.

Ans. 1. Make him welcome. Shew by your joy and cheerfulness in his presence that you count it your happiness to enjoy him. Let him see that you delight in him above all things, that you prefer him before your chief joy, that he is the head, the chief of your delights. Set him against all other things that worldlings rejoice in, Ps. iv. Shew that you count his presence a sufficient supply of all wants. Christ is better unto me than friends, children, riches, honours. These are miserable comforts if I taste not the sweetness of Christ in them; and there is enough in him to rejoice me when all these vanish. As too much delight in outward things does disparage Christ, so does sadness and uncheerfulness in the want of these things. Say, is not Christ better to me than all these? 1 Sam. i. 8, 'My soul shall magnify the Lord, and my spirit shall rejoice in God my Saviour.' Then do you magnify him when you count other things small in comparison of him. Then does your soul rejoice in him when you delight more in him than in all outward comforts. Thus to magnify him, thus to rejoice in him, is to make him welcome, and that is the way to continue him with you.

Ans. 2. Entertain him. He brings provision enough for you, will you provide nothing for him? It is true, indeed, you can provide nothing worthy of such a guest, but something he expects, and something there is he delights in and will accept.

When the three angels came to Abraham, how careful, how active is he to entertain them! Gen. xviii. It is the Lord of angels that comes to sup with thee; oh how careful shouldst thou be to provide that which he loves, wherein he delights! Why, what is that? I will but point at it. It is a humble, a broken, an upright heart. This he loves, this he delights in.

(1.) A humble heart. A heart humbled in sense of Christ's excellency and its own vileness. He beholds the proud afar off, but the humble he beholds with delight, and will delight to continue with it. See what sweet promises he makes thereto, Isa. lvii. 15. None so precious to Christ as those that are vile in their own eyes. He that is poor in spirit, though no man regards him, and though he do not regard himself, the Lord has a special respect to him, Isa. lxvi. 1. Those that have high thoughts, good conceits of their own righteousness, parts, performances, the Lord will overlook them, he stays not there; it is the humble spirit that he looks at, that he dwells with.

(2.) A broken heart. A heart broken from sin, and broken for sin; a heart that melts and bleeds, when it remembers how it has wounded, how it has dishonoured Christ; a heart that yields to Christ's motions, and receives his impressions. A stubborn, stony heart, that is insensible of sin, that is hardened against the word, that is not moved by all the melting manifestations of Christ's love, but continues in sinful ways, notwithstanding all the knocks of the word: this heart is an abomination.

Oh, if the Lord have broken your hearts, made them tender, take heed they be not hardened through the deceitfulness of sin. If you would entertain Christ with that which he loves, give him a broken, a contrite heart; this will be more acceptable to him than all sacrifices, than all the rarities thou canst provide, Ps. li. 16, 17.

(3.) A sincere heart. A true and upright heart. This Christ delights in. 'Thou lovest truth in the inward parts,' Ps. li. 6. He loves a whole, an undivided heart. That is a sincere heart that is wholly Christ's. Ἀνὴρ δίψυχος, ' a double-minded man' he cannot endure; one that has a heart and a heart; says he has a heart for Christ, when his heart is for the world; pretends Christ has his heart, when he has a heart for his lusts. He that will entertain Christ with a divided heart, divides himself from Christ. He will not endure the arbitrament of the harlot, ' Let it be divided.' If he have not all, it is as bad as if he had none at all. Give your heart wholly to Christ; if you entertain him with such a heart, he will like his entertainment, it is the way to have him stay with you.

Ans. 3. Let him have good attendance. If you be careless, disrespectful of him, how can you expect his company! Let every part of your souls wait upon Christ. When you tender him any service, offer up your souls with it. If you tender your outward man, without your souls, in ordinances where Christ feasts his people, it is as if you should bid your servant wait upon your guest, and withdraw yourself; this is a disrespect. Is not Christ worthy you should attend him in person? Take heed of these neglects.

Ans. 4. Let him have your company, be always in his presence. If you depart from him, wander after others, no wonder if he depart from you. Be always with him. How? Your minds with him, by frequent thoughts of him, Ps. cxxxix. 17, 18; your wills and hearts, by inclinations to him, the bent and tendency of them upwards, a bias leading you still; your affections on him, as the most lovely, delightful, desirable object, Ps. lxxiii. 23, 25; and with him in your daily converse; by ordering your conversation so as it may be a walking with God: Gen. v. 25, ' Enoch walked with God,' and so Noah, Gen. vi. 9. Labour to see him, to enjoy him in all, to act as in his sight, to order all for him, to dispose of all in subserviency to him.

2. *Branch of the exhortation.* To those that have not yet opened to Christ; to those who have not feasted with him. You will never have fellowship with Christ, you will never enjoy this happiness, you will never taste how sweet, how gracious the Lord is, till you admit him. He only sups with them that open to him. Oh then make haste to open.

Quest. But who are those that have not opened, that do not feast with Christ, that yet enjoy not fellowship with him? How shall I know whether this be my condition?

Ans. This we will briefly resolve, that the exhortation may be seasonable and forcible. You may know it,

1. By your appetite after spiritual enjoyments. Those that feast with Christ have a strong appetite to those spiritual dainties that he provides. He fills the hungry with good things. Do you hunger and thirst after righteousness, after holiness, after spiritual knowledge, after a clearer sight, a fuller enjoyment, of Christ? You know when you hunger and thirst after bodily nourishment there is a sense of emptiness; this emptiness of the stomach is a pain and anguish to you; you are restless till you be satisfied. Is it thus with your souls in reference to spiritual enjoyments? Are you sensible of a soul-emptiness? Is this your grief, your soul-affliction? Will nothing satisfy but Christ, more holiness, nearer communion? Do you pant and breathe after this in every ordinance? Can you truly say, ' As the hart pants after the water brooks, so pants my heart after God' ? Do you sigh and mourn in the sense of your soul's poverty and emptiness, Christ's withdrawings and estrangement? Is this the voice of your heart, ' Oh when shall I come and appear before him?' when will he appear, &c.? When carnal men think the Sabbaths and spiritual employments long and tedious, whereas they say, ' When will the Sabbath be done?' is it the voice of your soul, When will the Sabbath come, that I may see him whom my soul loves, that I may see his face, and hear his voice, and be satisfied with the pleasure? &c. Does your soul breathe after Christ in prayer? Do you desire the word as new-born babes, &c.? When you can withdraw from ordinances, think them tedious, have no more than some faint wishes after spiritual enjoyments, this argues Christ does not feast with you: ' He fills the hungry,' &c.; ' Ho, every one that thirsteth, come,' &c.

2. By your delight in the presence of Christ, and those spiritual enjoyments wherewith he feasts his people. If he feast with you, you will take such pleasure herein, as will dead your affections to unlawful pleasures, as will moderate your affections to lawful delights. If Christ feast with you, if you enjoy fellowship with him, the pleasures of sin are rank and unsavoury

to your souls. Those stolen waters which were formerly sweet, will now be as the waters of Marah; your stomach will rise against those things that formerly you have swallowed with delight. The word will be sweet to your taste. Secret prayer, and meditation, all those spiritual duties wherein Christ feasts his people, will be your delight. The provisions wherewith Christ entertains you will make you vomit up those forbidden morsels, wherewith sin and the world fed you. You will not henceforth count them sweet; you will have no more mind to return to sinful pleasures than to swallow up a vomit, or to wallow with the sow in the mire. If intemperance, good fellowship, uncleanness, unseasonable sports, or any way of wickedness, secret or open, be sweet to you, you may fear Christ is not yet come to feast with you; you have not tasted of those delights which are enjoyed in communion with him.

3. If Christ feast you, your souls will grow, thrive, and be well liking. This will be the fruit of these spiritual refreshments; they will make you more lively, strong, active, fruitful, in the ways and acts of holiness. You will grow in grace, &c.; go from strength to strength. Your souls will be as watered gardens, the fruits of the Spirit will flourish there. Your hearts, sometimes like a desert, will now be as Sharon; and that which was a wilderness, nothing but weeds, briars, and thorns—worldly, unclean lusts—will now be as the garden of God. The spices thereof will flow out: love, and zeal, and self-denial, and heavenly-mindedness, and contempt of the world. These will be on the growing hand, you will be outgrowing your distempers, prevailing more and more against corruption, and increasing with the increase of God. Oh, but where there is no spiritual life manifested in holy duties, no strength, no opposition, no effectual resolutions against prevailing and endeared sins, there is no sign that Christ is come in. Your souls would be in a better plight if Christ did feast them.

Thus you may know if Christ sup with you. And if the Lord bring these home to your consciences, the exhortation will be more seasonable. If you have not yet opened to Christ, if he do not sup with you, oh make haste to open. To stir you up hereto, consider the misery of those who have not this fellowship with Christ. If you have not fellowship with Christ,

1. You have fellowship with unclean spirits. These, though you perceive it not, feast with you, feed in you. The heart where Christ is not, is a place swept and garnished for Satan, fitted for his entertainment. There is no such refreshment to Satan in the world as the lusts of a carnal heart. These unclean spirits feed rank; your sins are their feast; it is their meat and drink to have you continue sinning. You cannot provide him any choicer delight than unmortified lusts. He sups with you till Christ come in. Your communion is not with the Father, but with him who rules in the hearts of the children of disobedience.

2. You have fellowship with the unfruitful works of darkness. Your lusts, proud, worldly, unclean, revengful, these feed on you, they are always gnawing upon the inwards of your souls. You feel it not indeed; no wonder, till Christ come you are dead. You have seen vermin crawling in, and feeding on a dead carcase; this is the very emblem of a soul without Christ. Unmortified lusts, like so many vermin, prey upon your souls. The worm that never dies breeds here; if Christ come not in and kill it, it will gnaw upon you to eternity.

3. You can have no fellowship with Christ hereafter. Those that acquaint not themselves with Christ by entertaining him, by communion with him here, he will not know them hereafter. If you admit him not, if he sup not with you here, he will say to you, 'Depart from me, I never knew you.'

MAN'S INSUFFICIENCY TO DO ANYTHING OF HIMSELF.

For without me ye can do nothing.—JOHN XV. 5.

IN the former verses there is a parable. A parable is a similitude; and in this, as in others, we have three parts.

1. Πρότασις, a similitude propounded, under three notions, the vine, the branches, the husbandman.

2. 'Απόδοσις, the similitude applied, to three parties, the Father, the Son, the elect; Christ the vine, the elect the branches, the Father the husbandman.

3. Εκθεσις, the similitude expounded and prosecuted, declaring the acts and offices of the several parties held forth therein: the acts of the Father, the husbandman, to lop and purge; of Christ, the vine, to support and nourish the branches; of the elect, the branches, to abide in the vine, and be fruitful. It is propounded in part, and applied, ver. 1; prosecuted in the rest. The acts of the Father, ver. 2, two, according to the distinction of branches: in respect of the unfruitful, ἄιρεσις; of the fruitful, καθάιρεσις; and the instrument by which he doth these acts, ver. 3; the acts and offices of the vine and branches, ver. 4 and 5.

I am the true vine. A vine; that to my members, which a vine is to its branches, give them life, strength, fruitfulness.

True. Not *vitis sylvestris*, a wild vine, either barren, or yielding nothing but wild grapes; but a choice fruitful vine.

Husbandman. How he resembles one, appears in the acts ascribed to him: ver. 2., 'Every branch in me that beareth not fruit, he taketh away; and every branch that beareth fruit, he purgeth it, that it may bring forth more fruit.'

He taketh away, ἄιρει. He detects their hypocrisy, so as they are no longer accounted branches.

He purgeth, καθάιρει, lops off that which is luxuriant. His instrument, ver. 3.; the word is his pruning-hook.

Clean, καθαροὶ, hence *catharist*. Take away the abuse of the word, it is the same with puritan, they differ but as Greek and Latin. No shame to be called a puritan, since Christ called his disciples so. It is an honour not to think one's self pure, but to be pure, whatever others think.

The acts and offices of Christ, ver. 4, 5, in that word *abide*.

I abide in you. The vine may be said to abide in the branches, by conveying juice, nourishment, whereby they subsist and flourish; which subtracted, they would be barren, wither, rot, and fall off. Christ abides in us by his influence, upon which depends our subsistence, life, strength, fruitfulness.

The acts and office of professors follow, ver 4, 5, *abide in me.*

Bear fruit. He urges one by the other. It is necessary, your duty, that which proves you branches, to bear fruit; but it is impossible you should bear fruit, except you abide in the vine. This he proves by the same simile repeated, ver. 4, and applied, ver. 5. Take the sense of the whole simile, and both verses thus: the branches cannot bear fruit without the vine; but I am the vine, &c., therefore abiding in me you may bring forth fruit; but, on the contrary (which is understood), not abiding in me, ye cannot be fruitful. He adds a reason in the text, 'for without me ye can do nothing.'

Obs. Men without Christ can do nothing; or, men out of Christ cannot do anything: 1 Cor. iii. 5, 'Who is Paul, and who is Apollos, but ministers by whom ye believed, even as the Lord gave to every man?' and 1 Cor. iv. 7. 'Who made thee to differ from another?' &c., Mat. xii. 34. I shall

1. Explain (1.) what it is to be without Christ; (2.) what is this impotency, *cannot do*; (3.) in what sense they can do nothing.

(1.) Without Christ; [1.] without union with Christ; [2.] without influence from Christ. Unless they be united to, assisted by Christ, they can do nothing. The first seems to be principally intended; for it is χωρὶς, not ἄνευ, and χωρὶς μοῦ is as much as χωρισθέντες ἀπ' ἐμοῦ, separated from, not united to: yet the other is necessary, and indeed inseparable. Where there is union, there is influence; and where there is acting, there is both.

[1.] Without union. Except ye be in him, as the branch in the vine, partake of his nature, virtue, &c; such a union as is held forth in this cup, a real, intimate, reciprocal, inseparable union: real, not seeming and in appearance only. There are some who are said to be in Christ, not because they are so, but because they seem so: ver. 2, 'Every branch in me that beareth not fruit.' If they had been really in Christ, they had not been fruitless, nor taken away. Those who seem but to be united, seem but to act; to seem to do only, is not to do. He that seems to do only, though he do all in appearance, doth nothing; if not really united, he can do nothing.

Intimate. Abide in me; not *by*, or *near*, or *with*, but *in me*. Appropinquation, conjunction, adhesion, is not sufficient; it must be insition, inhesion, implantation. Many may come near, sit down under Christ's shadow, join with him, cleave to him, yet be impotent, because without him; if not intimately in him, without him, and without him ye can do nothing.

Reciprocal. 'Abide in me, as I in you'; he in you, and you in him. Some may be in Christ, and yet not Christ in them. The elect, before regeneration, may be said to be in Christ; he is not in them, therefore they are as impotent as others. They were in him when he suffered, for he suffered as a common person, as their representative; even as we are said to be in Adam, sinning before we had a being, Rom. xv. 12. If Christ be not in you, as well as you in him, ye can do nothing.

Inseparable. Those are without Christ, who are not sure to be always in him; yet some are said to be in him who may be out of him. The members of the Jewish church were in Christ, else they could not be said to be broken off, Rom. xi. 20; but not inseparably. Faith only makes this union inseparable. They were tied to him by profession, external covenanting, but broken off for want of faith,—'they were broken off by unbelief, thou standest by faith,'—except you be inseparably united, your union is separated from acting, you can do nothing. This is in the text too. He says not, he that is in me, but 'he that abides in me.' Separable union is no union in the sense of the text; it leaves a man without Christ. To abide in Christ, and to be without Christ, are opposed in the text as immediate contraries; so that whosoever abides not in him is without him, no medium is allowed by Christ; and without him ye can do nothing.

[2.] Without Christ's influence, concurrence, co-operation, ye can do nothing. Not that general influence only, which is necessary both to the existence and operation of all creatures; for without this they would not do nothing only, but be nothing, sink into annihilation; this is it by which all live, and move, and have their being. But that special influence, by which, as head of the church, he enables those that are in him to act spiritually and supernaturally, in order to those supreme ends, his glory, &c., this influence supposes union; he concurs with none this way but those that are united to him; and union without this would not empower any to act; without influence, exciting, determining, fortifying, &c.

Exciting. The best principles and habits are as sparks in embers; they cannot burn until they be blown. They are as Peter asleep in prison, will not rise and walk, though the door be open, till the angel of Christ his influence awake them. No second cause can move till it be moved by the first; not grace itself, though more excellent than the rest. It is a creature, and therefore dependent, as in *esse*, so in *operari*. The apostle thought it necessary to stir up pure minds, 2 Peter iii. 1. He in so doing was a labourer together with Christ; he concurs, co-operates by this influence; without it ye can do nothing.

Determining. Souls rightly principled, if not indifferent to good or evil, yet indifferent to this or that act and object. This indifferency must be determined, else there can be no acting; no determinations but by this influence. If it could determine itself, it would be independent in acting. Nothing else can determine it, because nothing can have immediate access to the soul but Christ, and it is not determinable but by an immediate influence.

Though much be disputed against this determining influence, by some who advance the power of nature too much, yet I am forced to close with it by this reason: every particular act is decreed, Eph. ii. 10, else there could be no providence; and how should the soul meet with and be carried to the same acts that are in the decree, with all circumstances, except guided and determined to them by this influence? Our souls are like Ezekiel's wheels, indifferent to go or stand, to move below, or be lifted up above; they are determined to this or that motion by the spirit of the living creatures, by this influence that acts them. They are like clay in the hand of the potter, indifferent to be moulded into this or that form, determined by the hand and at the pleasure of the potter. Paul's comparison, Rom. ix. 21, holds, not only in respect of our state, but our actings: 'We are his workmanship, created unto good works,' Eph. ii. 10. There is a creation which respects acting as well as being; a creation unto good works to walk in them. A pen in itself is indifferent to draw a letter or a figure, or this or that form of either, the hand of the writer determines it; if this be withdrawn, the pen falls and blots. We are such instruments in the hand of Christ, he can draw what he pleases by us; but if he withdraw his hand, his influence, we fall, sin, blot, do nothing, or worse than nothing; as the pen draws nothing without the hand, so ye without Christ can do nothing.

Strengthening influence. 'I am able to do all things through Christ strengthening me,' Philip. iv. 13; therefore able to do nothing without Christ, 2 Cor xii. 9; his strength is made perfect in weakness, Eph. iii. 16, Col. i. 11; we can do nothing unless we be strengthened with might.

(2.) What is this impotency? In four degrees take its nature and latitude.

[1.] It is a privation of power, an absence, a total privation; an absence not in part and degrees only. It is not only a suspension of acts, as may be in sleep, but an absence of radical power: Rom. v. 6, 'When we were without strength, Christ died for us;' Exod. xv. 2, 'The Lord is my strength'; nor an absence of part or degrees of power, as in sickness, but a total privation, an absence of all power: Isa. xl. 29, 'He giveth power to the faint, and to them that have no might he increaseth strength.' Not such an impotency to act as is in a branch in winter to bear fruit, but such as is in a branch cut off from the vine, have not the least degree of spiritual power to do anything.

[2.] It is not only a total privation in respect of power, but it is universal in respect of the subjects of that power. Every part is impotent, deprived, and wholly deprived of all mind, will, memory, affections: Ps. cxxxviii. 3, 'In the day when I cried, thou answeredst me, and strengthenedst me with strength in my soul.'

[3.] It is not a mere impotency only, but an incapacity; not only want power, but incapable with any near capacity to receive it; not only as a branch cut off, yet green, for that may be engrafted; but cut off and withered, no capacity of fruitfulness, though implanted. The capacity is but either merely obediential, such as is in stones, to become Abraham's children; or at least very remote, such as is in dry bones, to be jointed and animated and made instruments of vital parts. The capacity is so remote, such a distance betwixt the power and the act, as nothing but infinite power can bring them together; that power which brought heaven and earth out of nothing, calleth things which are not as though they were; hence called a creation, 'his workmanship, created,' Eph. ii. 10; 'He that is in Christ is a new creature,' 2 Cor. v. 17, Eph. iv. 24.

[4.] There is not only absence and incapacity, but resistance; he is not able, and he is not willing to be able; without power, and unwilling to receive it. It is not only a physical, a want of power, but a moral privation, a want of will; both unable, and unwilling to be able, and unable to be willing. Unwilling, 'ye will not come to me,' John v. 40; hence on God's part, drawing, John vi. 44; striving, Gen. vi. 3; on ours, refusing, Prov. i. 24, Mat. xxiii.; resisting, Acts vii. 51; unable to be willing, Philip. ii. 13, 2 Cor. iii. 5.; we cannot think of being willing.

3. The extent of this impotency in this word οὐδὲν, 'can do *nothing*'; (1.) that they would do; (2.) that they should do; (3.) as they ought to do; nothing.

(1.) That they would do nothing, [1.] to avoid the least degree of misery; [2.] to attain the least degree of happiness.

[1.] To prevent misery, cannot satisfy justice, pacify wrath, avoid the curse, escape judgments.

First, They cannot without Christ satisfy justice. Justice requires perfect obedience; in want of it, death. That men cannot perform, that they cannot endure; it is eternal death, for the penalty is answerable to the fault. There is something of infiniteness in disobedience, at least objective; there must be something of infiniteness in the punishment: punishment is infinite in weight or duration; that which is infinite in weight a creature cannot undergo, it would sink him into nothing, therefore it must be infinite i continuance. What man is not capable of in weight must be supplied i duration. None can satisfy the demand of justice in point of perfect obedience, therefore all without other provision must die eternally.

The proper act of punitive justice, is to distribute punishment, to inflict the penalty due to disobedience, according to law. This the law according to which God proceeds with man, 'Do this, and live;' perform perfect obedience, and have eternal life; and in the negative, 'Do not this, and die;' fail in obedience, and die eternally. Now no man since the fall can perform perfect obedience, therefore justice is engaged to inflict eternal death on all.

Now, lest no flesh should be saved, mercy puts a favourable construction upon the law; dispenseth with personal obedience, and accepts of it performed by another, a surety, a proxy; so that, whereas the sense of the law, primitive and eternal, is this, Do this by thyself or another, and thou shalt live; satisfy the law by thyself or another, and the reward shall be life, otherwise thou shalt die; wisdom concurs with mercy, and finds out Christ as the fittest person to satisfy justice, both by obeying and dying, as most able, most willing to satisfy justice and glorify mercy. So that, by the mediation of these attributes, the rigour of the law is turned into the sweetness of the gospel, and runs thus: he that performs perfect obedience by himself, or by a mediator, Christ the righteous, he shall live; he that doth neither, shall die without mercy.

Now the former is impossible; no man can in his own person perfectly obey the law and thereby satisfy justice: and none but Christ can or will be accepted as a proxy, a surety. Therefore, all who are without Christ, who have not his obedience and righteousness imputed to them, must die without mercy, and the justice of God is engaged to see it executed. Justice is as a flaming sword, turning on every side to keep out those from the way of the tree of life, who approach without Christ his righteousness. Justice is our adversary, we must agree with it, give satisfaction to it in the way, in this life, else it will deliver us to the Judge, &c., Mat. v. 25, and we shall never come out, because it will never be paid. Revenging justice, as the avenger of blood, pursues all sinners; and there is no security, no city of refuge, but Jesus Christ. Vengeance hangs over your heads as a sword by a hair, and justice cries, as he to Elisha, 'Shall I smite him'? And if Christ interpose not, his blow will fall so heavy as it will sink you into hell.

Secondly, Nothing to pacify the hatred and wrath of God; all without Christ are exposed to these, and all the degrees of them. This severe affection in God is held forth in several degrees, and all of them bent against sinners without Christ.

Displeasure. Both persons and actions, all in them, from them. He vouchsafes no pleasing look, thought, word; he frowns, chides, smites, expresses displeasure every way: Rom. viii. 8, 'Those that are in the flesh cannot please God;' not they do not, but cannot. And this denotes not difficulty only, but impossibility: Heb. xi. 6, 'Without faith, it is impossible to please God,' whatever other accomplishments they have, or actions they do. And why? without faith and without Christ; he is well pleased in him, Mat. iii. 17, and with none but in him; no beauty in person, no loveliness in actions, nothing that can please him.

Anger. That is more than displeasure. He that is not well pleased is not forthwith angry: Ps. vii. 11, 'God is angry with the wicked every day.' No wonder; for everything they do, or speak, or think, is a provocation. So, as Christ in another case, Mark iii. 5, he looks round about on them with anger. Hos. iii. 11, 'I gave thee a king in mine anger;' those things that they desire are in anger.

Wrath. Sublimated anger, fury, the accomplishment of anger: Ezek. vii. 8, 'I will pour out my fury upon thee, and accomplish mine anger upon thee'! It flames, burns, and cannot be quenched, Jer. vii. 20. It is 'poured out,' Jer. vii., upon him and all his. The Lord never says, as Isa. xxvii. 4, 'Fury is not in me,' till you be in Christ. Wrath against their persons and services, Eph. ii. 3. 'Children of wrath,' born in it, to it, it is their portion, a rich portion, a treasury, Rom. ii. 5. 'It abides on unbelievers,' John iii. 36; 'revealed against their actions,' Rom. i. 18.

Hatred. This is more than anger in its height; as Aristotle, it is ἀνίατον, it is ὀυ μετα λυπῆς. It does βούλεσθαι τὸ μὴ εἶναι. Anger would make him smart that is the object of it, but hatred would destroy him. Anger is more easily allayed or removed than hatred; anger shews itself with some grief, but hatred with delight. God's love runs in several channels, but all his hatred is carried to sin and sinners. Christ is the Son of his love, and none partake of his love but in Christ.

Enmity. It is a deadly hatred, such as is betwixt mortal enemies: Luke xix. 27, 'Those mine enemies,' &c. Traitors, rebels to his crown and dignity: Rom. v. 10, 'When we were enemies.' No reconciliation without Christ.

Abhorrency. Both we and ours abominable; more than hateful persons, Tit. i. 16; in works deny him, being abominable and disobedient. Their services, those which God commanded. Prov. xv. 8, 'The sacrifice of the wicked is an abomination.' Isa. i. 13, 'Incense is an abomination to me.' Ver. 14, ' Your new moons and your appointed feasts my soul hateth, they are a trouble to me, I am weary to bear them.' Isa. lxvi. 3, 'He that killeth an ox is as if he slew a man, he that burneth incense as if he blessed an idol;' and what more abominable?

None can remove wrath but Christ. Eph. i. 6, He 'hath made us accepted in the Beloved.' 1 Pet. ii. 5, 'Spiritual sacrifices acceptable through Jesus Christ.' For his sake God calls them his people, and her beloved which was not beloved, Rom. ix. 25. It is he that reconciles, 2 Cor. v. 18, 19. He is the ἱλαστήριον, Rom. iii. 25; stands betwixt us and wrath. The law works wrath, Rom. iv. 15; he trod the wine-press alone. He only can make persons and services cease to be objects of wrath: 1 Thess. i. 10, 'Jesus which delivered us from wrath to come.' Rom. v. 9, 'Being justified by his blood, we shall be saved from wrath through him.'

Thirdly, Nothing to avoid the curse of the law of God. All that are out of Christ are under the law, and all under the law are under his curse; for the law blesses none but those who obey it perfectly, curses all that fail in the least: Gal. iii. 10, 'Cursed is every one that continueth not in all things which are written in the book of the law to do them! Every one that doth not all things is cursed, and continues so. It is a cursed state and condition, all in it are cursed, 2 Pet. ii. 14, ὑιοί κατάρας. An Hebraism ordinary in the Testament, sons, *i.e.*

First, *Destined* to the curse, as Judas, and the man of sin is called ὑιὸς ἀπωλείας, because ordained to destruction, 2 Thess. ii. 3. So he is בושׁ who is condemned.

Secondly, *Worthy* of the curse, as τέκνα ὀργῆς, Eph. ii. 3; and Son of peace, ὑιὸς εἰρηνῆς, Luke x. 6, *dignus pace.*

Thirdly, Actually *under* the curse, as ὑιοί φώτος, John xii. 36, &c.; or *filii contumaciæ,* Eph. ii. 2, the son of the curse.

Fourthly, *Most cursed,* as 2 Thess. ii. 3, ἄνθρωπος ἁμαρτίας, *i.e., peccato deditissimus,* most sinful, most cursed.

In every place, in the city and in the field, Deut. xxviii. 16, abroad and at home, where thou most blessest thyself, it shall enter as the flying roll, Zech. v. 4, Prov. iii. 33.

In every part, in body and soul, in every faculty and member, knees, legs, ver. 35; blindness, madness, astonishment of heart, ver. 28.

In every action, Deut. xxviii. 19, when thou comest in and goest out, ver. 19. The Lord shall send cursing, vexation, and rebuke in all that thou settest thy hand unto for to do, ver. 20.

In all relations, that which is dearest and sweetest, children: ver. 18, 'Cursed shall be the fruit of thy body.'

In all enjoyments: ver. 17, 'Cursed thy basket and store, fruits and cattle;' nay, the choicest blessings are cursed, Mal. ii. 2.

With every curse, spiritual and temporal, of law and gospel. The law curses all that want obedience, want works; the gospel all that want faith, without Christ, without both. The gospel-curse is more terrible, no avoiding, no repealing mercy; Christ himself cannot bless when it curses, or leaves under the curse.

Nothing but Christ can remove the curse, for there is no removing but by bearing; and no angel nor man can bear it, it would sink all into hell; not bear that which is due to one, much less what is due to all. If the Lord had not laid hold on one that is mighty, the heavy curse had pressed all into hell: Gal. iii. 13 'Christ has redeemed us from the curse of the law.' Rev. xxii. 3, 'There shall be no more curse, but the throne of God and of the Lamb shall be in it.'

Fourthly, Nothing to escape judgments. This depends on the former. Justice unsatisfied summons wrath. The curse is the sentence which justice passeth in wrath, and judgments are the executions of this sentence.

God's dispensations are judgments to all out of Christ. Not simply afflictions or chastisements (for these may be sent in love, and made subservient to happy ends), but judgments sent in wrath from a judge, not a father. There is a sting of vengeance in them till disarmed by Christ; they come to avenge the quarrel of the violated law. All dispensations are judgments; for, as all the ways of God are mercy to such as keep his covenant, Psa. xxv. 10, so are they judgments to these. As all things work for good to them, *etiam ipsa peccata; sic odientibus eum omnia cooperantur in malum, mala quæ fecerunt, quæ facere voluerant, quæ per alios jurarunt.* No question of those which are evil, *malum culpæ et pœnæ.* And it is clear of things indifferent, which receive impression of mercy or judgment from the principle or intention of God in dispensing.

Nay, those things which are good. *Immo bona quæ fecerunt, in illis non perseverando; vel quæ non fecerunt, omittendo; quæque acceperunt gratia Dei, abutendo.* Mercies in themselves and unto others are judgments, because not in love, nor to do them good. 'Judgment without mercy,' James ii. 13. No drop of mercy but through Christ, if you take it formally and strictly. Grievous judgments, spiritual, $νοῦς\ ἀδόκιμος$, &c. Insensible: when cry peace and dream of mercy, sudden destruction. There is no escaping judgment but by Christ. He only satisfies justice, he pacifies wrath; and, this done, nothing can be a judgment; their nature, their notion, is changed.

Obj. But did not Ahab escape a judgment, yet without Christ?

Ans. It was but deferred, 1 Kings xxi. 29. And but in part deferred, and but awhile; the deferring of it was a judgment, through his abuse of the forbearance.

Fifthly, Nothing to deliver from hell; the accomplishment of the rest.

He that can deliver from wrath temporal must deliver from this, else no deliverance.

All are as brands; must lie in fire to eternity if Christ pluck them not out. All will be drowned in this deluge of wrath that get not into the ark; all must perish by fire and brimstone that get not into this Zoar, or fly not into this mountain. He only can deliver your souls from death, &c.; no name under heaven by which ye can be saved but his alone, Acts iv. 12. It is Jesus only that 'delivers from the wrath to come,' 1 Thess. i. 13. No hill, no mountain, can cover from his wrath that sits on the throne. No man, no angel can secure, only the Lamb. Nothing but fire and brimstone without Christ; nothing but weeping and gnashing of teeth, nothing but everlasting burnings, nothing but shame, confusion, and utter destruction. It is he that trod the wine-press, there was none with him, Isa. lxiii. 3. It is he that drank of the brook in the way; 'in the way,' Ps. cx. 6, *i.e.* betwixt men and heaven. A great gulf, a vast ocean of wrath, curses, judgments, these keep all from heaven, and would carry all as with a violent stream to hell. Christ, to prevent it, he drinks of this brook, dries it up, makes the way plain and easy. But none else can drink it; none that ever drank could lift up their heads but Christ: it sunk them. 'There is no condemnation to those that are in Christ,' Rom. viii. 1; 'He that believes not,' is not united to Christ by faith, 'is condemned already.'

(2.) They can do nothing that they should, good spiritual; nothing [1.] that is formally so, [2.] dispositively so, that has a necessary connection with good of that nature.

[1.] Nothing formally so. In general, if they could do it of themselves, it would not be attributed solely to God, but so it is.

First, Not procure or act any grace. This cannot be done, except it be given from above: James i., 'Every good and perfect gift comes from the Father of lights;' if from men, it would be from below. Eph. i. 3, 'Blesseth us with all spiritual blessings in Christ;' Philip. i. 21, conversion, faith, repentance, love, hope.

First, Conversion. None can convert himself: Jer. xiii. 18, 'Turn thou me and I shall be turned,' says Ephraim, who else was as a bullock unaccustomed to the yoke; and the church, Lam. v. 12, 'Turn thou us unto thee, O Lord, and we shall be turned,' else not. There are two acts in conversion: 1. Passive, the work of the Spirit, infusing gracious qualities. It is properly a work, but metaphorically styled a voice or calling, yet an operative calling; also called preventing grace. And by this act of the Spirit we are united to Christ, before grace, both actual and habitual; for the habit is by this act infused, and herein man is become a patient. 2. Active, where, by the help of the grace received (Christ by his Spirit co-operating), we turn to God, unite ourselves to Christ, obey his call. That cannot be done without union to Christ, nor this without influence from him. We speak of the first, herein we are passive, can do nothing, no more than the air can enlighten itself without the sun; for it is called a turning from darkness to light, Acts xxvi. 18, or dead body raise itself; it is called a resurrection, so most expound, Rev. xx. 6, plainly, John v. 24, 25. It is Christ that is the resurrection, John xi. 25. No more than the world in a state of nonenity could create itself, it is a creation, Gal. vi. 15, 2 Cor. v. 17; no more than an infant can beget itself, for it is a generation; begotten again, John i. 13; no more than a stone can turn itself into flesh, Ezek. xxxvi. 26, and xi. 19.

Secondly, Faith. Cannot believe. This we have by Christ: Philip. i. 19,

'To you it is given in the behalf of Christ, not only to believe,' &c. Nothing must be attributed to us: Eph. ii., 'Through faith, not of ourselves; it is the gift of God.' All must be attributed to Christ: Heb. xii. 2, he is 'the author and finisher.' It is the gift of God indeed, may some say, but man may contribute something to obtain it; as riches are his gift, &c. No, says the apostle, it is so his gift as not of ourselves. But though all in faith be not, yet some part. No, it is all from Christ; he is the author and finisher. 1 Cor. xii. 3, 'No man calls Jesus Lord, but by help of the Holy Ghost.' But (may be) all men are not excluded, such only as are sottish, brutish, improve not nature and reason. No; all are excluded, says Christ: John vi. 44, 'No man comes to me except the Father draw.' Every man must be drawn, or else none will come, will believe; for coming is believing, John vi. 35. But (may be) this drawing is but suasion, some such act in God as supposes power in man to believe, if the duty be but declared and urged with moving arguments. No, it is a powerful drawing; God puts forth an infinite power in drawing. So impotent, so averse is every man to faith, as nothing can prevail but the working of the exceeding greatness of his mighty power; as great, as mighty as was requisite to raise Christ from the dead, and set him at his right hand, in despite of all the opposition that principalities and powers could make, Eph. i. 19, 20.

Thirdly, Repentance. Man, without Christ, cannot repent: Acts v. 31, 'Him has God exalted to be a prince and a Saviour, to give repentance.' It is Christ's gift. He gives it as a prince; to none, therefore, but his subjects, those who are in his kingdom, those in whom he rules.

Nothing can draw men to repentance but the regal power of Christ, that power which he exercises at God's right hand. For the acts of repentance are hatred of sin, sorrow for it, resolution to forsake it, and endeavour its ruin. Now sin is so transcendently dear, lovely, and delightful to a man out of Christ, as nothing but an infinite power can draw him to these acts. He loves it, delights in it more than anything in heaven and earth.

More than liberty. He gives up himself wholly, willingly to be its servant, its slave; when the jubilee is proclaimed, will have his ear bored.

More than time, strength, health, riches; spends all these upon sin. Experience tells us he is prodigal of these in whoredom, drunkenness.

More than his own body, members of it. Lusts are called members, Col. iii. 5; the principal members, eye, hand; most useful, right eye, right hand.

More than his soul. What is the reason the greatest part of the world lose their souls? Because they will not lose their sins to save them. The Lord makes this proposition, Whether will you lose your souls or your sins? The major part by far vote for their sins, and lose their souls merely on that account.

Sin is a man's self. 'Let a man deny himself,' *i. e.* his sins. It is dearer to him than his whole self, body and soul, and the eternal well being of both; he will suffer both to be cast into hell, and there be eternally tormented, rather than part with one beloved lust.

It is dearer to them than Christ, the Spirit, the Father, &c.

Now since every man naturally does thus doat, is thus mad upon sin, what can turn such transcendent love into hatred, such intense delight into sorrow? None but Christ his power. What can divorce a man from himself? What can make him with indignation cast away that which is dearer to him than eye, hand, soul, but the effectual working of infinite power?

Oh it is a mad, a dangerous mistake, to think you can repent when you list, and so defer it to your deathbed. Oh, repentance is not at your beck, it is the gift of God, and it costs him the expense of an infinite power to work it when you are in health, strength, and best disposed. What will it require when dying? will you put off such a difficult work till you have no strength? think to turn from sin when you cannot turn in your beds? It is Christ's gift, and he gives it to few; to them, before it is given, it is a peradventure: 2 Tim. ii. 25, 'If God peradventure will give them repentance.' We read not that ever he gave it any at that time but one. Will you leave your eternal salvation at an *if*, at a *peradventure?* It is ten thousand to one you never repent if you defer it. There is nothing to ground hopes on, much against it.

Fourthly, Love. One out of Christ cannot love Christ, neither *amore beneficentiæ* nor *complacentiæ*. Not for what he does; for no special favour, no spiritual blessing is vouchsafed but in Christ, Eph. i.; nor for what he is, for out of Christ he sees no beauty, tastes no sweetness, though there be nothing else in him; he knows him not, he sees no beauty nor comeliness that he should desire him. Christ is either a stumbling-block or foolishness; he never manifests himself but when he comes to make his abode, John xiv. 21, 23. Nor does he taste any sweetness in him; none taste the Lord as gracious but those that come to him as a living stone, &c., 1 Peter ii. 3–5. He must lie in your bosoms as a bundle of myrrh. No grounds of love, interest, likeness, love.

Fifthly, Hope. Out of Christ, without hope, Eph. ii. 12; Col. i. 27. 'Christ in you the hope of glory.' If you be not in Christ, he is not in you, and then no hope of glory. All other grounds, civility, morality, external acts of charity, piety, are but sand, and what then will become of the house? Mat. vii. 27; Job xi. 20, 'Your hope shall be as the giving up of the ghost;' no lively hope. Christ is the life of it: 1 Peter i. 3, 'Begotten again.' There is no more hope of heaven without Christ, than hope of a man's life that is giving up the ghost. Hope in Christ is as an anchor, Heb. vi. 19, 20, fastened within the veil, *i. e.* in heaven, upon Christ gone thither for that purpose, as the high priest into the sanctuary. All other hope is as a spider's web, Job viii. 13–15. The hypocrite, those who come nearest Christ, those who seem to be in him, who profess so to others, and sometimes think so themselves, yet because not in him, without hope; seeming union, seeming hope. Those that forget God, the proper character of those who are out of Christ and continue so; for if they did remember God, how dreadful, how terrible he is, a consuming fire, a revenging judge, an enraged enemy, they durst not so continue.

Secondly, Cannot subdue any lust. Jer. xiii. 23, 'Can the Ethiopian change his skin, or the leopard his spots?' &c. These may be painted or covered, but not changed. One out of Christ may restrain the outward acts, but not mortify the principle. There can be no formal opposition of sin in such a one, much less victory. Contrary qualities oppose one another in the same subject, as heat and cold. In water, the natural coldness strives with the heat it has from the fire, till it have reduced it to its natural temper; but when the whole subject is possessed by one quality, there is no contention. Sin possesses the whole soul, there is no room for grace until Christ make it; the strong man armed keeps the house, all is quiet, nothing to make opposition.

If there were any, yet no hopes of prevailing without Christ, he only is able to conquer sin; its power transcends all the power in heaven and earth but his. All the power of the creatures, the whole world of natural men, are subdued by it, and made its slaves. Sin reigns over all, the whole world lies in wickedness, fettered, captivated.

There is more strength in a saint to wrestle with sin than in all the natural men in the world; yet sin has been too strong for any saint that ever lived, it has foiled them, they have fallen one time or other.

There was more in Adam, while innocent, to resist sin, than in any saint since; for sin has a party within them, so as they are divided, weakened, and often betrayed by sin within to temptation without. But sin had no such advantage over Adam, yet it overthrew him.

The angels were far more able to withstand sin than Adam, had more excellent nature, more capacious of grace, and nearer to God; yet sin prevailed against them, cast them out of heaven into hell, transformed angels into devils, and keeps them in chains of darkness. The devil is as much a slave to sin as a sinful man is to him, led captive at its will; sin says to one, Go, and he goes, &c.

If neither reason, nor holiness, nor innocence, nor perfection, in man or angel, can resist sin, what power, then, is requisite to subdue it? Even the power of him to whom all power is given. It is he that leads captivity captive; it is he only that conquered all, and makes his people conquerors.

3. Cannot improve any ordinance, either to God's glory or their soul's good; not hear, pray, communicate.

Hear. They are deaf, Isa. xliii. 8, have ears, and are deaf. Compared to the deaf adder, Ps. lviii. 4, neither can, nor will hear. But deaf, and stop their ears. So stopped as none can open them but Christ. Isaiah, prophesying of the flourishing kingdom of Christ, chap. xxxv. 5, says, 'The ears of the deaf shall be unstopped.' Till Christ open the ear, and by it enter into the heart, till he speak a quickening, awakening word, all hearing is no hearing, to no purpose; though an apostle, an angel, Christ himself preach, it is not an engrafted word till it be an engrafting word; till then there is no ground to believe but it is the savour of death, 2 Cor. ii. 16.

Pray. How can they call on him of whom they have not heard? They cannot call Jesus Lord without the Spirit, 1 Cor. xii. 3; sure then they cannot call on Jesus. 'Behold he prays,' it is said of Paul, Acts ix. 11. He thought he prayed before, but he did not so in God's account. God counts that which you call prayer, without heat and life from Christ's Spirit, to be vain babblings, a profanation of his name, taking it in vain, no better than the howling of dogs, Hosea vii. 14. No odour sweet, but what Christ offers, Rev. viii. 3. It is else an abomination. It is an offering a strange fire, because not kindled from heaven. It is a wonder ye are not struck dead, burned, Lev. x. 2. Prayers are a sacrifice evangelical. It is essential to a sacrifice to be offered by a priest. Christ is the only priest under the gospel; those that offer without a priest may expect Uzziah's doom.

Obj. If prayer and hearing be so sinful, it is best to omit them.

Ans. Though a man without Christ be in such a dangerous condition, as whatever he doth be sin, yet some sins are more heinous. He sins in praying, but more not to pray; he sins in hearing, but more grievously in refusing to hear. Those services are so acceptable to God, as he is pleased to encourage and reward the resemblance of them, as in Ahab, Nineveh; may defer judgments here, and make future torments more tolerable; while they use the means, they are in the way wherein Christ works.

Communicate. Out of Christ they do it unworthily. The sinfulness and danger of that, see 1 Cor. xi. 29, 'eateth and drinketh damnation,' to judgment temporal, or eternal, or both. It is a sign and seal indeed, but a sign of God's indignation, and a seal of God's curse, and to some a seal of damnation. Those that are in Christ, eat judgment, if unworthily; those that are out of Christ, and continue so, eat damnation. God sometimes inflicts temporal judgments, yea, death itself, on saints: ver. 30, 'Many sleep.' But he will inflict eternal judgments, eternal death on others: ver. 27, 'Whosoever eat this bread, &c., unworthily, shall be guilty of the body and blood of the Lord,' *i.e.* guilty of some such sin as the Jews, who wounded the body, and spilt the blood of Christ; crucify him, or put him to an open shame. Guilty of high treason against the King of glory, prostituting him in a vile and shameless manner, as Heb. x. 29, 'Tread the Son of God under foot, and count the blood of the covenant an unholy thing.' Such communicating is most horrible profaning of the most precious blood of Christ. Out of Christ ye are no better, in God's account, than dogs and swine, Mat. vii. 6, Philip. iii. 2, Rev. xxii. 15. When they receive the body of Christ, *i.e.* that which represents it, it is cast under the feet of swine, and his blood given to be licked by dogs. Outrageous sinners, as much as they can, execute that on Christ which the Lord threatened on Ahab and Jezebel: 'The dogs shall eat Jezebel,' 'the dogs shall lick Ahab's blood,' 2 Kings ix. 10. This is to 'give children's bread to dogs,' Mat. xv. 26. He that comes hither without Christ, comes without the wedding-garment, Mat. xxii. 11. See his doom, ver. 13, 'Bind him hand and foot, and cast him into outer darkness.'

4. Cannot remove any spiritual distemper. Darkness out of their minds, hardness out of their heart, senselessness or terrors out of the conscience, disorder out of the affections. For the removing of these seem something like to miracles, and require such a power to effect them, as those acts which the Scripture relates as miracles, such a power to enlighten the mind, as at first to bring light out of darkness, or give sight to him that was born blind; as much to pacify a terrified conscience, as to still the tempestuous winds and raging seas; to mollify a hard, stony heart, as to bring water out of the rock; to order the affections, as to joint dry bones; to make a carnal fancy spiritual, as to turn water into wine; to subdue a rebellious appetite, as to cure the possessed with the raging spirit; to cast Satan out of the soul, as out of the body; to purify the heart, as cleanse lepers.

A miracle is when something is done, 1, *ex nihilo;* 2, *in subjecto inhabili;* 3, *sine mediis propriis;* out of nothing; in a subject altogether indisposed; without proper means.

Ex nihilo. These are such spiritual qualities as are created, not educed, *e potentia materiæ,* depend not on matter, as the sounder schoolmen.

Subjecto inhabili. If any disposedness, so remote, as no natural means, nothing but God, can bring into act. There is a total privation, both of act and power, *proxima,* and from such a privation there is no regress to the habit, but by extraordinary power.

Sine mediis propriis, such as have no native virtue or aptitude to attain the end, as clay to open the eyes.

The means used by God, 1, have no proper tendency to these ends and effects; all they have is by institution. They are not appointed because they are effectual means, but are fit means because they are appointed.

2. They have no efficacy but by divine influence. They have not any natural virtue in themselves; what they have is *ab extrinseco,* from divine assistance and co-operation. God appointed such on purpose to glorify his power, and take us off from dependence on means. What virtue in the foolishness of preaching to make wise to salvation; in the word to quicken, regenerate, sanctify? It was not Christ's word to the dead man, but his invisible power, that raised him, Luke vii., so to the sick of the palsy. It is but *verbum significativum* of itself, it is *factivum* by co-operation, signifies something of itself, but effects nothing without concurrence. It is but a passive, not a co-operative instrument. It works but *per modum*

objecti, and an object has no active power *per se* to work upon the organ; it is only an occasion of working, which some force in or about the organ makes use of (*Pemble*). Means that have a native power, when fitly and skilfully applied, do always produce their effects, but not when hindered by some extraordinary indisposition. The word, though most seasonably and skilfully applied, many times works nothing; that which makes it efficacious is absent, not in itself. Those work always, equally, in all alike disposed, not these. Therefore these being so like miracles, require an infinite power, cannot be removed but by Chirst. If there be a dark mind, it must continue so for ever, except Christ enlighten it. Christ was sent to this end.

3. Out of Christ men can do nothing as they ought. A clear demonstration. They can do nothing but sin, *Ergo*, either what they do is sinful, or if lawful in itself, yet they do it sinfully. Take *do* in its latitude, as comprising thoughts and words, and all sorts of actions, and they are sin or sinful.

(1.) Thoughts. They are thoughts of iniquity, Isa. lix. 7, yea, the most provoking iniquity, abomination, Prov. xv. 26. All, and always, Gen. vi. 5.

(2.) Words. No good word can proceed from an evil heart: Mat. xii. 34, 35, 'How can ye, being evil, speak good things? The evil man, out of the evil treasure of his heart, bringeth forth evil things.' The fruit will be like the tree, ver. 33. Ye cannot expect grapes of thorns, Mat. vii. 16. They will be vain, idle, poisonous, worldly, or worse. There must be a new root, a new stock, before there be good fruit; must be engrafted into the true vine before the words can be good grapes.

(3.) Acts, all kinds, natural, civil, religious.

[1.] Natural: eat, drink, sleep, sinful. 'What is not of faith is sin,' Rom. xiv. Applied by the ancients to prove that even eating, and every act of an unbeliever, is sin; though otherwise expounded now, it is true in this sense. Heb. xi. 6, 'Without faith it is impossible to please God;' 'Whether ye eat or drink, or whatever ye do, do all to the glory of God,' 1 Cor. x. 31. There is a command, it is a sin to violate it; but out of Christ men cannot avoid; so far from using natural things spiritually, as they use spiritual things naturally, to low base ends. Their table is a snare, a sin, what they eat ensnares them, Titus i. 15. 'Unto them that are defiled and unbelieving is nothing pure,' not the necessities of nature, not sleep or dreams, even their mind and conscience is defiled, much more their fancy.

[2.] Civil acts. Those which their particular calling engages to. 'The ploughing of the wicked is sin,' Prov. xxi. 4. By a *synecdoche* all their labours, buying, selling, working, a curse attends all. No curse where no sin; cursed because sinful. *Omnis vita infidelium peccatum est*, says Anselm, *et nihil bonum sine summo bono, i. e.* without Christ; all they have and do. Hence they are said to live, walk, dwell in sin, they abide in it; their whole life, all the acts of it; their whole course, all the steps of it are sin, Ps. i. 1. Their walking, their standing, their sitting: when they walk, it is in the counsel of the ungodly; when they stand, it is in the way of sinners; when they sit, it is in the seat of scorners; or if they scorn not holy ways, they despise them.

[3.] Religious acts. Those which may plead exemption, if any; acts of moral virtues are *splendida peccata*. *Etiam quod virtus videtur esse, peccatum est* (Ambrose). *Nec placere ullus Deo, sine Deo, potest* (Id.). Religious exercises, the sacrifice of the wicked, Prov. xv. 8. Acts of piety or charity, whatever comes under the notion of a sacrifice, is abomination; the sweetest sacrifice, incense, Isa. i. 13, the greatest abomination; compared to idolatry, Isa. lxvi. 3, because not in dependence upon, and in reference to, Christ.

Obj. The saints do sin in their best services; their righteousness is as a menstruous rag; *in multis offendimus omnes,* says James; therefore this seems not peculiar to men out of Christ.

Ans. It is true there are infirmities, defects, imperfections in the best; such as not answering the exactness of the law, requiring perfection, may be called, and are bewailed as, sins. But there is a vast difference betwixt their sinning and others', as will appear by a distinction. Acts may be called, and are, sins, or sinful,—

1. *Quoad substantiam,* or *materialiter;* when the act itself, abstracted from circumstances, is forbidden, as murder and adultery. And in this sense religious acts, in or out of Christ, are not sins; for the matter and substance of them is good and commanded.

2. *Quoad circumstantiam,* or *formaliter;* so that is a sin which is good in itself, if not well done, out of a good principle, in due manner, for right ends; for these, though accidental to an act, yet are essential to the goodness of it. Hence moral acts *plus debent circumstantiæ, quam substantiæ.* He that fails in any of these, makes the best act evil: *malum est ex quolibet defectu.* These are necessary ingredients to every good action; and to fail in any one, divests it of goodness. Now, there may be a double failing: through, 1, want, or total absence, as of light at midnight, no moon or stars; 2, weakness, or imperfection, as of light at twilight. We call things irrational that want reason, as beasts, properly; or that have it, but want the perfect exercise of it, as children, improperly.

This, then, is the answer: unbelievers want those things that are necessary essentially to make an act good, therefore their actions are properly evil. Believers have all the ingredients, but with imperfection, and in weakness; therefore their actions are not properly evil, but rather imperfectly good. Acts are good in themselves *in actu signato,* from the matter; but *in actu exercito,* and as acted by us, they cannot be good, without a good principle, a due form, a right end; without Christ, without all these. The want of any one makes an act evil, much more the want of all. Those that have not Christ, have none at all; and so their acts not at all good. Totally evil, not in the parts; want essentials, not degrees only; they do nothing as they ought, because,

1. No good principle; the stream rises no higher than the spring; not out of thankfulness, not out of love, nor out of respect to God's command, nor to the reward rightly apprehended; but out of custom, out of design to gain some temporal advantage; for the loaves, Mat. xxiii. 14, or to get applause; to be seen of men, or out of envy, Philip. i. 15; to remove some incumbent affliction, then seek him diligently, Hosea v. 15; to escape hell, out of fear.

2. Undue manner; not reverently, diligently, delightfully.

(1.) Irreverently. Not with self-debasing, God-exalting thoughts; without sense of vileness, which is visible in saints in all their approaches; as Abraham, Gen. xviii. 27, Isa. vi. 5; the publican, who stood afar off; the prodigal, unworthy, and the centurion; 'the four and twenty elders fall down,' Rev. iv. 10. High, awful apprehensions of God, his presence and glory. Though these may use the words, yet have nothing that answers them in their spirit, but have rude, common spirits, not as much respect as to an ordinary man, Mal. i. 14.

(2.) Negligently. Careless, with lips only, not with heart and strength; faint wishes, not strong desires, such as that, Ps. lxiii. 1, 'My soul thirsteth for thee,' &c., and xlii.; not δέησις ἐνεργουμένη, James v. 16, *operosa, actuosa,* wrought in, possessed with the Spirit. The possessed with evil spirits are called ἐνεργούμενοι. There is a holy possession; they have not such attention as that of the angels, 1 Peter i. 12; the same word, παρακύπτω, Luke xxiv. 12, John xx. 5, 8. Not such praises as David: 'Bless the Lord, O my soul; all that is within me, bless his holy name.' Their charity not παρόξυσμος, Heb. x. 24, but παράλυσις. There is a palsy in it, a deadness, a benumbedness; either cold or lukewarm, faint and heartless; not upon some particular indisposition, but its ordinary temper.

(3.) Unwillingly. Not willingnesses, free-will offerings, Ps. cx., but as a tax, grievous; the more spiritual and heavenly the employment, the more tedious; soon weary: Mal. i. 13, 'What a weariness is it! when will the Sabbath be done?' No delight; far from David's temper: Ps. lxxxiv. 10, 'A day in thy courts is better than a thousand.' They neglect opportunities; little in private or secret duties; draw back, as from that they have an averseness to.

3. No right end. This has a strong influence into the goodness of an act. *Non actibus, sed finibus pensantur officia:* not the acts, but the ends, give weight to a duty.

Not the general ends: 1, not to please God, but rather to please men; 2, not to glorify him, but to advance themselves; 3, not to enjoy him, content with duty without God.

Nor particular ends: to satisfy conscience, not to have communion with Christ.

Obj. But if men, out of Christ, cannot but sin in performing religious duties, it is best to omit them.

Ans. 1. By way of concession and caution. It is true; unregenerate men are reduced to a necessity of sinning, but it is through their own default. This is the great misery of that state, the greatest imaginable, that they can do nothing but sin. But it was man's sin that plunged him into this misery. God made man upright, and so he might have stood and walked, but he found out many inventions; and this is one of them, one of the worst, that he ensnared himself into a necessity of sinning. If he worship not God, he sins; because he is obliged to this, both by God's command and his own being. If he worship God, he sins; because he does it not from good principles, in a due manner, for a right end. If he pray not, he sins; because he is commanded to call on God, and thereby acknowledge his dependence on him. If he pray, he sins; because not with faith, fervency, &c. If he hear not, he sins, because God speaks to him; if he hear, he sins, because he mixes not the word with faith. If he serves not God, he sins, because God enjoins and expects service; if he serve him, he sins, because he serves him not in spirit. If he eat not, he sins, that would be self-murder; if he eat, he sins, because he doth it not to God's glory. Sin lies at his door, let him go backward or foward, he falls into it; but it was sin that brought him to it. Now, to neglect duty because he cannot perform it without sin, when his sin brought him to this exigence, is to add sin to sin.

Ans. 2. In such necessities, where evil is unavoidable, the less evil must be chosen. If you cannot but sin, it is better to be guilty of the least than the greatest sins. Now, it is a less sin to serve God amiss than not to serve him at all; better to do what ye can than do nothing; a total omission is a more heinous sin than an undue performance; better to offend in manner only than both in matter and manner; it is *bonum*, though not *bene*. There is a goodness in the acts performed, their matter and substance is good, though they want other ingredients of goodness. But omissions are purely evil, without any mixture of good; there is more contempt in total neglects, and so more provocation. You provoke God more by omitting prayer than by lukewarm, superficial performance; and so in hearing. The saints may allege, 'The men of Nineveh shall rise up in judgment,' &c., Mat. xii. 41. We may collect the nature of the sin by the degree of the punishment; the Ninevites' punishment shall be more tolerable, who performed but outward acts of religion, without inward affections, than those who would be brought to neither outward nor inward conformity; therefore omissions are more provoking sins than outward, though otherwise sinful performances. God, then (whatever he does now), will render to every man according to his works. It is better to pray as well as you can (though you cannot as well as you should) than not to pray at all; the omission is totally sinful, performance but partially; that is more wilful, this is in part necessary.

Ans. 3. If necessity of sinning were sufficient ground to omit religious acts, it is so also for omitting natural acts; if it be a reasonable plea for exemption from those, it is so also for exemption from these. We cannot eat, sleep, &c., but we sin, no more than we can hear and pray without sin; yet these are as necessary for your souls as those for your bodies; these as necessary as you are rational, as those as you are sensible; the necessity of sinning is equal. Now, since the reason is equal, yet men urge it unequally, for omissions in one kind, and not in the other: it is a sign that sinfulness, urged as a reason to omit holy duties, is but a pretence. The true reason is, their averseness to the holiness of the duties, not to the sinfulness that attends them.

Ans. 4. God rewards the outward performance though sinful, but there is nothing but wrath revealed against omissions; *Ergo,* no reason for it. Holy services are so acceptable to God, as he rewards the very resemblance of them, though but obscure. The lively actings of grace are so lovely in God's eye, as he seems to be pleased with the picture of them. It is manifest in Ahab, 1 Kings xxi. 29; and Nineveh, Jonah iii. 10; who had presently perished but for their outward humiliation; this procured a reprieve.

Reasons why a man out of Christ can do nothing.

Want of the principle of acting, defect in active faculties and members, no spiritual action without spiritual faculties, absence of active qualities and habits. What can a carcase do without a soul? He wants a soul, spirit. Or what can a soul do in itself (immanent acts) without faculties? or in the body (transient acts) without members? or by these, if altogether indisposed and disabled to act? Or what can faculties and members do without active qualities and habits, since they do nothing immediately but by the help and mediation of these? To use the metaphor in the text, 'What fruit can a tree bear without a root? or a tree rooted without branches? or by them broken and obstructed? or branches, if withered, without sap, not qualified? He that wants Christ wants that which is answerable in a spiritual sense to all these.

1. *Want of the principle of action.* The soul is the principle of action in a man, and the Spirit of Christ in a Christian, no act without. What the soul is to a man, that Christ is to a Christian, all imperfection separated. *Spiritus Christi forma ecclesiæ.* Gal. ii. 20: 'Nevertheless I live, yet not I, but Christ liveth in me.' Even as we say of the body it lives, yet not the body but the soul lives in it. The body separated from the soul is dead, so a man [out] of Christ is dead, Eph. ii. 1, Col. ii. 13. And what can a dead man do? Spiritual life is the result, the issue of the soul's union with Christ, as natural life of the soul's union with the body. Action cannot be without life, life cannot be without a soul. Every degree or kind of life springs from a soul suitable; vegetative, sensitive, rational life, from a vege-

tative, sensitive, rational soul. Now, as there is a degree of life above these, a spiritual life, so there must be a soul a degree above these, or something equivalent answerable to one, and this is Christ, who therefore is said to dwell in us by faith; this is the *copula*, and he is said to be our life, John xiv. 6, Col. iii. 4, and to give life, John vi. 33, to quicken, &c., so that he is a soul virtually though not formally; as necessary to the life and activity of a Christian as the soul to the life and actings of a man. No action without life, no life without a soul; neither without Christ.

2. *Defect of faculties and members, the instruments of action.* A man out of Christ wants spiritual faculties. He is wholly what Paul complains of in part, carnal, Rom. vii. 14. 'The carnal mind is enmity,' Rom. viii. 7; not only enmity but impotency, 1 Cor. ii. 14. No more apprehend spirituals than a blind man can see colours, therefore called blind, Rev. iii. 17; Isa. xliii. 8, 'Bring forth the blind people that have eyes.' Eyes they have indeed, but see not; for, being constantly fixed on lower objects, they can no more see spiritual objects than one eye can see both heaven and earth at once.

And as they want the prime spiritual knowing faculty, so the prime spiritual moving faculty. The will is carnal, there is a foreskin of carnalness upon the heart; it cannot move spiritually till it be circumcised, Deut. xxx. 6, Rom. ii. 29; Jer. ix. 26, it is old, gross; Mat. xiii. 15, fat; Isa. vi. 10, hard; Psa. xcv. 8, stony; Ezek. xi. 19, deceitful; Jer. xvii. 9, desperately wicked.

Though they have these faculties, yet they are wholly disabled for, and indisposed to, spiritual acts. What can a perforated memory retain? A sieve can hold no water. What can a seared conscience be sensible of to the soul's advantage? It is seared in part as to morals, wholly as to spirituals. If a body be organised, have members, yet if they be bound, obstructed, or maimed, how can they act? Man's faculties are bound, he is Satan's captive, fettered with sins, loaded with fetters, obstructed, no passage from heart or head, for active spirits; there can be no conveyance without union; *dissolutio continui*, maimed; the great fall we had in Adam broke all, put all out of joint. If a particular fall broke David's bones, Psa. li. 8, when he fell but from sense and degrees, but from one storey, much more this from the height of happiness and enjoyments. A failing may put one out of joint, as Gal. vi. 1. The word rendered restore, &c., is to set in joint, $\varkappa\alpha\tau\alpha\rho\tau i\zeta\varepsilon\tau\varepsilon$. How can a man walk with his legs broken, out of joint, or work with arms and hands wounded, maimed? A deadly wound we have by sin; men out of Christ are halt and maimed, Luke xiv, both Jews, ver. 21, and Gentiles, ver. 23, *mancos claudosque*. Nay, considered without a soul, they are no apter for action than those dry bones in Ezekiel's vision were fit for motion, Ezek. xxxvii., until the Lord caused breath to enter into them.

3. *Absence of active qualities.* As the soul cannot act without faculties, their instruments, so faculties cannot act without some qualities, which either concur as causes, or are required as necessary conditions, *causæ sine quibus non*, without which there can be no acts. The mind cannot discourse or argue without knowledge, nor apprehend without species, images, representations of its objects. The will cannot choose without liberty; the eye cannot see without its humours, or any that move without heat. Even so no spiritual act without a spiritual quality, and no such qualities without Christ. How can a man believe without faith, or mourn for sin without repentance, or be fervent in service without zeal, or expect happiness without hope, or affect union to God without love, debase himself without

humility, or submit in affliction without patience? These are formal acts, and cannot be expected but by their proper form, no more than the fire can burn without heat, or water wet without moisture, or the sun illuminate without light. It is impossible. There can be no spiritual act without such qualities, and no gracious qualities without Christ. Spiritual qualities are spiritual blessings, and the Lord blesses none out of Christ with these, Eph. i. 3. In Christ, *tanquam in capite, unde in membra manant,* he that is not a member is not capable. So in remote imperate acts. How can he mix the word with faith who hath none? How can he pray in spirit who is not spiritual? How can he sing with grace in his heart [who has no grace in his heart]? How can he serve the Lord with fear who is void of fear? How can he have his conversation in heaven who has no heavenly mind?

The soul is not only void of gracious qualities, but possessed with the contrary; no sound part from the highest faculty to the lowest. The mind, *quoad apprehensionem,* dull, blind; *quoad judicium,* wavering, erroneous, prejudiced; *quoad cogitationem,* vain, unfixed, independent, foolish, carnal. The memory receptive, retentive of evil, and that only; the conscience senseless or desperate, accuse when it should excuse, &c.; the will perverse, will when it should not will, rebellious, chooses when it should reject, rejects when it should choose, yields when it should resist, and resists when it should submit; the affections misplaced, disordered, immoderate, violent; fancy vain, carnal, brutish, no spiritual light nor holy order, nor due rectitude in any power of the soul till Christ come into it. Spiritual qualifications are part of his retinue: when he comes they attend him, when he is absent the soul is at a loss. Without these it cannot act spiritually, and cannot have them without Christ.

Use. This informs us of man's misery without Christ. One main design of the ministry of the gospel is to convince sinners of misery. Man will not come to Christ until convinced. 'The whole need no physician,' those who think themselves whole. Survey it as you love your souls, seriously meditate on it, let no thoughts thrust out these. Suffer yourselves to be convinced, be not afraid; it is safe, if not pleasing. To help you, observe my former method. This misery is positive, transcendent, perfect, unavoidable, increasing.

1. *Justice will be satisfied.* It is as dear to God as any attribute, it is himself. God will glorify it, and no way but by satisfaction; it will pursue the sinner, as Asahel did Abner, 2 Sam. ii. 19, 21. Is it nothing to be under the curse, all the curses of the law and gospel, heavier than mountains, more dreadful than all the menaces of men or devils; under wrath, fiery indignation, deadly hatred, as the wrath of a king, as the roaring of a lion? This wrath is heavier than a millstone about your neck. In danger of hell, but a step betwixt you and it! Your life is but a span. How can a man sleep upon a precipice? You are not certain of life for an hour, but sure of hell if you die out of Christ!

2. *Transcendent.* More miserable than sensitive and inanimate creatures; they act in conformity to God's will, and so declare his glory, and improve all the strength received to this end. Miserable man acts nothing for, but all against, God, is always cross to God and his designs. So the best is worse than the beasts that perish, the happiest more miserable than the worm or toad.

3. *Perfect.* Without mixture of happiness real; no degrees, no pledges, no hopes, no peace, but through false intelligence, mispersuasion; cry peace, peace, when sudden destruction cometh upon them, as on a woman

in travail. Inquire of peace, as 2 Kings ix. 18; when destroyers are at hand, Isa. xlviii. 22.

No safety. In the midst of enemies, deadly enemies, above, below, within, without. God incensed, the devil and all creatures ready to smite when God gives commission, and nothing suspends it but a provoked and abused patience. Oh what danger! Those are his greatest enemies whom he most trusts and loves, sin and Satan in his bosom; follows their counsels who thirst after his ruin; like Delilah to Samson, like Joab to Amasa, 2 Sam. xx. 9, 10.

No riches. Naked, famishing, yet without money, lie like Lazarus, but die like Dives; the state of their souls is like Lazarus's body.

No success. All tends to the ruin of their souls: it is worst when best. A successful sinner is like a ship carried with full sails against a rock; all gales of prosperity do but hasten you to hell, quicken your voyage thither; he is but made fat to the slaughter.

No pleasures. None that are truly delightful, but poisoned; gilded pills, please the eye and palate, but poison the stomach, and are bitterness in the end, as James iii. 8, it is said of the tongue, 'full of deadly poison.' There is death in the pot, nay, they are dead already, 1 Tim. v. 6, Rev. xviii. 7, 8.

No pledges. No relation to God that will afford comfort or advantage; not his children, but the children of the devil; they are of him as a father, his offspring, bear his image, receive a portion with him, that which is prepared for him and his angels.

Not friends, but enemies. In league with sin and Satan until in covenant; lie under the dint of terrible threatenings, Ps. xxxvii. 20, 'The wicked shall perish,' &c. Wound the head, &c., a deadly wound, Ps. lxviii. 21; consume as the fat of lambs, because exposed to his wrath, who is a consuming fire; Ps. xcvii. 3, 'A fire goeth before him, and burneth up his enemies round about.'

Not servants until members. Slaves of Satan, led captive by him at his will; servants of sin, Rom. vi. 16, inferior, worse than that which is worst of all things.

4. *Unavoidable misery.* They can do nothing for themselves; heaven and earth can do nothing, only Christ; will do nothing until in Christ: it cannot be avoided but by doing or suffering. To do, is impossible; to suffer, is intolerable; for sufferings of man, to satisfy, must be eternal. It is an ease in misery to hope for freedom. Here is no hopes without Christ, no promise, no attribute; faithfulness acts not but in performing promises; mercy will not run but in its proper channel, that is Christ; power cannot help without infringement of justice; justice is an enemy till satisfied; wisdom has found out no way for satisfaction but Christ, and if God cannot or will not, how can the angels, saints, or other creatures? They all say, as he, 2 Kings vi. 27, 'If the Lord do not help thee, whence shall I help thee?'

5. *Increasing wrath.* Swells bigger and bigger till it overflow. As the measure of iniquity fills, so the measure of misery, like Ezekiel's waters, Ezek. xlvii. 3, 4, to the knees, loins, and then unfordable. Adam left a treasury of misery to his posterity, and every child adds to it, every sin casts something into it; every thought, word, act, is a sin till in Christ. Oh the multitude of thoughts, what a black account! You think thoughts are free, but the Lord has manifested as much indignation against thoughts as actions. These destroyed a whole world at once, Gen. vi. 5; cast angels out of heaven; captivity, Jer. vi. 19; Simon Magus, Acts viii. 22; indignation at the last day, 1 Cor. iv. 5. Words, you say, are wind, but such

as will carry into the Dead Sea: Mat. xii. 36, 'Every idle word;' 'By words ye shall be condemned,' James iii. 6; 'The tongue is a fire, a world of iniquity, sets on fire the whole course of nature, and is set on fire of hell,' as it is kindled there, so it kindles it.

And acts of all sorts, Rom. ii. 5, 'treasure up wrath.' If the better sort of actions treasure up wrath, what do the worst? If, when you call on God, how much more when you swear and blaspheme? If acts of charity, much more acts of intemperance, drunkenness, &c. If, when you hear, much more when you neglect and contemn the gospel and revile the messengers of it. If in acts of justice, what in acts of direct fraud and oppression? If those cast in a mite, these cast in a talent. Oh misery! Justice is already exasperated, ye daily more incense it; God's wrath is already kindled, ye daily every moment add fuel to it; you are already at the pit-brink of hell, and every hour draw nearer to it, and heat the furnace of indignation seven times hotter. Better never have been born than live without Christ; better you had perished in infancy, than continue out of Christ; the longer ye live, the more miserable.

Quest. If it be such a misery to be out of Christ, how shall I know if I be out of him? Those that are not solicitous are certainly out of Christ.

Use. 2. Of examination. Try this whether you are in Christ; come to this trial as a business of great concernment. It is not a trial for your estates: you would be careful and solicitous there; nor for your lives only: there you would be attentive, serious. If one should tell you that the greatest part of this congregation were to be visited, though insensible of it, with a dangerous disease, those that did not discover it would certainly die, and should offer symptoms to discover it; would not every one be fearful, careful, diligent in attending? So it is here.

Signs from the nature of the union in general.

1. Separation from that which is at great distance from Christ; nothing is further distant from Christ than sin; he that is in Christ is separated from sin, in judgment, affection, practice; *judges* it dangerous, deformed, bitter, nothing more, not afflictions, &c. He that thinks sin profitable, lovely, pleasing, is out of Christ.

Affection. He sorrows, mourns in secret, weeps with a broken heart, as for an only son, Zech. xii. 10; shame, not in respect of men only, but God, as against mercy. Fear, not as it brings ruin, but as it separates from Christ, suspends his influence, &c. Hatred, not anger only; hate it as sin, all sin; seeks its ruin.

Practice. Avoids it, all occasions; flies from it as from a serpent; if once overtaken, seldom twice, with the same sin. He that lives in sin, commits the same sin often, drunkenness, whoredom, Sabbath breaking, cozening, omission of duties, public or private, is not in Christ. If you are in Christ, you do not absent from ordinances, frequent bad company. 2 Tim. ii. 19, the Lord will own none for his, nor should any profess the name of Christ, much less pretend to union with him, who departs not from all iniquity; from all, quite a great way, from the sight and occasions, Acts iii. 26. It is a blessed fruit of this union to turn from his iniquities, those wherein you have lived and delighted, 1 John iii. 6, οὐ ποιεῖ ἁμαρτίαν, *i. e. non dat operam peccato. Non simplex actio, sed cum studio et voluptate conjuncta;* if conscience condemn you of wilful and customary omissions or commissions, ye need no further inquiry.

2. *Likeness.* Where there is oneness, there must be likeness. He that is in Christ is one with him, therefore like him in graces, affections, actions; such virtues, and so exercised.

Virtue. 1 Peter i. 15, and ii. 9, as not of equality, but resemblance; contempt of the world, self-denial, humility.

Christ contemned the world. The world loved not him, nor he it; cared not for him, nor he for it; the riches, honours, pleasures of it were contemptible to him. What do ye most desire, that one thing only or principally? What do ye esteem? What do ye value yourselves and others by? What do you pursue in the first place? If it be the world, you are its children, not the members of Christ.

Self-denial. Christ sought not his own will, nor his own glory, John v. 41, John xiv. 14. What do ye when God's will and yours come in competition? What is your design, your interests, or his glory; pleasing and advancing yourselves, or honouring him?

Humility. Mat. xi. 29, those that are come to Christ have learned this. Are you cross, furious, impatient, revengeful, trample on inferiors, despise equals, undervalue superiors? Do you make yourselves a rule to others, and condemn those who are not of your mind and way, or it may be of your humour? Does your humility spring from the lowness of your outward condition, or sense of sinfulness, misery, spiritual wants, free mercy, unworthiness? Do you receive the word with meekness, as new born babes, willing to be guided, to submit to it? Acting with delight, do you count it your meat and drink to do the will of God? Have you such objects for your affections as Christ, delight in saints, in soul prosperity? &c.

3. *Propinquity.* Union implies this. Those that are far off from Christ are not in him. Are you continually with him by thoughts? These present Christ to us, and make us present with him. Are thoughts of Christ more frequent, delightful, consistent than of others? Is he not in all your thoughts? Do ye crowd out these? Are they strangers, or unwelcome? He is most where Christ is most, *i. e.* in his ordinances, in his banqueting house, sits down under Christ's shadow with great delight. How are you affected to the ordinances, praying, hearing? Are they dear, sweet, desirable? Is one day in the house of God better than a thousand, as it was to David? Ps. lxxxiv. 10. Do you thirst for the Sabbath ere it come? And why? Not for other respects, but Christ's presence? Do you omit wilfully, or upon small occasions? Are they tedious? Do you complain of length in others, and curtail yours? Is idleness or worldly employments more pleasing? 'When will the Sabbath be done?' Those that are united are always in him, with him, but this union and presence is not always alike manifested. The sense and comfort of it is to be found in ordinances, hence esteem, desires: 'When shall I come and appear?' Ps. xlii. 2, Ps. xxvii. 4.

4. *Adherence* to Christ. This is included in union; for it is not a corporeal, essential, or personal union, but rather moral and spiritual. And this union is better expressed by adherence than inherence; the soul spiritually cleaving to Christ, and clinging about him, and a strong tendency to more intimacy, fear of estrangement and separation. Does your soul cling to Christ, clasp about him, as ivy about the oak? If you have no strong inclinations after him, and resolutions to cleave to him, as in Ruth, chap. i. 16; if you are not fearful to offend, careful to avoid all unkindnesses that may alienate from him; if you refuse to hear, or answer not his call, accept not his invitations, slight his messages, reject his motions, refuse admission to him, can be content without his company; if anything else will please you in his absence, then you are not in him.

5. *Participation* of Christ. He that is in Christ partakes of the nature and influence of Christ, as the branch of the nature and sap of the tree, Rom.

xi. 17. A branch of a wild olive, grafted into a true olive, partakes of the root and fatness thereof, changes its nature, &c. If Christ be in you, there is such a change, as the Scripture expresses, sometimes by creation, 2 Cor. v. 17, Gal. vi. 15; by renovation, Rom. xii. 2, Titus iii. 5; by generation, Gal. iv. 19, John iii. 3; born of God, 1 John iii. 9; born of the Spirit, John xvi. Is Christ formed in you? Have you experience of the pangs of the new birth? Is there an universal change? Are old things passed away, and all things become new,—mind, apprehension? Can you see spiritual things more clearly? Col. iii. 10. Have you a new judgment of persons, things, state, actions? Is your conscience tender? Does it smite you sooner and more for small, secret evils, such as others make nothing of? Is your will pliable to good, inflexible to evil? Have you new intentions, resolutions, affections well fixed, moderated to lawfuls? Is your conversation not worldly, sensual, profane, &c.? Is it such as becomes the gospel, adorned with the fruits of holiness and righteousness?

6. *Sympathy* with Christ. Co-suffering, and sense of his suffering. He that is in Christ will be sensible of what is done against him. Christ's sufferings *for* men are finished, but his sufferings *by* men are still continued, blasphemies, reproaches, contempts, opinions and practices dishonourable to Christ. Those, then, who make Christ suffer, are not in him. Those who deny his glory, profane his name, contemn his words, slight his beauty and love, and the expressions of it, desert his ways of truth or holiness. Those who are not sensibly affected with these in others do not mourn in secret, Ps. lxix. 9, Rom. xv. 3, prefer it not before their own credit and interests. But such as are as tender of the honour and interest of Christ, as if it were their own, resent it, as though their own reputation and interest suffered thereby, are in him.

The ligaments and bonds of this union are uniting graces, faith and love. Faith unites Christ to us and love unites us to Christ. Christ dwelleth in us by faith, Eph. iii.; and we dwell in him by love, 1 John iv. 16.

Love. He that is in Christ loves him; he that is so near Christ, sees and tastes that which constrains him to love. This is a sure character of love which Christ gives, John xiv. 15, 'Keep my commandments.' This is not only a sign of love, but union: 1 John iii. 24, 'He that keepeth his commandments, dwelleth in him.' Is this your resolution, as it was David's? Ps. cxix. 106. When you read and hear as they, Jer. xlii. 5, 6, do you resolve sincerely what they did but feignedly? Do you labour to convince your judgments, make your hearts submit, and your lives conformable? What is your custom, after conviction and clear manifestation of God's will? Do ye forget, or neglect, run cross to it, put it off with excuses, say, The Lord is not so strict as you are made to believe; you see none so obedient, or time enough hereafter, or the Lord be merciful to me in this, I may be saved though I be not so punctual?

Delight. Ps. cxii. 1, 'Delighteth greatly,' &c.; as much as formerly in pursuing carnal designs. Is it your meat and drink to do his will? or are his commandments grievous, hard sayings, the land cannot bear them? Are all his ways pleasant, those commands that cross your interests, lusts, humours? Do you not overlook the least, nor excuse you from the most weighty, nor waive the strictest?

Faith. He that is not in the faith, is not in Christ. Now faith, to describe it in its lowest degree, is a consent to take Christ as God offers him. He offers him, not only as a Priest, but a King, both as a Prince and a Saviour. Are you as willing that Christ should rule you as save you? Do you desire as truly to be freed from sin as from hell? Is the filthiness of sin grievous, and not only the guilt and damnation of it? Do you desire holiness as truly as heaven; not content with pardon without purity? Is the dominion of sin as terrible as its wages? If you divide what God has joined in offering Christ, you have not received him; if you care not for Christ at all, or desire him only to save you from hell, can be content to live without Christ all your lives, and desire him only at death to free you from misery and wrath to come; if the sceptre, the yoke, the strict ways, the holy paths of Christ, be not desirable in your account, you have no reason to think you are in Christ. Resolve this question, If you might be assured that you should never be damned for your sins, would you leave sin? Or thus, If you might be saved without holiness, would you desire holiness? Would you follow it?

2. Characters from metaphors. That in the text, Christ is the vine, believers branches. By such means as you may discover a branch to be in the vine, you may know if you be in Christ. There are three signs; growth, pruning, fruitfulness.

(1.) *Growth*. That branch which grows not is either dead or separated from the vine. If you stand still, or run round in a circle of duties, without making any progress, if you grow not better every day proportionably to the means, mercy, light that you enjoy, you are not in Christ. You hear, that is better, &c., but are you improved by hearing? Do you hear with understanding, increase in knowledge? Does your light beget heat, kindle your affections? and do you manifest it in your conversation, walking answerable to the gospel?

You pray; but do you pray every day better, more fervently with the heart, from a sense of spiritual wants, so sensibly and importunately, as one ready to famish cries for bread, pinched with soul wants, as one fainting for thirst? Do you pray more spiritually; earnest not only for temporals, but spirituals; not only to be freed from hell, but to be made fit for heaven; as much for holiness as happiness? You have good motions sometimes, what becomes of them? Do you nourish them till they grow into resolutions? and do not these end but in endeavours? and are your endeavours visible in your life? Those that are in Christ grow daily in all things, Eph. iv. 15. Those that grow worse, or not better, or not in the best, in grace, in knowledge, from good materially, to good in principle and manner, are not in Christ.

(2.) *Pruning*, John xv. 2. The husbandman will not take pains to cut off luxuriances from branches that are withered or broken off, he prunes only those in the vine. Has the Father pruned you, cut off all inordinate motions from your hearts, and acts from your lives, or cut them so as they cannot grow? Are all actions exorbitant, such as become not a holy profession, cut off, separated from your conversation? 1 Cor. vi. 9–11; Eph. iv. 22. Is all corrupt communication cut off from your lips? Eph. iv. 29. Not profane, unclean, deceitful, but good, edifying, gracious. Are sinful thoughts, projects, reasonings, cut off from your minds? 2 Cor. x. 4, 5. If in Christ, all are subject to him, no speculative wickedness, no providing for the flesh, Rom. xiii. 14, no reasoning against Christ, &c. Are all inordinate affections cut off from the heart? Gal. v. 24. Have you no delight in sin, to act or remember it, no desire to return to Egypt, no lusting after the flesh-pots, no love to the world, no more than it hath to Christ? John xv. 19; Col. iii. 5–9. Are you mortified, crucified, dead to old lusts, take no more pleasure in them than Abraham in Sarah when dead? Gen. xxiii. 4. Would you have them dead and buried, not in hopes of a resurrection, but so as not to rise again? Are your lusts alive? Do you act them openly; or if there be some restraints upon outward acts, fear, or shame, or other carnal, selfish enforcements, do you nourish them in your thoughts. Do they live, and move, and command in your affections? Do covetousness, uncleanness, intemperance, pride, malice, &c., live within you, though they appear not as formerly in your lives?

(3.) *Fruitfulness.* That branch is in the vine that is fruitful, beareth not only leaves, but fruit, good, ripe, seasonable, and much. He is only in Christ that is fruitful, John xv. 2, 4, 5; filled with 'the fruits of righteousness,' Phil. i. 11; 'the fruits of the Spirit,' Gal. v. 22. He that is fruitful has every grace, and the exercise, the acts of every grace; both confidence and humility, hope and fear, joy and sorrow, spiritual poverty and contentment, heavenly-mindedness and diligence in his particular calling, love and hatred.

Acts. These are actually fruits; grace, but fundamentally. Without the acts of grace you are no more fruitful than a vine in winter. Many acts, much fruit.

Are you acquainted with the life of faith; not only faith to make you alive, but faith to live by? To live by faith is to make every act of life an act of faith; to pray in faith, hear, walk, work, eat in faith; act it on all its objects, attributes, offices of Christ, promises, relations, providences, experiences, functions of the Spirit, the person of Christ; in all its acts, recumbency, application, confidence. Do you cast yourselves, and the burthen of your affairs upon God, and there rest? What then means these torturing cares and indirect means? Do you use to apply promises particularly, do all in the strength of the promise? And rises it so high as triumph over dangers, doubts, difficulties? Can you trust him with all, for all temporals as well as spirituals, and upon disadvantage? Do you walk in fear, as seeing him who is invisible, with awful apprehensions, reverence, holy abasement?

Do you act it on all its objects; not only justice, but glory, mercy, purity, omnisciency? Do you fear, not only to suffer, but to offend; and that because it is a dishonour, contrary to his pure nature, and a base return for mercy?

Love. Do you know the constraints of love? Is there a vein of love runs in every act, to make it sprightful and lively? Do you hear his voice because you love him, seek his face because you love him, relieve his members because you love him, think and speak of him because you love him? Are you diligent in worldly affairs because you would be serviceable, and desire to be serviceable out of love? Are you diligent in holy duties because you would enjoy him, and desire to enjoy him out of love? Is your design and endeavour an act of love, in acts natural, civil, religious? Are you diligent in doing, and ready and cheerful to suffer, out of love? Is it your grief and affliction that you fall short hereof, and do you count it your happiness to be always under the constraints of love, to have your whole life influenced by it?

2. Metaphor. Believers are in Christ as stones in a building, whereof Christ is sometimes called the corner stone, Mat. xi. 42, Acts iv. 11, Eph. ii. 20; sometimes the foundation, 1 Cor. iii. 11; they are 'living stones,' 1 Peter ii. 4, 5. This affords three characters: 1. stedfastness; 2. dependence; 3. uniformity.

(1.) *Stedfastness.* A stone laid upon a sure foundation in a well compacted structure is not easily moved. One in Christ is stedfast, unmoveable, not tossed with every wind of doctrine, nor overthrown with every temptation. Do you yield to sins that have no visible temptation, as swearing; or to temptations at the first motion and assault, in judgment or practice? Are you overthrown by weak temptations, such as nature can resist, such as have no advantage from within? Do you fall frequently? Is your life a falling-sickness? or do you return to it when temptation returns? Loose stones may be removed at pleasure.

(2.) *Dependence.* Stones in a building depend one on another, all upon the foundation. Their strength is dependence. Is yours so? Do you live in continual dependence on Christ? Being sensible of weakness to bear Christ's yoke, do you run to him for support? In sense of difficulties in holy actings, sense of your impotency, convinced that no strength is sufficient, but some without, and that only in Christ; is your constant recourse to him upon all occasions for it? Is your life a leaning upon Christ; as the spouse? Cant. viii. 5. Do you make new applications to him in all your undertakings, sighing after him, resting on him? Do you do all in his strength?

(3.) *Uniformity.* It is a curious structure, a temple. In such buildings the stones are uniform; not one part rough and another polished, but all regular. Do you make conscience of all sins, all duties, to avoid the one, to perform the other? Do you not leave one sin to live in another, gross, secret, beloved, common? Do you not do one duty, and omit another, but do all public and private, and secret meditation, heart-searching examination, self-judging, secret mourning, strict watch over heart and ways, inward motions, and outward acts; not acts of common honesty only, but charity, by relief, and by counsel, admonition, and reproof? And acts of piety, do you not hear only, but attend, believe, remember, meditate, practise? Do you not pray only, but watch, trust, expect, and conform your life to your prayers? *Quicquid fit propter Deum, æqualiter fit.* What is done out of respect to God, is done equally, uniformly. He that does any part of his will sincerely for him, out of respect to him, will decline no part of his will, have respect to all.

Use of Exhortation. To get into Christ.

Motive. The strongest is necessity, here is the greatest. If you do not, you are most miserable; if you do, you are most happy.

The misery of not being in Christ appears from the former discourse; and further, from ver. 6, ' If a man abide not in me, he is cast forth as a branch, and is withered, and men gather them, and cast them into the fire, and they are burned.'

(1.) *Cast forth*, ἐκβάλλεται ἔξω. Cast out of God's favour, no good word, kind look, gracious act; out of his household, not his servants; he that commits sin is the servant of sin. Out of Christ's jurisdiction, not his subjects, but rebels, will not have him for their King; not his disciples, but Satan's, will not have him for their Prophet. He will not be their Priest; shall they have benefit by his sufferings, who continue to make him suffer? Nor shall they partake in his intercession; he prays for none but those that are in him, or in the way to him. ' I pray not for the world, but for those that thou hast given me out of the world,' John xvii. 9.

(2.) *Withered*, ξηραίνεται. No beauty, no more than we see in a withered stick; no life, dead, alienated from the life of God, Eph. iv. They live the life of the devil; no leaves, nothing to shroud from wrath, hide from justice; no fruit but fruits to death, pernicious fruit, such as endangers the tree that bears it; such as Deut. xxxii. 32, ' The vine is the vine of Sodom,' &c.; useless, Ezek. xv. 2, 3; obnoxious, Isa. v. 4–6; and good reason, for it dishonours God, ver. 8.

(3.) *Men gather them*, συνάγεται. As men gather dried sticks, so the devils gather wicked men. As good angels are employed about saints, so the devils about these. They are excommunicated in the court of heaven from society with angels and saints; delivered over to Satan, to be ruled and rewarded by him. He abides in Christ, in whom Christ's words abide. By the same reason Satan abides in them, because his words, his suggestions abide in them. 'His ye are whom you obey.' There are but two commanders in the world, the God of heaven, and the god of the world. He has soul-possession, if not bodily, dwells in them, and acts them: as the Holy Spirit acts the saints, so the evil spirits these. Satan 'works effectually in the children of disobedience.' They are gathered, and bound over by Satan to the great session.

(4.) *Cast into the fire*, εἰς πῦρ βάλλεται. This is the doom, and will be the end of all that continue out of Christ, barrenness entitles them to it: Heb. vi. 8, 'That which beareth thorns and briars is rejected, and is nigh unto cursing, whose end is to be burned.'

(5.) *Burn them*, καίεται. Keep them in the fire till they be burned. Those that continue out of Christ will not only be cast into the fire, but kept there burning; only with this difference from other withered branches, though they shall be always burning, yet they will never be consumed.

2. The happiness of those that are in Christ. Take all the branches in one bundle: that expression, 'If you abide in me,' &c., 'Ask what you will,' ver. 7, 'and it shall be given you,' a large grant as the heart of a man or angel can desire; not as Ahasuerus to Esther, v. 3, 'Ask to the half of my kingdom;' but what you will, heaven, or earth, or both, and all in both: if it be good, that is the only limitation, and this does not straiten the privilege, but enhance the worth of it. That which is not good, is not worth asking or giving. So the sense is this, 'Ask what you will,' if it be worth asking, if it be worth giving. Oh the sweetness, the largeness of this privilege, the happiness of those that partake of it! This grant, as it is large, so secure, the best security in heaven, the bond of Christ, his word, promise, obligation; no other condition of it but this, 'If you abide in me.' If a great prince, rich, powerful, should make such a promise, ask my son, my kingdom, my treasure, all that I have or can do; how happy would we think the condition of such a favourite! Nay, they have not only this happiness by way of promise, in words, *de futuro*, but actually, in hand, in words, *de præsenti*. 'All are yours, ye are Christ's, 1 Cor. iii. 23. Interest in him gives interest in all; union with him, possession of all. *All* is an exposition of *what ye will*. Man's desires are infinite, nothing will satisfy but *all*; therefore Christ, who is determined to enhappy all his, will satisfy their desires to the utmost, and gives all, all that heart can desire; himself, and all with him.

All that he is, as God; his attributes, essence, subsistence; as mediator, his offices, your king, priest, prophet, and the acts of it; as man, his mind; he is ever mindful of you, you are never out of his thoughts, Isa. xlix. 15. His heart, his affections, more tender and endeared than in any creature. Love, 'As the Father loves me,' John xv. 9, John xvii. 26; love not equally, but as truly, really, effectually, certainly, unchangeably. Delight, 'All his delight is with the sons of men,' Ps. x. 3, Prov. viii. 31. Compassion; for this end he assumed our nature, Heb. ii. 17. Joy, 'as a bridegroom over the bride,' Isa. lxii. 5. Oh what happiness! Surely this is the joy of heaven, yet you have it here.

All that he doth. His administrations on earth,' John xvii. 13, 19; his intercession in heaven, he now lives, &c. It is the end of his life in heaven.

All that he suffered. He was wounded for their transgressions; and that he purchased by sufferings, pardon, peace, grace, glory.

All that he hath, even from his throne to his footstool: Rev. iii. 21, ' To him that overcometh, will I grant to sit on my throne.' His footstool: Mat. v. 5, ' Blessed are the meek, they shall inherit the earth ;' ' He that overcometh shall inherit all things ;' not only peace, and plenty, and glory, but his peace: John xiv. 24, ' My peace I give unto you.' His fulness, the fulness of God, Eph. iii. 19, John i. 16, ' of his fulness.' His glory, John xvii. 22; his joy, ver. 11. All that he hath in heaven or earth, your Father, your portion; the Holy Ghost your comforter, teacher, John xiv. 26; the angels your attendants, your guard, Mat. iv. 6, Ps. xci. 12; the saints your brethren, your fellow-members, first fruits, Gal. iii. 28. Ye are all one in Christ Jesus, part of the same crop with those that are in heaven, only they are first reaped.

All in earth, 1 Cor. iii. 22, ' or the world, or life, or death, or things present,' &c.

All that he is, so far as it is communicable, and you capable; all that he doth, or can do, if good for you; ' no good thing will he withhold from them' that love him, Ps. lxxxiv. 11, and xxxiv. 10. All the difficulty is, whether can better judge what is best, God or ourselves. Oh what tempting happiness is he! Can the world, or sin, or Satan, promise or secure such things? ' Will the son of Jesse give you fields and vineyards? 1 Sam. xxii. 7.

Obj. But how shall we get into Christ?

Direct. The best I can prescribe is shewing the way by which the Lord brings men to Christ. No man comes except the Father draw him, and he draws by degrees.

1. *Illumination.* Opens the eye to see sin, sees it with another light; sets them in order before him, shews him the face of his soul in the glass of the law, the sins of his nature and life; leads him into every part of his soul and life, as he did, Ezek. viii., still greater abominations; brings to his mind sins past, and makes him possess them; opens the bag where they are sealed, lets him see what a woful treasure there is; shews him the number and weight, so that he sees cause to complain with David, Ps. xxxviii. 4, ' Mine iniquities are gone over my head; as an heavy burden they are too heavy for me.' Variously in degrees, not alike in all as to degrees.

2. *Humiliation* under the sense of sin's desert. Sees all the curses and threatenings bent against him, levelled at him, justice ready to discharge, wrath hastening justice; applies threatenings to himself, the soul that sins shall die, is cursed, condemned; conscience is awakened, sensible of the burden, groans under it; the sting of guilt pricks his heart, as theirs, Acts ii. 27; conscience is wounded, sometimes so deeply, as ready to faint; the burden of wrath lies so heavy, as makes him ready to sink. Hence horror, a degree of hell; fear, a spirit of bondage. Sees himself at the brink of hell, ready each moment to fall in. Herein the Lord proceeds with some variety; all are not humbled alike, some more deeply, some less; but all have some sense of their misery, so as to be apprehensive of an absolute necessity of Christ.

3. *Self-renunciation.* Renouncing his own righteousness, despairing that any thing he hath, or can do, will remove this misery, pacify wrath, expiate guilt, and counting all loss. Men convinced of wrath and misery are apt to inquire with the jailor, ' What shall I do to be saved?' and take up resolutions to pray, hear, &c., hereby to pacify God; but when he intends union, he takes away these rotten supports, to make way for Christ; convinces that nothing he can do is available; not the fruit of the body, nor rivers of oil; not good nature, well-meanings, holy duties; all are as men-

struous cloths; none but Christ. These must be pared off before there be engrafting.

4. *Hope.* Though he makes him despair of himself, yet he leaves him not to despair of God, raises some weak hopes from the mercies of God: 'He wills not the death of a sinner.' General offers of Christ: 'He came to save sinners,' to 'seek and save that which was lost,' and why not me? says the humbled soul. From examples in Scripture and experience, the Lord pardoned such grievous sins and sinners, who knows but he may pardon me? It may be he will. He cannot, dare not say at first, he hath pardoned, or will pardon; but it may be he will. From absolute promises, 'though their sins be as red as scarlet,' 'I will blot out their iniquities for my name's sake.' There is some hope concerning this.

5. *Desires after Christ.* These are virtually faith, when strong, spiritual, sincere, constant, insatiable. When I desire him, as one almost famished for bread, as the hart panteth for water, as one under a pressing burden for ease; as one dangerously wounded, and grievously pained, for cure; as one in danger of death, for life, 'skin for skin,' &c. Let me be poor, if I may have interest in Christ's treasures; let me be hated, persecuted of all, if Christ will pity me, love me; let me be banished from friends and comforts, if Christ dwell with me; let me be nothing, have nothing, if Christ will be mine; let God deny me what he will, if he give me Christ; let him dispose of me as he pleases for temporals, only let me live, let my soul live. Oh that I might have Christ, though I suffer, die, go through hell to him! These bring along with them,

6. *Consent to take him upon his own terms.* He thinks them propounded easy, embraces them with all his heart. No terms could be so grievous but he would accept them; he closes with Christ, clasps about him, resolves never to part. This is actual faith, and then actual faith makes us one with Christ, brings us actually to him.

Use. If those that are without Christ can do nothing, then they are deceived who ascribe to man's will unrenewed, such a power, as to that which is spiritual and saving, as is inconsistent with what Christ here tells us. They say man's will can do much herein, without Christ's special influence. Christ himself tells us, 'without him he can do nothing,' and the apostles after him, Eph. ii., Phil. ii. 13, 2 Cor. iii. 5. This is enough to crush that conceit of the power of free will, advanced first by the Pelagians of old, who were therefore branded as the enemies of the grace of Christ, and revived in later times by the Arminians, the Socinians, and the Jesuits, who all are zealots for it. And indeed it is of great moment, and of large influence. Luther called it *fundamentum totius papismi*, the groundwork of all popery. The words of Christ in the text are a full confutation of it. I need add no more to dissuade those from it who are tender of the honour of Christ, and the glory of his grace, but only to let you understand what it is, and help you to see into the inwards of it; for I cannot much fear that any amongst us will be taken with it, but because they do not well understand it; pride in the learned, and ignorance in others, are the great advantages of it.

I will therefore endeavour to open it to you as briefly and plainly as the matter will admit. The glory of Christ, the interest of souls (who are concerned to give him the honour of his grace) and the vindication of the text I have insisted on, require this of me.

Free will, in the sense of those who maintain it, is a power in the will to incline either way, when that which is supernatural and saving is offered as its object; a power and freedom in the will to choose or refuse, to yield or resist, to embrace or reject, as it list. So that this with them is twofold.

1. *To refuse or resist.* We say as to this, The will of a natural man may, and does, resist common motions or offers of grace, but not those that are special, viz., when the Lord puts forth the power of his grace with an intent to convert a sinner, then the will does not, cannot resist.

They say when the Lord and the power of his grace has done all that it can do, all that he is ever wont to do, the will ordinarily does, and always can resist it; so that if we will believe them, we must believe that when the Lord has done what he can, the will can do what it list. And so it must be free, so far as not to be subjected to the dominion and power of God; he cannot rule, or move it otherwise than it list; if it should be more than thus subjected to him, it would be destroyed. It is essential to the will to have a power to resist God, do what he can, unless he would take away the nature and being of it. This is the true visage of their opinion (in the first branch of it); if you will see it plain and naked, there needs no dirt to be cast upon it to render it odious.

2. *To choose, or embrace.* The will, they say, can incline to that which is spiritually and supernaturally good. They speak not of a capacity, which is not denied, but of an active power. A natural man, by the power of his will, as he can reject Christ, so he can embrace him; as he can resist converting grace, so he can yield to it as he will; the will can incline itself to this as well as the other. This is a true representation of their opinion in the other branch of it. Against which we say,

(1.) This is to deny original corruption (which is the foundation of all the doctrine of grace comprised in the gospel, for it all depends upon a supposal of the corruption of our natures), for if the will can incline itself to that which is spiritually good, it is not habitually inclined to evil only, it is not fixedly averse to supernatural good; and if we be not so inclined to evil, and so averse to good, our natures are not corrupted.

(2.) This is to deny the necessity of regeneration, which is the ground of all the benefits and privileges we have by Christ, the first stone in the structure, without which none of the other have place, for if the will can incline itself to spiritual good, it needs not regenerating grace to incline it; if it can incline itself to holiness, it needs no inward principle of holiness to incline it.

To solve this (that I may not conceal from you the best they have to say for themselves) they tell us, the will is not inclined but by the help of grace, that gives it power. But what is that which they call grace? Let that be minded. They say it is a common enlightening of the mind to discern the object, and a moral excitement or inviting of the will by arguments and rational inducements. Such grace, they say, the Lord affords to all indifferently, and it is all that he gives or does to the will of any one in order to conversion. Those that use this grace right, are converted; those that do not, are not.

To this we say, that such grace gives no strength to the will, but supposes it able already. He that holds forth a light to a man lying on the ground, and moves him with arguments to rise and walk, does not thereby give him legs, or strength, but supposes he has these already; so that his grace, such as it is, being supposed, still no room is left for original corruption, no need of regeneration; nor will Christ be the cause of conversion, the author of faith or holiness, and the efficacy of his grace shall depend upon the will of man. Grant the best they can allege, all these absurd and dangerous things must be allowed, if we will allow their opinion.

[1.] There will be no original corruption. For if the will be corrupted through original sin, that which helps it must take away the prevalency of this corruption; but such a grace as they tell us of, is of no such use or tendency; nor do they pretend that it heals the corrupted will, for they rather freely confess that there is no corruption in the will of a natural man.

[2.] The necessity of regeneration is for the implanting of gracious qualities in the soul, and especially in the will (that being the principal seat of all grace), that it may be possessed with the principles of faith, repentance, holiness; that by virtue of them it may be inclined to suitable acts; since, in every state, the will inclines according to the quality of it; nor can the fruit (the acts) be good, till the tree be good. But they do not pretend that their moral grace does implant any such gracious qualities or principles in the will; nay, they contend there needs no such quality in the will; the will can, and does, incline itself without it, and so no need of regeneration.

[3.] This, we say, makes Christ not to be the worker or real cause of conversion or regeneration, nor the author or giver of faith, repentance, holiness; which appears several ways; for since what Christ does for us this way is only, as they say, by this suasive or exciting grace,

First, He does not work conversion, but only invite to it; not *efficere*, but *suadere*. He is not the worker of it, but a persuader to it, and that for the most part ineffectually; moves the will so as it needs not to be moved, and commonly is not; effects not our conversion or regeneration, but only excites us to do it ourselves.

Secondly, This way (which is all they leave them) he neither gives the power nor the act.

First, Not the *power*, for suasive grace gives no more the power to yield than resist, but leaves the will, as they say, indifferent. Besides, this exciting grace supposes a sinner has the power already, and needs not giving, but only exciting. He that thinks it enough to shew a man his business, and persuade him to work, doth not thereby give him strength, but supposes he has it beforehand.

Secondly, He gives not the *act* or the willingness, for that which gives or works the act determines the will, or causes it to determine itself. But this which they call grace brings it only to the will's choice, and leaves it indifferent to act or not to act; and so, no more works the one than the other, and is no more the cause that it acts than that it acts not. They say God will convert us if we will (neither desires nor promises it absolutely), so that the will must be from us; but if we be willing we are actually converted, and so the act of conversion is from us.

(3.) This grace of theirs is given equally to all, and effects no more in one than another. Therefore Christ, in this respect, is no more the cause of conversion in these that turn to God than in these who are never converted; he works regeneration no more in those that are sanctified than in the unregenerate, *i. e.* he works it not at all, he is no cause of it. He gives faith and repentance no more to those who believe and repent than to those who persevere in impenitency and unbelief; he gave faith no more to Paul than to Judas; he gave repentance no more to Peter than to Simon Magus, *i. e.* he gave it not at all; for he does no more for any than this moral grace will do, and all have this alike.

(4.) This makes the efficacy of the grace of Christ to depend upon the will of man. That grace which they say is sufficient, if we will, becomes effectual; if we will not, it is of no effect. And so it is 'of him that willeth,' and not 'of God that shews mercy,' in making his grace effectual, Rom. ix. 16.

To help all this, some of them say there is another sort of grace, which they call subsequent and co-operating, by virtue of which they would have it thought that the Lord may be said to be the author of conversion. But this latter grace comes too late to be counted the cause of conversion, for, as they state it, it is not vouchsafed till the will have determined itself, therefore it is called subsequent. It concurs not with us till we are willing; the determination of the will is before it in order of nature. None have this grace (according to this method) but those who make right use of the former preventing grace; and right use is not made of that but when the will yields to the invitation, and gives its consent. Now, when the will yields and gives its consent, the soul is converted already; and so this grace which follows such consent cannot be the cause of conversion, unless that can be called the cause which is after the effect.

All that can be made hereof is this: the Lord by his grace helps to convert us when we are already converted; he gives us faith if we believe beforehand; he quickens us when [we] are already alive; he helps us to rise out of this state of sin and impenitence, when we are already risen! It is we that do the work first; he helps us in it afterward! If you can digest this, you may swallow their doctrine.

Thus have I truly shewed you what the patrons of free will hold and assert in opposition to the text. It exempts man's will from the dominion of God, it denies original sin, it leaves no need of regeneration, it takes from Christ the honour of being the author of our conversion, the giver of saving blessings; it subjects his grace to the sovereignty of man's will, so that it shall have no efficacy but as we list.

I need not lay any colours on it to make it look ugly. It detracts from Christ to exalt nature; it takes the crown from effectual victorious grace, and sets it upon the head of free will; it makes Christ and his grace in a manner needless, as to the restoring of our souls to life; it is but little that he does, and that to no purpose, unless we will. And if we will, we well nigh do it all ourselves. Thus must we conclude if we believe them. But if we believe Christ, without him we can do nothing.

Obj. If it be impossible to do anything out of Christ, then it is in vain to endeavour. If no possibility, why should we hope? If no hope, no endeavours; despair, or be careless.

Ans. 1. It is our duty to endeavour what is impossible by our endeavours to attain, so sin has made it; to avoid all sin, to perform perfect obedience, to love God with all the heart and strength. It is our duty to endeavour the continuance of those things we cannot possibly lose; *Ergo*, not absurd to endeavour the attainment of what is impossible. It was not possible that Herod should murder Christ in his infancy; yet Joseph used means to avoid it, fled to Egypt, was so commanded. It is not possible the elect should be seduced, fall away totally and finally; yet they are to use all means to prevent it. Necessity is a sufficient reason to act without further encouragement. A man in a river, ready to drown, will endeavour to save his life, though some should tell him it were impossible. There is a necessity where there is a command from God; now he requires, it behoves man to do his duty, and leave the success to God. Secret things do belong to God, Deut. xxix. 29; things future are secrets, events are future; present known duties belong to us. If it be not possible to attain happiness by our endeavours only, yet it is possible to attain it some other way. Do what he requires, and he will do what is best; leave him to find the way who made it.

Ans. 2. Though one out of Christ can do nothing spiritually good, yet he may do something preparatory. There are some things attainable by a natural man, which may be called preparations for Christ. Though they be not causes, nor necessary antecedents of conversion or union, yet are disposing occasions, and have a probable, though not a necessary, connection with these. Those that attain them may miss of Christ, but it is probable they will not.

This is great encouragement to endeavour; they are very desirable, and withal attainable. It is in his sphere, this should be his *palæstra*. I shall shew, 1, what these things are; 2, that one out of Christ may do them; 3, there is a probability they will succeed; 4, if they succeed not to the utmost, yet they are not in vain.

1. (1.) Knowledge of man's sinfulness and misery by nature out of Christ; sinfulness of nature and acts; misery, curse, wrath, present and to come. Knowledge of justice and the law: what that requires and forbids; and of justice, what it is ready to execute.

(2.) Conviction that he in particular is so sinful and miserable; wrought by application of what he knows in general to his own state: I am the man who am thus sinful, and therefore who am thus obnoxious to justice and wrath.

(3.) Sense of his misery. Letting his thoughts dwell so long upon it, till his heart be affected with what his understanding apprehends; till the notion beget affection, some sense thereof, fear of wrath, justice, threatenings, curses, lest they should be executed, sadness, consternation of spirit, dejection, humiliation of heart, and all high thoughts of his good and safe condition cast down, and himself laid with them in the dust, manifested by sighing under the burden of wrath, lamenting his sad condition.

(4.) Desire of freedom from this misery, serious wishes to be delivered from the wrath to come; not to come into that place of torment, not to dwell with everlasting burnings.

(5.) Believe that Christ only can free him; no name under heaven but this. Nothing that himself hath, or can do, or any other for him, can deliver him; none but Christ.

(6.) Diligent use of outward means where Christ is to be found: hear, pray, read, meditate, confer.

(7.) Outward reformation.

These are the preparations. Now,

2. That they are attainable by one out of Christ is evident, because such a one has all things that are requisite to attain them, which are three: 1, apt, fit means; 2, common assistance; 3, power to use the means.

(1.) He has fit means. *Fit, i.e.* such as have an aptitude (if made use of) to work these effects. The word clearly reveals man's misery, and Christ the only remedy. The word preached, and particularly applied, has an aptitude to convince of sin and misery in particular; and this seriously thought of, and imprinted by meditation, begets sense; from this sense springs desire of freedom, and desires beget endeavours.

(2.) He has common and general assistance. And this is enough (for these being but common works, do not require special assistance), he has it; because common assistance, whether by way of motion or co-operation, is never, or very rarely, denied either to rational or natural agents. If things requisite to an action be ready, and actually applied, and nothing hinder it but want of this divine assistance, the suspending of it is a miracle, which we can never expect. If fire do not burn combustible matter applied to it, it is a miracle, as we have an instance in Nebuchadnezzar's furnace. If nourishing meat, received and concocted, do not nourish the body, merely for want of this co-operation, it is no less miraculous. If the eye, rightly disposed, do not see a visible object conveniently placed, merely because divine influence is suspended, it is miraculous. And so if an intelligent man do not understand a plain discourse, merely because God concurs not, it is no less miraculous. And so in this case, if the means, apt in themselves to work these effects, do not prove effectual, when made use of, if there be no other reason but want of divine assistance, it is a miracle. There is no more reason to fear the want of common assistance, than to hope for miracles; no more ground to deny that, than to affirm this.

(3.) He has power to use the means; for nothing is required to the use thereof but the diligent exercise of reason. No man that thus objects will deny but he has the use of reason, and he cannot deny but he may be as diligent in the exercise of it about this object as about others. Reading, or hearing, and meditating on the word, will work the mentioned effects, and these acts are all within the reach of reason. To do these spiritually indeed requires a higher principle, but a common and rational exercise of these will attain these common works. Though without Christ ye cannot act spiritually, ye may act rationally. Ye may hear what is plainly delivered with understanding, and apply what is spoken in common to your own particulars, by the use of ordinary discourse, and remember what concerns your souls as well as what concerns your estate, and work what you remember upon your hearts, by serious thoughts and meditation; these acts are in the power of an ordinary understanding.

What, then, is the reason that when so many enjoy the gospel, so few reach these common works? It is not want of means, assistance, or power to use means; what then? It is woful negligence, and wilful carelessness; men will not hear, not so much as come; or if they do hear, yet not so much as to hear with understanding and remembrance; apply it not, keep it off as that which belongs not to them, or that which they are afraid of; meditate not, let it not stay in their minds, nor let their thoughts work on it.

This is the true reason why so many perish without excuse; they will not do what they can, and so provoke the Lord not to do for them what they cannot. This is the true, the only reason; others are idle or wicked pretences. And it is little less than blasphemy to accuse the decrees or providences of God as the causes, when negligence only deserves to be counted so. If a man have the use of his hands at command, and meat before him, would it not seem wicked and ridiculous if he should say he could not take the meat because he is not moved from above? When was such a common assistance ever denied? You have the word preached, and understandings capable; why do you not receive it? Is it not plainly because you will not? If a man eat, but force his meat out of his stomach before it be concocted, would it not be both wicked and absurd to say his meat doth not nourish, because God denies to concur with it, whenas the plain reason is his ejecting it? You here receive the bread of life; but by worldly cares and employments, you crowd it out of your souls before it be concocted by meditation; you stop reason in its working, will not employ it to meditate. It is not want of assistance, but want of will and care. You will not do what you can, therefore your destruction is of yourselves; God's justice is clear. This will stop your mouths at the day of judgment. Whatever the heathens have to plead, you will have nothing; but stand speechless, and hear that dreadful sentence passed without excuse. Will it be a sufficient plea to say you would not do what you could, because you could not do what you would; do nothing, because you could not do all; not do your duty, because you could not do what he has reserved in his own power; not obey him in things possible and easy, because he would not suffer you to entrench upon his prerogative? Oh woful plea, which will make your condemnation greater, and add to your torments! But, blessed be God, there is yet time to prevent this, and you see the way. Here is matter for your endeavours, you need not be idle and careless; yea, and here is matter of hope too. I say not, that if a man do what he can, God ought to give him grace, or will certainly; but only there is hope he will. You need not despair, as appears in the third answer.

3. Though there be no certainty that these preparations will bring you to Christ, yet there is probability they may; though the success of these endeavours be not certain, it is probable. Men count probabilities sufficient grounds to act upon, and indeed moral endeavours have no other encouragement; events are uncertain. But in affairs of the world, if there be one probable way, and no other visible, men never consult whether they shall take that course, but immediately, without delay, fall upon it with all their strength. So Benhadad, 1 Kings xx. 31, 32, 'Peradventure he will save thy life,' &c.; so the lepers, 2 Kings vii. 4, 'If they save us alive, we shall live,' &c.; so the Canaanitish woman, Mat. xv. 26, 27; all upon very weak probabilities. There is no certainty physic will cure a dangerous disease; yet because it is probable, a sick person will take it, though costly and unpleasing. No certainty that industry in a particular calling will make rich; yet because it is probable, men rise early and sit up late, &c. Here is as much probability for your souls, and it is of more concernment, and there is no other way visible that you can walk in.

The probability rises from many grounds.

(1.) It is God's ordinary way whereby he brings men to Christ. It is a great encouragement to a poor pilgrim that he is in the ready way home, though it be possible he may lose it; there is more hopes he may arrive there, than for him who never comes near, is out of it, and goes further and further from it. Those who have these preparations are in the way; those who want and neglect them are out and wander, what hopes of them? A poor prisoner lies in a dungeon many years, and like to do so until he die; a friend comes and shews him a way by which he may probably get out; it is possible the jailor may meet him, and prevent his escape; yet if he try, there is more hopes for him than those who love their dungeon and fetters, and will not stir, nor take a lively* course to escape. It is God's way, therefore hopeful.

(2.) It is a sign God is bringing such to Christ; not an infallible, yet a hopeful, sign, that God will give the end, when he stirs up any to use the means. It is a sign God intends salvation when he sends the gospel; but a more hopeful sign, and that which presages better and more particularly, when the gospel is improved, made use of by any to whom it is sent.

Those who use the means, though such as have but a probable connection with the end, have hopes; those who neglect them are desperate, have no ground to think they should attain the end. Shew us some token for good. There are several tokens: some portend infallibly, some but dubiously and probably. There is certainty from those, hope from these, neither from others.

(3.) These are nearer to Christ and happiness than others, *Ergo*, there is hope. The greatest part of the world are out of Christ; yet there is a latitude, some further off, some nearer. Christ says of one, 'Thou art not far from the kingdom of heaven,' Mark xii. 34. Some in the confines of it, some in another world, more hopes for them; some within sight of a city of refuge, others beyond Jordan. We may compare the kingdom of Christ to the temple; the glorified are in the holy of holies, the saints in the holy place, these under preparations in the court, there is more hopes they may get into the sanctuary than those who are in another country or a remote part of the land. There is more hopes, more encouragement for those that are nearer to Christ than for those that are further off.

* Qu. 'likely?'—ED.

(4.) These are more fit for Christ, more capable of grace than others: these preparations are a comparative capacity, though not absolute, so as never to miss of it; a material and subjective capacity, though not a formal; such disposing occasions as diminish the resistance though not abolish it, more easily reduced: abate something of it, though not quite expel and prevail against it; though all easy to God, yet to us some more, some less. A stone under the instrument of the workman is more capable of a form than a stone in the rock. The Lord indeed is a free agent, and ties not himself to preparations or dispositions, works where and when he pleases; the Spirit blows where it listeth; yet, a vessel in the sea, with sails spread, is in more hopes to get the advantage of a gale than one sticking in the sands without sails; these preparations are as sails spread. The impotent man that lay at the pool of Bethesda, John v., sensible of his infirmity, though he could not go into the pool when the waters were troubled, was more likely to be cured than those who were insensible of their diseases and did not come near the pool. Those that are thus prepared are sensible, and lie at the pool, there is more hopes, they are more capable, &c. Here is a capacity, though remote, more hopeful than none at all.

(5.) Few miscarry that go thus far, therefore there is hopes; few go thus far but go farther, are carried by God to Christ; few in comparison of those who go not so far, and of those who go so far and miscarry. The miscarriage of some merchants upon the seas doth not hinder others from venturing, because they see many grow rich thereby; but if they had no other way to subsist, though more should perish, they would adventure. We can do nothing, all for hopes of a subsistence; when necessity is the greater, the hopes are more; it is a duty necessary, not an employment out of choice. The most successful armies lose some in their conflicts, yet this discourages not the rest from hazarding all to conquer. We run no hazard here; we hazard none if we venture not;* and few perish in comparison of those who conquer; therefore great encouragement to endeavour; and if you do not, you are certain to perish, for anything you can do.

(6.) Those that miscarry are the causes of it themselves; they either despair, or relapse, or resist. The fault is man's.

Despair is very rare and unusual. The Bible, a history of four thousand years, tells us but of two, Cain and Judas. Yet there is more hopes of those that despair, than that senseless presumption affords any ground for, in which most live and die.

Relapse is the ordinary cause, when those who have gone so far omit, negligently perform, those duties in the use of which they arrived at such attainments. They embrace the present world with Demas, choke these motions, drown the voice of conscience, bestow so much time and strength on it as leave none for their souls; return to their vomit, base lusts, sensual pleasures, bad company, resist the common workings of the Spirit, provoke him thereby to add none special. The fault is clearly man's, none else can be accused. God moves not to evil, James i. 13, 14. He is not bound to prevent these miscarriages or their causes. None can oblige God but himself, and he has not engaged himself to anything in nature, or attainable by it. He cures not these distempers, yet he refuses not, but upon man's provocation and desert. He resists, or misimproves, or rejects, common grace and workings: is it not just with God to deny special, saving, irresistible? None miscarry but through their own default, may blame themselves, not God; therefore here is encouragement. If a band of soldiers should be assured that none should perish but those who run away, or revolt to the

* Qu. 'hazard more if we venture not'?—or, 'hazard none if we venture'?—Ed.

enemy, would not this be encouragement to fight to the last? So it is here. If a merchant should be assured that no adventurers make unsuccessful voyages but those who use means to sink their own ship, or those who, repenting their undertaking, return before they arrive at the place whither they are bound, would not this encourage him to adventure?

That you may perceive that what I speak concerning these preparations is far enough from their principles, who advance the power of nature or free-will, to the prejudice of free grace ;—

These preparations are not the cause of conversion 'or union, nor necessary antecedents, so that union and conversion should certainly and unavoidably follow these; nor parts or degrees of regeneration, &c., though steps to it; not *gradus rei, sed gradus ad rem;* nor spiritual or supernatural acts, but such as natural men may do with common assistance, such as is common to those who never are converted ; nor saving acts, such as pertain to salvation, or are necessarily linked with it, or with a title to it. Nor do they give power to a soul to believe, to turn to God, &c., if he will, yea, or power to be willing. Nor do they oblige the Lord to give Christ or spiritual blessings to such, either in point of faithfulness, as though he had promised it; there is no promise to such of grace to natural acts. Much less in point of justice, as though there were such worth in these to make it due; no, nor in point of equity, as though it were unreasonable, unequal, or incongruous for the Lord to deny regenerating grace to those who are under these preparatives. He may do what he pleases for all this; and what he pleases to do, either to give or deny, it will be highly equal and congruous.

4. Though these endeavours always succeed not to the utmost of what may be expected and desired, yet they are never in vain; for preparations are required and commanded, and industry to attain them is obedience. No man ever lost by obedience in small things; it has a recompense in itself: behold its reward is with it: there are advantages in it, though none should follow it. It is better to be in hell obeying than in heaven rebelling. There is so much sweetness and excellency in obedience, as makes it desirable, and worthy of our best endeavours, without respect to recompense. What greater excellency than conformity to the divine will? And there is no true pleasure in any acts but those that are conformable to it. When Paul says, 'If our hopes were only in this life, we were of all most miserable,' he speaks not his own, but the opinion of the world. For if there were no heaven hereafter, obedience would be a heaven, some part of happiness here. It is true of saints, and in proportion of others.

Yet there are extrinsecal advantages here and hereafter. It is observed that those who have searched after the philosopher's stone, though they have not found it, yet in the inquiry have discovered such rare and pleasing secrets in nature, as may countervail their pains and cost. So here, those that tend toward Christ in these preparatory works, though they find him not, yet have rewards that exceed their pains. Cyrus had temporal promises, Isa. xliv. 28, and xlv. 1, 13. Jehu, for his obedience in destroying idolatry, was invested in a kingdom, and had it established upon his posterity for four generations. Temporal blessings are the proper reward of temporal obedience. God thinks these below that which is spiritual and sincere, therefore saints often have not an equal share thereof with temporary believers: for the future, it has its reward, if not in perfect happiness, yet in more easy sufferings. 'It will be far more tolerable in the day of judgment for,' &c. If they enjoy not more, they shall suffer less.

AGAINST ANXIOUS CAREFULNESS.

Be careful for nothing.—PHILIPPIANS IV. 6.

THE beginning of the chapter consists of many exhortations. This is one now read. It has little dependence upon the former, that is obvious, unless with the two next before it, ver. 4, 'Rejoice in the Lord always.' Those that have interest in Christ ought to rejoice, and do so always in every condition; not only when their outward state is plentiful, and flourishing, and prosperous, but when it is like that of this apostle and the Philippians, low and afflicted, beset on every side with dangers, and exposed to all sorts of outward sufferings. They have cause for this joy always, because it is a rejoicing in God, who is an object that affords constant and continual occasion of rejoicing. If the world, or the most pleasing things in it, had been the object of their joy, it had been unreasonable here to have called for a constant rejoicing, it had been impossible to comply with it; the matter will not bear it, the world cannot, will not afford constant occasion for it. It is a variable and inconstant thing, and so are all the enjoyments of it; if we have them now, they will be gone ere long, or the comfort of them may vanish; if they please and delight us now, they may afflict and trouble us shortly, and bring us sorrow enough to dash all our worldly joy. But God is the same always, he varies not with the changes of the world, but is as delightful and joyous an object in affliction as in prosperity; we always find occasion of rejoicing in him, and therefore we may, we ought, to rejoice in him always. And that they may thus rejoice in the Lord, he advises them, ver. 5, to carry themselves moderately towards outward things; not to be much taken with them when they seem most pleasing, nor to be much troubled at them when they seem most afflictive; not to be much exalted when the world favours us, nor dejected when it frowns and crosses us; but to keep a temper, and avoid extremes, either of which damp or disturb spiritual joy. Τὸ ἐπιεικὲς seems to denote an equal carriage towards the world, an even passage through it, an indifferency towards the things thereof, whatever they be; as those who have their eye so much upon God, and so taken up with him, as to be little concerned in outward things, and the little circumstances of this life. The Lord is ἐγγὺς; can you be much taken with sensible things when the Lord is so near you? Can you see any object so lovely, so desirable, so delightful as he? Or if afflictions and sufferings be near, your condition troublesome, or persecutors powerful and violent, yet the Lord is near, a very present comfort, a very present help in such a time; he is at hand, ready to secure, or support, or refresh, or deliver; to make you gainers, rejoicers, more than conquerors; and therefore trouble not yourselves, be not careful or solicitous, only make your case known to him, that is all you have to do. He will take care of you and all your concernments, you need not be anxious about anything, ver. 6.

Obs. The people of Christ should be careful for nothing, μηδὲν μεριμνᾶτε, care for nothing, be not solicitously, anxiously careful for anything. As they need not, so they ought not give way to those cares which haunt and take up the minds of others. It is both their duty, and their privilege, and happiness. Indeed, there is little or nothing which the Lord requires of us but tends to our happiness. He shews not only his sovereign authority, but his infinite goodness, in those things which he enjoins us; and leaves us self-condemned and inexcusable if we comply not with his will, since it is his design, not only to have us shew our subjection, but to make us happy. All his commands tend thereto, and most of them (and this amongst the rest) directly and evidently, as will appear in the sequel.

For explication, let me inquire a little into the act and the object; what we are not to be careful for, and what it is to be careful.

1. For the former. The expression seems universal, but must be understood with that restraint which the Scripture elsewhere directs us to. *Nothing* here respects especially the concernments of this present life, the things of the world and of time. These are they about which we are in danger to take too much care; the concernments of our souls, the things of heaven and eternity, we are apt to be too careless and regardless of. The Lord uses a spur here; we need quickening, and are in danger to be too remiss, both as to the end and the means. The Lord calls upon us to take care of both, and we are to hearken to him accordingly, Deut. xv. 5, Luke x. 40, Titus iii. 8. Both the end and the way should be minded with great care; he excites and stirs us up to this; but where we are in danger to be too careful, there he uses a curb; and this is about the things of this life, for these he would have us not careful. These are the things intended in the text, and other expressions in Scripture point at them. What we are in danger of, what we are restrained from, is the cares sometimes of this world: Mat. xiii. 22, μέριμνα τοῦ αἰῶνος τούτου; and Mark iv. 19, μέριμναι, &c., sometimes of this life; Luke xxi. 34, μέριμναι βιωτικαι, the things which concern this life while we are in this world, earthly and temporal things, which are of no longer continuance nor further concernment than our present life. Nothing of this nature should be our care, we are not to be careful about any such thing. Particularly, we should not be careful about, (1.) getting and providing them when we want them, or have them not in such a measure and degree as we desire. Our Lord Jesus, in that excellent sermon which he made in the mount, insists most upon this; he stays not so long upon any other particular, and presses it with much force and variety of argument; Mat. vi. 25, 31, 34, where the word rendered, 'take no thought,' is the same all along which the apostle here uses, μὴ μεριμνᾶτε, be not careful, μὴ μεριμνήσετε, ye shall not be careful, either for plenty and superfluities, or for necessaries, food and raiment; there is no cause, no reason for carefulness to get either, as he argues admirably, and to the conviction of the dullest understanding, and the most distrustful heart.

(2.) About keeping, ordering, or securing them. Martha was too solicitous and careful in ordering the affairs of the family. Christ checks her for it, Luke x. 40. The rich man was careful how to keep his stores; he is branded as a fool for his pains, Luke xii. 17, 20, διελογίζετο ἐν ἑαυτῷ, he reasoned carefully, &c. We should not be solicitous and careful how to avoid losses and troubles, how to prevent or escape sufferings in our persons or outward concerns. The apostle in the text probably has a particular respect to this. The condition of the Philippians, exposed to dangers and sufferings, might make them subject to carefulness, how they should secure themselves and what they had. And so he thought it seasonable to mind them of their duty, to be careful for no such thing. The way of man, the way of flesh and blood, is to take much care in such a case. The way of God lies elsewhere; make your case known to him, and be at rest.

(3.) About deliverance when losses have surprised us, and troubles and sufferings are upon us. When this befalls us, a burden of cares is ready to fall upon us, we are apt to pull it upon ourselves. The Lord would not have us careful about this, he has better provided for us, Ps. lv. 22; and thus did the three faithful Jews ease themselves of that which would have oppressed others, Dan. iii. 16.

But are we to be altogether careless and regardless of the enjoyments or sufferings of this life, and have no more regard of them than Gallio had of the Jews' concerns? Must we 'care for none of these things'? Must we be neglectful of them, as the disciples thought that Christ might be, when in their danger they say to him, Mark iv. 38, 'Master, carest thou not that we perish?'

2. No, do not mistake; there is some care that is allowed, yea, enjoined and required, about these things, and there is a carefulness which is forbidden and condemned; and what the one and the other is, we are now to inquire. It was the second thing propounded for explication of this truth and the understanding of our duty; about the act, what it is to be careful in the apostle's sense, when he forbids it. And herein I shall proceed, (1.) negatively, (2.) positively. He does not prohibit all kind and degree of carefulness about the concerns of this life. There is a care which is lawful and necessary, of which take account in these severals:—

(1.) We may take notice of our outward condition, and the concernments thereof; we may make use of our judgment and reason, and employ and exercise them in discerning what our circumstances are, yea, and what they are like to be, Prov. xxii. 3, and xxvii. 12. It is part of Ephraim's censure, Hos. vii. 9, 'Strangers have devoured his strength, and he knoweth it not,' &c. We may and ought to mind and observe what we have, and want, what we have lost or are like to lose when trouble is near, and what we are in danger to suffer. These, and the like, we are to mind and consider, or else we are like to neglect those duties which depend upon the notice and consideration hereof, and which the Lord has suited to the several postures of our outward state. We shall not spiritually improve what is present; and all these things being under changes, we are like to be surprised and found unprepared for what comes next. What care a prudent observation hereof includes, is lawful and necessary, Prov. xxvii. 23.

(2.) We may have some thoughts about these outward things. Care is the exercise or employment of our thoughts about this or that, including the same motions which they have upon our other faculties; and some thoughts about these things are needful, and so some care. We may be reasoning, and advising, and thinking in ourselves of our enjoyments, how they may be duly preserved and well employed; of our wants, how they may be regularly supplied; of our dangers, troubles, sufferings, how they may be lawfully avoided, or patiently endured, or fruitfully improved, or seasonably removed. The apostle censures those who are careless in one of these cases, by which we may conclude of the rest, 1 Tim. v. 8, if any one, οὐ προνοεῖ τῶν ἰδίων, have not some provident care of his own concerns, as to outward things, he is far from being faithful.

(3.) We may have some sense of our external condition, such as may reach our hearts, and some way affect them, make some impression on them : in a temperate fear or hope, joy or grief, such as arises from the due and moderate employment of our thoughts about the things of this life. The apostle allows this, only bounds it, as the nature of these things requires, 1 Cor. vii. 30. And he would not have us insensible of afflictions, as those who have little or no regard of the hand of God therein, Heb. xii. 5, neither too great a sense, so as to faint under it; nor too little sense, so as to have little or no regard or care, which ὀλιγωρεῖν, the word there used, signifies.

(4.) We may use lawful means (so we do it lawfully, for measure, manner, and end) about these outward things, to preserve or procure the comforts of this life; to prevent danger, to keep off sufferings, or to be delivered out of them, we may have so much care, as will make us delight in such use of means. The Lord encourages it: Prov. xxi., 5 'The thoughts of the diligent tend only to plenteousness.'

It is not all care, you see, that is forbidden; what is it then ?

2. Positively. It is an excess of care. It is carefulness, an inordinacy therein. Which, what it is, and how it may be discerned, I shall endeavour to shew. The former in these particulars.

(1.) When they are too many. The mind is full of them, when not only some care, but carefulness; some thoughts, but thoughtfulness; a fulness of solicitous thoughts, and thoughtful cares; when the mind is wholly or near wholly taken up with them, and little or no room left for better, more needful, more profitable, more refreshing thoughts, those of higher and greater concernment; when more than are needful on any account, more than the condition of those things requires, or the quality of them deserves. If we would take our measures by the worth and value of these earthly things, a little care, a few thoughts, should serve their turn; they are of little moment, and of little continuance, and of small advantage or disadvantage, in comparison of that which should be our care indeed, and ought to be the main subject of our thoughts. Our minds are of a better temper, and were made for higher and nobler purposes, than to spend themselves upon such low and little matters, and to spin out their strength and spirits in care and thoughtfulness about them; there is an excess in giving way so much, and to so many of them; it is culpable and forbidden carefulness.

(2.) When they are tumultuous, and put the soul all into a hurry, and hale it into confusion and disorder. That is the import of the word τυρβάζη, whereby Martha's carefulness is set out, Luke x. 41. μεριμνᾷς καὶ τυρβάζη περὶ πολλά. When the thoughts about these things are not only too many, but like a confused multitude in a throng or crowd, where each one pushes, and troubles, and hinders one another, one can do nothing else when he is in it, and cannot easily get out. When they disorder, and disturb, and discompose the soul, and render it unfit for its proper work, though of greatest importance. When they put the soul into a commotion, and make it like the restless and troubled sea, or a vessel without anchor in a storm. A word of that import is used by Christ, when he is dissuading from this carefulness, Luke xii. 29, μὴ μετεωρίζεσθε. Let not your minds be tossed with these careful thoughts, like a ship at drift with the unruly waves. These are thoughts excessively careful, which disquiet and unsettle the mind, and like so many billows keep it in a tossing and restless agitation.

(3.) When they are perplexing and vexatious, when they in any degree reach the mind, and distend it, as is were, upon tenters; when they divide and rend it, as μέριμνα denotes, the word by which excessive care is so often expressed in Scripture. When the mind is anxious, and the heart thereupon in some pain and anguish, and sadder impressions made thereon than these outward things, however they go, can be any just ground or occasion of in those who make account their portion is not in this life, nor any part of their true happiness in things below.

2. In the next place, let me shew you how we may discern when our cares are excessive and inordinate, that we may the better know what are forbidden, and what we are concerned to avoid, and also wherein we have been guilty; that we may both bewail what is past, and be more effectually watchful for the future. We may be sure our care about the things of this life is excessive, and that is a condemned carefulness;—

(1.) When it is more for earth than heaven, more for the outward man and its concernments than for the soul; more for things of time, than those that are eternal. Opposites illustrate one another; and it is in opposition to this forbidden carefulness for outward things that our Lord Jesus gives that rule, Mat. vi. 33. Let this be your first, and chief, and great care; leave the care of the other to God. When this is not first, the other is before, or near it; and it is excessive indeed when it is either, when not much before or after it; when more careful to make sure of a good temporal estate, than to make our calling and election sure, very solicitous about a good title to earthly possessions, but take less care about a title to heaven, and interest in Christ.

More to thrive in the world, and increase in riches, than to grow in grace, or to get holiness planted and increased, and to get possession of more heavenly treasure. Very thoughtful about that, but more indifferent here. Careful of outward health, but more regardless of soul distempers and inward diseases, such as bring it to the gates of death. Curious in trimming and adorning the body (a little better-coloured clay), spend an hour or more, some days upon that; but take less care, and spend less time in ordering the soul, cleansing that from all filthiness, and putting it into a dress and posture fit to meet with God, even when approaching him in a solemn manner. When more careful to avoid sufferings than sin, and to keep out of outward danger than to keep out of temptation, and to secure our estates from wasting and decays than our souls from declinings and backslidings, and to be delivered from troubles and afflictions, than to be freed from selfish, carnal, and worldly lusts. This is a carefulness not only condemned, but such as to the greatest part of the world, yea, of those who live under the gospel, is actually damning.

(2.) When it hinders us from enjoying what we have; when so thoughtful to get more, or to keep what we have, or to secure it and ourselves from danger and trouble, will not let us enjoy with quiet and comfort what we have in possession. He is not like to rest quietly, who, when he composeth himself to it, has one that is still jogging, or haling him, or making a noise in his ears. When our thoughts, busy about these outward things, perform this ill office to our minds, and are still jogging them and buzzing in them, they deprive the mind of rest, they are then excessive.

If a man lie down, and his lodging be otherwise never so well accommodated, yet if there be thorns in his bed, he cannot lie easily. The cares of the world are compared to thorns, Mat. xiii. 22. When our thoughts lay our minds and hearts in an uneasy posture, and are still pricking them when they should be at rest, and make our enjoyments as a bed of thorns to us, there is a lamentable inordinacy in them. When the possession of outward things, which should be quiet and comfortable (else they are not enjoyed), is disturbed and embittered by carking disquieting thoughts, here is excess.

(3.) When it indisposeth us for holy duties; when we cannot break through the crowd of these thoughts to converse with God, or, if we do, yet too seldom, and with difficulty, and then come with souls discomposed, and these thoughts still follow us. When they should be quite shaken off and cashiered, they are still crowding in, when our minds should be wholly taken up with God; and they are still giving us diversion and interruption, and call off some part of our souls from him who expects them all, so that they are distracted and divided when they should be most united and entirely fixed on him, who will be sought with our whole hearts. They often hinder us from offering unto God, and when we can get leave of them to bring a sacrifice, yet these flies seize on it and spoil it. God likes not such offerings, no more than we like fly-blown meat. We come to pray, and when our minds and hearts should ascend up to God, these call them down, and carry them another way. We come to hear, and when the Lord speaks, we should attend him alone, and hearken to nothing else; but then these come, and knock, and buzz, and will be heard; and God, and what he speaks to us, is little minded. We set ourselves to meditate; oh, but our minds are prepossessed and taken up before with the concerns of this life, and they will not give way to thoughts of God and heaven and our eternal concernments, or they will mix with them, and make an untoward confused medley of heaven and earth, God and the world, in one lump, in one exercise. When these keep us from drawing near God, or from approaching him with cheerfulness, heartiness, entireness of mind and affection, or make us come with our loins ungirded, our souls draggling in the dirt of the world, and sweeping the dust after them, and raising a cloud of it, so that we cannot discern well where we are, or what we are doing, whether with God or with the world, whether we are minding him or it; or rather lose the sight of God, where he is to be most seen and enjoyed. When these cares bring us to this pass, then they are intolerably excessive.

(4.) When it is distrustful, arises from our not trusting God, or takes us off from depending on him, Isa. vii. 9, 2 Chron. xx. 20. To trust God with our affairs is the way to be established, to have the mind settled. When it is staggering and wavering betwixt fear and hope, and so unquiet and unsettled, this is from an excess of carefulness. When the soul thinks not itself sufficiently secured by the promise or providence of God, when he doubts whether the Lord is able, or whether he is willing, to provide for him and his, or to secure his concerns, or to dispose of all his affairs for the best, and so does not commit his way to him, but will look after it himself, and employs his thoughts anxiously about it, as though otherwise it could not go well, this is distrustful, and so sinful and excessive carefulness.

You will say we may, we must use the means, that is our duty. True, but do ye no more herein than is your duty? Over-doing is from overmuch carefulness and too little faith. And when you have done what is requisite herein, why are you so solicitous about the event, so thoughtful what will be the issue of your endeavours? That is wholly in God's hands, and belongs not to you, but to him. If you believe he will do anything at all, you must not doubt but he will take care of that which is properly his own work; and if he will take care of it, why do you so much trouble yourselves about it? Why do you not leave that to him which is properly his? Here your care crowds in where it has nothing to do, here it exceeds its bounds, from a distrust of God, where he is most to be trusted, and your minds and thoughts are very busy where you have nothing to do but to believe; where they should stand still and wait his pleasure.

(5.) When it hurries you to the use of unlawful or suspected means, such as are unwarrantable in themselves, or such as you may suspect to be so, or such as you are doubtful of; for though these be lawful in themselves, yet they are unlawful to you. It is excessive carefulness that pushes men on in such a course as is either evil, though they think it good, or good, if they think it evil; when so careful to keep what they have, as they will stretch their consciences rather than lose or hazard it; or to get more, that they will take some course to do it which they cannot justify, which the word or their own conscience allows not. So careful to avoid dangers and sufferings, as to dissemble, or equivocate, or decline some way of God, or take some unwarranted path to do it. So careful to get out of troubles, or to be eased from their present burden, as to venture out by some way that the Lord never opened. So careful for deliverance, that how it come (so they may but see it) they much care not. Rebekah and Jacob so careful to have the blessing, that they would get it by deceit rather than miss it. Jeroboam so careful to secure the kingdom to him, that he would set up false worship rather than run any hazard. Saul so careful not to fall into the hands of the Philistines, that he would sacrifice in a forbidden way, yea, and after go to the witch at Endor.

Such is excessive carefulness, which either draws into sin, or is a temptation to it. By this you may understand how we are not to be careful, what carefulness it is that is forbidden, and how it may be discerned. I have stayed the longer in the explication, because it is of a practical tendency.

In the next place, let me confirm this practical truth, and enforce it as your duty, by some considerations, which may serve both as reasons and motives for this purpose. The people of Christ should not be careful with such carefulness as I have described, for,

1. It is useless, it will not serve the turn; you will be nothing the nearer to what you aim at, for so much carefulness; it will not help you, it will rather hinder you from what you desire; and who that has the exercise of reason will make use of that which is no way useful for his purpose? This is one argument which the Wisdom of God (Christ himself) urges against it, Mat. vi. 27. You would count him a madman who would expect to grow taller by being thoughtful, or to lengthen his life by greatening his cares. Why, says Christ, you can no more reasonably expect to make provision for your life by such cares. This is no more the way to increase or secure your outward concerns, than it is to add a cubit to your stature: Ps. cxxvii. 2, 'It is vain to rise up early, to sit up late, to eat the bread of sorrows.' To cark and care is not the way to wealth, or the cause of it; those that take that course find they do it in vain, and are generally disappointed, ὅταν Θεος, since it is the Lord (so the words are to be read) who gives his people plenty, rest and comfort therein, though they never lose any sleep in seeking it.

This carefulness is not to keep what you have, or to get more; nor to secure you from dangers and sufferings, nor to bring you out of trouble; in vain will you seek these things this way: it is the blessing of God from whence these must be expected. Oh but, you will say, he blesses diligence. True, he blesses lawful diligence, but he never blesses this carefulness; and if any thrive or succeed, or get anything by it, without a curse, they have it some other way. This carefulness is the way to blast what you have, and what you get; to make it, or the comfort of it, wither, to curse it to you or your posterity; to endanger, instead of securing you; to strengthen your hands, instead of unloosing them; and to keep off deliverance, or make it prove no mercy, if you this way come by it. It is useless for these purposes, unless you count that useful which cannot expect a blessing.

2. It is needless; as it is of no use, so no need of it. It is not at all needful that you should trouble yourselves with such cares. Why so? Our Lord Jesus tells us (and it is another argument which he urges against this carefulness), Mat. vi. 32, 'For your heavenly Father knoweth that ye have need of all these things.' True, he knows all things, but what relief is that to me? Why, he is a father, the heavenly Father, and yours.

An earthly parent, who has but ordinary natural affection, if he know what is needful and good for his child, he will take care to provide it for him, if he be able; how much more will your heavenly Father do it, who as far exceeds the best parents on earth, not only in power, and wisdom, and riches, but also in love, and goodness, and bounty, as heaven is above earth; and far more, Isa. lv. 9, Mat. vii. 7 to the 12th; but I need not lead you to this by consequences; see what he says directly, to prove your care needless: 1 Pet. v. 7, 'Casting all your care on him; for he careth for you.' All that you may be tempted to be careful about is cared for already, by one who can infinitely better look after it than you yourselves, or any, or all creatures for you. What need is there, then, of your carefulness? If all the creatures in heaven and earth, angels and men, high and low, should faithfully engage themselves to take care of all your concerns; would you not think this a sufficient discharge of all your cares as needless? Oh but you have unspeakably more; that God, who is unspeakably more considerable than all the creatures in the world, has engaged himself to take care of you, that you shall want nothing that is good, that nothing shall befall you but what is really best for you; and to take such care of this, as to take care off from you; and is not your carefulness then needless? Since the Lord takes care of you, why is it not needless to trouble yourselves with these cares? Cannot he better dispose of all your affairs and concerns, than you yourselves can with all your care? Now if one that is better able to manage your business than yourselves should take it upon him, would not your hearts be at rest, and eased of the care of it? Would you not think it needless to trouble yourselves about it further? And does not the Lord take all your affairs upon him, when he bids you cast all on him? Cast, πᾶσαν την μέριμναν, all and every care upon him. And can any possibly take better order about all that you want, or desire, or fear, than the all-wise, and the all-mighty, and the all-sufficient, and the infinitely merciful God?

More distinctly, that carefulness is needless, appears,

(1.) By what he will do for you; of which before.

(2.) By what he has done for you. If he have done the greater things for you without your care, you need not be careful about the less, as though he would not do that without your carefulness. So our Lord Jesus argues: Mat. vi. 25, 'Take no thought for your life, what ye shall eat, or what ye shall drink; nor yet for the body, what ye shall put on: is not life more than meat, and the body than raiment?' You owe your life to him, he gave you that without your care; he formed your body, when you were not capable of taking any care about it; and will he not preserve the life that he has given, and uphold the body which he formed? Your care was not needful about the former, and there is less need of it about the latter, because that is less. You need not be solicitous about the lesser concerns of your life, how you shall be provided for in wants, or secured in dangers, or delivered out of troubles. He that took care you should have a life, and a body, and gave you the greater, he will not grudge you the less.

You took no care in the womb when you were there, how you should have life, or how you should be formed; you need take no more care now, than when you were in the womb. It was needless then, because the Lord took care of all, and he is as ready to take care of all your concerns now. You need not be so solicitous, lest he should think the less too much for his care, when the greater was not so.

(3.) By what he does for others. Other creatures, whom the Lord less regards than his children, need take no care for the concerns of their life or being; therefore those whom he more regards have less need to be careful. This is another consideration which infinite Wisdom suggests for this purpose, in one instance after another. Mat. vi. 26, the very fowls upbraid us for our carefulness, as needless trouble; they do not cark or moil, they have no need to do it, because the Lord takes care for the feeding of them; much less have we need to do it, whom the Lord has more regard of, and so takes more care for. This the Spirit of God sets forth to us more fully. There are but three things which such creatures are concerned in: how they shall be fed, and where they may rest, and by what means they may be safe; and the Lord takes care of all these. They are not, they need not be, solicitous about them; for their food: Ps. civ. 21, 'The young lions roar after their prey, and seek their food from God.' They teach us what we should do, they seek it of God, and we should make our case known to him, and not trouble ourselves with solicitous carefulness. The Lord fails not them, ver. 27, 28; he gives it them, and gives it in season, and gives it plentifully, and plenty of that which is good and desirable for them; and will he do less for those who are more to him, whom he has declared himself more concerned for? Need we fear that, or be solicitous about it? And as he takes care for their food, so for their rest and habitation. If we should be tempted to be careful about that, look up to these creatures, and by that which the Lord does for them, we may see it to be needless: ver. 16, 17, 'The trees of the Lord are full of sap; the cedars of Lebanon which he hath planted; where the birds make their nests: as for the stork, the fir-trees are her house.' And so for their safety, he has taken care they should be secured from danger: ver. 18, 'The high hills are a refuge for the wild goats; and the rocks for the coneys.' You may say, those that can help themselves need not take care; but what shall become of those who are destitute and helpless? If that be thy case, yet mayest thou learn, even by these creatures, that thy carefulness is not needful. As the Lord provides for all here below, so especially for those that are most helpless: Ps. cxlvii. 8. 9, 'Who covereth the heaven with clouds, who prepareth rain for the earth: who maketh grass to grow upon the mountains. He giveth to the beast his food, and to the young ravens which cry.' The meadows and lower grounds, they are refreshed and watered with the brooks and streams that run through them; but what shall become of the mountains? they are destitute of such advantage. The Lord provides for them also; he gathers the clouds and sends rain, and so they are refreshed and made to flourish. He causeth grass to grow there, where it could least be looked for, and whereby he provides for the wild beasts that feed there, whom men take no care of. The tame beasts, indeed, they take care of, as being useful to them; but if the Lord did not thus provide for the wilder beasts, they might starve, no other creature would take care of them. And so the young ravens, who being deserted by the old ones before they are able to help themselves, as soon as they are hatched, they would certainly perish, if the Lord did not take care of them, when they cannot do it themselves, and those who are most concerned would not do it for them. He gives them food when they cry out, as left utterly destitute. When you are tempted to carefulness, consider the ravens; our Lord Jesus sends us to them to learn this lesson: Luke xii. 24, 'Consider the ravens, for they neither sow nor reap, which neither have store-house nor barn, and God feedeth them.' Those whose condition is most helpless, and so seem to have most need to be careful, the Lord so provides for them, as they need not to take care; and need they take care, whom he is more engaged to look after? 'Doth the Lord take care of oxen?' says the apostle, 1 Cor. ix. 9. Doth the Lord take care of lions and ravens, of wild goats and coneys, &c., of beasts and birds? Does he take care for their food, their rest and habitation, their refuge and safety, for all their concernments; so that those who are most destitute and helpless amongst them need not be careful? And is there any need that they should trouble themselves with cares about their necessities or their dangers, for whom he has a more particular care, a more especial providence?

Our Lord Jesus shews how needless our solicitous cares are by another instance, in the plants and vegetables: Mat. vi. 28–30, 'And why take ye thought for raiment? Consider the lilies of the field, how they grow; they toil not, neither do they spin: and yet I say unto you, that even Solomon, in all his glory, was not arrayed like one of these. Wherefore, if God so clothe the grass of the field, which to-day is, and to-morrow is cast into the oven, shall he not much more clothe you, O ye of little faith?' The lilies, they toil not to make that grow of which clothing is made, nor do they spin it when it is grown up. They take no care, nor need they, the Lord clothes them. He not only makes them grow, but makes them flourish to such a degree, as 'Solomon in all his glory was not arrayed like one of them.' Now, says he (and it is the arguing of him in whom dwells all the treasures of wisdom and knowledge), if he made so splendid and rich provision for the withering grass, the soon fading flowers, of so little account with him, yea, with us, what then will he not be ready to do for those whom he much more regards and values? The lilies, the flowers, the grass, they need not care, and why? Because the Lord takes care for them; and if this be good reason, then sure those whom he takes more care of have less need to be careful. It is great vanity, if it were no worse, to trouble yourselves with that which is altogether needless; and carefulness about the concerns of this life is manifestly needless, upon many accounts, which we have from the mouth of Wisdom itself.

3. It is heathenish. Such carefulness about these outward things is no better than gross heathenism. This argument our Lord Jesus urges against it: Mat. vi. 32, 'About these things are the Gentiles solicitous.' It is the character of a heathen to be so careful about the things of this life, it smells rank of that blindness and infidelity in which the heathens are shut up. It should be as far from the disciples of Christ as heathenism is from Christianity; they more resemble the Gentiles than the people of Christ, who give way to such cares. It is heathenism in the professors of Christ's gospel, which is the worst and most intolerable. It signifies both heathenish thoughts of God, and heathenish apprehensions of things here below; both seem to be intimated in those words, ver. 32, 'For after all these things do the Gentiles seek.' Let us touch both.

(1.) It imports heathenish conceits of God, as if he were no God, or had no providence, or did not concern himself in the government of the world, or had no special regard of human affairs; as if he knew not what we wanted, or what we feared, or did not regard our necessities or dangers, though he knew them, but left us to shift for ourselves as well as we could, without any other aids and assistances than those of second causes. For if there be a God, a providence which reaches all things, and is sufficient for everything, but is more particularly concerned for those that are more nearly related to him; if this be apprehended and believed, hereby all this carefulness of ours is superseded. But where these cares prevail, it is not duly believed or apprehended, as it was not by the Gentiles. And therefore after these things they sought, and were so careful and solicitous about, as if they had had no God to take care of them. And it is for none but such heathens, who know not God, and believe not his providence, and mind not his faithfulness, and have no experience of his fatherly love, and particular care and compassions, to trouble themselves with these cares. It is for none but those, whose lamentable condition the apostle describes, Eph. ii. 11, 12, who are Gentiles, such as the Jews called uncircumcised, who were without the knowledge of Christ, far remote from the citizenship of Israel, strangers to the covenant of grace and promises of the gospel, and so without hope and without God in the world. If you would not shew yourselves to be too like to these, you must disband your earthly cares. They will signify you have heathenish conceits of God, like those whose minds the god of this world has blinded, and that the light of the glorious gospel of Christ (who is the image of God, and in whom we have the clearest discoveries of God, what he is in himself, and what to his people) has not shined into you. Much heathenish darkness and infidelity still covers your minds, if these cares trouble your hearts.

(2.) It imports heathenish thoughts and inclinations to things here below. Such a value of them, such an eagerness after the things of this world, as the Gentiles had. These were the most valuable things to them, and therefore these were their greatest care. 'After these things do the Gentiles seek.' Alas! they knew no better things, and so having the highest value for them, they would not commit the care of them to any but themselves, nor trust any with them, no, not God himself.

But have you such an esteem of earthly things? Are these your chief concerns, and so your chief care? Why, then, you are not only like the heathen, but worse than they; for you have seen, or might have seen (if your eyes had not been shut), better things: the glorious things of heaven, of Christ, of the gospel; things so far transcending all here below, so much more rich and precious, so much more pleasant and delightful, so much more necessary, durable, and advantageous, so much more excellent and glorious, as that the sight of them is abundantly sufficient to take down the value of all earthly things, and to lay them very low in your esteem, and so to make you little careful about them, little solicitous what becomes of them, at least well contented to leave the care of them to God.

Christ coming into the world brought life and immortality to light by the gospel, and discovered all the precious and inestimable things included therein, which were before folded up, and much hid from the world. And those who saw them effectually in that light, saw that in them which quite disparaged these earthly things to them, and made them no more to mind them, and to be no more careful about them, than toys and trifles, not worthy of their care and solicitous thoughts. You may see an instance of it in the primitive believers. When Christ, and pardon, and life, and glory was discovered to them by the apostles, how little did they mind the world, how little careful were they about their earthly enjoyments! Presently upon the view of those more excellent things, they 'sold their possessions, and brought the price, and laid it at the apostles' feet,' Acts iv. 34. Oh how far were they from troubling themselves with cares of getting more, who were so little thoughtful for the future, and so free and ready to part with that they had, Heb. x. 34. Here they shewed themselves Christians indeed, not sinners of the Gentiles, not heathenish worldlings, at a great distance from the heathenish temper of those who mind earthly things.

Christ has been long teaching you this. If you have not in some degree learned of him, you are so far in this heathenish darkness, and hearken rather to him who is the teacher, the god of this world, and blinds instead of enlightening those that follow him; but if you have learned Christ, and been taught of him, as the truth is in Jesus, he has shewed you that by the light of the gospel, which will make the things of the world to appear as loss and dung in your eyes, and not so worthy of that regard and care which the heathen, who knew no better, had of them.

If you would not shew yourselves of a heathenish spirit and temper in the midst of your profession of Christ and the gospel, after these earthly things you must not seek, and for them you must not be thus careful.

4. It is hurtful. It is not only needless and useless, that which will do you no good at all for the ends for which you use it, but it will do you much hurt, and more than all you are careful for, if it should succeed, will come to.

(1.) It will disoblige God, and take him off from caring for you in that particular manner, as he does for those who cast their care on him. It is so amongst men. They will not take the care of his affairs, who will not leave the care thereof to them. If the care of a business be left upon them, they are obliged; but if it be not, but the man takes the care of it upon himself, they are not engaged, they may leave it to him who will not trust them with it. So here, if you will cast your care upon God, he will take care of you and your concerns, but if you will not trust him with it, you may look to it yourselves, and take what comes, the Lord is disobliged. Jer. xvii. 5, 6, ' Thus saith the Lord, Cursed be the man that trusteth in man, and maketh flesh his arm, and whose heart departeth from the Lord: for he shall be like the heath in the desert, and shall not see when good cometh; but shall inhabit the parched places in the wilderness, in a salt land and not inhabited.' This is all you are like to get by letting your hearts depart from God in over-caring, and flying to this and the other instrument and means, viz., a curse, that will make your enjoyments like a wilderness, and yourself like the heath in it, which does not receive, or cannot expect any good from God. If you will cast your burden upon the Lord, he will sustain you, as he promises, Ps. lv. 22, but if you will not, you are like to fall under it; you have no assurance that your feet shall not fall and sink under the pressure. You disoblige the Lord, and that is a greater damage than your, and all the care of the world, can recompense.

*(2.) You lose in effect what you have, by this carefulness about it; you are like to lose the comfort and advantage of what you possess; carefulness, carefulness, like the lean kine, will devour it and eat it up all. What marrow and sweetness is therein, this is ready to suck it out all, and leave you nothing but a bare bone to gnaw on. Those outward things, which should be as refreshment and bread to you, it will turn it into ' the bread of sorrow,' Ps. cxxvii. 2; ' the bread of carefulness,' Ezek. xii. 18, 19. This will not suffer you to enjoy what you possess, and then you had as good or better be without it; you have nothing of it but the vexatious care and trouble. While Ahab was so careful for another vineyard, his whole kingdom was no joy to him, 1 Kings xxi. 4.

(3.) It will keep you from being the servants of Christ, so far as you give way to it. This is another argument of Christ against it, where he is levying so great force to subdue it in us: Mat. vi. 24, ' Ye cannot serve God and mammon.' The more careful you are about outward things, the less careful you will be to serve the Lord. The soul has not stream enough to run with any fulness towards both God and the world, and if the main current be not for God, he makes account he has none; he will count you servants of that about which you are most careful. Carefulness about these earthly things is not reconcileable with your faithfulness to God, and being true servants to him.

(4.) It corrupts the whole soul, the whole life. This is another reason which our Lord Jesus levels against worldliness and this carefulness for worldly things: Mat. vi. 22, 23, 'If thine eye be single,' *i. e.* if thy soul be freed from the mixtures of worldly cares and desires, the whole life will be lightsome; a spiritual and heavenly lustre will shine through it all; 'but if thine eye be evil,' if worldly carefulness and lustings are gotten in there, there will be nothing but darkness, a soul and life estranged from Christ, and remote from a strain and temper which is truly Christian; and instead of shining as lights in the world, there will be a walking on in the gross darkness of it.

(5.) It hinders the efficacy of the ordinances, and quite spoils them; it makes the word unfruitful, Mat. xiii. When the word falls upon the heart, and is about to put forth its force in the soul and in the life, these cares do as it were take it by the throat and strangle it, συμπνίγει, and so it becomes a dead letter, not καρποφερόμενον, not bringing forth fruit; it makes the prayers to be no prayers, a painted, not a real sacrifice; a mere piece of formality and hypocrisy; for when the lips draw near this draws away the heart, Ezek. xxxiii. 31, and when the heart is gone, the soul and life of the prayer is gone with it, and nothing left for God but a dead carcase: that which he counts no more a prayer, than we count a carcase to be a man. And it spoils our thoughts of God and heaven, and either keeps them out or mixes with them, and so makes us to have earthly thoughts of heaven itself, and worldly thoughts of the most high God.

(6.) It keeps us from joy in God, and disturbs our peace, that blessed peace we might have with God, that sweet tranquillity we might have in our own souls. Both these appear by the context. That we may 'rejoice in the Lord, and that always,' ver. 4, we must be moderate as to these outward things, ver. 5, and careful for nothing, ver. 6. Carefulness embitters the comfort which is to be had in outward enjoyments, and turns that into sorrow and vexation; it is more inconsistent with spiritual joy, 1 Tim. vi. 9, 10. They that will be rich, who make this their care, they give themselves many wounds, pierce themselves through with many sorrows. It is such a mischievous thing as cuts off or stops the pipes which should convey comfort to us both from the upper and lower springs, and will not let it pass to us either from heaven or from earth. If the apostle had been troubled with cares, either to avoid sufferings, or to get out of troubles, they would not have been matter of rejoicing and glorying to him.

It not only keeps us from joy, but will not let us have peace. This appears from the verse following the text. We must be careful for nothing, and trouble ourselves no further, but to 'make our requests known, that the peace of God,' &c. This is the way to have that sweet quiet and serenity of mind which is so transcendent a happiness. But the hurry of these cares will ruffle the mind and disquiet the heart, yea, and leave some guilt in the conscience too, which will not let it be at peace, and so hereby every part of the soul is robbed of its peace.

(7.) It involves those who give way to it in public calamities. When Christ is foretelling the dreadful ruin of Jerusalem, he warns those who would escape it to beware of these cares, as that which would bring them in danger of that terrible wrath, as well as other sins which are counted more provoking: Luke xxi. 34, 'And take heed to yourselves, lest at any time your hearts be overcharged with surfeiting and drunkenness, and cares of this life, and so that day come upon you unawares.' Where observe there is some intoxication in the cares of this life, as there is in excess of drinking. As an intemperate person is overcharged with too much drink, so is an intemperate soul overcharged with too much care, μήποτε βαρυνθῶσι. There is another sort of drunkenness besides that with strong drink: the heart may be overcharged and distempered with the cares of this life as well as with wine, and the effects are alike. He that is distempered with drink is not fit for business nor apprehensive of danger; mischief may come upon him, and often does, without any sense of it: so he that is distempered with the cares of this life, he is indisposed for the work which the Lord calls him to, and he is liable to judgment, and in danger to be surprised by it, and to have it fall upon him unawares. Take heed, says he, as of other stupifying wickedness, so of these cares, lest that day come upon you unawares, otherwise you are in danger to have the miseries of that day come upon you suddenly, unexpectedly, and so unavoidably. When God arises to execute judgment in a terrible manner, and to make the power of his wrath known in the execution, do not think that it will fall only upon notorious, flagitious persons, and that it will punish only luxury, drunkenness, and such excess of riot; even the cares of this life, however they are minced and counted no great provocations, may expose you to this wrath, and bring it upon you unawares, even when you look for no such thing. You know the calamities here threatened, and afterwards executed upon Jerusalem, were so grievous, as the like had not befallen any people under the whole heaven; and they are his disciples that he warns here: even they were in danger to be involved in these calamities if they were found entangled in these cares; and if they would endanger them, who can expect to escape that are under the guilt of them? You see how hurtful, how pernicious, how destructive this carefulness is.

5. It is very sinful, and shews there is much evil, very much corruption in the heart that gives way to it. It is a noisome, poisonous weed, and shews the soil is naught where it grows. To instance more particularly, it argues,

(1.) Unsubmissiveness to God, a heart not subdued to the divine will, not willing to have his concerns ordered and disposed of as the Lord thinks fit; and therein intolerable pride, self-confidence, and exalting its wisdom and will above that of God. Carefulness looks like a modest thing, but if you dissect and open it, it will be found big with such monsters as these are in the sight of God. Carefulness must have its own will, and its own way, and its own end, and is loath to submit to God in any of them. A submissive heart is content to have its concerns ordered, as to much or little, as to dangers or safety, as to sufferings or deliverance, as the Lord sees best and thinks fittest; he refers all to God, and rests quietly in his disposal; but when the heart is careful and troubled, it is because it cannot submit.

The Lord says, it shall go well with the righteous, in whatever condition they be; he will take care it shall be well, Isa. iii. 10. Oh but, says the careful heart, can it be well with me in such a want, loss, trouble, suffering? If the Lord should thus order it, I cannot think it would be well, and therefore I will take care it shall be otherwise; and so submits not unto the wisdom, and will, and way of God, but must have its own as better.

The Lord sees it good that such a one should be kept low, abridged of what he desires for himself and posterity, exercised with troubles and afflictions; but the man thinks it better to have the world at will, and to live prosperously, and thereupon will be careful about this, and submits not to those providences that cross him in it. Such stiffness and haughtiness, such crossing of God, and advancing of his will and judgment before the wisdom and pleasure of God, is this carefulness resolved into. One would think it were not such a devilish thing, but it is no better.

(2.) Unbelief and distrustfulness, and that by Christ's own arguing: Mat. vi. 30, 'If God so clothe the grass, &c., shall he not much more clothe you, O ye of little faith?' There is great unbelief, there is very little faith, where there is much care about our outward concerns. To trust in the Lord is expressed by casting our burden on him, committing our way to him, Ps. xxxvii. 5, and these are all one with casting our care on him, Luke xii. 28. He that will take the care upon himself will not, does not, cast it upon God, and so does not trust him; he will trust himself rather than trust God with his concerns. There is some doubting in such a heart, either whether the Lord be able or whether he be willing, to order his condition and affairs as they should be; and so he will not leave them to him, but look after them with all carefulness himself. Here is evidently a distrust of God.

When you meet with a man whom you fully trust with a business, you will not be further solicitous about it; but if you be still careful and anxious, it signifies you are not confident in him. And so it is here. This carefulness is from some doubtfulness lest your concerns in the hand of God should not be ordered as they should be, and this doubtfulness is inconsistent with that trust and confidence you should repose in God. Luke xii. 29, 'Seek not ye what ye shall eat or what ye shall drink, neither be ye of doubtful mind.' Where there is such solicitous seeking after these things, such thoughtfulness about them, there is a doubtfulness of mind concerning God; and where the mind is so doubtful, it is distrustful, there is little faith in it; Mat. xiv. 31, 'O thou of little faith, wherefore didst thou doubt?' As faith increases, cares will vanish; and as cares and doubts prevail, faith declines into distrust of God.

(3.) It argues much unmortifiedness; that we are carnal and sensual, and carnal and sensual lusts are unsubdued. From whence is such carefulness about earthly things? Is it not from our lusts, that are fed by these things, and live upon them, and would not be starved? There would be less carefulness about these outward things were it not to make provision for these. The flesh must be pleased, fancy and sense must be gratified; if our condition be not such as will serve for this, it is grievous to us. Therefore are we so careful and solicitous about our outward condition, lest it should be so ordered as to pinch the flesh. As our lusts die, our cares will die; but while these are so rife, they are too far from being mortified.

(4.) It argues a great inordinacy towards the world, an excess of affection to the things of it. Our hearts are much set upon that which we are so very careful about. If we did not too much love it, desire it, delight in it, we would not be so solicitous for it. If we did not too much fear losses and sufferings in our outward concerns, we would not perplex ourselves with care to avoid or escape them. Our care of any thing is answerable to our esteem of it and our affection to it. We are little solicitous about that which we have little or no affection for; we have little care of that which we contemn and despise; we would not be so careful about the world if the things thereof were contemptible to us. It is from our high esteem of, our great affection to, earthly things, that we are so careful about them. If we were crucified to the world, and the world were crucified to us, this carefulness for it would not be so strong. Where there is this crucifiedness to the world, there is an indifferency towards it and our outward condition. The heart is indifferent whether we have little or much, so we have but enough to be serviceable; whether we be high or low in the world, so we be but nearer unto God; whether we be afflicted or prosper, so that our souls do but prosper. And where we are indifferent in any case, we are not very careful which way it go, which way the Lord will dispose it, so that we are far from being thus crucified while we are so careful. This signifies not an indifferency but an inordinacy; and how sinful, how dangerous that is, we may judge by that of the apostle, 1 John ii. 15, 'Love not the world, nor the things that are in the world; for if any man love the world, the love of the Father is not in him;' Jas. iv. 4, 'Know ye not that the friendship of the world is enmity with God? Whosoever therefore will be a friend of the world is the enemy of God.'

(5.) It argues a neglect of heaven; that we are too careless, too regardless of the kingdom of God, and of the way, the only way that leads to it. This is intimated by our Lord Jesus in that place where we have such a rich treasury of arguments against this carefulness: Mat. vi. 33, 'But seek ye first the kingdom of God and his righteousness, and all these things shall be added unto you.' Those that mind heaven, and seek the kingdom of God as they ought to do, first and most, before all and above all, they will find something else to do than to trouble themselves so much about their earthly concerns. Those that mind these so much seek not that most, mind that too little. Where so much of the mind and heart is engaged and employed for outward things (as it is in careful persons), there will be little left for the kingdom of God and their heavenly interest. He that is over-careful for that cannot but have too little care of this; even as he that is too much taken up with his recreations and pleasures will neglect his business. The soul has not strength and vigour enough to lay out in any great measure upon several things, and so different as heaven and earth, ver. 24. If he be too much addicted to one of them, too careful to observe it, the other will be neglected, ver. 19, 20. If you be too careful to lay up treasure on earth, you will not, you cannot be careful enough to lay up treasure in heaven, and those Christ adviseth to shut out the one that the other may be admitted. And why, but because both cannot be entertained at once? The soul has not room enough for a due care about the heavenly treasure, if it be prepossessed with carefulness about earthly riches. If you mind earthly things your conversation cannot be in heaven, as is clear from the coherence of the apostle's discourse, Phil. iii. 19, 20, 'Whose end is destruction, whose god is their belly, and whose glory is in their shame, who mind earthly things, for our conversation is in heaven, from whence also we look for the Saviour, the Lord Jesus Christ;' $\pi o \lambda \iota \tau \epsilon \upsilon \mu \alpha$, our dealing and commerce, &c. You will drive no trade for heaven to purpose if you so mind and be so careful about earthly things. Merchants can drive a trade both in the East and West Indies, and mind their business at home too; and why? Because they do it by factors abroad. If they were to do all in their own persons, their trade at home would be as much as they could follow. You cannot manage your trade for heaven by factors; you must do that business in person if you will have anything done. If carefulness about your earthly concerns take you off from that, your trade for heaven is like to be lost. What would you have thought if Kish the father of Saul, when both his son and his asses were wanting, he should have been more solicitous about the asses than his son? 1 Sam. ix. 3, 5. It argues a viler temper in those who are so very careful about earthly things; they regard the asses so much, as that which should be dearest to them, dearer than relations or life, is little regarded. It argued a profane heart in Esau, when he would part with his birthright for a little pottage, Heb. xii. 16. He minded it not (though not only a civil but a sacred privilege) in comparison of that which would serve this present life, Gen. xxv. 32, 34, and so therein *flocci fecit partem futuri sæculi,* he set at nought his part in the world to come, says the Targum. Those that are so solicitous for what may sustain this present life, they too little regard the life to come and the concerns of it. It argues they are far from a heavenly temper, they are of a sordid, profane spirit, as Esau was.

6. It is foolish. It is great folly to be careful about the concerns of this life. This we may learn also from him who is wisdom itself: Mat. vi. 34, 'Take no thought for the morrow, for the morrow shall take thought for the things of itself; sufficient unto the day is the evil thereof.' Be not thoughtful for the future, how you shall be secured or provided for.

(1.) The morrow has burden, and trouble, and turmoil enough of its own, which you are like to find when it comes. You need not anticipate it, and bring it upon you before the time. It is a great folly to do so. Yet so you do, by taking the care of the morrow upon you to-day. You make a future trouble to be present. Is it so desirable as that you will not stay its time, but must needs have it beforehand? Is not this strange folly? Let the care and trouble of the morrow stay till the morrow come; will not that be soon enough? Those that have any wisdom will think so, and not so hasten the troubles of their life as to make those of one day to run into another, and to make those which would not come till the day after to leap into the day before, into the present day, by their troubling themselves with cares of the future.

(2.) But this is not all the folly of this carefulness. It will appear more fully by what he adds, 'Sufficient unto the day is the evil thereof.' Every day has its evil, *i. e.* its care, its burden, and trouble; and so much of this as is sufficient for it, as much as you can well bear. And would you have more than enough of this upon you, more than you are sufficient for, more of this evil than you can bear? Is this wisdom, or anything like it? Now, by carefulness for the morrow, for the future, you take the course to have more of this evil upon you than you are sufficient for; for when that of any one day is sufficient, by caring for to-morrow you add the evil of another day to that which is upon you already. By caring for the future, you bring the evil, the trouble of many days into one, when the burden of this day is heavy enough. You pull hereby many more burdens upon you than that of one day, even as many as the days come to, that you are anxiously careful for. It is great folly to charge yourselves with more than needs must, but so you do when you are solicitous about the future; for thereby you make the present (which is charged enough already) bear the charge and burden and trouble of the future also.

(3.) It is folly also, because there is a far better way to dispose of your temporal concerns than by taking such care and perplexing yourselves about them, a way that is easier and shorter, and pleasanter and surer, for the well ordering of them, than such carefulness will prove. And that way is opened in the text. 'But in everything, by prayer and supplication, let your requests be made known to God.' When anything is apt to perplex you and entangle you in these solicitous cares, instead of giving way to them, make your case, your request, known unto God, and leave it with him, commit it to him, cast it upon him.

[1.] This is an easier way. Would you compass your end more easily than by making a request for it? This is God's way. Is your way like it, which lies all along through troublesome perplexing cares? You would think him a man of much folly, and little under the conduct of any wisdom, who, when he might come to his end in a plain and easy path, would rather choose one that lies through briers and thorns and troublesome entanglements. Such is the way of carefulness; it is beset with that which is like briers and thorns to the mind; it is entangled and perplexed, full of trouble and vexation. But in the way of God you may have your affairs ordered for you with ease. It will give you no trouble nor disquietment. The Lord opens it for you, and calls you into it, because he would have you eased of what is troublesome. Use moderately the means he allows, and seek him in the use of them, and you need not trouble yourselves further, no occasion to be disquieted: Isa. xxvi. 3, 12, 'Thou wilt keep him in perfect peace whose mind is stayed on thee, because he trusteth in thee.' Thou wilt ordain peace for us.

[2.] This is a shorter way. The way of carefulness it is tedious, it is about, there is no end of it: cares for getting, for keeping and securing, for disposing the things of this life. It is folly to choose such a way when there is a shorter and more compendious way before you, and that which leads more directly to what you would come to, and is most desirable. What shorter way would you desire than to look up to God and make your requests known? The way of cares is tedious in itself; but being an indirect course, and such as the Lord approves not, allows not, he is provoked to make it and let you find it more tedious, as the passenger, that will not take directions from his guide, is like to wander and lose himself. You hear 'a voice behind you saying, This is the way;' but if you will not hearken to him, and follow his conduct, and be directed by him, but will be your own guides, he may leave you, as he did the Israelites, to wander in a wilderness, and be many years about that, which in few days, a little time, might be accomplished. 'They consumed their days in vanities,' Ps. lxxviii. 33. They spent their days and years, and themselves too, in the troubles of a wearisome wandering, and so may you do so too, and be harassed and worn out in bewildering cares, and that to little purpose; for,

[3.] This is a sure way; the other is far from being so. Now, no man who is not a fool will choose a way which is not like to bring him where he would be, when he has another before him which will assuredly do it. The way of God is not only plain and short, but sure. If you will walk in it, you may be sure either to arrive at what you desire, or at that which is better than you desire. You have the best assurance of it that can be given, the promise of God: Ps. xxxvii. 5, 'Commit thy way unto the Lord, trust also in him, and he will bring it to pass.' God undertakes he will bring it to pass, if you will commit it to him; and what greater certainty can you wish? Can there be any failing in that which God undertakes?

Oh but in your own way, the way of carefulness, there is nothing but uncertainties. What more frequent than for men to miscarry in that which they are most careful about, careful even to excess? You think the more care is taken, the more like to succeed; whereas many times it proves quite contrary. The more carefulness, the less success; God interposing, and crossing a way that is not his own, and blasting that which he likes not, and not suffering that to prosper which casts dishonour upon him. How solicitous were Joseph's brethren, lest their youngest brother should be advanced above them, according to the import of his dream! Yet the care they took to prevent it, proved the way to promote it; so far was it from answering their desires, that it directly crossed them. How careful was Saul to secure the kingdom to his posterity! He made it the business and design of a great part of his life, while he was king; but the issue was quite cross to his great and careful endeavours. How careful was Ananias to secure part of his estate! Yet, by the means his care put him upon, he lost both it and his life too. The Lord is engaged to disappoint such cares; and how can any be sure they shall succeed, when God is concerned to disappoint them? Mat. xvi. 25, 'Whosoever will save his life, shall lose it; and whosoever will lose his life for my sake, shall find it.' It holds true, as to our lives, so the concernments of our lives. He that is careful, in his own way, to secure his liberty, is like to lose it; or to save what he has, takes the course to be deprived of it; or to improve his estate, is more like thereby to impair it; or to preserve his reputation, takes the way to blast it.

Obj. But we see this carefulness often succeeds.

Ans. It does not succeed, when it seems to do. He that gets anything by it, if a curse go along with it, the seeming success is worse than a disappointment; and he that gets it not in God's way (as the way of cares is not) cannot look for a blessing. You can be sure of nothing that is truly desirable this way; you can make no account of anything, but the quite contrary.

[4.] Lastly. This is safer, a pleasanter, and in every respect a more happy way; and therefore it must be great folly to decline it, for a path in which no such thing can be expected. These, and the other particulars likewise, are evident by this one thing, that in this way the Lord is with you; in the other, you are left to and shift for yourselves. In this way you go leaning upon God; in the other, you lean upon your own understandings, and thoughtfulness, and puzzling endeavours. You are with God while you are in his way: Ps. lxxiii. 23, 'I am continually with thee; thou hast holden me by my right hand.' And while you are in his hand, you are safe, and cannot miscarry. Your course is comfortable and pleasant, being with God; it is blessed, and cannot be otherwise. Though it seems sometimes to lie through the valley of the shadow of death, yet, the Lord being with you in it, there is with you safety, and comfort, and happiness; for where is this to be had but in the presence of God? But being left to yourselves in your own way, what can be expected but danger, disaster, and misery? Judge you whether it be not great folly to choose such a way before that which is, in every respect, better, infinitely better.

7. It is incongruous to be so careful about these outward things: they do not deserve so much of your care; they are little worth, and it is very incongruous to take much care about that which is little worth. Particularly,

(1.) They are of little moment, they will not quit the care that they cost you; and that which will not quit the cost, you count not worthy of your care. Of how little moment they are, you may discern in these severals; that which will cost much, put you to great charge, and produce little when all is done, you count more worthy of your disregard, than much care; you think it lost on such things.

[1.] You are very little concerned in them; they are not the things which are your concernments indeed; whatever they are accounted by vain minds, your interest lies not in them, nor do they much concern it. And you think it not reasonable in other cases, to take much care, where you are little concerned. Your souls, and your eternal state, are very little concerned in these things; and here lies your interest, these are your concernments indeed. Much of these outward things threatens, and apparently endangers your eternal life: Mat. xix. 23, 24, 'A rich man shall hardly enter into the kingdom of heaven.' And again, 'I say unto you, it is easier for a camel to go through the eye of a needle, than for a rich man to enter into the kingdom of God.' If the Lord had said this of poverty or a straitened condition, we should have thought it reasonable to have feared it like death; yet who is afraid of riches, though the Lord have represented them so extremely dangerous? A small share of these outward things does not, of itself, endanger our souls, or everlasting condition. Lazarus was never the farther from heaven, for all his want, and afflictions, and poverty; Luke xvi. 22, 'The beggar died, and was carried by the angels into Abraham's bosom.' Oh, but though our souls and future life be not concerned in these things, yet this present life is very much; nay, but even this present life is very little concerned in much of them: Luke xii. 15, 'A man's life consisteth not in the abundance of the things which he possesseth.' The interest of your life consists not in having much of the world; for what is the interest of it, but that you may live healthfully, comfortably? And so we may live with as little of the world as the apostle Paul did; and what prince on earth lives so happily, so comfortably, as he did? That which you are careful for, is to have much for you and yours; to have more than is simply necessary, to have superfluities; but Christ tells you, that your life consists not in this, οὐκ ἐν τῷ περισσεύειν. Your life is little concerned in superfluities, and therefore you should not be careful for them, unless you will be so absurd as to take much care where you are little concerned. Those things are of very small moment, which are little considerable as to this present life, and less as to the life to come.*

[2.] There is little of reality in these things which you are so careful for; they are more in show, or fancy and opinion, than in reality. The good which we are careful to have in them, the evil that we are careful to avoid in them, is not so much really as in our conceits. He that has much, and uses but little, what more has he in effect, than he that has but little; what more real advantage, what more than in conceit?

What do delicacies and varieties contribute more to health and strength, than mean and plain fare? How then are they better, except in fancy? You may say, they are more pleasing; but if one can fancy the other to be as pleasing, it will be so, and there will be some reason to help the imagination, because that which is plain is really more healthful, and so in reason more pleasing.

What do great places, and power, contribute more to an happy life, than a low condition? What is the pomp and splendour of it, but πόλλη φαντασία an empty fancy, what show soever it make, how great soever it seem?

What real good is there in rich and gaudy habit, more than in that which is mean and common, since this will serve all the ends of clothing as well as the other? You will say one is more for ornament. But the judge of ornament is fancy; and therefore, that which is most comely to one seems ugly to another. The lily, the tulip, the peacock, outdoes all the gallantry of artificial habit, if you will but think so. 'Surely,' as Ps. xxxix. 6, 'every man walketh in a vain show. Surely they are disquieted in vain; he heapeth up riches, and knoweth not who shall gather them;' and embraces a vain show, as if it were a real good, and shews himself a very vain person, in taking so much care about that which hath so little of reality.'

The evil that we are so solicitous and careful to escape in these things is little, but what fancy and opinion puts upon them.

* No man can prolong his life, or make it more comfortable or happy, by possessing more than he needs or uses, D. *H.* [This marginal note has this signature D *H.* the former letter in the Roman, the latter in the italic character. The initials, therefore, probably stand for *Doctor* Howe, under whose auspices, and that of Matthew Mead, the sermons were originally published.—ED.]

Imprisonment seems a grievous evil, and what cares do some perplex themselves with about it! And yet a man can confine himself to his house, or to his chamber, for a long time; and if he do but fancy it, and have a good opinion of it, it will not be grievous.

So banishment seems grievous, and how careful are we to avoid it! Yet many can live for many years, often during life, in a strange country, for trade's sake; and why not on a better account? This would not be grievous, no more than the other, if there were but as good an opinion of it.

There is much of fancy in these things; they are evil or not, and more or less so, according to the opinion we have of them. And why should we trouble ourselves with so much care about such things, which have so little reality in them, wherein there is so little that is really good or evil? It depends upon imagination; you may think them out of what they seem to be, whether good or evil.

[3.] They will not answer the ends for which anything is worthy of your care; and what is that worth which will not answer the end of him who takes care of it? Men will not regard that which will not serve their turn, and think it absurd to trouble themselves about it. What do ye design in being so careful about these things? What would ye have of them? Is it pleasure, is it profit, that you aim at? Oh, but they rarely afford either of these, true pleasure or profit.

First, Will they help you to contentment? If they do not, they cannot truly please you; for what delight is there, or can there be, without contentment? Now, they are not apt, they art not wont, to satisfy those who have most of them: Isa. lv. 2, 'Wherefore do ye spend money for that which is not bread? and your labour for that which satisfieth not?' If they would give satisfaction, those who have the greatest confluence of them would be contented. But we find it is otherwise: Eccles. iv. 8, 'There is one alone, and there is not a second; yea, he hath neither child nor brother: yet is there no end of all his labour; neither is his eye satisfied with riches; neither saith he, For whom do I labour, and bereave my soul of good?' and v. 10, 'He that loveth silver shall not be satisfied with silver: nor he that loveth abundance with increase.' Will that please you that cannot content you, which will prove a troublesome, restless desire of more, instead of satisfying? And what is that worth that will not please you when you have it?

Secondly, Will they make you better? You have no real profit by them, unless they make you better. But when did you see any made better by having more? They debauch multitudes, and ensnare them in many foolish and hurtful lusts, and feed, and nourish, and minister to them; they are apt to clog the best, so that they move slowly in a spiritual course. They steal away their minds and thoughts from Christ and heaven, and divert or damp their affections to things above. All sorts are usually worse for them, but who is better? If they make you no better, you will be nothing the better for them; and who would trouble himself about that which he shall be nothing the better for? You are careful to escape afflictions and sufferings, but if you were freed from them, would it be better for you? Freedom from afflictions is often a grievous judgment; the souls of many suffer often for want of sufferings, and sometimes are utterly undone. David tells you it was good for him that he had been afflicted; but where does he, or any of his temper, tell you that it was good for him he was not afflicted? How unreasonable is it to be careful about that that you are like to be no better for! Or,

Thirdly, Will they make you happier? Are they any part of your happiness? How can that be, when those who have most of them are most miserable, and they that have had least of them have been most happy? If they would make you happy, there would be reason to make them your care; but since your happiness is not concerned in them, why are you so solicitous, &c.? Freedom from afflictions is counted a happiness, and yet this has drowned multitudes in perdition. And how often does the Spirit of God (who sure best understands what these things are) declare an afflicted state blessed! James v. 10, 11, 'Take, my brethren, the prophets, who have spoken in the name of the Lord, for an example of suffering affliction, and of patience. Behold, we count them happy which endure. Ye have heard of the patience of Job, and have seen the end of the Lord; that the Lord is very pitiful, and of tender mercy;' Ps. xciv. 12, 'Blessed is the man whom thou chastenest, O Lord, and teachest him out of thy law.' You see how little they tend to pleasure, profit, or happiness; and how little should they be in our care, which are of so little moment in these respects!

Fourthly, If the ends for which persons are commonly so careful for these things were gained, it will be worse than if they should miss them; success herein will be far worse than a disappointment. And is that worthy of our care, wherein a failure is better than success?

What are the ends which do commonly excite these cares, and which men are wont to propose to themselves in the careful pursuit of these things? Why take they so much care to escape afflictions and sufferings, and to get so large a share of riches, power, or greatness? Is it not ordinarily that they may live at ease, and fare deliciously, or go sumptuously, and gratify the flesh, or be in reputation and honour, and have more than others, and get above them, and look upon many as under them? And what is this (if we will judge truly of it) but pride, slothfulness, sensuality, and selfishness? And the more they have for the securing and maintaining of these, the more is their guilt, and the greater their condemnation. And should any be so careful to make themselves more sinful, and more miserable? Is this worth your care? Oh the lamentable delusion of the world, in being so careful to make themselves more miserable; in troubling themselves with cares for that which is not only (in the issue and tendency of it) nothing worth, but much worse than nothing! You see of how little or no moment these things are, and so how unworthy of great care. But this is not all.

(2.) They are of little continuance. If they were of more moment, yet if they were of small continuance, in reason you should not much care for them. But when they are of little worth, and of little continuance too, why should you be so very careful about them? But so they are; the time of them is both short, and, which is worse, uncertain. The things of this life are of no more continuance to us than our life is; the most of them commonly stay not so long. We see them vanish and die before us; we see an end of them ordinarily before our few days are ended. But if we had them for life, what is our life? is it not a bubble, a vapour, a shadow? You would think it childishness to see one very careful and solicitous about a bubble, a thing soon raised, and presently fallen and sunk. Who but a child would concern his cares in such a thing? Why, such a bubble is our life, and the enjoyments of life are more such; now raised, and presently gone: James iv. 14, 'What is your life? It is even a vapour, that appeareth for a little time, and then vanisheth away.' What if there be some splendour in this vapour, what if it please us? it will not do long. It is but a very short show, it is vanishing as soon as we begin to seek it; look on it again, and it is quite vanished. Such is our life; and the enjoyments of it appear for a little time, and then vanish, 'and the eye that saw them shall see them no more,' Job

xiv. 2. What if this shadow keep you from some inconveniences? It is but like the shadow of Jonah's gourd, a worm is prepared that will shortly (it may be the next day) smite it, and the gourd will wither, and the shadow (with the refreshment of it) will vanish. Are we sober when we trouble ourselves with cares about such vapours and shadows, such withering, vanishing things? They are but the enjoyments of a little time; if we have them now, they will shortly be gone; if they please us now, they will not please us long; and those that most please us, usually wither soonest: Isa. xl. 6–8, 'The voice said, Cry. And he said, What shall I cry? All flesh is grass, and all the goodness thereof is as the flower of the field: the grass withereth, the flower fadeth; because the Spirit of the Lord bloweth upon it: surely the people is grass. The grass withereth, the flower fadeth; but the word of our God shall stand for ever.' The apostle applies these expressions to riches: James i. 10, 11, 'But the rich, in that he is made low: because as the flower of the grass he shall pass away. For the sun is no sooner risen with a burning heat, but it withereth the grass, and the flower falleth, and the grace of the fashion of it perisheth: so also shall the rich man fade away in his ways.' The grass, or the stalk of the flower, is soon gone, that will be cut down or wither shortly. Oh but the flower, that which more pleases us, stays not so long; that is cropped, or sheds its leaves sooner. All is withering, all is gone; but usually that which we are most taken with is soonest gone. Oh, why should that which is of so little continuance be so much our care? The apostle, upon this account, thought them scarce worth the looking on: 2 Cor. iv. 18, 'While we look not at the things which are seen, but at the things which are not seen; for the things which are seen are temporal, but the things which are not seen are eternal.'

(3.) They are not only of short, but uncertain continuance. When we speak of continuance, we have but a short time in them; but if we speak of certainty, we have no time at all. We have no time certain, no, not a moment, in any of the concerns of this life; and this is reason enough why we should not trouble ourselves with cares about them. After all your care and trouble, when you look to enjoy them, the things may be gone. A tenant, if he have a lease of his farm, he may take some care of it; but if he have no time at all in it, but may be turned out the next day, the next hour, he can see no reason, he will have no heart, to take much care of it. It is thus with us as to all the concerns of this life; we have no lease of it, no time in them at all. The Lord of all may turn us out of this, and the other, and all the next hour, the next moment. And he has left us at such uncertainties, on purpose that we might see reason not so much to mind, not to be so careful about them: Prov. xxiii. 5, 'Wilt thou set thine eyes upon that which is not? for riches certainly make themselves wings, they flee away as an eagle towards heaven.' You would think him an absurd man who, when he sees an eagle in his field, would take great care how to fence it in there, whenas no fence can secure it, make it as high as he can. The eagle, when she list, will make use of her wings and fly away; she will do it certainly. Such winged things are the enjoyments of this life, they certainly make themselves wings. There is nothing so certain as our utter uncertainty of having them or keeping them. And is not our care lost upon that which we can never make sure to us for another moment?

Such reason we have, and so many motives, not to give way to this carefulness. Let me, in the next place, shew you what means are useful, and may be effectual, with the Lord's concurrence, to expel these cares, and secure us against this forbidden carefulness.

1. Get interest in God, and trust him. Study his all-sufficiency, and believe that he, above all, more than all, can satisfy all your desires, and entertain all your delights, and secure you against all fears; that there is in him all the good that is to be cared for in these outward things, and infinitely more; that he can communicate this good to you easily, plentifully, seasonably; that he can prevent, or divert, or remove all the evil you are solicitous to avoid, or be rid of, or else can turn it into good; that he is willing to do all this.

(1.) In general, believe the all-sufficiency of God, and get your interest therein cleared. View this well, and you may see enough therein to ease your minds of these cares, and to clear yourselves from the trouble of them. Is not he sufficient for you who is sufficient for all things, for all purposes? If he be, if you have enough in him, if you have more than those who have most in the world without him, if you have far more in him than the whole world comes to, what occasion have you to be careful about any more? Should he that has enough, abundantly enough, trouble himself with cares about more? Is not God all-sufficient enough for you? Dare you give way to a thought so dishonourable to him? Is he enough for thousands and millions of angels and glorified saints, enough for all the creatures of heaven and earth, and not enough for thee alone? And when thou hast so much more than is enough for thee, and all the world besides, shouldst thou be solicitous about more still? Should he, who has more than those who have most in the world without God, be still careful about earthly things? Should he who has a kingdom trouble himself about an acre or a foot of land? Why, all the fields, all the lands in the greatest kingdom on earth, are not so much, compared with what you have in God, as a foot, an acre of land is to such a kingdom. Should one who has treasure to the value of many millions, be careful and solicitous about a penny or a farthing? Why, all the treasure on earth is of no more value than a farthing, compared with the treasure and riches you have in the all-sufficient God. Should Ahasuerus, who had an hundred, twenty, and seven provinces, should Alexander or Augustus, who had got the empire of the world, trouble their heads about a molehill, or perplex themselves with cares about a trifle? Would not you think this notoriously absurd, and them little better than madmen? Why, all those provinces, all the kingdoms of the earth, the empire of the whole world, it is but a trifle compared with his estate who has God for his portion. If he be your possession and heritage, and yet you are perplexing yourselves with cares about these lesser trifles, when your eyes are opened, you will see cause to pass that censure upon yourselves (which the psalmist does in a like case): Ps. lxxiii. 22, ' So foolish was I, and ignorant : I was as a beast before thee;' 1 Cor. ii. 9, ' Eye hath not seen, nor ear heard, neither have entered into the heart of man, the things which God hath prepared for them that love him.' Has God prepared and laid up for you, as your portion, more than eye has seen, though it has seen all that the world can shew; have you more than ear has heard, though it has heard much more than the eye has discovered; have you more than has entered into the heart of man, more than you can think of, though you can think of more worlds than are in being? Is all this yours? And are you still carking, still caring, and are still perplexing yourselves about more, when you have so much already as the whole earth is nothing, and less than nothing and vanity compared with it? Sure you do not believe God and his all-sufficiency. If you had faith herein, and did but exercise it, your cares about earthly things would vanish. They would not stay, they would not appear, but where there is no faith, or very little: Luke xii. 28, ' If, then, God so clothe the grass, which is to-day in the field, and to-morrow is cast into the oven, how much more will he clothe you, O ye of little faith!' More particularly believe,

[1.] That there is all that is good in God; that there is in him all that is to be cared for or regarded; that you may have in him all the good that is to be cared for in these outward things; that there is in him infinitely more than these things contain or can pretend to; that all the good which you need take thought for, or are tempted to be thoughtful about, you may have it in him, whether you have these things or no. For all the good that is worthy of any care in earthly things, it came from him, he conveyed it into them; and therefore it is eminently in him. And there you may find it still, whatever become of these outward enjoyments; even as all the light and heat that is in the air at noon-day, it comes from the sun, and therefore is in the sun virtually and eminently, and there may be found, if there were none in the air; or as all the water that is in the cistern or pipes came from the fountain, and there you may have it, and more than these can contain, whether there be any in them or not. Now why should you be solicitous lest you should want these things, since all that is good in them, and any way desirable, all that you need care for, is to be had in God, and more and better than in them.

What are these things good for but to serve your necessities, or to serve you with conveniences and delights? Food, and raiment, and habitation are necessaries; we cannot live without them, and so think it excusable to be careful for them. But these you may have in God, when you are not, or cannot be, otherwise accommodated: Ps. xc. 1, 'Lord, thou hast been our dwelling-place in all generations.' So he was when they were in the wilderness, and had neither house nor home. Here David rested better than in his palace: Ps. lxxi. 3, 'Be thou my strong habitation, whereunto I may continually resort: thou hast given commandment to save me; for thou art my rock and my fortress.' To make use of the Lord for this purpose obliges him: Ps. xci. 9, 10, 'Because thou hast made the Lord which is my refuge, even the Most High, thy habitation, there shall no evil befall thee, neither shall any plague come nigh thy dwelling.' And who can dwell more safely, more pleasantly, than he who dwelleth in the secret places of the Most High, and abides under the shadow of the Almighty? ver. 1. And for food, he tells us, Mat. iv. 4, 'Man shall not live by bread alone, but by every word that proceedeth out of the mouth of God.' When we cannot have it, he can make up the want of it with a word. He can sustain life without bread, which in Scripture phrase includes all the necessaries of this life. He can make these things not to be needful, and order it so, that we shall need no more than we have. He can take away the necessity, and he that takes it away serves our needs better than that which does but from day to day supply them. If you take away my meat, God will take away my stomach, said that faithful woman. If I cannot have what I need, the Lord will not let me need it. And not to need these things is better than to have them, if the state of angels be better than that of frail indigent men: for that is the difference betwixt them and us; we have these things as needful, they need them not. And as for delights, he knows not God, is utterly a stranger to him, who believes not there are more and sweeter to be had in him than in the pleasantest things on earth: Ps. iv. 6, 7, 'There be many that say, Who will shew us any good? Lord, lift thou up the light of thy countenance upon us. Thou hast put gladness in my heart, more than in the time that their corn and their wine increased;' Hab. iii. 17, 18, 'Although the fig-tree shall not blossom, neither shall fruit be in the vines: the labour of the olive shall fail, and the fields shall yield no meat; the flock shall be cut off from the fold, and there shall be no herd in the stalls: yet will I rejoice in the Lord, I will joy in the God of my salvation.' When the very course of nature for ordinary preservation does fail, faith can see enough in the all-sufficient God not only to free him from perplexing cares, but to fill him with joy and glorying.

If you have God, you have all that these things are good for; all that you need care for, whether for necessity or delight, and so are no way concerned to be careful whether they come or go. So long as he goes not, whatever else go, you lose nothing, but what is still left you in him, and may be found there with wonderful more advantage. If a man have a great stock, a rich bank, he will not be careful though he have but little in his purse; he knows where to have more, and enough of it, whenever there is occasion for it. God is your bank, your treasury, all that riches is your own. What if you have not much money about you, much of these outward things to lug along you, you know where you have enough, it is not out of your reach, it may be had when you have occasion; why then are you so careful? If a man be stored with bars of gold, or jewels of great value, he is not careful though he have but little in small money. The things of this life are but like small money for present use. What if you have not much in pence, and such little pieces, so long as you have it in that vast and incomprehensible sum, the all-sufficient God, the total of which is beyond account, above all valuation, what need you be careful? Will not this yield you unspeakably more when there is occasion, than many bags full of single pence or copper money? In other cases you judge not of things by their bulk, but their value. Here is one thing you have (if God be yours) which is more worth than all other things together, and you may make more of it when there is need. It is virtually all, and comprises the good and advantage of whatever you care for. What, then, need you care for more? Oh if you did but see it, and know it, and believe it, you would dwell far from carefulness.

[2.] Believe that there is no good to be had from them without God. All the cares of the world can make nothing of them, can squeeze no drop of good out of them, unless he let it out. For as all the good that is in them is in him eminently, and so you need not care for them if you have him, so all the good that can be expected of them is from him dependently, and so they are not to be regarded without him. They can do you no good at all, they are not sufficient for it of themselves, their sufficiency for it is from him who is only all sufficient. Be as careful as you will to get as much as you can, and to keep it; yet you will get just nothing, but the trouble of your care and turmoil; nothing at all to be cared for unless he give it you. Now, if you did believe this effectually, you would not, by over-caring, provoke God to suspend that influence upon which all that is anything worth in them depends. The Lord can be as good to you as heart can desire, even without these; but these will be good for nothing without him. Meat and clothes, and rest, though you have more than enough, will not serve your necessities, will not keep you in health and strength, will not ease or cure you when you are ill. Pleasant things will not be delightful, will not so much as content you. Riches will not serve the end of riches, and when they do not serve their true end, they are far worse than well improved poverty: James v. 1–3, 'Go to now, ye rich men, weep and howl for your miseries that shall come upon you. Your riches are corrupted, and your garments are moth-eaten. Your gold and silver is cankered; and the rust of them shall be a witness against you, and shall eat your flesh as it were fire.' God has such a stroke in these things, that the creatures, though given in abundance, will not serve their proper uses when he says they shall not: Micah vi. 14, 15, 'Thou shalt eat, but not be satisfied; and thy casting down shall be in the midst of thee; and thou shalt take hold, but shalt not deliver; and that which thou deliverest will I give up to the sword. Thou shalt sow, but thou shalt not reap; thou shalt tread the olives, but thou shalt not anoint thee with oil; and sweet wine, but thou shalt not drink wine.' Haggai i. 6, 9, 'Ye have sown much, and bring in little; ye eat, but ye have not enough; ye drink, but ye are not filled with drink; ye clothe you, but there is none warm; and he that earneth wages, earneth wages to put it into a bag with holes,' &c. This was the issue of all their carefulness, when they neglected better things. They had enough to feed, and clothe, and make them rich, and yet they were in effect neither fed, nor clothed, nor enriched. God did but blow upon it, and all the good of these things, all that was to be cared for in them, vanished. If you did believe and consider this, you would see yourselves, your care so much concerned for the pleasing of God, that you would be little careful about other things.

[3.] Believe that he can communicate the good of all these things to us, though they of themselves cannot do it. And this he is all-sufficient to do, either by these things or without them. There is no restraint with him to do it either way. And though ordinarily he conveys it by these things, yet it is not at all difficult to him to do it without them. He can do this easily, plentifully, seasonably.

Easily. He can with the greatest ease give these outward things, or afford the comfort and advantage of them; he can do it with a word, with the turning of a hand. Let him but give the word, and it will be done: Ps. cxlvii. 15, 'He sendeth forth his commandment upon earth, his word runneth very swiftly;' Ps. cvii. 20, 'He sent his word, and healed them, and delivered them from their destructions, with the turning of a hand;' Ps. civ. 28, 'That thou givest them they gather; thou openest thine hand, they are filled with good;' and Ps. cxlv. 16, 'Thou openest thine hand, and satisfiest the desire of every living thing.' That which the things themselves cannot do, with all their abundance; that which we cannot do, with all our carefulness (satisfy us with the good of them), he can do more easily than we can open our hand. If we be careful to have these things, the good of them, without much trouble, faith will direct us where it may be had with ease; it will lead us to mind God, and not to mind nor be thoughtful about the things themselves.

Plentifully. He can fill, he can satisfy us with the goodness of them; not with the husks, which is all we can have without him, perplex ourselves with what cares we will, but with that which is desirable in them: Ps. civ. 28, 'Thou openest thy hand, they are filled with good;' Ps. lxviii. 10, 'Thou, O God, hast prepared of thy goodness for the poor.' 1 Tim. vi. 17, 'Charge them that are rich in this world, that they be not high-minded, nor trust in uncertain riches, but in the living God, who giveth us richly all things to enjoy.' He can give abundance of the good where there is but a little of the things; much contentment with it, much spiritual advantage by it; and upon that account, Ps. xxxvii. 16, 'A little that a righteous man hath, is better than the riches of many wicked.' And it is true in this sense, though it may look farther, when it is said, Luke i. 53, 'He hath filled the hungry with good things, and the rich he hath sent empty away.' He sends them away empty of the good of riches while they have them, and fills those with it who have them not. He can convey the marrow to others, and leave them nothing but the bare bone to gnaw on, which, how big soever it be (how bulky soever their estates are), is nothing the better, being but a bare and empty bone. If we be tempted to be careful for much of these things, which is so common as the best are in danger, this believed will help us to cease from this carefulness, and to apply ourselves to him, in whose hands alone plenty, and all the good of it, all that is to be cared for, is plentifully found.

Seasonably. When they will do us no hurt, when they would do us most good, when they are most needful, most useful. We know not the season, we mind it not. We would have these things, and are careful to have much of them at a venture; whether they will do us good or hurt we care not, but to take much care to have them, and our fill of them, whatever be the issue; as one in a fever, that will have wine, and his fill of it, though he die for it; he will have his appetite, indeed his distemper, gratified; come what will of it, whether it be safe or seasonable, he cares not. We consider not, we know not when it is safe, when it is seasonable; but the Lord knows perfectly, and can give it when the season is: Ps. civ. 27, 'These wait all upon thee, that thou may give them their meat in his due season;' and cxlv. 15, 'The eyes of all wait upon thee; and thou givest them their meat in due season.' Hosea vi. 3, 'He shall come unto us as the rain, as the latter and former rain on the earth.' He can give these, as he gives the first and latter rain, when it is most needful, and will be of greatest advantage.

This believed, would help us to eye God, and fix our minds on him, instead of fixing our minds on, and employing our thoughtfulness about, our outward concerns. This would teach us not to strain our souls with cares, in leaping greedily at the fruit which is above our reach; and observe the hand of God, which only can convey it to us seasonably, when it will be good for us, and worth the having.

This believed, that the Lord can give us the good of these things without them, will help us not to be so careful for the things themselves, for the good that is to [be] had by them, is all that is to be cared for in them; and this the Lord can help us to, whether we have them or no. When you have drawn all the spirit out of any herb or plant, you regard not the gross, dry, useless matter that is left, nor are solicitous what becomes of it. If you have the advantage and comfort which is expected from outward enjoyments, you have all the spirits of them, and this the Lord is sufficient to give you without them, yea, and to help you to as much of this in a little as in more of them. And this believed will help you to be indifferent as to the measure of these things, not to be careful or solicitous whether you have less or more.

[4.] Believe that he can secure you from whatever you are solicitous to avoid, or ease you of whatever you are careful to be rid of.

First, Losses, troubles, sufferings are wholly and uncontrollably at his disposing; he can prevent them when they are afar off and keep them so; he can divert them when they are near and turn them another way; he can remove them when they are upon you, for all of this nature that you are apt to be thoughtful about is in his hand, and all the instruments and circumstances thereof, and he can take whatever order therein he pleases. You are not careful about your concerns, when they are in such hands as you can be confident of. Have faith in God, believe but that all is in the best hands that they can possibly fall into when they are in his, and you will see no occasion to be careful. If you will but give God the pre-eminence above some creatures, and believe your affairs are better in his hands than in those persons that you can be confident of, your hearts may be at rest, all is as well as can be, unless it can be better than when all is at God's disposing. When a stone cannot move without the hand that you can trust, you will not be careful about what you may suffer by it. Why, all that may trouble you lies as still as a stone in the highway, and cannot move without the hand which you have so much cause to trust, which you have more reason to trust than your own : if you believe this, how can you be careful ? If the rod be in the hand that the child can trust and be secure of, he will not be perplexed about it. All that can afflict you is in the hand of God; if that be to be trusted, your minds may be at ease, there is not the least occasion to be anxious or perplexed ; believe but that God can secure you; that may hush your cares. The three faithful Jews found it enough for this purpose : Dan. iii. 16, 17, 'Our God is able to deliver us from the burning fiery furnace, and he will deliver us out of thine hand, O king.' This they believed, therefore they were not careful.

Secondly, He can secure you from the evil of afflictions, troubles, losses ; if they should come upon you, he can keep the evil of them far from you : Job v. 19, 'He shall deliver thee in six troubles ; yea, in seven there shall no evil touch thee.' When you are surrounded with troubles, he can take order that the evil of them shall not so much as touch you, Ps. xxiii. He can take a course that there shall be no evil to be feared; and where there is no cause of fear, there can be no occasion to be perplexed. There is nothing that in reason you can be careful to avoid but that which is evil ; believe but that God is sufficient to secure you from all the evil of troubles, and all occasion of carefulness will vanish. The evil of them, which we are so careful to avoid, is the smart, the sting, the damage, the grievance, we are apprehensive of; but the Lord can pull out the sting, and what need you then care for the serpent ? He can keep you from any damage by them, and what need you care what seems lost, if there be no damage by it ? He can ease you of the grievance, and why so careful to avoid that which will not be grievous ? He can take order that you shall not so much as smart by them. He can not only mitigate the evil you are wont to be perplexed about, and make it tolerable,—as 1 Cor. x. 13, 'God is faithful, who will not suffer you to be tempted above that ye are able ; but will with the temptation also make a way to escape, that ye may be able to bear it ;— but quite take it away. He can so order it that troubles shall not be troublesome to you ; that pressures shall not be heavy upon you, but go as lightly under them as if they weighed nothing ; that you shall not suffer by what others count great sufferings ; that you shall not lose anything which you need care for by your losses. If the evil be gone, there is nothing left that you need be careful about : and the evil the Lord can easily remove.

Thirdly, He can do you good by afflictions; not only free you from the evil of them, but make them good for you. He can render them as good or better for you, than freedom from them of itself is or can be. Believe this, and you will count it very absurd to be careful ; it is little better than madness to be careful to avoid that which is good, solicitous to escape that which will prove best for you. God is sufficient to do this. If you lose much of what you have, he can make the little that is left as good or better than the whole, as comfortable, as satisfying, as advantageous, yea, and yourselves more serviceable thereby than, it may be, you would have been with much more. It is not the quantity but the virtue of things that is to be cared for ; and the Lord can convey more virtue into a little than ordinarily there is to be found in very much, as you find more in a little spirits than in a great quantity of drugs. If the Lord can give you all the virtue of much in a little, what need you be so careful for much, unless the mere bulk and cumber of it be to be cared for?

And, as in losses and wants, so in other afflictions and sufferings, he can do you more good by them than you were like to have met with without them. He has done this ordinarily. Jacob's afflictions, which he met with in the loss of Joseph, proved a greater advantage to him and the whole family than if he had never parted with him: Gen. xlv. 5-7, 'Now therefore be not grieved, nor angry with yourselves, that ye sold me hither: for God did send me before you to preserve life: to preserve you a posterity in the earth, and to save your lives by a great deliverance.' If Jacob's care to keep Joseph with him had succeeded according to his desire, he and his family might have starved: Gen. l. 20, 'Ye thought evil against me; but God meant it unto good, to bring to pass, as it is at this day, to save much people alive.' He kept the Israelites so long in the wilderness, a place of much trouble and afflictions to them, that he might do them good thereby, Deut. viii. 15, 16; he led them so long in the valley of death, as it is called, Jer. ii. 6, to do them good. It was better for David, when he was persecuted and hunted as a partridge upon the mountains, than when he was upon his throne: Ps. cxix. 75, 'I know, O Lord, that thy judgments are right, and that thou in faithfulness hast afflicted me.' He did his people good by their captivity, the most grievous suffering that ever they met with, and the more, because it was not only the loss of their country, but the loss of the temple and the solemn worship of God: Jer. xxiv. 5, 'Thus saith the Lord, Like these good figs, so will I acknowledge them that are carried away captive of Judah, whom I have sent out of this place into the land of the Chaldeans for their good.' He did them that good hereby, which mercies, and deliverances, and his own ordinances were not effectual before to do; hereby he brought them to return unto him and acknowledge him: ver. 7, 'I will give them an heart to know me, that I am the Lord: and they shall be my people, and I will be their God: for they shall return unto me with their whole heart.'

I need not stay on particular instances; the apostle comprises all, Rom. viii. 28, 'We know that all things work together for good to them that love God, to them who are the called according to his purpose;' all afflictions and sufferings whatsoever, for of those he is speaking. He tells us, how that which we count so evil works for good: Heb. xii. 10, 'He chasteneth us for our profit, that we might be partakers of his holiness.' More of his holiness is so great a good as far outweighs all the evil, seeming or real, that is in any outward losses or sufferings whatsoever. Believe this, that he is sufficient to turn them into good, and it will take you off from such carefulness to avoid them. What pretence can there be for perplexing yourselves with cares for the escaping of that which is good for you? You may say, It is true, *if* the Lord will do this for me; oh, but you have no reason to question this, for,

[5.] He is willing, and you have all reason to believe that he is willing to do all this for you; believe that he is willing to communicate the good of these outward things to you, or the things themselves if they be good; this is all that is to be cared for. And this you may be sure of, if you count the word of the faithful God sufficient assurance: Ps. xxxiv. 10, 'The young lions do lack, and suffer hunger; but they that seek the Lord shall not want any good thing;' and Ps. lxxxiv. 11, 'For the Lord God is a sun and shield: the Lord will give grace and glory: no good thing will he withhold from them that walk uprightly;' and Ps. lxxxv. 12, 'The Lord shall give that which is good; and our land yield her increase.' You will not, if you be sober, be careful, lest you should be without that which is not good; you will not count that a want; and if your wants be no other, you are assured of a supply: Philip. iv., 'He shall supply,' he is willing to do it richly. You are no more concerned to be careful about this, than a child is, who has, and knows he has, an affectionate father, able and willing to provide for him. The Lord is more willing to provide herein for you than the best of fathers on earth. Would you desire more to free you from cares? Sure it needs not. Why, but you have more. The Lord is as much more willing to do it than any earthly parents, as the love of God exceeds the affections of men; as much more willing as the Father of mercies, and the God of all comforts, exceeds that bit of affection, that drop of love, which the narrow heart of an earthly parent can contain: Mat. vii. 11, 'If ye then, being evil, know how to give good gifts unto your children, how much more shall your Father which is in heaven give good gifts to them that ask him?' As much more willingly does he give as heaven is above earth. Do but believe this effectually, and you shall be ashamed, if not astonished, at the absurdness and unreasonableness of your cares.

And then as for afflictions, &c., he is not only able but willing to free you from them, or to secure you from the evil of them, which is all you need to care, or have any occasion to perplex yourselves about; and not only so, but to make them really good for you. All which he assures us of by many great and precious promises (which I must not mention now), he is willing to make them good; to make them prove best for you, in all respects, both in point of pleasure, and profit, and honour; all which are comprised in that of the apostle: 1 Pet. i. 6, 7, 'Wherein ye greatly rejoice, though now for a season (if need be) ye are in weariness through manifold temptations; that the trial of your faith, being much more precious than of gold that perisheth, though it be tried with fire, might be found unto praise, and honour, and glory, at the appearing of Jesus Christ.' Here is delight wherewith you may greatly rejoice, even in the midst of afflictions; here is profit, richer than that of gold, something much more precious and valuable; here is approbation with God, the greatest honour and glory, both at his appearing here and hereafter; and all this the issue of manifold afflictions, of fiery trials. But that the Lord is willing you should partake of so sweet, and rich, and noble advantage, he would not be willing you should suffer, no, not for a season. He is ready to make these not only good, but better for you than outward prosperity is wont to be, or of itself can be; and need you be so careful to avoid that which he will make better for you, than the condition you naturally most desire, better than a prosperous and flourishing state? Do ye think the apostle Paul, for all his sufferings, would have changed conditions with Nero, in the greatest flourish of his empire? Or, that Moses did not believe the Lord would make afflictions better for him than all the honours, or riches, or pleasures, of Egypt, when, Heb. xi. 24–26, 'he refused to be called the son of Pharaoh's daughter, choosing rather to suffer affliction with the people of God, than to enjoy the pleasures of sin for a season, esteeming the reproach of Christ greater riches than the treasures of Egypt'? The Lord is willing hereby to free you from that which is your greatest evil, your sin and corruption; which is the weakness, the disease, the poverty, the deformity, the misery of your souls. He has declared his will by his promise: Isa. xxvii. 9, 'By this shall the iniquity of Jacob be purged, and this is all the fruit, to take away his sin;' and Isa. i. 25, 'I will turn my hand upon thee, and purely purge away thy dross, and take away all thy sin;' and willing to make you hereby partakers of that which is the greatest good you are capable of on earth: that holiness, which is the health, strength, beauty, riches, life and glory of the soul, and fruitful therein, Heb. xii., 2 Cor. iv. Do you question his willingness here? Why, he is more willing you should have so much good by afflictions than yourselves are. You are afraid of this sovereign receipt, because it tastes a little bitter; like a foolish child, who will not take that to save his life which bites his tongue. The Lord is glad to force it on us; so much more ready is he to do us good thereby, than we are willing to have it. Believe but this, that he is so willing to make afflictions so good, so exceeding good, and you will condemn yourselves of childishness in perplexing yourselves much, and being so very thoughtful how to avoid them. These cares would find no place if faith were duly exercised: Ps. xlii. 11, 'Why art thou cast down, O my soul? and why art thou disquieted within me? Hope thou in God, for I shall yet praise him, who is the health of my countenance, and my God;' John xiv. 1, 'Let not your heart be troubled; ye believe in God, believe also in me.'

(2.) Get more submission unto God, if you would be freed from this carefulness.

[1.] Get judgment and will more subjected to the mind and will of God, so as to rest satisfied in that which he counts best for you. The Lord has assured his people that it shall go well with them, that he will dispose of their concerns for the best. If we did acquiesce in this, and were fully satisfied with it, and will and mind rested in it, we should be at rest from our cares; we should not be further perplexed about that which we were satisfied would be ordered for the best. The Lord has given sufficient ground in his word for our satisfaction herein; and we seem to be satisfied in general, and can say he will make all work for the best; and in particular cases, which are remote, and concern others, we make no doubt of it; but when we are tried in cases that more particularly respect to ourselves, and which touch us nearly, the unsubmissiveness of our souls unto God, in these dealings which he judges fittest for us, does presently bewray itself. Oh if I should meet with such a loss, lose such a relation, such a comfort, such a considerable part of a livelihood, how could it be well with me if such and such an affliction should befall me, so grievous, so wounding, which strikes deep into the interest of ease, or profit, or credit, or comfort? Then we fly off, and gainsay in particulars what we seemed satisfied with in general; and make that a question, which, before we came to be specially and deeply concerned, seemed unquestionable. Then we are ready to say (or to think at least) How can it be well with me if this should befall me? How can this be for the best, which threatens to ruin, to undo me; which comes upon me with open mouth, to swallow up my dearest comforts and concernments? Now we cannot submit to God, and yield up our judgments to that which he has so often declared; we cannot think it best, nay, we cannot think it good for us, though it be the dispensation of that God who has given us his word that all his dispensations shall be for the best. Here our judgments rise up against the mind and judgment of God, and what he thinks best and fittest for us we think worst of all; and accordingly we are anxious, and perplexed, and thoughtful, and full of cares how to prevent it, when such a providence approaches, or how we may remove it when it has overtaken us. Whereas, if our minds and hearts were but subdued to the mind and will of God, we would be satisfied with that as best which he thinks to be so; and so our cares would cease, and mind and heart would be at rest from the troublesome hurry of them.

Oh labour for this quiet, humble submission unto God; abhor that horrible pride whereby we prefer our own judgments before that of infinite wisdom, and advance our own wills before that of infinite goodness. See that mind and heart lower to God in all his dispensations, as most wise, and most good, and best of all for you, whatever they may seem to a proud selfish heart, or to a partial short-sighted mind. This you must do, if you would be freed from the sin and trouble of this condemned carefulness. If we will presume to make ourselves wiser than God, and to know better what is best for us than he, no wonder if our hearts be like the troubled sea, that cannot rest, if we be left to set ourselves on several occasions upon the rack of this carefulness.

[2.] Get your wills subdued to the will of God. If this were done, and our wills brought to a due subjection to the divine will, we should not be at all troubled or perplexed with cares; for, though we observe it not, our excess of carefulness is to have our own wills in this, and the other, and every thing that we are solicitous about. If our own will were not in it, and something therein lay not cross to that, we would not be troubled with cares or thoughtfulness about it.

Why are we so careful to get much for ourselves and ours; so thoughtful lest it should be lost or impaired, but because we would have a fair estate? That is our will, it is fixed and stiff for it. We cannot yield to be put off with a little, though it were the will of God so to order it.

Why are we so thoughtful and solicitous for the avoiding of afflictions and sufferings, or so very careful to get out of them when they are upon us, but because we would live easily, and pleasantly, and prosperously? This is our will, and is so much set upon it, that it cannot yield to a low and afflicted condition, though it were the will of God to dispose us in it. If we did but submit to his will, the care and trouble would be over; that which he wills for us would be welcome to us; we should not trouble ourselves with cares, either to prevent it before it come, or to escape it when it is upon us. You may see this in Saul: it was the will of God that David should succeed him in the kingdom; it was Saul's will that his own son should succeed him, and the crown not be removed from his family. Hence was Saul so afflicted with cares, after he suspected David should have the kingdom: hence was he so thoughtful how to make an end of him. His cares might bring or increase that melancholy, which is called (as some think) an evil spirit, or which an evil spirit made use of, to afflict him and trouble his spirit, 1 Sam. xviii. 8–10. If Saul could have submitted his will to God's, he had been freed from those cares, and the troubles of heart and life, which they brought upon him; but Saul would have his own will, rather than God's will should be done: this was the rise of his cares, and that which continued them during his life.

And thus it is commonly with us in other cases; when our carefulness is truly stated, the contest is betwixt God's will and ours. We may tremble that it should be thus, but so it is. We are careful to have our wills, with a neglect of God's will, nay, many times in opposition to it. Instead of being careful to have his will done on earth as it is in heaven, we are thoughtful how our wills may be done on earth, that we may have all that we will, and all as we will, whatever the will of God be. We would have his will yield to ours in this and the other, and that not to be his will which is so. We would have him will nothing but what we will as to our outward condition; or if he will anything that we like not, which suits not our inclinations, we will hinder it and have it otherwise, if all our care will do it. Oh what horrid pride is here, what rebellion against the sovereign will of the Most High! How do we attempt to cross God in our cares, and trouble ourselves with thoughtfulness to have our wills, though God's will be against it! Oh humble yourselves for this! Importune the Lord to give you hearts of flesh, such as will be tractable and easily wrought to a compliance with the divine will, to take away that stone rather than heart, which is in us naturally, that will break rather than yield. So far as the will of God is acceptable to you, so as yours can stoop to it though it cross you, so far you will not be anxious or careful. If you could submit to his will in all things, you would be careful for nothing.

(3.) *Live in the view of eternity.* Labour to walk still in the sight of your everlasting condition; let your eye be often on it; let your minds and thoughts be frequently taken up with that endless state which you must shortly enter on. Be still comparing your time here with that eternal condition that remains for you; consider how little or nothing it is in comparison, and that will help you to discover how small and inconsiderable the concerns of this present life are compared with those of everlastingness, and consequently how little to be cared for. You have that to look after, which is of so much more importance than the things of this life, as far exceeds them, as that vast incomprehensible eternity exceeds a little moment. Oh believe this effectually, consider it seriously, and you will find something else to do than to trouble yourselves so much with cares about concerns of so inconsiderable a moment! Why was the apostle no more careful about the things of this life, why no more troubled about them? why no more thoughtful to avoid afflictions and sufferings, or to get rid of them? He gives you this account of it: 2 Cor. iv. 17, 18, 'For our light affliction, which is but for a moment, worketh for us a far more exceeding and eternal weight of glory; while we look not at the things which are seen, but at the things which are not seen; for the things which are seen are temporal, but the things which are not seen are eternal.' His view of those eternal things made things of time seem nothing to him, not fit to be the concern of his care, scarce worthy to be looked on. A due prospect of eternity would help us more to overlook the things of this life, and to look upon ourselves,* our cares, as very little concerned in them. He that has his eye much fixed upon that, when he looks downward, will be ready to think he sees nothing. What are the atoms, the motes, that we see stirring about us in the light, to one that, with the help of an artificial glass, has been viewing the sun and the heavenly bodies? The things of time are no more to those of eternity than these motes are to the sun or the whole heavens. Let these motes dance on; what are we concerned in them, unless to keep them out of our eyes, out of our hearts and minds?

A traveller that has but a night to stay in a place, he will not be very solicitous about his accommodation; he will take it as he finds it, considering it is for so short time; he must be gone the next morning. You would think him little better than a madman who would take as much care about his inn as he does about his own dwelling house. Why, such is our case in this world, and so we should think of it. We are strangers and pilgrims, we are in a journey, we are seeking a country; our habitations are but as an inn, and our enjoyments as the accommodations of it; and our abode herein is not so much, compared with eternity, as a night's lodging. Whether they please us or please us not, we need not much care, since it is for so short a time; we must be gone, as it were, the next morning. Ps. xlix. 12: 'Man being in honour, abideth not,' בל ילין he shall not stay, he shall not lodge a night. Alas! what need he care whether he be in honour or not, whether he have little or much, since it is for so little a while, since he is not to abide in that condition so much as a night comes to? It is not so much in respect of everlastingness. Be not careful about it; take it as it comes, since

* Qu. 'our sorrows'?—ED.

you must be gone out of it so very soon. Would you think that traveller in his wits, who, when he is but to stay in his inn so few hours, would busy himself to stuff his bed and pillow with thorns, so that, when he can but rest a while at best, he may not be able to rest at all? Thus you do when you trouble yourselves with the cares of this life. Our Lord Jesus expresses them by thorns. When you must rest no longer, will you take the course not to rest a short night? Your stay here is not so much to eternity as a night. Ps. xc. 2, 4, 'A thousand years in thy sight are but as yesterday when it is past, and as a watch in the night.' If a thousand years be but to eternity as a watch in the night, the space of three or four hours, and that passed over insensibly in sleep, what is our life, which is but so small a parcel of a thousand years? The fourth part of a night is but a very little thing. Oh but it is not so much, it is but as yesterday, and yesterday when it is past is nothing. This life is no more expressly: Ps. xxxix. 5, 'Thou hast made my days as an handbreadth, and mine age is nothing before thee; verily, every man at his best state is altogether vanity.' If our life be as nothing to everlastingness, what are the concerns of it? If this were believed and considered, would that be so much our care, which is no more than nothing in the account of God?

Let those infidels trouble themselves with the cares of this life who think their souls shall last no longer than their life; but you that believe you must live hereafter more millions of years than there are minutes in your whole life, yea, more millions of ages than there are minutes in a million of years, what do you think your life here is to that, of such an astonishing continuance, of an endless, an everlasting duration? Can you conceive it to be like anything more than a moment? And why are you so careful, why so much concerned about the accommodations of a moment, of a minute? What if they please you or please you not; is it any great matter, since it is for so short a time? What if they be not such as you could wish; will they not serve well enough for a moment? May you not be indifferent how it fares with you for such a very little while? Oh, but the concerns of eternity, of a condition that will never, never have an end, that will be never nearer to an end after it has lasted millions and millions of ages; oh sure this should be your care, and so much your care, that the things of this life should have little of it in comparison, little or nothing in comparison of them, because they are little or nothing compared with them, of little or no continuance comparatively, and so of little or no consequence.

That emperor made himself ridiculous to the world, who, giving out that he had a design to conquer a kingdom, and taking care to raise a vast army, and marching them many hundred miles, in the end employed his soldiers only to gather cockles. You declare your design to be for a kingdom, an everlasting kingdom; you must strive, and wrestle, and combat to compass it. Here lies your business, here should your care be employed. If, instead of this, you turn your cares upon the things of this life, you fall a-gathering cockles or picking straws, instead of seeking that kingdom; the things of time are of no more value than straws in comparison of it.

PRAY FOR EVERYTHING.

But in everything by prayer and supplication, with thanksgiving, let your requests be made known unto God—PHILIP. IV. 6.

THE apostle having forbidden the Philippians to be careful, he shews them what they should do instead thereof. He shews them a better way to obtain what they or others are apt to be careful about, than all such forbidden carefulness would prove. Instead of troubling yourselves with cares for anything, apply yourselves to God by prayer in everything.

Obs. The people of God should have recourse to him by prayer in everything.

For explication, let us inquire into the act, the extent, the manner of praying. What we must do, and wherein it must be done, and how we must do it.

1. For the act. It is prayer, expressed here by four words, προσευχὴ, asking of God, or, as it is rendered, prayer; δέησις, supplication; εὐχαριστία, praise or thanksgiving; αἰτήματα, petitions or requests. For the opening of which, you know there are two principal parts of prayer, petition and thanksgiving, the asking of what we would have, and the due acknowledgment of what we have received. When we take notice of what the Lord bestows, and are affected with the riches and the freeness of his mercy therein, and out of an hearty sense thereof gratefully acknowledged; this is, εὐχαριστεῖν, to give him thanks, which is one chief part of prayer, that which should not be omitted. When we would pray, as he requires, our requests should be joined, μετ' εὐχαριστίας, with thanksgiving. The sense of our wants, pressures, sufferings, should not drown the sense of his mercy and bounty expressed towards us. Eagerness after more should not make us overlook what he has done for us already; but while we beg, we should also be thankful, having as much occasion for this as the other.

Then for petition, the other part of prayer, that is here, αἰτήματα, the several requests we make, or petitions we put up, and προσευχὴ, and δέησις, denote the same. He uses more words to express the same thing, as the Hebrews were wont to do (whose manner of speech he much uses) to signify frequency or vehemency; to mind us that we should be very much and often in this duty, or that our hearts should be very much in it when we are about it.

We need not inquire how these two words may be distinguished; it is like the apostle intended no more than I have expressed. But if we will be so curious, one of them may denote the object of our prayers, προσευχή is πρός τόν Θεόν εὐχή, a request directed to God. To whom shall we address ourselves if we would be relieved, or supplied, or delivered? Let your requests be made known to God, πρός Θεόν. Others may be unable or unwilling to help; it may be a wickedness, or it may be to no purpose to seek to them; but God is able and willing to relieve, he has made it your duty to apply yourselves to him, and to none else without him. The other may denote the subject of our prayers; δεησις, rendered supplication, is from δεόμαι, to want. That which we are to request of God is what we want, be it something which we have not, or more of that which we have, if it be needful for us, that which we want indeed. We may seek it of God; it is both our duty and privilege to do it; he both encourages and commands it. It is a principal part of prayer, to which there are so many promises, for which there are so many precepts, to spread our wants before God, to make them known to him. Not that he knows not what we want before we declare it, Mat. vi.; but this is the way, most for his honour and our advantage, to have supplies. 'He will be sought unto,' Ezek. xxxvi. 37. We must seek him, and not formally, and as of course; but as those who are sensible what they want, and who it is that only can relieve us, make all known to him.

2. For the extent of it. 'In everything;' so we must both pray and praise him, both make our requests, and give thanks, in everything; but here seems some difficulty, as to both, which I will endeavour to remove.

(1.) How can it be our duty to give thanks in everything? There are many cases, wherein it may be a question, whether they require thankfulness; several, which seem to call for humiliation rather than thanksgiving. But this in general may be determined, whatever our estate or the circumstances of it be, so far as there is any mercy to be discerned therein, so far we ought to be thankful, yea, though there be much of anger and divine displeasure there. And thereby we may resolve the particular cases wherein it is questionable, whether it is our duty to be thankful, and how it can be so.

[1.] When we are under afflictions, are we to give thanks for personal grievances? Yes; there is something in them for which we may, we ought to be thankful. But how? Not for the afflictions considered in themselves, for so they are not joyous, but grievous. But if they be for righteousness' sake, then are they blessed dispensations, then they are occasions of joy, and so of praise, Mat. v. Then they are gifts, special favours, and so oblige us to thankfulness: Phil. i. 29, 'Unto you it is given in the behalf of Christ, not only to believe on him, but also to suffer for his sake.' Yea, when they are chastisements, and occasioned by our miscarriages, yet then we may and ought to be thankful, because they are no more, not so much as we had deserved, and had reason to fear; not so many, not so grievous, not so continued. When we lose something, had it not been for that mercy (which we should be thankful for) we had lost all. When we suffer in one particular, we might have suffered in all, in soul, body, estate, relations, altogether. When it is but a rod, it might have been a scorpion; when it lies but on us a while, it might have oppressed us all our days, and made our whole life a life of sorrow and affliction. But they are not so much as others suffer. What are our sufferings, when greatest, to those of Christ, though he was innocent, not, as we are, covered with guilt? What are our afflictions to the sufferings of others, who are as dear to him, and have less provoked him? What to theirs, who, by the Lord's testimony, were such, of whom the world was not worthy? Heb. xi. And because they proceed from love, and shall have a merciful issue, if not for the grievance of them yet for the rise, and for the effects of them, so far as they are sanctified, to make you partakers of his holiness, to bring forth the fruits of it; so far as you have his presence, and are supported under them, and enabled to demean yourselves under them as children, to bear them with patience, submission, the exercise of faith, hope, and other graces requisite in such a state; and because, where we have one affliction, we have a thousand mercies. And should the sense of one, though sharp, drown all these, especially a few of them? Some one of them is more just matter of praise and rejoicing, than all the afflictions in the world of sorrow and dejection. You are in troubles, but you are not in hell; and why not there, but because his mercy towards you is infinite? The Lord has taken this or that from you. Oh, but hath he taken his loving-kindness from you? Has he divorced you from Christ? Has he cut you off from hopes of glory? Has he extinguished his grace in you, or taken his Holy Spirit from you, or shut you out from the covenant of grace, or separated you from his love? Rom. viii.

[2.] When public judgments are inflicted, that calls for mourning and lamentations, what place then for praise and thanksgiving? Why, so far even then we are to be thankful, as the Lord remembers mercy in the midst of judgment. We then have occasion of thanksgiving, because he inflicts no more judgments, pours but out some one vial, when he might pour out all together; because he makes not those inflicted more grievous and intolerable, more spreading and universal, more destructive and ruining; because we are secured and preserved, we escape when others fall; because it does but scorch us, when it might consume us, Lam. iii. They could see occasion of thankfulness in the midst of those calamities, which had burnt their temple, destroyed Jerusalem, laid their country desolate, and carried the inhabitants into captivity; they could discern mercy and compassions through all this, and so far as this can be discerned, there is cause of thanksgiving.

[3.] When we are under temptations. An hour of temptation is a time of fear and trembling, yet even then we have cause of thanksgiving. So far as the temptation prevails not; so far as we are strengthened to resist it; so far as it is not too violent to be borne or withstood; so far as we escape the danger; if we do not quite escape, so far as we take warning by it, and are made more watchful, and stand more upon our guard, and are more humbled in the sense of our own weakness, and led to more dependence on the Lord our strength, and fear and hate that more to which we were tempted, and are more resolute against it. 1 Cor. x. 13, 'There hath no temptation taken you but such as is common to man; but God is faithful, who will not suffer you to be tempted above that ye are able; but will, with the temptation also make a way to escape, that ye may be able to bear it.' So far as the Lord's faithfulness, his mindfulness of his covenant, appears in any temptations, whether for good or to evil, so much cause is there of thanksgiving.

[4.] When we fall into sin. That is the hardest case; yet here we ought to be thankful, not because we are left to sin, for that is cause of sorrow and deep humiliation, but because he leaves us not to sin more, as we would do were it not for his gracious restraints; because the Lord does not leave us, does not cast us off when we sin; because he proceeds not more severely against us for sin; because we do not die in it; because he does not cast us off, and cause us to perish in the very act; because he gives any time for repentance, or any heart for it. Here is matter of thankfulness, since he is so highly provoked by sin; since he might so easily satisfy his just displeasure in destroying us; since he might do it with advantage to his glory, the glory of his justice, and might prevent further provocations, and more dishonour; or because he over-rules this desperate evil, to occasion any good; or works any cure of this deadly poison, as he can do. And thus you see how we may give thanks in everything, even in those wherein it is hard to see any occasion for thanksgiving.

(2.) As there is some difficulty in respect of thanksgiving, so in respect of prayer, whether we may apply ourselves to God in everything particularly; and that which the text leads me to, whether we may make our requests known to him for temporal things, the concerns of this world. With some, this seems questionable; μὴ προσελθῆς Θεῷ ὑπὲρ εὐτελῶν πραγμάτων, says Chrysostom, make not thy address to God for small things; *injuriam magno Deo facit, qui parva petit, parva autem sunt omnia temporalia*, says Savonarola. But such sayings must be understood as intending a restraint only, not an absolute prohibition, since by warrant from Scripture we may pray for what is there promised, and 'godliness has the promise of this life,' 1 Tim. iv. 8. And these are some of the things that the text directs us to pray for. We are not to be careful for the things of this life, but instead thereof, make our requests known in everything; as in other things, so in these. We have both rule and example for this in Scripture. Our Lord Jesus directs us to pray for our daily bread; so Jacob: Gen. xxviii. 20, 'And Jacob vowed a vow, saying, If God will be with me, and will keep me in this way that I go, and will give me bread to eat, and raiment to put on,' &c. And Agur, Prov. xxx. 8, 'Give me neither poverty nor riches: feed me with food convenient for me.' They may be sought, but with limitation.

[1.] Not principally; for they are not the things that we are principally concerned in, Mat. vi. 33. The kingdom of God, and the righteousness of it, things eternal and spiritual, are to be sought principally, first and most, above all, more than all, as being of far greater value and consequence, of greater necessity and importance. We may far better fall short of the things of this life, that may trouble us for a time; but to miss the other, will be our misery for ever, and of greater value. The other are but loss and dung in comparison, of no considerable value; and so we should be far from seeking them principally.

[2.] Not for themselves, but in order to better things; not to serve ourselves of them, but to be more serviceable by them, to do more good with them; not to please our senses, but to help us the better to please the Lord; not because they suit our inclinations, but to enable us to do the will of God, and that work which he has set us to do. As the apostle desired a prosperous journey, Rom. x. 10, not for the journey's sake, as though he loved or delighted in that, but that he might have thereby an opportunity to do more good. To seek these things for themselves, profit for profit's sake, or pleasure's sake, is to seek them as God only should be sought, and so to idolize them.

[3.] With submission. These things are not good for all, in every degree. We know not whether they will be good for us, nor what measure of them may be best. We must not seek them peremptorily, as those that have a mind to have them at a venture, but with a reserve if they may be good for us; and these must be submitted to the will and wisdom of God, who only knows it. *Illi committite, ut si prosint, det; si scit obesse, non det.* Refer it to him, either to bestow them if he see it good, or deny them, if he know they will not be good. The all-wise physician knows better what is good or hurtful than the distempered patient.

We are not to seek outward things as we may seek faith, repentance, pardon, holiness, growth in grace, power against sin. These are absolutely necessary to our happiness; it is his will his people shall have them; he has declared it in his word, and promised them without reserve ; and therefore so we may beg them. But outward things are not absolutely necessary to salvation ; we may be happy without them, or such a measure of them ; we know not but it may hinder instead of promoting our happiness. They are not promised absolutely, and therefore should not be so sought.

Those things which tend but to our well-being in spirituals, as comfort, assurance, and highest degrees of holiness, are not to be sought but with submission, much less these which tend but to our well-being in temporals. 'Not my will but thine be done,' said our great pattern. And David herein shewed himself to be a man after his own heart : 2 Sam. xv. 25, 'And the king said unto Zadok, Carry back the ark of God into the city ; if I shall find favour in the eyes of the Lord, he will bring me again, and shew me both it and his habitation.' He referred it wholly to the will of God, whether his outward condition should be prosperous or no. So much for the act and the extent of it. The mode or manner of praying is, the

3. Third particular propounded, how we must pray. Take an account of this in these severals.

(1.) Pray much and often. That we are enjoined, when he bids us pray in everything. We must pray whenever we have occasion ; and everything gives us occasion for some request. We have occasion to pray, from what concerns our eternal state, our spiritual state, and our outward conditions, occasions to pray from everything. We have either wants or fears, which respect every state ; and therefore frequent, constant occasions to pray, and so we should be much and often in this duty. It is called for in the like expressions : Eph. vi. 18, 'Praying always with all prayer and supplication in the Spirit, and watching thereunto with all perseverance, and supplication for all saints.' What is here implied, is there expressed, $\pi\rho o\sigma\varepsilon\upsilon\chi\acute{o}\mu\varepsilon\nu o\iota$ $\grave{\varepsilon}\nu\ \pi\alpha\nu\tau\grave{\iota}\ \kappa\alpha\iota\rho\tilde{\omega}$, praying always whenever opportunity or occasion is offered ; this is offered frequently, continually. And so we are enjoined to continue in prayer : Col. iv. 2, 'Continue in prayer, and watch in the same with thanksgiving ;' to 'pray continually without ceasing,' 1 Thes. v. 17, Luke xviii. 1. The meaning of these expressions is not that we should do nothing else but pray, that this should take up all our time, and we should be every moment in this employment, but that we should be much and often in it. We should still keep a praying temper ; we should always be disposed to it, always ready for it when occasion is offered. No employment should wear off this temper, or indispose us to this duty. As when the apostle says, Rom. ix. 2, 'I have great heaviness, and continual sorrow in my heart ;' not that the acts and expressions of his sorrow were never discontinued. We know he was often rejoicing upon other occasions, but their sad condition had made a lasting impression of grief upon his heart, which he was ready and disposed to express when occasion was offered. Though the act of prayer be intermitted, and discontinued through other employments, yet the disposedness to it should last ; the heart should be ready for it whenever there is occasion and opportunity. Such a continual disposition and readiness to pray, is, as we call it, an habitual praying ; and in this respect we may be said to rejoice always, evermore, 1 Thes. v. 16, Philip. iv. 4. So to pray always.

But that is not all. As we must be always ready to pray, so we must frequently shew this readiness, this habitual frame, by praying actually ; we must do it every day ; it must be our daily employment, our daily sacrifice. As the priests might be said always to sacrifice, because they constantly offered sacrifice, evening and morning ; or, as Mephibosheth is said to eat meat with David continually, 2 Sam. ix. 7, because he did eat with him at his set meals; so we, that we may answer these commands which require us to pray continually, must have our times for prayer every day; as they had for their sacrifice, and we and they had for their daily meals.

But this is not all neither: we have many times repasts and refreshments besides our set meals; and they had many other sacrifices besides those offered evening and morning, some extraordinary, and some upon particular occasions. So should we, besides our ordinary and daily addresses to God, make our requests known in an extraordinary manner when we have extraordinary occasion, public or personal. We should apply ourselves to him at any time (besides those seasons which we daily observe) when we have more particular and special occasion. We must take all occasions to offer our requests which the providence of God offers us, both those that are continued and in course, and those that are emergent, and bring special reason for it. In everything, both of this and that nature, our requests must be made known, and so much and often, such a frequency as may be called a continuance in prayer.

(2.) Pray carefully. Instead of being careful about other things, be careful in this. Pray carefully; take care how you perform this duty: shew this care about prayer in everything you pray for. Not that you should pray with anxiousness, solicitousness, perplexity, but that you should not pray carelessly. This care in praying is expressed by watching, frequently joined to this duty in Scripture: Col. iv. 2, 'Continue in prayer, and watch in the same with thanksgiving;' Eph. vi. 18, 'Praying always with all prayer and supplication in the Spirit, and watching thereunto with all perseverance;' 1 Pet. iv. 7, 'Be ye sober, and watch unto prayer.' There must be diligence and care in praying. We must be watchful about it, as that which requires our care. We are careful about that which keeps us waking and watchful. Watchfulness denotes the importance of that which we watch, and some danger in it, and the sense of both. It is of some consequence that we think ourselves concerned to be watchful about. We should go about this duty as a matter of great importance. We should be sensible who it is with whom we have to do, of what importance it is to make an address to the great God, and of what importance our necessities are which we spread before him. If we pray with sleepy, drowsy, listless hearts, we slight the great God, and slight our own necessities, our own interest, and slight a duty wherein both the Lord and ourselves are so much concerned. If we go about this duty with a sleepy soul, we offer to God a dream instead of a real supplication; we affront him, and shew a wretched disregard of our own concernments, and therefore we should awake ourselves when we come before God; as Deborah, Judges v. 12, 'Awake, awake, Deborah; awake, awake, utter a song;' David, Ps. cviii. 2, 'Awake, psaltery and harp, I myself will awake early;' and Ps. lvii. 8, 'Awake up, my glory,' &c. We should stir up ourselves to lay hold on him; we should rouse mind and heart, graces and affections, that all may be stirring and active, and not shut up in a careless, drowsy listlessness. This is to watch unto prayer, this is to be vigilant and careful about it.

Further, it denotes danger. When we are watchful, we apprehend some danger, and this is signified when watchfulness in prayer is called for: Mat. xxvi. 41, 'Watch and pray, that ye enter not into temptation;' Mark xiii. 33, 'Take heed, watch and pray;' Luke xxi. 36, 'Watch ye, therefore, and pray always.' There is danger, for there is temptation attends our prayers. There is danger lest our minds and hearts should wander from God, when they should be fixed on him. There is danger lest such distempers seize on, and cleave to our souls in praying, as may turn our prayers into sin; so there is danger lest our prayers should miscarry. We should be apprehensive of the danger, and so watchful to prevent it, to avoid it. Careful and vigilant that we enter not into the temptation to which we are subject when we pray; watchful to espy it, that we be not surprised; to resist it, that we be not overcome; that though it attack us, it may not carry us along with it, we may not enter into it. Vigilant to prevent wanderings and distractions, those loose vagaries of our vain minds and hearts into which they are apt to run when they should be most fixed, and have that before them which should wholly take them up, as Abraham watched his sacrifice; vigilant and careful to discern and shake off inward distempers, which are wont to mix themselves with our prayers, and spoil them.

(3.) Pray earnestly. It is the property of the Hebrew tongue to express vehemency, by joining divers words of the same signification together. The apostle being a Hebrew of the Hebrews, usually follows that style; and that may be one thing intended here, by adding divers words of the like signification to express prayer. He would have us to pray with some vehemence and earnestness, as Elias did; his vehemence in praying is so expressed, James v. 17, προσευχῇ προσηύξατο, he prayed vehemently, as Luke xxii., 'With desire have I desired,' i.e. greatly, earnestly, vehemently desired. Our hearts and affections in prayer should not only be roused, but extended; drawn out in some earnestness: not only awakened, but warmed; there should be a spiritual heat and fervour in them. We should be 'fervent in spirit' when we are thus 'serving the Lord.' Pray as the church for Peter, Acts xii. 5, προσευχὴ ἐκτενὴς, fervent prayer was made; the same word 1 Pet. iv. 8, ἀγάπην ἐκτενῆ; and so it is said 'the tribes served God,' Acts xxvi. 7, ἐν ἐκτενείᾳ, 'in fervency,' or, which is all one in effect, with souls stretched to him. Prayer is ἀνάβασις τοῦ νοῦ πρὸς Θεὸν, the ascent of the soul to God; and therein the soul should stretch forth itself to the utmost to get near unto God. To pray lazily, slothfully, is to pray as though we prayed not; and that will have answerable returns from him, will provoke him to hear as though he heard not, to regard our requests as though he regarded them not. He that begs coldly bespeaks a denial; may be used like an idle beggar; too lazy not only to work, but to seek relief. The Lord, if he love you, will whip you out of such intolerable sloth.

It is earnestness the Lord expects in prayer, such as is expressed in Scripture by crying out of the depths, Ps. cxxx. 1, by mighty cries, Jonah iii. 8, strong cries, Heb. v. 7, such as those of a woman in travail, Isa. xxvi. The soul should cry, as pained with its spiritual wants, inward distempers and corruption, as one in anguish till delivered.

By striving: Rom. xv. 30, 'Strive together with me in your prayers to God for me;' such as wrestlers use when they put forth all their strength, use all their might to prevail.

By wrestling. So Jacob wrestled with God, Gen. xxxii. 26. And herein his wrestling consisted, Hos. xii. 4, he 'wept and made supplications;' he prayed earnestly, affectionately; his heart melted and run out in his supplications.

If we would take care to pray thus, the other carefulness wherewith we trouble ourselves would be needless; this would do our work both for the things of time and eternity: James v. 16, 'The effectual fervent prayer of a righteous man availeth much.'

(4.) Pray spiritually; with spiritual intentions, and by the Spirit's influence.

[1.] With spiritual intentions. Look that your aim and end be right in all you seek. It cannot be right unless it be spiritual. Even in our worldly business our end and design should be higher than the world. A Christian should not have such ends and designs as a natural and worldly man hath in his earthly affairs. How far should we be from such ends in holy and spiritual employments. Our prayers will be such as our ends are, carnal, and selfish, and earthly, if our intentions be such; for the form gives the denomination, and *quid forma in naturalibus, id finis in moralibus;* what the form is in natural things, that the end is in moral acts. If the end in praying be carnal or worldly, it is a carnal and worldly prayer, no more fit to be offered unto God than an unclean beast was to be offered in sacrifice. ' It is as the cutting off a dog's neck, or the pouring out of swine's blood, an abomination in the sight of God,' Isa. lxvi. 3, 4. When you pretend to be best employed, it is to be doing evil before his eyes, and to choose that in which he delights not: James iv. 3, ' Ye ask, and receive not, because ye ask amiss, that you may consume it upon your lusts.' They asked amiss, because they missed the right end. The ends we should aim at are the honouring of God, pleasing him, enjoying communion with him. These we should principally aim at in seeking either spiritual or temporal things. If we seek spiritual gifts, that we may be more eminent than others, and accordingly respected, applauded, admired, this is to be little better than Simon Magus, Acts viii. 9. Such prayers may be the issue of the gall of bitterness. Those that are in the bond of iniquity may be enlarged in making such requests. If we seek more grace, higher degrees of holiness, out of respect to our reputation, or merely for our own ease and comfort, instead of seeking and worshipping God in such prayers, we do but seek ourselves.

When we desire health, that we may live pleasantly; or long life, that we may long enjoy the comforts of this world; or plenty, that we may have enough to gratify the flesh, and lay out upon our pleasures; or riches, for those low and common ends for which worldly men desire them; or outward prosperity, that we may not be troubled with sufferings, grievous to flesh and blood; or public deliverance, for our own safety and welfare or success, that we may have our wills upon these we have suffered by: this is not to pray spiritually. The Lord counts not such requests to be prayers, though for the object they be directed to him, and for the manner be fervent and affectionate. The Lord accounts things to be such as their end is. That which is an act of obedience in itself may be no better than murder in his account, when the end is not right; as Jehu's killing of Ahab's children; God enjoined it, 2 Kings x. 30; yet he obeying only for his own ends, God will avenge it of him as if he had been a murderer, Hosea i. 4. So sacrifice, though he required it, is resented by him, as if no better than the killing of a man, Isa. lxvi. 3. And prayer likewise, if not for spiritual ends, instead of proving an acceptable sacrifice, will be counted an abomination, Prov. xxi. 27.

[2.] Pray by the Spirit's assistance; seek it, wait for it; do nothing that may check or restrain it, and give any impediment to it. Rely not upon inward abilities, or outward helps, real or pretended, so as to disengage that blessed Spirit, ready to help his people in praying when they are sensible of their want of his assistance, and look up to him for it. Be not like those who do shut their eyes because they have spectacles, or do tie up their legs, if not cut them off, because they have got crutches. When you have a better help, do not disoblige it by preferring or confining yourselves to a worse. Depend upon him alone who can help you to make requests in everything; do nothing which may provoke him to withdraw or suspend his assistance. Look upon this alone as your sufficiency for this duty, which are not sufficient of ourselves to think a good thought, much less to offer up a good prayer, a spiritual sacrifice. The Lord will not have it offered with common fire, of your own or others' kindling. You must fetch fire from heaven if you would sanctify the Lord in your approaches. Look to the promise, Zech. xii. 10, 'I will pour upon the house of David, and upon the inhabitants of Jerusalem, the spirit of grace and supplication; and they shall look upon him whom they have pierced,' &c. Prayer should not be the issue of models and exemplars only, no, nor of habits and qualifications within; but should flow from the spirit of grace and supplication. So in the primitive times, they are required to pray accordingly, προσεύχεσθαι ἐν πνεύματι, Eph. vi. 18; ἐν πνεύματι ἁγίῳ, Jude, ver. 20; by the Spirit, by its help and assistance; so that the prayer may be said to proceed from him. Those who like not to hear [of] praying by the Spirit, confess from hence, that so they prayed in the apostle's time; but they would have us believe it was a miraculous and extraordinary gift, such as was not to continue, and it is not now to be expected or pretended to; but I think they mistake. By praying in the Spirit in these two texts cannot be meant an extraordinary gift, such as those of healing, prophesying, tongues, &c.; for not to take notice that such a gift of prayer is not mentioned amongst those that were miraculous and extraordinary, where we have a particular account of them, Mark xvi., 1 Cor. xii. 8–10, xiv.; but this we may insist on as granted by them. Yet as all extraordinary gifts were not confined* upon any one person except the apostles, so no one extraordinary gift was bestowed upon all and every believer; and so that which all partaked of was no extraordinary χάρισμα, grace or gift. But this for praying was bestowed upon all believers, as appears by the texts alleged; for all the believing Hebrews, all that were sanctified, to whom Jude wrote, ver. 1, are required thus to pray, ἐν πνεύματι ἁγίῳ; and all the converted Gentiles at Ephesus,' to whom Paul wrote, are exhorted to exercise this gift, Eph. vi. 18; and all other believers in them are called to do it, if the epistles be of general concernment. Now, it could not be their duty to exercise it if they had it not, or might not have had it; and if they all had it, it was an ordinary gift, and continued to the church in all ages. These precepts oblige us as much as them, and it is as much our duty to pray in or by the Spirit as it was theirs. We are still to pray by the assistance of the Spirit; but how does the Spirit help us therein? What assistance are we to look for? We may learn that by the apostle: Rom. viii. 26, 'The Spirit helpeth our infirmities: for we know not what we should pray for as we ought; but the Spirit itself maketh intercession for us with groanings which cannot be uttered.' This assistance is expressed by two words, especially συναντιλαμβάνεται, he helps our infirmities or weaknesses. Ἀσθενείαις, ἀσθενοῦντες ἀντί τοῦ ἐν ἐνδείᾳ ὄντες, says Favorinus: weakness is from some want. We are in some want as to several things requisite to praying: want of judgment to discern what we should pray for; what is best for us we know not, he helps that. And so want of memory: he minds us of what is most needful, most seasonable, when otherwise we might pass it over; it is promised. So want of affection, holy and lively motions, the languor and sickness of the soul, the dulness, listlessness, deadness of it, that is, many infirmities in one. So want of expression too, which will more appear by the other word ὑπερεντυγχάνει, which signifies to act for one, as an advocate for his client. The Spirit of God advises his people, intercedes for them, as it were petitioning, or, as they say in our courts, moving for him, or drawing up his petitions or motions, dictating what he shall move for, and how, and in what form and words. And this is it which the apostle

* Qu. 'conferred'?—Ed.

declares here; this is the way whereby the Holy Ghost helps our infirmities in prayer. Thus it is that he makes intercession for them, by dictating what, τί, and how, καθὸ δεῖ, in what manner, for what things, with what expressions; helping them both to matter, affections, and words. Thus Grotius explains the word, a man of great esteem with those who differ from us herein, *est advocatorum*, &c. It belongs to advocates, who dictate petitions to their clients; and is ascribed to the Spirit of God, *quia preces ad Deum nobis dictat*, because he dictates to us the requests we offer to God. And so to pray in the Holy Ghost, Jude 20, is with him to pray *dictante Spiritu Sancto*, the Spirit of God dictating, suggesting to us what and how.

But of the Spirit's assistance in prayer, more hereafter. Let us in the mean time be sensible, when we are going to pray, of our great need of it, our insufficiency without it; let us labour to engage it for us by all means, especially by depending on him for it. Let us hearken to his motions, and follow his dictates, and yield to what he suggests, and not grieve, nor quench the Spirit of grace, nor put restraints upon him, nor any way provoke him to withdraw and leave us to ourselves, or to our own seeming abilities, but real weaknesses, our own lazy inventions and devices. When we come to the throne of grace, if the Spirit be not there our advocate, our plea will avail nothing. Our prayers cannot be spiritual without the assistance of the Spirit; and unless they be spiritual, they will not be fit to be offered unto that God who is a Spirit, and will be worshipped in spirit and truth.

(5.) Pray in faith. This is frequently called for, and made the condition of effectual and prevailing prayers: Mark xi. 24, 'What things soever ye desire, when ye pray, believe that ye receive them, and ye shall have them;' James i. 16, 'Ask in faith, nothing wavering;' Mat. xxi. 22, 'All things whatsoever ye shall ask in prayer, believing, ye shall receive.' Our whole life should be a life of faith, Gal. ii. 20; by virtue of this, we should walk with God and man too: 'We walk by faith,' 2 Cor. v. 7; and should hear with faith, if we will hear to purpose, Heb. iv. 2; and so pray in faith, if we would prevail.

But what is it to pray in faith? It requires particular application, a fiducial recumbence, or a general persuasion.

Use. Since this is our duty, let us take notice of it, let us observe it, and make our requests known, and that in everything. Pray, and pray much and often, and pray carefully, and pray earnestly, pray spiritually, and in faith; and thus pray in everything. I might enforce this duty with many motives, but I intend not to stay on it. Mind these two.

1. It is most honourable to God, is as much for his glory as anything we can do. We can speak nothing more high and excellent, more noble and glorious of anything than this, that it honours God. This excels all, because it is the end of all. Everything is more valuable as it promotes this sovereign end; and therefore prayer is most valuable, because it most advances, and tends most to honour God. We can add nothing to the essential and absolute glory of God; this is δόξα ἀκίνητος καὶ ἀναλλοίωτος, a glory which is infinite, to which nothing can be added. We have no way to glorify him but by declaring or acknowledging him to be glorious, giving a testimony to his glorious perfections and excellencies. Now, there is nothing we can do does more declare the glory of God than prayer; nothing that acknowledges more of his excellencies, and gives a clearer testimony to his glorious perfections. This gives him the glory of his immensity and omnipresence, acknowledges he is everywhere, applying ourselves to him wherever we are. His omniscience: acknowledges he knows the desires of our hearts, and understands best of all what is best for us; his power: acknowledges he

can do whatever we would have him, exceeding abundantly above all that we can ask or think; his goodness: that he is willing to hear such vile creatures, to supply, relieve, support, deliver, save to the utmost; his dominion: that he has right to dispose of all things as his own; his providence: that he rules and orders all, good and evil, small and great; his justice: that he is ready to revenge his elect that cry; his truth and faithfulness: that he is mindful of his word and promise, the ground of all our requests; his all-sufficiency: that there is enough in him for us, to satisfy, enhappy whatever our condition at present happen to be; more in him than in all things, since we seek to him more: Ps. l. 23, 'Whoso offereth praise glorifieth me.' That which is said of one part of prayer is true of the whole, he that offereth praise glorifieth him. If we would honour him much, glorify him in everything, let us in everything make our requests known.

2. It is most advantageous to us.

(1.) It is an universal expedient, that will avail us in everything; the Lord would not direct us to use it in everything, but that there is nothing in which it will not stand us in stead. The advantage of other things is particular: one is good for this, another for that purpose, but prayer is good for all. The efficacy and advantage of it reaches as far as the Lord lets forth his omnipotency. Prayer can prevail for anything that the Lord will employ his power about. This can prevail for the supply of all wants, redress of all grievances, security from all fears, deliverance from all troubles, the satisfying of all our desires. It can prevail with that great God who can do whatever he will in heaven and earth, who has all creatures, all things, at his beck: Hos. xii. 3, 4, 'By his strength he had power with God, yea, he had power over the angel, and prevailed.' That which can prevail with him who can do all, can do all at the second hand. This can prevail, not for small things only, but the greatest, not only for earth but heaven: Deut. iv. 29, 'If thou seek the Lord thy God, thou shalt find him; if thou seek him with all thine heart and all thy soul.' For Christ, Prov. viii. 6; for the Spirit, Luke xi. 13: 'How much more shall the Father give the Spirit to them that ask him?' Rom. viii. 32. It can prevail not only for easy things, but the hardest, that which is most difficult, and bring relief in cases that seem most desperate, can do more than the whole power of nature. Prayer has wrought miracles, and if it do not so still, that is not because it is less powerful, but because the Lord thinks not fit they should be done: Joshua x. 12, 13, 'Then spake Joshua to the Lord, in the day when the Lord delivered up the Amorites before the children of Israel, and he said in the sight of Israel, Sun, stand thou still upon Gibeon; and thou, moon, in the valley of Ajalon. And the sun stood still and the moon stayed,' &c. Peter was in prison, the king resolved to have his life; he is secured by armed men, by iron gates, by chains and bolts; his case seems desperate, his escape hopeless, to sense or reason impossible; but prayer is made for him, and this brings him out in despite of all, and conveys him out of danger through a train of miracles, Acts xii. 4, 5. It is the readiest expedient, always at hand; the easiest and shortest way, and the surest; never fails, is never in vain.

(2.) It is a ready way, always at hand; you need never be to seek for this, as you may be for other means of supply and relief. All others may be out of your power, above your reach, but you need not be at a loss for this, which is *instar omnium*, and will stand you instead of all else. In such a destitute condition you may pray; when you are without riches, without liberty, without strength, without health, without friends; when you can neither help yourselves nor others can help you; yet then you may pray, and so engage the Lord to help you. When you are in the depths, sunk below the reach of other relief, then you may pray: Ps. cxxx. 1, 'Out of the depths have I cried unto thee, O Lord!' When you are environed with calamities, so straitly besieged by them as no supply, no relief, can get in to you, then you may relieve yourselves by prayer, as David did in such a case: Ps. cxvi. 3, 4, 'The sorrows of death compassed me, and the pains of hell got hold upon me; I found trouble and sorrow. Then called I upon the name of the Lord: O Lord, I beseech thee, deliver my soul!' Or if you were in as forlorn a condition, as Jonah in the whale's belly, where neither he nor any creature else could afford any help, yet then you might pray, as he did, Jonah ii. 1, 2, 7, 10. He that can pray needs never be at a loss, however the world goes. He has the key in his hand which can open all the treasures of heaven, and let him in to all the riches of the goodness of an all-sufficient God. The violence of men may take estates from you, but they cannot take away the spirit of grace and supplication; they may shut out friends from you, but they cannot shut you out from access to God by prayer; they may bereave you of liberty, but not of liberty to pray; they may cast you into prison, but there you may be as much enlarged as anywhere; they may take from you public opportunities, but you may pray in private, in secret; they may watch your mouths, but your hearts may pray; you may be too weak to work, to follow your callings, but scarce too weak to pray; not able to go abroad for help, but then you may go to God with your requests. You may be too weak to speak, to move your lips, but then your hearts may move, and therein lies the heart and soul of prayer, 2 Kings xx. 1, 2, Isa. xxxviii. Prayer is an expedient ready at all times, on all occasions, to bring you in what supply and relief you need.

(3.) It is a short and easy way: no more but ask and have, seek and find, Mat. vii. 7. There may be difficulty and trouble in other ways of relief, but what show of either in this? Could your hearts desire an easier way to compass what you desire, than by making your requests known? Jehoshaphat's enemies were like to prove too hard for him; he could not levy an army sufficient to deal with them, but he could lift up his eyes to God and pray, and that did his work; a few words prevailed against a huge army: 2 Chron. xx. 12, 'O our God, wilt thou not judge them? For we have no might against this great company that cometh against us, neither know we what to do; but our eyes are upon thee.' When you know not what to do, when you can do nothing, do but pray, which you may easily do, and the rest shall be done to your hand. So it was to him, ver. 17, 23. The poor woman in the Gospel, that had taken a costly and tedious way for relief, Mark v. 25, 26, she applies but herself to Christ, and without further trouble or expense, her grievance is removed, ver. 29; so, Mat. xvii. 15, 16, 18, 21, that which nothing else can effect may be thus done with ease. When Naaman liked not the prophet's way for his relief, what say his servants to him? 2 Kings v. 13, 'If the prophet had bid thee do some great thing, wouldst thou not have done it? How much rather, then, when he saith to thee, Wash and be clean?' If the Lord had bid us do something difficult and troublesome to get our wants supplied, our fears scattered, our grievances redressed, would we not have done it? How much more when he bids us but make our requests known? You have not money at command, you can make no friends, you can get no interest in great persons, you can raise no armies; these are too hard for you. Oh, but can you pray? Is that too hard for you? Why, this that you may so easily do will do more for you than all the other can do. This can do all for you that you need desire, and may not this be done with ease? The Lord does not require you should consume your bodies or waste your strength in praying; put but up your petitions, let but your hearts go along with it, you need not trouble yourselves to write it, no, nor to express it in words, when your weakness will not afford expressions. The Lord hears the language of the heart, and knows our meaning when we cannot utter it; Rom. viii. 27, 'He that searcheth the hearts knoweth what is the mind of the spirit.' Oh what an easy way has the Lord opened unto us for an universal supply and relief to us in all cases! How inexcusable shall we be if we walk not in it!

(4.) It is a sure way, an expedient that never fails, of such efficacy that it was never used in vain: Isa. xlv. 19, 'I said not unto the seed of Jacob, Seek ye me in vain;' Ps. xxii. 4, 5, 'Our fathers trusted in thee, they trusted, and thou didst deliver them. They cried unto thee, and were delivered;' Ps. ix. 10, 'Thou hast not forsaken them that seek thee,' He has never been wanting to them that seek him; he will never disappoint them, never suffer them to seek him in vain. Your labour and pains may be in vain; your designs and projects, your care and thoughtfulness, your endeavours for yourselves, and others' for you, may be in vain. But your prayers, if prayers indeed, will never be in vain. Oh, where will you meet with an expedient that will never fail? Such an admirable engine is prayer, never used in vain. The disciples fished all night and caught nothing, John xxi. 3; but they never prayed a night, or an hour, and catched nothing. This net is never spread in vain, we may be confident of it, 1 John. v. 14, 15. We have all the assurance of it that can be desired, the very best security that heaven and earth can afford, the word of the true and faithful God, his truth and faithfulness engaged for it, who is truth and faithfulness itself, and that in many great and precious promises. Martha says to Jesus, John xi. 22, 'Whatsoever thou wilt ask of God, he will give it thee.' He has vouchsafed to give us the like confidence as to whatever we shall ask, John xv. 7, 'If ye abide in me, ye shall ask what ye will, and it shall be done unto you.' John xvi. 23, and Mat. vii. 7, &c. Prayer will either be answered or rewarded; it will either procure the thing we desire, or something as good, or something better. If it be not returned on those you pray for, it will be returned with a blessing upon yourselves, Ps. xxxv. 13.

GOD'S END IN SENDING CALAMITIES AND AFFLICTIONS ON HIS PEOPLE.

By this therefore shall the iniquity of Jacob be purged; and this is all the fruit to take away his sin.—ISAIAH XXVII. 9.

IN the former part of this chapter, the Lord by the prophet expresseth his wrath and severity against his people, enemies* and oppressors, and his mercy and favour to his people: that in terrible threatenings; this in gracious promises, both repeated in variety of expressions again and again.

He begins with the former, ver. 1, where he threatens to do severe and terrible execution upon the oppressors of his people, under the notion of leviathan and the dragon, or the whale in the sea, *i. e.* upon the greatest and most potent of them; those whose power seems irresistible, who devour all before them, as the whales do the smaller fish; upon them altogether, uniting their forces and complicating their interests. *Leviathan a* לוה *addere, copulare;* signifying an addition of many creatures united in one.

Ver. 2. Here is his favour to his people, he would make them like a vineyard of red wine; bring them into a flourishing, a fruitful condition. They should bring forth the best and most acceptable fruit, red wine being the best and strongest wine in that country. Their state should be matter of praise and joy; *sing.*

Ver. 3. Under the notion of water, he promises whatever was requisite to make it flourish and fructify. There should be no drought to hinder its thriving; 'water it every moment.' Nor should anything violently break, or privily creep in to hurt it: 'I the Lord will keep it;' he doth and will do it 'night and day;' 'every moment' of both.

Ver. 4. 'Fury is not in me' towards my vineyard; my people having humbled themselves, and reformed what was a provocation to me, I am at peace with them. But if there be briers and thorns in my vineyard, where there should be nothing but the choicest vines, such as bring forth pricks instead of grapes; tear, and rend, and wound, instead of bringing forth fruit acceptable to God and man; such as are both barren themselves and pester the vineyard, and hinder it from being fruitful: these I will consume and burn up together.

Ver. 5. So will I proceed against those that are as briers and thorns in

* Qu. 'people's enemies'?—ED.

my vineyard, those that are as hurtful plants, or fruitful* weeds, unless they take the course to make peace with me ; unless they lay hold of my arm, ready to destroy them, and apply themselves to me in ways and means that may pacify me.

Ver. 6. He adds another promise of establishing and multiplying his people, and making them fruitful of a multitude of converts and plenty of fruit.

Ver. 7. Whereas it might be objected, that the Lord seems to have no such peculiar favour for his people, since he doth so severely judge and chastise them ; it is here shewed that there is a vast difference betwixt his proceedings against them and others ; he does not smite and destroy them as he does his and their enemies. And the difference is more punctually declared in the two next verses.

Ver. 8. He corrects them in measure, his love moderates his displeasure. When it shooteth forth, or when he casts them forth as disobedient children, he doth not cast them off or utterly reject them.

When he debates with them by judgments, he remembers mercy, which considers their relations and their weakness, and favourably proportions their sufferings accordingly.

When the most boisterous wind, as is the east wind, is raised, which might scatter and utterly dissipate them, he allays it so as it does but fan and winnow them.

Another difference is in the text. The Lord has quite another end in chastening his people and judging their enemies ; he proceeds against these with an intent to destroy them ; against his people with a design to purge and refine them. ' By this,' &c.

So that here we have the end and use of the chastenings and afflictions wherewith the Lord exercises his people, viz., the purging of their iniquity and taking away their sin. And the instance here is, in that which was the capital crime of Israel and Judah, the sin to which they were before the captivity most addicted, viz., idolatry, worshipping false gods, or the true God otherwise than he had appointed. ' When he maketh,' &c. ; when the altars erected for sacrifices in the high places shall be utterly demolished, the stones of them beaten as small as chalk, or limestones to make lime or parget of ; the groves also and images cut down and demolished. The end and fruit of the Lord's judging and chastening them, was the destroying of idolatry, the instruments and monuments of it : under the chief sin, comprising the rest.

Obs. The end of those calamities and afflictions which befall the people of God, is to purge out their iniquity and to take away their sins ; their troubles and sufferings are to purify their hearts and to reform their lives. That which is aimed at in the sad dispensations they are exercised with, is mortification and reformation ; the removing of sin, of all sorts thereof, both sin and iniquity, from all parts, both heart and life.

Nothing is more evident in Scripture than this truth, and it is most frequently declared. We shall instance in some few places for many : Isa. i. 25, I will turn my afflicting and reforming hand upon them, and by the calamities inflicted will destroy those that are incurable, and refine the rest both from more gross and more specious evils, both dross and tin. 1 Cor. xi. 32, Ye are chastened of the Lord, that those sins which are the cause for which the Lord condemns the world, may be removed, and so your condemnation prevented.

Hence it is that outward calamities and afflictions are expressed by a fire and a furnace, such as are used for the refining of metals, and the consuming or separating of that dross which doth debase them. Isa. xlviii. 10, His

---

* Qu. 'unfruitful' ?—ED.

people being not yet sufficiently refined, he had made choice of a furnace of affliction further to purge them more thoroughly; Isa. iv. 4, the filth, *i. e.* sin, which made them filthy and loathsome in the sight of God; and blood, *i. e.* all manner of defilement and pollution. Ezek. xvi. 6, Hos. vi. 8, 'By the spirit of judgment,' *i. e.* by judgments inflicted on them; 'By the spirit of burning,' *i. e.* by the fire of affliction, which, as the fire of a finer, burns up and wastes the baser parts of the purer metal; and sometimes they are expressed by a wind or a fan, whose end and use is to cleanse the floor, and separate the wheat from the chaff, ver. 8 and Mat. iii. 12.

This is it which is more or less aimed at in all sorts of sufferings, not only in those which are for correction, but also in those that are for trial or for righteousness' sake.

1. Those that are for correction called παιδεῖαι; the proper end of these afflictions is the amendment of the afflicted. The Lord makes his children smart for sin, that they may be afraid of it, and no more venture on it. He lets them fall into trouble, or lets calamities fall on them, that they may fall no more into sin; this is evident by the texts fore-quoted. The Lord aims at this, not only in the execution, but in the threatening of chastisements: Rev. iii. 19, 'Be zealous,' be no more lukewarm. That was the sin for which he threatens to chastise Laodicea: 'And repent,' *i. e.* reform, and abandon those evils which provoke me to severe proceedings. He intends this in shewing and shaking the rod.

2. Those that are for trial, called δοκιμασίαι. Their principal end may be for to try the truth or strength of grace; to discover or prove our faith, love, patience, sincerity, constancy; but that it is the only end, appears not. The mortifying of sin and taking away iniquity may be intended in this also. We find both these expressed together in Scripture, as jointly intended in afflictions and sufferings. Those that are to try and prove the people of God, are also to purge and refine them, Dan. xi. 35; shall fall into calamities, brought on that people by Antiochus, specified ver. 33; and this not only to try them, but to purge them and cleanse them; so chap. xii. 10, and Zech. xiii. 8, 9. Not only to try them, as gold is tried by the fire, whether it be the precious metal it is taken for, but to refine them as silver is refined, which is put into the fire, and continued there till the dross be wasted or wrought out of it.

3. Those that are for righteousness' sake, called διωγμοί, persecutions. That which moves wicked men to persecute them may be their righteousness, while that which the Lord aims at in leaving them to persecution, may be the taking away their sin. Those sufferings which befell the believing Hebrews were trials, and are called chastenings; yet were inflicted by their persecutors for their profession of Christ, and faithfulness to him; but that which God intended therein was what a father aims at, or should do, in correcting his child, Heb. xii. 5–7. *Ad hoc corripit, ut emendet*, says Cyprian, lib. iv. epist. 4, when he is giving account for what sins persecution befell them in his times, and what design the Lord had therein, *vapulamus itaque ut meremur*, &c. The Lord corrects his children by the hand of persecutors, that he may reform and amend them, that by this their iniquity may be purged.

For the further confirmation of this truth,

1. In general it is evident in Scripture, that the Lord aims at the good of his people in afflicting them; and intends to do them good by whatever calamities befall them: Rom. viii. 28, 'All things,' afflictions and sufferings especially; for it is spoken with a particular respect to them. This was the Lord's design in all trials, calamities, and sad dispensations, wherewith the

children of Israel were exercised in the wilderness, Deut. viii. 15, 16, Jer. xxiv. 5. That complication of calamities which befell the Jews in the captivity, was designed and ordered for the good of the faithful. They lost their estates, all being a prey to the soldiers; their relations, many of them falling by the sword; their liberty, being prisoners and captives; their country, being carried into a strange land; yea, the ordinances of worship, the temple being destroyed; yet all these dreadful losses were for their good.

Now, which way such evils may prove good to the people of God, we may learn by that of David, Ps. cxix. 67, 71. Before he was afflicted, he was a transgressor, he took liberty to leave God's way; but by his afflictions he was taught to keep it; he had learned thereby not to transgress.

Indeed, we cannot well imagine how afflictions should possibly do us good, if they did not help us against sin; for this is it which withholds good things from us, both spiritual and temporal, or hinders them from being good. Holiness (upon which spiritual and eternal mercies depend) cannot thrive, but as sin declines; and temporal blessings can scarce be blessings, unless we be helped against sin; the more outward enjoyments we have, the more snares, if sin be not mortified and avoided.

2. The Lord, in afflicting his people, proceeds not as a judge, but as a Father. A judge punishes offenders, because justice must be done, the law must be satisfied; others must be deterred from breaking the laws, and many times, by the death of the delinquent, so as to leave no place for his reformation.

But a father corrects his child that he may make him better, that he may offend no more; not because he would shew himself just, but because he is affectionate, and would have that avoided, which might impair his affection, or hinder the course of his love and delight. And under this notion doth the Lord represent himself, when he chastises his people: Prov. iii. 11, 12, ' He corrects whom he loves;' and because he will love, he chastens; that sin which is displeasing and hateful to him, may be avoided; and so his people may continue the children of his love and delight. By affliction, therefore, would he have their iniquity purged; he would have this to be the fruit of it.

3. This appears by the nature and properties of an end in three particulars, which we may apply to the Lord, according to our imperfect way, conceiving of him, as he gives us leave, after the manner of men.

(1.) That is an end which sets the agent a-work, and excites him to act. *Finis movet efficientem ad agendum.* The purging and refining of his people is assigned in Scripture as the motive or reason why the Lord takes this course, Jer. ix. 7, and Ezek. xviii. 30–32. Therefore will he judge them, that they may turn from their transgressions, and cast them away.

(2.) The end gives measure to the means; *media mensuram et modum accipiunt ex fine*, Arist. Pol. i. cap. vi. Means are used in such measure and degree as will be sufficient to effect the end, and no more, nor otherwise. The Lord afflicts his people in such measure and manner as may be effectual to purge their iniquity, &c., ver. 8. As a physician proportions what he administers according to the nature of his patient's distemper, and the quality of the humour that is to be purged; such ingredients, so much of them, and no more than he judges sufficient for the cure; so doth the Lord, as it were, exactly weigh and measure what afflictions, and what proportion and degree thereof, may serve to mortify sin, and reclaim his people from it.

If less will serve, he ' stirs not up all his wrath,' Ps. lxxviii. 38, and lays a restraint upon the wrath of men too, Ps. lxxvi. 10, cxxxviii. 7.

If less will not serve the turn, he lets out more; if a gentle fire will not refine them, he heats the furnace, Jer. ix. 7, makes it hotter, and melts them.

(3.) When the end is attained, there is no more need, no more use of the means. The Lord, when the iniquity of his people is purged, will no more chasten and afflict them for that end and purpose, Isa. x. 12. When he has sufficiently chastised his people, so as the end for which he chastened them is accomplished, he will make no more use of oppressors to afflict them. When his children submit, and give ground to hope they will offend no more, the rod shall be burned. The Assyrian, called his rod, ver. 5, shall be so dealt with, ver. 16, 17. When his people are sufficiently humbled and reformed, there shall be no more yokes nor burdens, ver. 27.

Use. For exhortation; to advise in the fear of God, to comply with his end in judging and afflicting us. The Lord hath been judging his people many years; he hath made his power known, even the power of his wrath in judging us. He hath followed us year after year with terrible judgments. He hath revealed his wrath from heaven against our apostasies and rebellions, by sword, by plague, by fire, yea, and by famine too; and such a famine as expresses more wrath than any of the rest: those ruining us only in our outward concernments, but this threatening ruin to our souls; and is the more grievous judgment, because the generality are less sensible of the danger and grievousness of it. He has given the sword a commission to eat flesh and drink blood; and, as if the wrath of man had been too little, he has armed the powers of heaven against us, and sent destroying angels to make havoc amongst us, and to cut down thousands and ten thousands in city and country. And after all these instruments of wrath, as if they had not done enough, he himself has appeared against us in a posture yet more dreadful; we have seen him march against us, and pass through us as a consuming fire, devouring our strength, our riches, our glory; laying all our pleasant things desolate, and making such terrible devastations, as may strike every one that sees, or hears, or that thinks of it, with horror and trembling.

Now, what is the Lord's end in all this? Why, if he have mercy for the nation, and design not our utter ruin, by this should our iniquity be purged; and this should be the fruit of all, to take away our sin.

Nay, he has been judging professors amongst us; he has been visiting his own people, not in such a way as he visits those with whom he is well pleased; they have seen the day of a severe visitation; they have had their share in the public calamities, and a great share thereof has been the portion of many; they have not escaped the displeasure of God, and the wrath of man has been more bent against them than others. Those that observe the Lord in the way of his judgments, cannot but take notice that many of them have seemed more particularly pointed at those who profess him.

And besides our share (whatever it has been) in national sufferings, he has been visiting us with more particular and personal chastisements. He has been breaking us with great breaches; his hand has made breaches, not only in our congregations, but breaches in our families; sad breaches in our dear relatives; great breaches in some of our estates; large breaches in our liberties, our soul liberties. He has broken us with breach upon breach, Job xvi. 14; and some of us may say, our breach is great like the sea, who can heal us?

And after all that is come upon us, shall we wipe our mouths, and say, We are innocent, we have not so much offended him as others, we have not so highly provoked him? Shall we justify ourselves, and condemn the Lord's proceedings against us ? Shall we think he has no controversy with us, when he is pleading it so severely ? Shall we say he is at peace with us, when he has been contending with us, and is so to this day ? When we see for all this his anger is not turned away, but his hand is stretched out still, shall we imagine he is well pleased with us, when his displeasure is so evidently revealed from heaven against us ?

O no, far be this from us. Surely this nation has highly provoked God ; surely his people have provoked him. The provocations of his sons and daughters are not small, if they be not greater than those of others. The hand, the rod of God speaks this ; the many, the sharp rods wherewith he has corrected us, speak this aloud, if our consciences be silent or asleep.

This being our case, the truth before us shews us what is our great duty at this day, the duty of the nation, the duty of the people of God especially. Though others will not see when God's hand is stretched out, what it points at, yet they should see. Though others will not regard, yet they should lay it to heart, and apply their minds, and consciences, and souls to it.

The end of all that is befallen us is the purging of our iniquity ; and what does the Lord expect from us, but to comply with this end, in mortifying sin, and cleansing our heart and life from it ? Those sins especially, for and by which we have suffered, this is it which the word, which the providence of God now calls us to, and hath made it so much our duty, as I know not whether anything else can be more, or be so much the duty of all sorts at this day.

If, after all that has come upon us for our unfruitfulness under the means of grace, when the axe has been laid to the root, again and again, and we have been so often in apparent danger of being cut down, or of being left desolate of the means by which our souls should live, we still continue barren ;

If, after all, &c., for our worldliness, we will still so highly esteem earthly things, and affect them, and pursue them as worldlings do, and seek them for such ends, and convert them to such uses, as the custom is ;

For our neglect of holiness in the power of life, and exercise and growth of it, we will still content ourselves with a slothful, easy, cheap, fruitless profession of it, and be more indifferent whether we have more or less of it than we are to outward things, and much better content with a little holiness, than with a little of the world, and less concerned whether our souls thrive or no, than whether we thrive in our earthly affairs ;

If, after all, &c., for our pride, folly and vanity, we will still be more vile this way ;

If, after all, &c. for our contentions, divisions, decay, and loss of brotherly love, we will not seek union with, nor express love to one another, in lesser differences, but live in open contradiction to so many express precepts of the gospel, and let envy, strife, bitterness, wrath, malice or ill-will, and evil-speaking continue, and continue in these, and such like, the apparent works of the flesh ;

If, when the Lord has laid any of us aside for unserviceableness, &c., we labour not for a more serviceable temper ;

If, after we have lost such mercies, opportunities, advantages, by our unthankfulness, murmuring, repining ; the dread of having our carcases fall in the wilderness, bring us not to an effectual sense of our sin ;

If we still remain proud, selfish, carnal, unprofitable, unmortified, unrefined : if we continue under the guilt of these, and other sins, for which the Lord has been contending with us ;—

Our guilt will be exceeding great, and our danger such as I cannot easily express. Let me endeavour it in some particulars, which may serve as motives to enforce this duty of complying with the Lord's end, in afflicting and bringing calamities upon us.

1. Otherwise our calamities are like to continue; the Lord may wear out this generation in his displeasure; he may cause our carcases to fall in the wilderness, and swear in his wrath that we shall never enter into his rest. So he did with the Israelites, when what befell them in the wilderness did not purge their iniquity. We shall shew ourselves hereby to be such as they were, 'a people that err in our hearts, and have not known his ways,' Ps. xcv. 10, 11—the ways that he leads us to by afflictions, nor the way that would lead us out of them speedily and comfortably. This will move the Lord to come to that severe resolution, 'I will deliver you no more;' for this was it which brought him to that resolution against the Israelites, when neither former deliverances, nor present oppressions, took away their sin, Judges x. 11–13, Isa. ix. 12, 13. If our transgressions and iniquities be upon us, we may pine away in them, Ezek. xxxiii. 10, and languish under fears, restraints, distractions, calamities, all our days. Thus we may make our condition desperate, and deliverance hopeless; and propagate our miseries to our posterity, and leave them the sad heirs of what our sin has brought upon us.

There is no way of mercy out of trouble, but by leaving the sin which brought us into it; no ordinary way, &c., Isa. ix. 12, 13.

2. This may increase the affliction upon you, add more weight, and put more sting into it; this may strengthen your bonds, and make your yokes heavier, and less tolerable. Whenas your fears and troubles are but by fits, and with some intermission, this may raise them to, and fix them in, a continued paroxysm.

If less will not serve to purge your iniquity, you may expect a larger dose, that which will prove more bitter, and in the working, may make you sick at heart. Those that have but lost one or two dear relatives may be bereaved of all, and left to weep for their children, so as not to be comforted, because they are not.

Those that have but seen the flame at a distance, or been but frightened, or a little scorched with it, may have it kindle, and break forth round about them.

Those that have but lost part of their estates, if this take not away their sin, may be stripped of all, stripped naked, as some have been, and set as in the day that they were born, and made as a wilderness; as the Lord in like case threatens, Hosea ii. 3.

Those that have but been threatened by the sons of violence, or a little disturbed, may be given up into their hands, or delivered up to their will; and not only see, but feel, the paws of those lions which before they did but fear.

Those that have but been straitened as to spiritual provision, and only not fed with the hand they desired, may have no hand at all left to feed them.

It is the Lord's ordinary method, when a gentler fire will not purge and refine, to make the furnace hotter.

3. This may multiply your afflictions, and make them come in upon you as waves and billows in a storm, so as you may have cause to complain with the prophet, Ps. xlii. 7, the depths above and the depths below, the displeasure of God and the wrath of men, may correspond to pour out themselves upon you as it were waterspouts; as though they called one upon another, and did conspire as it were to overwhelm you. If one will not be effectual to purge your iniquity, God may try another and another; yea, seven times more, and it may be all at once. You see what the Lord threatens, Lev.

xxvi. 18, 21, 23, 24, 27, 28. The stubborn child, that will not yield to his father's will when he is correcting him, must expect to be scourged again and again; he cannot escape many lashes. You know your heavenly Father's will in chastising you is to purge your iniquity and take away your sin, to quicken you to a more vigorous proceeding in a course of mortification. Now, since you know his will, if you do it not, you leave nothing for yourselves but a fearful expectation of many stripes, of multiplied afflictions and calamities.

4. This may bring more grievous evils upon you than any you have yet met with, outward calamities. The little finger of what this incorrigibleness will bring upon you, may be heavier and more intolerable than the loins of all you have yet suffered. You have been chastised with whips; but if this do not take away your sin, beware lest the Lord do not make use of scorpions. You are warned of this by the advice that Christ gives to one who had been under a great affliction, John v. 14. Those that will sin more must suffer more, whatever they have suffered already. How grievous soever that seems to be which is past, if it purge not thine iniquity, there is something worse yet to come.

Why, you may say, Is there any worse judgment than the sword? Is there anything more dreadful than such a plague as has been destroying us? Is there anything more terrible than such a fire as was consuming us? Our hearts tremble within us, and horror surprises us, when we do but think of the woes that are past; can there be anything worse yet to come? Indeed, there would be no fear of it, if by these our iniquity had been purged; but if these have no such effect upon us, we are in danger to know by experience that the Lord's treasures of wrath are not yet exhausted, there is but a little thereof in comparison yet spent upon us; the vials of his indignation are not yet emptied; we have but yet had a taste thereof; the worst of all, the dregs, are at the bottom, and these we expect will be poured out upon us if our sin continue. Oh that we could with fear and trembling labour to prevent it, by complying with the Lord's end in what is come upon us already, so that by this our iniquity may be purged!

5. The Lord may give you over, and refuse to correct any more. You are in danger of this if the Lord find that former corrections are in vain, and in vain they are if they attain not their end; and their end they cannot obtain if they do not take away your sin.

It seems a condition acceptable to flesh and blood to be without afflictions and sufferings; but to those who judge of things as they are indeed, and as the Scripture represents them, for the Lord to refuse to afflict when afflictions are needful, signifies one of the highest degrees of divine wrath, and is a more dreadful judgment than any of those outward calamities which the Lord calls his sore judgments; sword, famine, pestilence, fire, speak not more indignation in God than this.

When a man gives over a stubborn child, after all correction has done no good upon him, and says, I will whip him no more, I see it is in vain, all that I have done is to no purpose, there is no hopes of reclaiming him, let him go on and take his course; the condition of that child is more sad and lamentable than of such a one as his father corrects most severely: 'As many as I love, I rebuke and chasten,' Rev. iii. What affection has he for those whom he will not rebuke? &c. : 'Blessed is the man,' &c., Ps. xciv. 12, 13. Their condition seems cursed whom he will not chastise, Heb. xii. 7, 8. If they be his children whom he thus forbears, yet he deals not with them as his own children, he has not at this time, in these circumstances, so much favour for them, but as the children of strangers whom a man will not trouble himself to correct.

When the Lord is expressing the highest indignation, he doth it in threatening to judge and punish those no more against whom his wrath is kindled, Isa. i. 5, Hos. iv. 14–17.

6. He may leave you to spiritual judgments. This usually is the issue of not improving outward calamities, and is the dreadful consequence of the Lord's forbearing to inflict. Outward afflictions are his rods, but these are his swords; and when upon incorrigibleness under those, he takes up these, his wrath is raised to the height. Formerly he fell upon their outward concernments, which are less considerable, now he falls upon their souls; the iron enters into their souls, and the more dangerously and mortally because insensibly. That wrath begins here which will burn to the bottom of hell. When he gives stubborn souls up to blindness of mind, hardness of heart, searedness of conscience, vile affections and lusts, and a reprobate sense, oh these are the first-born of the second death. No greater severity, short of hell, than in the inflicting of these.

Yea, but does he inflict these upon any that belong to him?

Ans. The not improving of other afflictions may provoke the Lord to leave his children to spiritual judgments, and to some measure and degrees of these now mentioned, and to others also more woful than any outward calamities. This may provoke the Lord to bring upon his people a famine of the word, as he threatens, after other judgments had been ineffectual, Amos viii. 11–13. Not a scarcity, but a famine, and that more dreadful than a famine of bread and a thirst for water, so that they shall run to and fro, &c., and the virgins and young men shall faint and swoon for thirst.

2. Or if the word and ordinances be continued, this may provoke him to deny his presence and concurrence, to withdraw his Spirit, and withhold his influences, upon which the power and efficacy of them depends; so that the staff of bread shall be broken while it is in their hands, and the ordinances become dry breasts, so that they can suck nothing but wind out of them which are appointed for spiritual nourishment, Isa. lxv. 3, 4. Oh what a curse would you think it, if all you eat or drink should neither strengthen, nourish, nor refresh you! But this is worse, it is a curse upon spiritual blessings.

3. Or this may provoke him to leave you to backslidings, and inward decays and declinings, and to smite your souls with a spiritual consumption; so that inward strength shall waste away, grace shall wither, and holiness hang the head like a blasted flower. You think a consumption of the body worse, though less sensible, than the stone or gout. What, then, is a soul-consumption? You think poverty, or the loss of an estate, a great affliction; oh, but to grow poor unto God, to have your spiritual substance wasted, and your heavenly treasure consumed, that is a more terrible stroke to those who are taught of Christ to pass a true judgment of things.

4. This may provoke him to give you up in some degrees to your hearts' lusts; to fall into some gross sin, and wallow in it, as Solomon into false worship and sensuality; or, which I fear is too ordinary, and the sad case of too many amongst us, to indulge themselves in such sins as are less reproachful amongst professors: habitual lukewarmness in serving the Lord; indifferency as to their spiritual and heavenly interests; loose, careless, unwatchful walking tolerated; selfishness, unserviceableness in their places, sensualness, and flesh-pleasing, and worldliness, sinking deep and sticking fast in the mire and clay of it.

To be left to these evils is a more grievous judgment than to be given up to the hands of our enemies, or to be left to fly before them, which yet seemed less tolerable to David than a destroying pestilence.

5. Or this may provoke him to give them up to some hardness of heart, and searedness of conscience, in some degree; so that though their sin be often reproved, and the danger thereof discovered, yet reproofs make no impression, conviction will not fasten. If it be a way they are fastened to by affection or interest, they will not believe it is a sin, or such a sin as they need be severe against; especially if they can get some fig-leaves to hide its shame, some pretences to excuse its sinfulness. If they can but believe it will not damn them, say what you can against it, it will not prevail. Such stiffness against convictions of sin, and the like untractableness as to duty, is the symptom of an insensible conscience and an hardened heart; and to be given up to it is a spiritual judgment of a dreadful importance.

6. Or this may provoke him to send a spirit of delusion, which may lead you out of the way of truth, and seduce to relinquish part of that faith which should be earnestly contended for by the saints; or to give you up to a spirit of wantonness and unsobriety, so as to disrelish those wholesome practical truths, and that teaching which tends most to the promoting of the power of godliness in heart and life, and would lead you up to higher degrees of holiness, self-denial, mortification, crucifiedness to the world, and all spiritual fruitfulness; and to dote upon trifling questions, frivolous opinions, vain imaginations, the niceties of this or that way and persuasion, empty notions, strains of fancy, which make neither mind, nor heart, nor life better. This is a kind of spiritual frenzy, a delirium, a soul-dotage; and you count not only a furious, but a trifling, frenzy to be a lamentable distemper in nature, much more lamentable in a spiritual deliration.

7. Or he may be provoked hereby to send a spirit of terror. When other scourges will not serve the turn, he may wound the conscience, Job vi. 4, and give you those wounds that are intolerable, Prov. xviii. 14. He may kindle a hell in your souls, and set that worm a-gnawing there which is some of the torture of hell itself. He may make you *Magor-missabibs*, terror round about, a terror to yourselves, a terror to others, while himself is a terror to you. Wherever you look for comfort, ease, relief, you may be disappointed: Ps. lxxvii. 3, 'I remembered God, and was troubled.' The thoughts and remembrance of God, of Christ, of heaven, of the promises, instead of relieving you, may add to your trouble and torture. All the springs of comfort may run nothing but waters of Marah; the bitterness of death may be in them. The Lord's loving-kindness is better than life, Ps. lxiii. 3; to be bereaved of the sense of it is therefore worse than death. Oh what is it then to be under the terrors of the Lord!

Oh, if the terrors of the Lord be dreadful to you, take heed you be not found under the guilt of not improving more tolerable afflictions. Take heed you continue not under this guilt. You are in the highway to spiritual judgments, if outward calamities do not take away your sin. It is the Lord's method to proceed higher and higher in the demonstrations of his anger, and to let out more wrath (as he doth in these judgments), when lesser significations of his displeasure are not effectual.

7. This is the way to be rejected of the Lord; for those that are not his to be rejected wholly, for those that are his to be in part rejected, Jer. vii. 28, 29. Those that receive not correction, *i.e.* who yield not to what is required and intended in correction, their case is to be bitterly lamented; such being rejected of the Lord as the generation of his wrath. So Jer. vi. 29, 30. All the means the Lord has used for the refining of this people are in vain, all his labour is lost. Though he has blown up the fire in the furnace to such an heat as the bellows themselves are burnt by it, though the

lead (used then, as now quicksilver is used, in the fining of silver, to melt it more easily, and with less waste) be quite consumed, yet the founder melteth in vain; all is to no purpose. The wicked things, or, as in the Hebrew, wickednesses, are not removed from them. Refuse silver shall they be called, such as will not pass, but will be rejected in payment. The Lord hath rejected them as dross, not silver, or that which has too much dross in it to be current.

Though he will not utterly reject those that belong to him, yet if they be not refined by their afflictions, he may deal with them as if he utterly rejected them. He may proceed against them as against those whom he utterly rejects, so as no eye may be able to see any difference; as in the captivity, to which this rejecting refers, no difference was to be seen between those that were better and those that were worst.

Though they lose not the relation of children, yet he may treat them as though they were not his children, as though he were not their Father; nay, as though he were an enemy, Isa. lxiii. 10, Jer. xxx. 14, 15. Because their iniquities were increased, when by their afflictions they should have been taken away, though he do not disinherit them, yet may he leave them without hopes of inheriting; so that it may be all one as to their apprehensions, as if they were disinherited; nothing may be left them, in their own sense, but a fearful expectation of judgment.

8. This provokes the Lord to bring destruction. This endangers your ruin, the ruin of your country, the ruin of yourselves. This exposes to national desolation, or personal destruction, Isa. i. 5; and the issue of revolts after smiting, ver. 7. As temporal judgments, when not improved, end in spiritual, so spiritual judgments end in ruin, Isa. vi. 9–11, Zeph. iii. 7, 8. He that learns not righteousness by public judgments, so as to be thereby more refined and mortified, he doth his part to bring utter ruin upon the place and country where he lives. This desolation of it, when it comes, may be charged upon him. Those that should stand in the gap, and make up the hedge, do hereby make the breach wider, and pull away that which might put a stop to the current of ruining wrath. If this land perish, those that might have saved it, by complying with God's end in judging us, have destroyed it, by not improving judgments for this end. And it is no wonder that those whose hand makes way for destroying judgments, whoever they be, do perish by them. Even those that have interest in God may be ruined and cut off by this sin, and may perish for it. Those that reform not themselves and their families, when they have real admonitions from heaven to do it, may have Eli's doom, though they have special relation to God, as Eli had. Those that are of the Lord's planting, and by the hand of affliction have been lopped and pruned, and yet continue barren, or have wild grapes found in their branches, the Lord, when he lays the axe to the root of the tree, may cut them down as well as others; they may fall by this sin. And it is not more comfortable to die for righteousness' sake than it is dreadful to die in and for sin. And though the Lord may rescue their souls from everlasting miseries, when they fall by the stroke of temporal wrath (as some of the Corinthians fell, 1 Cor. xi.), yet will they be saved so as by fire, and escape the wrath to come very narrowly, even as firebrands plucked out of the fire.

Oh then, if you would not plunge yourselves into this misery, look that by this your iniquity be purged, otherwise there is great danger of the Lord's high displeasure, and the severest acts and expressions of it. But this is not all, though this be terrible. There is danger also of great and heinous guilt. It is a crime of an high provocation, not to be mortified and refined by calamities and afflictions, whether common or personal; there is much to aggravate it, and render it exceeding sinful.

(1.) It is a double disobedience. The Lord calls upon you by his word to purge out and put away sin. When this is not effectual, he summons you to do it by judgments and afflictions. He calls for it both by his word and by his rod. He requires it by a word, that you may see, Jer. ii. 31; and by a rod, that you may hear, Micah vi. 9. To yield neither to one nor the other is to add disobedience to disobedience. Not to comply with his word, clearly discovering this to be your duty, and frequently urging it on you, is heinous disobedience. But to stand out against it, when it is enforced with the rod, is plain rebellion. If a prince enjoin a subject to do this or that, and he refuse, that is a disobedience that will not easily escape without some mark of his displeasure. But if hereupon he raise a force, and begirt the house or castle of such a subject, and threaten to batter or storm it unless he yield, to stand out in that case will be rebellion. So it is in this. Here is one provocation added to another, and the latter worse than the former, Zeph. iii. 2. Not obeyed, and which is more, and doubles the guilt by an addition of something worse, 'she received not correction.'

(2.) It is a strange boldness and impudence not to put away sin, not to cease from it, when the Lord is smiting for it, and declaring his displeasure against it by real rebukes; such are branded in Scripture as those that know no shame, Zeph. iii. 5. How does that appear? Why, the Lord warned them by judgments, ver. 6, yet they received not instruction, but still corrupted their doings, ver. 7. And as those that have a whore's forehead, Jer. iii. 3, because she was not brought by the chastisement mentioned to put away her sin, therefore, says he, 'thou hast a whore's forehead,' &c.

What impudence would you judge it for a servant, who has been beaten for his faults, to tell his master, while the rod is in his hand, he will not leave it, he will do it again. While you do not purge your hearts, and reform your ways, after chastenings for this purpose, you tell the Lord, while the rod is upon or over you, you will not be mortified or refined. This is the language of your hearts and ways.

(3.) It is madness, spiritual folly with a witness. As if one who has drunk poison, should spill the antidote that should secure him from the mortal danger thereof, instead of vomiting up that which so endangers him, yea, and should be ready to swallow down more, when that already taken is still working in his bowels. Sin is worse to the soul than poison to the body. Not to receive correction is to refuse the antidote, and so to let the poison work on, yea, to heighten the mortal danger of it by new additions. It argues stupendous foolishness, and such as is inveterate, and almost past cure, if the rod will not cure it, Prov. xxii. 15. If the rod will not fetch it out, it is fast bound up indeed. The bond of this folly and iniquity is exceeding strong, little hopes anything will break it if the hand of God upon his children do it not. It is desperate and incorrigible folly, that will not be removed by severe handling, Prov. xxvii. 22.

(4.) It argues great hardness and obduration, and signifies he is very much hardened in those evils for which the Lord corrects him, when his chastising hand does not conquer and prevail against them, Jer. v. 3. It is for those who have made their faces harder than a rock, not to receive correction, but to refuse to return when the Lord has been striking and consuming them; it is a sign not only of natural, but contracted hardness. Such was that stigmatised in Ahaz, 2 Chron. xxviii. 22, 'This is that king Ahaz.' Here is a hardened wretch indeed, here is a signal instance of obduration to sin more in or after distress. It is some stiffness not to yield to the word, Zech. vii. 11, 12, even this makes way for great wrath. Oh but to stand out against the hand of God too, not to be pliable nor tractable, when we have been under the mighty hand of God, this speaks obduration with a witness. If that be as the adamant, this is harder than a rock or flint, the issue more dreadful.

(5.) It argues much affection, a heart greatly in love with it, when he will not leave it, whatever it cost him; when the smart of one scourge after another will not make him leave his hold of it; when the rod, though in the hand of God, will not drive him from it; when he cleaves to its breasts, though there be wormwood upon them, and the Lord has embittered it by afflictions; when he will not quit its embraces though plague sores be upon it, and the marks of divine displeasure are plainly visible.

That love to sin is so far from being mortified, that it is predominant and greater than the fear of any other evil, when he will endanger the loss of relations, liberty, estate, life, yea, the favour of God and the pledges of it, gospel, and ordinances, and his presence in them; when he will run all hazards rather than quit it; expose himself to temporal calamities or spiritual judgments, yea, run upon destruction itself rather than leave it.

(6.) It is brutishness, worse than that of the horse and mule; for these you may restrain from mischief by bit and bridle; you may hedge up their way with thorns, and keep them within compass. But those that are not mortified, reformed, by afflictions, they break through the hedge, though of thorns, as afflictions are called, Hos. ii. 6.

When Balaam's ass saw the angel of the Lord standing in the way, and his sword drawn in his hand, she turned aside out of the way, and would not be forced into it, Num. xxii. 23. What brutishness is it to venture on in a way when the Lord stands to stop it, as it were, with a sword in his hand; yea, after ye have been wounded by it, and felt the weight and sharpness of it!

Hence, those who are not reduced and reformed by afflictions, are expressed in Scripture by dromedaries, wild asses, Jer. ii. 23, 24; untamed heifers, Hos. iv. 16; bullocks unaccustomed to the yoke, Jer. xxxi. 18.

(7.) It argues great pride; a heart lifting up itself against God; not only pride in carriage towards men, but in deportment towards the Most High. When the soul is truly humbled, it yields, submits, to whatsoever the Lord would have him leave, or whatsoever the Lord will have him do, Acts ix. 6; and in this pliableness to the will of God, doth the nature of true evangelical humiliation most consist.

But pride is in its exaltation yet unbroken, when it will not leave that temper, those ways, and designs, and actions that the Lord would have him leave; when he does not yield, submit, and stoop to the divine will herein, though the Lord himself has been laying weight upon him. All the Lord's dispensations have not yet humbled him; he is yet stout against the Almighty; nor is pride hid from his eyes, till he be withdrawn from his purpose, Job xxxiii. 17.

(8.) It is contempt of God, and argues that there is no fear, or little fear, of God in the heart; for when should the fear of God shew itself, but when the Lord is angry, and appears terrible? And how should it appear, if not in leaving that which has provoked God to anger, and at which he has been actually expressing himself displeased? Not to leave sin, when the Lord has been judging you for it, is in effect to say, I will take my own course, let the Lord do what he will, let him do what he can with me for it. The Lord reads and hears such language in your hearts and ways, when they are not refined and reformed by judgments and chastenings. This is to despise the chastenings of the Lord, and to make nothing of his severity; to slight the Lord himself, when he will least endure it; when he is executing judgment, and expects you should submit and stoop to his will with fear and trembling.

(9.) This is to affront God, and run cross to his design, and defeat his end, in these proceedings. If a person observe not exactly the letter of a law, yet if he satisfy the end and design of it, he will be in equity excused; but a punctual observance of the words, if the end of the law be crossed, will leave him a transgressor. But if you be not more mortified and refined by afflictions, you run cross, both to the plain words of God, and to his design in these dispensations, and affront him every way, walk as contrary to the great God as may be.

(10.) It argues the person is incurable, and the case hopeless, for this is one of the last remedies; and when the last fails, nothing more is to be hoped for. Food and sleep are the first means for the support of health and life, but when these will not serve, we use physic; but if physic also be ineffectual, the case is desperate. The word and ordinances should purge and mortify us, and take away our sin; but if these do it not, the Lord makes use of his afflictions and sharp dispensations, these are his physic; but if these fail too, which is the last remedy, what hope is there then left?

You see by these particulars our danger; how dreadful it is for those that have been exercised with public judgments, or personal chastenings, not to be purged or refined thereby. If sin, so great a sin; if the wrath of God in such expressions of it be not feared, it is to those who are past fear. Make it appear that you are far from such a desperate distemper, by complying with the Lord's end in what has befallen us. Make that your great business, which the Lord has made so, by improving what has come upon us, so as this may be the effect, to take away sin.

There is another consideration by which I would enforce this great duty, and that is the advantage we shall reap by complying with the Lord's end in bringing afflictions and calamities upon us; and,

1. The putting away our sin, and the purging our iniquity, is in itself so great an advantage, that this alone, duly considered, may be sufficient to lead us to a full and cheerful compliance to the will of God herein. For what is sin? It is our poverty; it is the sickness and languor of our souls; it is a noisome and a pestilent disease; it is lameness, and blindness, and impotency; it is a monstrous and loathsome deformity; it is a dungeon, with fetters and vermin; in a word, it is misery. It is really as great an evil to our souls as these are to our bodies. It is so represented in the word of truth. It is all these, it is more, it is worse than all these; and what an advantage would it be to be rid of such a horrid, a hideous evil as this.

It is the worst poverty, that which makes you poor towards God, poor and naked in his sight, in his account, who sure can best judge what is riches and what is poverty. He counts them miserably deluded who think they are rich, while their iniquity continues, and judges them poor and naked, however their goods be increased, if their sin be not done away; so Christ, of Laodicea, because of her lukewarmness, that one sin, Rev. iii. Now what an advantage would a poor man count it, to be freed from this poverty and nakedness! This you may gain by putting away your sins; you are freed from the most wretched poverty.

Sin is the soul's sickness, a mortal disease which has been the death of millions and millions; a noisome and destructive disease; a leprosy, a plague, a cancer, a gangrene. In Scripture language it is no better, it is worse. The purging of your iniquity is the purging out of such a pestilent humour, the freeing of you from such a loathsome and dangerous disease; and would you not count it a happiness to be raised from such a sickness, to be rid of such a leprosy: a great advantage to be cured of the plague, the plague of the heart, a soul gangrene?

If your child, or a dear relative, were blind, or lame, or dumb, or otherwise impotent; if he were frantic, or lunatic, or a natural fool, what would you give to have them freed from such a misery? The case is your own; sin is worse than these to your souls, if you will believe the report of the Holy Ghost concerning it in Scripture. It makes you lame, blind, impotent; it is the most stupid foolishness, the highest frenzy and madness, only you may be cured at an easier rate: do but put away your sin, and the cure is wrought, the work is done, your soul is made whole. Thus you may be freed from the most ugly and monstrous deformity, that which makes you loathsome and ugly in the sight of God, which he (in whose love and delight your souls are infinitely concerned) doth not only hate but abhor.

Thus may you be freed from the most miserable restraint, the most dismal and nasty dungeon; thus may you shake off your fetters, and be rid of the vilest vermin; only by quitting your iniquity, and putting away your sin. Do but this, and so far as it is done you are discharged of all misery and wretchedness.

Oh, if our souls and consciences, if our families or congregations, if our religious or civil assemblies, if our country, if the world were but purged of iniquity, which pesters, troubles, disorders, confounds all, what a happy change would there be! Men would be like angels, who are now, for want of this, like brutes or devils; earth would be like heaven, which is now, through sin, the unhappiest region in the world next to hell; our commerce in the world would be a communion with God, while now we converse together as fools or sharks, as foxes or tigers, either over-reaching, or vexing, or preying one upon another. Oh, if ungodliness, and unrighteousness, and unsobriety were put away, there would be a new heaven and a new earth; there would be a new, a happy face of things everywhere; there would be a face of heaven, of the peace and order and happiness of heaven, upon our souls and consciences, upon our families, upon our assemblies, upon our country, upon the world. Alas, that the world will not be persuaded to be so happy upon so easy terms! But shall those who profess themselves children of light, shall the people of God be guilty of such madness and cruelty to themselves and others? Shall nothing, no, not the hand, no, not the rod of God, lead them, so far as they can, to rid the world of these miseries, and to possess all, so far as they can reach, of these blessed advantages? Oh be persuaded to purge iniquity out of your hearts, lives, families; to endeavour the rooting of it out from the place where you live, and from every place that your influence can reach. Be exemplary herein as to your own persons, and the great advantages you will gain and enjoy thereby may induce the world to follow you herein; or however you shall not lose your reward. To be rid of sin yourselves (so great a misery, all miseries in one), is a most rich blessed advantage.

2. This is the way to deliverance; a sure, a speedy way to be delivered, and that in mercy too. To be delivered from the grievances and afflictions that are upon you, and from those that are approaching; from what you feel, and from what you fear. Afflictions are but the means to purge your iniquity; the taking away your sin, that is the end of all this. When the end is once attained, no wise agent will further make use of the means; there is no need of them. When your iniquity is purged, the Lord will see no need of continuing what afflicts you for that purpose; and he who afflicts

not willingly, nor delights to grieve his children, will not afflict and grieve them needlessly.

When the child submits, and gives hopes he will offend no more, the rod is laid aside, the father's severity gives way to the expressions of his love and compassion. And so the Lord represents himself, Jer. xxxi. 18–20.

When the metal is sufficiently purified, and the dross wasted or wrought out, the furnace is no further useful, the finer sees no need to keep it in the fire. Oh, if our iniquity were once purged, the Lord would quickly take us out of the furnace; nor would there be any danger either of continuing longer in it or of having it made hotter.

Not only the wisdom and mercy of God, but his truth and faithfulness, makes this sure to us; for he has promised it frequently, 2 Chron. vii. 14; which is an answer to Solomon's prayer, chap. vi. 26, 27, and xxx. 6, 8, 9. If we turn from our evil ways, then will the Lord heal, though the wound seem incurable. Though our breaches seem great, like the sea, and such as none can repair, yet will the Lord heal them, certainly, speedily, mercifully.

Oh if we were in a capacity for such a mercy, if our iniquity were but purged, how soon would he give over this sharp course of physic we have been under! If this work were but accomplished upon mount Zion, how soon would he lay aside the sharp tools we are apt to complain of! If our iniquity were but taken away, how soon would he put an end to the days of blackness and thick darkness! How soon would this day of judgment and calamity clear up into a day of mercy and salvation! How certainly would the day of a gracious visitation dawn upon us once again!

Yea, if the generality of the nation should not be purged, yet if those who have interest in God should comply with this his end in judging and chastening, if their sin be hereby taken away, possibly the Lord might be prevailed with by them, and for a few in comparison might spare the whole. The holy seed may be the substance of support of it, as Isa. vi. 13. We see the Lord would have spared Sodom for ten righteous persons, Gen. xviii. 32. And though that may be thought a special favour (granted at the importunity of Abraham, an extraordinary person) to spare so many for so few, and so may not pass for a common rule; so that ordinarily from thence we might draw a like conclusion; yet that in Job seems more general, Job xxii. 30, for (as it may be read) 'The innocent shall deliver the island.' There is such pureness in those who are refined by the furnace of affliction, and they may pass for innocent whose sin is thereby taken away. So Jer. v. 1, if there be any considerable number purged from the common iniquity. So Isa. lxviii. 8, that people is expressed by a vine, so withered or barren that the vine-dresser may be ready to cut it down as dead, yet if one spy in it some cluster that may afford wine, there may be hopes, since it is not quite dead, it may be recovered, and so the whole vine and branches may be spared for a good cluster; hereby signifying that the generality may escape for those few that are upright.

So that this is the way, not only to procure deliverance for yourselves, but others; not only for your persons and families, but for cities and countries. It is the way to become saviours, *i. e.* to prevail with the Lord to appear as a God of salvation to the community against whom he otherwise would proceed as a destroyer.

But if the end of God be not herein complied with, especially by those from whom it is most expected, a deliverance in mercy is hopeless. We make it desperate, and leave ourselves or others no expectation of it in an ordinary way, and according to those rules by which the Scriptures shew us the Lord commonly proceeds.

It is true indeed the Lord is not confined to rules, nor ties himself to walk in the common path. He may save and deliver a people, as it were, by prerogative. And so he did Israel, while their iniquity was not purged, 2 Kings xiv. 25-27, by Jeroboam, who did evil, and departed not from it, ver. 24.

(1.) But this was not in mercy, nor was it lasting. It was rather a reprieve than a deliverance. The advantages thereof (such as they were) were but of short continuance. In the next chapter, you may see them all in blood and confusion.

(2.) And to be delivered from outward afflictions, if sin be not taken away, either before or upon deliverance, is but to be reserved for greater calamities. Sin still remaining will curse and blast temporal deliverance, and the fruits of it, and will make it appear in the issue that there is little or no mercy therein, how specious soever they may seem. So that what we call deliverance by prerogative is not a deliverance in mercy, if the sin of a people be not taken away, either before it or by it; for this brings a curse upon such deliverance, as it does upon other temporal blessings. The Lord threatens it for this sin amongst others, Mal. ii. 2. Not laying to heart God's judgments and chastenings; not giving glory to him, by answering his end therein, and turning from sin, will make freedom from such calamities, if it be a blessing in such a case, to be a cursed blessing, such as will bring more misery than advantage.

(3.) And if such a deliverance as is neither durable nor merciful were desirable, yet have we no ground to expect it; for faith must be grounded upon common rules and ordinary promises, not upon extraordinary proceedings, and looks (when it would have firm support) not at what the Lord *may* do, by prerogative or absolute sovereignty, but at what he *hath declared he will* do. Faith can have no encouragement at all from what is merely possible; it looks for some certainty, and acts not but upon a sure word. Now it is only possible the Lord may deliver a people, when their sin is not taken away, but it is highly probable he will not, he has declared so much against it. It is only certain he will deliver those in mercy whose iniquity is purged, for the promise of it is to them, and to them alone. If, then, by the calamities you would be freed from, your iniquity be purged, if this be the fruit, &c., you may be certain of deliverance, if it be good for you, and of that as soon as ever it will be so.

3. Hereby you will gain that which is better than deliverance, even this very thing. The purging of your iniquity is better than any outward deliverance; for sin is worse than afflictions and calamities. That is clear in Scripture, in reason, and even in the judgment of those whose practice contradicts it. There is that in sin which is more hateful, more dreadful, more grievous and afflictive in itself, and to those who have either spiritual sense or true judgment, than there is in afflictions. It is far and incomparably the greater evil, and therefore freedom from sin, though but in part, is far better than total freedom and full deliverance from outward calamities.

If the Lord should defer deliverance, yet if thereby he purge you more and more from sin, he shews you more mercy, and does that which is better for you than if he should presently deliver you, he is more kind and gracious to you than if he should fully repair all the losses and breaches that afflictions has made upon you. It be unquestionably better to be freed from a greater evil than from a less.

Moreover, the more iniquity is purged the more does holiness increase; these being such contraries, as the exclusion of one lets in the other, and the declining of one is the advance of the other. And the one gains as many degrees as the other loses. As darkness vanishes, light increases; and as sickness is removed, health and strength is recovered. So as sin is expelled, holiness grows. Hence in some places of Scripture the purging of iniquity is the fruit and end of afflictions and chastenings. In other places, the increase of holiness is the fruit thereof, Heb. xii. 10. So that by improving afflictions for the taking away sin, you will partake more of holiness. That is the advantage you will reap thereby, and it is so rich and considerable as all the advantages of outward deliverance are not to be compared with it. For holiness, it is the health, the strength, the beauty, liberty, safety, the riches, the dignity, the comfort, the life, the happiness of the soul, either formally or efficiently; it either is these, or brings these to the soul. And those who will judge of things as Christians, and not as worldlings or sensualists; those who will not be carried away with the common error and delusion of them whose minds the god of this world has blinded, will judge the health and strength of the soul to be the best health, &c., and that which makes the soul rich, more valuable than all earthly riches, and so an increase of holiness far more desirable than the advancement of their outward estate; and that which adorns, honours, and advances their souls in the sight of God, incomparably better than all worldly honours, dignity, or preservation; and that which makes the soul free, more than that which frees the body from restraint, &c. They will count these soul-advantages so much better as the soul is to be preferred before the body, or outward concernments.

Now, outward deliverance brings you but these lower and less considerable advantages, restores health or strength to the body, repairs your estates, or makes you rich on earthly accounts, or brings you to a freer, safer, or higher condition in the world. But afflictions, though they be continued, if they be improved for the purging iniquity, and consequently for the increase of holiness, they make your souls strong and healthful, they make your minds truly free, and great, and noble; they render you lovely and honourable in the sight of God; they enrich your souls with heavenly treasure, with the riches of God, in comparison of which worldly wealth is but thorns or thick clay, loss and dung, riches falsely so called; they bring you peace, and comfort, and happiness, of which otherwise there is nothing but a dream or a shadow in the world, and over and above they work for you a far more exceeding and eternal weight of glory, 2 Cor. iv.

And therefore it is unquestionably true, and past all doubt to those who pass a true judgment of things, that to improve afflictions for the purging of iniquity is incomparably better than deliverance from afflictions. And therefore if the day of deliverance be so much desired, much more should you desire and endeavour to comply with the Lord's end in judging and afflicting, so as hereby your iniquity may be purged, since this is far better, and incomparably more to be desired than what you so much desire.

Let me in the next place lay down some rules and directions, the observance of which may be helpful to promote the Lord's end in judging and afflicting, so as by this iniquity may be purged.

1. Set yourselves against all sin, not against this or that particular evil, which conscience, or the word, or providence may more directly point at, but against every sin. For though afflictions may help you more against one than another, yet they are not less improved* unless they help you more or less against all sin. The words in the text are general, and so laid down as they may reach all sin and iniquity. The fruit of affliction should be the purging iniquity, the taking away of sin without exception. *Et ubi lex non*

* Qu. 'not rightly improved'?—ED.

distinguit, non est distinguendum: where the law makes no exception, we must make none. We must overlook no sin if we would comply with the rule before us. And that we may not be partial, let me instance in some that we are too apt to overlook.

(1.) Set yourselves not only against sin of life and practice, but against the corruption of your natures, that which is all sin in one, the nursery, the spawn of all; that in which all particulars do as it were live, and move, and have their being, Mat. xv. 18, 19. Out of the corruption of the heart, as from a fountain, flows all the impurity of words and actions. You may stop up one current of sin, and another, but to little purpose, while the fountain still runs freely. It will overflow or bear down the dams you make to stop it, or find another passage when you have done all you can. If you do nothing to dry up the spring in the heart, to divert or dam up this or that passage in your practice will be to little purpose: Mat. xii. 33–35, while the tree, while the heart is evil, the fruit will be so. The evil treasure in the heart must be exhausted, else the product thereof will be evil things; that which is in the life will be dross while the heart is not refined.

The avoiding of some particular evils is but to pare the nails, which will grow again; but the mortifying of thy natural corruption is to go about to cut off the arm. This is to make sure work, that once cut off, can grow no more.

(2.) Set yourselves against a sinful temper of heart, not only against sinful acts. For such a temper is worse, more provoking, more dangerous, though it be less sensible than many evil acts; as a constant sickly temper is worse than a fit of the toothache, yea, than fits of the stone or gout, though the pain there be more acute and afflictive. A worldly, carnal, selfish, slothful, or lukewarm temper of heart, is far worse than some particular acts of worldliness, selfishness, sensuality, or lukewarmness. For the temper is fixed, and is a continued sin; the acts are transient. The temper is fruitful, being a pregnant disposedness to more and more acts suitable to it. The acts have no such pernicious pregnancy, and the Lord judges of us more by the bent of the heart than by some particular acts. He, the bent of whose heart is towards the world, the riches, pleasures, dignities of it, will be a worldling in the account of God, rather than he who sometimes by the force of temptation is hurried into a sordid act. And so of the rest, he whose heart is bent to please the flesh, &c., and the temper being less sensible, and not so much taken notice of, is the more dangerous, because the less watched and opposed, and the cure of it less minded and endeavoured.

Accordingly, the Lord proceeds severely against churches and persons, not only for wicked acts, but for a sinful temper, which is very apparent in what he threatens Laodicea, Rev. iii. 15, 16. It is a lukewarm temper that he so thunders against, it being so loathsome to him that for it he threatens to ease himself of her, as that which he nauseates and abhors, as we do that which we are sick of. This might be ruin to some in whom it was predominant; and in those whom he loves, and where it was not so prevalent, it could not escape without rebukes and chastenings, ver. 19. And the end thereof was not a desisting from this or that act only, but the change of their temper. 'Be zealous therefore and repent,' *i. e.* bewail, abhor that odious temper, and get it turned into one quite contrary. And thus must you do if you would comply with God's end in rebukes and chastenings, not only quit your old practices, but your former sinful temper. Instead of a worldly temper, get one that is heavenly, so that the bent of your hearts may be for the things above, that heavenly treasure; instead of a selfish temper, get one that is self-denying, that which will incline you to seek and mind the things of Christ, not your own things, and to resign up yourselves entirely to the serving of Christ's interest; instead of a carnal, sensual temper, that which is spiritual; instead of a slothful temper, that which will make you active and industrious, and laborious for Christ, for your souls and heavenly interest; instead of a lukewarm temper, that which will be zealous for God, and against sin, though you suffer for it; ardent in love and desires to Christ, fervent in spirit in serving him.

(3.) Against those sins, not only which you know at present, but against those which you shall know, and ought to take notice of as sins, though they have escaped your notice hitherto. Not only against those which you are convinced of to be sins, and your sins, but these also, for which you have sufficient means of conviction, though they have not been, or are not effectual. The rod has a voice. One thing that the Lord principally calls a people to, by judgments and afflictions, is to search and try their ways, to find out what evil is in them; and when afflictions and sufferings are continued, and drawn to a great length, notwithstanding prayer, and some other means used for the removal of them, their continuance is sometimes because the evils for which God is angry are not reformed, sometimes because they are not discovered and discerned. Those who suffer by them, do not take notice of them, are not or will not be convinced of them; and therefore those who think their fears, pressures, or sufferings of any kind, tedious and continued beyond their expectation, and are apt to cry out, 'How long, Lord,' &c., have a clear call, and are highly concerned, in answer to it, to search diligently, to search and try, to search again and again, whether there be any evil, any provocation in their hearts or ways which they have not observed, or not sufficiently taken notice of. They are not to content themselves with a superficial view, that which first offers itself; nor with former inquiries, though there have been some diligence in them; nor with common apprehensions of themselves or others concerning the ground of God's controversy. They may suspect they have not been inquisitive enough, or have been partial, or suffered false love, or the reputation or multitude of those who have concurred with them, or something or other, to hinder them from discerning some evil for which God is angry, and so ought to make a more impartial and stricter inquiry after it, and to give all diligence in the use of all appointed means to make a further discovery.

If this be our case, this is the course we ought to take. If, after all the means which have been used for freedom from what afflicts us publicly or personally, we find the Lord's anger is not yet turned away, but his hand is stretched out still; if our hopes have deceived us, and our expectations have been frustrate; if after some little reviving in our troubles, fears are renewed, and the clouds still return after the rain: we have hereupon some ground to suspect, that the cursed thing which troubles is not yet discovered, and that we do not yet discern the cause why the Lord is contending with us; and therefore are highly concerned to make a more strict and diligent search after it, and to resist and avoid whatever may have hindered us from conviction.

And great reason we have to engage ourselves thoroughly in such a course, if we consider but this only, that the Lord has proceeded against a people, yea, and destroyed them, for sins which they have not discovered, which they have not been convinced of (only sufficient means being offered for their conviction). Many have been ruined for their sins, which they have not known, being not willing, or not careful enough to know them.

We may see this in the ten tribes, and the account given of their ruin, 2 Kings xvii. 9. Secretly; *Hebr.*, They hid, or covered, or cloaked what they did. There were some specious and plausible pretences, wherewith what they did was covered; so that the sin and the sinfulness of it did not appear. Hereby it came to pass, that their sin was a secret to themselves. The act was open, public, visible (their high places, their images, their worship, which are the particulars immediately mentioned); but the sinfulness thereof was a secret. The excuses and pleas wherewith it was cloaked kept them from discerning it; they seem to have been ignorant or unconvinced of that sin, and yet they were ruined for it, ver. 23.

Wrath came also upon the other two tribes, upon the like account, for sins which they were not convinced of, the sinfulness of which they did not know or believe. That which principally hastened their ruin, was false worship, Jer. xliv. 21, 22; and yet even after the desolation of temple, city, and country, hereby we find them so far from being convinced, that this was their sin, that they ascribe what good they met with to the practice of it, and what mischiefs befell them to the forbearance of it, ver. 15, 17, 18, 19, where it is expressed by what they confirmed themselves against conviction: the approbation of their betters, the authority of the ancients, the example and concurrence of their rulers in all their cities, and the measures they took of the providence of God, in dispensing to them good or evil.

Yea, that which was the utter ruin of God's ancient people the Jews, their crucifying of Christ, was not known to be a sin by many of those who concurred to it. Therefore the apostle says, They did it ignorantly, Acts iii. 14, 15, 17; they were not thoroughly convinced that Jesus was the Messiah, though there was evidence enough to convince them, because they did not duly search into and observe it, so they sinned ignorantly, not knowing it was a sin, or such a sin. That was the condition of most of them, and yet for this that people was utterly rejected, and wrath came upon them to the utmost.

So that the Lord may proceed against a people, and often does it, for sins that they know not to be sins, and of the sinfulness of which they are not convinced. The ground of his controversy with them (when he is ready to destroy them), may be that which they little think of. They may be extremely endangered by that wherein they do not imagine their danger lies; that sin may be the great provocation, which they discern not to be their sin.

And therefore if you would comply with God's end in judging and afflicting, it may not be enough to put away the sin that you know, but you must search after those you yet do not know, and attend to the means which he offers for your conviction, and be careful to avoid whatsoever might hide a yet not observed sin from your eye, or might turn your eye from it, or might make you stiff against conviction. Use all means which may help you to a further discovery; you are called to it in a special manner. If you have reformed what is discovered, and yet the Lord's anger is not turned away, search your hearts and ways, even those that you have not suspected. Make use of the words as your light; hearken to conscience; observe your afflictions, what they seem to point at. Commune with your friends, with those that are disinterested; neglect not the charges of those that differ from you, no, not the reproaches of enemies, especially be importunate with God.

I have the longer insisted on this, because all things considered, it is to be feared, that the ground of the Lord's controversy with his people at this day, is either not fully discerned, or at least not removed.

(4.) Set yourselves not only against the outward acts of sin, but against the inward motions; not only against complete sin, but the embryos of sin; against it in its inward formation, when it is but breeding, or you find it first stirring, before it be brought forth, and be exposed to open view. Oppose it as soon as God sees it to be sin, before it appear in the sight of the world. A man may live so as the world can charge him with no sin; and yet there may be a world of sin in his heart, &c. An inward act or motion may be sinful, though it never appear outwardly; but there are many outward acts, which, without some inward sinful motion, would be neither good nor bad, but indifferent. Hezekiah's shewing his state and riches to the ambassadors of Babylon, might have been, as to the outward act, inoffensive, if some inward motion of pride or the like evil had not tainted it; but thereby it was rendered so sinful, as the Lord dreadfully threatens it, Isa. xxxix. 5, 6, 7; and so David's numbering the people, 2 Sam. xxiv. Nay, the best outward acts, those that are most holy, most eminent and exemplary, most extraordinary and heroical, by some inward irregular act and motion, may be quite spoiled and turned into sin. So was Jehu his reformation perverted; and so may the giving of all our goods to the poor, or the giving of our bodies to be burned, if the inward motions of the heart be not right in such outwardly glorious actings or sufferings, be quite depraved and sullied in the sight of God.

The sinfulness of outward acts is derived from inward and unlawful motions, Mat. xii. 35. Cleanse the heart, or else even the avoiding of outward sinful acts will be unclean; hence verses 33, 34, Luke vi. 43.

(5.) Set yourselves not only against sins that you are tempted to at present, but against those that you may be tempted to, though now you do not find them stirring, nor in motion, 2 Kings viii. 13. You should oppose yourselves where there is danger; now, we are many times in more danger of sin when we find it not stirring, and observe it not tempting us, than when we are aware of a temptation. It is found by experience, sin often gives the most dangerous and deadly assaults, after some cessation, after it has lain still and quiet, as though it would stir and tempt no more, as though it were subdued, and the heart and power of it broken.

(6.) Set yourselves not only against your own, but against your othermen's, sins. If you could avoid sin in your own persons, yet you may sin by others. If it were so, that you should never act sin personally, yet you may be guilty of others' sins, guilty either as principals or as accessories; and when you are but accessories, you sin, though not equally as when you act it.

You may be guilty of the sin when others are the actors of it, by commanding and ordering: so Saul of Doeg's, 1 Sam. xxii. 19; David of Joab's, 2 Sam. xii. 19. When you incense or provoke, as Jezebel did Ahab, 1 Kings xxi. 7; when you allure or entice, as the harlot, Prov. vii. 21, and those, Prov. i. 10, 11; when you counsel or advise, plot or contrive, as Jonadab of Amnon's, 2 Sam. xiii. 6; when you consent or approve, as Ahab to Jezebel, 1 Kings xxi. 19, Rom. i. 31; when praise or commend, Isa. v. 20, excuse or defend, Prov. xxiv. 24; when empower or capacitate, as 1 Tim. v. 22; though without any intention or suspicion that they will so employ their power.

So negatively, by not hindering it; so Pilate, Mark xv. 15. By not informing, declaring that it is sin, as false prophets, false worship. By not dissuading, reproving, correcting; so Eli, 1 Sam. iii. 13. By not removing the occasions; this was the blot in the character of the good kings of Judah, they take not away high places, 2 Kings xii. 3. By not mourning for others' sins; so Ezek. ix. 4, 6, only the mourners were to be delivered; those that mourned not, though they were not actors of those abominations, were to fall by the destroyer. By this it is evident, that not only your own, but your other-men's sins, may expose you to afflictions, yea, to destructive calamities. And Eli is a pregnant and dreadful instance of it; upon him and his family such judgments were poured down, as made the ears of those who heard thereof to tingle. And this not for the sins which himself acted; but for those which he restrained not, when he might and ought to have hindered the actors. So that we comply not with the Lord's end in afflicting and judging us, though our own sin be taken away, if we do anything to promote sin in others, nay, if we do not what we ought, and all that in us lies, to hinder others from sinning; if we do not reform, not only ourselves, but our families, our relations, and all over whom we have any power or any influence; and if we do not mourn and humble ourselves, and afflict our souls for what we have not power to reform.

(7.) Set yourselves against sin, not when it appears in its own colours, but when it puts on a disguise. If we would answer the Lord's end in chastening, we must not only put away sin when it shews its native face, which is so ugly and odious as it will affright an awakened conscience, but when it puts on a mask, and hides its ugliness with fair colours. When there is danger that sin may have no more entertainment, it will borrow a better habit, that it may procure a new admission. Sin is like the devil its father; he would not appear to our first parents in his own likeness, but in a serpent, which was then a harmless and sociable creature. So after, he would not offer himself to Saul in his own shape, but in the habit of Samuel. So sin uses not to appear in its own colours; for then, where there is anything of an enlightened conscience, men would not dare to meddle with it. Satan clothes it in another habit; and when one is worn out, or the Lord enables us to see through it, it takes another, and turns itself into any shape rather than it will be quite excluded. If you would have this to be the fruit of afflictions, the taking away of your sin, you must reject it in every appearance and habit; not only when it is apparently a work of darkness, but when it is transformed into an appearance of light.

It may be you are afraid of worldliness, as it is declared in Scripture to be no better than whoredom, drunkenness, or idolatry. Oh but take heed of it, when it puts on the fair colours of diligence in a lawful calling, or necessary providing for family and posterity!

It may be you abhor false worship when it appears, as it is, to be an invading of God's prerogative and an advancing of man's will and wisdom before that of Christ. Oh but take heed of it, when masked with the pretences of order, decency, reverence, and submission to our betters!

It may be want of love to the brethren is dreadful, when branded as a damning sin, and a sign of an unregenerate state. Oh but take heed of it, when coloured with zeal for the truth, or for a way we count best; and they, as dissenters or opposers, fancied to be unworthy of our love, and the acts and expressions of it!

To find our own pleasure on the Lord's day, and to neglect duties of religion in private or families, you may count, as it is, a great profaneness; but take heed of this profaneness in another garb, beware of being less conscientious under a pretence of gospel liberty.

You know to despise Christ's messengers is to despise Christ; you will be afraid of this. But take heed of despising them under other disguises, as legal teachers, or ministers of the letter, or men of low ordinary gifts, or under any other mask which Satan may help you to.

Jeroboam would not bring in idolatry in an Egyptian dress, to imitate them, as in the wilderness, that was too gross, too coarse; but masked with reason of state, necessity, and conveniency, 1 Kings xii. 26-28.

2. Set yourselves against some sins more especially. As afflictions and judgments should help us against all more or less, so, if we duly improve them, we must make use of them to help us against some sins especially, viz. those that are most dangerous; those that we are in most danger of, and those that we are judged or corrected for. To instance in some particulars; if you would comply with God's end in afflictions and calamities, so as by these your iniquity may be purged,

(1.) Set yourselves especially against mother sins, those which are most pregnant, which give life, strength, and motion to many others. If you would have all sin taken away, if you would have this to be the fruit, &c., be careful to take away those that maintain all. Besides natural corruption, the root and body of all (of which before), there are some main branches, some cardinal evils observable, upon which the rest of our sins are but as it were dependents, are but sprigs shooting out of the main arms of this tree of sin and death. Now, the principals being suppressed, the other, if they fall not of themselves, will with more ease be quelled.

These are as it were the vital parts of the body of sin, which, wounded and mortified, the rest would quickly expire. These are Satan's strongest holds, which command all about them; demolish these forts, and the rest will easily be brought under. The other are but ministering sins, the servants of these. Now, as when the dragon was cast down his angels were cast out with him, so cast down the master sins, and the rest, the retainers, will fall with him.

Unbelief. That is the root in a manner of all sins; that which supports, conveys sap and life to them; that which cumbers the ground, hinders anything from thriving near it, that might hinder the growth of sin. Labour to pluck up this root of bitterness, and the branches will wither; but lesser sins will never die, though they may be restrained, till unbelief be plucked up.

Besides this, the principal mother sins are those mentioned by the apostle: 1 John ii. 16, 'The lust of the flesh,' sensuality, the affecting to gratify the flesh, our bodies with ease and pleasure. 'The lust of the eye,' *i.e.* covetousness, the affecting of riches, worldly profits and advantages. 'The pride of life,' the affection of a carnal and selfish excellency. Set yourselves principally against these three, and the overthrow of them will be the ruin of that army of lusts which war against your souls; for the rest are maintained, have their strength, support, and activeness from them.

Intemperance, incontinence, slothfulness, an immoderate affecting of ease, sleep, pastime, and the numerous evils that have their rise and dependence hereupon, are removed, when sensuality, the lust of the flesh, is taken away.

Then for covetousness or worldliness, called the lust of the eye, what a multitude of sins doth this breed, and nourish, and set a-work! Injustice, oppression, unfaithfulness in words or oaths, fraud, deceit, simulation, dissimulation, neglect of soul and heavenly interest, omission, or slight performance of holy duties, perplexing cares, mercenariness: all these, and many more, issue out of this one cursed womb. Now by killing the dam you starve the young, this loathsome brood will languish; kill this master-sin, and its numerous retinue and dependents will be undone.

So for pride; this is a radical sin, the branches of it are self-dependence, self-conceit, carnal confidence, presumptuous curiosity, self-seeking, ambition, hypocrisy, contempt of others, self-magnifying, ostentation in words, actions, fashions, entertainments; discontent, contention, disdain, detraction. Pluck but up this one root of pride, and all these, and many more, will die and wither. Reformation of some particular evils is but like Samson's shaving his locks, which in time did grow again. If Delilah would have made sure work, and prevented the recovery of his strength, she should have plucked it out by the roots. Indeed, the mortifying of these capital evils, unbelief, sensuality, worldliness, and pride, is as the cutting off the head. There is little danger of the growing of these lesser evils, which are but as the hair, when that is done. You untile the house in other attempts; but by bending your main force against these supporters of the rest, you pull down the pillars of it.

(2.) Set yourselves especially against those sins which you are most subject to. You may judge of it by these severals, which I will but name. Observe what evil your constitution or complexion most inclines to, what your calling or course of life, your employment, or want of employment, most exposes you to; what has formerly most commanded your affections, your love, delight, desire, zeal, &c.; or what custom has most riveted you in; or what you are fastened to by your interest, credit, or profit, or ease, or safety. This sin you may look upon as the champion of the rest, that which gives them heart and strength, which encourages and sets them on. If this fall, the victory over the rest will be easier; even as when Goliath was slain, the Philistines fled.

The king of Syria knew of what consequence Ahab's death would be to the obtaining of the victory; Jehoshaphat and the men of Judah were but his dependents, and would follow, and be involved in his success, good or bad; and therefore he adviseth, 2 Chron. xviii. 30. Many other sins are dependents on these; it leads, acts, employs, enforceth them; let these be taken away, and the rest will scarce stand out against you.

(3.) Set yourselves especially against the sins of the times. There is no complying with God's end, if you do not utterly abandon these. They are so visible, I need not mention them. Atheism, apostasy, perjury, unfaithfulness to God and men, advancing mens' advices before divine appointments, profaning his day, name, worship, all that is truly holy; uncleanness, intemperance, violence, contempt of the gospel, rebellion against, putting away the word of life; abuse of his messengers; and others, which may be discerned without any troublesome search. For this people declare their sin as Sodom, and it is heightened with impudence, universality, incorrigibleness. Oh keep at the greatest distance from these, touch not with them in any degree. Avoid not only these abominations, but the appearance of them; be neither actors nor partakers herein, if you have any regard of complying with the Lord's end in judging us.

(4.) Set yourselves against those sins especially, which are less disgraceful amongst professors; such as custom and opinion has made less reproachful, whatever they be in themselves, and in the sight of God, than the gross pollutions of the world. Let me instance in some: eagerness after the world; indifferency towards holiness, the growth, power, and life of it; superficialness in holy duties; unfruitfulness under the means of grace; unteachableness under the rod; unserviceableness in their places; an unbridled tongue; loose, careless, unwatchful walking: passionateness, pride, selfishness, unpeaceableness, envy, strife, debate, malice, revenge, evil-speaking, detraction, and many others, too rife amongst professors.

Some of these are as heinous in themselves, as great sins in God's account, and as much branded in Scripture, as those which are counted the spots of the wicked, swearing, uncleanness, drunkenness; and the special aggravations which burden all the sins of sons and daughters, make them all grievous provocations.

But because they are too common amongst professors, we are too apt to make light of them; we give them more allowance, and count them less reproachful; and so are in danger to overlook them, when God is calling us to purge them out, and dealing with us by his providence to take them away.

If you would comply with God's end, take special care that these be abandoned; judge of them, not according to common opinion, but as the Lord judges of them, and think yourselves as much concerned to free heart and life from these, as you think others concerned to abandon idolatry, whoredom, or drunkenness.

(5.) Set yourselves especially against those evils for which the Lord judges and afflicts; these, above all, should be regarded by those who would answer the Lord's end, &c. If all others should be put away, and these only retained, the Lord's end would not be answered; though he would have all iniquity purged, yet his hand is more particularly against these, and so should ours.

Now that we may comply with the Lord's design against these sins, it is necessary that we should discern them, and endeavour to make a discovery of them. In order hereto, observe in general, that there may be, and ordinarily is, a concurrence of many sins to the bringing of common judgments, or sharp and long afflictions, though some sins may contribute more than others hereto. We may be long a-ripening for his judgments and severe dispensations. A continued evil course, made up of divers sins, is ordinarily precedent to this; though, when we are ripe for it, some particular act or acts may occasion the Lord to put in the sickle, and forbear no longer. And those particular provocations, upon which judgment breaks out, and affliction seizes on us, as they are sometimes more, so they may be sometimes less, heinous than those, or some of those, that prepared and disposed us at some distance for such severity.

As a child may somewhile, by several faults, provoke his father to correct him, before he will take the rod, though upon some particular offence he may resolve to bear no longer, but scourge him presently, though that offence be not always the greatest; he may mind him, while he is correcting him, of others which made way for that severity, and designs the reforming of others, as well as of that particular, upon which immediately he made use of the rod.

And, therefore, when we would discover evils, for which the Lord is judging or correcting us, we should not look only at this or that particular, which might have the next hand in bringing an evil day upon us, but at those also that have been preparing and ripening us for it at some distance; for the influence of these may be as great, though more remote, in procuring the evils that afflict us; and the Lord's designs in dealing severely will not be answered, unless both these and the other be taken away. And, accordingly, I would have you make use of the directions I shall give, to help you in the discovery of those sins and iniquities, for which the Lord has been judging and afflicting us; and therein I design principally a discovery of those evils amongst professors, which have had these woful effects upon us.

If you would discern what the sins are, for which the Lord hath been, and is, contending with us, the observance of these particulars may be helpful.

1. Search for them. If you would make a discovery, you must make a

search, and pursue it personally, diligently, thoroughly. The church, in her lamentable condition, thought herself much concerned to take this course, Lam. iii. 40.

Personally, our ways. There is something of the accursed thing hid in every of our tents. Each of us is, more or less have been, an Achan to ourselves, and the place where we live. We may say, I, and I have troubled. Each of us should search our own tent, our own hearts and ways, and not put off this duty to others, as more guilty than ourselves. We should not be smiting others with the charge of this and that guilt; but every one smite upon his own thigh, and say not, Oh what evil has such and such a person or party done? But what evil have I done? The Lord's judiciary or correcting hand has reached us all one way or other, and found us all guilty, and so we should find ourselves, if we would have a stop of severe proceedings.

Diligently. Throughly, every corner of our souls, the most secret recesses of our hearts; all the parts of our lives, all our designs, all our actings, all our ways, even those that we have not suspected, those that have passed for innocent, or better than innocent. That which seems to be best in the vessel may raise the storm; even in a Jonah may more cause of it be found than in the heathen mariners. That which threatens the wreck of all, may be there where we little imagine it to be, and may be that which we have no suspicious thought of, and which, it may be, we have thought it a crime to suspect. Who, before the discovery, would not have thought it a sin to have suspected Jonah as the malefactor rather than the profane mariners? Search, therefore, everywhere, everything; that which we count best may have a provocation in it.

2. Beware of those things which may hinder you from discerning those sins, and being convinced of them; which may shut your eye or divert it; which may make you unwilling to see, willing to overlook, resolve not to be convinced, or loath to yield to conviction. There are many things of this nature and tendency, which you are to avoid and resist, which you are to observe, and be watchful that they do you not this disservice.

(1.) *Self-love.* That blinds the eye, keeps it close shut, will not let it see that which is odious and loathsome in himself, that which disparages and is a just occasion of ill reflections upon himself; makes him loath to see what should make him vile in his own sight; unwilling to see that which would trouble, disquiet, affright him; or to take notice of what might be a just cause to judge, condemn, pass sentence against himself as a common incendiary, a troubler of the community where he lives; makes him readier to see a mote in another's eye than a beam in his own, and to censure and condemn any rather than himself. Self-love will see all ruined rather than see itself the cause of it; and fancy the ground of it anywhere rather than where it is, when it is at home. Self-love will be blind where you are concerned to be most quick-sighted: this must be suppressed, mortified, and what remains of it not at all consulted with or hearkened to, if you would discover the evil.

(2.) *Subtlety.* To find out pretences and arguments for the hiding and covering of sin, and to manage them so as to stave off conviction, and to answer or evade whatever tends to fasten it. Naturally there is such a subtlety in us, and we are prone to make use of it; and many times art is added to nature, and joins fig-leaves together so artificially, as the nakedness of sin is covered, and the shame of it hid from our eyes. Thus the Israelites, those of the ten tribes, so cloaked and covered their sin that it was a secret to them, they discerned it not to be a sin, 2 Kings xvii. 9; *Hebr.*, they covered or cloaked what they did. They had such pleas and arguments for their false worship, it was so cloaked and disguised thereby, that it did not appear to them to be a sin: the sinfulness of it was a secret.

Saul was a notable artist this way. The prophet had much to do to convince him that a plain act of disobedience was a sin, 1 Sam. xv. 3. There is the command. Saul and the people destroy all the persons, but only Agag, and all the cattle that were vile and refuse, ver. 9. Hereupon he is confident he had not sinned, ver. 13. And when Samuel tells him, that the bleating and lowing of the cattle was sufficient to confute him; for God had commanded to destroy all, and he had spared some, ver. 14; he shifts off this very speciously and plausibly, ver. 15. The best only are spared; and these not for our own use, but for the honour and service of God, to sacrifice to him, and express our thankfulness for so great a victory. And if this were a fault, the people did it, not I. Upon this he confidently justifies himself, and persists in it, after Samuel had said much for his conviction, ver. 20; and when he could no longer hold out in justifying the act wholly, yet he has something to allege, which might excuse and extenuate it, ver. 24.

We need not wonder, when men are still as subtle to deceive themselves, and have the advantage of much more art than the world had of old, that arguments are mustered up, to make good and justify so many sins; and that it is so exceeding hard, in many cases and circumstances, to convince persons of their sin.

If you would discover the sins for which God judges and afflicts us, you must get a willingness to be convinced, and not seek evasions, nor catch at fair pretences, nor study arguments tending to prove your sin is no sin; nor accept of them from the invention of others.

(3.) *Pride.* A good conceit of themselves, an over-weaning opinion of their own holiness, uprightness, or innocency. This makes men very backward to believe that they are guilty of such evils as provoke the Lord to severe proceedings, and apt to think, conclude, the cause of such severity is in others rather than themselves.

This blinded the pharisees. Of all the sects among the Jews in Christ's time, they had the reputation of greatest holiness. They thought themselves, and were thought by others, to be the most eminent for piety and righteousness; and this made them stiff against whatever was urged, by Christ himself, for their conviction.

And this hindered Laodicea from the sight of that for which Christ had a controversy with her, Rev. iii. 17. She made account she was rich, &c., and this hindered her from the knowledge, from the sight of that which was her sin and misery. 'And knowest not,' &c.

And this hindered the Jews of old from discerning their sin and sinfulness, when the prophet set it before their eyes; they thought themselves better than any people in the world, the only people of God, honoured and privileged by him above all others; and they had ocular demonstrations of it, the temple of God amongst them; and with this they answer (though it was but a lying, a deceiving allegation) all that the prophet made use of for their conviction, Jer. vii. 4. And hence it came to pass, that all which the prophet alleged for the discovery of their sin was to no purpose, ver. 13.

(4.) *Interest.* There is nothing more conceals sin; nothing so much hinders men from discerning and being convinced of their sin, than interest. When such a way helps him to riches and dignity, and supports him in such a state; or when it ministers pleasure to him, and is the solace of his life; or when it secures him, keeps him safe; and if he should leave it, himself and outward concernments would be evidently exposed and endangered. Oh, he will see anything rather than see this to be his sin. He will use all shifts, find out a hundred evasions, rather than yield to conviction here. And any plea for it will seem of more force than the most cogent argument against it.

The world has one instance of the power of interest for this purpose, which is so pregnant, as I need add no more.

It is as evident, as can be expected in anything of that nature, that there is a horrible degeneracy in church-government, worship, and discipline, amongst the Romanists, and those who follow them. It is palpably quite another thing than that which was primitive and apostolical; there are other ordinances, other officers, other administrations of worship and discipline, than what were appointed in Scripture. The apostasy of latter times herein is so great and so plain, as it may seem matter of astonishment that any should in the least doubt of it. And yet there are multitudes who plead, and argue, and dispute, and fill whole volumes with defences of such a degeneracy, and revile and persecute all that will not yield to them, *i.e.* those that will not be persuaded that midnight is noon-day. Now, what is it that does thus blind and infatuate them, but interest? They, by their new officers and administrations, gain riches, and honours, and power hereby. This furnishes them with arguments, this helps them to answers and evasions, as to whatever is brought from Scripture for their conviction. And this makes them resolute to believe (say what you will to the contrary) that darkness is light; and so continues the Christian world in such a dreadful apostasy, from generation to generation. Oh the fatal, the stupendous, the pernicious power of interest! That one argument of Demetrius, Acts xix. 25, ' Sirs, ye know that by this craft we have our wealth,' was of more force with those of his temper than all the reasonings of the apostle Paul himself to the contrary. Oh how hard was it to let them see idolatry in a practice so much for their interest!

Those that would discover the sin, for which the Lord judges and afflicts, must be disengaged from the power of worldly and carnal interest. This makes conviction always difficult, sometimes impossible.

(5.) *The judgment or example of those whom we reverence*, and have an high esteem of. It will not be easy to believe that to be a sin in us, which is countenanced by the judgment or example of those who are got high in our opinion; by their antiquity, or by their authority, or by the greatness of their parts and accomplishments, or by their exemplary holiness, or by their known conscientiousness in other things. And yet it is possible that the Lord may proceed against us for some evil, that has most of these, or all of these, to countenance it, and to secure it from being thought what indeed it is, a provocation in the sight of God. It may be you may have the judgment and practice of many of the ancients, of the best of your ancestors, for it. You may have the approbation of your rulers, of your betters, of your greatest, or of your dearest relatives, of your teachers for it. It may be the judgment of some of greatest parts, learning, and other accomplishments; such as you may think best able to discern betwixt things that differ, and to judge what is good and what evil. It may be the practice of some that are really holy, and truly conscientious in other particulars; and yet for all this, it may be a sin, and a ground of God's controversy with you. But how hard will it be to believe it, and to be convinced that it is so, against such a stream, so powerful to bear down all before it which tends to conviction!

The Jews' provocation was great, and brought dreadful evils upon them; and yet they would see no evil in it, notwithstanding all that the Lord, by the prophet, said to discover it; because they had the judgment and practice of those whom they did most reverence to defend it, Jer. xliv. 17, 19, their ancestors, and rulers, and husbands. How many sinful mistakes, in opinion and practice, are defended to this day by the authority of the ancients, those who were learned and holy, besides the plea of their antiquity.

The Pharisees, by such means, shut their own eyes and the eyes of others, so as they could not see sin in the grossest unbelief, John vii. 48; as if they had said, Can that be a sin which neither those of greatest authority, nor those of greatest reputation amongst us for wisdom, learning, and holiness (such were the pharisees in those days) judge to be a sin, nay, which they judge to be a duty? Or can that be a duty which persons of such eminency every way do judge to be a sin?

The difficulty will be greater, and it will be more hard to believe that to be our sin, when multitudes of those whom we count most conscientious concur with us therein. And yet so it may be; possibly the Lord may contend with us for something, wherein we have the concurrence of many who are truly conscientious. And therefore if we would discover the evils for which the Lord afflicts, we must follow no other rule in judging thereof but what he has prescribed. To the law and to the testimony; examine hearts and ways by that, not by the judgment or example either of the greatest or of the best; for these may deceive, yea, it may be, blind and delude us, and instead of being a light, may shut us up in darkness, and hinder us from discovering what we are so much concerned to discover.

(6.) *Dissension.* When a people are divided, and split into parties, and the differences pursued with heat and animosity, they are apt to transfer the guilt, each party from itself, to those from whom they are rent, and to have their eyes so intent and fixed upon the guilt of those whom they affect not, as to overlook their own. In this case Ephraim is against Manasseh, and Manasseh against Ephraim, and both against Judah. Each party will charge the other, and both will be ready to charge a third, but no one to take the guilt to itself. And so the end of afflictions and calamities is in danger to be lost amongst them; whiles, though all suffer, yet none will cry Guilty as to himself; but though they smite one another, and God is smiting them all, yet none smites upon his thigh, and says, ' What evil have I done, to bring this evil day upon us?' Whereas the Lord's judging and process against them all argues all to be guilty, and the guilt to lie amongst them all, in each party some of it. And the way to know the total of God's charge against us is to observe the particulars wherein each party is guilty, and to put them all together, inquiring after them, and yielding to conviction in the severals, without partiality.

If you would pursue this concernment successfully, passionately,* take heed of addicting yourselves to a party. Besides other mischievous consequents of it, it tends much to hinder you from discerning your sin, and the sin of those you give up yourselves to, when the Lord for it is proceeding against you jointly. Those that give up themselves to a party are under a strong temptation to be, as in other cases, partial, so also in finding out their guilt. For what self-love does to a person, that such a love, a little further extended, doth to a party: blinds the eye, and will not suffer it to see its guilt, nor take an impartial view of it, nor pass a true judgment upon it, or a just sentence against it.

Oh take heed you be not so keen against others as to have no edge left against the evils that are your own, or those of your own way and persuasion.

(7.) *Prejudice* against those who are ready to tell us of our sin. The

* Qu. ' dispassionately '?—ED.

truest information, the most faithful discovery will be lost on us if we be prejudiced against those that offer it. This will hinder us from believing it, make us misinterpret it, tempt us to reject it. Ahab's soul was closed against all conviction from Micaiah, when he declares that he hated him, 1 Kings xxii. 8. And the Jews were hardened against all Jeremiah's endeavours to make known their sin, and convince them of it, when they had received this prejudice against him, that he sided with the Chaldeans.

If you would know your sin, look upon him as a friend, whatever he be otherwise, that will make it known to you, Ps. cxli. 5.

(8.) *The exceeding vileness of others* may hinder us from taking notice of our own sinful distempers or miscarriages. When gross and horrid wickedness exceedingly abounds in the place and times where we live, we may be apt to think that there is no other cause of the judgments there executed, and so professors may be tempted to overlook the more refined evils that are amongst themselves, and consequently may take little notice of that which is in great part the ground of God's controversy. The sins of sons and daughters, though not in their own nature so horrid and grievous as the wickedness of the debauched world, may, by reason of special aggravations, whereof the sins of others are not capable, be great provocations in the sight of God. Though they pass not for crying sins, yet may they cry aloud in God's ear. He may resent them as abominations, though we make light of them, and may proceed severely against professors for them, as those whom he abhors, Deut. xxxii. 19, Amos. iii. 2. He had chosen them, above all on earth, to be his peculiar people, and admitted them into a covenant with himself singularly gracious, and therefore the sins which he passed by in others, he would punish most severely in them. And therefore we have little reason to be so severe against the sins of others, as to let our own escape a severe inquisition and censure.

These are some of the impediments which may hinder us from finding out the sins for which the Lord hath been judging and afflicting us. If we would discover them, these must be removed, avoided, rested.* We must take notice of them, as evils like to obstruct us in our course of complying with the Lord's end, and must be watchful against them.

3. Listen unto conscience. It has light and power to make you know your sin. It is God's officer, his deputy; he has placed it in your breasts for this purpose, to discover sin.

Conscience hath the light of a rule. The κοιναί ἔννοιαι, common notions of good and evil are planted in it. Hence that of the apostle, Rom. ii. 14, 15. The Gentiles, which had not the law of Moses, yet in that they had a conscience, they had a law discovering what is good and what evil. And where this implanted law is obscure or defective (the tables of it being much broken by the fall), it may be repaired, and the defects of it supplied by the written word. So that there is a light in it to discover what is sin, what is evil.

Also it hath the office of a witness, and brings in evidence for or against a person, according as he hath demeaned himself towards the rule, Rom. ii. 15. And it is called συνείδησις, which is a man's knowing that he hath done, or not done, what the rule requires; and so is a witness for or against him, either pleading for him as not guilty, or accusing him as a transgressor. Now the way to know your crime is to inquire of your accuser; if you would have a discovery, and want evidence, hearken to the witness, that which God has appointed to perform this office within you.

* Qu. 'resisted'? or 'arrested'?—ED.

It hath also the authority of a judge, and passeth sentence according to evidence, 1 John iii. 20, 21, οἴκειον δικαστήριον, *Naz.*

The whole process of conscience, in the execution of its several offices, for the discovery of sin, you may discern in such a syllogism. Whosoever doth thus and thus, sins against God (this it manifests as a law or rule); but thou hast done thus and thus (this evidence it brings in as a witness), therefore thou hast sinned against God. (There is its sentence as a judge.)

You see conscience is every way furnished to help you to the discovery of sin; make use of it accordingly. Get it more and more enlightened, that it may give true and full direction. Beware it be not corrupted with false principles, that the rule be not made crooked, and bended to favour you in any evil. And order it so as it may prove a true and faithful witness; let it not be bribed, nor overawed, nor cut short; hear it out, give it liberty and encouragement to speak the whole truth. Let it not be baffled, as modest witnesses are sometimes by wrangling advocates. Observe its first reports, take them in their genuine sense, before they be perverted, darkened, eluded by the arts and sophistry, the shifts, cavils, evasions of corrupt and deceitful hearts, which would deal with the plain witness of conscience, as cunning lawyers are wont to do with the evidence that makes against them.

This is the way to have conscience help you to a true judgment concerning the sins for which you are afflicted.

4. Hearken to others. Neglect not the help of any who may be serviceable for this discovery; and there are many who may contribute to it, friends, strangers, different parties, yea, your enemies; but especially those who are called to the guidance of your souls. *Plus vident oculi, quam oculus.* The more eyes, the better and the fuller discovery. That which escapes your sight may be obvious to another; he may have a more discerning faculty, and better advantages, and may be freer from those impediments which hinder your prospect.

There is a special obligement upon friends to be helpful to one another herein. The laws of friendship require a discovery of that which endangers one another. You would count him unworthy the name of a friend, who knowing a thief or an incendiary to lurk in your family, with a design to kill, or rob, or burn your house, would conceal it from you, and not acquaint you with it on his own accord. There is no such thief, murderer, incendiary, as sin: it more endangers us, and those concernments that are more precious than goods, or house, or life; and that most endangers us, by which the Lord's anger is already kindled against us. Silence or concealment in this case is treachery. He is the most faithful friend, and worthy of most esteem and affection, that deals most plainly with us, in reference to the discovery of our sin. He that is reserved in this case is but a false friend, a mere pretender to love, whereas, indeed, he hates his brother in his heart, Lev. xix. 17.

And because this act of love, though most to be valued, is too unacceptable to our perverse natures, we should provoke and encourage one another to this office; when we are together, this we should commune of, especially in a day of affliction. This should be one of our principal questions and inquiries, Oh wherefore is the Lord's anger gone out against us? What is the cause that it is not yet turned away? We should get every one to declare, and mark every one's opinion concerning it.

Hearken to strangers. Their judgments are more to be regarded, because they are not concerned in our interests, or in our differences, or in our sufferings. And those that are disinterested may pass the truest judgment; they have less bias to mislead them; and therefore, if we have opportunity to know it, their opinion should not be neglected concerning the cause of our calamities or afflictions.

Hearken to those who differ from us. They may be less partial to us than we to ourselves, and are under less temptation to spare us than we to spare ourselves. If the evils were observed, with which the differing parties amongst us do charge each other, and the sum of each charge put together, out of the whole might be made a better collection of the ground of God's controversy with us all, than each party will make for itself. Those that differ from us may, and will see that in us that we cannot or will not see in ourselves. Therefore, the way to understand fully why the Lord contends with us, is to take notice, not only of what we see ourselves, but what others may see for us, and charge us with, examining impartially how far their charge is just.

The accusations of enemies are not to be neglected. You may have heard of one who, intending to wound his enemy, lanced an imposthume, which otherwise might have been mortal to him. We are prejudiced against what comes from an enemy, as being the issue of hatred and malice; but even malice sometimes speaks a truth when it will serve a turn; when it tends to the disgrace and disparagement of the accused, and may render them odious; and that which discovers our sin, though it tend to our shame, serves our turn as well as theirs. We are not so much to regard whether they charge us maliciously, as whether they charge us truly; and so far as their suggestion is true, from what mind soever it proceeds, and whatever design they have in it, let us make use of it for our conviction, and so turn the poison into a medicine.

When Judah and Israel were in the field, ready to join in battle one against the other, Abijah, the king of Judah, declares to Jeroboam and his followers, the sin which they took no notice of, 2 Chron. xiii. 8, 9. If Jeroboam had made right use of this discovery, though it was the accusation of an enemy, it would have done him far better service than his army of eight hundred thousand mighty men.

5. Reform what evils you know already, if you would have a discovery of those you know not. Proceed against them effectually, till they be mortified in the heart, and cut off from the life. A good improvement of what light we have is the way to have more. That promise is of large extent, and may reach this case: Mat. xxv. 29, Mark iv. 25, 'Him that hath,' *i. e.* who duly uses and improves what he hath, 'more shall be given.' And as in truths, the practice of what we know, is the way to know more, according to that of Christ, John vii. 17, so in reference to sin, he that purges out that which he discovers, shall not want discovery of what the Lord would have purged out by afflictions; but if you tolerate any sins which you know, this may provoke the Lord to deny you the knowledge of what you suffer for. Such abuse and non-improvement of light may justly be punished with darkness. Those who make themselves like idols in one respect, so as to have hands and act not against the sin which they see, may be left to be like idols in another respect, so as to have eyes, yet not to see the sin which they smart for.

6. Observe carefully the judgments and afflictions which are upon you, or upon the place where you live. There is sometimes such a similitude betwixt the judgment and the sin, that he that knows the one may know the other. A strict observance of the calamity may help us to discern the sin which brought it. There is often a proportion between the sin and the punishment, either in the substance thereof, or some remarkable circum-

stance; particularly, this is observable, 1. Sometimes in the things wherein we suffer. Babylon made herself drunk with the blood of the saints, and she must have blood to drink, Rev. xvii. 6, and xvi. 6. King Asa puts the seer into prison, and the stocks (see the same word, Jer. xx. 2, and xxix. 26), and he is struck with a disease in his feet, 2 Chron. xvi. 10, 12; Adonibezek cut off the thumbs and great toes of others, and he himself had his thumbs and toes cut off, and by the likeness of his sufferings is led to the sight of his sin, Judges i. 6, 7.

Sometimes in the parties or instruments by which we suffer. David sins in his indulgence and inordinate affection to Absalom, and Absalom is made the instrument to afflict him.

Sometimes in the time. When Belshazzar is drinking in the vessels of the temple, and praising his gods of gold, &c., and at the same hour appears the sentence for his ruin, Dan. v. 4, 5.

Sometimes in the measure. The rich sensualist affords not Lazarus the crumbs of his table, and he himself is denied drops of water, Luke xvi.

Sometimes in the manner. Jacob comes, as the elder, to Isaac, and deludes him; and Leah comes, as the younger, to Jacob, and so he himself is deluded.

7. Make use of the word. Nothing comparable to that, for its virtue and power to discover sin, and convince you of it. It is a clear, a searching, a convincing, an undeceiving light. Your own hearts and consciences may delude you; others may abuse you, and be too favourable or too severe, may represent you better or worse than you are; but the word will not deceive you; nor, if you make due use of it, will it suffer you to be deceived. It will help you to discern that which yourselves or others will not, or cannot, otherwise see: Heb. iv. 12, 13, 'mind and spirit.' It will discover a difference betwixt those things which are most hard to be distinguished, the mind and spirit. It will help you to discern those things that are best, $\dot{\alpha}\varrho\mu\tilde{\omega}\nu$, the nerves, the least parts, and those things that are most secret, and have most to fence them from our sight: the marrow, that which is within, not only the skin and the flesh, but the bones. It will not only discover your actions, but your thoughts and imaginations; the most secret plots and contrivances, the most retired motions and workings of mind and spirit, $\varkappa\varrho\iota\tau\iota\varkappa\dot{o}\varsigma$ $\dot{\varepsilon}\nu\theta\upsilon\mu\dot{\eta}\sigma\varepsilon\omega\nu$ $\varkappa\dot{\alpha}\iota$ $\dot{\varepsilon}\nu\nu\omicron\iota\tilde{\omega}\nu$. It is a critic in discerning these. It will help you to an exact and accurate judgment of the most obscure and subtle devices of your hearts; and, ver. 13, there is nothing so small, so secret, so disguised, so concealed, but this will bring it to light, and make it manifest. 'All are naked and open to the eyes of that' $\pi\varrho\dot{o}\varsigma$ $\dot{o}\nu$ $\dot{\eta}\mu\tilde{\iota}\nu$ $\dot{o}$ $\lambda o\gamma\dot{o}\varsigma$, 'of which we are speaking.' As all the secrets, the entrails, the inwards of a sacrifice were exposed to the eye of the priest, when he had flayed it, and cut it down the back, and laid it all open, $\tau\varepsilon\tau\varrho\alpha\chi\eta\lambda\iota\sigma\mu\dot{\varepsilon}\nu\alpha$, &c. It will flay off all coverings and pretences, which hinder you from discerning your sin, or being convinced of it, 1 Cor. xiv. 24, 25. These are his sins, even the secrets of his heart, made manifest to himself by the convincing power of the word.

There are three parts of the word especially useful for this purpose.

(1.) The commands or injunctions. Observe what it requires, what it forbids. In this respect it is a rule; and that is *index sui et obliqui*, discovers both your duty and your sin. If you would discern the crookedness of a thing, you bring it to the rule. Bring your hearts, the motions, the designs, the temper of them, to this rule, if you would see what crookedness the Lord is correcting in you. What was the temper of your hearts before affliction seized on you? What was the bent, the designs, the contrivances, the language, the posture, the motions of it? Whither did the stream of it run? Upon what was the face of it set? Compare these with the rule; you may thereby see what was wrong there, and what called for the rod, and what occasion the Lord had to make use of it.

Bring your lives, your actions, your ways to the rule; call to mind how they were ordered before trouble came. The word may, and will, if duly observed, point at that which is your troubler, Rom. vii. 12. It is 'holy, just, good.' And that which is so helps you to discern what is not so in the sight of God, and consequently what he is angry at, and why he expresses his anger in afflictions and chastenings.

The word is compared to a glass, James i. 23–25. If you would see what spots the Lord would have washed off, what defilement and pollution he would have purged, look into the glass, view your hearts and lives there, and do it, according to the import of the word there. Content not yourselves with a glance, a transient view, but παρακύψας, bend down to it, as one that would take pains to see, and has a mind to take all the advantages this glass will afford for a full self-discovery.

(2.) The threatenings. These may contribute very much to the discovery of the sins by which we suffer. In order hereto, observe what is threatened in the word of God, and for what; what calamities or judgments are denounced, and for what sins. If the judgments or afflictions be upon us that we find threatened, and the sins be amongst us for which they are threatened, this will be a good ground to conclude that those are the sins for which we are judged and afflicted. To instance in two or three, which may lead us to the sight of some sins, for which in all probability the Lord hath proceeded against us.

2 Thes. ii. 10, 11. Here some are threatened to be given up to strong delusions; and the sin for which this terrible judgment is threatened, is not receiving of the truth in the love of it, and taking pleasure in unrighteousness; *i. e.* in false and unrighteous conceits and opinions, such as are not according to truth and godliness.

Now what a spirit of delusion has seized upon many, even multitudes of professors, is too evident. That it has intoxicated them, and made them reel from one thing to another, as drunken men; and that many are fallen by it, fallen foully from the ways of truth and holiness, and from sober and wholesome principles. And the delusion is strong, and continues on them to this day; all means and dispensations have not been effectual to break the bonds of it, and to bring them to themselves. That this judgment is inflicted, and abides so, is visible; and it is one of those we should most tremble at, as being both a dreadful judgment and a high provocation. And hence we may come to the discovery and conviction of the sin for which it is inflicted. The truth has not been received in the love of it. The truths of the gospel, leading to holiness and mortification, have not been cordially and affectionately received, have not been admitted in the power and efficacy, have not been practically entertained nor rooted in the heart. That seems to be one sin for which the Lord has a controversy with us, and which he has been pleading severely in the way forementioned, by sending strong delusions.

Another threatening, Mat. xiii. 12, Mark iv. 25, Luke xix, 26, where those that have not (*i. e.* who improve not what they have, as appears by the following verses) are threatened to have it taken away. We had opportunities for the beating down of sin, promoting of holiness, advancing of Christ's interest; large opportunities for the winning of souls, defeating of Satan, enlarging the kingdom of our Lord Jesus. We had advantages for reforming what was amiss in worship, discipline, practice, for the rooting out every plant, &c., for the conforming of all according to the pattern in the mount.

Have we lost these opportunities for our own or others' souls, wholly or in part, or are in danger of it? Are we bereaved of those blessed advantages we had for reformation? What sin is it that has bereaved us? What is the cause the Lord has taken, or is taking from us that which we have? Why, what can we pitch on with more probability than the sin for which this is threatened? We did not faithfully improve what the Lord entrusted us with while we had it. Here is another chief ground of the Lord's controversy; it seems to be.

Further, the Lord threatens that who are not faithful shall be deprived of the means of fruitfulness, Isa. v. 1–7; and that the gospel of the kingdom shall be taken from those who bring not forth the fruits of it, Mat. xxi. 43; and elsewhere the unfruitful are threatened to be cut down, Mat. iii. 7, 8, 10, Mat. vii. 19; and more fully in a parable, Luke xiii. 6, 10.

Now, have we been in danger to be cut down by one destroying judgment after another? Have many been cut down round about us? Has the rain been withheld in its season? a restraint upon that which should make our souls fruitful? Does the Lord by his providence threaten to take away the hedge, and break down the wall that has secured us, and so leave us to be eaten up and trodden down? Are we in danger to be laid waste, left as a wilderness not pruned nor digged? Has the Lord seemed to lay hold on the gospel of the kingdom, and been moving and removing it, as though he would take it away? What is the cause of all this? We need not be to seek if we will observe these threatenings. We see that which brings such a calamity is unfruitfulness, and it is observable.

(3.) Scripture relations; the account we have there of the course of providence, and the Lord's proceedings with others. If, in several dispensations, he has dealt with us as he dealt with others in like circumstances, probably it is upon like grounds; if we suffer in some proportion as others have suffered, probably we have sinned as they sinned. To give but one instance, which possibly may lead us to the sight of a great provocation, and that which had a great hand in procuring and prolonging our troubles and afflictions.

Has the Lord proceeded with us as he did with Israel in the wilderness? When we were almost in the sight of Canaan, are we brought back again to so great a distance from it, as we may seem nearer Egypt than the land of promise?

Let us inquire, then, if our sins have not been somewhat like theirs. Have we not been unthankful for great deliverances, great mercies? have we not undervalued them, and made no answerable returns for them? have we not given way to discontents in the midst of all occasions of thankfulness? have we not murmured and repined when we had manna enough, and all provisions and advantages for our souls without restraint? have we not quarrelled with our condition, if not with the providences of God, because they have not suited with some particular humour or interest? Oh the horrid unthankfulness of this generation! Because we wanted something we desired, or some interest was not gratified, or some instruments liked us not, we fell into distempers much like theirs in the wilderness, and suffered ourselves to be transported with ungrateful and unreasonable discontents, so far as all we enjoyed were sacrificed thereto. Oh how justly may the Lord swear in his wrath that we shall never enter into his rest; that our carcases shall fall in the wilderness; that our eyes shall never more see what we would take no thankful notice of!

Oh how did we undervalue mercies, and such as obliged us to higher degrees of love and thankfulness than any people in the world were obliged to! The greater the mercies, the more intolerable the contempt of them. So it was in Israel, and so expressed, Ps. cvi. 13-16, 21-27. Oh what was it that we despised not?

8. Apply yourselves by prayer to God for the discovery of those sins, for which he judges and corrects. Beg of him light, direction, and conviction; all other means will signify nothing without his concurrence and assistance. He makes the discovery by means; they will discover nothing to purpose without him. The sufficiency and efficacy of means is from him; your due use of them, and success in using them, depends on him. You can do nothing by them, they will do nothing for you without him. Acknowledge his all-sufficiency in this, as in other things; and the insufficiency of whatever else you may be apt to depend on. Make it appear that you use the means in obedience to him; yet your dependence is only on him; your expectation of success alone from him.

Seek him accordingly. 'Cause me to understand, O Lord, wherein I have erred'; 'make me to know my transgression and my sin,' as Job xiii. 23. Search me, and try me; enable me to search and try myself, impartially, diligently, narrowly. Help me against whatsoever might blind my eye, or divert it, or contract it. Enlighten conscience, and awaken it; as it is thy officer, let it be thy voice, and represent faithfully thy charge against me. Direct others; bless the word, that it may be a searching, convincing light. Order all and concur with them, that I may understand wherefore thou contendest with me, and with thy people, and with these nations.

Be importunate, as apprehensive of the great importance thereof. How much you are concerned to have the Achan, the accursed thing discovered; and how dangerous it is to have that escape your notice which is the ground of this controversy. Give him no rest till he make known to you, both what ripened and disposed you at some distance for this severity; as also what had a nearer hand in bringing those evils upon you; both what prepared the rod, and what provoked him more immediately to make use of it; both what raised the clouds, and dissolved them into showers of displeasure, and still continues the storm; both what moved the Lord to anger, and to express his anger so many ways, and to draw out the expressions of it to such a length; wherefore it is that his anger is not yet turned away.

Pray fervently for this, and pray in faith. You have great encouragement to come to the throne of grace for this with confidence, 1 John v. 14. Now that is according to his will, which he has made your duty—to seek the knowledge of your sin, these sins especially. And he has promised, those that seek shall find. Seek this with a sincere and fixed resolution to put away every sin you shall discover; and there is no doubt but he will help you to the discovery. That is according to his will which he is willing you should do; but he is willing you should know the sins for which he judges and corrects. Whether he proceeds as a father or as a judge, you may be confident of it, he is willing you should understand wherefore he proceeds against you. What judge will conceal from a delinquent the crime for which he is arraigned, sentenced, and penalty inflicted? What father is unwilling to make known to his child the faults for which he chastises him? So he may lose his end in correcting him. That which he aims at is the reforming of what has offended him; but the child is not like to reform it if he do not know it. And so it is here, the end why the Lord afflicts is to take away your iniquity; but how shall you put it away if you do not know it? As sure as the Lord is willing to have his end in chastening you, so sure is he willing to let you know why he chastises. And therefore you may beg the knowledge of it in faith, and with confidence that he will not deny it, since there is so much ground to believe that he is willing to grant this request.

And, 2, You may apply yourselves to Christ with as much confidence also; for it is his office, as he is the great prophet, to instruct his people in their great concernments. And are they not greatly concerned to know wherefore the Lord is angry with them? Is it not of great importance to them to answer the Lord's end in smiting them; and so understand that without the knowledge of which they cannot answer it? It is Christ's office, as he is prophet, to make known his Father's will, whether signified by his word, or by his rod; and you may be confident he is willing to perform his office.

And, 3, You may address yourselves to the Spirit of God, with the like exercise of faith; for he is sent for this purpose, to convince of sin, John xvi. 8, ἐλέγξει. He will convince the world of the great sin for which he has a controversy with it; and make it evident that unbelief is the sin for which he judges them; and he will not be wanting to his people in that which he performs to the world. It is his office to convince them of the sin for which God contends, to make their sin evident; so as πασαν ἀπολογίαν ἐκκόπτει, to leave no defence, no covering to hide it from them.

Encourage your faith hereby, and exercise it in prayer. So may you prevail with God to bless the use of the other means specified; so as thereby you may discern, and be convinced of those sins personal or national, for which the Lord hath been judging and afflicting.

And so much for this great inquiry, so necessary to be insisted on; that we may comply with the Lord's end in proceeding against us. Let me proceed to some other directions which may be helpful to this purpose.

9. Make use of judgments and afflictions, to engage your souls thoroughly against sin; whatever in them is troublesome, afflictive, grievous; whatever is hateful, dreadful, terrible, make account it is from sin; charge it all upon sin's account. Whatever is of this nature in the world, it is from sin; if it be so in itself, sin made it so, and it had never been so to you, were it not for sin. And *quod efficit tale, est magis tale.* Are you bereaved of dear relatives? Weep you for children, and the loss of other endeared friends, because they are not? Why it is sin that killed them; this was the death of them all. This is the grand murderer, and has been so from the beginning. Distempers, diseases, to which we ascribe their death, are innocent in comparison; there had been no such thing in our bodies, in any of our families, or in any part of the world, but for sin. This bred them, brought them, employed them; they had never done any execution but for sin. This alone made diseases, and made them mortal. If their death be grievous and bitter to you, let the bitterness of their death be upon sin.

Are you impoverished? Sin has bereaved you. Are you laid low? Sin has tumbled you down. You charge the fire, you cry out against incendiaries; but this is the fire that has consumed so much of our riches and glory; this is the great incendiary. Had it not been for sin, no instruments would have attempted it; no matter have been receptive of it. This kindled it; this blew it up into those dreadful flames; this carried them on with rage, fury, so as they despised all opposition. To this we owe our ruins, our desolation; the sight, the report of which, has struck those that saw, yea, those that heard thereof, with horror and astonishment.

Oh! if poverty, if the loss of estate, the ruin of families, be grievous to us; what is sin? whose hand is in all this, whose hand has done all this, and without which it could never have been done.

Is a plague dreadful, such a one that sweeps away thousands in a week? Oh! but there had been no plague in the world but for the infection of sin; and sin is more pestilent, more contagious, more destructive. No plague like that of the heart. Where the other has destroyed its thousands, this has destroyed its ten thousands; this has infected the whole world; and all that perish die of this plague.

Is persecution grievous? Why, this is it that makes men persecutors; yea, this is it which made him a devil, who acts and inspires them. Of an angel of light, this made him a fiend of darkness; and it is by the mediation of sin that he engages his instruments in hellish designs, to extinguish the light.

Had it not been for sin there had [been no plagues, no judgments, no calamities, no afflictions, no distempers in our souls, no diseases in our bodies, no complainings in our streets, no lamentings in our families. There had been nothing afflictive, nothing troublesome; no, nor fear of any such. This, this is the Achan, the troubler, &c. This is the burden and grievance, this is the sting and poison of all. Take an account of all that afflicts you or others, cast it up exactly; and then discharging all other things as innocent, charge all upon sin. Make such use of troubles and afflictions to engage your souls against sin, so you will be disposed effectually to purge out your iniquity, and put away your sin, and so comply with the Lord's end in judging.

10. Content not yourselves with any opposition of sin, unless it be universal. If you would comply with God's end in what has befallen you, or is approaching you, so as to have iniquity effectually purged and taken away, the opposition you make against it for this purpose must be universal, not only in respect of the object; you must not only set yourselves against all sin, of which before; but in respect of the subject, oppose it with all your faculties. All that is within you must be set against it. The opposition must be in and from every part; not only in the conscience, but in the will and affections; not only in some part of the mind, but in the whole heart, the whole soul, and in every power thereof. Rest not till you find a party against sin in every part, till you feel each faculty of your souls like Tamar's womb, twins struggling.

11. Think it not enough to avoid or oppose sin, unless you get it mortified. The purging of iniquity, and the taking away of sin, imports no less than the death and burial of sin; the putting it to death, and the burying it out of your sight. Unless you endeavour this, you answer not his call by afflictions, you come not up to what he designs therein.

When he puts his people into the furnace, he would have their dross not only loosened, or a little parted from them, but thoroughly wrought out and purged, and so wasted and consumed. If it be not wrought out and wasted, it may mix with the better metal again in the cooling, and so the fire and furnace will be to little purpose.

The Lord would have your iniquity purged, so as you should return no more to your vomit; and sin taken away, so as it should no more be found, as formerly, in heart or life; but this will not be; you are not secure from it, unless sin is mortified, and iniquity subdued.

The Philistines did not continually invade the Israelites, they were not always making inroads upon them; yet because they are not quite subdued, Israel was always in danger; often miserably foiled, and their land wasted. Content not yourselves to force this enemy to yield to a cessation, but make it your design to break its power; be still labouring for a fuller conquest, that it may not only be still and quiet, but may have no power left to be otherwise.

The heathen could oppose some gross sins, and abstain from the acts of them: the Spartans from drunkenness; Socrates from passion; Alexander from incontinency; the Romans, many of them, from perfidiousness. But notwithstanding, their iniquity was not purged, their sin not taken away, because they were not mortified; but 'those that are Christ's have crucified,' &c., Gal. v. 24, Col. iii. 5. This is it that he calls for, by his word and by his rod. This is it he principally aims at in calamities and afflictions; not only some avoiding of sin, but the purging of it out, the taking it away, *i.e.* the mortifying of it. Whatever you do against sin less than this, you comply not with God's design; by this alone, and by nothing without this, will you answer his end. And therefore on this we shall insist a little, and shew how it may be effected.

If you would subdue your iniquity, and mortify your sin,

(1.) Get mortifying apprehensions of it. Labour to possess your minds and judgments with full and effectual persuasions that sin is such a thing as is not fit, as is not worthy, to live; that you are highly concerned not to suffer it to have a being in heart or life; that you should not in any reason, that you cannot with any safety, tolerate it or endure it should have life or being; that it is most worthy, of all things in the whole creation, to be utterly ruined and exterminated. That this may be the vote of your judgment, Away with such a thing from the earth! Away with it out of my heart, life, out of the world, for it is not fit that it should live! As they, Acts xxi. 22.

The Spirit of God in Scripture leads you to such apprehensions of sin, and lays down clear grounds to raise them, and to fix them, and to carry them on to full and powerful persuasions, such as should thoroughly engage us to mortify them. It represents sin to be such a thing as should be in all reason put to death, and denied a subsistence, and proceeded against with that severity, Deut. xiii. 8–10, which was to be used against the seducer.

It is declared to be an enemy, a mortal enemy, to your souls, and all your dear concernments; an enemy in arms, in actual, in continual war against you, 1 Peter ii. 11, James iv. 1. It is not only so to you, but an enemy to God, to mankind, to the whole creation; a public, a desperate, an irreconcilable, a cruel, deadly enemy. And should not such an enemy be persecuted to death?

It is a monster eminently, $\dot{\alpha}\mu\dot{\alpha}\rho\tau\eta\mu\alpha$ $\tau\tilde{\eta}\varsigma$ $\varphi\dot{\upsilon}\sigma\epsilon\omega\varsigma$, the most ugly peccancy, horrid exorbitancy of nature. Nay, that which transforms every soul and spirit that gives it entertainment, into monsters; so it has dealt with the fallen angels, it has turned them into monstrous fiends; so it has dealt with the souls of men, they come into the world without eyes, or feet, or hands, or hearts for God, monstrously defective. It has perverted and misplaced all the parts and faculties, as if head were lowest and feet highest; a monstrous dislocation! If the effects of it be so prodigious, how monstrous is sin itself! And should such a monster be suffered to live? Oh if it were but seen in its own shape and colours, how would the children of men run upon it, to root it out of the earth!

It is a robber. It robbed our first parents, and in them all mankind, of the image of God, of all the heavenly treasure they were possessed of, of the inheritance they were born to. It left nothing but sorrow and misery; fathers and children, all mankind, were hereby quite beggared and utterly undone. And when the Lord had taken a course to repair all this, yet still it is attempting to rob us of all that is precious to us; of grace, of the means of grace; to rob us of our peace, our comforts, our hopes of glory. It would leave us nothing but beggary and misery here, and hell hereafter. Should such a robber live?

It is a traitor to Christ, to his crown and dignity. It would overturn his throne, throw down his sceptre, trample on the ensigns of his sovereignty. It will not have him to rule over us; and should not such a traitor die the death, which suggests and acts treasonable things against Christ?

It is a ravisher of souls; draws away conjugal affections from Christ; gets into the marriage-bed; forces them to commit folly in the sight and presence of Christ, without any regard of the eyes of his jealousy; prostitutes them commonly, openly to the world; yea, to Satan himself, 2 Cor. xi. 2, 3, James iv. 4.

It is a witch. Indeed, the mistress of witchcrafts; a sorceress, as the expression is, Nahum iii. 4. It practised sorcery upon the Galatians, chap. iii. 1. It was by means, through the mediation of sin, that they were bewitched so as to take error for truth, and truth for error. And others are practically bewitched thereby, so as to call evil good and light darkness, to count that their glory which is their shame, that their refreshment which is poison, that gain which undoes them, that their happiness which ruins them. So they conceive of things, so they act, as those that are bewitched; as such who are under the power of sorcery, which is *illusio sensuum*, an abusing of the discerning faculty, so as things appear to be contrary, or quite otherwise, to what they are. Now, Exod. xxii. 18, a witch was not to be suffered to live.

It is a murderer; it sheds the blood of souls. Satan, who is called 'a murderer from the beginning, John viii. 44, has murdered none, from the beginning to this day, but by this instrument. This kills every way, temporally, spiritually, eternally. This has been the death of all that have died any of these ways from the foundation of the world to this moment, and will continue this more bloody practice while it continues. And should not such a murderer be executed? Should it not die without mercy?

In the text, when the Lord would have iniquity purged, it refers either to purging by fire or physic. If the former, it implies that sin is dross, that which debased the soul, once of the finest and purest metal, and makes the Lord look upon it as vile and refuse, to reject it as reprobate silver; such as will never pass with him unless it be refined, such as he will never accept on any account until it be purged. And should you endure such an embasement of your souls, and of such dangerous consequence?

If to physic, it insinuates that sin is a malignant humour, a disease, that which breeds and continues all the soul's maladies; which, unless it be purged, the soul can never have health. It will still keep it under pains, weaknesses, languishments; and will, in fine, make it sick unto death. And should this have a being, a quiet abode, within you? It is desperate folly to forbear it.

And when the Lord would have sin taken away, that denotes it as a filthiness, not to be endured in our sight; like those garments, to be taken away, Zech. iii. 3, 4. Those filthy garments were his iniquity; and in the original it is excrementitious garments. Iniquity is to God, and should be to us, as the filthiest excrements, as the mire wherein a sow wallows, as the vomit of a dog, as the stench of an open sepulchre, as the putrefied matter of an ulcer. And is not such a thing to be removed far from your sight, far from all your senses? You have no patience, you will be restless, until it be done.

The Scripture thus sets forth sin to us, that hereby such apprehensions of it might be formed in us as of that which is not to be endured, not to be suffered to have life or being. We should make such use of them; and when our minds are effectually possessed with such apprehensions of sin, then is it mortified in our minds. This is the way whereby the judgment purges iniquity, and puts away sin. And this will contribute much to the mortifying of it in all other parts; for the judgment is the *primum mobile* in the soul, the wheel that first moves, and sets the rest on motion. According as your apprehensions and persuasions concerning sin are, such will the motions in your hearts and lives be against it.

(2.) Get mortifying resolutions. Get your hearts resolved against sin; to prosecute it to the death; to engage all the strength you have, and can procure, in such a prosecution of it; resolve not to spare it; not to forbear it in the least; not to tolerate it, nor suffer it to have any quiet abode in any part of heart or life; not to enter into a parley or treaty with it; not to yield to any cessation, much less to make any peace with it, no more than the Israelites with those whom the Lord had devoted to destruction, Deut. xxiii. 6. Resolve to ruin it, to expel it out of your hearts, and cut it off from your lives. Make use of the mortifying apprehensions forementioned to raise you to such resolutions; let them be full and effectual, fixed and unwavering resolutions.

Full. That the main strength of the will may be in them. Not such as leave the heart in suspense, or in an indifferent posture, or a little inclinable, but carrying it down, as it were, with full weight, into such determinations against sin. Rest not until you find this the bent of your hearts, and that which is prevalent and predominant in them.

Effectual. Not some faint, powerless tendencies of the will, which excite not the other faculties, put them not upon actions and endeavours; but such as will engage them in the use of all means for the effecting of what is resolved on. Get your hearts wound up to such resolutions, that may be as a spring, setting and keeping all in motion, Ps. cxix. 106, 48. That which he has resolved on, he vigorously pursued.

Fixed. Not wavering; not off and on; not by fits only, when some sermon, or some affliction, or special occurrence has made some impression; not like Ephraim, of whom the Lord complains, Hos. vi. 4. But this should be the settled temper of the heart: the face of it should be constantly against sin; and when you find them varying or declining, all care and diligence should be used to renew and reinforce them, to raise them again, and keep them up in their full force and vigour.

Make use of judgments and afflictions (according to a former direction), of the grievousness or bitterness of them, to draw your hearts to such resolves for the ruin of sin; make use of what you have found most effectual heretofore for this purpose; or, if those you have used prove less powerful, try others; leave nothing unattempted that the Lord affords for this end. Look upon it as your interest to have sin ruined; as that wherein your safety, your comfort, your happiness, yea, the life of your souls, is wholly concerned. If you destroy not sin, it will ruin you; if you kill it not, it will certainly be your death. And when will a man be resolute, if not in such a case, when he must either kill or be killed? It is according to what was said to Ahab, 1 Kings xx. 42: 'Thus saith the Lord, If thou let go out of thy hand the sin which he has appointed to utter destruction, thy life shall go for its life.' Oh then, if thou intendest thy soul shall live, resolve to prosecute sin to the death, and be peremptory in the resolution.

When the will is thus resolved against sin for the death of it, sin is already mortified in the will, the sentence of death is passed against it; it is בן מות condemned to die; and the will having the command of the other faculties and the whole man, it will be brought to execution. The work of mortification is in a fair way to be carried on universally; and though it be not fully executed at present, yet the Lord, who judges us by the bent of our hearts, and the prevailing tendency of our wills, will judge one so resolved against sin to be so far a mortified person. This is the way whereby the will purges iniquity, and puts away sin; and that which contributes most to the purging and putting it away everywhere from the soul and from the life.

(3.) Get mortifying affections; such are the affections of aversation, which carry the heart from sin, or set it against sin: *e. g.* anger, indignation, revenge, fear, shame, sorrow, hatred; whereby the soul moves from or against sin, as the most offensive, the most provoking, the most dangerous, the most shameful, the most hateful evil. These affections should be bred, and nourished, and strengthened; you must kindle them, blow them up into a flame, and keep them flaming. You should not bear with yourselves in the want, or in the weakness, or in the declining or decay of them. These affections, thus upheld, will be the death of sin; it cannot live in a heart where these are kept up in life, and strength, and action: these will distress it, wound it, starve it; these will be crucifying it; these will drag it towards the cross, and be as so many nails, to fasten the body and members of it to the cross. Particularly,

[1.] Anger. Let sin be the object, the chief object of your anger, Eph. iv. 26. Then, to be sure, you are angry and sin not, when you are angry at sin, when that is the cause and the object of your anger. Our Lord Jesus, the spotless pattern of meekness, was angry at sin, Mark iii. 5. Those kinds or degrees of anger which are vicious or culpable towards other objects, or upon other occasions, are your duties and excellencies in reference to sin. You may be, you must be, soon angry, ὀργίλοι; and much angry, πικροί; and long angry, χαλεποί.

First, Anger should kindle at the first appearance of sin. We should not think of it without something of this passion. The best men are ὀξύχολοι, soon angry, and easily provoked against sin. That which is a weakness in other cases, is a perfection or a degree of it here. We should be slow to anger at that which offends us only, but not slow to anger at that which offends God. Our souls should be as tinder, and take fire at every spark of sin. He that is soon angry in his own cause, for his own petty concernments, dealeth foolishly, Prov. xiv. 17; such anger resteth in the bosom of fools, Eccles. vii. 9; but he that is not hasty in his spirit to anger against sin exalteth folly. The more quick your anger is against sin, the more speedy will be the execution, the mortifying of it. Get a spirit apt to be angry at sin, and use means to provoke it.

Secondly, Be much angry at sin, and not content yourselves with a low degree of anger; get it raised into wrath and indignation. There is no such danger of transgressing the bounds of moderation here as in other cases; that is immoderate anger which is more than the cause requires or deserves; but the fiercest wrath and the highest indignation of God is not more than sin deserves; and does it not then require and deserve all ours? Let it be against sin purely, against our own sins principally, or against the sins of others, not their persons. And then, if it be great wrath, it is not too much Moses, a person meek above all men on earth, was kindled into wrath by the sight of sin, Exod. xxxii. 19, his anger waxed hot at first sight of sin. A little anger will not do much against sin; the heart that purges it out must be wroth with it, it should be taken away with indignation.

Thirdly. Be long angry. Even for ever; angry so as never to be appeased. It is no sin to be implacable here, nay, it is your duty. The sun must go down, and rise, and go down all thy days upon thy wrath against sin. Such an anger will not serve the turn as is ἴατον χρόνῳ; when it is a mortifying affection, it is ἀνίατον, an unappeasable anger. Anger at other things must be allayed, suppressed, extinguished; but against sin it must be nourished, heightened, settled, digested into malice. For though it be a wickedness in other cases, yet malice against sin is a virtue, a duty; you cannot be too malicious against sin, you cannot bear it too much ill will.

There is an holy anger, a sanctified malice, which is singularly useful for the expelling of iniquity and mortifying of sin. Turn all your anger, wrath, malice, into this stream against this object. Whatever is apt to provoke you elsewhere, you may see it all in sin; nothing so offensive, nothing so injurious, nothing more affronts you, nothing so much wrongs you in your dearest concernments. When you are apt to be angry at other things or persons,—Such a one has thus and thus abused, wronged, affronted, vexed, troubled me; so causelessly, so disingenuously, so continually,—turn your eyes, your thoughts, from that, and look upon sin, and say, Oh, how much more has sin done against me, yea, against God? How much more cause have I to be angry at sin? Oh, I do well to be angry at it, even to death. So you may make it a mortifying affection.

[2.] Fear. We are willing to be rid of that which we fear, and ready to use all means, take all occasions to put that far from us which we are afraid of. And the more dreadful and terrible it is, the more dangerous it appears, the more forward we are to get it removed, and the more eager to have it at the greatest distance from us. If you would have sin purged out and put away, get your souls possessed with a fear of it, and so represent it to your souls as you may see cause to fear it more and more. You will not suffer that to have a quiet abode in your hearts which you are greatly afraid of. Look then upon sin as the most dreadful, the most formidable evil in the whole creation. So it is in itself, so it is declared to be. You have the word of God for it; believe the report of God concerning it; believe all the experience of the world, which has found it so; believe that which you have all reason to believe.

That is most dreadful, most the object of our fear, which is most dangerous. Now sin is transcendently so; so dangerous, as nothing else in the world deserves to be thought or called so in comparison. This is the root from which all dangers grow. One thing may be dangerous to our health, another to our estates, relations, liberty, life. Oh, but sin endangers all. Nothing is safe where sin has place. This hazards our temporal, our spiritual, our eternal concernments; this strikes at all. Nothing could hurt us; nor men, nor devils; nothing could endanger us, if sin did not open their way. If sin did not expose us, our enjoyments, our liberties, our comforts, our hopes, were all safe, we need not fear what man could do unto us. The foot of pride could not come near us, the hand of the violent could not remove us, nay, could not shake us. But what is the wrath of men, poor inconsiderable worms like ourselves? This, and this alone, exposes us to the wrath of the great God; this, and this only, can cast both body and soul into hell. We fear where no fear is in comparison; we fear a prison, but what is that to hell! We fear the loss of estate, of relations, of liberty, of life, but what is the loss of God's favour, of heaven, of soul and body for ever? It is sin only that brings us in danger of such a loss.

In fine, whatsoever is dangerous, whatever is dreadful to us, sin made it so. It had not been so in itself, or not so to us, but for sin; and therefore sin is more to be feared than all we fear. There had been, there would be, no cause of fear if sin had not been, or if it were once put away.

Is it fearful to have your souls dwell amongst lions? Why, but it is sin that transforms men into such creatures, it is sin that gives them the fierceness of lions. Take away this, and they are tame and harmless creatures; a lamb may play with them without danger; you may put your hand into the mouth of a tame lion without fear, you might lie down by them securely were it not for sin.

Are afflictions, losses, sufferings, calamities dreadful? It is sin that first let these into the world; it is sin that still exposes you to them; it is sin that embitters them and makes them grievous; it is sin that withholds those comforts which would quite drown the afflictive sense of any outward suffering. And what would there be in it to be feared, if the afflictiveness of it were gone? When sin is taken away, the bitterness of these is past.

Is death terrible to you? Why, but 'the sting of death is sin,' 1 Cor. xv. 56. You would not fear to have a bee fly into your bosom if the sting were gone; it would hurt no more than an innocent fly.

Is hell dreadful to you? Oh, but it was sin that made hell; this digged the bottomless pit, this bred the worm that never dies, this kindled that fire that never goes out; this feeds those flames, those burnings, and makes them intolerable, and makes them everlasting; but put away sin, and there is no fear of hell to you.

Is the wrath of God terrible to you? Oh, but no part of the creation had ever known any such thing as wrath in God had it not been for sin, Eph. v, 6, Rom. i. 18, Col. iii. 6.

You see nothing is to be feared but for sin; so this is to be feared above all, nothing else in comparison. This, this is the one thing to be feared, without which nothing else is dreadful. Believe but this effectually, and according to the evidence you have of it, and you will be as active to purge iniquity, to put away sin, as you would be to rid yourselves of all your fears, and of all that is fearful.

[3.] *Shame.* This is another affection which will contribute much to the mortifying of sin; that which we are truly, greatly ashamed of, we are not only content to be rid of it, but active to get it removed, and put away far from us.

Look upon your sin as your shame, your greatest, your only shame in comparison, as that which is the shame of the whole creation, the most shameful thing in the world.

Are you ashamed of a filthy garment, of a loathsome defilement, of a monstrous deformity? Why, sin is more so in the sight of God than any of these, than all these together are in our eyes. It is a greater shame to you than if you were all besmeared with excrements, than if you were overspread with scabs and leprosy, than if you had no sound, no straight, no comely part in your whole body, but all crooked, or ulcerated, or monstrously misplaced and dislocated. Thy soul, as sin has used it, is a more shameful sight in the eye of God.

Are you ashamed of such weakness or folly as would render you ridiculous or despised by all you converse with? Oh, but sin is the most shameful weakness, the most absurd folly, in the account of God, of angels, and of men too, that are truly judicious, and so it is branded by the Spirit of God in Scripture.

Are you ashamed of that which all the world would cry shame of: of betraying those that trust you, dealing unfaithfully with those that rely on you, of being ungrateful to those who shew you greatest kindness, of abusing and wronging those who deserve best of you, of dealing disingenuously with those who most oblige you, of being sordidly penurious where you should be most bountiful, of cheating and defrauding those who refer themselves to you? Do your hearts rise against such unworthy practices? Would you blush to be charged with any of them, even though you were innocent? Oh, but there is no man deals so unworthily, so shamefully with another, as you deal with God in sinning against him. All the treachery and unfaithfulness, all the fraud and injustice, all the ingratitude, all the disingenuousness, all the baseness and sordidness which you cry shame of in the world, is to be found in sin; you are guilty of it all towards God when you sin against him. Any one of these is shameful alone; but all these meet together in sin, and whatever else calls for shame. Believe this, and work it upon your hearts, till you find them rising against sin as the most shameful evil. This will make you willing to have it crucified, forward to do execution on it yourselves, when you are sensible that the purging your iniquity is the purging of your shame, and the taking away of sin the taking away your reproach.

[4.] Grief and sorrow for sin. This is another mortifying affection which will hasten the death of sin. We seek redress of that which is a grievance to us, and will take pains to be eased of it. Oh, if sin were the grief, the sorrow, the affliction of your souls, you would count the purging of it out, the taking of it away, a great, a merciful deliverance. No less than it would have been to the Israelites to have had those nations driven out before them, which were as pricks in their eyes, and thorns in their sides, and a continual vexation to them in the land where they dwelt, Josh. xxiii. 13, Num. xxxiii. 55. The Lord thought the foresight of this might be enough to quicken them to drive them out in all haste; but when they felt what was foretold, they ran all the hazards of war to drive them out and be delivered from them.

Oh, if sin were such a grief and sorrow to your souls, such a vexation to your hearts, as it should be, and as it gives you occasion enough to find it, you would count no outward deliverance comparable to a deliverance from sin. You would freely engage your whole strength in a war against it for to drive it out; you would be restless till these pricks were pulled out of your eye, and these thorns plucked out of your sides, till that were taken away which is your grief and vexation.

And should not sin be such a grievance to you? It is so to God. It grieves him at the heart, Gen. vi. 6, Ps. xcv. 10, Amos ii. 13; it was so to Christ, Mark iii. 5, Isa. liii. 3, 4; it is so to the Spirit of God, Eph. iii. 4; it is so to men who have a sense of what is grievous, 2 Peter ii. 7, 8; it is so to the whole creation, Rom. viii. 21, 22. Is it so to all? And shall those who should be most sensible of it be only void of sense? Whatsoever is a grievance to us is either pain or loss, *pœna damni* or *sensus;* either the loss and want of some comfort, or some sharp suffering. For sufferings, this brings them all, this sharpens them all; for losses and wants, this bereaves us of what we lose, and this intercepts the supplies of what we want; and this makes holes in the cisterns, and lets our comforts run out, and then stops the pipes, that no more can run in; this lays an obstruction at the spring head, Isa. lix. 1, 2.

If sin were not grievous, because it is a grief to God, a Father of such love and indulgence; because it is so grievous to him who bore our griefs; because it is such a grief to the Spirit our Comforter; yet since it is the cause of all the grievances that befall us, we have cause enough on this account to resent it as the most grievous evil, that which should above all things raise our grief and command our sorrow. Believe it to be so, and so work up your heart as you may find it to be the grief and affliction of your souls indeed; and then you will be forward and active to be eased of it, you will think it your happiness to have it purged out and taken away; you will see cause to make it the business of your lives to get it mortified.

[5.] Hatred. This of all other affections has the most powerful and effectual tendency to the mortifying of sin. This will not suffer you to be satisfied with anything less than the death of it. That is the nature of hatred, as the philosopher shews, when he is declaring the difference betwixt anger and hatred, Rhet. lib. ii. cap. ix., ὁ μὲν γὰρ ἀντιπάθειν βούλεται ᾧ ὀργίζεται, ὁ δὲ μὴ εἶναι, he that is angry would have him utterly ruined, would leave him neither life nor being. And again, ὁ μὲν πολλῶν ἄν γινομένων ἐλέησεν, ὁ δ' οὐδενός, he that is angry may relent after the inflicting of some severities, but he that hates has no mercy. This hatred will have sin die without mercy. Get but your hearts possessed with hatred of sin, and then it is dead already in the heart, and this will pursue it to the death everywhere.

To excite this affection, look upon it as that which is truly hateful, as that which has all in it that is hateful, as that which has nothing in it but what is hateful.

It is truly hateful, as being wholly and perfectly evil; a direct contrariety to the chief good; opposite to his nature, to his will, and so hated of God, Ps. xlv. 7. He hates sin infinitely, cannot endure to see it; and he hates it only, nothing but sin, or nothing but for sin. He hates it irreconcilably; he may be reconciled to the sinner, but never to the sin, nor to the sinner neither, unless he leave sin. That must be extremely hateful, which God, who is love, cannot but hate.

Sin has all in it that is hateful. We hate that which is ugly, though it be not hurtful; we hate that which is mischievous, though it be not ugly; but sin is both ugly and mischievous; nothing more, nothing so much in the whole creation.

It has nothing in it but what is hateful. It is a mere compound of ugliness and mischievousness, without the least alloy or mixture of anything comely or commodious. A toad, though the hatefullest of creeping things, has something in it, which separated from the poison, is of physical use, but sin is nothing at all but poison. The devil himself, how hateful soever, yet as he is the workmanship of God, is so far good, but sin has nothing in it of God's workmanship, nothing in it in any sense good; it is the spawn of the devil, and of him, not as he is a creature, but as he is a devil, and so has nothing in it but what is purely evil, and absolutely hateful. It has not the least touch of comeliness, not anything that may pass with excuse, not anything that is tolerably evil, nothing but what is to be utterly abhorred, Rom. xii. 9.

Get your hearts so affected towards sin, as that which is so hateful, and to be abhorred; get a true, an active hatred of sin. And that will be the death of sin, will lead you readily to purge it out, and so to comply with the Lord's end, &c. Nourish in your hearts this hatred of sin by a frequent view of the hatefulness of it; keep up this affection lively and active, and sin will have much ado to live by it.

[6.] Revenge. This, though severely forbidden and condemned in other cases, is called out by the Spirit of God against sin, and commended where it appears against it, 2 Cor. vii. 11. There was in the Corinthians, in reference to the sin amongst them, not only sorrow, fear, indignation, but also revenge. And such an affection there should be in us, inclining our hearts, and making us eager to come even with sin, to render it evil for evil; to deal with it according as it has dealt, or would deal, with us; to be avenged of it for the mischief it is continually plotting and acting against us;

to starve it, as it would starve our souls; to weaken it, as it wasted us; to wound it, as it has wounded us; to ruin it, as it would destroy us; to be the death of that which would bereave our souls of life; to leave it no provisions, no supports, no hopes, as it would have made our condition helpless, and comfortless, and hopeless; to spare it no more than it has spared our souls; to persecute it as restlessly, as unweariedly, as it pursues us. Such an affectation,* you see, is the highway to have sin mortified, to purge it out as it would have had the Lord to have rejected us, and to turn it away as it would have provoked God to have put us away.

(4.) Get mortifying graces, three especially, love to God, and faith in him, and fear of him. These exercised will have a powerful influence upon heart and life for the mortifying of sin, will carry you on effectually to compliance with the Lord's end in afflicting, will help you mightily to purge it out, and take it away.

[1.] Love to God: Ps. xcvii. 10, 'Those that love the Lord will hate evil.' And the more they love him, the more they will hate it; and the more degrees of hatred, the more degrees of mortification. The more it is abhorred, the more, and the sooner it will be mortified. This will turn the wheel upon sin with a quick motion. When love prevails, it will not let you drive on heavily in a course of mortification; it will make you diligent, active, and unwearied in the use of means for this purpose. It will not suffer you to think the labour and pains requisite hereto grievous. You see the power of love in Jacob: says he to Laban, Gen. xxxi. 40, 41; all this hardship he endured, and for many years together, yet love to Rachel made him think the hard measures easy, and the tedious years as a few days, Gen. xxix. 20.

[2.] Faith. If these devils be not cast out, it is because of our unbelief, Mat. xvii. 19, 20. Other means cannot, the principal cause will not, without faith, Mat. ix. 22, Acts iii. 10.

[3.] Fear of God. There is an inconsistency betwixt the fear of God and sin, they cannot dwell together. Where sin reigns, it leaves no place for the fear of God; and where the fear of God prevails, it will leave no place for sin: Prov. iii. 7, 'Fear the Lord, and depart from evil.' 'The fear of God is the beginning of wisdom;' and wherein that wisdom consists, the wise man tells us: Prov. xiv. 16, 'A wise man feareth, and departeth from evil;' depart from it as far, and as fast as they can, as from that which is hateful to them, Prov. viii. 13. It is visible in Job's character, that this is the proper effect of the fear of God, Job i. 1.

Labour for this fear of God, to get it implanted, strengthened, and exercised, so as you may go out against sin continually under the influence of it. Not a fear of aversation. which makes one shun what he fears, such as was in our first parents, Gen. iii. 8, 10, and in the Israelites, Deut. v. 24, 25. They were afraid, and durst not come near to God, but wanted the due fear of his majesty, ver. 29, the virtue of which is to keep us from departing from God, Jer. xxxii. 40. That is the fear of God which tends to the mortifying of sin; an obsequious fear, a fear to dishonour what we reverence, to offend what we love, to lose what we highly value, and to suffer by what we would enjoy.

If you fear this dishonouring of God, this will lead you to mortify sin, as that which alone is a dishonour to him, and robs him of his glory, and lays him low in the minds, hearts, and ways of the children of men.

If you fear offending God, this will lead you to purge sin, which alone displeases and provokes him; this alone he dislikes and is distasteful; this

* Qu. 'assectation'?—ED.

alone he hates and abhors. Sin it is that affronts him, slights his authority, thwarts his designs, crosses his will, breaks his law, makes nothing of his commands or threatenings.

If you fear the withdrawing of his presence or the sense of his favour, this will lead you to mortify sin. For it is sin that makes him depart and leave you; it is sin makes him hide his face, and frown on you, Isa. lix. 2.

If you fear, lest he should not only be, but shew himself displeased, by threatenings or executions, this will lead you to mortify sin; for this is it alone which he threatens. This is it for which he afflicts you, in inward or outward concernments; this withholds those influences upon which the life, strength, growth, fruitfulness, and activeness of your souls depends; this draws out his hand to inflict public calamities and personal chastisements. Your sufferings past, and fears of what is approaching, you owe to sin. Judgments and afflictions should make you fear him: he is a strange child who will not fear his father more, when he has smarted by his displeasure. And if you fear his displeasure, this will quicken your proceedings against sin as the cause of it.

If you fear further severity (and such a fear may be filial; for if a servant may fear wrath in a master, much more should a child fear the wrath of his father), this should lead you to mortify sin. 'Sin no more, lest a worse thing come,' John v. 14. Sin, that has brought already that which is so dreadful to us, will bring something yet worse if it be not mortified That which is past is but a spark in comparison of the flame that it will kindle hereafter, Heb. xii. 29. If we let sin pass unpurged, unmortified, as others do, he will be 'a consuming fire' to us, as well as to others. Knowing therefore the terror of the Lord, let us be persuaded to purge out iniquity, and put away sin.

Now to raise this fear. There is scarce anything in God, but a serious view and consideration of it tends to possess the soul with such a fear of him, as may engage it to mortify sin, and to get it purged out. Let me touch some particulars briefly.

The glory and excellency of God. When Isaiah had a vision of the Lord in his glory, Isa. vi. 1–3, this made him look upon his sin as intolerable; he cries out of it, as one undone by it, ver. 5. He is restless till it was removed, and taken away, and purged, ver. 6, 7. The Lord is an infinite glory, and sin is the thing that provokes the eyes of his glory, Isa. iii. 8, Deut. xxviii. 58. Get due apprehensions of the glory of his majesty, and you will judge it intolerable to have that continue in your hearts or lives, which is such a provocation in his most glorious eye. It will quicken you to get such provoking uncleanness purged out, and quite taken away; you will be afraid to have it found about you. That glory will strike you with a fear of affronting it, by that which is so insufferable, so utterly opposite, so provokingly contrary to it.

The almighty power of God. That should strike our souls with a great fear of him, καὶ φόβος τῶν δυναμένων τι ποιῆσαι, Arist. Rhet. lib. ii. cap. x. We fear those that are potent, powerful to do us good or hurt, though they be but men like ourselves; how much more should we dread the mighty God, before whom the united powers of all creatures are but as the might of ants or worms to us? The power of God is laid down in Scripture as a ground of fear, Jer. v. 22. Those that will not fear such a power are hardened rebels, ver. 23, or senseless wretches, ver. 21; Ps. lxxvi. 4–7. Will you provoke such a power to anger, before whom, provoked, no creature, how mighty soever, can stand? Why, if sin be not mortified, if it be not purged and taken away, you retain that which incenses him; you offer that to the sight of the great and mighty God continually, which is such a provocation to him.

The holiness and purity of God. He is 'glorious in holiness,' Exod. xv. 11. This was one of those glories, Isa. vi., which struck the prophet with such a fear, and gave him such a sense of the impurity of sin, and his uncleanness by reason of it, that he thought it unsufferable for him to stand before God, and himself incapable of being employed by him, till his iniquity was purged and taken away. Hab. i. 13, his holiness is such he cannot endure the sight of sin, Rev. iii. 15. You keep that in his sight which is intolerable for him to see; while you do not purge it out, and get it taken away. If you do not mortify it, you keep that alive in his eye which he loathes and abhors to see. The fear of God, where it is, will not suffer this; and due apprehensions of his glorious holiness will excite in you such a fear.

The omniscience of God, Ps. cxxxix. 1, 2, 3, &c. This duly considered, will strike you with an holy dread of the divine majesty, such as will hasten the death of sin. If there be something very offensive, to one whom you otherwise stand in awe of, yet so long as you can hide it out of his sight, you fear not. Oh but there is nothing hid from God, nor can be. The secrets of your hearts are no secrets to him; they are as plain and open to him as the highway is to you. That which no other sees, or can see, is as visible and conspicuous to him as if it were writ with a sunbeam; every secret evil is an open wickedness to his eye. That which you act or think in most secret retirement, is no more concealed from him than that which is openly proclaimed. All is manifest in his sight, all are naked and open to his eyes, Rev. ii. 23, 1 Chron. xxviii. 9. You can take no course with sin, but you will be an offence and provocation to God unless you mortify it. There is no hiding of it, no hopes of concealment, no way to avoid this, but by purging it out, &c. This you will do if you fear God; and due apprehensions of his all-seeing eye will make you fear him. God is ὅλος ὀφθαλμός, all eye; and such an eye as sees all things.

The immensity of God. His is everywhere, Ps. cxxxix. 7–13. He that stands in some awe of one when he is present, may less regard him when he is absent; and sometimes absent he will be, and so the fear abated and remitted. But God is never absent, nor can be; he is always as present with thee as thou art with thyself. He is as much with thee in secret as when thou art in public; as much with thee in thy closet as in the street; as much present in thy heart as he is in heaven (though in another manner). He possesseth the reins; he is always as near thee as thy heart; as intrinsic to thee, as much within thee, as thy very soul is.

So that if sin be not mortified, if it be not purged out and taken away, take what course thou wilt with it, act it where thou wilt, imagine it but never so secretly, it will always be in God's presence. Thou wilt always provoke him; as that servant would provoke thee who would still lay some dunghill or some carrion in thy bedchamber, or in thy closet, or some loathsome thing or other always in thy way. If thou fearest God, thou wilt not use him thus; this will put thee upon purging out sin, and if thou believest his immensity, thou canst not but fear him.

His dominion over us. He has full and absolute propriety in us, and power over us. We are his, not our own, as much as any work of our hands is ours. He may dispose of us as he pleases. Shall I not do with my own as I will? We are in his hands, as clay in the hands of the potter; he may form us for his use, or he may break us; and none can say unto him, What dost thou? Now this is a just ground of fear, φοβερὸν ὡς ἐπιπολὺ τὸ ἐπ' ἄλλῳ εἶναι. He that is in the power of another is fearful of him. We are nothing so much in the power of any other, and therefore should fear nothing like him, Mat. x. 28. It is perfect madness, such as speaks the absence of fear and wit, to retain that which will be a continual offence and provocation to him, who may do with us what he list; but this you will do, this you will retain, if sin be not mortified, &c. The fear of God, where it is, will not suffer this; and there will be fear, where there is a sense of his absolute dominion over us.

His righteousness. That is another ground of fear, Job xxxvii. 23, 24. He will not afflict without just cause, but he will afflict where there is such cause. He renders to every one according to his works. The rule by which he proceeds is his law, and his proceeding according to that law is his righteousness. He is able, as we shewed before, and he is willing. His righteousness makes him willing to express his displeasure, when he has just occasion; and occasion he will ever have till sin be mortified. So that the neglect of this will lay you continually under imminent danger, δῆλον γὰρ ὅτι βούλονται τε καὶ δύνανται ὥστε τε ἐγγὺς εἰσὶ τοῦ ποιεῖν, Arist. *ibid.* That which any are willing and able to do, is ready to be done; so that God's displeasure is always *in præcinctu*, always ready to break out against you; yea, more and more of it, than has yet seized on you, while sin is unmortified. If there be any fear of God, or his displeasure, it will quicken you to the mortifying of it. And where there is a due sense of his righteousness and justice, there will be this fear.

The goodness of God also should excite this fear, and gives it a most advantageous rise in any ingenuous temper, Hosea iii. 5. Those that have tasted how gracious the Lord is, and have had experience of his infinite goodness, will be afraid to dishonour, offend, or provoke him, else they are of a base, disingenuous spirit. The highest expressions of goodness and mercy should raise this fear of offending to the height, Ps. cxxx. 4; even common favours oblige the soul to such a fear, Jer. v. 24, Ps. lxxii. 5, and iv. Has the Lord forgiven those injuries and affronts, against which his just indignation might have flamed forth for ever? And shall I harbour that which will again affront and provoke him? An ingenuous spirit recoils from this as a thing frightful and shameful. Does he withhold no good thing from me? And would he have me but to part with sin, to put away this one thing for his sake, as that which his soul hates? And shall I not get this put away? This is fearful disingenuousness. The goodness, the forgiveness, yea, the common bounty of God, is apt and proper to beget, in those who are acted by the free Spirit of Christ, such a fear as will be the death of sin.

The judgments of God. These, indeed, are not the first, nor the principal grounds of the fear of God; but yet, in their place and order, even those should teach us that fear of the Lord which hastens on the work of mortification; and if we learn it not thereby, those judgments are not duly improved by us, Ps. cxix. 118–120, and Eph. iii. 5, 7; and that none may suspect it to be a legal temper, Rev. xv. 3. This should be the effect of judgments upon others; much more, when they are amongst and on ourselves, and we involved in them, according to that, Luke xxiii. 40. It is the voice of severe proceedings to every of us; wilt thou not set thyself against sin, when it has brought thee into the same condemnation? When God is smiting sin with the sword of justice, he teaches us, and, as it were, guides our hands to wound it with the weapons of mortification. Shall we dare to spare it or harbour it, when we see God himself severely prosecuting it? If we fear God, we will not dare to do it; and when will we fear, if not when he appears terrible? We should learn righteousness by his judgments, Isa.

xxvi. 9; and mortifying of sin is the first part of this lesson, without which the other can never be learned to purpose.

Make use both of those other perfections of God and also of his judgments, to possess you with awful apprehensions of God; and walk under the sense and power of such apprehensions, so as they may influence you in your actings and endeavours against sin, for the purging of it out, and getting of it taken away. The fear of God is destructive of sin; it will not suffer you to think yourselves safe, unless sin be mortified.

(5.) Mortifying means, those which the Lord has appointed for this end. Make use of those weapons wherewith the Scriptures furnish you; use them daily, carefully, conscientiously, diligently; let it be the business and design of your lives. Look upon it as part of your work every day, and make account you have not done the work which God calls you to, and employs you in every day, if you have not done something against sin. Every day should help on the work of mortification, but especially days of affliction; then, if ever, the work should go on apace, otherwise they will be days of blackness indeed.

Let this be your chief care, as being your great concernment. Make conscience of it, as that which you are highly obliged to; and what you do against sin, do it with all your might, with all diligence. Imitate the apostle, 1 Cor. ix. 26. Paul did not use such weapons as were only for exercise, such as they call *lusoria;* he did not make a flourish, and only beat the air, with an intent only to shew his skill, not to hurt his adversary; he did not *ventilare*, but *pugnare;* he did fight in good earnest, as for life and death; his weapons were such whereby he might kill sin, and get it quite subdued, ver. 27.

More particularly, [1.] make use of the word. That is a most powerful engine for the overthrowing of sin; it is called 'the sword of the Spirit,' and the Lord has put it into your hands on purpose to do execution upon sin. It is one of those weapons which are 'not carnal, but mighty through God to the pulling down of sin's strongholds, casting down imaginations, and every high thing that exalteth itself against the knowledge of God, and bringing into captivity every thought to the obedience of Christ,' 2 Cor. x. 4, 5.

Every part of the word is powerful, and should be made use of for this purpose.

First, Commands; such as that, Isa. i. 16; and that, Col. iii. 5. There is authority in such commands, engaging us to fight when we would draw back, or loiter, or spare ourselves; and so sin is cut off from the advantages it might here gain upon us.

And there is encouragement in them. They are like the voice of a general, calling on his troops to charge; this rouses their courage and spirits, especially when they know he will second them, and is never wont to come off without victory.

And there is a virtue goes along with the commands, to a heart that will comply therewith, empowering to do what is commanded. It is not a bare, empty word; but a word of power and efficacy, through the concurrence and assistance of the Spirit enabling to do what it enjoins: 'He said, Let there be light, and there was light,' his word effected what he said; 'He sent out his word, and healed them,' Ps. cvii. 2; 'He commanded, and it was done,' Ps. xxxiii. 9. His commands to us will be as effectual, through the working of his Spirit and power, when we make due use of them.

Let the command be often in your minds; lay your hearts and consciences under the authority of it; comply with it, as if you heard his voice, and had it from his own mouth; as though you heard him thereby calling on you to charge, as though you saw him ready to second you, and make you assuredly victorious by his successful conduct. Remember, it is he that calls upon you, who will stand by you, and make you more than conquerors, if you flinch not, and betray not yourselves.

Secondly, The threatenings. These are as a sacrificing knife at the throat of sin, as corrosives, threatenings against sin. These shew it is condemned to die; they are the sentence of death passed by the Lord upon it; and hence you may be assured he is ready to assist you in the execution. Threatenings against those who do not mortify it: Rom. viii. 13, if you do not die to the flesh, you shall die. A threatening believed and applied close to the heart, and kept there by serious and severe thoughts of it, deads the heart to sin. It quells inclinations to it; quashes thoughts of harbouring or sparing it; confutes all the promises and flattering pretences of sin, by which it pleads for life and further entertainment; makes them appear to be lies and delusions; and shews, that not what sin offers or makes fair show of, but the quite contrary, will come to pass, and must be expected; and so cuts off all hopes and expectations of any true pleasure, or real advantage, or anything else desirable, to be had by sin; by which hopes it maintains itself, and is kept alive in deluded souls. And when these expectations are given up, and these hopes expire, the heart of sin is broken, and the heart of the sinner dies to it; and so far as the heart dies to it, so far sin is mortified, for its life is bound up therein. There is enough in the threatening so to embitter sin as no delight can be taken in it; it holds forth the wrath and displeasure of God as that which will be the issue of sin, instead of any advantage which it deceitfully offers, and so leaves you not the sight of anything for which sin should be suffered to live; but shews all reason why it should die, presses the soul against it, enforces and hastens to the execution of it. Even in the heat of temptation, a threatening duly apprehended and thought on would be as water to a kindling fire; it checks it, damps it at first, and continuing to pour it on, in fine, will extinguish it.

Believe but the threatening, and you will not believe, you will not regard what sin pleads for its life. The reason why it escapes and is forborne, is because we believe sin rather than God; the threatening, if mixed with faith, would lead sin to execution, without delay, without mercy.

Thirdly, The promises. These contribute much to the mortifying of sin, 2 Peter i. 4, 2 Cor. vii. 1. The promises have not only the force of an argument, but a real efficacy to this purpose; they have a powerful influence upon the children of promise, in their engagements against sin. These raise their spirits, heighten their courage, inspire them with resolution; and how much courage and resolution will prevail, even in those who are overpowered with strength and numbers, the world is full of experiments. These give them full assurance of divine assistance, of present relief when they are distressed, of all refreshment when they are ready to faint, and of a glorious issue of the conflict in victory and triumph. Here they may have a vision of the Lord of hosts engaging with them; of the Captain of their salvation, Jesus, ever victorious, leading them on; and of his Spirit teaching their hands to war and their fingers to fight the Lord's battles; such as are so unquestionably. In them you may hear the voice of God himself, speaking to you comfortable and encouraging words indeed, Isa. xli. 10–15.

Here is ground enough of confidence that we shall overcome, if we endeavour it. And then what glorious things they are assured of who overcome! Rev. ii. 7, 17 and iii. 5, 12, 21. Here is enough, considered and believed, to strengthen the weak hands and the feeble knees, and to raise the faintest to such a height of courage as will bear down all opposition.

And further, the promises out-bid what sin would bribe us with to spare it; and shews that in comparison there is nothing it tempts us with but trifles, shadows, and vain empty shows; that it would defeat us of the inestimable treasures in the mines of the great and precious promises, and put us off with a feather or a bauble; and so they engage us to proceed against it, as an unparalleled cheat and a pernicious deceiver.

[2.] Cut off the provisions of sin. Those by which it is nourished and maintained, kept in life and strength, and enabled to hold out against you. When an enemy is strongly seated, so as there is no storming nor undermining him, the way to subdue him is to fire his stores, cut off his water, intercept his convoys and provisions. Such a course should you take against sin; if you would subdue it, you must starve it, Rom. xiii. 14. Observe what it is that kindles lust, maintains sensuality, upholds worldliness, nourishes pride, or any other evil that you are subject to, and let these be removed. Gratify not your corruptions herein, and you take the course to starve them. Take away the fuel, and the fire will go out.

Use 2. For information. From hence we may give an account why troubles and afflictions befall the people of God. This is it which has much amazed both those that were acquainted with God, and the heathen too; that those who are best meet with hard measures in this life. But considering that those who are best are not perfect, and that there is a mixture of evil in those that are good, and that afflictions are the means to free them from that evil, it need be no wonder that the best are afflicted. The providence of God is not hereby impeached, but rendered more glorious; the wisdom and goodness of it is herein conspicuous. It is not because the Lord regards not human affairs, or cares not what befalls his creatures, but because he has a special care of his people, and sees it needful, considering what the complexion of their souls is by reason of sin, to exercise them with afflictions. He does it not without cause, he has a design therein suitable to his infinite wisdom. This end is expressed in the text; it is to purge their iniquity, &c. Sin is as rust upon their spirits, it must be filed off, and this cannot be done ordinarily without sharp tools. There is chaff mixed with the wheat, corruption with their graces; there needs a rough wind to separate them. There is dross in the best metal, there needs a furnace or a fining pot to work it out. There are distempers in their souls, which impair their health, and endanger spiritual life; there is need of physic to purge them out. Afflictions are such physic, administered by the great physician of souls for this end, that hereby their iniquity may be purged.

2. And from hence we may give an account why their afflictions are their ordinary fare; so that it is the complaint of some, which was the Psalmist's, lxxiii. 14, 'All the day long have I been plagued, and chastened every morning.' Sickly tempers must have a physical diet; to purge spring and fall will scarce secure some from the malignity of their distempers. The Lord knows our frame, and sees what is usually needful for every temper; and when he afflicts most frequently, he does no more than needs must, than he sees requisite for the purging of sin.

3. We may see also from hence why the troubles of the righteous are many, and why they are grievous. It is because less is not enough to attain the end. A gentle purge will not move every body, and that which works not may do more hurt than good. A wise physician will give that which will work, though it make his patient sick at heart in working. Is it not better he should do it than let him die? A father that will not have his

child undone will give many stripes, when fewer will not serve the turn. When a slower fire will not serve the refiner's end, he heats the furnace hotter and hotter. The people of God are not 'in heaviness through manifold temptations,' but 'if need be;' as the apostle expresses it, 1 Peter i. 6. And need there is, if fewer and easier will not purge our iniquity.

4. We may learn also from hence why troubles and afflictions are continued, and drawn out to a great length, why means for removing them are ineffectual, and hopes of deliverance is blasted. Why is the metal kept long in the fire, but because it is not soon refined? The Lord 'afflicts not willingly, nor grieves the children of men;' he delights not to protract our troubles; it is we that prolong them, because we continue unpurged, unrefined, unmortified. He shews us the way to shorten, and put an end to them quickly. Let us but comply with his design, and get our iniquity purged, &c., and deliverance will come speedily. The God of our salvation will come, and will not tarry. It is we that make him slow, and obstruct the way of deliverance; and if we should still delay, if he should cause our carcases to fall in the wilderness, if he should cause us to consume our days in troubles, it is because, Jer. vi. 29, 'the bellows are burnt, the lead is consumed by the fire,' but we are not purged.

Use 3. For instruction. If the end of afflictions be the purging of iniquity, this teaches,

1. Patience and contentment under afflictions. No reason to murmur or repine, or to give way to any sallies of impatience, or expressions of discontent, whatever our troubles be, how many, how sharp, how long soever. Will you not be content the Lord should cure you, and proceed in that method which his wisdom sees best and most effectual for that purpose? While you are under afflictions, you are under cure; and is it not better to be under cure, though the method seem unpleasing, than to be left languishing under soul distempers without remedy? Such lancing is painful. Oh, but what is the end of it? It is not to let out your blood, but to let out your corruption. Should you not be content to submit to any course of physic to free you from desperate distempers, when infinite wisdom prescribes it too? 'The cup that my Father gives me,' &c., John xviii. 11. What though it be a cup of trembling, and flesh and blood shrinks at it? Yet it is a Father that mingled it. Though the ingredients be bitter, they are wholesome. It is to free you from the danger of deadly poison; such poison is that iniquity which the Lord hereby is purging out. He is hereby whipping out of you that folly which is bound up in your hearts. Oh, that is a foolish child indeed, of no understanding, who had rather have his folly than the rod, that had rather be ruined than smart a little.

2. Cheerfulness under afflictions. Let not your spirits sink under them, though they may be heavy and tedious. Bear up cheerfully; faint not when you are rebuked, fall not into despondency. Look to the Lord's end in all severe proceedings; though affliction in itself be grievous, yet the end thereof is not so, that is matter of joy rather, 2 Cor. iv. 16. What though the receipt be bitter, it is to make me well; it is to heal my languishing and diseased soul; it is to purge out that which is my greatest misery.

3. Thankfulness. If the Lord should correct us merely for his pleasure, we ought to be contented; but since he chastens us for our profit, we ought to be thankful. Oh what cause is there of thankfulness, when we are assured that we are chastened of the Lord, that we may not be condemned with the world; that he chastens us that we may be thereby freed from that corruption for which the world will be condemned, and which would be our condemnation also if it were not purged out; to chasten us, to make us

smart a little; thereby to free us from the greatest, the most dreadful, the most deadly evil; to free us from sin, an evil incomparably worse than the extremity of all outward sufferings; and to free us from condemnation, in comparison of which all the calamities of this life are but as the prick of a pin. Oh, who would not be thankful for such a cure in such a way! The most afflicted condition on earth, ordered for the purging of sin, is incomparably a greater mercy than the most prosperous and flourishing condition in the world with an unpurged soul. Oh bless the Lord for those wounds, how deep soever they pierce into your estates, health, liberty; if they let out the corruption of your hearts, if they take away your sin, you will see cause to bless the Lord for them to eternity.

4. To love the Lord. Even his chastening of us should provoke to love him; for he afflicts us not to satisfy his anger, but to do us good; to purge our iniquity, *i. e.* to free us from the very worst of evils. So that he afflicts us not as an enemy, but as a father; not because he hates us, and would be revenged of us, but because he loves us, and would render us capable of more and greater expressions of his love, by freeing us from that which renders us unlovely, and abstracts the current of his loving-kindness. Herein are those affectionate expressions verified, 'As many as I love,' &c. So infinite is his love, that it breaks forth where we could least expect it, even in judgment he remembers mercy; even when we think him most angry, when he makes us smart, he is expressing love; he is taking away our sin, and therewith our misery. Now, love calls for love again: 'We love him, because he loved us first.' We are obliged to love him, wherever he shews love to us. If we love not him that we find loves us, we are worse than publicans; for they, the worst of sinners, do so.

Oh let us love him, not only because he spares us, because he showers down mercies on us, because he sent his Son to die and suffer for us, but because he makes us suffer, because he afflicts us out of so much love as to take away our sin. Oh he has not such a love for the world, as he has for his children, when he seems most severe in afflicting them.

5. To trust him. He has declared that by this our iniquity shall be purged, that this is his end and design in afflicting. Let us then believe that this is his end, and that it shall be accomplished; let us believe that it shall be to his afflicted people according to his word, that by this our iniquity shall be purged, that 'this shall be the fruit to take away our sin.' A soul that duly values so great a mercy, as the subduing of his iniquity, and the mortifying of his sins, will be ready to say, Oh, if I were but sure that this would be the issue of my sufferings and afflictions, I should not only be patient and contented with them, but would be cheerful under them, and thankful for them, and love the Lord for inflicting them. But this is my fear, they will not have this effect upon me. Why, but what assurance can you desire to encourage your faith, and to secure you from this distrustful fear, more than is here given you? You have for it the word of him who is truth itself, on his part; heaven and earth shall perish, rather than one tittle of it shall fail of performance, if you be not wanting to yourselves; if you walk in the way laid open to you, and use the means I have given an account of; if you wait on the Lord, and keep his way, assuredly his word will be made good, 'By this shall your iniquity be purged; and this shall be the fruit, to take away your sin.'

THE CONVICTION OF HYPOCRITES.

Many will say to me in that day, Lord, Lord, have we not prophesied in thy name? and in thy name have cast out devils? and in thy name done many wonderful works? And then will I profess unto them, I never knew you: depart from me, ye that work iniquity.—MAT. VII. 22, 23.

THESE words are part of Christ's sermon on the mount. The latter part of it he applies for conviction, the conviction of hypocrites, those that pretend to be what they are not. These are of three sorts:

1. These are so apparently, both to themselves and others, who pretend they are Christians, but are so no further than in outward profession. They bear the name, but express not the thing; such as the apostle speaks of, who profess they know God, &c., Tit. i. 16; profess they love Christ, but in their actions crucify him; live in known sins, in visible wickedness: so as their own consciences may testify to themselves, and their conversations do testify to others, they are no Christians indeed; they have nothing of the reality, and they are a reproach to the name. There is a visible contradiction betwixt the words whereby they profess it, and their actions and practices.

2. Some are so apparently to themselves, but not to others. Those wh have the outward lineaments, but want the soul of Christianity; and either are, or easily may be, conscious to it. Such an hypocrite is a stage-player in Christianity. He outwardly acts the part of a Christian, has his words, and garb, and gestures, and actions; but look within him, and he is quite another thing. The description of hypocrites which Christ gives us, agrees exactly to him: outwardly he is like a whited sepulchre, but within full of dead bones and rottenness. He has a form of godliness, but denieth the power thereof.

3. Those that are so apparently neither to themselves nor others, but are so really, and in the sight of God. They may account themselves sincere Christians, for some slight resemblance; and they may be so accounted by others, for their outward conformity to the laws of Christ, and yet in Christ's account they may be workers of iniquity, such as he will not own hereafter as his people. Of this last sort are the hypocrites in the text. He spoke these words for the conviction of such, and so we shall endeavour to handle them. In pursuance hereof, we observe three things: 1, their presump-

tion; 2, their plea; 3, their doom. Their presumption; they persuade themselves that heaven is theirs. They put in their plea for it at the bar of Christ; argue with him as though it were not equal, not just, that they should be excluded, so confident are they of salvation. Hence,

Obs. Many think themselves sure of heaven, when it is sure they shall never come there. Many are persuaded they shall enter into heaven, whom Christ is resolved to shut out of it. This is clearly implied in the text; yet because it is but implied, I shall not much insist on it; and it is not that which I principally aimed at. Only it will be necessary to take notice of the grounds of this woful mistake, that they may be avoided. And they are such as these:

(1.) *Ignorance and inadvertency.* There are many who know not, or at least consider not, what is necessary to bring a soul to heaven; where the way lies, and what Christ requires of those that would enter into it. They consider not that there must be regeneration; that 'unless a man be born again, he cannot enter into the kingdom of God;' that there must be a new creation; that the new Jerusalem is only for new creatures. There must be an universal change in every part of the soul, in the whole course of their lives; that old things must pass away, and all things become new; new heart, and new way. There must be a holiness in the life, growth, power, and exercise of it; that 'without holiness no man shall see the Lord.' There must be self-denial; a denying of their own wisdom, will, humour, interests. A renouncing of the world; they must be crucified to the world; they understand scarce what it is to be crucified. Mortification; they must mortify the flesh with the affections and lusts; die daily. A taking up the cross: that if any man will come after Christ, that it may cost him tears, sighs, bonds, imprisonment, his estate, his relations, his limbs, his blood, his life, and all; that he must be fully resolved to be at the expense, whenever there is occasion; that it requires all diligence, 2 Pet. i.; that he must strive, and break through all difficulty, what sweat and toil soever it cost to crowd in, Luke xiii. 24; that he must wrestle, employ all his strength, Eph. vi. 12.; that he must run, put out all his might, so run as he may obtain; that he must fight, be in a continual war, fight the good fight; that he must beat his body, 1 Cor. ix. 27; that he must take heaven by force, if he will have it. If they did know and consider this, they would not be confident of heaven, when they are strangers to these things which are required of all those for whom heaven is intended.

(2.) *Negligence, slothfulness.* If they know these things, yet will not take the pains to examine their state by them, they will not be at the trouble to compare their hearts with the rule. They will not spare a few hours seriously to inquire whether they come up to what the word requires.

Alas, for the wretched carelessness of men as to their own souls, and their everlasting state! One that seriously observes, would think that the greatest part of people amongst us are either atheists or madmen; either they believe not that there is a God, or that the Scriptures are his word; or that their souls are immortal; or that there is a state of everlasting misery or happiness for every one after death; or that there are evidences in the word, by which they may know whether they shall be eternally damned or saved. Either they believe not these things, and so are plain atheists; or if they believe there is such a God, and such a soul, and such an eternal state, and such a word wherein they may have directions to know whether their souls are bound for heaven or hell, would they not make use of these directions? Would they not spare some hours to examine seriously whether heaven or hell be their portion? Would they not do this presently? Would they not do it seriously, as a matter of eternal life or death requires, if they were not madmen indeed, if they were not quite bereaved of all spiritual sense and reason?

No; rather than they will thus trouble themselves, they will take it upon trust that they shall go to heaven, when, alas, they have no ground for a trust but what Satan suggests, or their own deceitful hearts prompts them; and thus they hang the whole weight of eternity upon a cobweb; and thus they pin the everlasting concernments of their souls upon a shadow, as though it would hang there safe enough, where it can have no hold at all. Would any do this but a madman? What! trust without trial in a matter of eternal consequence to body and soul. What need I put myself to this trouble? I will trust God with my soul, say some; what need I take any care further? But alas, wretched creature! this is not to trust God, but to trust Satan with the soul; and oh what a woful account will he give thee of it one day! Now, when men are so careless of their souls, when they will not trouble themselves to inquire after their eternal state, no wonder if they be so wofully mistaken as to promise themselves heaven, when nothing but hell is reserved for them.

(3.) *Self-love.* This possesses men with a good conceit of themselves, a good opinion of their souls' condition; so that if they come to examine their state, or be called to try it in the public ministry, they come to the work prepossessed. Self-love will not suffer them to deal impartially with their souls; they catch greedily at anything that seems to make for them, and are careful to stave off everything that would make against them; or, if they cannot yet put such a favourable construction on it, as partial men will do when they are resolved to defend a bad cause, they look upon that word as an enemy, that would shake the rotten pillars of a false hope. They deal with it as the prophet did with the king's messenger, make sure to shut him out. As self-love makes them flatter themselves, so they would have the word of God to flatter them; they love not plain, searching, awakening truths; they will have a good opinion of themselves, whatever be said to the contrary. They say, as Laodicea, that they are 'rich and increased,' &c., though Christ in the ministry say the contrary, they are 'poor, wretched,' &c. Though this be plainly manifested, yet self-love makes them both unable and unwilling to discern it. A blind man cannot judge of colours; and self-love blinds them, they cannot judge of the complexions of soul, whether the features, the characters of heaven or hell be on it; care not for looking in a true glass lest the visage of their soul, if truly represented, should trouble them. Satan blinds one eye, and self-love closes the other, and the deceitfulness of sin seals both. No wonder if they call darkness light, &c.; no wonder if they fancy themselves in the way to heaven when they are in the high road to hell. The blind leads the blind, you know what will be the issue; no wonder if when they think they shall be safe ashore in heaven, and their feet near the very banks of happiness, at that very moment they are falling into the ditch.

(4.) *Misapprehensions of God.* If light and conviction proceed so far as to discover to a sinner that he comes short of the rule, and that what the word calls for, as necessary to salvation, is not to be found in him; if he cannot misapprehend his own state any longer, rather than he will quit his vain deceiving hopes, he will misapprehend God and think him more merciful than the word represents him. It is true, says the sinner, in this case, the rule is strict and the way to heaven seems to be strait, and much is required of a sinner that he may be saved, and I am to seek in this or that; but God is merciful, and he may save me, though I find not this or that which seems to be required. Though I allow myself in this or that sin, and fall into it now and then, why it is but a little one, and God is gracious, he is not so strict and rigid as some would make him. What though I be not so strict and precise as some others, must none be saved but such as they? God forbid. Though I come not up to the rule, God is gracious, he may dispense with me, I may be saved as well as the best of them.

But alas, poor deluded sinner! if here be all thy hopes, thy case is hopeless. Will God be so merciful as to contradict himself and go contrary to his word? Will he shew thee so much mercy as to neglect his truth? Will he save thee when he cannot do it without making himself a liar? Doest thou not tremble to see that thou hast nothing to bear up thy hopes of heaven but plain blasphemy?

If thou find not what he requires as necessary to salvation, if he should save thee without it, he should deny himself, abandon his truth. Dost thou think he will make himself no God that he may make thee happy? Oh, how sad is thy case, when even as thyself has stated it, thou hast no hopes of heaven, but upon such terms as the very thought of them deserves hell for ever!

(5.) They have many *vain and insufficient pleas* for their salvation. (That leads me to the second part of the text.)

2. The hypocrite's plea. That is express. They have many things to allege for themselves why they should be admitted into heaven. Let us survey them a little.

Their first plea is in the word LORD: that includes much. It is of the like import as the same word, ver. 21. This denotes that they did acknowledge and profess Christ, acknowledge him as their Lord, and profess him zealously, so some explain it; or that they did pray unto him, that they prayed frequently and fervently, as the doubling of the word, *Lord, Lord,* intimates, and that they did believe on him as their Lord. They had some faith, either of assent, affiance, or both. So Chrysostom and others. *Vid. Maldonat.*

Have we not prophesied? &c. Here is their next plea; and prophesying in Scripture is preaching: 1 Cor. xiv. 3, 'He that prophesieth speaketh unto men, to edification, exhortation, consolation;' or praying: Gen. xx. 7, 'He is a prophet, and when he shall pray for thee;' or singing: 1 Chron. xxv. 1, so probably it may be taken, 1 Cor. xi. 5; or foretelling things to come: that is the ordinary acceptation of the word; or for explaining the prophetical writings.

Now, if we take it in its full latitude, their plea is fuller: they had preached Christ, explained the prophecies concerning him; they had prayed to him, and sung his praises; and by his Spirit had foretold things to come, for the confirmation of his truth and doctrine.

And in thy name cast out devils. By the power of Christ they had dispossessed Satan, and in a miraculous manner cast him out of those bodies that he had possessed. And this was not the only wonder they had done for Christ; they had done many more. *And in thy name,* they had done works for him, many works, and many wonderful works; not *mira* only, but *miracula;* works truly and properly miraculous, beyond the whole power of nature.

Thus much they had done for Christ, and all this in his name, by his authority, in his strength, for his glory. Whatever they intended, these works did tend to glorify him in the world, and that eminently and extraordinarily; all this they allege for themselves, and they allege them truly. Christ objects not against the truth of their plea, but against the sufficiency of it. Though all this was true, yet it was not enough to make them capable of heaven, and there he excludes them.

Obs. Many shall go far towards heaven, and yet never reach it. They may go far in the ways of Christ, and yet miss heaven in the conclusion. This is evident in the text. Here are many who had professed Christ, and been zealous professors; who professed him not in word only, but had really worshipped him; had been much in hearing, preaching, praying, praising him. Nor did their religion consist only in outward acts, they had believed on him too; nor was their faith without works, it was accompanied with many works, with many wonderful works; and yet for all this, when they shall come to allege these things at the day of judgment for their admission into heaven, Christ tells us here that he will shut them out, he will disclaim them, and profess to them that he knows them not, *i. e.* that he never loved them, never approved them; he will command them to depart from him, and give them their portion with the workers of iniquity. There needs nothing more for evidence to this truth. But the

Question here will be, How far may professors go in the ways of Christ, and yet come short of heaven?

I shall resolve this according to the method of the text, by endeavouring to shew how far they may go both in ordinaries and extraordinaries.

1. In extraordinaries.

(1.) Revelations, dreams, visions. God may reveal himself by dreams and visions. It is no peculiar privilege of the godly which is promised, Joel ii. 28; Acts ii. 16, ' Your old men shall dream dreams, and your young men see visions.' For dreams, it is evident in Nebuchadnezzar, to whom the revealer of secrets, as Daniel speaks, by dreams made known what should be hereafter. His dream arose not from an ordinary cause, it was sent from the Lord, the revealer of secrets. The subject of his dream was not ordinary, but secrets and things future; even the most remarkable acts of providence that should come to pass to the end of the world: the rise, periods, and revolutions of the world's monarchies, and the erecting of the kingdom of Christ: the stone cut out without hands, Dan. ii. 34, which should crush all the kingdoms of the world, and raise his throne upon their ruins. Here is a remarkable revelation, almost comparable to any mentioned in Scripture. Another you have, Dan. iv. 4, 5. Pharaoh also had a revelation by a dream. Gen. xli. 25, 28; and when Saul complains that the Lord answered him not either by dreams or prophets, it implies that he did reveal himself by these before he was cast off, 1 Sam. xxviii. 6. This is confirmed, Deut. xiii. 1, 2.

For visions, we have a clear instance in Balaam, the wizard or enchanter, who used to seek for enchantments, Num. xxiv. 1; even to him did the Lord reveal himself by visions. God came unto him, chap. xxii. 9, and conferred with him, and revealed to him both what he should say, and what he should do, ver. 12, 20. He had the vision of an angel, ver. 31. So chap. xxiii. 4, 5, God met Balaam, and put a word into his mouth. Two several immediate revelations we have in that chapter, and two, chap. xxiv. whereto the preface is observable: ver. 23, ' The Spirit of God came upon him, and Balaam took up his parable, and said, The man whose eyes are opened,' &c., ' which heard the words of God, which saw the vision of the Almighty, falling into a trance, but having his eyes opened;' and ver. 16, ' Which knew the knowledge of the Almighty.'

(2.) The gift of prophecy. Those whom Christ shuts out of his kingdom, and will take no notice of them, and had this plea for themselves, ' In thy name have we prophesied.' It is known that Saul was at best but an hypocrite, yet, 1 Sam. x. 10, 19, 23, ' the Spirit of the Lord came upon him, and he prophesied.' Hence the proverb, ' Is Saul also among the prophets?' And there is scarce a clearer prophecy of Christ at such a distance than that of Balaam's, Num. xxiv. 16, where he also foretells the ruin of several nations, Moab, Edom, Amalek, the Kenites, Assyrians, and Romans, and who should ruin them, which the event has proved true, 1 Kings xiii. 21, 22.

(3.) The power to work miracles. They may do signs and wonders, heal all diseases, cast out devils, yea, it is possible for them to remove mountains. For proof, see Deut. xiii. 1, 2, 'If there arise amongst you a prophet, or a dreamer of dreams, and gives thee a sign or a wonder, and the sign or the wonder come to pass, saying, Let us go after other gods.' Idolaters may do these. They may also cast out devils. This they plead whom Christ will not own: 'In thy name have we cast out devils, and in thy name done many wonderful works,' Mat. vii. 22. Yet what they were appears by Christ's profession, ver. 23, ' Depart from me, ye that work iniquity.' The children of the unbelieving Jews had power to cast out devils, as appears by Christ's question, by what power they cast them out. Mat. xii. 24, 27. The disciples tell Christ they saw one casting out devils in his name, and rebuked him. That it is possible for those who are not godly to have a miraculous faith, so as to remove mountains, is evident, 1 Cor. xiii. 2, for we cannot suppose the apostle would argue from an impossibility. But we need not make use of suppositions, since it is express that Judas had power to work miracles; for, Mat. x. 1, ' Christ called his twelve disciples,' whereof Judas was one, ' and gave them power against unclean spirits, and to heal all manner of sickness, and all manner of diseases.' We cannot doubt but Judas was one, since he is named amongst them, ver. 4 and Mark iii. 17, immediately after Judas named, he adds: ' These twelve Jesus sent forth, and commanded them to heal the sick, cleanse the lepers, raise the dead, cast out devils: freely ye have received,' &c.

(4.) The gift of tongues: 1 Cor. xiii. 1, ' Though I speak with the tongue of men and angels.' *Donum linguarum in summo gradu quale esset, si quis omnibus linguis loqui possit.* For these are not saving gifts, and therefore may be given to those who shall never be saved.

By the way, observe a delusion in those who prefer these before saving graces, and by the appearance of those will be drawn to embrace errors, whereas it is wholesome advice, which we find in the epistle to Hero, ascribed to Ignatius, πᾶς ὁ λέγων παρὰ τα διατεταγμένα, κᾂν ἀξιόπιστος ᾖ, κᾂν σημεία ποιῇ, κᾂν προφητεύῃ, λύκος σοι φαινέσθω. And after, κᾂν ψωμίσῃ τα ὑπάρχοντα πτωχοῖς, κᾂν ὄρη μεθιστᾷ, κᾂν παραδῷ το σῶμα εἰς καῦσιν, ἔστω σοι βδελυκτός.

2. In ordinaries.

(1.) In knowledge they may go far. This we may discover in the text; it is included in the word *prophesy*; for whether we take it for teaching and publishing the truth, or foretelling things to come, it necessarily supposes and imports knowledge. And this knowledge may be,

[1.] *Great* for the extent of it. It may reach many truths that are out of the reach of many sincere Christians. Their minds may grasp more of truth than the understanding of others is capable of; may admit more light than others can let in. They may dig further into the mines of truth, and make greater discoveries. No question Judas knew more than many of those he preached to, though we may suppose some of them sincerely converted. If he had not known more than his hearers, he had not been, διδάκτικος, apt to teach, fit to be their teacher. And Christ, who would have this to be observed as a qualification in those that we choose, would not himself choose one destitute of it.

But that their knowledge may be exceeding great, the apostle puts it out of question, 1 Cor. xiii. All knowledge they may have, and yet want charity (saving grace), and have nothing that accompanies salvation, ver. 9 ; all, *i. e.* knowledge in a high degree, of a large extent. They may know not only all necessary truths, those that are vital and radical, being the foundation of religion, but those which raise the structure, and tend to edifying; nay, those which are for the finishing and completing of an intelligent Christian, which tend to make him a thoroughly furnished and accomplished man as to his intellectuals.

All knowledge is a large expression, and will reach thus far and farther, without stretching; he may far outgo a true saint in the largeness and extent of his knowledge; know much more clear and evident, solid and convincing. He may apprehend truth not only truly, but clearly, distinctly, evidently; so as the clearness of his conceptions may convince his conscience, and satisfy his judgment of the truth he apprehends. His notions may appear in his mind with such a clear ray of evidence as may scatter all doubt, leave no room for question or contradiction. He may be able to convey his notions clearly to others, so as to convince and satisfy them. A sincere soul, as to many things, may be much in the dark compared with him.

Such a clear, convincing knowledge may be in them who apostatise, &c., Heb. vi. 4. These expressions, which the Arminians would have to be so many characters of true believers, that thereby they may prove the apostasy of the saints, may all be applied to Balaam, a wizard, and no saint. The Holy Ghost ascribes the like things to him.

Enlightened. 'The man whose eyes are opened,' Num. xxiv., 'who knew the knowledge of the Almighty,' ver. 16; 'tasted of the heavenly gift,' *i. e.* of Christ. Unbelievers may taste him, believers only feed upon him. Balaam had some foretastes, some foresight of Christ; for he prophesied of him, and that as clearly as any at such distance. 'Partakers of the Holy Ghost:' the Spirit of God came upon him, ver. 2, 3. The gift of prophecy: 'tasted of the good word of God.' He had tasted of the gospel, the best word of God; his prophecy is evangelical, a prophecy of Christ; good, because it brings good tidings of great joy. 'Powers of the world to come;' hence his desire, 'Let me die the death of the righteous,' Heb. x. 26, ἐπίγνωσις; after they have made such a clear discovery of the truth as convinces judgment and conscience, and brings it to an acknowledgment that it is the truth, and worthy of acceptation, entertainment, approbation; and yet for all this clear knowledge they are evidently hypocrites, else they could not sin that sin, nor incur that doom.

[2.] *Divine* as to the object of it; divine matter. They may have great and clear knowledge of the things of God, of the truths of Christ, of the doctrine of the gospel; not only of those truths that are more common and obvious, but of the more mysterious and subtle parts thereof, those which are called the mysteries of the kingdom, *arcana imperii*: Mat. xiii. 11, 'To you it is given to know the mysteries of the kingdom of heaven.' Mysteries of God: 1 Cor. iv. 1, 'Let a man account of us, as of the ministers of Christ, and stewards of the mysteries of God.' The apostle's discourse, 1 Cor. xiii. 2, implies that he who has no true grace, may know all mysteries, all gospel mysteries. *Mysterium est sacrum arcanum*, a divine secret; such as could not have been known but by divine revelation; such as no light of nature, no human understanding, could have ever reached, had they not been brought down by the Spirit of revelation. He may see far into these mysteries; he may have access unto the most retired of those secrets; he may wade far into the deep things of God, as if all were fordable. Those things which are δυσνόητα, difficult to others, may be easy to him.

As for speculative points, there is no question. They may soar aloft in those notions, and be as eagles in the clouds, when a sincere soul may flag, never rise to so high a pitch, and be more apt to admire them than able to follow them.

As for truths questioned, intricate controversies, they may decide them with clearness and satisfaction, when others do not understand the terms, or think the arguments against the truth unanswerable, or are nonplussed, and gravelled in the difficulty and abstruseness of the things.

As for practicals, they may resolve those cases of conscience with ease and evidence, when an upright heart is sadly entangled, and sees no clear or safe way out.

As for experimentals, though they have but this knowledge at the second hand, yet they may have more at the second than those of experience have at the first. By experimental discourses, and conversing with experienced Christians, they may come to great attainments in this kind. They may draw the lineaments of a new creature so exactly, and to the life, as though they had a pattern thereof in their own souls. They may give such an account of the work of grace, as you may think they were transcribing their own hearts, and that their expressions were but copies of some original there. They may hold forth the conflicts betwixt the flesh and the spirit, as though the combat were in their own quarters, as though they had really felt some such thing as you hear. They may express the actings of grace in such and such a duty, such an occasion, under such a temptation, in such a manner, as you would think nothing could teach them, but their own experience. They may have the exact idea, the true notion of these things in their heads, when there is nothing of all this in their hearts.

As for textual divinity, the understanding of the Scriptures, they may excel herein. They may overcome those difficulties, which some obscure places make impassable and unfordable to others. They may understand not only the words and phrases, and so become masters of the letter of the Scripture; but they may, with a great sagacity, find out the sense and meaning of the Holy Ghost, and may outstrip many herein who have the Holy Spirit dwelling in them. The apostle's expression, *all mysteries*, will, I think, bear me out in all this, if experience did not witness it. And, indeed, being on a ticklish point, in a slippery place, I will not venture to go without hold; and that which I will lean upon all along shall be Scripture, in its expression or consequences, or else clear reason and experience. They may, with a great happiness, find out the meaning of prophecies, which are for the most part the darkest parts of Scripture; for in the text it is said, 'Have we not prophesied?' and 1 Cor. xiii. 2. And if they may have the gift of prophecy to foretell things to come, which is rarer and further out of our reach, sure they may have the gift of prophecy to explain what is foretold, this being more common and ordinary.

[3.] Spiritual as to the author of it, such as proceeds from the Spirit of God. They may attain their knowledge, not only by their pains and industry in searching after it, not only by reading, study, conference, &c.; but the Holy Spirit may dart this light into them, either in the use of means or immediately, Heb. vi. Those who were never in a saving condition, are said to be enlightened. And who it was that enlightened them, we may learn by another clause in that verse, 'partakers of the Holy Ghost.' They partaked of the Holy Ghost, because they were partakers of the light, and other gifts and operations of the Holy Ghost. They did partake of him, as he communicated himself to them, and this was one way he enlightened them; not only in a common way, as all light and knowledge in the world may be said to come from the Father of light, and as Christ is said to enlighten every man that comes into the world, viz., by implanting in their minds that light which we call natural, and with a common concurrence with the endeavours of those that are industrious, helping them to an increase and improvement of that light: for this he vouchsafes, as he is God and Governor of the world. But he enlightens them in a more special and peculiar manner (though not the most peculiar) as he is Mediator, and the great Prophet of his church, sending his Spirit (in the execution of his prophetical office) to spread abroad a divine light in the minds of some who enjoy the gospel, whereby they may discover the deep things of God. The Spirit of God may come upon such a man as Balaam, or Saul, or Caiaphas, and may shine into their souls, if not ordinarily now with a prophetical light, yet with an evangelical light, to discover to them the secrets of Christ, and the mysteries of the gospel, and the things of the world to come. You have all these in that verse: the gift of God, *i.e.* Christ, as some; and the word of God, *i.e.* there is the precious mysteries of the gospel, &c. They may partake of the Holy Ghost, and be thereby so enlightened as to see these things, and so see them as to taste them; they may by this light discover the excellency, goodness, sweetness, of these things, so clearly and convincingly as if they did taste them. Such a light, such a knowledge, they may have from the Spirit of Christ, in that respect a spiritual knowledge, and yet have their portion in outer darkness.

[4.] Operative. Their knowledge may be in great measure effectual; it may have a mighty efficacy both upon their souls and lives, both upon heart and affections, and upon their conversation; it may have an influence both upon inward and outward man, powerful to change both in some degree.

The inward efficacy of it may be clearly collected from that of James ii. 19. The devils have such a clear knowledge of God as they cannot but believe what they know; and this knowledge, which brings them to believe, makes them tremble; here is the efficacy of it, it works fear and horror. Now why knowledge may not work this in men as well as devils, I apprehend not; and why it may not work other affections as well as fear, no reason can be assigned; and I shall shew how the affections in particular may be moved, in the next head.

Now since this knowledge may have such power upon the affections, and seeing affections are but the acts and motions of the will, it follows that it may have some efficacy upon the will. Now the will being the great wheel that, moved, sets all the parts of the whole man on motion, it is hence evident that their knowledge may be operative upon the whole man, it may have a working influence upon every faculty within, upon every part and member without. For the inward efficacy of it we have said sufficient at present, it may excite fear, hope, joy, sorrow, &c.; and as it may make some alteration within, so may it effect a reformation without. The apostle expresses this evidently, 2 Pet. ii. 20, he speaks of some apostates here, who, therefore, were in a damnable condition, and yet had 'escaped the pollutions of the world,' the sinful abominations of the wicked world, and the means whereby they escaped is the knowledge of Christ. The light of this knowledge did discover their former evil ways to be so sinful and abominable that they fled from them, ἀποφύγοντες, as one would fly from an ugly fiend; they so fled from them, as they seemed to have made a real escape from the evils of an unconverted state, ver. 18, ὄντως. See here the efficacy of this knowledge as to reformation of life; it may make them not only avoid sin but fly from it, to fly from it as from a pollution, as though they loathed and abhorred it; not only to go but to fly from it, as we do from that we are greatly afraid of, and to fly so far, so fast, as one would think it could never overtake, one would hope they had made a clear escape. Such, so powerful may be the knowledge of those that are no better than hypocrites; thus far may they go in knowledge, it may be so great, clear, &c., and yet Christ may profess even to these at the great day, 'I know ye not.'

Let not ignorance take encouragement from hence. If such knowledge will not bring a man to heaven, to what purpose is it to labour after knowledge? Say not thus; methinks this should rather strike ignorant persons with fear and trembling. If so much knowledge will not bring a man to heaven, how far art thou from heaven who hast so little, none at all? If these whose knowledge brings them so near it, within sight of it, shall not enter, how far are you from it who come not near them, who shall fall short of it? If he who stays a mile off the palace cannot lodge in it, can he expect to lodge there who stays twenty miles short? If those who come so near to heaven as they can discover it, take some view of it, come within sight, shall yet never enter, how can they look to enter who stay ten thousand miles off, who stay in the suburbs of hell? Such is ignorance; you are so near hell as you are within the shadow of it, hell overshadows you. Darkness and the shadow of death are joined in Scripture. Ignorance is spiritual darkness, the very shadow of eternal death. There is but a small partition between you and hell. Hell is outer darkness, and ignorance is inner darkness; it is the very next room to hell. Oh consider your sad condition. Will you stay far short of those who fall short of heaven? If those who come so near Canaan as they can descry it, so near it as they taste some of it, shall yet fall in the wilderness and never enjoy it, how can they come to Canaan who will not stir out of Egyptian darkness? How can you come to the land of promise, come to heaven, who stay in your ignorance, that which is worse than Egyptian darkness, and a condition further from heaven than Egypt is from Canaan? A man with thus much knowledge may possibly perish, but an ignorant person shall certainly perish, Isa. xxvii. 11.

Quest. But if they may go so far in respect of knowledge, wherein does their knowledge come short of that which is saving? Wherein do they differ? How may they be distinguished, so as I may know whether my knowledge be saving, or only such as hypocrites may have?

Ans. I shall endeavour to distinguish all along betwixt that which is common, and that which is saving, lest this doctrine, which is so necessary for the conviction of counterfeits, may not be hurtful to any soul that is sincere in the least degree, to trouble or disquiet them, whom the Lord would not have troubled; but I shall be brief in this part, because the text leads me not directly to it.

Their knowledge comes short, in that it is not, 1, truly experimental; nor, 2, practical, thoroughly efficacious.

1. *Experimental.* They may have more natural knowledge in the letter; know more of the nature of divine objects, more distinctly, methodically, and vent it more plausibly. A great difference, as betwixt the knowledge which a naturalist has of manna, and an Israelite. He, by reading and discourse, knows more of the nature and effects of it, but he that hath tasted it, fed upon it, knows it more feelingly, satisfyingly, inwardly. 'Taste and see that the Lord is good,' Ps. xxxiv. 8; 'If so be ye have tasted that the Lord is gracious,' 1 Pet. ii. 3. A formalist knows God in his nature, attributes, subsistences, operations; notionally, by reason, revelation, but not experimentally; knows what he is in himself, not what to him and in him: as the Israelites knew the land of Canaan before they came to it, but far otherwise when in possession of it; as the knowledge of Balaam prophesying of

Christ, and Simeon having him in his arms; Zaccheus from the tree, and in his house.

The godly know God's attributes experimentally, acting within them. Omnipotence enabling them to believe, Eph. i. 19; subduing lusts, overcoming the world. If there were no other arguments *ab extra* to prove it, this would be sufficient to convince them. Omnisciency, by detecting the heart's deceitfulness, discovering secret sins, pride, hypocrisy, self-will; immensity, by God's special presence in their hearts, acting, supporting, comforting; mercy, infinite grace in pardoning sin. They know Christ experimentally in his offices: as priest, saving them from guilt; as prophet, enlightening them; as king, conquering sin, the world, Satan. The Spirit in its functions, convincing, regenerating, uniting, helping infirmities, sealing.

Formalists know these, but not within them; know he is almighty, but have not felt him so, &c.

2. It is not *efficacious*. True saving knowledge is transforming knowledge, changeth the subject into the likeness of the object. This light leaves a lustre, a beauty behind it, as the sun. It is a heavenly vision, a vision of God. Now the sight of God assimilates: 'We shall be like him, for we shall see him,' 1 John iii. 2. It is effectual in the mind, does spiritualize it in others; as the sun more lightsome, but nothing cleaner and sweeter on a dunghill. In the conscience, makes it tender, sensible. This light makes those characters appear, which custom in sin wears out; so as the conscience can put them together, and thereby frame its charges, accusations for sins past, though small in ordinary account. And its warnings and prohibitions against sin for the future, makes sin as a prick in the eye, not as wounding only, but as polluting. In the will, inclines it to the object known, according to the clearness of the discovery. A great sympathy betwixt these faculties. The will must either not move at all, or move as it knows. When the beams of Christ's beauty shine in the mind, the will leaps to him, embraces him: 'Come in, thou blessed of the Lord.' In others there are some languid motions, faint inclinations. It brings not the will quite off from other things, so as to close fully with Christ. It may move the scales, and bring the will to some indifferency, to some stand, but it brings not full weight, swaying down the will to full resolutions for Christ. There is something in the other end of the balance, some gainful or delightful lust, that doth counterpoise whatever the light discovers of Christ, and keeps the will from a downright determination to sell all for him. In the affections, light and heat are inseparable; divine light in the mind conveys a heat into the affections. As this heat melts the will into the will of God, so it kindles the affections into holy flames, love, desire, zeal, joy, when the object is good; dissolves it into fear, sorrow, shame; raises in it hatred, indignation, when the object is evil. Light is always hot; but the direct beams are not so hot as the reflected. The beams of a formalist's knowledge are not reflected; his mind refracts them. It is like the sunshine in winter, it may give some lustre and refreshing to the earth, and may thaw and mollify the outside, but at night all is frozen up; it makes not the plants grow, or the earth fruitful. In the life it is practical, makes him active. There is a conformity betwixt life and light, knowledge and practice. He lives up to his light, detains not truth in unrighteousness. He does what he knows. 'If ye know these things, happy are ye if ye do them,' John xiii. 17. He is obedient to the heavenly vision; he dares not do that which he knows to be sinful, nor omit that which he knows to be his duty.

The formalist's knowledge is weak and partial, may restrain him from the pollutions of the world; but saving knowledge will avoid that in which the world sees no pollution.

2. They may go far in respect of graces and affections; the Holy Ghost may work in them such graces, stir up in them such affections as have a great resemblance with those that are saving. They may in these respects partake of the Holy Ghost; for there are some whom the apostle tells us may be partakers of the Holy Ghost, and yet have nothing in them that accompanies salvation; and may shew it by falling away, and turning apostates, Heb. vi. 4, 9. They may be partakers of the Holy Ghost upon this account, because the Holy Ghost may make them partakers of many spiritual gifts and common graces, such as are highly valuable in themselves, and exceeding useful and profitable unto others, and much for the ornament and comfort too of those that have them; and though they be not saving, have no necessary connection with eternal life, yet they are very like to, and have a near affinity with, saving graces; so as it will be very difficult to distinguish them, and to make the difference evident to a soul under doubts and jealousies of its spiritual condition: so like they are, that they sometimes go under the same name in Scripture, and are held forth to us under the same expressions. Those who have no saving grace may yet taste of the powers of the world to come, may have some tastes of that glory and happiness that shall be revealed. They may taste of the good word of God, some tastes of the sweet and precious things of the gospel; they may taste of the heavenly gift, have some tastes of Christ, frequently called 'the gift of God,' John iv. 10. They may taste that the Lord is gracious, but yet not as true believers taste; for they taste Christ so as to let down what they taste, as a hungry man eats his meat, or a man ready to faint with thirst tastes his drink; they let it down with delight and greediness. So do true believers receive what they taste of Christ: they let it down as a choice delicacy; they retain and digest it. It is turned into nourishment, and proves life, and health, and strength to their souls. These taste Christ too, but it is with some disrelish; so as they either spit out what they taste, or let it down so sparingly, that it proves no advantage as to spiritual life and health; or vomit up again what they have let down, as not agreeing with their foul stomachs, with their unpurged hearts, which they make visible in their apostasies.

However, some tastes they have, and that from the Holy Ghost; by him also they are enlightened (as before), and partake of him, not only in respect of illumination, but also as to some kind of sanctification; not that which is saving, but that which is very like it, Heb. x. 29. Those who fell so wofully, so desperately, as to tread under foot the Son of God, are said to have been sanctified.

We need not, I think, restrain this to an external church sanctification; as if they had been said to be sanctified because they had separated themselves from the world to come to the church, and to partake of the privileges thereof, whereby they were visibly dedicated and set apart unto God.

Nor to a reputed sanctification, as though they had been only sanctified in the opinion of others, who, judging charitably, took them to be inwardly holy, because they were so outwardly, having a visible holiness in their conversations.

For there is a sanctification besides these, which is inward and real; not in outward expressions only, or in the repute of others, and yet is not saving, how much soever it resemble it. There may be in such as those whom the apostle speaks of a real change, a change in the soul, a change in every part of the soul, so that every part may be in some measure changed, and so far sanctified; and yet not savingly changed, renewed, sanctified, though, for the near resemblance betwixt them, many may mistake the one for the other.

There may be a change in the mind: that which was formerly darkness may be now full of light; as before.

In the conscience. It may be awakened to a sense of sin which was asleep before; some tenderness, before seared. It may be more faithful in accusing for sin, and restraining from it; in suggesting that which is good, and spurring on the soul to the practice of what is well-pleasing in the sight of God, 1 Tim. i. 19. They had a conscience in some kind or degree good, else they could not have put it away.

In the will. There may be new inclinations, a strong current of the heart may run another way, in a new channel, some tendencies towards God and things of heaven. Such a change there was in Uzziah, wrought by the ministry and instructions of Zechariah: 2 Chron. xxvi. 5, ' He was to seek God.' Something must be added to make up the sense, and the least that can be added is, ' He was inclined to seek God;' and there was some strength in his inclinations. And therefore some render it, ' He gave himself to seek God.' He was freely addicted to it, and his inclinations were acted; and yet, look on him in the latter end of this chapter, and you will find grounds of jealousy that his heart was not upright with God.

There may be new purposes and resolutions. Experience tells us this, That an unregenerate heart may be bended to excellent resolutions, and yet shew what it is by starting off, and returning, like a deceitful bow, to its unbent posture. How many under afflictions or convictions, under impressions of fear or apprehensions of death, will resolve as much, and as well, one would think, as any out of heaven could do? How often were the Israelites brought to such resolutions; and how often did they express them by engaging themselves solemnly in covenant with God; and yet the Lord complains, Ps. lxxviii. 57, that ' they turned back, and dealt unfaithfully: they were turned aside like a deceitful bow.'

There may be new designs and intentions; designs for God, for his worship, his ways, for what tends to his glory. So it was in Jehu; a design for reformation against the idolatry of Baal. He gives it out, it was for the Lord. And good Jonadab, much taken therewith, engages in it. Yet Jehu shewed his hypocrisy sufficiently afterwards. Thus, and much more, may the will be changed.

In the affections. He may love that which he formerly hated, and dislike that which he formerly loved; he may be grieved for that in which he before delighted, and that may please him which before was his grievance; he may desire that which before he avoided, and may shun that which formerly he desired; he may esteem that which he formerly contemned, and slight that which once he highly valued. This I shall clear and prove particularly afterwards.

Briefly, the Spirit of God may move upon the face of the soul, before it be formed into a new creature, and may raise therein divers motions truly spiritual and holy; such motions there may be in it, though not of it. They cannot be called the acts of such a soul, because they have not their rise from it, nor have due entertainment in it. Even as when Satan raises wicked motions in a regenerate heart, suggestions tending to blasphemy, self-murder, or the like; if these rise not from the heart, and meet not with consent and entertainment in it, these are counted not the acts of that soul, but the acts and sins of Satan, who injects them. So we may say of those spiritual and heavenly motions that the Holy Ghost raises in an unregenerate soul, they come immediately from the Spirit, are his act, the soul is passive in them; they owe not their holiness to the heart wherein they are, but to the Spirit from whom they come.

Thus there may be holy motions in an unholy heart; and as a regenerate person, finding such wicked suggestions in his heart, may charge himself with them as his own sins, and thereupon may draw sad conclusions against himself, so an unregenerate person, finding such spiritual motions in his soul, may challenge them as his own acts, and from thence may conclude that he is sanctified savingly, when there is no just ground for either.

Thus much in general. Proceed we now to shew particularly what graces and affections there may be in hypocrites. There may be,

1. Some kind of repentance. It is said of Judas, Mat. xxvii. 3, that 'he repented himself.' And the men of Nineveh have this testimony from Christ himself, Mat. xii. 41. There was some reality in their repentance, something that deserved the name, else Christ would not have so called it; there was no gross dissimulation in it; and yet, not long after, they relapsing into their evil ways, the Lord appoints the prophet Nahum to denounce their utter destruction. And from hence some collect, that (at least as to the generality) it was not saving repentance.

More particularly, they may go far as to the several acts of repentance.

(1.) Confession. This is one act of repentance which the Lord calls for in returning sinners, Jer. iii. 12, 13. Now, such as are not in a saving condition may confess their sin, and confess it particularly, and aggravate it in their confessions, and take shame to themselves in the acknowledgment of it. So the Israelites, who provoked the Lord to swear in his wrath, &c., confess their sin, Num. xiv. 40. And Saul, 1 Sam. xv. 24. So Judas confesses his sin, and that in public; he specifies, contents not himself with a general acknowledgment, I am a sinner, but I have sinned in doing this; and he sets it out with its heavy aggravations, I have betrayed, betrayed blood, betrayed innocent blood, Mat. xxvii. 3. Cain cries out of the weight and grievousness of his sin. So Pharaoh acknowledges his sin, condemns himself for it, and justifies the Lord, Exod. ix. 27.

(2.) Sorrow for sin. That is another act of repentance; they may mourn for sin with its attendants, bewail it bitterly; the sense of it may be the grief of their hearts, the affliction of their souls; they may express exceeding much sorrow for it. The Israelites, after their sin in the golden calf, being convinced of it, and threatened for it, they mourned, Exod. xxxiii. 4, and put off their ornaments, thereby acknowledging themselves worthy to be debased and stripped naked of all that was precious to them. And, after their murmurings, Num. xiv., it is said, ver. 39, 'they mourned greatly,' and yet they continued a people of provocations, see ver. 44. Ahab, when the prophet Elijah had convinced him of, and threatened him for, his sin, he expresses an extraordinary sorrow for it, and that in the most significant expressions, I meet with none that goes beyond him, 1 Kings xxi. 27.

He rent his clothes. Thus they used to express their greatest sorrow; thus did Jacob express the grief and anguish of his soul, when he apprehended that his dearest child was devoured and torn in pieces, Gen. xxxvii. 34, 35. Here was an extraordinary sorrow, and he thus shews it. And so does Ahab express his.

Sackcloth upon his flesh. Not over his other garments, but next his skin; this was another expression of exceeding grief. Jacob thus expresses the greatest sorrow that ever seized on him. Ahab seems to go one step further, he lay in sackcloth, he wore it night and day; as he walked, so he slept in it.

And fasted. So they were to afflict their bodies when they were called in an extraordinary manner to afflict their souls; they hereby manifested soul-affliction.

And went softly. This was a sign of grief and mourning, Isa. xxxviii. 15. Such was Ahab's sorrow, and such were the testimonies of it. Nor was all this merely hypocritical, only in show and outward appearances; there was real inward grief in the heart, in some degree answerable to these expressions. There was no gross dissimulation, for it is said, and it is the Lord who testifies this of him, 'He was humbled before the Lord,' ver. 29. It was not only before men, outward expressions may serve for that; there must be some inward soul humiliation, that a man may be said to be humbled before the Lord. If it had been nothing but dissembling, the Lord would not have so much countenanced it as to have reproved* him for it. The Lord saw so much reality in it, as he thought fit to exempt Ahab in great part from what he had threatened, ver. 29.

Pass we to Judas. His grief and sorrow was more grievous to him than death; and what sorrow can be greater, more grievous than that? His sin sprung such grief and anguish in his soul, as drowned the sweetnesses of life, and overflowed all the comforts of his life; they were all under water, so that he saw nothing why he should desire to live in such anguish of heart, and so he sought ease and refuge in death. A sorrow more bitter and grievous than death, is sure an exceeding great sorrow. Yet such was that of Judas.

They may express this sorrow by abundance of tears, and pour them out in great plenty. So did the Israelites in Mizpeh, 1 Sam. vii. 2, 6. Their heads were the fountain from whence they drew this water, and that which they poured out before the Lord was their tears; and that which raised this flood of tears was their sins: 'We have sinned,' &c. And yet this was the people who did that which in the very next chapter is recorded to be a rejecting of God. Such sorrow was found in the generality of the people, ver. 5, 'all Israel;' and yet what they were, as to the generality of them, is apparent all along in their story, Heb. xii. 17.

Such may be their sorrow, and may prevail for pardon. Some kind of pardon it may procure, even that which the Scripture calls so sometimes; not a dissolving of their obligation to eternal sufferings, but a deferring thereof, and a freedom from temporal sufferings. The Israelites, where they are said to mourn so much, had such a pardon, Num. xiv. 20, so Ps. lxxviii. 37, 38. There may be such a sorrow as may obtain such a pardon, in those whom Christ will at last condemn.

(3.) Hatred of sin. This is essential to repentance, and is accounted a certain evidence of that which is saving; yet there may be some hatred of sin in those who are not in a saving condition, Rom. ii. 22. Abhorring is an high degree of hatred, yet there may be an abhorring of one sin, together with an allowance of another, which is inconsistent with a saving state. Judas could hate profuseness. Prodigality, it seems, was odious to him, Mat. xiv. 3–5, this was the object of his indignation, and yet what a character is given of him upon that expression, John xii. 5, 6. Jehu hated the false worship of Baal, if pursuing of it to destruction be a testimony of hatred, 2 Kings x. 26, 27, 30, yet his heart was not upright. Some hate pride, haughtiness, disdainful supercilious carriage; others lasciviousness, uncleanness, open profaneness; others superstition, human inventions and innovations in divine worship; others errors, schisms, heresies. And we see injustice, oppression, passion, fury, unmercifulness, cruelty, dissembling, and hypocrisy seem generally hated. Yea, further,

* Qu. 'reprieved'?—ED.

It is possible there may be a falling out with a bosom sin, and that which has been much loved may be no less hated. See it in the Jews.

Idolatry seems to have been their beloved sin, their *peccatum in deliciis*, that to which they were most addicted for many generations; yet after the captivity we may discern in them a special hatred of this sin above others. They would die rather than suffer an image in their temple, so far were they from worshipping them. When Pilate attempted to set up the statue of Tiberius in the temple, the Jews exposed their necks to him, and told him they would choose death rather than suffer it. And the like resolution they shewed upon the like attempt in Caligula's time, as Josephus relates. So that they might truly be said to abhor idols. Here is some hatred of sin in them, and yet who more unbelievers, more impenitent?

(4.) Resolution against sin. This is a principal ingredient in true repentance, yet some resolution against sin there may be found in formalists. I think we may rationally conclude that if Judas, after he had felt what burden and anguish there was in his sin, had been in a condition to act it anew, he would rather have chosen death than that act; for we see he chose death to free him from the anguish of it, and he does what he can to hinder the progress of it; tells his tempters that it was a sin, a bloody sin, and throws back the money, which was the price of his treason. Do ye think he would have been tempted to that wickedness? Can we think his heart was not fully resolved against it? And why may not others under like sense of sin be as much resolved against former evil ways, and yet be as far from saving repentance as he?

What an high resolution was that of Balaam's against disobedience? Num. xxii. 17, 18, 38. Balaam's bosom sin in all probability was covetousness, 2 Peter ii. 15, and here is a temptation that suits his temper exactly, strikes the right string. What would not a covetous man do for an house full of gold? &c. Yet this is his resolution notwithstanding.

What Nineveh's repentance was I shewed before. This was one part of it, they were resolved to turn from their evil ways; they were not only resolved to do it, but they did it; the Lord saw that they did it, Jonah iii. 10. And which is much, for that sin which probably reigned most amongst them, and so particularly specified, the violence which was in their hands.

Thus far they may go in a way of repentance, such confession, sorrow, hatred, resolution.

Quest. But if they may go thus far in a way of repentance, wherein do they fall short? Who is there goes further? If this be not repentance unto life, which has such confession, sorrow, &c., where is it to be found? Wherein is such a repentance defective?

Ans. This I will give you a short account of, that while I intend the necessary conviction of some, I may not leave others under unnecessary scruples. But briefly, this being not the design of the text, yet so as this design may not miscarry.

Let us then take a short view of these acts of repentance, and shew their defects in formalists, so as thereby those that are sincere may have the comfort of their sincerity, discerning wherein they go beyond them.

For confession. That is no evidence of saving repentance, but as it proceeds from hatred of sin, is accompanied with sorrow, and seconded with resolutions against sin. The trial must be by these, not by the outward act; for herein a hypocrite may go as far as any. Without these, confession is but as sounding brass or a tinkling cymbal; a sound that signifies nothing of sound repentance, that which accompanies salvation. Proceed we then to those acts wherein the distinction may be discovered. In the next place,

Their sorrow is defective upon a threefold account.

(1.) They mourn not for sin, but its consequents. Not as it is sin, a violation of law; not as it is an irregularity in the sight of God, contrary to God, his pure essence, holy will; not as it is evil, a privation of good, opposite to holiness. They love not good as good in itself; nor can hate evil as evil. As they delight not in that which is spiritually good, because it is spiritual, so they mourn not for that which is sinfully evil as it is sinful; not for sin itself, but the train of sad consequences.

(2.) Not for consequents in reference to God, but themselves; not as it displeases, dishonours him, tramples on his authority, advances the creature above him; burdens him, crosses his designs, grieves his Spirit, gratifies Satan, wounds Christ. If mourn for his displeasure, rather for the effects of his displeasure than because he is displeased; because he will shew himself displeased, than because he is so; because he will make it appear to their smart and loss that he is grieved.

(3.) Not in all its consequents in reference to themselves; not as it defiles the soul, deprives it of his beauty, strength, health; debars it from communion with Christ; keeps it at a distance from God; makes it more uncapable of grace; hardens it, disposes it to more sin, leaves the seed behind; indisposes it for holy duties, makes it unserviceable to God.

But as it is exposes to wrath temporal, eternal; contracts guilt, leaves horror; deprives of outward mercies, liberty, health, riches; makes obnoxious to hell.

Their hatred of sin is defective, comes short of that which is essential to true saving repentance, in that,

(1.) It is not extended to all sin. They hate not every evil way. The Jews hated idolatry, but not sacrilege, Rom. ii. 22. They hated gross sacrilege too, they were far from breaking or robbing their temples; none more zealous for the temple. As many formalists amongst us, very zealous for God's house, for the externals of worship, the outside of religion, and think themselves far from sacrilege upon this account, while they make no conscience of robbing God in another way; defrauding God of that spiritual service, that soul worship, which is indeed the soul of worship, of highest value with him; and the outwards of religion of no other account than a dead carcase without it.

Sincere hatred is universal. He that truly hates any hates all. Now formalists may hate gross sins, but those which the world counts small they will have a toleration for, some or other; this is but a little one, I may live in it without danger.

They may hate open wickedness, but they hate not secret sins. Their hearts do not rise against the secret motions of sin which arise in their hearts; they do not abhor these, nor loathe themselves for them.

They may hate a sin which is generally hated, which is cried down by the times, and abhorred by the people amongst whom they live. They may be carried down with the stream thus far. But they will scarce hate a sin that is in credit, countenanced by the times, encouraged by the example of those that are great or many; or if they hate such a sin, it will be because they love not those whose sin it is.

They may hate an unprofitable or an expensive sin, which is like to bring them in no revenue of profit or pleasure; but scarce will they hate the sin of their calling, that which they have lived by, and has been as a right hand unto them, to bring them in riches or pleasures.

They may hate a sin from which their nature is estranged, which is contrary to their temper and complexion, but they will not hate the sin of their constitution, that to which they are carried with an eager and delightful propensity.

(2.) They hate others' sins rather than their own. Judas could hate an appearance of profaneness in another, but not that real covetousness that was in his own heart. Jehu could shew some hatred of the idolatrous worship of Baal, but yet retain the idolatrous worship of Jeroboam; hate the idolatry of the house of Ahab, but continue an idolatry of another kind in his own house.

(3.) Their hatred is rather directed against the persons than the sins of others. Who would not think the scribes and pharisees were zealous haters of Sabbath-breaking, when their jealousy was so quick-sighted, as they would spy it where it was not, even in the disciples, and Christ himself? Yet it was not the sin, but the man they hated: We will not have this man to rule over us. This man was the mark at which their hatred shot; the sin was but the blind, or the stalking-horse.

(4.) They hate rather the effects of sin than sin itself. They hate shame and reproach, sorrow and suffering, terrors and anguish of conscience, torments of hell. These are real evils in their apprehensions, and they may really hate them as the effects of sin, and yet not hate the sin itself.

(5.) It is not hearty. They hate it not with all their hearts, neither does it reach the heart of sin. They may hate some of the excrements of sin, pare its nails, or shave its hair, as the Israelites were to do with the captives they intended to marry; or possibly they may cut off some members, but they would not the main body; they spare the life of the old man. They may lop off some branches, but they strike not at the root. Their hatred does not reach the corruption of their natures; they loathe not that, they pursue not that to the death with mortifying endeavours; they confine it indeed that it break not out into outrageous acts, but they do not crucify it. If their hearts did hate it, they would pursue it to the death, nothing else would satisfy.

Their resolutions are defective.

(1.) In their rise. They rise not from an inward, universal change. Not from a principle of holiness, but from apprehensions of present ruin and destruction, as Nineveh; or from terrors and anguish of soul, as in Judas when upon the rack; or from the power of restraining grace, which keeps them from resolving to sin, rather than helps them to full resolutions against it, in which case their resolutions are rather negative than positive. Thus it was with Balaam, Num. xxii. 18, 38. He says not, I will not, but I cannot; he had a good mind to it, but the Lord overpowered.

(2.) Continuance. They abide not, they are not followed to full execution. The cause from whence they rise is not constant, and that being removed, they vanish. They flow no longer than they are fed by their spring from whence they rise; and that is not like those waters which spring up to eternal life. It is but a flash of fear or terror, or anguish, which passes away like a land flood, is quickly gone, and so the resolutions fall with them. When they are come off the rack, you hear no more of their resolutions, at least you see nothing of them in their practice. So it was with the Ninevites. So with Balaam. Their goodness is like the morning cloud. Nothing more ordinary. David apprehended this danger, it is like, when he puts up that prayer for the people, who then seemed well resolved, 1 Chron. xxix. 18.

They may go far in respect of faith. They may have a faith so like to that which is saving and justifying, as they themselves may take it to be the very same; and others too may judge it to be the faith of God's elect, even those that have the spirit of discerning. Simon Magus believed, Acts viii. 13. Such a faith he had, and so expressed it, as Philip and the church took him to be a true believer, and accordingly admitted him to those privileges which are peculiar to true believers, and which they could not lawfully communicate to him, but that upon some sufficient ground they may account he had true faith. Those that received the word into stony ground believed, Luke viii. 13. Such a faith they had, as by the description of it, seems not to differ from saving faith (that of the good ground) save in the root; the difference is not apparent, it lies under ground; those that will discern it must dig for it. The discovery of it must be referred to time, or the day of trial; till then it is not easy, if it be feasible.

There are four several acts of faith, each of which do claim to be the saving, the justifying act. And there are many strong pleas put in by divines of great note to make good the claim; and undoubtedly one or other of them cannot fail of it. Now such as these in the text may go far in them all, and so far as it will be no very easy matter to discover wherein any other may go further. The acts are assent, consent, dependence, assurance. We will endeavour to shew how far they may proceed in every of them.

1. *Assent.* They may have that faith which is placed in assent. And some there are who place saving faith herein, whose names or arguments I will not trouble you with; but keeping close to the matter, shew what this assent is, and in what degree it may be found in temporaries. Assent is an act of the mind, judging that which is propounded to be true. And faith in this acceptation is an act of the judgment or understanding, giving credit to the doctrine of Christ, judging it to be the truth. Such a faith, such an assent hypocrites may have, and that without dissimulation. They may believe the doctrine of Christ, assent to the truths revealed in Scripture, close with them as divine truths. Yea, after some strugglings and reluctancies from temptations, to doubting and unbelief, the power of these truths may become victorious, so as to triumph in the mind, and captivate the judgment to an obedient assent. More distinctly and particularly this assent may be.

(1.) Universal. He may believe all the truths contained in Scripture, so far as he is acquainted with them, and he may be acquainted with more than those that are true believers. He may know more than most of those who have learned Christ as the truth is in Jesus, and consequently he may believe more than they; his faith may grasp those truths which they have not yet reached. As his knowledge may be more extensive, so his faith may be more comprehensive. In this kind of faith he may go as far as the apostle expresses his progress, Acts xxiv. 14. Paul was confident that Agrippa had so much faith, Acts xxvi. 26, 27.

He may believe all things contained, both in the law and in the gospel, and that not only implicitly, but expressly, so far as they have come within the reach of his apprehension, and there are none that expressly believe any more.

He may believe, not only matters of fact there related, but matters of faith there propounded; not only what is obvious to sense, or may be discovered and proved by reason, and confirmed by experience; but that which is far out of the reach of sense, above the discovery of reason, without the encouragement of experience, even such things as depend wholly on revelation.

He may believe that the relations are true, both of things ordinary and miraculous; all the commands are just, and the prophecies shall be fulfilled; all the promises accomplished, all the threatenings executed. There is no question but the devils may believe this, James ii. 19. They believe it, and are affected with it; much more such men who live under the hopes, the light, the power of the gospel.

(2.) *Supernatural.* Such a faith as could never have been engendered merely by the light and power of nature; such a faith as has its original from heaven, and is inspired by the Holy Ghost. For there are two ingredients which make up this faith: the one is light to discover the truths that are to be assented to; the other a power inclining the mind to give its assent. Now both these they may have from the Holy Ghost, both the discovering light and the inclining power, both this illumination and this inclination. And we have proof of both in that Heb. vi. 4. Those who had nothing accompanying salvation were enlightened, there is the former; and tasted of the heavenly gifts, there is the latter; and both from the Spirit of God; for in respect of both, they are said to be partakers of the Holy Ghost, in the third expression. By heavenly gifts some understand Christ, many understand faith. Indeed, those expositions are not inconsistent, both come to one; for it is by faith that Christ is tasted, and this faith is a gift, a heavenly gift; the Holy Ghost bestows it, by giving light to discover the truths of Christ, and by inclining the mind to assent to them, and close with them. In both respects this faith or assent is not a work of nature, it is not an act of natural strength; it is not of themselves, it is the gift of God; a heavenly gift, a supernatural act.

(3.) *Divine.* They may have a divine faith, not only in respect of its original and efficient, but in respect of its ground and foundation, The ground of their faith may be a divine testimony, it may be raised upon a divine foundation, viz. the truth of God. They may ground the credit they give to the doctrine of the gospel, not only upon probable reason, which is the ground of that assent we call opinion; nor upon evident reason, the ground of that assent we call knowledge or science; nor upon human testimony, the ground of human faith; but upon divine testimony, which is the proper ground of divine faith. They may believe the truths revealed in Scripture upon this ground, because they are persuaded that God, who cannot lie, has revealed them. To believe the truths of God, upon the account of the truth of God, is a divine faith. Thus the Israelites, a great part of whom were no better than those in the text, believed the Lord, and his servant Moses, Exod. xiv. 31. Seeing that miraculous work, they then believed what Moses had declared to them, being persuaded that it was from God; they gave credit to Moses's message, being convinced he had it from God, whom they believed to be truth itself.

(4.) *Firm.* They may stedfastly believe all the truths necessary to salvation without doubt or wavering; they may count it a high wickedness to call any of them into question; they may be so confident of the truth of Christ's doctrine as to trust their salvation thereon, and be ready to hazard their lives for a testimony thereto. The apostle tells us, Rom. iii. 2, that unto the Jews, many of whom were but Jews outwardly, were committed the oracles of God, and they received and preserved them accordingly; they had no more doubt thereof than of an oracle, than of an oracle of God, questioned it no more than that which they were persuaded was uttered by the mouth of God, Heb. x. 26. Those who may fall into that unpardonable sin, may come to such an acknowledgment of the truth, as proceeds from a conviction, that beyond all doubt it is the truth indeed; that is the import of ἐπίγνωσις. They may arrive at a great height of confidence concerning Scripture truths; so did the Jews, who were only so in name, Rom. ii. 19.

(5.) *Approving.* This assent may be accompanied with a high approbation of divine truths; they may not only account them true and faithful, but worthy of all acceptation; not only good, but the best; the most certain, worthy to be received with confidence; the most comfortable, worthy to be received with joy, Luke xviii. 13; the most blessed and enhappying, worthy to be received as the words of eternal life, John v. 39; the most excellent, and so worthy of their best affections and endeavours, of their highest esteem and approbation, Rom. ii. 18. Being instructed out of the law concerning the will of God, he discerned such things therein as he approved as most excellent.

2. *Consent,* another act of faith. Consent to take Christ as he is offered; this is the heart's receiving of Christ, and this receiving is called believing, John i. 12. To believe on Christ to adoption, &c., is to receive and consent to take him, is the soul's receiving of him; for the heart, before shut up against Christ, by consent is opened to let him in. Hence many define justifying faith by this consent, or acceptance of Christ as a Lord and Saviour.

Let us inquire how far such as these in the text may consent to take Christ as their Saviour, as their Lord.

That they may be willing to take him as their Saviour is out of question; ready to accept of him for the benefit of his satisfaction and purchase; willing to have Christ, to satisfy justice, appease wrath, remove the curse, deliver them from hell; willing to have Christ for pardon, peace, adoption, glory; content to have the gift of righteousness, redemption through his blood, forgiveness of sins, and an inheritance amongst those that are sanctified. Experience assures us many, otherwise utterly strangers to the life of faith, are willing to accept of Christ as a Saviour.

But can they consent to accept of him as their Lord, to be at his command? as their king, to be governed by his laws? Here it seems to stick; let us see how far they may come off. Here are some in the text who acknowledge Christ to be their Lord; who profess subjection to him as their Lord; who worship, who serve him as a Lord; who had done many eminent, extraordinary, wonderful services for him; and this in the name of Christ, by his authority, through his power, to his glory. If you will not believe them when they profess zealously that Christ is their Lord, they will shew you their faith by their works, many and wonderful; they will convince you by miracles. Yet Christ disowns them.

Others, though they cannot reach extraordinary, yet will give you ordinary proof in abundance, that they do consent to have Christ for their Lord, and to be governed by his laws.

They may yield as much satisfaction unto Christ, as kings demand of their subjects; they are ready to obey the laws of Christ, so far as obedience is required to the laws of princes; and what would you have more to shew them good subjects? They may go as far in a visible observing of Christ's laws as any believer on earth; they may submit to all his ordinances, not only the royal law, but positive institutions; as the primitive Christians, they may continue stedfastly in the doctrine of the apostles.

They may be ready to practise all known duties, and to avoid all open known sins, not one pollution of the world to be seen in them; they may forbear the gratifying of a beloved sin, a darling lust, rather than disobey Christ, as Balaam, Num. xxii.; nay, upon the signification of Christ's will and pleasure, they may turn from such a lust, even from a reigning sin, as the Ninevites, Jonah iii.; thus far they may accept of Christ as their Lord; thus near they may come to that faith which consists in a consent to embrace Christ as their Lord and Saviour.

3. *Dependence.* Something of this faith of dependence temporaries may have, John ii. 23; those with whom Christ would not trust himself are said to believe in his name. To believe in the name of Christ, *credere in Christum*, is more than to believe Christ *credere Christo*. To believe him is but to give credit to his word; but to believe in him, denotes some dependence on him. The devils may believe him, but I find not that they are said to depend on him. This is expressed by a singular phrase in the New Testament, a preposition, ἐν, εἰς, ἔπι, being added to the verb πιστεύειν, a phrase not used by other Greek authors; no, nor by the Septuagint; but it is frequent in the New Testament, and that in compliance with those expressions in the Old Testament, which holds forth faith in such phrases as denote dependence. To trust in God, or to believe in him, is to rely on him, to rest, to stay, to lean on him; and since the Holy Ghost does most frequently express faith in such like terms, I think it is a good argument to persuade that the nature of that faith, which the Scripture so much commends and calls for, even that faith which is saving and justifying, consists in dependence. Let us see, then, how much of this may be attained by formalists, how far they may proceed towards a faith of dependence. Phrases there are by which the Holy Ghost expresses this faith of dependence, or trusting in God; and if the faith sometimes ascribed to unregenerate men be held forth in the very same expressions, we may safely collect that some such thing as this faith of dependence, some degree towards it, or some near resemblance of it, may be attained, acted, expressed by those that shall not be saved. Proceed we then in this way, which will be both clear and safe, though narrow, and but little if at all traced. To trust or depend on God is

(1.) To *cleave* to him, Deut. iv. 4. It was now forty years since their coming out of Egypt, the unbelieving generation were fallen in the wilderness; those that remained expressed more faith, and are therefore said to cleave unto the Lord. To cleave to God is to trust in him, as is evident, 2 Kings xviii. 5, 6.

Now, such professors as we have in the text may have something of this faith of adherence. Such as these are said to cleave unto God: Josh. xxiii. 8, 'As ye have done,' &c.; he speaks of the generality of the people, and yet there were strange gods amongst them, chap. xxiv. 23. Though idolatry was not tolerated publicly, yet had they idols which they worshipped in secret. No better are they, Jer. xiii., who yet are said to have cleaved, ver. 11, and yet they were disobedient, ver. 10. By virtue of that kind of faith, by which they have their adherence ascribed to them, they seem to cleave so to God, as though they were glued and soldered to him; for רבק, which comes from the word rendered *to cleave* (in the forequoted places), signifies glue and solder, as Isa. xli. 7. This may be the reason why such professors are said to be in Christ, John xv.; they may have such a faith as gives them some kind of union; they may so cleave to Christ, as they may be said to be in him.

(2.) To *stay* on him, Isa. x. 20; Isa. l. 10; Isa. xxvi. 3, 'Thou wilt keep him in perfect peace, whose mind is stayed on thee.' Now, this is ascribed also to those that are not in a saving condition, Isa. xlviii. 2, נסמכו; these made the Lord their support, they stayed up their hearts on him (as Ahab is said to be stayed up in his chariot), 1 Kings xxii. 35; yet what they were, see ver. 4. It is the same word by which David expresses his faith, Ps. lxxi. 6, and Ps. cxii. 7, 8. Some faith like this they may have, and so act it, as if God was their trust, as if Christ were the stay, the support of their souls.

(3.) To *lean* on him. To lean is to trust in Scripture, Isa. xxxvi. 6, Prov.

iii. 5. And thus the spouse her faith in Christ is expressed by leaning on him, Cant. viii. 5. And some such thing may be found in those that are not in a saving state, Micah iii. 4; what they were, see verses 9, 10. These would lean upon the Lord as a God that owned them, and be confident that in this posture, leaning, trusting, they should be safe: 'No evil can come upon us.' They lean upon God as a weak man leans upon a staff. The word is שָׁעַן; and from thence comes מִשְׁעָן, a staff. Even wicked men may thus lean upon Christ as if he were their rod and their staff, their comfort and support; lean upon him that they may be upheld by him, that they may not fall into hell and eternal misery, and may be confident thereupon that no such evil shall befall them.

(4.) To *rest* on him. Thus is the faith of Asa expressed, 2 Chron. xiv. 11. Such as these in the text may rest in God, 2 Chron. xxxii. 8; they rested on the words of Hezekiah, which indeed were the words of God; and to rest on the word of God, is to rest on God himself. Thus did that people, who some few years (about ten or twelve) after are said to do worse than the heathen, chap. xxxiii. 9, 10; such as these may rest on God, may rest on God in a promise. Look upon the words again, and you will find that they contain a promise, chap. xxxii. 7, 8. Here is a promise, an absolute promise too, which is many times found more difficult for faith to apply and rest on than a conditional; yet on these words, on this promise, they rested; they applied it to themselves, and rested on it, and thereby supported their hearts in this extremity, when they saw ruin and misery seem to approach; so that hence it appears, that those who are not in a state of salvation, may rest upon Christ, and that in a promise. We shall give more evidence to this in the ensuing discourse.

(5.) To *rely* on him. So Hanani the seer expresses it, 2 Chron. xvi. 7, 8. Asa did trust God before he did rely on him, and had the reward of his faith against the Ethiopians; but now his faith was to seek, he trusted the king of Syria rather than God; which is expressed by his relying upon him, and not relying upon God. Those that are worse than Asa, are said to rely upon God, 2 Chron. xiii. 18. Now, Abijah was one of those that are said to rely upon the Lord. Indeed, he is the man who expresseth this faith or relying on God; and you may find very remarkable actings of this faith from verses 5 to 13, and such as may become the best of believers, and yet Abijah was far from uprightness, 1 Kings xv. 3. Such a man as this could express his relying on God, and have the Lord's testimony that he did so; yea, and make the covenant of God the foundation of his faith and reliance, and act it all along upon the promise. Yet thus it was, the covenant, the promise, is the groundwork on which he begins to raise his confidence, ver. 5. The promise he intends is expressed, 2 Sam. vii. 16. This promise he applies; he relies on it with confidence that the Lord will perform it, even when an army of eight hundred thousand men were in his view to cut off all hopes from the promise, and when he had but half so many to resist them; yet then the promise helps him to such a height of confidence, and to such high expressions of it, as I know not where we shall meet with higher. And if you observe, they have all some reference to the promise.

So that here you have another proof that unregenerate men may rely upon God, may depend upon Christ; and that in the promise, pleading the covenant of God, and applying the promise to themselves as the ground of their trust. Let us offer a little more proof of it.

The men of Nineveh believed God, Jonah iii. 5. One would think it a wonder that they should thus believe; the God of heaven was a strange God to them, they had other gods of their own, whom they accustomed to serve and worship; the God of Israel was a strange God, and the prophet was to them a strange man. They had no experience of him; why should they trust him? We are not apt to believe strangers in matters of such importance; yet they believed, at least they had a legal faith; that which they believed was the threatening, ver. 4. Now, it seems far more easy for those who live under the gospel, though unregenerate, to apply a promise, than for those of Nineveh to believe a threatening; there seems more difficulty to apply a threatening than a promise. In applying a threatening, we are like to meet with more opposition, both from within and from without. From within, for a threatening is like a bitter pill, the bitterness of death is in it; no wonder if that hardly go down. From without too, Satan will be ready to raise opposition; he is afraid to have men startled, lest the sense of their misery denounced in the threatening should rouse them up to seek how they may make an escape. He is more sure of them while they are secure, and will labour to keep off the threatening, lest it should awake them who dream of peace and happiness while they are sleeping in his very jaws.

But now, in applying a promise, an unregenerate man ordinarily meets with no such opposition. Not from within, for the promise is all sweetness; the promise of pardon and life is the marrow, the quintessence of the gospel. No wonder if they be ready to swallow it down greedily. And Satan will be so far from opposing, as he will rather encourage and assist one who has no interest in the promise, to apply it; for this he knows will be the way to fix and settle them in their natural condition. A promise misapplied will be a seal upon the sepulchre, make them sure in the grave of sin, wherein they lie dead and rotting.

And therefore if unregenerate men may apply a threatening, which is in these respects more difficult, as appears they may by the example of the Ninevites, and by the experience we have of divers under the spirit of bondage, why may they not be apt to apply a promise, where they are not like to meet with such difficulty and opposition?

Further, is it not more easy to believe a promise for pardon and happiness, than to believe a promise for a miracle? But natural men, such as in the text, may apply a promise for a miracle. They may have a faith of miracles; so had these in the text, so had Judas; the apostle supposes it, 1 Cor. xiii. Now, a faith of miracles depends upon a special promise, whereby God reveals his will to have such a wonderful work done by them. They believe it, depend upon him for it, and it is done. If unregenerate men may apply a promise for a miracle, why may they not apply a promise for mercy? This is clear enough; and by this time you see how far they may go towards a faith of dependence. They may cleave to God, stay, lean, rest, rely on him; and that in the application of a promise.

4. *Assurance* (that passes for another act of faith), which is a persuasion of a personal interest in God, and a title to Christ and his benefits, with a confidence that he has right to them, and has, or shall have, possession of them. Lutherans and foreign divines generally place saving faith in such a persuasion, and so were many of our own wont to do; and some, that make it not the vital act, that which justifies, yet make it an eminent act of justifying faith. This grace embracing Christ, and depending on him, is faith in its infancy; but this grace ascertaining and persuading, is faith in its growth and proficiency, in its state and triumph. They make it a high attainment of faith to arrive at such assurance, such a persuasion.

Let us inquire how near hypocrites may come to this. And I shall make it evident, (1.) that they may have a persuasion of their personal interest in God, and their title to heaven; (2.) that this persuasion may be strong, and stand unshaken against all opposition; (3.) that it may continue, and hold up, even to the death; (4.) that it may be grounded, established upon those grounds, which have a very near resemblance of those that are the supports of God's elect.

(1.) That they may have such a persuasion, will be clear both by Scripture and experience. Those that are strangers to God, may be persuaded of a personal interest in him; those whom Christ will utterly disown, may be confident of a title to him as their Lord and Saviour; those who are heirs of hell, children of wrath, may persuade themselves that heaven is their portion. The first of these is the foundation of all the rest. Covenant interest in God is the first link in that golden chain which reaches from time to eternity. All blessings, positive and relative, temporal and eternal, are linked to it. He that persuades himself that God is his God, lays hold on the first link, which draws all the rest, he may easily persuade himself that all are his, 1 Cor. iii. 22, 23.

Now in Scripture I find many no better than these in the text, who claim interest in God, and confidently speak God to be their God. Balaam the wizard could do this, Num. xxii. 18; he takes it for granted that the Lord was his God, yet he was an enchanter, and gave that pernicious counsel whereby the Israelites were joined to Baal-peor, Num. xxv. 2, 3. There seems to be more weight in Abijah's speech; he asserts it with more spirit and confidence, grounds it upon God's covenant with them, and their keeping covenant with him, 2 Chron. xiii. 10. As if he had said, As for you, O Israelites, ye have forsaken God, broke covenant with him, you can have no confidence to claim interest in him, or expect any success or blessing from him; 'but as for us, the Lord is our God, and we have not forsaken him.' And who is this that is so confident of his interest in God? See 1 Kings xv. But he speaks this to Israel. Israel is more confident, and pleads this to God himself, Hosea viii. 2. Here is a particular application, which should be the act of faith only, 'My God.' And it is grounded upon the covenant; they plead covenant interest in God, wherein he had engaged himself to be their God, and they to be his people. In the Hebrew, Israel is the last word in the verse; and Jonathan's Targum to make out the sense, adds, 'Israel thy people.' And this is the form of the covenant, Deut. xxix. 12, 13, 14. Grounding their confidence hereon, they lay claim to the Lord as their God in covenant: 'My God.' And who are they that speak thus in the language of faith? that speak in Thomas's language, when he most expressed his faith? Why they are such as, ver. 1 and 3, had transgressed God's covenant, and trespassed against the law, and that had cast off the thing that is good.

The Jews who set themselves against Christ, were settled in this persuasion; Christ himself could not beat them out of it, John viii. He insinuates that they were slaves to sin and Satan, ver. 33; expresses it, ver. 35; they answer, They are free, they are Abraham's seed, ver. 33; he grants they are Abraham's seed by natural descent, but insinuates that they had a worse, another father, upon a spiritual account, vers. 38, 39, 41; they reply, they are no children of fornication, they had no father but one on a spiritual account, and God was their Father. Here was their confidence, which they will retain, say Christ what he will; they counted themselves the children of God, and so expected the love and portion of his children.

They may be persuaded that Christ is their Saviour, and that he redeemed them. So those wretches, 2 Pet. ii.; they are said to be bought or redeemed by him, because thus they presumed, this was their persuasion. And so some take it, and not without warrant from Scripture, for the Holy Ghost speaks so in other places, of things as if they were really so, when they are so only in the opinion and persuasion of men: 2 Chron. xxviii. 23, 'He sacrificed unto the gods of Damascus, which smote him.' Not that they really smote him, but that he was so persuaded. As in the former place, they are said to be bought or redeemed by him; not because Christ did really redeem them, but because they were so persuaded.

They may be persuaded that heaven is theirs, and that eternal life shall be their portion: John v. 39, 'Search the Scriptures, for in them ye think ye have eternal life.' They made account to have eternal life, and they gathered this from the Scripture; and so were the more confident and assured of it, because they thought they had Scripture ground for it.

It remains to shew wherein this faith is defective, wherein it comes short of that which is saving and justifying. And this I shall endeavour to discover in those acts which are most apt to occasion scruple and trouble, to those that are sincere but weak believers. But this very briefly, because I have fully discoursed of faith upon another subject,* and the text leads me rather to a detection of hypocrisy, than a discovery of sincerity. Yet this must be briefly discovered, lest that be mistaken, and so the main design of the text miscarry.

1. Their consent has a double defect.

(1.) As to the act, it is but a semi-consent; imperfect, not full; some tendencies, no peremptory motions; some inclinations, no absolute resolutions; convinced, not persuaded; almost persuaded, not altogether, $\dot{\epsilon}\nu \ \dot{o}\lambda\dot{\iota}\gamma\omega$, open half way to Christ. They would enter the marriage chamber, but not strive to enter; would purchase the precious pearl, but not come up to the price; would drink of the water of life, but thirst not; hunger not after the bread of life, though they see some necessity of it.

(2.) As to the object, they consent not to take whole Christ; they will embrace him as a Saviour, &c. But will they accept of him as their Lord and King? Why, yes, they may go far in yielding subjection to him as their Lord; but then they will not have him to be an absolute Lord. They like not an absolute subjection; they would have his sovereignty limited in this or that particular, where it seems to entrench too far upon that liberty which some lust or carnal interest desires. His way must be a little enlarged, made a little wider in one place or other, it seems too strait, too narrow; his yoke must be made a little lighter, it pinches too much upon that which is dear to them in this or that particular; whereas a sincere believer counts all the ways of Christ pleasantness, even when they are straitest, and give least room to the flesh. The yoke of Christ, when it is laid on him in his full weight, he accounts it easy and his burden light. His sceptre, how massy and weighty soever, is precious to him as gold, more precious than fine gold; if he might have a dispensation in this or that, he would not be exempted.

They will accept of Christ to save them, but will they have him to sanctify? Why, yes, some kind, some degree of sanctification they would have; but not thoroughly sanctified, not wholly mortified. How Christ comes, and so how he must be entertained, the prophet shews us, Mal. iii. 2, 3. There are some hypocrites, ver. 1, who impatiently desired Christ, and expostulated with God, why he was so long in sending him; but little did they think he would come in such a way as is here described, as a refiner's fire, and as fuller's soap. If Christ would come with a pencil and draw a face of holiness upon their conversations, they would be willing so to entertain him; they are willing to have some tincture of holiness there, and to have it

* *Vide* A Treatise of Faith. [Vol. I. of this edition.—ED.]

garnished with the most specious acts of religion, and plausible works of charity.

Or if he would draw the lineaments of sanctification upon the surface of their souls, they can well enough endure such a superficial work. Let that be gilded and adorned as much as he will, they will not stand with him. For any tincture in the surface, either of heart or life, for a superficial change in either, if that will serve his turn, it will serve theirs too; they are content, upon these terms he may come and welcome. But to come as a refiner's fire, to burn up their lusts, to consume all their dross, and utterly to dissolve the old frame of nature, to melt their souls, so as to make them run into a new mould, they like not this. As this seems harsh and painful, so there will be waste and loss in refining, they are apt to think it needless. There is some dross which is as precious to them as silver, why should this be consumed? They like their old frame too well to have it quite dissolved. Would it not be enough to have it furbished and gilded over? Must it be quite melted? Must this be the work of their lives, to make use of Christ as fire, to be continually consuming their lusts? Must that which is so dear to them pass through the fire? Must they be always improving the purifying virtue of Christ as fuller's soap, to wash out the stains and spots of sin, some of which they count their beauty and delight? Must this be their daily care? and must they be at this trouble continually all their lives? And will not Christ come and be entertained upon any other terms? Why, then, who may abide the day of his coming? who may abide it? Why, not any hypocrite in the world. He is a sincere believer, indeed, that will embrace Christ when he comes as a refiner's fire, that will not shrink and shrug at the heat and painfulness of it; but will admit it into the very inwards of his soul, and there nourish it till it have consumed whatever is offensive to Christ, how dear soever it has been to him.

2. Dependence on God, resting on Christ in a promise. This makes as fair a show of saving faith as anything can do. Wherein falls it short? Why, it is defective on this account, because it is not accompanied with that self-resignation which is either essential to faith, or inseparable from it, Luke xiv. 32. A hypocrite may rely upon Christ, but he will not resign up himself wholly to him; and that will appear in one, or all of these three severals.

(1.) In point of performance. He will not comply with the whole will of Christ discovering his duty. Indeed, if ye ask him in general, if he be willing to do whatever Christ requires of him, it is like he will affirm it peremptorily and with confidence. He himself may be deceived herein, as well as deceive others, while he stays in generals; for *dolus latet in generalibus*.

But come to particulars; it may be you may mention a thousand particular duties to him, and he may be willing to submit to them all. You may easily miss that duty which he sticks at, when possibly it is but one duty or two among ten thousand that he cannot digest; but if ye be directed to hit right, and inquire of that duty which pinches upon his credit, and will expose him to disgrace and reproach, if he be popular, and affect vain-glory and applause, if that be his humour;

Or which entrenches upon his profit, makes a breach in his estate, hazard his impoverishing and undoing in the world; if he be covetous and inclined to the earth, if that be his complexion;

Or which robs him of his ease and pleasure, and cuts him short of those delights, wherewith he has been wont to make his life sweet and comfortable; if he be slothful and sensual, if that be his temper:

Inquire of such a duty, are ye willing to do this now when Christ calls for it? This will puzzle him; here will he stick. He will either plead, Sure this is not a duty, Christ is not such an hard master as to require that which will tend to disgrace me, or undo me, or make my life uncomfortable; or if ye convince him it is a duty, why, then he must be dispensed with; I will do whatever else the Lord would have me, only in this, the Lord be merciful to me: 'The Lord pardon thy servant in this thing,' as Naaman said about his going into the house of Rimmon, 2 Kings v. 18: herein the hollowness of his heart, the unsoundness of his faith, may be detected. See it in Abijah, he who makes such a flourish with his faith as few true believers go beyond him, 2 Chron. xiii. It is said of him, 1 Kings xv. 3, 'His heart was not perfect as David's.' Now wherein lay the uprightness or perfectness of David's heart? See that Acts xiii. 22, πάντα τὰ θελήματα. That was the index of David's uprightness, and this was the index of Abijah's hypocrisy; his heart was not perfect like David's; he would not fulfil, &c. His faith was not accompanied with a full resignation of himself to the will of God.

(2.) In point of relinquishment. He is not willing to part with every sin. There is some sin or other has deeper root in his heart than his faith. Ask in general if he be resolved to abandon every sin, and he may express his resolution with a great deal of confidence. Come to particulars; and if you specify ten thousand sins to him, he may be severally resolved against them all.

But lay your hand upon the head of his bosom sin, that which is rooted in his complexion, or commended to him by example and custom, or endeared to him by some harvests of pleasure or profit that he has reaped by it, ask him, Shall this sin be crucified? Here he is at a stand. Either he will contend it is no sin, and you will hardly fasten a conviction on him; or if he cannot avoid it, to satisfy conscience, and keep up some hopes of heaven, he will be content to proceed against it, as though he intended its death. He will imprison it, confine it; it shall never see the light, never break forth into open act; and there it shall have but prisoner's fare, he may cut off much of those large provisions that he has formerly afforded it; nay, he may bring it sometimes to the block, as if it were for execution. He may be drawn to those mortifying duties, which, if they were heartily managed, might be the death of it. Ay, but when the axe is falling upon its neck, when the sacrificing knife should go to its throat, he cannot find in his heart to do it. When it says to his heart, as Benhadad's servants pleaded to Ahab, 'I pray thee, let me live,' 1 Kings xx. 32, he cannot but spare its life, whatever come on it. Here is the unfaithfulness of his heart; notwithstanding all his shows of faith, he has some lust or other that he will not resign up to death for Christ. Thus it was with Herod: he 'did many things;' the ministry of John brought him a great way, and a little is much for a king; but when John touched his Herodias, he touched him to the quick; there he flies off. Many things he did, but this one thing he would not do. Thus it was with Abijah, that famous instance of a temporary faith; he did not leave that sin which was commended to him by the example of his father, 1 Kings xv. 3.

(3.) In point of suffering. He is not willing to part with all, to suffer all for Christ. Indeed, while sufferings are not in view, ask him, Are you content to have Christ accompanied with poverty, disgrace, displeasure of friends, hatred and persecution of enemies, imprisonment, banishment, tortures, death? And while these sufferings are at a distance, he may seem as resolute as any; but when it comes to trial, he falls off. A temporary faith has not root enough to stand in such storms. See this in the stony ground: Luke viii. 13, 'In time of temptation they fall away.' What temptation this is, see Mat. xiii. 20, 21, 'persecution and tribulation.'

But can I have no evidence of my sincerity till such a trial?

Why, yes; the former particulars may suffice for that. Indeed, it is possible that an hypocrite may not be discovered to others, no, nor to himself, till the fiery trial; but that is much through his own default, not making a strict and impartial inquiry into the state of his soul. If he did, he might discover his heart to be in league with some sin or other; and that would be a sufficient discovery both of the unsoundness and unstableness of his faith, that it is not sincere at present, nor will hold out for time to come. Whereas a true believer may make use of the contrary, as an evidence both of the sincerity and stability of his faith; both that it is sound, and that it will abide the fiery trial; for I take this for a sure rule, established upon good reason, he that will part with his most endeared sin for Christ, will be ready to part with his life for Christ, when he shall be called to it.

Proceed we now to those other graces and affections which hypocrites may, in some measure and degree, seem to partake of.

3. They may have some love to God; some affection to Christ, some love to the people of God; yea, to holiness and the ways of God.

(1.) Some love to God, which may be raised upon such grounds as this: they may apprehend God to be good in himself. The heathens gave him the title, not only *maximus*, but *optimus;* not only the greatest, but the best good: the *summum bonum*, the chief good. The Platonists make him τὸ ἀγαθὸν, the idea of goodness, goodness in perfection, in whom there is a concurrence of all perfections, a confluence of all things amiable and excellent. A natural man may apprehend him to be so good, as other things deserve not the title of good compared with him. This we may infer from Christ's discourse with the young man: Mat. xix. 16, Since thou dost not conceive me to be God, why callest thou me good, knowing that none is good but God? None comparatively good; none good as he is, originally, essentially, perfectly, unchangeably. Now goodness is the proper object of love; and an object duly propounded to its proper faculty will draw out some act or motion to it. As an hateful object, propounded as most hateful, does usually raise some motion of hatred, so an amiable object, propounded as most amiable, does usually raise some motion of love.

Further, they may apprehend him to be the fountain of goodness, not only to be good in himself, but to be the author of all good to others. So does Plato describe God to be good, and the cause of good. The light of nature leads men to subscribe to that of James, chap. i. A natural man may discover not only goodness in God, but riches of goodness, and that distributed, and that duly expended and laid out upon the sons of men; and the apostle tells us, this discovery is such, as does lead, &c., Rom. ii. 4; nay, it does not only lead, but draw (it is not καλεῖ, but ἄγει). Now, how does it draw? How is goodness attractive but by virtue of love? In this manner, what cause have we to love him, who is so rich in goodness? And how should it grieve me to have offended him, whom I have so much cause to love?

Moreover, they may apprehend that all the good things they enjoy do come from God; that they are parcels of that treasury of those riches of goodness which are in God. Laban, though an idolater, and that in dark times, could see and acknowledge, that what he enjoyed was from the blessing of God, Gen. xxx. 27. Now here is a stronger engagement to love, when God is apprehended, not only good in himself, and good to others, but good to him. This we find will beget some love in the brute creatures; no wonder if it raise some motions of love in the more apprehensive sort of men; who, notwithstanding the fall, have yet this advantage of beasts, they can apprehend a good turn, an engagement to love more clearly, and have more ability to reflect upon the Author of it.

Further, they may conceive the blessings they enjoy proceed from the love of God, Ps. xliv. 3. They may conclude, because he blesses them, he therefore loves them; and this is a strong engagement to love, even upon the worst of men, Mat. v. 46. The worst of men cannot resist such an engagement. The publicans will return some love for love. And may not natural men, apprehending strongly that God loves them (and has many ways expressed his love to them), make some return of love again?

Lastly, they may conceive they have a special propriety in God, believe that he is their God. Now propriety, though it be but in fancy, is a great endearment; we are apt to love our own things. I have proved before, that hypocrites may be confident of their interest in God; let me but add one text more, Rom. ii. 17, 'Thou art called a Jew, and restest in the law, and makest thy boast of God.' He speaks to those who were but Jews outwardly, *nomine tenus*, one who had nothing but the name; yet such a one can rest in the law, *i. e.* trust in it, for to trust and to rest upon are the same in Scripture phrase; he trusted in the law. Now the first words of the law are, 'I am the Lord thy God.' This he believed, and of this he boasted, that the Lord was his God; and he was not alone in this. Now propriety is a strong engagement of affection.

Upon these accounts a hypocrite may have some love to God. And that we may not rely upon reason, see if the Scripture hold not forth as much. Jer. ii. 2, the day of their espousals was when the Lord took them to be his people, and brought them out of Egypt, and led them through the wilderness. Then the Israelites had some kindness for the Lord, some love to him. And yet then what a character does Moses give of them, Deut. ix. 6, 24.

They may have some love to Christ too, and that upon the grounds premised. There is more of the loveliness of Christ discovered in the gospel than the light of nature can discover of the attractive goodness and excellencies of God. There is love in its triumph, in its highest exaltation, displayed before the sons of men; such expressions of love as one would think might force love from the devils, could they but persuade themselves of any interest in it. But now there are some hypocrites who can be confident they have interest in it, they are the objects of it; all this love, and the expressions of it, were for them; this I proved before. They can believe that Christ lived and died, &c., for them. And will not this be enough to command some common affection, to draw out some motions of love to Christ? See Mat. x. 37, 'He that loveth father or mother more than me is not worthy of me.' This expression implies that there are some who may have a kind of love for Christ, while they have a greater love for other things; such as think him worthy of some love, and yet are unworthy of him, and so never shall have saving benefit by him. Those Jews in the prophet seem passionately affected to Christ, Mal. iii. 1. The same word is used to express the affection of Shechem to Dinah, Gen. xxxiv. 19, who refused not the hardest terms that could well be propounded, so that he might have her to wife, see ver. 3. Such an affection these Jews seemed to have for the Messiah, and yet what they were, see ver. 7, and chap. ii. ver. 17.

They may love the people of God. See this in Herod, Mark vi. 20. He reverenced John, had an observant respect for him, delighted to hear him, and was exceeding sorry when Herodias had compassed his death. All which argue his love to John; and the reason of it is observable: he affected him because he knew he was a just and a holy man. A hypocrite may respect a holy man because he is holy. And further, John was a severe, a searching preacher, a sharp and impartial reprover of sin; one who would not spare the king himself, would not baulk the bosom sin of Herod; told him plainly what none of his courtiers durst tell him, It is not lawful for thee to have thy brother's wife, ver. 18; and yet for all this did Herod thus affect him.

So that a hypocrite may affect a searching minister, one who uses to ransack his conscience, to enter into his bosom, and there to wound his darling sin. Such a minister he may reverence, he may take pleasure in him, and delight to hear him. Herod was none of the highest flown hypocrites, yet could he reach such a pitch. What may those do who are of a more refined strain, when a tyrant, an adulterer, could do this?

They may have some love to holiness and the ways of God. Holiness is an observance of the law of God, for this is the rule of holiness. Now the light of nature, with a little help from Scripture, can discover that a general due observance of the law of God would bring such order, concord, contentment into the world as would make it a new world, transform it into a kind of paradise, and restore the golden age. And is not this sufficient to render holiness, or, which is all one, an observance of the law of God, lovely and amiable?

Ephraim, in the prophet, is said to love the ways of holiness, Hosea x. 11. This, well understood, does evince our purpose. To understand it, observe, that walking in the ways of God, in the paths of holiness, is in this chapter, as in many other places, set forth in terms belonging to husbandry, by ploughing, sowing, reaping, thrashing, as verse 12. In this verse it is set forth by threshing (for their way of threshing was a treading out the corn with the feet of oxen or heifers). To tread out the corn, applied to Ephraim, is to walk in the ways of God, and this Ephraim is said to love. She had some love to the ways of holiness, yet far she was from holiness itself, as appears by the Lord's complaint, ver. 13; so that, though she loved to walk in the ways of holiness, yet there was scarce a footstep of holiness to be found in her. It was some extrinsecal consideration that endeared holiness to her, of which I shall give you an account presently; for the distinction betwixt this love and that which is sincere and saving, lies in the text before us, and therefore we will offer it to your observation before we proceed further.

A hypocrite may love the ways of holiness, but it is not the holiness of those ways that he is in love with, but some outward advantage that he meets with, as he walks therein. This is notably held forth in the phrase of treading out the corn. It was forbidden by the law to muzzle the mouth of the beast that trod out the corn, Deut. xxiv.; so that the heifer was feeding all the time she was treading, and this was it that made her like the work. It was not the labour, but the food, that she was in love with; if her mouth had been muzzled, she would have liked her work no longer, she would soon have been weary of it. Upon this account did Ephraim love the ways of God, as any hypocrite may do; while they walk therein, they reap some outward advantage thereby, some gain and profit, some credit and applause, some temporal blessings, of which godliness has the promise. It is not godliness itself, but some attendants of godliness, that they were in love with. While they are fed with these, they will love to tread the corn, love to walk in the ways of holiness; but it is not the work that they love but these wages. Let them but be muzzled, let but these outward advantages be subtracted, and they will quickly grow weary of the way of holiness.

As for their love to the people of God, it is but some slight affection, which a carnal respect or interest, when there is occasion, will over-rule and command out of doors. We see it in Herod; his respect and affection to Herodias prevailed in him against the very life of John the Baptist. And though they may seem to love them because they are holy, so as their love may seem to be grounded upon their holiness, yet indeed their holiness comes in but at the second hand. The first and chief ground of their affection and respect is something else, to which holiness is made subservient.

We may see this in Herod also. It concerned him to keep up his respect and reputation with his people. And the people they had an high opinion of John, as a just and holy man; they counted him a prophet, Mat. xiv. 5. And therefore was Herod concerned to countenance him, and shew him some affection. And so the first ground of Herod's respect to him was his repute amongst the people; his holiness was but considered as the ground of the people's respect.

As for their love to God and Christ, it is not ingenuous, nor superlative.

(1). They love God not for himself, because he is good, but because he does good. Love him for the loaves: John vi. 26, 'You seek me not because ye saw the miracles, but because ye did eat, &c., and were filled.' Self-love is the rise of this love; now the streams rising no higher than the spring, it must be base love. (2). It is not a love of union. Not from a love to be near him, with him, in him, in his presence, here and hereafter, in ordinances, and in heaven. (3). It is not a love of complacency, because they are pleased with God above all, with all in God; and all that comes from him, works, word, mercies, afflictions, threatenings, promises. It is not a love to be like him, 1 John iv. 17. (4). It is not transcendent. They do not love him more than all, wishing more good to him than all, preferring him and his will before all, Mark x. 37, Luke xiv. 26. He does not apply all his faculties to love, and manifest love, Deut. vi. 5.

4. They may have some desires, like those which are found in the people of God, nearly resembling those desires which are as the pulse of an holy soul, by the feeling of which we are wont to judge of its spiritual temper and constitution. Their desires may be drawn out after heavenly and supernatural objects; they may have some desires after heaven and salvation, after Christ, the author of salvation, after those ways which lead to it.

(1.) They may desire heaven, that glory and happiness, those joys, and that rest which remains for the people of God. We see this in Balaam, Num. xxiii. 10. He knew that the death of the righteous was but a step to happiness, and that the end of their life here was the beginning of eternal life. Such a death, such an end, he desires; such as would instate him in eternal happiness.

The heathens had some apprehensions of that happy immortality which succeeds the death of righteous men; that the soul, in a state of separation, would be happier than in conjunction here with the body; and this future state some of them have desired rather than life. Nonnus reports of Cleombrotus, that lighting on Plato's *Phædo*, his dialogue of the soul, and learning there that the soul would be happier when parted from the body, he was so transported with desires of that happy, immortal state, that he forthwith deprived himself of life to enjoy it, ἔρριψε ἑαυτόν ἀπὸ τοῦ τείχους καὶ τέθνηκεν.

If an heathen could be so transported with desires of happiness, who saw it so little, and had his hopes of enjoying it, no wonder if temporary professors do long for heaven, when it is so clearly discovered, when life and immortality is brought to light by the gospel.

They may desire Christ, the author of salvation; they may apprehend him to be the way, the truth, and the life; and so may desire him as the true way to life. The stiff-necked Jews did long for Christ, they did ardently desire the coming of the Messiah; as he was the desire of all nations, so in especial manner the desire of that nation, as expecting he would be the glory of his people Israel, Mal. iii. 1, 'Whom ye seek, whom ye desire,' בקש, it signifies a desire expressed by prayer, and the use of means for the attaining what is desired. Thus did they desire. It is true, that which much engaged their hearts to long for the Messiah, was an expectation of his coming as a glorious temporal monarch; but this was not all, they expected more from him than is comprised in such a notion, as appears by that of the woman of Samaria, John iv. 25. Certainty of all things concerning the worship of God as the way, and salvation by him as the end, as appears by the preceding discourse in the former verses. And we see the foolish virgins, they expected the coming of Christ, they waited for his glorious appearing to consummate his marriage with his espoused people; they prepared for this, trimming their lamps, and going out to meet him; they desired his coming that they might enter with him into the marriage-chamber, that where he was, they might be also; they express the importunity of their desires, as in the former ways, so by knocking and calling.

They may have some desires to know the ways of Christ, to be acquainted with the way that leads to life, and some desires to walk therein, Isa. lviii. 2; they seek him daily; and what do they seek? they ask of him the ordinances of justice; they would be acquainted with the righteous ways and holy ordinances of God; they behaved themselves as those that desired to know the ways of the Lord, to be acquainted with his will, as those that had a mind to walk in his ways and comply with his will; yet they were but hypocrites in their most specious actings, vers. 3, 4. But we have a notorious instance of this in the address of those Jews to Jeremiah, xlii. 1–3; they all here unanimously and importunately desire to know the will and way of God; and, if any words whatsoever could be an infallible sign of the motions of the heart, we might collect from their words that they desired to know the way of God out of a design to walk in it; for they call God to witness, in a solemn manner, that this was the bent and resolution of their heart, vers. 5, 6; yet they were hypocrites in all this, as we see, ver. 20.

5. They may have some joy and delight in that which is spiritual and heavenly, some joy in spiritual objects, some delight in holy employments, some rejoicing in the gospel, in Christ, in their interest in Christ, in the ways of Christ; and these are the chief objects of this affection of the people of God, of that joy which is unspeakable and glorious. Hypocrites may have like acts upon the same objects.

(1.) They may rejoice in the gospel; it may be a joyful message to them, and so they may receive it; they may entertain it, welcome it, as tidings of great joy; they may hear it with joy and gladness; so did Herod, Mark vi. 20. The phrase seems to import such an affection as the psalmist expresses, Ps. cxxii. 3. Those whom the apostles admitted into the church are expressed by the character, Acts ii. 41. Herod had such an affection, something very like it, for the Holy Ghost holds it forth in the same phrase, Mark xii. 37. Herod and such hypocrites may rise up in judgment against such amongst us who are so far from hearing the word gladly, as they care not how little they hear of it, who rather loathe this manna, with the Israelites seem cloyed with it; think they should have too much, if they should have as much as is offered; so far are they from receiving it gladly. How far do these come short of heaven, who come so far short of hypocrites? They can receive the word with joy, and rejoice in the light of the gospel; so did those Jews, John v. 35; yet such as came short of life, ver. 40. Though John was a plain, severe, a searching, a convincing teacher, a burning and shining light, that both searched and scorched their consciences, yet they embraced his doctrine with joy, and rejoiced in it; so the stony ground, Mark iv. 16; Mat. xiii. 'With joy.'

(2.) They may delight in Christ. If John Baptist, who was but Christ's harbinger, was welcomed with joy by temporary professors, well might they entertain Christ himself, whose harbinger he was, with rejoicing; if John, who was but as the morning star, was looked upon with delight, how much more the Sun, Christ himself, the Sun of Righteousness? 'Light is sweet,' Eccles. xi. 7. Light is sweet to the eye of the body; so is spiritual light to eye of the soul; it is a pleasant thing to behold the light of life, the Sun of Righteousness. It is so even to some hypocrites; it was so to the disobedient Jews, though they saw him but afar off, at some hundred years' distance; though they had but such glimmerings as could be in the sky so long before the rising of this Sun; some dawnings thereof in prophetical Scriptures, shadowed with much darkness; yet even such appearances of Christ was their delight, Mal. iii. 1. The Angel, the Mediator of the covenant of grace, in whom, and for whose sake, that covenant of life and peace was made, and in whose blood it was sealed and ratified; in him, in this messenger, they delighted. So those who had nothing accompanying salvation, tasted some sweetness in Christ, Heb. vi. 4; there is heavenly sweetness in Christ the heavenly gift, and this they tasted, and the taste of it could not but be sweet and delightful; they tasted something herein like the joys of heaven, and therefore are said to partake of the powers of the world to come; and yet these, for all the sweetness they have tasted in Christ, all the delight they have taken in him, may fall off from him, and so shew that at the best they were no better than hypocrites.

(3.) They may rejoice in their interest in Christ, a supposed, presumed interest; for such as is real they have none. That hypocrites may have persuasions of their title to Christ and his benefits, I shewed at large, &c.; that the result of this persuasion may be joy and rejoicing is so evident as needs no proof; as he that has found the pearl of great price will rejoice, so he that does but persuade himself he has found it, may be surprised with rejoicing; for, indeed, it is the apprehension, not the reality, that is the immediate cause of joy. He that has real interest in Christ, yet not apprehending it, may go mourning all the day long: while he that is a stranger to Christ, yet presuming upon a title to him, may rejoice as one that finds spoils; and, indeed, a hypocrite may far exceed a true believer upon this account; he may have a spring-tide of joy, it may flow and fill its banks, when the comforts of a sincere soul are at a low ebb, Job xx. 5, 6. Though his joy be but short, yet it is great, what it wants in time is made up in measure; it is a joy like that of a triumph, and what is comparable to that? puts his soul into a triumphant posture, so as his excellency mounts up to the heavens, and his head seems to reach the clouds; so that, carnal Jew, Rom. ii. 17, $\kappa\alpha\upsilon\chi\acute{\alpha}\sigma\alpha\iota\ \grave{\epsilon}\nu\ \Theta\epsilon\tilde{\omega}$, thou gloriest in God. He gloried in this, that God was his God. The word imports a jetting or strutting of the neck; when the spirit is elevated, and moves in a triumphant posture, then it glories. David's soul was in such a posture when he breaks forth into those expressions, Ps. xxxiv. 2, 'My soul shall make her boast,' &c.; by the same phrase does the apostle express this formalist, he boasts, he glories. Comfort is more than peace, and joy is more than comfort, and glorying is more than joy; it is joy in its highest exaltation, joy exulting, making the spirit jet and strut as one marching in triumph; such may be the rejoicings of a formalist. His soul is so full of joy as it cannot be contained, but breaks out into triumphing shouts, and songs, and exaltation. That is the import of the word, in Job xx. 5.

(4.) He may delight in the ways of God; may rejoice, not only in his privilege, but in his duty. We have this twice expressed in one verse, Isa. lviii. 2. They not only delight to know, but to do; demean themselves as those who delight both to find out the way to God, and to walk in it; they delight to approach; yea, and the ways wherein they delighted was that wherein the flesh takes no delight. One of them was a duty which tends to macerate and humble the body, and afflict the soul; for that is the instance immediately adjoined, ver. 3, 'Wherefore have we fasted, and thou seest not?' &c. So Ezek. xxxiii. 31, 32: 1, they come frequently; 2, attend devoutly; 3, hear with delight. They took pleasure in the prophet's sermons, as in a most delightful song set off with exquisite music.

But now their delight is defective, in that it is,

(1.) In something external, not in divine objects themselves. In the saints, not because holy, strict, but because kind, affable. In ministers, not as God's instruments to regenerate, search the heart, discourage sin, but as learned, eloquent, plausible delivery, sweet deportment; in the gospel preached, for notions perfecting the intellectuals, not as it teaches to deny ungodliness; in prayer, not as enjoyment of God, communion and communication, but as it gets them applause, upholds credit, satisfies conscience.

(2.) It is in general confused. Descend to particulars, it vanishes. In the gospel offering Christ as a Saviour, with pardon, reconciliation, liberty; but come to the terms upon which Christ is offered, denying self, taking up the cross, &c., they go away offended.

6. They may have some zeal for God and his concernments. Zeal is an affection which much honours God, and is much honoured by him. The Lord expresses an affectionate resentment of the zeal of Phinehas for many generations, Num. xxv. 11, 13; Ps. cvi. 30. Zeal, when it is of the right stamp, is a character, not only of a true, but of an eminent Christian. Now such professors may express much zeal; it may flame as high (sometimes higher) as that which is kindled from heaven. To give you an account of this more distinctly, in some particulars,

(1.) They may have zeal towards God; not only for themselves and their own interests, but for God. So had Paul before his conversion, and the Jews while unconverted. We may take the apostle's word for both, Acts xxii. 3. He gives this testimony, not only of himself, but of those who then persecuted him. His zeal was drawn out, not he says towards his own reputation, and advantage, preferment, but towards God. So says he of these Jews here, and so he testifies of them, Rom. x. 2. They had, even the rejected Jews, they had a zeal, he says; he says not a zeal of their own carnal interests and worldly concernments, but 'a zeal of God,' such a zeal as engaged the apostle's heart, drew out his desires after them, obliged him to pray for them, ver. 1. Their zeal is assigned as the cause of all this, ver. 2. It was a zeal of God, according to the best of their knowledge.

(2.) They may be zealous for reformation, zealous against false worship. See this in Jehu, 2 Kings x. 16. Here is zeal made visible by action, and so confident as it dare expose itself to view: 'Come, see.' Offers itself to the test of Jonadab. And it is zeal for the Lord. Zeal, when it is not for

God, is but wildfire; when it is not in the cause of God, it is out of its place; like fire in the thatch, not in the chimney, more apt to consume the house than to be serviceable to it. 'It is good,' Gal. iv. 18. Now he was zealously affected in a good thing; it was a business wherein the Lord employed him. It was zeal against sin, against false worship, against the idolatrous worship of Baal; a zeal which consumed the place, the means, the instruments of that false worship; a zeal for reformation, which the Lord rewards with a kingdom to him, and his posterity for some generations, ver. 30. And yet Jehu was not sincere for all this, see ver. 31. But whatever he was, his zeal for reformation, and against corrupt worship does bear witness against, and condemn that lukewarmness and indifferency of many amongst us as to reformation and purity of worship. It is a lamentable thing to see so many ready to fall back to those old corruptions; forward to return to their vomit, to lick up that superstition which the Lord in a sharp course of physic had brought us to disgorge. A lamentable thing to see such lukewarmness and indifferency as to the worship of God refined from its old dregs, and reformed according to rule; to see this even in those that should be of a better temper. Such indifferency when we are engaged for reformation by all that is solemn and sacred; such indifferency, as though reformation had cost nothing, no prayers or tears, no treasure or blood, no hazards or sufferings; such indifferency as though those old corruptions had been no ground of God's controversy with us; no ground of former persecutions, banishment, imprisonments, and sufferings of all sorts to those of whom the world was not worthy, as though the precious gospel of Christ itself had not been apparently hazarded thereby; such indifferency as will be determined by a worldly interest, so as this shall turn the scales for a corrupt way, those antiquated corruptions; and that, notwithstanding the word of God, the principles of reformed churches, and all our engagements be put in the other end of the balance, these shall be no weight against a worldly interest, a carnal respect. Sure this is to be bewailed and laid to heart. I confess a sincere soul may be overswayed by a worldly interest in a particular act; but beware when this becomes a temper, when it is predominant, when it is constantly or commonly prevalent; then it is of sad importance. Whatever things or relations we secure thereby, we hereby forfeit our relation to Christ; he will not own such as his disciples. In Christ's account we miscall such when we call them Christians; their proper name is worldlings; the denomination should be regularly from that which is predominant.

But not to digress. If Jehu be condemned, notwithstanding his zeal for reformation, how shall such lukewarmness and indifferency as to the worship of God escape?

(3.) They may be zealous for the ordinances and institutions of God. As against false worship, so for the true worship of God; as for reforming worship corrupted, so for continuance of worship reformed. Paul, before his conversion, was exceeding zealous for the ordinances, Gal. i. 14; the ordinances delivered by God to the fathers. So it is taken by interpreters, and not restrained to pharisaical traditions. He was zealous for those institutions which were established by the law of God, for which the believing Jews were zealous, even after their conversion, Acts xxi. 20.

(4.) They may be zealously affected to the people of God, zealous for their salvation. So were the false apostles for the believing Galatians, Gal. iv. 17. The apostle commends Epaphras for his affection to the Colossians in a like phrase, Col. iv. 13. The false apostles had a great zeal for the Galatians; they were zealous for their salvation; they endeavoured to bring them into that way which in their judgment was the only way to salvation. They mistake the way indeed, and therefore he adds, 'but not well.'

Yet formal professors may know the true way, and then there is no reason but they may shew as much zeal therein for the salvation of others as these false teachers did for the Galatians.

7. They may have some fear of God. To fear God is the most signal character of the people of God in Scripture. Yet some fear of God may be found, even in those that have no saving interest in God; nay, some fear of God may be found in devils, James ii. 19. Here is fear, and that which proceeds from believing; here is a great fear; and such as is effectual, manifests itself by trembling.

But this fear, you may say, arises from apprehensions of wrath and justice; it is a legal, a servile fear. It is true. But there is a fear that springs from apprehensions of mercy and goodness; an ingenuous fear, such as the prophet speaks of, Hosea iii. 5. Now some such a fear as this we find in the Israelites, those who for their rebellions against God fell in the wilderness, and were not suffered to enter into the land of promise, Exod. xiv. 31. Here is a fear accompanied with faith; they believed and feared; here is a fear arising from the Lord's mercy and goodness, vouchsafing them a gracious and miraculous deliverance from the hands of their enemies. This is mentioned immediately before, ver. 30. Here is a fear attended with joy, breaking forth into the praises of God, chap. xv. ver. 1. And we find it repeated, Ps. cvi. 11, 12. Here seems to be that happy concurrence, that sweet mixture of joy and trembling, whereby the soul is kept in that temper which is the best, a middle temper, then it is upon the right bottom; fear moderating the excesses of joy, that the heart be not too much exalted; and joy alleviating the pressures of fear, that the soul be not too much dejected. Such a temper as the Lord himself delights in, and calls for, Ps. ii. 11. The Israelites had some semblance of this; they feared, there is their trembling; and sang his praises, there is their joy. But what were this people, whose temper seems so excellent? The words immediately following discover them to be no better than those in the text, vers. 13, 14. They soon forgot them; indeed as soon as their song is ended we find them murmuring, Exod. xv. 24. But three days interposed betwixt that seeming excellent frame of spirit and this detestable distemper, betwixt this fear of God, and this mutiny wherein they murmured against him. So speedily did all their faith, their joy, their fear end in a mutiny.

Further, the fear of God may be exceeding great in natural men. So it was in those mariners, who used to be most fearless, Jonah i. 10; when they apprehended the nature of the prophet's sin, and saw the effects of it, then were the men exceedingly afraid. Though Jonah tells them, ver. 9, he feared the Lord, yet they seem to be possessed with more fear of God than Jonah. Even natural men, upon some occasions, may express more fear of God than a prophet, than some eminent servant of God, when under a temptation. But here their fear seems to be from apprehension of danger, and so more servile; see ver. 16. You will see a fear of a more ingenuous strain. Now, the storm was over, the sea was becalmed, the danger was past, deliverance appeared, and that as the consequent of their prayer; and yet now they feared the Lord, and that with a great fear (as it is in the Hebrew), such as is accompanied with acts of worship, and resolutions of praise and obedience. Such a fear of God may be in heathens (for I find not any divines determine that they were converted, nor find I any certain ground in the text for such a determination). Now, if such an affection may be in heathens, strangers to God, and the discoveries of God in Scripture, what may there be in those who may see God by the light of Scripture, and live under the discoveries of God, both by the law and the gospel?

8. They may have some contempt of the world; yea, a high degree of it. This seems to be the property of the Lord's redeemed, those who are redeemed from the earth by the blood of the Lamb. But yet some men of the world may despise the riches and honours, the pomp and vanities, of the world; they may reject them, relinquish, deny themselves the possession and enjoyment of them, forbear the pursuit of them. They may look upon the most splendid things in the world as things below them, unworthy of their thoughts, affections, or endeavours. There seems to be the greatest allurement, the strongest temptation, the subtlest snare in riches. Here is a snare which few seem to escape; the people of God are here too much entangled, therefore I shall insist on this most, and shew how natural men may despise, refuse, and trample upon riches; and demonstrate this, not in words only, but in their practice. Peter, in the name of the rest of the disciples, seems to boast of their relinquishing the world for Christ, Mat. xix. 27. His speech has reference to the young man too much in love with the world, who would part with Christ rather than his possessions. Ay, but, says he 'We have left all.' This was an argument of great self-denial and contempt of the world, to forsake their houses, and what estates they had, to follow Christ, in a poor, despicable, afflicted condition, but this they all did; he speaks it in the name of the twelve. And to the twelve Christ applies his answer, ver. 28. Now, Judas was one of these; he had forsaken all as well as the rest. A Judas may shew such contempt of the world, as to abandon and relinquish all he has in it.

Paul was not a whit behind the very chiefest apostles in self-denial and estrangement from the world. Who is there that could less regard earthly things than he, who was crucified to the world, and minded riches no more than a dead man? And yet see the false apostles would out-vie him in this very thing. Whereas he received maintenance from the churches to which he preached, they would receive none, they would preach gratis; and forced the apostle to do so also, that he might cut off their occasion of glorying, as if they were greater contemners of the world than he, 2 Cor. xi. 12.

Would we not take it as a great argument of contemning the world, if we should see a rich man sell his estate and bring the price of it into a common treasury for the maintenance of others, reserving only a part of it to himself? Would ye not take this as an evidence of an heart not valuing riches? Would it not prove a shrewd trial, if professors amongst us should be put upon such an act? Yet Ananias and Sapphira did thus much, Acts v. 1, 2. They sold their possession, brought the price of it to be disposed of for the relief of others, and they would not be the disposers of it themselves neither, as those that are most liberal would desire to be in such a case; they lay it down at the apostles' feet, they reserve but a part of it for their own use.

Ay, and they did this voluntarily; it was a free act; for, as appears by verse 4, there was no necessity laid on them to sell their possession, or part with so much of the price of it. They might have kept it unsold, or kept the price of it to their own uses, and yet have continued in communion with the church, not have been judged unworthy of the apostles' fellowship. There was no decree made by the apostles, no injunction laid upon the primitive Christians, to sell or alienate their possessions; for Peter clearly sheweth that Ananias might justly have kept his own, in land or money. It was a voluntary act, and so is a greater evidence of a less esteem of his possessions.

So that hence it appears, an hypocrite may so little value riches as to sell his whole estate, and dispose of the greatest part of it for the relief of others; so far they may contemn the world.

There is an appearance of some contempt of the world in that deluded generation amongst us, which we call Quakers.

The papists, whom they herein follow, and by whom they seem in most things to be influenced, come not short of them in this. The retirements, abstinence from meats and marriages, voluntary poverty, and other severities observed in some of their stricter orders, is looked on as a contempt of riches and pleasures. But if this were real and not counterfeit, if we saw a lively face of this amongst them, and were not deluded with a vizard, yet would they have no great cause to boast, since

The Essenes, a superstitious sect amongst the Jews, and no better than half pagans, could vie with them herein. Indeed, the Papists are but their apes; as in other monastical observances, so in this shew of contemning the world, as Plato and Josephus represent them, they had more of this in reality, and little less in appearance. But to mention nothing but what is to our purpose, besides their abstinence from sensual pleasures, they so little valued riches, as none was admitted into their society but he must part with all his possessions; and so they lived together, as not any one of them had anything of his own.

Nay, this is to be found in mere heathens. The Lacedæmonians, the gallantest and most powerful state in Greece, when Greece was in her greatest flourish, lived in a visible contempt of riches and other vanities which the world much admires, and that for many years together.

Let me give you some particular instance, wherein this contempt of the world has been visible amongst heathens. It is observed, that some of the gallantest men wherewith the more refined part of the heathen world has been honoured, have lived in extreme poverty; and that not out of necessity, but out of choice; not because they wanted opportunities to make themselves rich, but out of a contempt of riches, and because they thought it better to want than to enjoy them.

It is reported of Epaminondas (the great Theban general, the gallantest commander that Greece ever bred, and who by his brave conduct had raised Thebes, a contemptible state before, to be the most powerful city in Greece) that the condition wherewith he contented himself was so low and poor, as it afforded him but one sorry coat; so that when he sent this to the fuller, he was glad to keep house till it was returned, for want of another. It is like he could not want opportunities to enrich himself in those great wars wherein he commanded in chief and was always victorious; but, as they represent him, he was so far from seeking riches, as he would not accept of them when they sought him; for besides other rich offers which he rejected, when the king of Persia presented him with a large quantity of gold ($\pi o \lambda \grave{u}$ $\chi \varrho \acute{u} \sigma \iota o \nu$, says Ælian), he would not accept of the present. We would look upon him as an elevated soul in these days, as one raised high above the world, who would not stoop to such a golden offer.

Phocion, a man so eminent for abilities in government both in peace and war, as he was forty-five times chosen governor of Athens, yet is reported to have lived all his time in the lowest poverty; and this he did voluntarily and out of choice too. For when Alexander sent him an hundred talents (which in our account amounts to nineteen thousand pounds, a vast sum in those days), and besides this, the choice of any one of four cities in Asia for a constant revenue, he refused both the one and the other. Why, says he to Alexander's messengers, does the king send me such a rich present?

Because, answer they, he counts thee the best and most upright man in Athens. And why then, replies he, will he not suffer me to continue so? οὐκοῦν ἐασάτω μὲ τοιοῦτον εἶναι. Insinuating that it was more difficult to be a good man in the midst of riches than in the lowest poverty, and intimating that this was the end why he preferred poverty before riches.

Let me but add one more, it is that famous cynic, whom they represent speaking in a strain something like Scripture language : that he was a pilgrim, a wanderer here; that he was not at home while he was in the world; that he was absent from his country; that he was poor, poorly clad, and had nothing but from hand to mouth; and yet no less contented with this poor condition than Alexander with the empire of the world, vid. Ælian, p. 125. He would not change this poor estate for one more plentiful, though it were in his choice ; for when that great monarch offered him what he would desire, he desired only that he would stand out of his light. So little did he value these things of the world, which others value more than their souls.

I could easily cloy you with such examples, but I forbear. Indeed, I use not to trouble you with foreign instances, but this part of my subject seems to require it, and the usefulness of them may make up an apology, if any be needful. We may see something herein that may provoke Christians to emulation. How should we be ashamed to admire these things so much, which the light of nature discovers to be so contemptible ; to lay out so much of our thoughts, time, endeavours upon riches, which the heathens counted not only unworthy of their hearts and endeavours, but of their acceptance. However, by this it is plain, that there may be a contempt of the world in those whom Christ will not own.

They may go far in a way of obedience ; make a great progress towards heaven in respect of their practice. What they have of religion and godliness, may not only be notional but practical ; such as consists not in some light and knowledge, some inward heat and affection only, but which may make a great, a fair appearance in their practice, both in their addresses to God and in their dealings with men, in public and private, in acts of holiness and righteousness.

There may be a visible holiness in the face of their conversations, a visible conformity to the rule of holiness, a visible compliance with the revealed will of God, both as to moral and positive preceipts. Their lives and deportment in the sight of the world may be both blameless and beautiful. So was the outward carriage of the Pharisees, by Christ's own testimony, beautiful without, Mat. xxiii. 27. He searches the heart and could see what was within ; that which was visible was beauty, and such as got them the repute of very holy men. So far as one man can judge of the acts of another, their obedience may seem as good as the best, and we being to judge of men by their acts, they may be reckoned amongst the best in their generation. Thus they may live, and thus they may die ; live as saints and die as martyrs, in the account of others and in their own account too, and yet, in the judgment of Christ, may be no better than workers of iniquity ; no better than these in the text, and in the end have no better reward.

But not to stay in generals, a distinct and particular account hereof will be more satisfying and convictive, and this way I shall lead you to a discovery, a prospect of a formal professor in his utmost obedience, by three steps.

(1.) There is a negative obedience, in not doing that which is evil ; this consists in an observance of negative precepts, and appears in avoiding sin, declaring* what the Lord forbids.

Qu. 'declining'?—Ed.

(2.) There is a positive and active obedience, in doing that which is good; this consists in a conformity to positive precepts, and appears in the practice of those duties which the Lord commands, a performing of those acts of morality, charity, or godliness, which are enjoined in the law or the gospel.

(3.) There is a passive obedience, which consists in suffering what is inflicted, either for the profession or practice of what is according to the mind and will of God, either for the profession of his truth or obedience to his will, in case upon trial we resolve to obey God rather than man.

Now formal professors may go far in each of these, in avoiding what is forbidden, doing what is commanded, and suffering for their faith or practice. I will shew this particularly, and when all is put together, you will see that the same will amount to no less than what I delivered in the general account.

[1.] They may go far in avoiding sin, there may be a notable exactness in their negative obedience, strict in avoiding what is offensive to God. I shall lead you to the height of their progress herein by these several degrees.

First, They may avoid gross sins, shun that wickedness which is the practice of the profane world, so as no such blots shall be seen in them as are too visible in the lives of others. Such a representation we have of the Pharisee, Luke xviii. 11: he was far from being plunged in that wickedness which other men are sunk into; his spot was not the spot of the publican. This was the temper of that sect generally; their avoiding of gross sins, such as were condemned by the letter of the law, was the ground of their confidence that they were righteous. They were not so bad as others, and therefore thought they were good enough. And this was the occasion of the parable, ver. 9. This sect, whom Christ will condemn, may go thus far, ver. 14. The apostle speaks of some who had escaped the pollutions of the world, and yet were far from escaping hell, 2 Pet. ii. 20. They had got out of the puddle wherein the profane world does wallow, and yet afterward returning to their vomit, shew their natures were never truly changed; they were dogs still, by running back to the mire shew they were never thoroughly washed, never truly sanctified.

Secondly, They may avoid the open commission of smaller sins. Not only such as civil men are afraid and ashamed of, but such as the world will scarce count sins, will not easily be convinced they are sins. It is known that the Jews, at that time when they rejected Christ, were so far from worshipping idols, as they would not suffer any image in their temple; so far from profaning the name of God by wicked oaths, as they forbore the use of it in their common discourse, lest it should be profaned; so far from breaking the Sabbath by following the works of their callings, or spending any part of it in sports or recreations, as they scrupled works of necessity, lest these should be a profanation of it.

Paul, while unconverted, says he was blameless as to the observation of the law, Phil. iii. So he was not only free from gross acts of profaneness, but from smaller acts of disobedience before men; he had been blameable, if he could have been charged with these. The way wherein he was engaged, held forth the most accurate strictness to the eye of the world, and, therefore, did avoid the open practice of smaller sins, Acts xxvi. 5, κατὰ τὴν ἀκριβεστάτην αἵρεσιν τῆς ἡμετέρας θρησκείας. The apostle speaks of some drawn to apostasy, who had clean escaped, 2 Pet. ii. 18, ἀποφυγόντες. They did not only avoid sin, but fly from it. They fled so far and so fast, as they seemed to have made a clear escape; they seemed to have broke all the snares, great and small, else they were not quite escaped. If we see a bird entangled in any part, if she stick but by one claw, we say not she is clean escaped. These in the text, as to outward appearance, were quite got out of the net; they seemed not less or more entangled, were not openly inveigled in any sinful practice, greater or less. Such an escape may hypocrites make from open sins, more and less heinous.

But no wonder if any of the Jews (their light being such, as the rest of the world compared therewith was darkness) made conscience of smaller sins, since we see that the light which the heathen had, led them to make conscience, not only of their words and actions, but even of their looks and glances. Pericles, his speech to the Tragedian, is memorable to this purpose; he taking Sophocles tardy upon this account, perceiving his eye too much taken with a beauty that passed by him: One in your place, says he, should not only restrain his hands from covetous practices, but his eyes also from wanton looks, *Valer. Max.* p. 212. If such conscientiousness was to be found in heathens, whose consciences might easily be asleep, being so much in the dark, how much more tenderness may there be in professors under the gospel, whose light is like that at noon-day, whenas that of the Jews was but as twilight, that of the heathens but as star-light? How does this condemn a great part of those who go under the name of Christians!

Thirdly, They may be careful to avoid some secret sins, such as the eye of the world can take notice of; they may be careful to avoid sinful thoughts, yea, sinful dreams, more excusable than thoughts, because less voluntary. Epiphanius, relating several severities and hardships to which the Pharisees inured themselves, as to their lodging, and the posture wherein they slept, assigns this as their end therein, διὰ τὸ δῆθεν μὴ σωματικόν τι παθεῖν, to prevent nocturnal pollution, that no impure dream might occasion any outward involuntary defilement, *vid. Casaub.* p. 44.

The heathen could see this, that a righteous man would avoid secret sins as well as open. Notable is that of Plato, ὁ δίκαιος ἀνήρ κἄν τον Γύγου λάβη δακτυλιον ἵνα μὴ ὁρᾶται, &c. A just man will not do an unrighteous act though he could do it invisible. What their practice was in secret is not discernible, and therefore instances of this kind cannot be expected; but this was their principle, which Ælian thus lays down, p. 414. He is a bad man, not only who does wrong to others, ἀλλὰ καὶ ὁ ἐννοήσας ἀδικῆσαι, but who thinks of doing them wrong. Now we may reasonably suppose that their light leading them to this, some of them would follow it; for so we find they did in other cases. But the light in those that live under the gospel is more clear and strong as to the discovery and condemning of secret sins, and no doubt but it may procure some compliance in inward acts, since we see it carries all before it as to those acts that are outward and public.

Fourthly, They may avoid the occasions of sin; not only sin itself, but the occasions of it; they may shun these themselves, and they may remove them from others.

Thus Jehu not only removed the idolatry of Baal, but the occasion of it; he did more herein than some of the good kings of Judah; though they removed idolatry out of the temple, would not suffer it there; yet they tolerated the high places, as the Lord often complains. But he destroyed the very place of that false worship, 2 Kings x. 27. He both broke the eggs, and pulled down the nest, that idolatry might be hatched no more there.

It is reported of some of the Pharisees, that they wore hats so deep as to cover their eyes; and others of them, when they went abroad, would shut their eyes, lest through those windows, the occasions of sin should glide into the heart. If there was such strictness amongst the Pharisees, whom Christ so much condemns, how shall that looseness amongst us escape the damnation of hell! *Mihi timorem illa incutiunt.* These things make me afraid, says Nazianzen; lest when we should exceed the Pharisees, we be found worse than they; lest there be more reason to call us serpents and a generation of vipers.

But to our purpose. No wonder if formal professors may avoid occasions of sin under the gospel; since the Pharisees seemed careful to shun them under the law.

But what shall we say, if such strictness may be found amongst heathens? Ælian relates this of Clitomachus, that when any act of the brute creatures, which might be incentive to lust, was offered to his view, he would forthwith turn aside from it; and if at a feast he heard any immodest discourse, he would immediately rise and quit the company. This was much for a heathen. May we not expect more from those that live under the gospel? Formal professors have much more light, though they have no more grace.

Moreover, they may not only shun the occasions of sin themselves, but they may be careful to remove the occasion of sin out of the way of others; yea, when that cannot be done without their own damage and prejudice. Valerius Maximus gives us a pregnant instance thereof in a heathen, Sparina, a young man exceeding beautiful, perceiving that he was therefore much observed, and fearing the consequences of it, he disfigured his face, lest his beauty should prove a snare to others. *Deformitatem sanctitatis suæ fidam, quam formam irritamentum alienæ libidinis esse maluit*, p. 224. He had rather have his deformity an argument of his own purity, than beauty to be an incentive of uncleanness unto others. May not this heathen condemn such amongst us, who are so far from disfiguring themselves, lest they should prove a temptation to others, that they will disfigure themselves to seem more beautiful, and will patch up a beauty rather than want one, whatever be the consequences of it? How can those who have less conscience than heathens have more hopes than heathens! But though we have some worse than heathens, under the vizard of Christians, yet some we have will go as far as they in this particular, as to the shunning occasions of sin, and yet may come as far short of heaven as they who live without hopes of heaven in the world. Hypocrites may both shun and avoid sin.

Fifthly, They may be careful to avoid the appearance of evil, not only sin itself, and the occasions of it, but the very appearance of sin. Idolatry seems to be a sin to which the Israelites and Jews were most addicted; you may find this all along in the Old Testament. This seems to have been the beloved sin of that nation for many ages. But after the captivity, when the Lord had made them smart for it under many sufferings, they so much abhorred idolatry as they would not endure any appearance of it. Josephus gives us a remarkable instance to this purpose. Herod had built their temple in a most magnificent manner; over the great door thereof he placed a large golden eagle. This was no idol, no image either of the true or of any false God. Ay, but it was an image; the Jews looked on it upon this account as an evil appearance; so they took umbrage at it; it was an eyesore to them. Thereupon a company of them conspire together, and down they throw it to the ground. They would rather hazard their lives than endure such an appearance of evil. And indeed it was not only the hazard, but the loss of their lives; Herod burned them quick for this act. Thus zealous formalists may be even against the appearance of evil.

Sixthly, In reference to the avoiding of sin, they may use divers mortifying exercises; such as tend to tame the flesh, to beat down the body, and so to weaken sin. They may cut off those provisions for the flesh, whereby the lusts thereof are gratified, nourished, and so fulfilled. They may abridge themselves of those lawful comforts, which are so apt to be abused for the advantage of the flesh, and are so ordinarily abused by the best when they take their full scope therein. They may deny themselves those delights which the flesh so much desires, and which prove snares to the people of God, when they are not very watchful, cautious, and spiritual, and keep not a strict hand and a vigilant eye over their hearts in the use of them; I mean the delights we take in relations, meat, lodging, apparel, and habitation. Formalists may deny themselves much in these; may neglect them, and content themselves with mean fare, hard lodging, plain habit, poor habitations. They may displease and cross the flesh herein, keep it down, and disable it from acting those lusts, to which these outward things are supports and incentives. They may afflict the flesh with much abstinence and many austerities, which seem to have some tendency to starve and mortify it. The Pharisees were much in fasting, humbling, and afflicting their bodies, Luke xviii. 12. Twice a week was their constant practice, besides their occasional fasts: Luke v. 33, 'Fast often.' And then they abstained from all kind of nourishment from evening to evening. But the abstinence of the Essenes, another sect amongst the Jews, was greater. If we compare our fare with theirs, their whole life may seem to have been a continual fast; they content themselves with one meal a day, only a supper, and then they had no other drink but water; no meat, but bread and salt. Another dish some of them had, but that was only hyssop, and those that used it were counted more delicate than ordinary.

The papists boast much of their fasting, but the strictest popish fast is a feast compared with the Essenes' best fare. So abstemious they were in their diet, and their habit, lodging, houses were answerable; all carried a great appearance of contempt of the world, and neglect of the body. That is the apostle's phrase, Col. ii. 23. And some think he there represents to us these same people. 'Touch not, taste not, handle not,' was their rule, and so was their practice; they lived at a distance from the delights and softnesses of the world, and so little gratified the flesh as they seemed plainly to neglect it, ver. 23. These things had a specious show of wisdom, *i. e.* of holiness; for so wisdom is sometimes taken in Scripture. Much of holiness consists in self-denial and mortification, and there is an appearance of these in this neglect of the body, when it is not in any honour, no respect had of it, the flesh, for its satisfaction in outward things.

[2.] They may go far in positive and active obedience; as in avoiding that which is evil, so in doing that which is good. Their conversation may not only be clean from the blots and pollutions of the world, but adorned and beautified with the visible acts of holiness and righteousness. They may seem exact and conscientious in acts of piety towards God, and acts of righteousness towards men; they may go far in the outward performance of those duties which the Lord requires, and has appointed to be the visible way to heaven.

The evangelist gives Herod this testimony, that he did many things when he heard John, Mark vi. 28. Now, he that considers what education and examples Herod had, even the worst that could be, what his place and state was, the evangelist calls him a king; what his snares and temptations were, those that are common to great men, and some peculiar to him; may reasonably judge that it will be more easy for a private person (not in such circumstances as he was) to do all (as to the outward act) than for him to do many things, and yet as far from heaven as he, Mark x. 17. And, indeed, some there were amongst the Jews so exact as to the duties of the first and second table, that they thought they were obedient in all, omitted nothing which the law required. This you may see in the young man coming to Christ in the Gospel; he was one of prime nobility and great possessions. Luke calls him a ruler, ἄρχων; he shews his zeal in running to Christ; he shews an honourable respect to Christ in kneeling to him (much more than many of his quality) acknowledging him a teacher sent of God. He shews great care of his soul in his inquiry; he propounds no frivolous question, such as the Pharisees did; his inquiry is after eternal life, how his soul might attain it. Christ frames his answer according to the form of the question; if thou wilt have life by doing, Mat. xix. 17, 'Keep the commandments.' Why, he had kept all these, and that from his youth; observed these commands, as to the letter of them, and the outward acts required therein; he is confident he never violated any of them since he had the knowledge of good and evil. Now I am apt to think that he spoke as he thought, and was verily persuaded he had done as much as he said (not understanding the extent and spiritualness of the commands) : for it is said, ver. 21, 'Jesus said unto him, If thou wilt be perfect, sell all that thou hast, and give it to the poor, and thou shalt have treasure in heaven.' Christ would not have been so affected therewith if he had grossly dissembled. He had been so careful in an external observance of the law, as he thought he had omitted nothing; and yet was far from the eternal life he inquires after; for he leaves Christ (though sorrowful) rather than he would part with his possessions.

But this young man did not understand how much the law required. It is like the apostle Paul, before his conversion, was more knowing; yet he professeth, that while he was unconverted, as to his observance of the law, he was blameless, Phil. iii. 6. So exact and punctual was he in obeying the law, that as none could blame him for any open commission of sin, so none could blame him for any omission of duty, as to those acts that were then acknowledged to be sins or duties; he was unblameable in both respects; he had not been blameless if he could have been blamed for either. And yet for all this righteousness, which seemed so spotless, if he had not found another righteousness besides that of his own, that of the law, he had been lost.

But though he was so strict in his obedience that man could not blame him, yet his own conscience might blame him. Conscience will accuse those who are so exact as men cannot at all charge them. Was he unblameable in his own conscience? See for that, Acts xxiii. 1. Here he professeth solemnly, in a great assembly, that he had lived in good conscience, in all good conscience, and that before God, and this all his life long; not only in the Christian, but in the Jewish religion, not only after, but before his conversion; for so far both interpreters and the words carry it: ' until this day.' He had all his days, unto that very day, acted sincerely and uprightly, according to his conscience. He walked conscientiously while he was a Jew. He did not act that which conscience condemned, nor did he decline that which conscience enjoined him, and yet if he had died in that state he had gone to hell. Thus conscientious may such be, who shall never enter into heaven.

But we have more* formalists in acts (that are outward) of righteousness towards God and men. Many not only go as far as ordinary sincere Christians, but even as far as the apostles, the holiest and most exemplary Christians, 2 Cor. xi.; so did the false teachers amongst the Corinthians, ver. 13–15; as to a visible form and specious appearance; as to the outward lineaments of godliness; as to the external acts of holiness, self-denial, mortification, contempt of the world, they were even as the apostles of Christ. The Corinthians did so take them, though they were the most knowing, dis-

* Qu. 'mere'?—ED.

cerning, intelligent people amongst the primitive churches. They were so much taken with them, as the apostle is put to argue them out of this delusion. Even as Satan (says he) may assume such a shape, and make a glorious appearance of heavenly light and holiness, as he may be taken for an angel of light and glory; even so those, that are no better than the ministers of Satan, may in their outward actings put on such a beautiful form of holiness and righteousness as they may be taken for the ministers of righteousness, yea, for the very apostles of Christ. There was such an appearance of light and holiness in these false teachers, it shined so bright in the eyes of the Corinthians, as it cast a shadow upon Paul himself, though he was not behind the very chief of the apostles. We see in this epistle he is hard put to it to continue in the esteem and affections of the Corinthians; so far did these false teachers seem to exceed him.

But let me give you a more particular account of this. They may go far in acts of morality, charity, piety, and religion.

First, For acts of morality. Not only carnal Jews and formal Christians, but the very heathens have made a strange progress herein. They have some of them gone so far, as I know not who can go beyond them, staying in the outward act.

For temperance; abridging themselves in those delights which the flesh so much affects, not gratifying it at all. Examples before.

For continence. Some, even men, not yielding a jot to the most tempting allurements that impudence could devise; as they report of Zenocrates, Valer. Max. p. 212; and some women preferring their chastity before their lives, as they relate of Hippo, p. 316, who, being taken by an enemy's fleet, cast herself into the sea lest she should be defiled.

For mercifulness. Those that ruled over Israel, after the division, had that repute; so the servants of Benhadad, 1 Kings xx. 30, 31; though we cannot find one good king, one godly man amongst them.

For truth and faithfulness. Some have valued their word more than what is dearest to us in the world, more than liberty and life itself. So they report of Attilius Regulus, rather than he would break his word, he would part with relations, country, liberty, and life too; yea, and did thereby expose himself to a most cruel death.

For liberality, the noblest kind of it, in a generous expending of their estates for the service of God, and the promoting of his worship, we have an instance of it in those Israelites, whose carcases for their sin fell in the wilderness. When Moses invited the Israelites to contribute towards the building and furnishing of the Lord's tabernacle, they offered their precious things so freely, as he was glad to restrain them, Exod. xxxvi. 5-7. Here was liberality, indeed, that must be restrained by proclamation; and yet this was the people who would give their golden ear-rings also to make a molten calf of, Exod. xxxii.

Araunah, though a Jebusite, and one of no great quality, if we may guess by his thrashing, yet was free as a king when there was occasion for the service of God, 2 Sam. xxiv. 22, 23.

Cyrus, though an heathen, sent for the service of God in the temple at Jerusalem, five thousand four hundred vessels of gold and silver, Ezra i. 11.

Herod was a noble instance hereof, though a prodigy of wickedness otherwise. He built the temple of God at Jerusalem; and made it more large, sumptuous, and magnificent than that of Solomon's was, if we may believe Josephus, who saw it both standing and destroyed.

For patience. We find those who have borne their great losses thankfully, and have suffered wrongs and injuries, without seeking any revenge.

I might produce many examples, but I will desire your patience for two only. Nonnus reports of Antisthenes, that suffering shipwreck, and having all his estate cast overboard, he cried out, εὖγε ὦ τυχη χαριν σοὶ ὁμολογῶ, &c., I thank thee, O providence, that thou hast taken away all that I had, even to my threadbare coat; εὐχαρίστως φέρων τὴν ἐσομονὴν αὐτῶ πενίαν, he took his future poverty with thankfulness. To bear injuries without seeking revenge, is by some counted such a virtue as the heathen could not attain; yet Phocius (if truly represented) seems to have expressed it; he having done many great services for his country, and they most unworthily rewarded him with a violent death: when he was about to suffer, left this injunction to his son, That he should not revenge his death upon his persecutors, Ælian, p. 335. This was much in an heathen; but more may be expected from professors of Christianity, who have greater engagements, and a higher example of patience.

For justice, we might present you with many memorable instances from foreign relations, but since Scripture affords one sufficient, I shall go no further. We may find justice appearing most impartially in Saul, though otherwise a hypocrite, 1 Sam. xiv. Saul being in pursuit of the Philistines, adjures the people, lest the execution should be slackened, not to taste any food till evening. Afterward the Lord not answering him, ver. 37, he concludes some of them had broke that engagement, and resolves, whoever it was, he should die. Upon a scrutiny, it appears to be Jonathan, his son and heir-apparent of the crown. Who would not expect but that he should now relent? No, but he is impartial, even Jonathan himself shall die, ver. 44. And, but that the people overpowered him, he had been as good as his word, ver. 45. Thus impartial may formalists be in the administrations of justice, so as that natural affection, the strongest temptation, may not prevail with them to spare their dearest relations obnoxious. I should be tedious if I should lead you to the utmost extent which they may reach in moralities, but these may suffice for a taste, and by this you may judge of the rest.

Secondly, They may go far in acts of piety and godliness, those acts of worship which are directed unto God, and tend much to his honour when duly performed, prayer, hearing the word, meditation, sanctifying the Sabbath.

For *Prayer.* An act of divine worship, which the Lord so much requires, so much encourageth, which has so many promises, so many privileges, which is so pleasing to God, so prevalent with him, when ordered according to his will. They may be much in prayer, and shew much affection in it; they may pray long, and pray often, and pray affectionately, so as they may seem to keep pace herein with the best of God's people, so that none but the Spirit of God can discern anything, but that they pray by the Spirit, and that the Spirit of supplication breathes and speaks in them.

They may pray long, persist in the duty with much perseverance. Three of the evangelists tell us of the Pharisees' long prayers, Mark xii. 40. And Christ blames them not because their prayers were long. He requires it of us on some occasions, and it was his own practice, he continued in prayer all night, Luke vi. 12. We are to 'continue instant in prayer,' Rom. xii. 12; Col. iv. 2. But then it is blameable when in pretence only, and for a wicked design. When a man is weary of a full meal, a bit and away is best with him, it argues a weak or a distempered stomach. It is a sign of a carnal heart, to be soon weary of this spiritual and heavenly employment. 1 Thes. v. 17, the apostle bids us pray continually. The Pharisees, as Epiphanius represents them, did seem to comply herewith; they did pray συνεχῶς, give themselves so much to this duty, as if they prayed without ceasing. Nor were they alone in this. We meet with a sort of men in church history who, taking the words of Christ, Luke xviii. 1, according as the letters found, not in the true and sound sense, ascribed so much to prayer, and continued so much in it, as they were denominated from this duty, were called *euchetæ* or *precatores*, prayers or suppliants, yet for other wickedness mixed herewith, were excluded from communion with the church, and ranked amongst heretics. This about the fourth age after Christ. Formalists will be much and long in prayer, especially under affliction, Hosea v. 15, early, or as some render it, diligently. He that is diligent will be at his work early, and continue at it till it be late. I might give you some instances in heathens who have continued whole days, whole nights, in prayer, but I forbear.

They may pray often, it may be their frequent exercise, their daily employment. So did those formalists seek God, Isa. lviii. 2, *jom, jom, i. e.** as the phrase in Scripture is used, constantly, incessantly, frequently, every day, in a constant and continued course, without intermission. We are often at that wherein we delight, and they may delight in prayer, delight in approaching to God, ver. 2. The Pharisees prayed often, as they stayed long at it, so they came frequently to it, Luke v. 33. We find them at it at all times, night and day, in all places; in the temple, Luke xviii. 10; in the synagogues, and in the streets, Mat. vi. 5; in their houses too, and in their chambers. Though they affected public prayer much, yet they are reported to have been much at it in private, in secret. They gave themselves so much to private prayer at home, says Epiphanius, that they deprived themselves of sleep, to gain more time for it, that they might watch unto prayer. He relates several devices they used to awaken them to this duty, and keep them vigilant. Some of them, when they were forced to compose themselves to rest, would hold a ball of brass in their hand over a basin, that, falling when they fell asleep, the noise thereof might awaken them to their devotion. The apostle enjoins us, Col. iv. 2, to 'continue in prayer, and watch in the same,' so that these Pharisees seem to comply exactly with the rule.

They may pray affectionately. There may be a great appearance of zeal and fervency, of ardent desires and much importunity, meltings of heart and enlargement of spirit. They may be so much affected in prayer, as though they were transported, carried up in this duty, as though they were in a rapture, a divine ecstasy; their spirits may be so raised, so elevated, as though they were not in the body.

I shall clear this gradually to you as it is propounded. The ingemination of the word, *Lord, Lord*, in the verses before the text, denotes zeal in their acknowledgment of Christ, importunity in their addresses to him. Those formalists represented to us by the Psalmist were earnest in their inquiries after God, fervent in seeking him when his hand was upon them, Psalm lxxviii. 34. The word שחר, translated, *early*, signifies earnest and vehement importunity: They sought God with earnest desires, importunate fervency, and yet they were but hypocrites, vers. 36, 37.

The Ninevites cried mightily unto God, Jonah iii. They did not only pray but cry, and they cried mightily; they sent up strong cries, so strong as they pierced the heavens, reached the throne of grace, came up before God, and prevailed with him, so much as that he repented of the evil that he had said he would do unto them, and he did it not, as we have it, ver. 10.

So the Jews (though what the generality of them was, is well known) express heart-meltings and enlargements in their prayers under affliction, Isa. xxvi. 16. 'Poured out;' it is a metaphor taken from water, of which men are not

---

* That is, יום יום, *day by day*.—Ed.

sparing when there is occasion, pour it out freely and largely. In Scripture phrase, when persons are said to pour out their spirit or their prayer, it implies a large drawing out of their spirits and affections, with plenty of sobs and tears, *vid. Engl. Annot usque fin.* Their hearts were melted, and run out together with their words; their souls seem as it were dissolved, and poured out in their prayer. A prayer. The word לחש signifies a soft, sweet, lowly speech, such as takes the heart more than the ear (*vid. Leigh*); such a prayer as has more spirit and fervour in it than words and language. For raptures, it is a strange story which Nonnus, a Christian author, relates of a heathen philosopher, that in the winter time he continued in prayer all night long, παννύχιος εὐχόμενος; and though the season was so exceeding cold, yet he was so trausported, τοσοῦτον μετάρσιος γέγονε τὴν ψυχὴν, his soul was so transported, as his body was not at all sensible of the cold. We need not stumble at it, if those whose conversations be otherwise offensive, pretend to raptures and transportments in prayer; it seems this is no more than may befall a heathen. Satan, who can so transform himself as he shall be taken for an angel, whereas he is a devil, can so transport a person as he may seem to be in heaven, rapt up above the body, when he is indeed sunk into sin, and abides in the suburbs of hell. And he can do this so cunningly, with such artifice, as it shall be taken for the act of the Spirit of God, for the extraordinary working of the Spirit of supplication. And upon this account the prayers of a hypocrite may sometimes seem to be divine ecstasies, heavenly raptures; his soul in prayer may act at such a rate of freedom and elevation, may so soar aloft to such a height as though the clog of flesh and sense were shaken off, as though the soul were set free from its dark and heavy commerce with the body, as though it were already in glory, and acted and spirited by the immediate vision of God. Satan has played many such pranks as these in the world ere now, and they tempt him to do it who prize raptures and ecstasies more than a settled spiritual frame of heart, who look more after visions and revelations than that good old way and that sure established rule. But enough of this. You may see how much formalists may be in prayer, and how much affected therein.

For *hearing of the word.* Formalists may hear diligently, attentively, with delight and pleasure, with fear and trembling, with resolutions to obey it, with a great compliance and submission to it; some fruitfulness and active obedience, so as to be enlightened, convinced, restrained, reformed; they may be led by it so far, as it will be hard to discern who may go further.

We learn, by the parable of the sower, that three parts of men will hear, though but one in four hear savingly; three to one that hear the word of life fall short of eternal life.

They may hear frequently, in season and out of season. They may watch daily at the gates of Wisdom, and wait at the posts of her doors; they may be as diligent herein as the best, Ezek. xxxiii. 31; they may flock as diligently, sit as attentively as my people, as the best of the people of God; those that care not how little they hear, neglect opportunities when they are offered, fall short of formalists, are a degree lower than hypocrites; and yet Christ burdens these with so many threatenings, heaps woes upon them, as one would think might sink them into the lowest part of hell; yet it seems contemners of the word will sink lower.

They may hear with joy and delight. So did the perverse Jews hear John Baptist; so did the common people hear Christ; so did the stony ground receive the seed.

They may hear with fear and trembling. It is a commendation of the

Corinthians, that they received Titus with fear and trembling, 2 Cor. i. 15; yet a formalist, a heathen, may tremble at the word. So did Felix the judge tremble before the prisoner, Acts xxiv. 25.

They may hear with resolutions to obey. So did the Israelites hear Moses, Exod. xxiv. 3, Deut. v. 27; yet the Lord suspects them, as is intimated, ver. 29. So they heard Joshua, xxiv. 16, 18, 21, 24. Who could seem more resolute for God? Who could express higher resolutions to serve him? Yet how they served him appears almost in every page. So they promise to hear Jeremiah, xlii. 5, 6.

They may hear it, so as to comply far with it. They may give some answer to the call of God therein; they may be in some degree fruitful, and may reap some fruit by it; their minds may be enlightened, their judgments convinced, their consciences awakened, their affections moved, their wills inclined, and their lives reformed, and their souls persuaded, almost persuaded, to a thorough close with Christ, as Agrippa; in a word, all that light, those affections, that obedience in all its several acts and degrees, may be the fruit of their hearing the word; it may bring them to do much, to suffer much, to leave much for Christ; they may be brought to work, to do many works, many wonderful works.

For *meditation*. A duty of high excellency and singular advantage; but too much neglected by those who should most delight in it. It argued an excellent spirit in David, that he made the law, the word of God, his meditation day and night. Can a formalist do this? Why, even the Pharisees did attempt it; they used means apt to keep the law in their minds and thoughts, day and night; they did more herein than others. Two things Christ mentions, which were used for this purpose in the day time, phylacteries and fringes, Mat. xxiii. 5. The phylacteries, as is generally agreed, were little scrolls of parchment, wherein part of the law being written, they wore on their foreheads, and left arms' wrists, that thereby they might always be put in mind of the law; and thence they derive the word from $\varphi v \lambda \acute{a} \tau \tau \omega$, *to keep*, because hereby the word was to be kept in their thoughts, conservatories of the law. The rise of them is supposed to be from that command, Deut. vi. 8, Exod. xiii. 9, 16. Now, some of the Jews, supposing such schedules of remembrance were here enjoined, did use them in a less form; but the Pharisees wore them broader, as a sign of more care to keep the law in their thoughts always, than others had. The other means was fringes or borders of their garments; and this was of God's own institution, Num. xv. 38, 39. You see them here prescribed for this end, that it might give them frequent occasion to remember and meditate on the law. Now, the Pharisees did not only wear these as others, but enlarged them, as though they desired to have the word more in their minds and thoughts than others; nay, as a severe monitor, they used to wear sharp thorns in those fringes, *acutissimas in iis spinas ligabant*, says Hieronymus, that these pricking them, whether they walked or sat still, the pain might bring the law ever and anon to their thoughts with a sharp and quick remembrance. This for keeping the word in their minds when they were up; then, at their lying down, Epiphanius tells us that some of them used to lie upon boards no larger than an handbreadth, that being subject to fall, their falling might awaken them to thoughts of God and his word.

I shall conclude this head with the testimony of Philo the Jew, concerning the speculative Essenes. He says the exercises wherein they spent the day was prayer and meditation; and therefore, as he calls them $εὐχέται$, supplicants or prayers from thence, so from the other, $\vartheta εωρητικοί$, or meditators, having their name from that which was the great employment of their lives.

Thirdly, Thus I have shewed you what a way formalists may proceed in acts of morality and religion. Let us now view them in their acts of charity, wherein I shall be brief.

That Ananias and Sapphira should sell their possessions, and dispose of them to the relief of others, seems an high act of charity; it would be so looked upon, if such an act could be seen in these times; but Crates, though an heathen, went farther: he parted with all, if they represent him truly, ἔῤῥιψε τῶ δημῶ, he threw all he had amongst the people (says Nonnus), expressing withal why he did it; Crates will keep none of his possessions, lest they should keep possession of Crates.

But we need no other testimony, that of the apostle is so pregnant, 1 Cor. xiii. 3; he supposes that it is possible for a man to give all his goods to the poor, and yet have no charity. This seems stranger, that where there is the greatest charity in the world's account, there should be no charity at all in the sight of God. What greater act of charity can there be in the world, than for a man to bestow all that ever he has on the poor? Yet so charitable he may be, and yet have no charity at all; he may do thus much who has not the least dram of saving grace. An hypocrite may give all his goods to the poor, and when he has done, have no other reward but what the workers of iniquity shall have. The Pharisees were much in giving alms, they gave them freely and solemnly, and yet were rejected.

Thus I have helped you to a discovery of formal professors, in the acts, and degrees, and extent, of their negative and active obedience.

Thirdly, Let us now view them in their sufferings, and see how far they may proceed in passive obedience; that is the third and last part of our undertaking.

Active obedience is far more easy than passive. Many may be ready to do much for God, and yet unwilling to suffer anything; the flesh rises up against sufferings with all its might, as most unpleasing, yea, destructive to it; many, while the world smiles and shines upon them, may flourish in their profession of, and actings for, God, flourish like a green bay-tree; but a storm of persecution will blast and overthrow them. Those hearers resembled by the stony ground, who rise up to such an height of faith and joy; yet, when persecution arose, they fell away. Here is the greatest trial.

May hypocrites stand out in persecution? may they resist unto blood? may they be willing to suffer for God? Why, yes; they may not only do, but suffer, suffer for the cause of God; suffer much, yea, suffer as much as any; they may suffer loss of estate, suffer loss of all dearest relations, suffer tortures and imprisonments, yea, suffer death too.

First, They may suffer in their estates, suffer the spoiling of their goods; endure the loss of all rather than disobey God, or do an act that they do but conceive to be unlawful.

To waive other proofs, it is known that the Jews would suffer their goods to be spoiled, and all they had to become a prey to the enemy, rather than make resistance on the Sabbath-day, because they conceived that resistance (in any case but for life) was a breach of the Sabbath. This was their principle many hundred years since, when the observation of the seventh day was a duty, and they retain it still, for anything I know; and a formal Christian may go as far, in like cases, as a carnal Jew.

Secondly, They may endure sufferings in their dearest relations, the death and tortures of their dearest children. This to some would be almost as great a trial as their own death and sufferings. David's expression speaks as much for him: 'O Absalom, would God I had died for thee!' Thus much formalists may suffer willingly. Those hypocrites offer it, Micah vi.

6, 7. The prophet had been upbraiding them with their ingratitude, unworthy dealing with God. They, to quit themselves of such an odious charge, make large and free offers of what they would do for God: they would think nothing too dear, nothing too much, so that they might please him; they would give him plenty of burnt-offerings, thousands of rams, and oil in excessive abundance; or if he were less pleased with these sacrifices, they would sacrifice their first-born to him; they would offer up their children, the dearest of their children, as a burnt-offering unto God. This, to me, is the plain meaning of the expression. Nor need it seem strange that they make such an offer; for it was a custom not only to offer it, but to do it, Ps. cvi. 38. Even Ahaz, in whose reign Micah prophesied, made his son a burnt-offering, 2 Kings xvi. 3, made his son be burned alive. This is it which they profess themselves willing to do; they will do as much for God as Abraham was ready to do, offer up their Isaac, their first-born. And, indeed, why might they not be as willing to endure this for God, as others amongst them were to do it for idols? And yet methinks there scarce can be any suffering more grievous than this, which these formalists seem so ready to endure, not only the death of their children, but the burning of them quick.

Thirdly, They may suffer tortures, bonds, imprisonment. Sozomen, in his Church History, lib. v. cap. x., gives us a remarkable instance. He tells us one Basius, an Encratite (which sect the ancient church excluded from their communion as heretics), for opposing idolatrous worship in Julian's time, was grievously scourged, racked, and tortured, all which he endured with such courage and patience as astonished his tormentors, and after all was cast into prison, where he continued till Julian's death. Thus much he suffered, and that in a good cause, for opposing idolatry, the common cause of the primitive sufferers; and this too before his conversion, for he was not converted to the true faith till the churches had peace. So that a man destitute of saving grace, may suffer grievous things in the cause of God, and that with courage, patience, and perseverance.

Fourthly, They may suffer death too, die as martyrs, and yet not die in the Lord. The Marcionites, whom the ancient churches counted an execrable sect for their opinions and practices, yet gloried in their martyrs. So did the impostor Montanus and his followers, as Eusebius, *Hist.*

There were some amongst the Donatists (who had no communion with the ancient churches). There were some called Circumcelliones, who were so desirous of martyrdom, that they would force men to put them to death.

Not to mention what Josephus reports of the Essenes, a sect amongst the Jews little better than half pagans, they endured the most exquisite torments even to death, rather than they would speak evil of Moses; rather than they would do this, or eat any forbidden meats, they were content, with wonderful patience, to be tortured, burned in the flames, cut in pieces, torn asunder with all kind of torments, *vide Montan.* So to say nothing of the Martyrians, of whom *vide Baron. Epit.*

We need no other proof but the apostle's testimony, 1 Cor. xiii. 3. He supposes it possible that a man may give his body to be burned in the cause of God, and yet have no true charity, no saving grace; he may yield himself to death, to that most cruel death by fire, may be willing to be sacrificed in the flames, and yet not have a spark of true grace in his soul.

So that upon the whole survey of a formalist's obedience, you see he may live in the world like a saint, and go out of the world like a martyr, and yet be entertained by Christ as a worker of iniquity.

Use 1. For conviction. The light of this truth discovers that the greatest part of those who enjoy the gospel of the kingdom have no title to heaven, the kingdom promised in the gospel. For this inference is clear, if many may go far towards heaven, and yet be excluded out of heaven, which is evident in the text, then those who go not so far as those many, and those who will go no further than those many (of whom Christ speaks), shall certainly come short of heaven.

Now this is the sad condition of most of those who live (I say not only of those who live without Christ, and without God, and without hope in the world; those forlorn outcasts of the earth, who sit in darkness and in the shadow of death, on whom the light of the gospel, the light of life, shines not) under the gospel. More particularly, this is the woful state of ignorant persons, profane wretches and formalists. These are far from heaven, even such of them as seem to themselves and others to be nearest; they are not in the state of salvation, whatever good opinion they have of their eternal state; the former, because they go not so far as those hypocrites in the text; the latter, because they go no further. Those who continue ignorant, or profane, or formal, whatever they promise themselves (and such are apt to promise themselves most, who have least reason), will find no better entertainment from Christ than those in the text, Christ will profess to them, &c. Many who have dreamed of heaven and happiness all their life, will be awakened at death or judgment with this voice of thunder, Depart from me, you have no part in me; no part in heaven, in happiness, that is prepared, purchased by me. Your portion lies elsewhere, with other companions, with the devil and his angels; in another place, in everlasting fire. Christ speaks this now in mercy to warn you, to awaken you while you have time to prevent it. He will speak it then in judgment, then it will be too late; his judgment will be irrevocable, it will be followed with sudden and immediate execution. Oh that to-day you would hear his voice, while it is called to-day, before that terrible day comes; before that dreadful voice cut you off from Christ, from heaven, from all hopes of either, and that for ever! And that this voice of Christ now may be better heard, I shall deliver it distinctly and particularly.

1. To ignorant persons. You that make it not your business to acquaint yourselves with Christ, his truths, his ways, you that will not know him here, he will not know you hereafter; you who say to Christ, either in words or actions, Depart from us, we desire not the knowledge of thy ways, Christ will profess to you, and say, Depart from me, I know you not. What more equal than this proceeding? Your own consciences may justify him. Why should he take notice of you then, who take so little notice of him here? It is evident from the text. Christ will be thus severe in proceeding against affected ignorance, and there is little ignorance amongst us, in the midst of so much light, but that which is wilful and affected. If so much knowledge as hypocrites have will not find the way to heaven, how shall they find the way who continue in the blindness and darkness of ignorance? If those who arrive at such a height of knowledge will come short of heaven, sure those whose ignorance keeps them far below these will never reach heaven. Hypocrites may have much knowledge, Rom. ii. 18–20; so much knowledge they may have, and knowledge is necessary to salvation. If they shall not be saved who have that without which there is no salvation, how can they be saved who want it? The inference is so clear as ignorance itself may see it. But if so clear a consequence do not speak it, you may hear the Lord speak it directly and positively. There is no salvation for you without knowledge. If you be ignorant, you shall perish. Those that are knowing *may* perish, but those that are ignorant *must* perish. There is no avoiding it, nothing else can be expected. Ignorance will end in destruc-

tion, Hosea iv. 6 ; rejected by him here, rejected by him hereafter ; destroyed temporally, destroyed eternally. No destroyer like ignorance; plague, famine, and sword, do not bring so many to the grave as ignorance brings to hell. They perish; this is the Lord's voice in the Old Testament, and it is the voice of Christ too in the New Testament, 2 Cor. iv. 3. He says not, they may or they will perish, but they perish, this is their present state, they are condemned already. While they thus continue, there is no hopes, for what hopes for any sinner, but either in the mercy of God or the undertaking of Christ? But neither mercy nor Christ will relieve ignorance, the Lord cuts them off from hopes in both. Mercy itself will not save them; Christ will be so far from being their Saviour, as he will be their destroyer. The Scripture is express in both, Isa. xxvii. 11 ; there is no hopes in mercy, nor is there any in Christ. He who saves others will destroy them, he who has compassion on others will inflict terrible vengeance on them. See it dreadfully denounced, 2 Thes. i. 7–9, If there be no hope for the hypocrite, who has knowledge, sure there is no hope for these persons that want knowledge ; no hopes, unless they bestir themselves to get out of that darkness and shadow of death where ignorance confines them.

2. Profane persons are hereby excluded from heaven, whether their profaneness consists in commissions of gross acts of wickedness, or in the omission or neglect of duties of holiness. Thus many whom Christ tells us shall not enter into the kingdom of heaven, were of a more refined strain than the profane world; both their profession and practice speaks them better. And if Christ will shut those out of heaven that are better, sure he will not admit those that are worse ; if no unclean thing shall enter into his kingdom, sure there will be no room for profane persons ; no uncleanness so loathsome in God's eye as profaneness. Those who continue in the practice of known sins—lying, swearing, Sabbath-breaking, uncleanness, drunkenness, injustice, worldliness,—these are workers of iniquity with a witness. If Christ shut those out of heaven who work but iniquity in secret, so as none but his own eye sees them, sure he will never suffer them to enter who are workers of iniquity in the eye and view of the world. He who is of purer eyes than to behold iniquity on earth, will never endure to see such workers of iniquity in heaven.

Hypocrites have escaped the pollutions of the world, they have got the start of these, and yet shall never reach heaven; how shall they reach it then who stay so far behind hypocrites, and lie entangled in the toils of Satan, even into the suburbs of hell? Hypocrites seem righteous in comparison of profane persons; now, 'if the righteous shall scarcely be saved, where shall the ungodly and sinner appear?' Where but at Christ's left hand? The consequence is evident; but if Scripture consequence will not convince, hear what it speaks directly: Gal. v. 19–21, 1 Cor. vi. 9, Eph. v. 5, 6.

There is a profaneness also in omitting, neglecting holy things, spiritual employments; neglecting and slighting the worship of God in public or private. Esau is called a profane person upon this account, Heb. xii. 16. Before the priesthood was instituted under the law, it was the privilege of the first-born to be the administrator of holy things; they performed acts of worship in private families or public assemblies, they offered burnt-offerings and peace-offerings, Exod. xxiv. 5. When it was said Moses sent the young men to offer, the Chaldee paraphrase renders them בוכרי, the first-born. Esau, by parting with his birthright at so easy a rate, to which this privilege was annexed, slighted the worship and service of God, and so comes to be counted a profane person. Those are profane persons who slight, neglect the service of God in public or private, who set not up the worship of God in their houses, who instruct not those under their charge, who pray not in their families; when this is their duty and privilege, part with it for nothing, are more profane than Esau in this respect. Those also who neglect the worship of God in public, are weary of the word and prayer, care not how little they hear, once a day is enough for public service though that day come but once a-week; these are worse than those in the text; they are further from heaven than hypocrites, whom Christ professes shall never come there; for they may be diligent in acts of worship, public and private, as before. Some are apt to think their eternal state safe enough if they be not guilty of commissions, if they avoid gross acts of sin, though they omit, neglect holy duties; but, alas! they will find it otherwise. Oh that they would consider it before it be too late! The day is coming when Christ will pronounce the sentence of condemnation upon the profane world for omissions, Mat. xxv. 45, 46. If there be no heaven for the hypocrite, certainly there is none for the profane person. He goes not so far towards heaven as those that come short of it, and therefore sure he can never reach it.

3. Formalists are not in the state of salvation; those who are neither ignorant nor profane, but have a form of knowledge and godliness without the power of it, the outward lineaments of righteousness without the life of it, and rest in this as an evidence of a saving state; such as these, if they rest there, will never reach heaven, because they go no further than those in the text, whom Christ professes shall never come there. Whatever confidence they have to be saved, and whatever be the grounds of their confidence, they are never like to enter into the kingdom of Christ, unless they advance further. The truth, as I have opened it, discovers both the vanity of their confidence and the vanity of those grounds upon which it is raised, viz. their own righteousness.

The Scripture is so clear against ignorance and profaneness, so clear, that no unrighteous person shall enter into the kingdom of heaven, that none who will open their eyes, or whose consciences are any way awakened, who can be satisfied about their eternal state unless they have some righteousness or other to rest on.

Satan, who goes about every way seeking how he may devour souls, by stratagem as well as plain force, since men will have a righteousness, he is content, provided they rest in such a one as will not deliver them out of his clutches. He can so order the righteousness of men, as it shall be a strong hold in their way to keep them out of the kingdom of God, persuading them to sit down in such a righteousness for salvation as is not sufficient to save them. Thus does he delude formalists. No stronger delusion than this, none more subtle, more hard to be discovered; and yet scarce any more common and ordinary. The apostles, especially Paul, bend themselves much to the detection of this delusion; so does Christ: it seems to be his design in the words before us. The Jews of old, the professors of Christ in all ages, have been apt to split themselves on this rock; it has slain its thousands, yea, its ten thousands. More particularly, there is a threefold righteousness, which the more refined sort of men ordinarily rest on, the insufficiency of which, as to salvation, appears sufficiently from what this text has afforded us.

(1.) A negative righteousness. Many think they are righteous because they are not so unrighteous as others, conclude their condition good because they are not so bad as other men. They are no atheists, no idolaters, no profane swearers, no gross Sabbath-breakers, no murderers, adulterers, extortioners; they blaspheme not God, profane not his name, deny not his truths, persecute not his people; they do no wrong, oppress or defraud no man. There is none can charge them with any such unrighteousness, and therefore conclude they are righteous. Not so profane as others, therefore holy; not so worldly as others, and therefore fit for heaven; no open workers of iniquity, and therefore servants of righteousness; they have escaped the pollutions of the world, and therefore shall escape hell; as though hell were only provided for gross wickedness, as though it were a place for none but publicans and harlots. This is the reed upon which some men rest, as though it were strong enough to uphold their souls from falling into hell; but, alas! it is a broken reed, those that lean on it will find it so. It will break under you, and let you sink as low into hell as the Pharisees and hypocrites; for indeed this is no other righteousness but that of the Pharisees; nay, it is not so much as a gross hypocrite may arrive at. The Pharisee in the parable, against whom Christ passeth sentence, had this, and more, Luke xviii. 11, 14.

(2.) A moral righteousness. Some, because they are not only free from gross vices, but adorned with moral virtues, conclude their condition safe and good, and their hopes of heaven well grounded, because they are chaste and continent, temperate in the use of outward comforts, just in their dealings, candid and ingenuous in their deportment, contented with their condition in the world, and liberal to those that are in want, free for good uses, compassionate to the afflicted, patient in bearing wrongs, &c., make these the ground of their confidence that Christ will admit them into heaven. But those that build on these, build on the sand, for here is no more than may be found in heathens; and therefore such who go no further, have no better grounds for their hopes of heaven than those whom the apostle leaves hopeless, Eph. ii. 11, 12. These in the text went far beyond such, and yet Christ professes they shall never reach heaven.

(3.) A religious righteousness, consisting in the performance of holy duties, in public, in private, in secret. They are diligent in hearing the word, in season and out of season, frequent in meditation, much in prayer and fasting, careful to read and study the Scripture, forward to discourse of the things of God. Many make these their refuge, and think herein to secure themselves, conclude they are safe as to their eternal condition; whereas indeed this is but a refuge of lies. Many may shroud themselves herein who shall never take sanctuary in heaven; for this is no more than the righteousness of the Pharisees, who were strict in observing the Sabbath, &c.; and Christ declares that to be insufficient, Mat. v. 20.

Examine your state, inquire what are your hopes, and what are the grounds of them. If you have no better foundation for them than such a righteousness, you may read your condition in the latter end of this chapter: ver. 26, 27, 'He that heareth these sayings of mine, and doth them not, shall be likened unto a foolish man, which built his house upon the sand: and the rain descended, and the floods came, and the winds blew, and beat upon that house; and it fell, and great was the fall of it.'

Use 2. Instruction to the people of God. This teaches you care, caution. If a hypocrite may go so far, you that dread the state and the reward of hypocrites, be careful to go further.

Be careful so to walk and act as if you cannot have the testimony of men, yet you may have the testimony of God and of your own consciences, that you do really exceed and outstrip formalists. This concerns you as much as your assurance of heaven comes to. If you come short of them, nay, if ye be but near them, if you do not leave them out of sight, Satan will be apt to suggest that you are no better than they, and so shall fare no better at the last day. And how oft has this suggestion prevailed with sincere souls? To prevent this,

1. Be diligent. Shake off a slothful, lukewarm temper; that is very like the hypocrite's habit. Content not yourselves with a lazy profession. You that live the life of God, be not satisfied to live at such a cheap and easy rate of duty to him; decline not those duties that are painful, chargeable, or hazardous. It is a diligent hand that makes rich, that brings riches of assurance, such riches as Satan cannot easily cheat you of, by charging you as hypocrites. Diligence is the spiritual part of duty, is an attainment that a hypocrite cannot reach. If you would make sure work, you must give all diligence, 2 Peter i. 10. If ye do this, though you may be shaken with such a temptation, yet you shall not fall, ver. 11,—'abundant entrance.'— Laziness and slothfulness in the ways of God, will leave you so near the hypocrite's quarters as you may be taken to serve under the same commander. Frame not to yourselves a religion made up of ease and indulgence. 'Strive to enter in at the strait gate;' hypocrites may *seek* to enter, but you must *strive*. A hypocrite may have *some* diligence, you must give *all* diligence. He will *walk* a great way, you must *run* if you would outstrip him. He will seek the kingdom, &c.; you must seek it *first* and most, before all, above all, more than all. He may skirmish with his lusts, you must beat them down, subdue them, crucify them. He may put forth his hand to the kingdom of God, you must offer a holy violence to it, and take it by force. Be diligent in spiritual duties, especially the spiritual part of them: that is the way to leave a hypocrite behind you.

2. Content not yourselves with a small, a weak measure of grace. Small things are not easily discerned, and what you cannot easily discern, you will hardly be able to distinguish. It is no easy matter to distinguish hypocrisy in its height and elevation, from grace at its lowest ebb. Riches of grace occasions riches of assurance. There is but little difference as to their estates betwixt a poor man and a bankrupt. Grace, when it is weak and low, does but ordinarily afford weak and low assurance. Assurance is from the testimony of the Spirit; now the Spirit witnesses, together with our spirit, and our spirits give testimony, according to the measure, workings, and evidence of our graces. If it be weak and low, assurance is weak and low, and so more easily dashed out of countenance by the specious flourishes of a formalist. A hypocrite will not mind growth in grace; indeed, it is to no purpose to bestow culture, or water that which is not planted.

3. Keep grace in exercise; it is best discerned when it is in motion. View the outside of two watches, and how will you know whether of them wants a spring, if neither of them be in motion? Exercise of gifts may gain you credit, but it is exercise of grace that alone will gain you comfort in reference to your sincerity. A hypocrite will be much in exercise of gifts, but as to the exercise of grace he is at a loss; and where he is at a loss, there must you find sincerity.

4. Take heed of concluding your sincerity from insufficient grounds, upon anything that may be found in a hypocrite.

(1.) You must not ground it on extraordinary acts, visions, or revelations, or miracles, or raptures. If you had dreams, visions; if you had the Spirit of prophecy; if you could speak with the tongue of men or angels; if you could cast out devils or remove mountains, these would not argue a saving state; these are but common dispensations, vouchsafed sometimes to heathens, sometimes to hypocrites.

(2.) Nor upon any outward act, how glorious, how heroical soever. There is not any outward act that can be performed by a godly man but a hypocrite may do it; no outward act of obedience, how eminent soever, ordinary or extraordinary, but a formalist may come up to it. Even that renowned obedience of Abraham, in attempting to sacrifice his only son, was not only attempted, but acted by his posterity, when they were degenerated into idolaters. A slave may do as much outward service for his master as a child for his father, sometimes more, as having more strength for servile work. It is true, there is a vast difference as to the affection with which, and the end for which, these two work, but this is inward, and so invisible. No difference in the outward work, which is visible, but that which is to the child's disadvantage, who may want ability to do as much, though he have a mind to do more.

(3.) Nor upon every inward act, though holy and spiritual. There may be holy motions in an unholy heart. The faculties wherein saving grace acts are the understanding and the will. The memory and conscience are but the same understanding under distinct notions, and the affections are but the motions of the will. Holiness acting in the understanding can hardly be distinguished from what is to be found in the minds of hypocrites, except by the influence which such intellectual actings have upon the will. In the will, then, we must chiefly look for a distinction. And the two prime acts of the will afford two characters which are never found imprinted on a hypocrite, the *velle*, or election of the will, as it respects God, the greatest good; the *nolle*, or aversation of the will, as it respects sin, the greatest evil.

[1.] The will, savingly sanctified, gives God the pre-eminence, makes ease, credit, pleasures, profits, honours, relations, enjoyments, hopes, and all, stoop to him.

[2.] It hates every evil way.

Where these are found in truth, the condition is saving, and the person will be owned by Christ, when he professes to others, 'I know ye not.'

SOUL IDOLATRY EXCLUDES MEN OUT OF HEAVEN.

For this ye know, that no whoremonger, nor unclean person, nor covetous man, who is an idolater, hath any inheritance in the kingdom of Christ and of God.—EPH. V. 5.

THE apostle, in the former chapter, and the beginning of this, we find exhorting the Ephesians to holy walking. He proceeds herein positively, ver. 1, 2. The argument is, 'Hereby ye shall be followers of God.' Ye are his children, dear to him upon many accounts; and it becomes children to follow, to imitate their father; to follow him, though it be not *passibus æquis*; to follow him at a distance, though ye cannot come up to him: ver. 2, 'Walk in love.' The argument drawn from the love of Christ, the most forcible argument to a member of Christ: 'The love of Christ should constrain,' &c. It answers all objections. How? Love those that hate, revile, disparage, &c. Christ died for enemies. Walk in love, Christ died in love. To die is more than to walk.

2. Negatively: ver. 3, the argument, 'It becometh saints.' Those that are separated to God as his in peculiar, should be so far separated from these pollutions as they should not name them, but as they name that which is shameful and abominable. They should be so far from committing them, as they should not mention them without detestation.

Ver. 4. He extends it not only to their actions, but to their words; not only worldly, filthy, blasphemous talking should be avoided, but 'foolish talking, that discourse which is vain, idle, unedifying; not only that which is foolish, but that which is counted witty. Scurrilous, abusive wit is not convenient for saints. He uses that very word, εὐτραπελία, by which Aristotle expresses one of his moral virtues. By which we may perceive the dimness of the light of nature in those who saw clearest. Those that have no better guide may mistake a vice for a virtue.

He adds the reason, ver. 5; argues *a concessis*, 'This ye know;' a covetous man, and the like may be understood of the rest, is an idolater, and no idolater hath any inheritance, &c.

Not only the covetous, but the unclean, are idolaters; for the apostle, who here makes covetousness to be idolatry, counts voluptuous persons idolaters also, where he speaks of some who make their belly their God, Philip. iii.

Indeed, every reigning lust is an idol, and every person in whom it reigns is an idolater. 'The lust of the flesh, the lust of the eye, and the pride of life,' *i. e.* pleasures, and riches, and honours, are the carnal man's trinity, the three great idols of worldly men, to which they prostrate their souls; and giving that to them which is due only to God, they hereby become guilty of idolatry, according to that remarkable speech of Cyprian, (Serm. de jejun. et tent.) *Diaboli in regno genu flexo concupiscentiæ suæ idolum quisque colit.* In Satan's kingdom, every one bowing himself to his lust worships it as an idol. That this may be more evident, that covetousness, uncleaness, and other lusts are idolatry, let us consider what it is, and the several kinds of it. Idolatry is τὸ λατρεύειν τῇ κτίσει παρὰ τὸν κτίσαντα, Rom. i. 25, to give that honour and worship to the creature which is due only to God. Or as Nazianzen, Orat. 33, μετάθεσις τῆς προσκυνήσεως ἀπὸ τοῦ πεποιηκότος ἐπὶ τα κτίσματα, to transfer that respect which is due only to God, from him to the creature. There is some honour, some worship, which is proper to God alone, Isa. xlii. 8, Mat. iv. 10, Isa, xlv. 23. Now when this worship is made common, communicated to other things, whatever they are, we hereby make them idols, and commit idolatry. Now this worship due to God only is not only given by heathens to their false gods, and by papists to angels, saints, images, &c., but also by carnal men to their lusts. For there is a twofold worship (as all agree) due only to God, internal and external.

1. External, which consists in acts and gestures of the body. When a man bows to, or prostrates himself before, a thing, this is the worship of the body; and when these gestures of bowing, prostration are used, not out of a civil, but a religious respect, with an intention to testify divine honour, then it is worship due only to God.

2. Internal, which consists in the acts of the soul and actions answerable thereto. When the mind is most taken up with an object, and the heart and affections most set upon it, this is soul worship, and this is due only to God. For he being the chief good, and the last end of intelligent creatures, it is his due, proper to him alone, to be most minded and most affected; it is the honour due only to the Lord to have the first, the highest place, both in our minds and hearts and endeavours.

Now according to this distinction of worship there are two sorts of idolatry,

1. Open, outward idolatry, when men, out of a religious respect, bow to or prostrate themselves before anything besides God. This is the idolatry of the heathens, and part of the idolatry of papists.

2. Secret and soul idolatry, when the mind and heart is set upon anything more than God; when anything is more valued, more intended; anything more trusted, more loved, or our endeavours more for any other thing than God. Then is that soul worship, which is due only to God (and that which he most respects and calls for) given to other things besides him. And this is as true, as heinous idolatry, as the former, though not so open, discernible, nor so much observed.

And it is this secret, this soul idolatry which the apostle intends, when he calls voluptuous men idolaters, Philip. iii.; and when he calls covetousness idolatry, Col. iii. 5; and when he styles unclean, covetous persons idolaters in the text. Hence,

Obs. Secret idolaters shall have no inheritance in the kingdom of God. Soul idolatry will exclude men out of heaven as well as open idolatry. He that serves his lusts is as uncapable of heaven as he that serves, worships idols of wood or stone.

Before we come to confirm and apply this truth, it will be requisite to make a more clear discovery of this secret idolatry, the most that are guilty of it not taking notice of their guilt, because they account nothing idolatry but what is openly and outwardly so. In order thereunto, observe, there are thirteen acts of soul worship; and to give any one of them to anything besides the God of heaven is plain idolatry, and those idolaters that so give it.

1. *Esteem.* That which we most highly value we make our God. For estimation is an act of soul worship. *Cultus et veneratio denotant præcipue internam rei excellentis æstimationem,* worship is the mind's esteem of a thing as most excellent. Now the Lord challenges the highest esteem, as an act of honour and worship due only to himself. Therefore to have an high esteem of other things, when we have low thoughts of God, is idolatry. To have an high opinion of ourselves, of our parts and accomplishments, of our relations and enjoyments, of riches and honours, or those that are rich and honourable, or anything of like nature, when we have low apprehensions of God, is to advance these things into the place of God; to make them idols, and give them that honour and worship which is due only to the divine Majesty. What we most esteem we make our god; if other things are of higher esteem, ye are idolaters, Job xxi. 14.

2. *Mindfulness.* That which we are most mindful of we make our God. To be most remembered, to be most minded, is an act of worship which is proper to God, and which he requires as due to himself alone, Eccles. xii. 1. Other things may be minded; but if they be more minded than God, it is idolatry, the worship of God is given to the creature. When ye mind yourselves, mind your estates and interests, mind your profits or pleasures more than God, you set these up as idols in the place of God; when that time, which should be taken up with thoughts of God, is spent in thoughts of other things; when God is not in all your thoughts, or if he sometimes be there, yet if other things take place of him in your thoughts; if when ye are called to think of God (as sometimes every day we should do with all seriousness), if ordinarily and willingly you make these thoughts of God give place to other things, it is idolatry.

If either you do not think of God, or think otherwise of him than he is: think him all mercy, not minding his justice; think him all pity and compassion, not minding his purity and holiness; think of his faithfulness in performing promises, not at all minding his truth in execution of threatenings; think him all love, not regarding his sovereignty: this is to set up an idol instead of God. Thinking otherwise of God than he has revealed himself, or minding other things as much or more than God, is idolatry.

3. *Intention.* That which we most intend we make our god; for to be most intended is an act of worship due only to the true God; for he being the chief good must be the last end. Now the last end must be our chief aim, *i. e.* it must be intended and aimed at for itself; and all other things must be aimed at for its sake, in a reference, in a subserviency to it.

Now, when we make other things our chief aim, or main design, we set them up in the stead of God, and make them idols; when our chief design is to be rich, or great, or safe, or famous, or powerful; when our great aim is our own ease, or pleasure, or credit, or profit and advantage; when we aim at, or intend any [thing] more, or anything so much, as the glorifying and enjoying of God: this is soul idolatry. And oh, if men would impartially search their hearts, and examine their intentions, how much idolatry might they discover, which is not now taken notice of!

4. *Resolution.* What we are most resolved for we worship as God. Resolvedness for God, above all things, is an act of worship which he chal-

lenges as due to himself alone. To communicate it to other things, is to give the worship of God unto them, and so to make them gods. When we are fully resolved for other things, for our lusts, humours, outward advantages, and but faintly resolved for God, his ways, honour, service ;

When we resolve absolutely for other things without limitation or restriction, and but conditionally for God, upon such and such terms ; to serve him, so as ye may serve yourselves too ; to seek him so as to enjoy your lusts with him ;

When resolve presently for other things, but refer our resolves for God to the future ; let me get enough of the world, of my pleasure, of my lusts, now ; I will think of God hereafter, in old age, in sickness, on a death-bed : these are idolatrous resolutions ; God is thrust down, the creatures and your lusts advanced into the place of God ; and that honour which is due only to him you give unto them. This is unquestionable idolatry.

5. *Love.* That which we must love we worship as our God ; for love is an act of soul-worship, *idem est*, προσκυνεῖν καὶ φιλεῖν. To love and to adore are sometimes both one. *Quod quis amat, id etiam adorat,* that which one loves he worships. This is undoubtedly true, if we intend hereby that love which is superlative and transcendent ; for to be loved above all things is an act of honour, worship, which the Lord challenges as his due in peculiar, Deut. vi. 5. In this the Lord Christ comprised all that worship which is required of man, Mat. xxii. 37. Other things may be loved, but he will be loved above all other things. He is to be loved transcendently, absolutely, and for himself ; all other things are to be loved in him and for him. He looks upon us as not worshipping him at all, not taking him for a God, when we love other things more, or as much as himself, 1 John ii. 15. Those that are φιλήδονοι μᾶλλον ἢ φιλόθεοι, 'lovers of pleasures,' 2 Tim. iii. 4, they make their pleasures, their bellies, their god, Philip. iii. 19 ; those that love their riches, the things of the world, more than, or equally with, God, they make these their gods, worship a golden calf : this is the idol in the text. Those that love their relations, &c., Mat. x. 37, Luke xiv. 26, those that love themselves more than God, idolise themselves. Love, whenever it is inordinate, it is an idolatrous affection.

6. *Trust.* That which we most trust we make our god ; for confidence and dependence is an act of worship which the Lord calls for as due only to himself. And what act of worship is there which the Lord more requires, than this soul-dependence upon him alone? Prov. iii. 5, 'With all thy heart.' He will have no place there left for confidence in anything else ; therefore, it is idolatry to trust in ourselves, to rely upon our own wisdom, judgments, parts, accomplishments ; the Lord forbids it, Prov. iii. 5.

To trust in means or instruments. The church disclaims this, Ps. xx. 7 ; as also Ps. xliv. 6, 'I will not trust in my bow.' Asa is branded for dependence on physicians, 2 Chron. xvi. 12.

To trust in wealth or riches. Job disclaims this, and reckons it amongst those idolatrous acts that were punishable by the judge, Job xxxi. 24. David joins this and the disclaiming of God together, Ps. lii. 7 ; and our apostle, who calls covetousness idolatry, dissuades from this confidence in riches, as inconsistent with confidence in God, 1 Tim. vi. 17.

To trust in friends, though many and mighty, Jer. xvii. 5. He fixes a curse upon this, as being a departing from, a renouncing of, God ; an advancing of that we trust in to the room of God, Ps. cxlvi. 3. These are such idols, when trusted, as those who have eyes, &c. ; hence, Ps. cxviii. 8, 9, 'Better to trust,' &c. As in the mighty, so in the many, Hos. x. 13. Idols are called lies in Scripture ; such are these, &c., Isa. xxxi. 11. The idolatry of this confidence is expressed, in that the true God is laid aside. Trust in the creature is always idolatrous.

7. *Fear*. That which we most fear we worship as our god; for fear is an act of worship, *est adoratio quæ timorem significat* (Thurasus Nicen. 2). He that does fear, does worship that which is feared, which is unquestionable when his fear is transcendent. The whole worship of God is frequently in Scripture expressed by this one word *fear*, Mat. iv. 10, and Deut. vi. 13; and the Lord challenges this worship, this fear, as due to him alone, Isa. li. 12, 19. That is our god which is our fear and dread, Luke xii. 4, 5. If you fear others more than him, you give that worship to them which is due only to God; and this is plain idolatry; hence the fearful are reckoned amongst idolaters, and the same sentence denounced against them as against idolatry, in the text, Rev. xxi. 8. Those, therefore, who fear other things more than God; who are more afraid to offend men than to displease God; who fear more to lose any outward enjoyment, than to lose the favour of God; who fear outward sufferings more than God's displeasure; who had rather sin than suffer; more afraid of troubles in the world, than of losing peace with God; those whom the sight of man will more restrain from sin than the all-seeing eye of God; who will venture to make more bold with God than men, and stand in more awe of others than God: they stand guilty of idolatry, that which is here threatened.

8. *Hope*. That which we make our hope we worship as God; for hope is an act of worship; *qui sperat, adorat*, that which we make our hope we worship, and worship is due only to God. It is his prerogative to be the hope of his people, Jer. xvii. 13, Rom. xv. 13. When we make other things our hope, we give them the honour due only to God; it is a forsaking of the Lord the fountain, and advancing of broken cisterns into his place, hereby worshipping them as God only should be worshipped. Thus do the papists openly, when they call the virgin mother, the wooden cross, and saints departed, their hope; and thus do others amongst us, who make their prayers, their sorrow for sin, their works of charity, or any acts of religion or righteousness, their hope; when men expect hereby to satisfy justice, to pacify God's displeasure, to procure heaven. Nothing can effect this, but that which is infinite, the righteousness of God; and this we having only in and from Christ, he is therefore called our hope, 1 Tim. i. 1; ' our hope of glory,' Col. i. 27. Those that make their own righteousness the foundation of their hope, they exalt it into the place of Christ, and honour it as God; and to honour anything as God, is evident idolatry.

And so it is, not only in expectation of eternal glory, but outward happiness. When our principal hope is in friends, riches, &c., it is idolatry; for this is to worship them instead of God. And Job ranks it with that gross idolatry of worshipping the sun or moon, Job xxxi. 24, 29.

9. *Desire*. That which we most desire we worship as our god; for that which is chiefly desired, is the chief good in his account who so desires it; and what he counts his chief good, that he makes his god. Desire is an act of worship; *Est adoratio quæ desiderium significat*, that we most adore which we most desire; and to be most desired is that worship, that honour, which is due only to God. To desire anything more, or so much as the enjoyment of God, is to idolise it, to prostrate the heart to it, and worship it as God only should be worshipped. He only should be that one thing desirable to us above all things, as to David, Ps. xxvii. 4. Those that desire corn, and wine, and oil, more than the light of God's countenance, the favour of great men more than the sense of God's love, and to live in mirth and jollity, in abundance of worldly enjoyments, rather than holily in spiritual

communion with God; to be rich in the world, rather than to be rich towards God; those that desire anything in heaven or earth, as much or more than they desire God, are idolaters, such as the apostle threatens.

10. *Delight.* That which we most delight and rejoice in, that we worship as God; for transcendent delight is an act of worship due only to God; and this affection, in its height and elevation, is called glorying. That which is our delight above all things we glory in it; and this is the prerogative which the Lord challenges, 1 Cor. i. 31, Jer. ix. 23, 24. To rejoice more in our wisdom, strength, riches, than in the Lord, is to idolize them. To take more delight in relations, wife, or children, in outward comforts and accommodations, than in God, is to worship them, as we ought only to worship God. To take more pleasure in any way of sin, uncleanness, intemperance, earthly employments, than in the holy ways of God, than in those spiritual and heavenly services wherein we may enjoy God, is idolatry. Thus those who take most pleasure in drinking or eating, make their bellies their god; and those who most delight in fulfilling their lusts, be it a worldly, or an unclean, or a revengeful lust, they exalt their lusts above the God of heaven, and worship them; and this is a more heinous idolatry than to fall down and worship the sun or moon, angels or saints, because these are more worthy of honour than base lusts; nay, it is worse than to worship the devil, since Satan himself, being a creature, is not so vile as the lusts of men. And yet this is the common sin of unregenerate men, and the whole world of them lies in this idolatry, worshipping not only the creature, but their base lusts, before the God of glory.

11. *Zeal.* That for which we are more zealous we worship as god; for such a zeal is an act of worship due only to God; therefore it is idolatrous to be more zealous for our own things than for the things of God; to be eager in our own cause, and careless in the cause of God; to be more vehement for our own credit, interests, advantages, than for the truths, ways, honour of God; to be fervent in spirit, in following our own business, promoting our designs, but lukewarm and indifferent in the service of God; to count it intolerable for ourselves to be reproached, slandered, reviled, but manifest no indignation when God is dishonoured, his name, Sabbaths, worship, profaned; his truths, ways, people, reviled. This is idolatrous; for it shews something is dearer to us than God; and whatever that be, it is an idol; and thy zeal for it is thy worshipping of it, even with that worship which is due only to God.

12. *Gratitude.* That to which we are most grateful, that we worship as God; for gratitude is an act of worship, *est adoratio quæ gratiam notat*. We worship that to which we are most thankful. We may be thankful to men, we may acknowledge the helplessness of means and instruments; but if we rest here, and rise not higher in our thanks and acknowledgments; if the Lord be not remembered as him, without whom all these are nothing: it is idolatry. For this the Lord menaces those idolaters, Hosea ii. 5, 8. Thus when we ascribe our plenty, riches, to our care, industry; our success to our prudence, diligence; our deliverances to friends, means, instruments, without looking higher, or not so much to God as unto these, we idolize them, sacrifice to them, as the prophet expresses it, Hab. i. 16. To ascribe that which comes from God unto the creatures, is to set them in the place of God, and so to worship them.

Thus you see wherein this secret idolatry consists, and how many ways we may be guilty of it. Many more might be found out, but I shall but add this one. Then we are guilty of this idolatry,

13. When our *care and industry* is more for other things than for God.

No man can serve two masters. We cannot serve God and mammon, God and our lusts too, because this service of ourselves, of the world, takes up that care, that industry, those endeavours, which the Lord must have of necessity, if we will serve him as God; and when these are laid out upon the world and our lusts, we serve them as the Lord ought to be served, and so make them our gods. When you are more careful and industrious to please men, or yourselves, than to please God; to provide for yourselves and posterity, than to be serviceable unto God; more careful what you shall eat, drink, or wherewith be clothed, than how you may honour and enjoy God; to make provision for the flesh, to fulfil the lusts thereof, than how to fulfil the will of God; more industrious to promote your own interests, than the designs of God; to be rich, or great, or respected amongst men, than that God may be honoured and advanced in the world; more careful how to get the things of the world, than how to employ them for God; rise early, go to bed late, eat the bread of carefulness, that your outward estate may prosper, while the cause, and ways, and interests of Christ have few or none of your endeavours, this is to idolize the world, yourselves, your lusts, your relations, while the God of heaven is neglected, and the worship and service due unto him alone is hereby idolatrously given to other things.

Argument 1. Such idolaters are not in covenant with God. It is the covenant of grace alone which gives right and title to the kingdom. Those that are not in covenant, have no title to heaven; and those that have no right nor title to it, shall have no inheritance in it. They are not in covenant; for the very first article of the covenant is, that we take the Lord for our God, and that we have no other gods but him. But idolaters have many other gods. Their hearts never subscribed the covenant of grace; they are in league with other gods, with the world, the flesh, their lusts. No entering into covenant but by renouncing of these. Till then, ye are in covenant with hell and death; no title to the inheritance, no hopes of it.

2. Such idolaters are not yet born again, are not yet converted; and without the new birth, no inheritance in the kingdom; those only are heirs of this kingdom, who are born of God, who are born again. The Lord Christ affirms this twice together, to make it sure, and affirms it with a double asseveration, John iii. 3, 5. No receiving this inheritance till conversion, till turned from darkness, from the power of Satan, who engages all his power to continue sinners in the service of other gods, Acts xxvi. 18. No entering the kingdom except ye be converted, Mat. xviii. 3. Now conversion is, the apostle tells us, 1 Thes. i. 9, a 'turning from idols;' not only from those with which men commit open, but secret idolatry. Till the heart be turned from idols, till this secret idolatry be renounced, there is no conversion; and without this no salvation, no inheritance in the kingdom of God, &c.

Use 1. *Information.* This shews us the misery of a great part of the world; nay, of the greatest part of Christians; nay, of many of them who have escaped the gross idolatry of pagans, or apostate Christians. Not only open, but secret idolatry, excludes from any inheritance in the kingdom of heaven; and this secret idolatry is so common, as the disciples' question will not be unseasonable. Alas! 'Then who shall be saved?' Where is that heart in which some idol is not secretly advanced? Where is that soul that does not bow down to some lust or vanity? Where is that man that does not give that soul-worship to the creature which is due unto the Creator? Some there are, indeed, though few, that are not defiled with this idolatry; but they are none of this number who are yet in the state of nature. Every natural man, let his enjoyments, privileges, accomplishments, be what they will, is an idolater. He that is not converted, changed, born again; he that lives in any known sin, be it uncleanness, or covetousness, or pride, besides the visible guilt of these gross sins, he is a secret idolater; and no idolater shall have any inheritance in the kingdom of God.

Quest. Whether may the regenerate be guilty of this secret idolatry? Whether may those who are truly sanctified give this soul-worship to other things, which is due only to God? It seems difficult to determine this either way, the reasons being weighty for both, affirmative and negative; for,

If it be denied, what shall we say to those many instances which Scripture affords, whereby it is too evident that the people of God may fall into incest, drunkenness, murder, adultery, denying of Christ, nay, idolatry itself? Solomon is a sad example hereof, yet he a chosen vessel. The name *Jedidiah*, given him by the Lord, tells us he was beloved of God; yet he, 1 Kings xi. 7, 8, &c.

But if it be granted on the other side, other difficulties occur; for how can this be consistent with the state of grace, since the sincerity of that state consists in this very point, that the interest of God be advanced in the soul above all other interests? Besides, this is a plain breach of the contract with Christ, for secret idolatry is spiritual adultery. It passes under this name ordinarily in Scripture. Other failings a husband may endure in his wife; but such unfaithfulness tends to dissolve the conjugal covenant. And this in the text is not the least difficulty: for how can they retain a title to the inheritance under this guilt, since the apostle is peremptory, such shall not inherit the kingdom? &c.

Ans. Take the resolution of this difficulty in these three conclusions:

1. There is an aptness and propenseness, in those that are sanctified, to this idolatry as to other sins. Man's corrupt nature is the nursery, the seed-plot of every sin, and this amongst the rest. The fruit of our first sin in Adam is the corruption of our natures, which consists in a proneness, a disposedness, to all abominations, idolatry not excepted. Grace being imperfect in this life, does but correct this corruption in part, it does not extinguish it; it weakens this disposition to idolatry, it does not abolish it. Those natures that are most sanctified on earth are still a seminary of sin; there is in them the roots, the seeds of atheism, blasphemy, murder, adultery, apostasy, and idolatry. Though the virtue of these roots of bitterness be weakened by renewing grace, yet it is not quite lost; the old man abides in those that are most renewed, and it is furnished with all its members; though they may be weakened, maimed, mortified, yet not one of them is quite perished. And what these members are, the apostle gives us an account, and reckons this very idolatry amongst the rest, Col. iii. 5. He writes to those that were sanctified, and yet he speaks of this and the rest as their members: 'Mortify your,' &c. This is a member of the body of death, which has place in the most sanctified heart on earth; though it be mortified in them, yet is not annihilated. This disposedness to idolatry remains more or less in the best, while the body of death remains; and this we part not with till the soul part from the body.

This is idolatry *in semine*, in the seed and root of it, the proneness of our depraved natures to it. We may call it virtual idolatry; and of this the regenerate are guilty, and will have cause, while they live, to bewail their guilt.

2. They may be guilty of idolatrous acts and motions. This proneness and disposedness to idolatry may come into act; this root of bitterness may sprout and bud; this seed of idolatry in their natures may fructify, and bring forth too much of this cursed fruit; this member of the body of death

may act and move. The old man is not dead in those that are sanctified, though it be dying, and while it is alive, it will move, it will be in action more or less, some time or other. And that the saints may be guilty herein, the reason is here evident. The apostle calls covetousness idolatry here; and voluptuousness idolatry, Philip. iii; so far therefore as any be guilty of covetousness, &c., so far they may be tainted with idolatry. But the regenerate may be guilty of covetousness, not only in respect of proneness and disposedness to it, but actually; chargeable with covetous acts and motions, and therefore with idolatrous acts and motions.

And if in this particular, so in the rest formerly specified; for wherein does the idolatry of covetousness consist, but in this? That it is an inordinate, an immoderate love of riches. Now if love in the renewed may be inordinate, so may other affections, desire, delight, zeal, fear, sorrow; there is like reason for all. And if there may be inordinacy in these motions of the will, there may be the like in the acts of the mind. And therefore the regenerate may be guilty of idolatrous acts and motions, both in mind and heart.

3. They are not guilty of habitual idolatry, as unrenewed men are. The Lord has the habitual pre-eminence in their hearts, when other interests are actually advanced, as a king may keep his throne, when rebels may prevail in part of his dominions.

They are not habitual idolaters. They yield not [to] these idolatrous motions knowingly, willingly, constantly, as others do; they are not tolerated, allowed; they are not unresisted, unlamented; they offer not themselves thereto, but are surprised by them; they are against the constant bent of their hearts, against purposes and resolutions, against prayers and endeavours.

When they discover these motions, they are astonished at them. They loathe and abhor, they judge and condemn themselves for them; they bewail and lament them, they are their grief and soul affliction; they fly to the blood of Christ for pardon, to the power of Christ for strength against them, and are diligent in the use of mortifying duties to get them subdued; they cry to the Lord with strong cries, as the ravished virgin was to cry out, to shew it is not by consent, but violence, that these prevail. There is a resistance, not only from conscience, but the will, even when it too far consents.

So that these inordinate motions, though idolatrous, are not the idolatry of natural unrenewed men; it is not reigning habitual idolatry. And so the difficulties objected are overcome; for it is this reigning habitual idolatry (not that which is virtual, not that which consists in some inordinate acts and motions resisted, bewailed, pardoned) which is inconsistent with sincerity of grace, which is that spiritual whoredom with which a covenant with Christ cannot consist, which excludes from the inheritance of the kingdom. Of this the regenerate are not guilty; with the two former they may be tainted.

Use 2. *Examination.* Try whether you be guilty of this soul idolatry or no. Idolatry is (according to its *etymon*) a worshipping of idols. It speaks two things, worship and idols. Therefore, that we may make a full discovery of it, let us inquire both after the objects and the acts; search both what are those idols that are worshipped, and what are those acts of worship that are given to them. And to stir you up to this examination, let me premise these two things, the danger and secrecy of this.

1. The danger. It is a sin will endanger your loss of heaven, make it exceeding difficult, or altogether impossible. If one should tell you of some mischievous person lurking in your house, with an intent to murder you, or

set your house on fire, &c. The apostle tells you of something more mischievous; that which is more dangerous, and nearer to you; that which will endanger the loss of an inheritance, of a kingdom.

2. The secrecy of it calls for diligent search. Nothing more common or more concealed. How common is this soul idolatry in the soul of every unsanctified man! There are chambers of imagery (to allude to that in the prophet, Ezek. viii. 12), idols set up in every room, in every faculty of man's soul, which he worships in the dark, in secret; so much in the dark, as others cannot see it, himself will not acknowledge it. None more ready to disclaim it than those who are most guilty; take it for a groundless and injurious slander if any charge them with idolatry. They acknowledge the true God, and have none, worship none but him, whatever pagans and papists do. This is the confidence of most. They know of no idols, are conscious of no idolatry, whereas in every corner of their hearts there are multitudes of idols; and the most acts of their souls are idolatrous worship of those idols. They are apt to say, as Jacob to Laban of his idols: Gen. xxxi. 32, 'With whomsoever thou findest these gods, let him not live;' whereas they are hid in every man's tent, covered in the stuff, hid so secretly as an ordinary search will not discover them, so as to convince the party of his guilt.

Yet, though few will own it, nothing is more common. And therefore it is necessary something be spoken in order to conviction, that ignorance may not be pretended; that men may come to the knowledge of this sin; that you may see it, be ashamed of it, be humbled for it, see a necessity of Christ his blood to wash away this crimson sin; or if men will not see, they may be left without excuse. Search: 1, idols; 2, worship.

1. Every man in the state of nature makes an idol of himself; exalts himself when he should advance God; minds himself more than he minds God; aims at himself, when he should aim at God: rests in himself, when he should depend upon God; loves himself more than God; honours himself more than God; seeks himself more than God; would have that ascribed to himself, which is to be ascribed only to God; would have himself eyed, admired, praised more than God. Self-conceit, self-love, self-seeking, they are all secret strains of idolatry, and ourselves are naturally our own idols.

Nay, further, he makes every part of himself an idol.

2. He makes his understanding his God, by preferring his own wisdom before the wisdom of God; making his own judgment his guide, and not the word of God, which infinite Wisdom has prescribed as our rule and guide; quarrelling at providence, as though he knew what is more good, more fit for him than God himself; as though he could dispose things more wisely than infinite wisdom. How ordinary is this, both in respect of public and private dispensations! If I had had the disposing, the ordering of those affairs, of this or that event, it should have been otherwise ordered, it should have gone better with the church, with the state, with myself! So relying upon his own understanding more than the wisdom of God; depending on, and being more confident of, his own projects and contrivements than on the providences of God.

3. He makes his own will his God; idolises it, by preferring his will before the will of God. This ye do when ye will not submit to the will of God in suffering what he inflicts; when ye will not obey the will of God in doing what he commands, in avoiding what he forbids. You hereby set your wills in the place of God's. To instance:

It is God's will you should accept Christ upon his own terms. You will not; you break his bands, &c.; count his burden too heavy, his yoke not easy.

It is God's will you should live holily, according to the rule of the gospel. You will not; you count it too strict, too precise, brand it, &c.

It is his will you set up his worship in your families.

It is his will you avoid swearing, Sabbath-breaking, drunkenness, uncleanness, break off these sins by repentance. You will not. Do ye not evidently herein prefer your wills before the will of God, and thereby idolise them? Here is a double guilt in every such sin, indeed in every known sin; here is both disobedience, not doing the will of God, and idolatry, preferring your own will before his. Such rebellion is as the sin of witchcraft; such stubbornness is as iniquity and idolatry, as Samuel to Saul, 1 Sam. xv. 23.

4. He makes his fancy, his senses his gods; idolises them in seeking to please his fancy, his senses, rather than God. How common is this! When that preaching which is most pleasing to God will not please men, but that which most gratifies a vain, a wanton fancy; when men will displease God rather than displease their eye, in turning it from ensnaring objects; displease God rather than turn away their ear from filthy and unclean discourse; rather than not gratify a brutish sense, in lascivious gestures and wanton dalliance; rather displease God than put themselves to the trouble of making a covenant with their eyes, and keeping a strict watch over their senses: hereby you shew you had rather please your senses than please God. And what is this but to advance them into the place of God, and idolise them?

5. Others make their belly their god. Of this, Philip. iii. 19; do more for their bellies than they do for God; care more what they shall eat or drink, than how they shall serve or honour God; aim more at their own ease, and the commodities of this present life, than they regard God or the life to come; make it their end rather to provide for this than to provide for their souls. This is to serve their bellies instead of God. Such idolaters are epicures, whose language is, Let us eat and drink, &c.; life is short, therefore let us be merry while we live. Such idolaters are gluttons and drunkards. All inordinacy in this kind has a tincture of idolatry. Such idolaters are the poorer sort of people, who are immoderate in caring for the things of this life. The apostle thus explains this idolatry, when he adds, 'who mind earthly things,' &c. Such idolaters are the richer sort, when they will spend more on superfluities than they are willing to lay out for God, grudge to lay out so much for the refreshing the poor members of Christ, maintaining the gospel, or other religious uses, as they will ordinarily spend in a feast. Such are those who will offend God rather than not gratify their appetites. In a word, such are those who make it the main end of their callings, employments, endeavours, to provide for themselves plenty. This is to serve their bellies, not Christ, of which the apostle, Rom. vi. 8. And to serve this instead of God is to advance it into the place of God, to idolize it.

6. Some make their pleasures their God. Either sensual pleasures, of which before, or intellectual pleasures. Whatever the heart immoderately delights in, whether objects of sense or objects of the mind, he makes it an idol. The apostle prophesies of such idolaters in the text, 2 Tim. iii. 4. Thus men offend, not only in unlawful pleasures, but those that are indifferent. To instance in recreations; when men spend that time in recreations which should be spent in serving God, either in duties of general or particular callings, this is to serve themselves more than God, to be lovers of pleasure more than lovers of God.

7. Men make their credit their god, preferring their credit and repute in the world before the honour of God. This idolatrous humour was the cause

why the Jews rejected the Son of God, John v. 44; 'They loved the praise of men,' John xii. 43. This appears, when men will not endure a reproof for sin, though it proceed out of zeal to the glory of God; when they can better endure to hear and see God contradicted in the lives and words of men, than to have themselves crossed or contradicted in a word or deed; when they can more patiently see God dishonoured, than hear themselves disparaged; when it grieves not men so much to see Christ undervalued, neglected, as themselves slighted and disrespected; his word, ordinances, messengers, contemned, despised, as their own parts, judgments, disesteemed or disparaged; can pass by affronts, indignities offered to God, but their hearts rise against those who diminish their own reputation amongst men. When men make it more their aim to be well accounted of, well reported of in the world, than that God be glorified, Christ advanced, and the gospel adorned, this is to prefer their own reputation before God's glory, and to idolize it. When men do their good actions to be seen of men, make a show of more outwardly than there is within, are more zealous, active, enlarged, in the view of the world than in secret, when God only sees; this shews they seek their own repute more than the honour of God, and so make it their idol, advancing it into the place of God.

8. Men make wealth and riches their god, when their hearts and minds are more set upon the things of the world than upon God. Then is this world idolized; and this the Scripture calls again and again idolatry. Nothing more evident and common, and yet nothing more difficult, than to convince men of their guilt herein. But if you will impartially answer these questions, you will see reason to suspect yourselves, and cry guilty, and bewail your guilt herein.

(1.) Do ye not value these things more than the light of God's countenance?

(2.) Do ye not love them more than holiness, than spiritual riches, the riches of Christ?

(3.) Do ye not desire the increase of them more than growth in grace?

(4.) Do ye not delight in them more than in communion with God, fellowship with Christ?

(5.) Do ye not grieve more for disappointments herein than God's withdrawings?

(6.) Are ye not more affected with worldly crosses than soul distempers?

(7.) Are ye not more afflicted with wants of these things than spiritual wants?

(8.) Are ye not more eager in seeking these than following after God?

(9.) Think ye not earthly enjoyments to be greater security than the great and precious promises?

(10.) Are not the thoughts of them more pleasing, welcome, than the thoughts of heaven and of Christ?

(11.) Do ye not esteem others more for these than for their interest in God?

(12.) Are not these your hope and confidence of security against an evil day?

(13.) Do not these employments make you omit holy duties, or cut them short, or perform them in a careless, heartless manner, hereby serving God as though ye served him not, as though ye cared not to enjoy him?

(14.) Do not your hearts stick so fast in this thick clay (as the prophet calls it), as you can scarce raise them towards God in prayer or heavenly thoughts?

(15.) Do ye prize these more, out of any other respect, than because hereby you may be most serviceable to God?

(16.) Are ye not more careful to increase or preserve them than to employ them to the utmost for God? If it be thus in any of these respects, much more if in all, it is too evident your hearts and minds are carried idolatrously after this world, it is too much your idol. You mistake if you think all is well, while you covet not that which is another's, or seek not to get them by unlawful means. If you be innocent herein, you may yet idolize the world in all the fore-mentioned respects, and many more than I can now mention. This may suffice to discover their sin, to those who are willing to know it.

9. Some make their relations their god, idolize husband, or wife, or children, by setting their affections more upon them than upon God; and this appears when they take more comfort in them, rejoice more in their company, than in the enjoyment of God; when they are more impatient of their absence than of God's departings, hiding or concealing himself from their soul; when more afflicted for the loss of them than for the loss of God's favour, in the comfortable sense and effects of it; when more fearful to part with them than to live at a distance from God; when more careful for their comfortable subsistence than that they may be serviceable to God. This is to prefer them before God, to idolize them.

10. Some make their friends and allies their god. When they rely more on them than on the Lord, they idolize them. Judah is charged for thus relying on Egypt, Isa. xxxi. 1, 3. When they depend upon these for counsel, advice, for help, assistance, for supplies or provisions, more than they rely on God for these, they are idolized.

When the heart is borne up with cheerfulness and confidence, while these outward dependences are afforded, but when they are removed, sinks into perplexities, discouraged, it appears in this case that these are more your confidence than God, that these are preferred.

11. Many make their enemies their god, when they fear man more than God, 1 Peter iii. 14, 15. When we fear him that can only kill the body, more than him who can cast both body and soul into hell, then God is not sanctified, *i. e.* he is not worshipped. That worship which is due unto God only is given unto man. When men are immoderately troubled, disquieted, perplexed at apprehensions of danger to their liberty, estates, lives, from men, not being so apprehensive of danger to their souls from the justice of God; when venture rather to provoke God than to provoke a man of power; when the wrath of a powerful enemy is more dreadful than the wrath of the almighty God; when ye are more startled at the threatenings of men than those threatenings that are denounced against sin by the word of God: then men are exalted above God, and our enemies are idolized.

12. Some make the creatures their god, so are guilty of idolatry (to waive other instances) when they swear by the creatures. Swearing, in Scripture, is frequently put for the worship of God, as being a special part of his worship. (And so it appears, what horrible profaneness it is, to swear by the name of God vainly, rashly, customarily, as many ungodly persons use to do in common discourse.) So it is used, Deut. x. 20, Isa. xix. 18, for worship in the New Testament, Isa. lxv. 16, Jer. xii. 16. We profess that to be our god by which we swear; for an oath is an invocation of God, as a witness of the truth sworn, and a punisher and avenger of falsehood. Now, invocation is a part of worship; and, therefore, when we swear by anything but God, we worship it as God, which is plain idolatry; hence that fearful expression which should strike terror into all guilty of such swearing, Jer. v. 7.

Thus it is idolatry to swear by the saints departed, by Mary or Peter; idolatry to swear by the rood or mass; a popish, idolatrous custom too common amongst us. This is to swear by the idol of the papists, and so to acknowledge it as our god. See how dreadfully the Lord threatens a sin just like this, Amos viii. 14. Sin is the idol of Samaria, who, in their revolt from the true God, worshipped the God of Israel, in the similitude of the creatures set up in Dan and Bethel; as the papists do in other resemblances. Those that swear by this idol, the Lord threatens they shall fall, &c. And is it not as great a provocation to swear by the popish idol, the mass, the rood? It is idolatry to swear by the light, the heavens, fire, or other creatures; the sin of the Pharisees, for which Christ reproves them, Mat. v. 34. To swear by the name of God, as men do in common discourse, is high profaneness. To swear by any but God, is idolatry; for that by which ye swear, is worshipped as God only should be worshipped, and so idolized.

13. Men make Satan their god, giving that to him which is due only to God. Indeed, when any idol is set up, and worshipped with the soul, or with the body, then the devil is worshipped, 1 Cor. x. 20; and what he speaks of the Gentiles, is spoken also of the Israelites, Deut. xxxii. 17; hence Jeroboam's idols are called devils, 2 Chron. xi. 15. It is like they intended to worship God in their idols; but, in the Lord's account, it is a worshipping of devils.

More especially, Satan is idolized, when men go to wizards, cunning men, as ye call them, such as are in covenant with the devil. This is forbidden, and joined with the abominable idolatry of Moloch, Lev. xx. 6; it is expressed by a phrase, by which the Lord uses to express idolatry, to 'go a whoring after.' This sin was Saul's ruin, 1 Chron. x. 13, 14. To inquire of these, is to inquire of the devil instead of God, and so to prefer him before God; horrid idolatry!

But this idolising of Satan is more common and universal than this consulting of wizards. Something of this idolatry is to be found almost in every sin; for then we idolize Satan, when we obey him rather than God; which appears when we yield to his suggestions and temptations rather than to the commands of God in his word, rather than to the motions of his Spirit in our hearts. This is to obey Satan, this is to serve the devil rather than God; and his servants ye are, whom ye obey; that is the apostle's rule. Now, by becoming his servants, you advance him into the place of God, giving him that service which is due only to God; and so he is called the god of this world, 2 Cor. iv. 4. Not that he is so, but because sinners, by serving and obeying him, by entertaining his suggestions, yielding to his temptations, do, in reference to this obedience, make him so. When Satan is obeyed rather than God (as he is in most, if not in every, sin), then he is preferred before God; and Satan is made the idol which you worship.

14. Men make their lusts their god, when they serve their lusts rather than God. As it is idolatry to serve and worship the creature more than the Creator, Rom. i. 25, so it is idolatry, and much more abominable, to serve our lusts more than the Creator, these being the vilest things in earth or hell. There is a service due only to God, Mat. iv. 10, and when we yield this service to our lusts, then we serve them as God only should be served, when we serve them absolutely. That this may be clear, observe there is a twofold service: 1, absolute, which is without reference and subordination to another, and this is due only to the God of heaven; 2, relative, when we do service to others, but in reference and subordination to God. Thus we may serve one another, as we are exhorted, Gal. v. 13. But this service of others must be in reference to God; we must serve them for God, as the apostle directs, Eph. vi. 7.

Now, we cannot serve our lusts, in reference to God, nor for his sake;

these are quite opposite, no way subordinate; and therefore, if we serve our sin at all, we serve it absolutely, as God only should be served, which is plain idolatry. We cannot serve the Lord in serving our lusts; no man can serve these two masters; and therefore, so far as we serve sin, we are the servants of sin, not of God; it is our idol. So the apostle, Rom. vi. 16, 17; that is your god which you thus serve; and, therefore, they serve divers gods, who serve divers lusts, Titus iii. 3; Rom. vi. 12, 13.

But when do men thus serve sin? Why, always, when they 'obey it in the lusts thereof;' when they obey their lusts rather than God; when they yield their members instruments of unrighteousness unto sin, rather than instruments of righteousness unto God; when yield to the motions of corrupt nature, rather than the commands of God Then ye serve sin, as God only should be served. Examine, then, whether guilty.

When a worldly lust moves you to lay out your thoughts, endeavours, affections, upon the things of this world, and the Lord commands you to use the world as though you used it not, to rejoice, love, &c., which of these is obeyed?

When the flesh prompts you to uncleanness, intemperance, and that either speculative or actual; and the Lord commands ye to suppress these motions, and mortify the flesh: which of these is obeyed?

When corrupt nature moves you to revenge, to use means to come even with those that have wronged you; and the Lord commands you to love your enemies, to return good for evil: which of these do you obey?

When a proud, ambitious lust tempts you to slight, undervalue others, to prefer yourselves before them; and the Lord commands you to be vile in your own eyes, to prefer others in honour before yourselves: which do you obey? If these lusts be obeyed before the Lord's commands, you prefer your lusts before God, you shew yourselves servants of sin, rather than servants of the God of heaven. You idolize, &c., when you delight more in gratifying these lusts than in the service of God. When you take more care, more pains, to make provision for the flesh, to fulfil the lusts thereof, than to comply with the will of God, in using all means to mortify these lusts, you serve your lusts rather than God; you render that service which is due to God unto those lusts that are viler than any toad or serpent; you make your sin your God. And if it be thus, how common then is this abominable sin of idolatry! how innumerable are those idols which men set up in the stead of God! If, not only as the prophet upbraids the Jews, 'according to the number of your cities,' Jer. ii. 28, but according to the number of your relations, of your senses and faculties, nay, according to the number of your lusts, which are as sand on the sea, &c., so are your gods. O enter into your own hearts, search them out, be ashamed of them; fly to Christ for pardon of them, for strength against them. See here the horrid sinfulness of a corrupt nature, how it swarms with idols, how it is wholly idolatrous, and from hence see the necessity of a Saviour, of pardoning, mortifying, renewing grace.

2. We have searched out this idolatry by inquiring after those idols which are worshipped instead of God, let us search after it further by inquiring what acts of soul worship they are which are given to these idols. Hereby the guilt of this secret sin will be more fully discovered, and the examination tend more to conviction. These acts of worship are many. Examine,

1. What are your apprehensions. The Lord being infinitely and most transcendently glorious and excellent, he challenges our highest apprehensions, as due only to himself. If he be not in our judgments preferred above all things, he is not worshipped as God. Whatever is advanced above

him, or equally with him, in our esteem that is idolized. Now because this in general will be denied, examine it by these particulars. *In generalibus latet dolus.*

(1.) What knowledge do ye most affect? The soul will be prying into that which it counts most excellent. The angels, 1 Peter. If ye be without the knowledge of God, if ye desire it not, Job xxi. 14. If ye study not this more than anything in the world, count it not most excellent, so as to count other things dross, Philip. iii. If ye can better be without this knowledge of God in Christ than without the knowledge of those things that concern your health, estate, repute in the world; if more industrious, &c.

(2.) What is it you would most appropriate to yourselves? What is it you most endeavour to make sure of? That which a man accounts most excellent, that he will labour to make most his own. Give ye all diligence to make sure your friends, your estates; and are you negligent to make sure your interest in God? Think ye no assurance too much there? and can ye be content to live at uncertainties, content yourselves with weak hopes and probabilities here? A sign, &c.

(3.) What is it you admire? Can you admire worldly excellencies, while the discoveries of Christ affect you little? Can you admire the parts, the achievements, the labours of others, while ye have low thoughts of God? Are ye better pleased to have yourselves admired than the Lord extolled? A sign God is not highest.

(4.) What do ye most praise? That will be most praised which you apprehend most excellent. Are ye much in the praises of God; often speaking such things of him to others as may endear him to them, as may raise their esteem of him? Take ye all occasion to speak great things of his name; or are ye much in the praising of men, means, instruments, little in praising God? Can ye rejoice more to hear yourselves praised, extolled, than ye do in praising God? A sign God is not praised as he ought.

(5.) What do ye glory in? That which ye count most excellent will be your glory. Do ye glory in your wealth or friends, in your parts or performances, in your wit or strength, in anything or all together, as much as in God? Jer. ix. 23, 24, Gal. vi. 14.

(6.) What do ye value others for? Because they are great, or wise, or rich, or powerful, or fair? Do ye esteem them for anything more than for their interest in God, or their resembling of him? A sign God is not highest.

(7.) Are you willing to part with all for God? A man will be ready to lose all rather than that which he esteems more than all. He in the parable resolved to sell all he had, that he might purchase the pearl of great price. Paul counted all things loss, Philip. iii. 8; the disciples left all to follow Christ. If you be not willing to part with riches, embrace poverty, when Christ calls for it; part with relations, hate father and mother; part with ease, accept of sufferings; part with credit, welcome reproaches, for Christ's sake; you have higher apprehensions of others. He that 'will not leave houses and lands,' &c., Mat. x. 37, 'is not worthy of me.' Not worthy, because he has not worthy thoughts of him, prefers other things. So it is evident, when men will part with Christ rather than their sins; will not leave deceit, worldliness, intemperance, uncleanness for Christ; Christ is undervalued, these are idolized. The worship which is due only to God you pay unto them; thus this idolatry will be manifest by your apprehensions.

2. What are your thoughts? Much of the inward worship of God consists in thoughts of him. That which your mind is most set upon, that which your thoughts are most taken up with, that you worship as God; where your treasure is, there will your hearts be also; that which your

thoughts do chiefly run upon, that is most precious to you, that you ordinarily make your chief good. David was a man after God's own heart; why? His thoughts, his heart, ran most after God: 'My soul thirsteth for thee; I remember thee upon my bed, and meditate on thee in the night-watches,' Ps. lxiii. 6; 'I have set the Lord always before me,' Ps. xvi. 8; 'When I awake, I am still with thee,' Ps. cxxxix. 18; 'Yea, I am continually with thee,' Ps. lxxiii. 23. Hereby he shewed he had no other gods but the God of heaven, as he professes: 'Whom have I in heaven but thee? and there is none in earth that I desire besides thee,' ver. 25. Hereby he manifested he was not in the number of those idolaters that are far from God, that go a-whoring from him, of whom he speaks, ver. 27. Try by this if you are not in this number.

(1.) If you have any thoughts of God, are they not few and rare? Do ye not forget God? Are ye not unmindful of him whole days, whole nights together? Do not the thoughts of other things take up your hearts, and leave no room for thoughts of God, even when you are called to meditate on him? Are there not some, of whom for the most part we may say, God is not in all their thoughts; who live a great part of their days without God, without thoughts of God in the world? The mind is in the mean time employed, though God be not the object of it. That which is entertained when he is excluded, that takes place of God, is set up as an idol; and those thoughts which are due to God, are the idolatrous worship of this idol.

(2.) Are not thoughts of other things more pleasing, more welcome, than thoughts of God? find they not easier admission and freer entertainment? When the mind is right for God, it is of David's temper, Ps. cxxxix. 17, 18. These were precious guests to David; so precious, he knew not sufficiently how to value them. And though they were more in number than the sands, yet did he not grudge them entertainment; they had free admission into his soul: 'Continually, night and day, I am still with thee.' He reckoned this amongst his chief treasures. Are not you of another temper? May ye not truly say, How precious are the thoughts of my worldly comforts and enjoyments to me! how sweet are the thoughts of revenge to me! how delightful are the thoughts of forbidden pleasures to me! whenas the thoughts of God, of glory, of Christ, of spiritual things, are a burden. By this you may know what god you serve; whether the world, your pleasures, your lusts, vanities, or the God of heaven. What thoughts fill you most with contentment and comfort? What are your greatest refreshment? If thoughts of God be most delightful, then you serve, you worship him; if thoughts of the world, &c., be most pleasing, most welcome, then you serve, you worship them, Ps. xciv. 19. What are the objects of those thoughts which are the comforts, the delight of your souls, &c.?

(3.) What thoughts are most abiding, most fixed? Are the thoughts of God passant and fleeting, when other thoughts make their abode with you? Do vain thoughts lodge within you, when thoughts of God and heavenly things give but a short visit, and away? Are these your inmates, dwell in your minds as at home; when those are but strangers, and have scarce encouragement to sit down, or make any stay in your souls? Why, then, it is suspicious, the objects of those thoughts that are so consistent are advanced into the place of God; they have that worship which is due only to the God of heaven.

3. What is your last end, your chief design? God being the chief good, should be the last end; and to be chiefly aimed at, most intended, as a principal act of soul-worship, due only unto God as the last end. Now, most men have other ends; God is not the last, the chief. But how shall this

be known, since few or none will acknowledge it? It may be discerned by the effects and properties of the last end.

(1.) It excites the agent; *finis movet ad agendum.* It stirs up to actions, and may be assigned as the chief reason of our actings. Try, then, by this. You are in continual action and motion one way or other, what is it that sets you on work? what is the principle of your motion? why do you drudge and toil, take such care and pains, go to bed so late and rise so early? Is it that you may be great or rich? is it that you may live in plenty or pleasure, and leave enough for posterity? Is this all? or is this the chief motive that sets you a-work? Why, then, God is not your end, other things are advanced into his place. Otherwise your chief motive would be, in all your cares, labours, that ye might honour God, that ye might please him, that your employment might be more serviceable to him. These would be your aim above all, but that other things are above God in your intentions.

(2.) It directs the agent; *dat ordinem mediis.* If God be your end, you will be ordered by him, so as to move to that first which is next to himself. You would give that the pre-eminence which is best, which is next to the last end. Try, then, by this: do ye not prefer worldly employments before spiritual, prayer, meditation, self-examination, &c.? Do ye not seek riches, pleasures, more than holiness? Do ye not neglect to seek the kingdom of God and the righteousness thereof? Do ye not mind the world more than your souls? Must spiritual duties be content with the second place, or no place at all? Would ye not omit a spiritual duty rather than lose a worldly advantage? Is not heaven less regarded than earthly things? If thus, it is evident God is not your last end; something else takes place of him, is idolised, and aimed at more than God. If the Lord, as the last end, were your motive, director, you would move first and most to those things, to those employments, that have most affinity with him, most spiritual, most heavenly advantage.

(3.) It regulates the agent; limits him to those means only which serve to attain the end. He that makes riches his end, will not be prodigal or careless; for these tend not to promote his design, but are destructive to it. He that makes credit, honour his end, will not be seen to act those things which tend to his shame or reproach; his end restrains him from these; those means are only chosen which are subservient. So if it be your chief end to honour, please, enjoy God, you will not live in any known sin; for this is utterly inconsistent with, quite repugnant to, this end. Nothing dishonours, displeases, deprives of God but sin; those therefore that allow themselves in any evil way whatsoever, it is impossible God should be their end. It is evident they give this worship to something else besides the living God, and herein are idolaters.

(4.) It moderates the agent; *finis dat modum et mensuram mediis.* It prescribes bounds to the use of means, so as one shall not exclude another. If God were your end, if ye aimed at him above all, you would not be so eager after earthly things, and so lukewarm in holy duties. You would not be so industrious for your bodies, and so careless of your souls; you would not be so forward for outward advantages, and so backward for God. While it is thus, &c.

(5.) It facilitates; *finis dat amabilitatem mediis.* It makes the means lovely and pleasing which tend to advance it. If the Lord be your end, then the ways of God will be the ways of pleasantness. Then it will be your meat and drink to do his will. The duties of mortification will not seem so harsh and difficult. You would not be so backward to, so weary of, prayer, hearing, reading. Meditation of God and spiritual things would be delightful. Self-examination, communing with your hearts, would not be tedious. Strict and holy walking, watchfulness over your hearts and ways, would not be looked upon as your bondage. While it is otherwise, God is not your end, some other thing does displace him in your hearts, and is preferred before him.

(6.) It compensates the agent. When attained, it is counted a sufficient recompence for all the care, pains, labour taken in pursuing it. If the Lord be your end, whatever you get by your endeavours, nothing will quiet, will satisfy you, but the Lord himself. Suppose you get a competent estate by your industry in your callings; suppose you have compassed your designs in point of credit, or profit, or other outward advantage: if you rest in this as a sufficient recompence, it is a sign your chief aim was not God. For when he is your end, nothing will quiet you, except you enjoy more of God in the increase of your enjoyments. If when your endeavours succeed in the world, you say with him, 'Soul, take thy rest,' applaud yourselves in outward successes, rest here, look not beyond these outward things, though ye enjoy no more of God, though ye are hereby no more serviceable to him, though ye bring no more glory to him, then the Lord is not your last end, other things are more aimed at, more intended, and the worship due only to God is given to them. Thus you may discover this secret idolatry by your ends and designs.

He that makes Christ his chief aim, if at length he finds him whom his soul loveth, this quiets his heart, whatever he want, whatever he lose besides. He counts this a full recompence, for all his tears, prayers, inquiries, waitings, endeavours.

4. What are your supports? What do ye depend upon in troubles and perplexities, in fears and dangers, in wants and necessities? That which your souls rely on you worship as god. For soul dependence is an act of worship due only to God: Philip. iii., 'Worship God in the spirit.' They who have confidence in the flesh, worship not God in the spirit; they give this spiritual worship to something besides God. But since every one will be ready to disclaim this, and profess that their trust is in God, and him only, let this be examined in these severals.

(1.) Do ye not sometimes make bold to use unlawful means? Do ye not use some indirect course to compass your ends, to obtain your desires, or free you from trouble? Why do men step out of those callings wherein providence has disposed them? Why do they use unwarrantable practices in their callings, lie, deceive, oppress, dissemble? Why do they use lawful means unlawfully, immoderately? Why so eager upon worldly things, as to neglect God, heaven, their souls? Why? But because God is not their support; and when the soul is not stayed upon him, it relies upon something else idolatrously. This was Saul's sin; the apprehension of an apparent danger from the Philistines put him upon that which the Lord had forbidden, 1 Sam. xiii. And for this the Lord cast him off. More inexcusable are they who use indirect courses, when they have no such temptation; who, to get a small advantage, will be unjust, unfaithful, unrighteous; care not to defraud others, so they may gain by it; come short of the heathens in point of true and just dealing. Nothing more evident than that the Lord is not your confidence, when ye use such practices. You idolize something else. Isa. xxviii. 16, 'Makes no haste.'

(2.) Do ye not seek less unto God, when your affairs are hopeful, prosperous, and means visible to accomplish your designs? Are ye not then less in prayer, not so frequent, not so instant, not so importunate, not so fervent in spirit? Are ye not more careless, more indifferent? This is a sign means and instruments are your support, rather than God. Where there is much confidence in God, there will be much seeking to him; for this is the vital act of confidence. Who is there, even amongst those who make conscience of seeking God constantly, that are not less in this duty, less hearty, zealous, enlarged, when their affairs prosper, and are like so to continue, than when they are in fears, danger? This argues the heart is something taken off from God, and stays more upon the creature.

(3.) Do not your hearts sink into perplexities and discouragements, when outward means fail, when your wanted supports are removed; when you are in want, and see none to relieve you as formerly; when you are in troubles, and see no means of deliverance; when you are in fears and dangers, and see no outward securities? Are your hearts then troubled, perplexed? Is such a condition too heavy for you? Can you not bear up cheerfully under it? Why, this argues those outward means now removed were more your support than God; otherwise he continuing still the same, your hearts would stay upon him, and find repose and security there, when all outward supports fail. So with David, Ps. lxxiii. 26; and the prophet, Hab. iii. 17–19. This is the proper season for acting of faith, Isa. l. 10.

5. What are your expectations? To expect that from other things which only is to be expected from God, is to give that to them which is only due unto God. Soul expectation is an act of inward worship, Ps. lxii. 5. Try by this. Do ye not expect heaven for your harmless carriage or good deeds? Do ye not expect pardon for your prayer, or mournings, or purposes not to sin? Do ye not expect your good duties will be accepted, merely because they are (as you think) well performed? Now what is this, but to expect from your performances what only should be expected from Christ? Do ye not expect contentment and satisfaction from the creatures, from outward comforts plentifully, peaceably enjoyed? Whereas nothing can satisfy the soul of man but God only. Would ye not expect happiness from things below, if ye might enjoy them according to your hearts' desire? Is not this to expect from the world and outward enjoyment what only can be found in enjoying God? Do ye not expect your ends, merely because ye use the means, without looking further; expect knowledge, because you read or study; expect a competency in the world, because you are frugal, diligent, careful; expect your undertakings will succeed, because you manage your affairs with prudence, and follow your business with industry? Do ye not expect all these without looking to God for them? Oh no, every one will say, this will be universally disclaimed. Oh, but if you expect not these things but from God, why do not ye seek God for them? How is it that ye neglect prayer in your families, and when you go about your employments? How is it you do not frequently lift up your hearts to God, and send up your desires to heaven for success, for a blessing? How is it that you are so negligent in prayer, when you are diligent in using outward means? If ye did expect these things from God, you would seek to him heartily, constantly for them, and your hearts would be as busy, as diligent, as earnest in praying as you are in following your other business, Isa. xxxvi. 37. Would your friend think you expect anything from him, if you never seek to him for it? Men's neglect of seeking God, or careless heartlessness in seeking him, shews plainly their expectations are more from something else than from God. Thus may you discover this secret idolatry by your expectations.

6. Where are your affections? Upon what do ye most fix them? That on which you most set your hearts and affections, that you worship as God.

Examine, then, whether your affections be idolatrously placed more upon other things than God. Instance in love, fear.

(1.) What do ye most love? If ye love anything more than God, or equally with him, you are guilty of this idolatry. Idolatry is ordinarily called whoredom and adultery in Scripture. The apostle answerably calls those who immoderately love the things of the world, adulterers and adulteresses, James iv. 4. Love of these things is idolatrous. She is an adulteress in soul who loves another more than her husband. So is he a soul adulterer, and so guilty of spiritual adultery, who loves anything more than God.

Oh, but you will say, God forbid that we should love anything more than God; he is not worthy to live that does not love God, love Christ, above all. This is generally taken for granted. Oh that it were not a general mistake! That we may not be deceived, try it thus.

[1.] Do ye love holiness above all other accomplishments in the world? Otherwise ye cannot love God above all things; for this is the image of God, the nearest resemblance of him upon earth. Now those that hate holiness, that scorn it under the names of puritanism, preciseness, they hate God indeed, whatever affection they pretend in word. Naturalists write of a beast that bears such an antipathy to a man, as he will tear and rend his picture. Those that manifest such antipathy to holiness, the image of God, do really hate God, however they disclaim it; and since they hate him, if they love anything in the world, they love it more than God.

[2.] Do ye love the people of God above all others? Those that are born of God are holy, strict, exemplary in their conversation. If these be not loved above others, others are loved more than God, 1 John v. 1, and iii. 20. If these be the objects of your love, you will choose them before others for your companions; they will be the men of your counsel, of your delight, your eyes will be upon the faithful, Ps. ci. 6, whereas vile, profane persons, you will avoid them; you will take no pleasure in their society. Those that hate, scorn, reproach, revile the people of God, inasmuch as they do it unto them, they do it unto God. They shew how they are affected unto Christ, by their disaffection to his members. If you hate these, represent them under what notion you please, you hate God; so far are ye from loving him above all others. Profane persons are the professed enemies of God; if you delight in their society, your hearts are joined to those whom the Lord hates, &c.

[3.] Do you hate sin, every evil way that ye know to be evil? Otherwise ye love not God at all, Ps. xcvii. 10, Ps. cxix. 104. If ye delight in sin, willingly act it, live in it, notwithstanding the Lord forbids, threatens, hates it. Deceive not yourselves, if there be any truth in the word of God, the love of God is not in you. He that will not leave his sin for God, loves his sin better than God, idolizes it, gives that worship to his lusts which is due only to the God of heaven.

[4.] Do ye endeavour to obey Christ impartially? John xiv. 21, 23, 'If ye love me, keep my commandments.' He will do whatever he commands, how unpleasing soever it be to the flesh; how prejudicial soever it may prove to him in the world; however it cross his carnal humours and worldly interests; how inconsistent soever it be with his own ease, credit, advantage; how great, how small soever. He that lives in the neglect of any known duty, loves not God so much as that which moves him to neglect it. That has the pre-eminence, and is preferred before God.

[5.] How do ye bear the absence of Christ? Love is *affectus unionis;* it affects union, more of his presence, more intimacy, nearer enjoyment.

Because he is most near in his ordinances, therefore he prizes, loves, longs for them; because he is nearer in heaven than in the ordinances, therefore he loves, longs, for the appearing of Christ. By this ye may know. Can ye not tell what it is to enjoy Christ, to be near him, to have communion with him? Can ye live contented at a distance from him, so be it you have but outward comforts in abundance? Can ye better endure the withdrawing of Christ than the absence of some endeared relation? Can you better dispense with the loss of his favour, in the comfortable sense of it, than the loss of wife, children, lands, goods? Would you offend Christ by sin, rather than suffer for him? Why, then other things have more of your love than Christ, and so are idolised. Thus discover idolatry by love.

(2.) Whom do ye most fear? There is so much of the worship of God in fear, as I told you, it is ordinarily put in Scripture for the whole worship of God. That which you most fear, that you worship as God; and if you fear anything more than God, you shew yourselves herein idolaters; but how shall it be discovered that we fear others more than God? Why, by these particulars:

[1.] Are ye not loath to reprove men for sin, lest ye should offend them? To admonish them when they offend God, lest ye should incur their displeasure? Do ye not connive, if not countenance it? Are ye not silent, if ye excuse not the sins of familiars, or others, lest by rebuking sin ye should exasperate the sinner against you? What is this, but to fear men more than God? When the fear of men is more powerful to hinder from performing that which God commands, than the fear of God is to move you to the practice of it, do ye not choose herein to offend God rather than man? more afraid to displease them than displease God?

[2.] Do ye not decline the profession of those truths, the practice of those duties, which profane men do jeer and scoff at, such as will expose you to their taunts and reproaches? What! be so strict, so precise, pray by the Spirit, repeat sermons, scruple at such and such small matters, play the dissembler! These are the reproaches of a profane world. Does the fear of this hinder you from any holy duty, from strict conscientious walking? Why, then you fear men more than God.

[3.] Are ye not more afraid to suffer than to sin? Do ye think it folly to be so scrupulous as to hazard your liberty, or estate, or life, rather than do what is unlawful? Would ye take liberty to sin rather than lose your liberty? strain your conscience rather than venture your estate? dispense with yourselves in omitting some known duty, or denying some truth, or admitting some unwarrantable practice, rather than endanger your life? Why, then, it is clear you fear something more than God. He that is not more afraid of sin than any loss or suffering whatsoever, is more afraid of something else than God, and so idolizes it.

[4.] Is not the threatenings of men more dreadful to you than the displeasure, the power, the threatenings of God? If men in power should send a pursuivant, and denounce to you, that in case ye are guilty of swearing, Sabbath-breaking, &c., he would see you put to death, and seize on your estate, would not this message daunt ye, startle ye, make ye tremble? Why, the God of heaven sends you many such messages. He has again and again threatened eternal death to many sins that you are guilty of; yet you tremble not, you little regard it. Is it not plain, then, that you fear men more than God? Is not this such idolatry as is here threatened with the loss of heaven?

[5.] Are ye not more bold to sin in secret than in the view of the world? Are ye not careful to restrain sinful thoughts as well as scandalous acts?

Are ye not more fearful of such acts as the law of the land will punish, than such as the law of God condemns, such as are reserved for the tribunal of Christ? Are ye not afraid to sin, when no eye sees you but the eye of God? Do not soul-sins, secret lusts, inward corruptions, afflict and trouble ye? Why, then, it is apparent you fear something else more than God. You give that worship unto others which is due only to God, which is the soul-idolatry here threatened.

7. Examine by your elections; what is your soul's choice, when Christ and the world, Christ and the flesh, come in competition? That which you choose as the greatest good, that you make your god. If you choose Christ, then the Lord is your God; if you follow the flesh, embrace the world, then these are your gods. This choice of them, as the greater good, is that worship (and a principal act of worship it is) due only unto God; and when the flesh and the world carry it, they are idolized.

These are the great competitors for the soul of man, Christ, and the world, and flesh. That interest which prevails, the soul bows down to it, worships it as God should be worshipped. They are both importunate suitors, and offer great things to win the soul's consent; and that which it chooses it worships.

The flesh attempts the soul thus: If thou wilt follow me, live after my dictates and motions, close with my suggestions, make provision to satisfy me, then thou shalt live in ease and pleasure, gain many advantages in the world, avoid that trouble, those dangers, that persecution, that reproach and scorn, which the zealous followers of Christ cannot avoid.

Christ moves the soul thus: If thou wilt choose me, thou shalt have pardon, and peace, and life. 'He that findeth me, findeth life,' Prov. viii. 35. Thou shalt be freed from wrath, justice, hell; thou shalt have interest in all those glorious things that I have purchased with my blood. With such offers does Christ importune the soul in the gospel to accept of him.

Now, which of these prevails with you? Which of these offers seems best? Which motion do ye yield to? I know there are few or none but will be ready to say, it is Christ that I choose, I renounce the world and the flesh; the offers of Christ are gracious, and I have been always ready to yield thereto; God forbid that I should choose or prefer any thing before my Saviour! This is generally taken for granted; but, alas! it is generally mistaken, otherwise Christ's flock would not be so little, and those that are saved so few. Many suppose they choose Christ, while they embrace an idol. And this is the fatal mistake, the ruin even of most who enjoy the gospel. But how shall this be discerned? Why, Christ has discovered this clearly, if men were willing to see, if they had not rather be deceived than be at the trouble to examine by the rule. The soul that chooses Christ is willing to accept of him upon his own terms; this is the touchstone, &c. He that will not take Christ upon his own terms, his heart did yet never choose him. But what are Christ's terms? See Mat. xvi. 24. Now, do they deny themselves who will not deny a lust for Christ? Do men deny themselves, when self-love, self-seeking, self-pleasing, is so predominant, so visible? Do they take up the cross who lay it upon others? Are not they far from choosing to suffer for Christ rather than sin, who will sin when they are not tempted to it by fear of suffering? Do they follow Christ who walk contrary to him, who decline his ways as too strict, too precise; who brand zeal as madness, holiness as hypocrisy, circumspect walking as needless preciseness? Such do plainly refuse Christ, and choose their lusts and the world before him. That choice of Christ is only real and sincere, when the soul takes him, not only as a Saviour, but as a Lord. Try, then, by this. Are you as willing to be commanded by Christ, as to be saved by him—to submit to his laws, as to partake of his benefits? Do ye desire him as much to make you holy as to make you happy—as much for sanctification as for salvation—as much to free you from the power sin as from the guilt of it—not only that it may not damn you, but that it may not have dominion over you? If you do not choose Christ for this, and in this manner, you choose him not at all. 'Tis plain, while you would have Christ for your Saviour, something else is your god. The interest of the flesh and world prevails, and this you choose as a greater good in life, though ye would be saved by Christ at death.

8. Examine by your inclinations. Your souls are always in motion. Now, whither does this motion chiefly tend, whither are they bound? The inward worship of God does much consist in the motion and inclination of the heart towards God. When it moves most towards him, and but to other things as helps and furtherances in the way to him, then he is worshipped as God. But when the heart moves more to other things than to God, those things are idolised, and that worship is given to them which is due only unto God, which is the idolatry we are now inquiring after.

Feel, then, the pulse of your souls; observe their motion, that ye may know whether or no it be idolatrous. Whither do the inclinations of your hearts most carry you? Which way do they most move, and to what objects? Do they move most towards heaven or towards the earth? towards Christ or sin? towards the enjoyment of God, or towards outward enjoyments? towards spiritual objects, grace and glory, holiness and heavenly communion with Christ, or towards carnal objects, your relations, sensual pleasures, earthly advantages? If your hearts work more after these, these are your idols, and these inclinations are idolatrous. The idolatry lies here in the degree; it is lawful to move towards these outward things; but when the heart is more carried after them than after God; when it is inordinate, then it is idolatrous. Now, that you may discern in what degree your inclinations are, observe these severals:—

(1.) Is your motion after God absolute, and your inclinations to other things but subordinate and relative? Are your hearts carried after these outward things for God? Move your hearts towards them, that by the help of them you may move faster after God? When your inclinations are drawn out after relations, is it principally because they have special interest in, or some resemblance of, God? When you move towards the world, is it principally that you may be more serviceable to God in your generation? If not, you idolise them. If your hearts move to these things for themselves absolutely, and not in reference to God, because they are like him, or because therein you enjoy him, or because thereby ye may better serve him; if not thus, your inclinations are idolatrous, your hearts hereby run a-whoring after them, as the Scripture uses to express idolatry.

(2.) Are your inclinations after God stronger than after other objects? Is there more life and vigour in your motions heavenward? Are they not more easy, more ordinarily, and with less displacency, obstructed and diverted, than those other things? Is the bent of your heart after God, when you are employed about worldly things? Is it not the affliction of your souls, that they move no faster, no more forcibly, towards Christ and glory, and that they are so easily turned aside to vanities? Can you say with David, 'My soul followeth hard after thee'? If your inclinations be strong to the world, your relations in it, employments or enjoyments in it, when weak and faint after God, these inclinations are idolatrous.

(3.) Are your inclinations after God more effectual than after other things?

This will be discovered by your prayers, by your endeavours. The soul that moves effectually towards God breathes out many sighs and prayers and tears after him, is ever reaching at him, stretching out itself to meet him, to lay hold of him, to apprehend him. When he seems to withdraw, it follows him with strong cries and mournful complaints, 'How long, Lord, how long, &c.; O, when shall I come and appear before thee!' Now, then, if, when thou find not the comforting and quickening presence of God, yet, notwithstanding, you are still and silent in this sad condition, either pray not, or stir not up yourselves to pray with fervency, importunity, but content yourselves quietly in your ordinary way; why, then, it is evident your hearts are moving after something else more than God. So for your endeavours. If you can be diligent, careful, industrious in worldly business, but slack, negligent, careless in the ordinances, it is suspicious your inclinations are more after other things than God, which is idolatrous.

9. Examine by your fruitions. What is that in which you take most contentment, complacency, that which gives you most satisfaction? What is your sweetest and most delightful enjoyment, in which you rest best pleased? To delight in the Lord above all things is a special act of soul worship, due only unto God. When you delight in anything more, in anything so much as him, you give that worship due only to God unto other things, which is the idolatry here spoken of. If any enjoyment be more pleasing, satisfying, than the enjoyment of God, you erect an idol in the place of God. Examine: are not the ways of sin, intemperance, uncleanness, revenge, worldliness, more pleasing than the ways of holiness, wherein ye may walk with God and enjoy him? Do ye not more delight in earthly success, abundance, prosperity, than in the light of God's countenance, sense of his favour? Take ye not more contentment in worldly vanities than spiritual enjoyments? Take ye not more comfort in relations, wife, children, &c., than in communion with God and fellowship with Christ? Are not sensual pleasures more delightful than those which arise from spiritual and heavenly objects? Are not recreations or worldly employments more pleasing than those duties, exercises, wherein the Lord may be enjoyed? If they be, it is too evident the Lord is not your chief enjoyment. The heart is more taken, pleased, satisfied with something else than with God, which is to idolise it.

To examine this more punctually.

(1.) Can we rest satisfied without assurance of interest in God? Can we be content without the sense of his love? Can we be quiet in his absence? Are ye satisfied when ye find not the presence of God, the comfortable and powerful effects of it in your souls? Do ye rest in outward accommodations, health, plenty, friends, when ye have no certainty that the Lord is at peace with you? Do ye rest in the performance of spiritual duties, though ye find not the presence of God in them? Content with ordinances, though ye find not, enjoy not God in them? Why, then, God is not your chiefest enjoyment; something else does please you as well, if not content you better. You may see this in a familiar instance. The infant's most pleasing enjoyment is the breast; if it want this, nothing else will quiet it. Offer it heaps of pearl or mines of gold, nothing will content it without the breast. So it is with the soul that makes the Lord his chiefest enjoyment; nothing can content, quiet his heart, but the presence of God, the sense of his love, the power of his Spirit, the effects of his presence in his soul in spiritual light, life, strength, activeness, comfort. Outward comforts are unsavoury to him if he find not, enjoy not the Lord in them. The pleasures of the world are bitter to him while he misses his chief delight. He will sigh in the midst of others' mirth while the Lord, the joy of his soul, is removed. The ordinances themselves seem empty, when he sees them not filled with the glory and power of the Lord's presence. As she, 'What do all these avail me?' Give him riches, or honours, or friends; let corn, and wine, and oil increase; his heart is not quiet. What will all these avail me if the Lord be absent, hide his face? If you be satisfied with other things, without regarding whether God be present or no; contented though God be absent, though in part withdrawn.

(2.) Are ye not backward to spiritual communion with God? more hardly drawn to those duties, exercises, wherein ye may enjoy him, than to some other enjoyments, some other exercises in the world? Do not your hearts hang back from secret prayer, meditation, exercise of faith? Find you not yourselves much more forward to some other things? Oh, if the Lord were your chief delight, your sweetest enjoyment, you would be more eager, more forward to follow after him. You need no enforcements; you go on your own accord after the world, your relations, your pleasures, recreations; and do ye need so many motives, persuasions, inducements, enforcements, to draw you to God? Why, then, have ye not cause to fear something else has more of your hearts? The fruition of something else is sweeter than that of God. This soul-worship is misplaced.

(3.) What cheerfulness find ye in drawing near to God in those ways wherein he is to be enjoyed? How cheerful are we when there, where they most delight to be! How pleasant is the fruition of that which is their joy! Can you be thus pleasant and cheerful in the company of friends, in the employments that tend to your advantage in the world, and yet so dull, untoward, heartless, in those services wherein ye may draw near to God, as though ye were cloyed with them? move here as if ye were out of your element; drive on heavily in these ways, as though the wheels were off, and come to these duties as to a meal with a full stomach? It is suspicious you delight in something more than God, give that worship to something else which is due only to God.

(4.) Are you not easily drawn from God? Are you not less discontented with a diversion from God than from some other things on which your hearts are set? That which you will easily part with, you are not much pleased with. Will not a temptation to take you off from close walking with God, prevail sooner than a motion to leave some sensual delight, ensnaring vanity? Can ye be more fixed and constant in other enjoyments and delights, but more easily, more ordinarily removed from God? This argues some distaste, some dislike of spiritual enjoyments. When the apprehension of such a pleasure, such an advantage, will be more powerful to turn ye aside from God than the promises of the word, the motions of the Spirit, and former experiences are to keep you close to him, this argues the Lord is not your most delightful enjoyment. Men do not easily part with that which is their chief delight; and if the Lord be not, something else is; and whatever that is, it is an idol.

(5.) Neglect ye not that which would make ye capable of the fullest enjoyment of God? Do ye not neglect holiness? Are ye not content with some low degrees of it? Is it your design, your endeavour to come up to the highest pitch of it? There is no seeing, no enjoying God without this. And the more of this, the more of God is seen, the more enjoyed. When this is in perfection, the enjoyment will be perfect. When this is weak, enjoyments will be small, and at a distance. The soul that counts the Lord his sweetest, most delightful enjoyment, will never think he has enough of him, and therefore will be ever labouring for that which will make him capable of more. If an opinion of holiness will serve your turn, or the beginnings, the principles of it, without the life, strength, exercise, increase of it, it is suspicious; you place not your happiness in the fruition of God; and if not in him, then it is in something else; and whatever that be, it is an idol.

Use 3. Exhortation. Be exhorted, in the fear of God, to avoid this idolatry. It is the apostle's exhortation, with which he closes his epistle, 1 John v. 21. Search it out, else how can it be avoided? Make use of the directions in the former use for that end at large delivered. If you discover it not, since such a discovery has been made thereof, it is because you will not see; and then henceforth this abominable sin in you is wilful, and yourselves inexcusable, and the justice of God clear, if any perish for it.

When you have found it, bewail it. Bewail it with sorrow proportionable to the heinousness of the sin. Use it as an aggravation of your other sin, wherein, for the most part, there is a mixture. It may be thou art not an open blasphemer, an actual murderer, or a wretched apostate, but art thou not a soul idolater? Nay, there need no question be made of this. Go then in secret and blush before the Lord, and take shame to thyself, and be humbled for it, humbled deeply, for it is an high provocation.

Fly to Christ for pardon. O that this might be the issue of all delivered on this subject, to drive ye to Christ; not only to beget in you some slight ineffectual apprehensions of some need of a Saviour (with which too many content themselves to the ruin of their souls), but to possess you with deep apprehensions of an absolute necessity of him, of his blood. Nothing else can wash off the deep stain of this crimson sin. One act (though ye be guilty of millions) of this idolatry, will be enough to sink you into hell, enough to kindle the everlasting wrath of God against you; that wrath which will burn for ever, which will burn so as none can quench it, except the blood of Christ be applied to that purpose. See into what a sad condition this sin has already brought ye. Hereby,

1. You have forfeited an inheritance. It is not some parcel of your estate, some of less value, worth less consideration, but your inheritance, your whole inheritance, and that for ever. For a man to lose his whole inheritance is a great, a sad loss; but this is it you lose by this sin. 'An idolater,' says the text, 'shall have *no* inheritance.'

2. Oh, but it may be the inheritance is little worth, and then no great matter if it be lost. Oh no; it is a rich, a large, a glorious inheritance you lose hereby; it is no less than a kingdom. The loss of a crown, the loss of a kingdom, sticks deep. Oh what hazards will not men run to save a kingdom! Their treasure, their blood, their lives, yea, and the lives of thousands, will men lose rather than lose a kingdom. Why, this is it you lose by this sin, no less than a kingdom. 'An idolater shall have no inheritance in the kingdom.'

3. Oh, but it may be it is some inconsiderable kingdom, some petty jurisdiction, then the loss is not so great. Oh no; it is the loss of the kingdom of God, and that is more than the loss of all the kingdoms of the earth. It is not the kingdom, the empire of a Cyrus, or of a Cæsar, or of an Alexander, or Othman, but it is the kingdom of God. You lose hereby such a kingdom as the empire of the world is but a span, a mote, yea, nothing, compared with it. Oh, what dreadful bloody conflicts there have been for the empire of the world! how many millions have been sacrificed to secure it! And will ye lose the kingdom of God rather than sacrifice this sin? The retaining of this sin will be the loss of that. So the text, 'An idolater shall have no inheritance in the kingdom of God.'

Oh, but though this loss, this hazard, be exceeding great, yet it may be avoided; though I continue in this sin, yet is there no hope in Christ? May not he admit me into this kingdom notwithstanding? Oh no; Christ has no kingdom for such; he never purchased a kingdom for those that will continue in this sin. Christ, who has made way for others to the kingdom, will himself shut soul-idolaters out of it. The text tells us this too, 'No inheritance in the kingdom of God, of Christ.'

Obj. But is this certain? Is this dreadful loss unavoidable? May it not be otherwise? Oh no; to dream of such a thing is madness; nothing is more certain. The apostle is in nothing more peremptory; mind the words, he says, 'An idolater shall not,' &c. He speaks not doubtfully, as of a thing uncertain, that may be or may not be. He says not, peradventure an idolater *may* not, but he *shall* not. As sure as the word of God is true, as sure as the apostle was directed by the Spirit of God, without all peradventure, a soul idolater shall have no inheritance, &c.

Obj. But is not this strange doctrine, to speak at this rate, of soul, of secret idolatry, a sin so common as few can acquit themselves of it; to say that all guilty of it shall certainly have no inheritance, &c. Is not this strange doctrine?

Ans. If it be strange, it is ignorance makes it so, for in the apostle's time it was a known, an acknowledged truth; there was no question, no doubt, made of it. The first word of the text tells us this, 'This ye know.' As if he had said, You certainly know, you undoubtedly acknowledge this; you make no question, no doubt of this, 'No idolater shall,' &c. No idolater, that is so habitually, perseveringly, shall. This idolatry, though it be secret, though it lodge in the retired chambers of the soul, though its pavilion be darkness, and no eye see it but the all-seeing eye of God, yet if it be not forsaken, lamented, resisted, subdued, it leaves no title, no way to the inheritance. Methinks this should be a sufficient dissuasive from this sin, a loss so great, so irreparable, so certain. This should effectually stir you up to search out this sin, to seek pardon of it, to get power to subdue it, to expel it. But further to stir you up against this sin, consider

2. How it is represented in Scripture, in what colours the Holy Ghost sets out idolatry.

(1.) It is called the worshipping of devils, not only in the Gentiles, 1 Cor. x. 20, but also in the Jews, Deut. xxxii. 17. Yet these, in their idolatrous service, did not intend to worship devils, no, nor to worship their idols; but, as the papists pretend, to worship Jehovah, the true God, in those representations, as appears, Exod. [xx. 4 ?]. Now, what a horrible abomination is it to worship the devil! Samuel, when he would aggravate Saul's sin to the height, tells him it was like the sin of witchcraft and idolatry, these being the worst of sins. Yet, if we compare these, idolatry seems worse than witchcraft, for witchcraft is but a compact with the devil, but idolatry is a worshipping of the devil; now, is it not worse, a greater abomination, to worship than to make an agreement with him?

(2.) It is called whoredom and adultery, Judges ii. 17; 'Went a-whoring,' &c., 2 Chron. xxi. 13, Jer. iii. 9; idolaters are called the 'children of whoredoms,' Hosea ii. 4, and iv. 12. It is spiritual adultery. The Lord can no more endure idolatry in his people, those that profess him, than a man can endure adultery in his wife; other failings may be borne with, but this calls for death or a divorce. Hence the Lord, where he forbids this sin, he adds this reason, Exod. xx., 'For I am a jealous God.' This provokes the Lord to jealousy; he will no more endure a competitor in his worship than a husband will endure a partner in the affections and enjoyment of his wife. He is a jealous God.

(3.) This is the principal character of antichrist. Babylon, the seat of antichristianism, is not called the tyrant of Babylon, nor the heretic of Babylon, but 'the whore of Babylon,' the mother of fornications and abominations, with whom the kings, nations, and kingdoms of the earth commit fornication, Rev. xvii. 5. Babylon,—mystery. It is a mysterious spiritual whoredom; her great abomination is whoredom in a mystery, opposite to the great mystery of godliness, the mystery of the true worship of God. Now, is it not a dangerous thing to have the least character, the least part of the mark of the beast, that mark by which the Lord has designed her and her partakers out to most dreadful and remarkable destruction?

(4.) The Lord does most severely, most dreadfully threaten and punish idolatry above other sins. You may read the heinousness of it, in the grievousness of Israel's, of Judah's sufferings for it, Daniel ix. 12. 'Under the whole heaven,' &c. The word confirmed hereby was the threatenings executed for this sin, than which the Lord threatened no sin more, none so much, by his servants the prophets. He punishes not only the idolaters themselves, but even their posterity to many generations after them, for this sin, according to the tenor of that threatening, Exod. xx. 5; and the Jews are so apprehensive of it, as to this day they have a saying, That no judgment befel the Jews for those many hundred years after they left Egypt but there is an ounce of the golden calf in it.

Obj. But this was gross open idolatry, worshipping of images; it was not this secret, this soul idolatry; the Scripture speaks no such thing of that.

Ans. This secret and soul idolatry, is in some sense worse than open idolatry; and, therefore, those Scripture expressions setting forth the vileness and danger of that, may be applied to humble us under the sense of this. That this may appear, and mistakes may be prevented, remember wherein these two sorts of idolatry do consist. It is open gross idolatry when that outward worship, which consists in the gestures of body, bowing, prostration, &c., is given in a religious way to others besides God. It is secret idolatry, when that inward worship, which consists in the acts and motions of the mind and heart, are given to other things besides God. Now, when both inward and outward worship together are given to the creatures, that is the worst of idolatry of all; then the sin is complete in all the dimensions of its guilt. But now, if we compare these two sorts of worship apart, it is far worse idolatry, when inward worship is given to other things than God, than when outward worship only is communicated to them. And in this sense I say, that secret soul idolatry is worse than that which is gross and open, and that in divers respects.

1. The Lord more respects inward worship than outward, the acts and motions of the soul, than the acts and gestures of the body. 'My son, give me thy heart.' 'The true worshippers shall worship the Father in spirit,' John iv. 28. It is inward, spiritual, soul worship, which the Lord most requires, most respects, most delights in, is most honoured by; and therefore it is a greater provocation to give this soul worship to other things than that of the body. It is worse idolatry for the soul to bow down to a lust, than for the body to lie prostrate before an idol.

2. Even in worshipping God, a man may be excessive in outward acts and expressions, in the motions and gestures of the body; but there can be no excess in the inward acts of worship. Ye cannot love God too much, nor trust, fear, desire, delight, nor have too much esteem of him, and this argues a greater excellency in, a greater necessity of this inward worship,

than of that which is outward, and therefore a greater provocation to give that soul-worship unto others, than this of the body.

3. The objects of secret idolatry are worse than those of open idolatry, the idols worshipped are more vile, more abominable; and, therefore, the idolatry more to be abhorred. For the idols here worshipped, the objects of soul-worship in this secret idolatry, are for the most part the lusts of men. Now, there is not the basest creature that ever the blindest of the heathen worshipped, that is so vile as our base lusts. There is no creature so mean (not such as the Egyptians worshipped) but has some goodness in it, Gen. i., something of worth or use as it is a creature; but there is no goodness at all in the lusts of men, nothing but what is altogether and upon every account most abominable, and that in the eye of God, who judges of things as they are, and so judges righteous judgment. He looked upon all that he had made as good, even the meanest of his creatures; but he cannot endure to look upon men's lusts, he is of purer eyes than to behold iniquity; so vile, so loathsome, so abominable, so full of provocation, he cannot look upon them but with indignation. Now for men to give that divine honour, that soul worship which is due only unto the Majesty of heaven, unto their vile abominable lusts, must needs be more heinous, more intolerable, than if it were given to the works of God's hands, than if it were given to the sun or moon, yea, or to wood and stone, yea, or to toads and serpents; for these are better, have more worth in them than our lusts, for they are the works of God's hands; whereas your lusts are the loathsome issue of filthy impure hearts.

When your lusts have more of your hearts, thoughts, delight, desires, love than God, it is worse idolatry upon this account than if you should bow to a sun or moon, than if you should lie prostrate before a toad or serpent.

Obj. But some may say, If we did make vows or prayers, if we did burn incense, or offer sacrifice to our lusts, then might we be charged with this idolatry; otherwise the censure seems to want good ground.

Ans. I have instanced at large in many acts of worship besides these, which are due only to God; and it is idolatry to give any one, not only these. But as for this objected, see if there be not something answerable to these, nay, something exceeding these acts of worship given by men to their lusts.

1. As for prayer and invocation. If the desires of your hearts be more after the fulfilling of your lusts, and making provision for them, than after the pleasing and honouring of God, why then, you pray more to your lusts than unto God. For if the desires of your souls be not after God, as they cannot be while your lusts prevail, why, then, that which you count praying to God is but the carcase of a prayer. Your lusts have that which is the soul and life of prayer. For the essence of prayer consists in the ardent desires of the heart, the expressions and gestures are but formalities and circumstances, not at all regarded by God except in displeasure, when the other is absent, Isa. xxix. 13. This was no praying; but Hannah's was without expressions, 1 Sam. i. 13, 15.

2. As for vows. If you purpose and resolve to live in sin, and follow the motions of your lusts, is not this a mental vow? This is equivalent to, and has the strength and firmness of, a vow, and is stronger than any resolution for God can be, while the strength of sin is unsubdued.

3. As for sacrifices. If you give up yourselves to any way of sin, you sacrifice more thereto than the cattle of a thousand hills. A man given up to a lust, he sacrifices his time, his strength, his enjoyments, his parts, his

endeavours, his thoughts, his affections, nay, his soul thereto. And are not these more valuable than the sacrifices of bulls or goats? than any sacrifice of that nature in use among the Jews or Gentiles, Ps. li. 16, 17. An heart broken, *i. e.* subdued to God, ready to yield to his will in all things, is a sacrifice to God. So is a heart subdued to a lust, ready to yield to its motions, it is a sacrifice to it; such a sacrifice as God requires for himself, and would be well-pleased with it, if it were offered to him; better pleased than with all external sacrifices.

Obj. But what does this concern the people of God already in covenant? Though they may be guilty of some inordinate, *i. e.* idolatrous motions, yet are not they hereby brought within the compass of this threatening. They cannot lose their title to the inheritance, that which they were ordained to, that which they are born to. 'The foundation of God standeth sure,' &c. 'Whom he has predestinated,' &c.

Ans. Be it so. They fall not directly under the threatening; yet does it sometimes concern them. If it did not, yet are there other weighty considerations that should make this sin dreadful even to God's people.

1. Though it make not their possession of the inheritance impossible, yet will this make it exceeding difficult. The apostle gives direction, 2 Peter i. 11, how an entrance may be ministered abundantly into the everlasting kingdom. Though the people of God, giving way to these motions, may possibly have an entrance, yet not abundantly ministered. It is one thing for a man to creep into his inheritance; another to be carried with full sail into it. The apostles speak of some that shall be saved, but so as by fire, 1 Cor. xiii. 15; though they may escape this threatening, yet very hardly, with much danger and difficulty; even as out of the fire he shall be, מצל מאש, as a firebrand. The Lord Christ makes it such a difficulty as is next to an impossibility, Mark x. 23, &c. Now to prevent a mistake, he tells them, it is not the having, the possessing of riches, but the idolizing of them, trusting in them, ascribing that to them which is due only to God; which makes it thus exceeding difficult for those that have riches, &c. And there is the same reason of all other things inordinately affected. He that inordinately loves, fears, delights, desires, esteems anything in the world, it will be exceeding difficult for such a one to enter. And lest any should make light of it, he further expresses the difficulty by a comparison, ver. 25. There is but the difference of a letter betwixt κάμηλος, a *camel*, and κάμιλος, a *cable;* and this latter way some render it, 'It is easier for a cable,' &c. Take it which way you will, it speaks a difficulty impossible to be overcome by the power of man. And so he explains it, to allay the disciples' astonishment, ver. 26, 27. It is possible only to almighty power, which alone can so disengage the heart from riches and other objects, as it shall not immoderately affect them, inordinately love, desire, prize. There is no other way possible to heaven, but by subduing this idolatrous humour of trusting in, idolizing of, riches. And the same is true of any other object whereon the mind, the heart, is more set than upon God: 'It is as easy,' &c.

If you give way to these inordinate motions, affections, &c., you will find the way to heaven, like the Israelites' way to Canaan, tedious, difficult, dangerous. It was idolatry made it so to them. The Lord might have brought them a short, a safe, an easy way, to the promised land, and made it a journey of as few days as it was years; but their idolatry, with other sins, provoked the Lord to swear in his wrath, &c. And this very thing, both sin and punishment, is proposed as ensamples to us, lest, being ensnared in their sin, we should fall by their punishment, fall in the wilderness, and come short of Canaan, 1 Cor. x. 6, 7, 11, 12. If this shut not the people of God out of his rest, yet it may make your way thither exceeding woful and perilous, exceeding difficult and hazardous; it may bring ye back into the wilderness, when ye are in sight of the land of promise; may dash your hopes, darken your evidence, and make your way on earth a dry and comfortless desert, a perilous and howling wilderness.

2. This will blast the prosperity of your souls, endanger the life of holiness, keep ye back from the power of godliness, bring your souls into a consumption, keep them in a languishing condition, even near unto the gates of death. And what greater miseries can befall a servant of God in this world? Oh, if we could look upon things with a spiritual eye, these distempers would be more dreadful than outward sufferings. When anything in the world is inordinately, *i.e.* idolatrously minded and affected, it is a soul disease, like to those diseases of the body which draw all the spirits and nutriment to the distempered part, and leave the rest weak and languishing in a consumption. While ye love other things inordinately, you lose your first love to Christ; while ye are so eager after the world and other vanities, you must needs be lukewarm in the ways of God; while ye are so active after a soul-idol, you cannot but be barren and unfruitful towards God. And how dangerous are these distempers, how odious to the Lord, how severely does he threaten them!

This idolatrous plant will suck away all the juice and sap of your souls, and leave grace to wither and languish. It cumbers the ground wherever it takes place, and makes all about it barren.

There is no coming up to the power of godliness, to the vigorous exercise of grace, to the lively actings of holiness, no access to intimate communion with God, where this is tolerated. And what is the life of a Christian without this, but a shadow of death? If the hearts of lukewarm, formal, backsliding professors (who abound everywhere) were searched, some such imposthume would be found there, some lust or vanity idolatrously affected, imposthumating their hearts, and eating as a cancer; nor can our souls ever prosper, but will still be backsliding, till the ulcer be lanced. And are not such distempers dreadful, which bring the soul so near to apostasy? Should not this be a forcible motive?

3. If you continue in this guilt, you may be sure some sharp affliction will befall you. If the Lord have any love to you, he will not lose you: 'As many as I love, I chasten,' Rev. iii. Either he will pluck that from you which ye immoderately value and affect, or else he will so embitter it to you as you shall find by sad experience that it is an evil thing and a bitter that thou hast forsaken the Lord thy God, to set up other things instead of him, Jer. ii. 19. He will make this very wickedness to correct thee, and thy backsliding hereby occasioned to reprove thee; he will turn those idolized comforts into gall and wormwood, and convey a sting into that which thy heart, with such delight, embraces. If thou fall not in the wilderness (as habitual idolaters), yet will he turn thy idols into serpents; so that instead of the comforts thou expectest to refresh thee, thou shalt find a sting to wound thee. The Israelites' sufferings for idolatry and other evils are proposed as ensamples to the people of God, 1 Cor. x. If thou expectest to enjoy thy idol quietly, thou art deluded; if thou belong to God, he will make thee smart for it. If you will not speedily put away these spiritual whoredoms out of your sight, the Lord will strip ye naked, and make ye as a wilderness, Hosea ii. 3; see chap. v. 6, 7.

4. The Lord will withdraw himself from you. There must needs be an eclipse when the earth gets betwixt you and the sun. You will find the

light of his countenance clouded when such gross vapours, such lusts, such inordinate motions abound. The Lord is a jealous God; if he do not send you a bill of divorce, yet ye shall have little of his presence; he will be separated in part, though not totally and for ever. And oh how sad will your condition be, if outward afflictions and spiritual desertions should meet together! If the Lord, for your idolizing the things of the world, should leave you destitute of them; if ye should fall into poverty, disgrace; if cast off by friends and relations, too much valued; if he should cast you into languishing sickness, and then wound your conscience, drop bitterness into your spirits, and set his terrors in array against you; if you should cry to him in this condition, and he refuse to hear you; if seek him, and he not be found of you; if he should send you to the gods that ye have served; if he should bring to remembrance your idols, your credit, riches, pleasures, sports, company, relations, and say to you, as to them, Judges x. 13, 14, Go and cry to these idols that you preferred before me, let them deliver you, let them speak peace to you, let them save you, let them free you from the wrath to come, let them secure you from going down into the pit. You have slighted, undervalued, cast off me when you prospered; and do ye come now to me when ye are afflicted? Nay, go to the gods that ye have chosen. You thought them more worthy of your thoughts, affections, hearts, than me; make much of your choice, eat the fruits of your doings, I will have nothing to do with you: Oh what a dreadful condition will this be? There is but even a span betwixt hell and it. Now, by continuing under this guilt, you are in the high way to this woful condition, you are posting towards it. Oh remember it before it be too late.

Quest. But since this soul idolatry is so dangerous to all sorts, how shall it be avoided? What means may we use, to escape out of this dangerous snare?

Ans. For satisfaction to this, observe these directions.

1. Get new natures. All other means will be ineffectual without this. The regeneration of the soul is the only way to the destruction of this sin. The first beginnings of spiritual life, are the first pangs of death to soul idolatry; and as grace increases, as holiness grows, so does this sin decay. It ceases to be habitual and reigning, when the principles of grace are first implanted; and as holiness, which is Christ's interest in the soul, grows stronger and stronger, so the interest of the flesh and world, wherein the life and power of this sin consists, grows weaker and weaker. They are as the house of David and Saul. This is the woful misery of an unrenewed condition; and oh that it might be laid to heart by those whom it concerns! While ye are in the state of nature, unconverted, not sanctified, not born again, you are unavoidably idolaters. It is reigning and habitual, and so damning, and destructive, till ye be regenerated. Sin has the throne, Satan has the sceptre, every base lust and vanity takes place of God, of Christ, in your hearts. Whatever ye love, ye love it more than God. Whatever ye trust, delight in, desire, esteem, the god of this world is your god, and the lust of the flesh, eye, pride of life, is your trinity. God has no place in your minds and hearts, or but an inferior place, a place unworthy of him, below your lusts, vanities, relations, enjoyments. God has no true worship from you; that which is due to him is given to other things; and so it will be till you have new hearts, till old things pass away. Oh what a woful condition is this! Be convinced of it. Cry unto God for the spirit of regeneration, for those new hearts which he has promised. Till then, you are, you will be, such idolaters as have no inheritance in the kingdom.

2. Mortify your lusts. It is the apostle's direction, Col. iii. 5. If we

inquire, as the apostle James in another case, from whence comes this soul idolatry? we may answer, as he, James iv. 1, 'Comes it not hence, even of your lusts that war in your members?' Here is the spring-head of this abomination. Stop up this, and the motions, the streams thereof will fail. When Delilah would destroy Samson, she inquired wherein his strength lay. Why, the strength of this idolatry lies in unmortified lusts; except ye cut these off, ye will never prevail against it. Oh that instead of those vanities, to which Satan diverts so many professors from the great concernments of their souls, this might be your care, and study, and design, to die daily. Be much in mortifying duties: 1, Search out your lusts, get more acquaintance with the distempers of your hearts; 2, Be ashamed of them; 3, Acknowledge them, with all their aggravations, be humbled for them in the sight of God, frequently, seriously; 4, Cut off the occasions which nourish, support them; 5, Beat down your bodies, and bring them into subjection; rather forbear lawful liberties, than yield any encouragement to your lusts by them; 6, Cry unto God for strength against this great multitude; look on them as more dreadful than an host of armed enemies; as more dangerous, more pernicious; say as Jehoshaphat, 2 Chron. xx. 12; 7, Bewail them as your greatest afflictions; 8, Act faith on Christ crucified, and by the power of it draw crucifying virtue from him; it is through his strength only that you must conquer. The life of this sin is bound up in the life of unmortified lusts. Crucify these, die daily unto them, and this sin will die, will fall with them.

3. Get right apprehensions of the things of the world. An overvaluing of outward things is the birth and food of this soul-idolatry. The motions and affections of the soul follow the dictate, the judgment of the understanding; if this be corrupt, no wonder if they be inordinate. The judgment is the spring of the soul's motion; if that be out of order, no wonder if all the motions of the heart be irregular. Whence is it that we immoderately love, desire, delight, trust, outward things, but because we overvalue them, apprehend more in them than there is? Let your thoughts often represent to your souls the vanity, emptiness, uncertainty, dissatisfaction, deceitfulness, unprofitableness of your choicest worldly enjoyments, and the vexation of spirit that attends them, and converse in the world under the sense of these apprehensions. Look upon them, as the Spirit of God represents them, nay, as experience testifies of them, and the ground of idolizing them will be far less. Consult with the best experience, and stand to its verdict. What did Samson or Solomon find in beauty, or Haman in honours, or Judas in his money, or the rich man in his full barns and exceeding plenty, or David in his dearest child, or Job in the wife of his bosom and choicest friends? Oh miserable comforts, miserable comforters! Are such things worthy to come in competition with God? Think seriously of these things, judge of them as they are, use them as though ye used them not. When you are crucified to the world, then will this sin languish, then will the strength of it be weakened.

4. Let your hearts be especially jealous of lawful comforts; these are the most dangerous snares. Because we apprehend least danger in them, herein we are most secure, and therefore the sooner surprised. Because we may lawfully follow our callings and worldly business, therefore men take liberty to follow them too eagerly, engage their minds and hearts too far upon them, and that before they are aware of it.

Because we may lawfully love friends and relations, we are less watchful to avoid excess in our affections. Because recreations are lawful, therefore we are apt to take liberty to exceed therein. Because we may take comfort in outward enjoyments, therefore we are more apt to let out our hearts to them, as if they were our chief comforts; especially when our employments border upon spiritual things, we are apt to think we cannot be too inordinate, whereas spiritual things themselves may be carnally used. And the extreme here is more easy to them that are conscientious, than in things apparently evil. Oh, how many who escape the gross pollutions of the world, and are far from excess of riot, are miserably ensnared in the inordinate using and affecting of lawful things! Here we lie most open to Satan; therefore, if ye would avoid this idolatry, be most watchful and jealous in these things.

THE CHILDREN OF GOD SHOULD NOT BE PARTAKERS WITH OTHERS IN THEIR SINS.

Be ye not therefore partakers with them.—Eph. V. 7.

Having given you a general account of the eighth verse, before I take a more particular view of the words, I thought it not amiss to take notice of a very useful and necessary truth, which this seventh verse offers unto our observation. It is this:

Obs. The children of God should not be partakers with others in their sins. Those that profess, &c., and would be accounted followers of God as dear children, should be careful not to partake with others in their wickedness.

The first thing ye should be careful of, is to avoid personal sins; the next, not to be tainted with the guilt of other men's sins.

If you would walk as becometh saints, ver. 3, it is not enough not to act sin yourselves, not to be principals in sinning; you should be fearful to be accessory to the sins of others. It is the apostle's advice to Timothy, 1 Tim. v. 22. Avoid not only the acting of sin thyself, but also a partaking with others' sins. If thou couldst live free from personal guilt, yet thou mayest contract guilt enough by other men's sins to make thee liable to condemnation.

The marrow of this truth lies in knowing how and in what ways we may be in danger to be partakers of other men's sins. Unless this be known, it will not, it cannot be well avoided; and therefore I will endeavour to shew how many ways ye may be guilty in others' sin, guilty of that evil which other men act; how ye may be accessory to that sin wherein others are principals. This may come to pass very many ways. To help your memories, I shall reduce as many as I have observed (for all I will not undertake to find out) to six heads, most of which are pregnant, and include in them many particulars.

Ye may partake of others' sins, by practising, concurring, causing, occasioning, countenancing, not hindering the sins of others.

1. By *practising* the like evils. The apostle seems especially to intend this. Commit not the like sins; act not like the children of disobedience. They are guilty of fornication, vers. 3 and 4, take heed ye tread not in their steps: 'Be ye not,' &c. 2 Kings xvi. 10: King Ahaz, going to Damascus, saw an altar there, and sent the pattern of it, that Uriah the priest might

build one according thereto; and it is said, 2 Chron. xxviii. 23, that 'he sacrificed unto the gods of Damascus.' Here is an evident partaking in those idolaters' sin. Those that give us the best account of that mysterious book, expound that place, Rev. xii. 2, so as by the Gentiles they understand the papists. And these are called Gentiles, because guilty of the like superstitious, idolatrous worship with the Gentiles, in their worshipping of images, and praying to souls departed. They hereby so far partake of their sins as to partake of their name. That is a remarkable instance, Mat. xxiii. 34, 35. The Jews, by persecuting and killing the servants of Christ in their time, became guilty of the blood of God's servants, shed by their fathers in former times. That is the best account we can give why the Lord would bring upon that generation all the righteous blood that had been shed in all generations. By acting the like cruelty with their fathers, they did shew their real approbation of their forefathers' sins. This made them accessory to sins committed before they had a being, so far as they were to suffer for them also, not only for their own personal wickedness. Imitation is a participation; and this clears the justice of God in visiting the sins of fathers upon their children. If children imitate their fathers they partake in their sin; no wonder then if they partake of the plagues due to their fathers' sins.

Some take this as an excuse, &c. But you see how the Lord takes it. If you imitate the sins of ancestors, the Lord may not only charge the guilt of your personal sins, but the guilt of your forefathers' sins, upon your souls. Who would not tremble to hear the Lord Christ threaten to charge the guilt of all former generations upon that one generation? If ye be imitators of them, you are in some sense partakers with them; and so the Lord may justly punish you for them.

Hence we have both precept and example, to confess the sins of our fathers. Command, Lev. xxvi. 39, 40. Example of David, Ps. cvi. 6; of Jeremiah, iii. 25; of Daniel, ix. 5, 6. Now, why confessed, but that they may be forgiven? And forgiven to whom? to forefathers deceased? No, by no means, there is no forgiveness after death. But that they may be forgiven to the living. And why forgiven to them, but that they may be guilty of them. Guilty, then, ye may be of fathers' sins; and how more evidently than by imitation? To imitate is to participate.

2. By *concurring*. A concurrence, though it be but partial, may make thee guilty of sin as an accessory, whoever be the principal in sinning.

Now there may be a sinful concurrence; you may partake of others' sins, by concurring with them, divers ways, and so be guilty of that sin which others act.

(1.) By contriving. When sin is contrived, there is concurrence of the head, though not of the hand. Thus Jezebel was guilty of Naboth's murder, though the elders and nobles of the city were the actors in it. It was her plot, 1 Kings xxi. 9, 10. The guilt of his blood was upon her soul, though her hand was not imbrewed therein; and therefore the Lord threatens that in the very place that was the occasion of her murderous plot the dogs should eat her, ver. 25.

Thus David was guilty of Uriah's death, though Joab was the actor, and the Ammonites the executioners, 2 Sam. xi. 15.

Thus Rebekah of Jacob's dissembling. She contrived it, to defeat Esau, though he was the actor. And if he smarted for it in so many hardships after, she had her share in his chastisement.

Always the contriver is chargeable with a great part of the guilt, if not the greatest. If thou plottest and contrivest how to defraud, how to disparage, defame, how to be revenged, &c. Whoever effect what thou plottest, though thy hand be not in it, though thou be not seen therein, the Lord, who is the searcher of hearts, will charge the sin upon thy soul.

(2.) By consenting. Where there is consent to sin, there is a concurrence of the will, though not of the outward man. This consent is always guilty, whether it be free, so Saul was guilty of Stephen's death, Acts viii. 1; or whether it be extorted, so Pilate was guilty of Christ's death, though the Jews seemed to overrule him thereto; or whether it be tacit, and shewed no way but by silence, *qui tacet, consentire videtur*. If, when anything that is unlawful is propounded, thou givest consent any way, though but as it were unwillingly and with reluctancy; yea, though it be but by silence, that sin is thine, the Lord will charge its guilt on thee, whoever act it.

(3.) By inclination. Where there is an inclination to an unlawful act, there is a concurrence of the heart, though the outward man act not. If thy inclination be such, thou couldest wish in thy heart such or such a wickedness, which others act; though thou dost not contrive it, nor expressly consent to it, nor contribute anything to bring it to pass, yet thy heart is with the actors of it, thou hast a good mind it should be done, this is enough to bring the guilt of it upon thy soul. Instances of this must be sought in our own hearts; it is hard to find them elsewhere, because inclinations are not known but by outward expressions, and so without these are not related. That of Shimei comes near it. It is like he did not contrive Absalom's rebellion, or David's sufferings thereby occasioned, nor is it probable that he was called to give his consent, nor do we find him joining with Absalom in the war, yet his words shew it was the inclination, the desire of his heart, that all this evil should befall David; and this had been enough to make him guilty in the sight of God, though he had never broke forth into such expressions before men. If thy heart be inclined to that which others act in an evil way, even this, if there be nothing else, taints thee with the guilt of their evil actings. The Lord passes sentence according to the motion of the heart, though men judge only outward actions. 'He that lusts after a woman, has committed adultery with her in his heart.' He that desires revenge, does murder the man in his heart, though another do the act without thy consent or knowledge, thy heart concurs, because that is its inclination. And he that concurs with a sinner, so far partakes of his sin.

(4.) By rejoicing. When a man is glad that an unlawful act is done by others, he concurs in affection, though not in action. Thus was Ahab guilty of Naboth's blood. He did not contrive his death, the plot was Jezebel's; nor did he execute it, the fact was done by the nobles and elders of the city. Nay, for anything appears, he knew not of it till it was done; but when he knew of it, he was not sorry for it. His cheerfulness, readiness to take possession, shews he was glad enough that Naboth was dead, 1 Kings xxi. 16. And this makes him so guilty, though he was neither plotter nor actor, as the Lord charges him with killing Naboth, ver. 19, and the threatening falls heaviest upon him, vers. 21, 22.

If thou art glad when others do wickedly, this will make thee guilty of their wickedness. If thou art glad at the losses, disgraces, sufferings of those thou lovest not, though thou be not the oppressor, or the slanderer, or persecutor, though thou art not otherwise than in affection instrumental herein, yet thou art guilty hereof.

(5.) By sentence and vote. He that gives his vote that an unlawful thing shall be done, though others do it, he is guilty of it. Here is a verbal concurrence, though not real. Thus Saul was guilty of Christians' death, Acts

xxvi. 10. His sentence made him guilty, if he had no way pretended to execution. The apostle advises Timothy to beware he partake not of men's sins this way, 1 Tim. v. 22, 'lay hands,' *i.e.* admit no man to the ministry, suddenly, without due examination, without sufficient evidence that he is fitly qualified for that high calling. 'Neither partake,' *i.e.* if others joined with thee, will sin in admitting unworthy persons, and will vote them suddenly into the ministry, who are suspected of scandal or insufficiency; concur not with them, lest hereby thou be partaker of those other men's sins. So it is ordinarily taken; a verbal approbation of that which is unlawful, any expression which shews a liking of that which is sinful, brings a man under the guilt of that sin, whoever act it.

(6.) By assisting. He that contributes anything to the promoting of sin, though he be not the principal actor of it, brings the guilt thereof upon his soul. Thus was Saul also guilty of Stephen's death, Acts vii. 58. He did not cast stones at Stephen; so far as the relation acquaints us, he only kept the clothes of those that stoned him. Yet, promoting this sin but thus far, he made himself guilty of it. Here is a real concurrence, though but partial and inferior.

So Demetrius, and the rest of the silver-smiths, that made shrines for Diana, if they had not joined in the idolatrous worship of that idol, yet their craft tending to promote it in others, had been sufficient to involve them in the guilt of idolatry, Acts xix. 24.

So those tradesmen amongst us, who make use of their professions to nourish pride, drunkenness, voluptuousness, helping them to what they know will be so abused, bring upon themselves the guilt of these sins. Whatever such seem to get hereby, they will find a dreadful score hereafter, when they must be accountable, not only for their own personal sins, but for the sins of multitudes, which, by the abuse of their professions, they have nourished and promoted.

(7.) By communicating in the profits or pleasures of sin. When men are willing others should continue in sin, for the unworthy advantages they reap thereby. Thus panders are guilty of whoredom, though they personally act not uncleanness. So receivers are guilty of theft; 'cast in thy lot amongst us, let us all have one purse;' partaking of the gain, they partake of the sin: Ps. l. 18, 'When thou sawest a thief, then thou consentedest with him, and hast been partaker with adulterers.' So are they, who, for the pleasure they take in uncleanness, care not how many write immodest lines, or speak immodest language.

The masters of the damsel who was possessed with a divining devil, had rather she should have been still in his possession, than they dispossessed of the gains they got thereby; and so were hereby accessory, both to the devil's wickedness, and the damsel's misery.

Thus are they guilty of practising with the devil, who have recourse to those that practise by him; to wizards, or, as ye call them, cunning men. By seeking to these for the recovery of things lost, or the discovery of things secret, you are accessory to their witchcraft, and tainted with the guilt of that league which they have made with the devil, by virtue of which they come to that craft after which you inquire. Which practice, of seeking to wizards, is so clearly condemned, so severely threatened, in Scripture, as none dare use it but such as are ignorant of the word of God, or such as do not regard it. But I may meet with this hereafter. Thus, you see, these seven ways ye partake of other men's sins, by concurrence with them, which is the second general I propounded.

3. By *occasioning* the sins of others. When we give others occasion to sin, and that may be done many ways.

(1.) By evil example. One sin of an exemplary person may occasion many. When magistrates, or ministers, or parents, or masters of families, or any one eminent in the account of others, makes bold with that which is evil, it is a pregnant sin, has many in the bowels of it. We may say of it, 'Behold a troop;' it goes not alone, it has many followers. Such cannot sin at so easy a rate as others, one evil may bring the charge of a thousand upon their souls. Peter's failing in Judaizing, conforming to their ceremonies, withdrawing from the Gentiles, to the infringement of Christian liberty, it involved many in his guilt, and so himself in the guilt of many, Gal. ii. 12, 13. To this day, some encourage themselves in wickedness by the examples of Noah, Lot, David. It was thought wonderful that Abraham should have issue at an hundred years of age. Ay, but evil example is more fruitful; it can occasion sin many hundred, some thousands, of years, after it first appears in the world. Our first parents' sin is fruitful to this hour. Thou knowest not but the bad influence of thy sin may operate many years after thou art dead. Masters of families, and parents especially, should consider this. Those that are under you have their eyes upon you. They are more apt to be led by example than precept; they will do as they see others do before them, not as you bid them, but as you lead them. If parents be given to swearing, tippling, gaming, whoring, scoffing, contention, superstition, &c.; advise your children as much, as seriously as you will; you shall find one ill example do more hurt than a thousand wholesome admonitions will do good. Thy sin may lead others to hell, thy children's children when thou art dead; and will not that which sinks them burden thee? One sin may this way bring along with it the guilt of many thousands.

(2.) By the offensive use of things indifferent. When a professor will go to the utmost line of his liberty, in the use of things lawful in themselves, but of the lawfulness of which others are unsatisfied, this is to stand on the edge of the hill (as Chrysostom calls it). One that is strong possibly may stand there safely; but a weak one thereby encouraged to follow him, may be carried headlong. Is it not better not to go so high, than to endanger the ruin of others by following thee?

Two great questions there were of this nature in the apostle's time; the apostle gives many cautions in the use of liberty about them. One was, whether it was lawful to eat things sacrificed to idols. The intelligent sort of Christians then were persuaded to eat them, when sold in the shambles, or used in civil feasts. The weaker sort did not so well understand their liberty herein, were not satisfied that it was lawful. Now see what advice he gives to the intelligent, 1 Cor. viii. 8. This is indifferent, and you have liberty to use them, to eat these things; but, ver. 9, if one that is not satisfied be encouraged (by seeing thee use this liberty) to eat with a doubting conscience, the use of thy liberty becomes a stumbling-block to the weak, occasions him to fall into sin, by doing that which he is doubtful of.

Another question was, about the indifferent use of meats, whether it was lawful to eat what was forbidden by the ceremonial law. The more knowing Christians were satisfied of its lawfulness; the weak sort doubted. The apostle gives the like caution in this case, Rom. xiv. 20. Why evil? Since it was lawful in itself, why, says he, it is evil to thee, because it occasions sin in others. It caused the weak to stumble; they, following the practice of the strong, when they doubted of the lawfulness of the practice, did stumble, did sin, doing it with a doubting conscience, for, ver. 23, he cautions them in using all things that are lawful; this may be an occasion to others of doing many things unlawful, and their guilt this way will reach thee.

The apostle advises to avoid all appearance of evil. *Quicquid male fuerit coloratum.* For that which has but a show of evil in itself may occasion a real evil in another, and so he that committed but evil in show may be tainted with a real guilt.

(3.) By scandalous sins, either in judgment or practice; for these are not only abominable in themselves, and the occasions of sin in others by example, but also in a more dangerous and dreadful way, by strengthening the hands of sinners, and opening their mouths to blaspheme.

Those that are guilty of the licentious opinions and practices of these times, besides that guilt, heavy enough to sink them deep into hell, they also contract the guilt of the blood of those souls, who are hereby hardened against the ministry of the word, against the providence of God, in their old profane superstitious courses. They contract also the guilt of that blasphemy, whereby the name of the great God is dishonoured, and the holy ways of Christ disparaged. This is your preciseness, and this is your Reformation! See the issue of it. Is it not better to keep in the old way, than to run mad in the new? So profane persons cry out, so blind wickedness casts dirt upon the strict profession of Christ and his holy ways, because some apostates have left the way that was too good, too strict for them. But the Lord will judge righteous judgment, and stop the mouth of profaneness in his own time. In the mean time, woe be to them to open it, that put these words into profane mouths, and give occasion to such blasphemies. Offences must come, but woful will it be, both for those that give them, and for those that take them.

David's sins were highly sinful in themselves, but there was a sinfulness, besides those heinous facts, which the Lord would not pass by, when he pardoned them, 2 Sam. xii. 13, 14. David's adultery and murder drew along with it the guilt of blasphemy; not that he blasphemed, but because he occasioned others to do it; and for this he must smart, and so must they, &c.

Take heed of scandalous evils: they usually occasion greater sins than themselves, and bring upon the actor a greater guilt than that of his personal acts.

(4.) By provoking. He that says or does that which provokes another to sin, is at least the occasion of it; and hereby, besides the guilt of the provocation, brings upon himself the guilt of the sin to which the sinner is provoked. Hence the apostle advises so often to beware of this, Gal. v. 26, Eph. vi. 4. It does not cease to be sin, because you are provoked to it; no, it is more sinful, because more sin therein, both the provoker and the provoked. The Lord shews who provoked Ahab, when he is aggravating his sin; so far is provocation from extenuating a sin, 1 Kings xxi. 25. He that provokes another to pride, by overvaluing expressions; or to lust, by filthy speeches; or to wrath and revenge, by incensing words; or wordliness, by covetous suggestions, he brings upon himself both the guilt of these sins, and the effects of them, whoever act them.

(5.) By ensnaring. Those whose garb, gestures, words, are as snares, may justly be accounted occasions of sin, and so guilty of those iniquities wherein they ensnare others. We read of the whoredoms of Jezebel, 2 Kings ix 22. And no wonder, since we read of her painting, ver. 30. Where there is the occasion, usually there is the sin; every one avoids not the snare. Tamar's whorish habit and posture was the occasion of Judah's sin, it was a snare to him, Gen. xxxviii. 14. Her guilt was double, both involved in the guilt of her own wickedness, and that of his, which she thereby occasioned. The apostle shews what direct snares, dangers, there are in words to occasion sin, 1 Cor. xv. 33. Corrupt, immodest, and such like evil communication, it is as sparks scattered amongst powder, a wonder if none take fire, if this be not an occasion of kindling an hell of lust, or other wickedness in the hearts of the hearers. But while this kindles others, he that throws abroad such sparks shall not escape scorching; the guilt is chargeable upon him as the occasion.

(6.) By leading others into temptations. So not only the devil, but men, therein like him, occasion sin, and draw the guilt of others' wickedness, so occasioned, upon themselves also. There are incarnate tempters, and such who do but expose others to temptations. So those that engage others in the company of debauched, unclean, drunken companions, are accessory to their wickedness if the temptation prevail. So those that lead others amongst seducers, if they catch infection, are answerable for it, even as he that leads another to a pest-house, if he die of the plague, is accessory to his death.

Those that present tempting objects to others, if they take, occasion the sin, and are guilty as well as the actor.

Thus was Eve guilty, not only of her own, but of her husband's sin, Gen. iii. 6. Thus men partake of others' sins when they occasion them, and occasion them by leading others into temptation.

(7.) By shewing opportunities to sin. This is evidently to give occasion, and so to partake. Thus Judas was guilty of crucifying Christ, by shewing the Jews an opportunity to apprehend and crucify him. Thus the Ziphites were guilty of Saul's intended cruelty against David, by shewing him an opportunity to execute it, discovering where he was hid, 1 Sam. xxiii. 19, 20. So those that shew others opportunities to fulfil their lusts, or satisfy their revenge, or get unjust gain, or gratify any other lust, are thereby accessory to their sin, and partakers with them.

(8.) By affording matter of sin to others, that which they know or suspect will be sinfully abused, hereby occasion their sin, and partake in their guilt. Cyprian, lib. iii. ep. 16, writing to the elders and deacons of the church, reproves them sharply for admitting some to communicate before they sufficiently testified their repentance; tells them hereby they furthered the ruin of such sinners, *ut magis pereant, et plus cadant;* and that the elders thus admitting such were hereby many ways guilty, *erunt autem rei qui præsunt*, &c. They contracted guilt, by not shewing the danger of such communicating, by not hindering such from it. As those who are grossly ignorant, or evidently live in gross sins, do, by intruding, eat and drink their own damnation, so those that admit such are hereby accessory to their damnation, and guilty of their profaneness. As when a dish or a potion, which will prove healthful to some, poison to others, is promiscuously offered to all, he that offers it is accessory to the death of those that are poisoned by it. Nor can this guilt be avoided by any, till a course be submitted to, by which, according to Scripture rules, it may be known competently who are fit, who are unfit, to whom it may be the seal of life, to whom it may be the savour of death.

If you be fearful of being accessory to the temporal death of any, should not we be fearful of being accessory to the eternal death of any?

So those also that afford others matter, which will be abused to drunkenness, gluttony, &c., they are thereby guilty of the intemperance of others, being this way the occasion of it.

(9.) By not removing the occasions of sin. He that can and may remove those things which are the occasions of others' sins, and does not, is thereby the occasion of other men's sins, and so partaker with them.

The Lord has a controversy with divers of the kings of Judah, because the high places were not taken away, not because they did worship there, but because they being not removed, others did worship there, 1 Kings xv. 14, Asa; 2 Kings xii. 3, xiv. 4, xv. 4. The continuance of them was the occasion of others' sin, and they who had power, not removing them, did thereby partake of others' sins, and are therefore charged, condemned as guilty.

Things lawful, if indifferent (not necessary) when they are abused, and become occasions of sin, should be taken away. The brazen serpent, when the Israelites abused it to idolatry, though it was set up by Moses, and reserved as a monument, a memorial of their deliverance from the fiery serpents in the wilderness, yet when it became an occasion of sin it was broken in pieces, and Hezekiah is commended for breaking of it, 2 Kings xviii. 4. When the love feasts in the primitive church were abused to intemperance, the apostle regulates them.

Many indifferent things abused by the papists to superstition are upon this account excluded in the reformed churches, and retaining of some such amongst us, we find by experience has been of very ill consequence, and some can read the guilt of those who would not remove them, in the late sad providences wherewith this land has been exercised, though others will not open their eyes to see, nor their ears to hear the rod, and he that appoints it.

When costly apparel becomes an occasion of pride, or delicate fare an occasion of intemperance, &c. Those that have power, magistrates, parents, should reduce them to necessaries, who abuse superfluities, else they are in danger of a participation in others' guilt. I might exemplify this in many particulars.

(10.) By authorising. When those are put into such place and office, as they are not fit, not qualified for, those that are instrumental in calling them thereto are accessory to their sinful miscarriages in the managing thereof.

This is evident, especially in the great callings of magistracy and ministry; and guilt may be herein contracted, either by interposal of authority in magistrates, or by the intervening of election and votes in the people. When places, which require men fearing God, hating covetousness, dealing truly, are filled with irreligious, covetous, unjust officers, those that are instruments to promote such are accessory to their sins.

So for ministry. It was Jeroboam's brand that he made priests of the meanest of the people, 1 Kings xii. 31. When people choose one scandalous in his life, erroneous in judgment, insufficient, unqualified in other respects of his life or holiness, they are guilty of the blood of their souls thereby endangered, though he be principal therein.

Accordingly, some give account of the apostle's words formerly quoted, 1 Tim. v. 22. Take heed of admitting such into the ministry, who are unworthy, unqualified, not apt to teach, not able to convince gainsayers, not exemplary in their lives, not holding the form of wholesome words. And be not partaker; for hereby, if thou authorise, admit such, thou wilt be partaker of their sins. If any perish through their ignorance and insufficiency; if any be tainted with their errors, superstitions; if any be led to or encouraged in wickedness by their evil example: it is the sin of the blind, profane guides; but thou hereby wilt be partaker of their sin, and accessory to the ruin of those souls, for he is the occasion who brings in the cause. Their blood will be principally required at their hands, but in the second place at thine, who was instrumental to bring such into place: of them as the cause, of thee as the occasion, of them as principals, of thee as accessory; of them as actors, of thee as partaker. This is the tenth way of being guilty of others' sins as an occasion, which is the third general way of partaking of other men's sins.

4. By *causing*, He that is the cause of another's sin, partakes thereof; not only as an accessory, but many times as a principal. Now one may be the cause of another's sin many ways.

(1.) By commanding. He that commands, enjoins another to do that which is unlawful, is the cause of his sin, and so sometimes more deeply guilty than the actor; especially if the obedience to those commands proceed rather from the authority of the commander than from the disposition of him that obeys. This holds both in public and private.

In public; so those that enact things evil and unwarrantable, by laws and edicts, they involve themselves in the guilt of all that obey them. This is the highway to make sins national, and so make whole nations ripe for judgment; both magistrates and people being hereby tainted with guilt of rebellion against God. Hence the Lord denounces a woe against such decrees, and threatens desolation for them, universal calamities, of equal extent with the guilt, Isa. x. 1, 3.

Such were the statutes of Omri, whereby he enjoined the people to walk in the ways of Jeroboam, Micah vi. 16. Omri was dead, and so was Ahab, yet the people's observances of their wicked injunctions are called the works of the house of Ahab. Ahab and his house were answerable for the people's offences herein, as though they had been Ahab's works. Why, Omri and Ahab's statutes were the cause of the people's sin, 1 Kings xvi. 25, 26. Micah prophesied in the days of some kings, who repealed the wicked statutes of Omri; yet the statutes and works of Omri and Ahab are still remembered, and desolation threatened. If a people will observe idolatrous or superstitious customs, though the laws enjoining them be repealed, yet will the Lord remember the guilt of such law-givers, and bring desolation upon the observers of them: 'That I should make thee a desolation.'

This is true also in private commands; thus Saul was guilty of the murder of the priests, and the destruction of Nob their city, by commanding Doeg to execute that cruelty, 1 Sam. xxii. 18, 19. And there we have an example, shewing what must be done in case things unlawful be commanded, ver. 17. A king is not to be obeyed in unlawful commands; disobedience in this case is obedience in the sight of God.

Thus David was guilty of Uriah's death, for though he did but give the command, yet he is charged with the sin as much as if his own hand had murdered him: 2 Sam. xii. 9, 'Thou hast killed.'

So when masters command their servants, or parents their children, to lie, or to defraud others, or to profane the Sabbath, &c., both they sin in obeying, and the commanders are guilty in their disobedience; they are the cause of their sin by commanding, and so partake in their guilt, yea, are principals herein.

(2.) By threatening. He that threatens another, that he may thereby fear him to do that which is unlawful, is the cause of his sin, and so principal therein. Thus was Nebuchadnezzar guilty of all their idolatry, who were drawn by his threatenings to bow to his golden image, Dan. iii. 6. This threatening involved him in the guilt of all the people, nations, and languages that fell down, &c. One word, one sentence, may make a man guilty of millions of sins.

Thus persecutors are guilty of the grievous crime of those who fall off from the ways of truth and holiness, and also of the destruction of those who are hindered from entering into those ways, for fear of what they threaten. So some wicked men will threaten their children, or those that depend on them, if they will be so strict, precise, conscientious, so much in praying, reading, following sermons; if they will not walk in the same ways of looseness, superstition, with their fathers, they shall not have their favour, their countenance, nor share in their estates; they shall be cast off or disinherited. Now, if hereby they be drawn off from ordinances, holy duties, society with the people of God, strict or holy walking, they shall die in their sins, but their blood will be required at the hands of those whose threatenings was the cause of their sin.

(3.) By counselling and persuading. He that gives another evil counsel is guilty of his sin, if he bring it into action; or if it go not so far, he is guilty so far as it proceeds towards action. Whatever sinful influence thy persuasion has upon any one, thou art tainted with the guilt of him whom thou persuadest or counsellest. Thus Jonadab was guilty of Tamar's ravishment, though Amnon was the ravisher, because he was the counsellor, 2 Sam. xiii. 5. He counsels him to take this course to satisfy his lust, and so is equal in the guilt. Thus Ahithophel was guilty of Absalom's incest, because he advised him to it, 2 Sam. xvi. 21. Thus Athaliah was guilty of Ahaziah's wickedness, because she was his counsellor, 2 Chron. xxii. 3–5. A counsellor to sin is a partaker of the sin to which he advises; a persuader to wickedness is a principal therein, as being the cause thereof.

(4.) By alluring. He that entices another to that which is sinful, by promising any advantage in sinning, or proposing hopes of profit, pleasure, or credit thereby, so far as his enticements are effectual to draw others to sin, so far he sins with them. For this see Prov. i. 10, if they entice thee with hopes of gain, as ver. 13.

So the strange woman allures with hopes of pleasure, Prov. vii. 18. The force of such allurements, that they are cause of sin, ver. 21; such enticements have cast down many wounded, yea, many strong men have been slain thereby, as ver. 26; these are the way to hell, going down to the chambers of death, ver. 27. Such enticers, by destroying others, bring the guilt of their ruin upon their own heads.

So when they allure others in hopes of secrecy,—none shall perceive it, none shall be the wiser;—or in hopes of safety,—men shall not know, and so have no occasion to censure or punish, shall never find it out;—and God is merciful, he will not be so strict, so severe, as to damn his creature for one sin, for such a sin;—or by the example of others,—such and such, better than thou have done the like or worse things, and why shouldest thou scruple at it?

Satan, the master of this art of enticing, proceeded at first in such a method, in alluring to the first sin, as sinners have since learned of him: Gen. iii. 4, 'Ye shall not surely die.' Here he promises safety, notwithstanding the Lord had threatened it with death, yet he assures them of safety, no such danger for all this, &c. He proceeds, ver. 5, and promises advantage, your eyes, &c. He promises advancement too: ' as gods.' See how cunningly the arch-enticer baits his hook, and then see how it takes: ver. 6, 'Good for food,' there is the profit; 'and pleasant,' there is the delight.' 'To make one wise,' there is an higher advantage. Here is the effect of one enticement; they sin, the whole world sins in them, and the allurer sins in all, and so is cursed above all. The enticer to sin is always involved in the guilt of the sinner, and so in his suffering.

(5.) By deriding. Scoffing at scrupulousness and conscientiousness in avoiding sin. Jeer and abuse men because they follow not such practices, use not such language; because they fear an oath, or keep not company, or observe not their unwarrantable customs. Brand such as precisians or hypocrites, and so by discouraging a holy care to avoid sin, do what they can to make men careless in sinning. I remember not an instance of this nature in Scripture, neither amongst the Jews in the Old Testament, nor amongst Christians in the New. The more it is to be lamented that such wickedness should be found amongst us, as the history of so many hundred years does not afford an example of. Such scoffers do what in them is to open a floodgate of sin in others, and overwhelm themselves in the guilt of it, Isa. xxviii. 22.

(6.) By boasting of sin. Some there are who are risen up to such a height of desperate wickedness, as they will sometimes brag of it, and glory in their shame. 'Why boastest,' &c., Ps. xciv. 4. Some will boast of their uncleanness, that they have defiled others; of their intemperance, that they are strong, Isa. v. 22; of their exceeding and overcoming others in drinking; of their craft and deceit (or wisdom, as they call it) in circumventing and over-reaching others; of their contentiousness, in wearying, silencing others.

Now this boasting of sin as though it were their glory, may be an encouragement, an inducement to embolden others in such wickedness, and so by causing others to sin, though their own guilt be unsupportable, they burden themselves, their souls, with the guilt of others.

(7.) By hiring others to sin. Thus Satan assaulted Christ: 'All these things,' &c., Mat. iv. 8, 9. Thus the Jews were guilty of betraying Christ, by hiring Judas to betray him. So are they guilty of perjury who suborn witnesses, as Jezebel in the case of Naboth. It is reported of the wicked Arian bishops, that when they could not otherwise prevail against Athanasius, that zealous defender of the truth, they hired a lewd woman to come openly into the council and accuse him of committing filthiness with her. In this case, she was the false accuser indeed, but they were principally guilty of the false accusation.

So those that encourage, reward others for publishing slanders, or raising false reports of those they love not, whoever be the instruments, the guilt will be charged upon them who plainly, or by interpretation, do as much as hire them.

So are those guilty of witchcraft who reward such as practise with the devil for discovery of secrets, or recovery of things lost; such rewarding is a hiring of them still to be familiar with the prince of darkness.

So Judah was doubly guilty, both in his own person and in Tamar's; both by committing lewdness with her, and hiring her to it.

Thus you see how many ways we may partake with others in their sins, by causing them. This is the fourth general.

5. By *countenancing* the sins of others. He that is a countenancer of others' sins, is a partaker of other men's sin; and that sometimes of sins past, sometimes of future sins. Now ye may countenance the sins of others, and so be accessory to them, many ways.

(1.) By defending them. He that defends, secures sinners from censure and punishments; does countenance them, and so partakes with them. Thus the Benjamites were guilty of that horrible wickedness which was committed by the men of Gibeah. The sin of one town involved the whole tribe in its guilt, because when justice was demanded against those sons of Belial, they refused to deliver them up to justice, they engaged themselves to protect, to secure them from punishment, Judges xx. 12–14. Now, what was the issue? As they made the sin of those sons of Belial their own, by appearing in the defence of it, so the punishment of those sons of Belial fell upon them. That numerous tribe, which consisted of so many thousands, were all destroyed, man, woman, and child, except six hundred, ver. 47. It was but the inhabitants of one town that were the actors of that wickedness, but all the towns, cities, and inhabitants were destroyed for this sin, because all partaked of it by defending it.

That sin which thou defendest by word or deed thereby becomes thine, whoever be the actor of it. Those that defend blasphemers, would not have them censured, proceeded against, thereby become guilty of their blasphemy.

Those that plead for such as the word of God censures, be their wickedness in judgment or manners, they are accessories to it, tainted with the like guilt, in danger of the same punishment.

(2.) By justifying others' sins. Denying that to be sinful which the word condemns, and that to be error which is contrary to gospel truth. Thus do some justify not only the wicked, but their wickedness, which, how sinful it is, the Lord declares, Prov. xvii. 15. If ye quit those whom the Lord condemns, plead for that against which the Lord has given sentence, be it with what arguments or distinctions soever, it is an abomination; it is so in itself, and it is withal a partaking of those sins of others, which are hereby countenanced.

Those that call evil good, or darkness light, or error truth, or superstition devotion, or will-worship religion, or cruelty justice, there is a woe denounced against this, Isa. v. 20. Christ foretells of some that would count the persecution of the apostles the doing of God good service, John xvi. 1. And some call that popish superstition, in placing holiness in times and places, where the Lord never placed it, an act of religion; count the doctrines and traditions of men the worship of God, as the Pharisees; abstinence from marriage holiness, and abstinence from meats, mortification. The apostle has another name for it, 2 Tim. iv. 1–3.

So some justify the calling in question of truths clearly revealed, under the notion of love to the truth, fear to be deceived.

So others justify many gross errors under the notion of new discovered truths, plead for a boundless licentiousness under the notion of Christian liberty, or liberty of conscience; so some call the impudence of others good breeding, and the profuseness liberality, a joining with drunken companions good fellowship.

Now suppose ye be not personally guilty of such wickedness in judgment or practice, yet if ye justify them in others under such names or notions, in these or the like ways, giving them terms improper for them, colouring them over as good, which are in themselves evil, this is a countenancing them. Whoever be the actors, this makes you accessories. If thou justify those that sin, thyself art condemned as guilty of that from which thou wouldst acquit others.

(3.) By extenuating of others' sins. Those that make sin less than it is, and excuse it when it should be aggravated, when those that are guilty are insensible of the guilt and sinfulness of their evil, this is a dangerous countenancing of sin, and that which makes the excuser guilty with the actor. So some, too much inclining to popery, will excuse the papists; their idolatries must not be counted superstitions, and their heresies but errors in smaller matters. So amongst carnal people, petty oaths must be counted but idle words and thoughts free, and riotousness and uncleanness tricks of youth. Many distinctions, pleas, pretences, excuses, are found out to mince and lessen sin, when the least is great enough to sink body and soul into hell. Some excuse it from custom; he does but as others do, and shall he be singular? from age, he is but young, and youth will have its swing; from nature, we have all corrupt natures, and it will break out one time or other; from example, they do but as our forefathers before us, and shall we be so uncharitable as to think them damned? from education, excuse ignorance, they are not book-learned, want the means; from intention, though he have done ill, he means no hurt; from calling, excuse the neglect of their souls, much ado to live, and 'he is worse than an infidel that provides not,' &c.; from event or success, it proves well, and he prospers notwithstanding, and therefore God is not much offended, Jer. xliv. 11.

These, and many other fig-leaves, do men find out to cover the deformity; and though they make use of them to hide their own for the most part, yet sometimes, especially if they be concerned, they will find some for others.

It is true it is a duty to cover the failings and infirmities of others, but then they must be failings indeed. We must not make that small which is great, nor excuse them who are too ready to excuse themselves, and make little of that which they make nothing of.

To excuse sin in the presence of the sinner, when he is not sensible of, not burdened with his guilt, is to countenance his sin, and to encourage him in sinning, and to make thyself accessory to his wickedness. To excuse sin before those who are like to make use of it, so as to continue in impenitency, or to make bold with that which is extenuated and excused, is a most dangerous countenancing of sin, tending not only to make others guilty, but thyself with them.

(4.) By commending. When others are applauded for their sins, then is sin countenanced in a high degree; *e.g.* when those that will not forgive injuries, engage themselves in unjust quarrels, public or private, are commended as men of valour and courage; when wicked politicians are cried up for men of singular wisdom; when approaching to God by mediation of saints and angels is commended for humility, and men's inventions in the service of God is applauded as voluntary worship and free-will offerings; when rejecting of ordinances is cried up as a less formal, more spiritual way of worship; when curious and dangerous opinions are admired as deep and profound mysteries, Rev. ii. 24. The doctrines which Jezebel, who called herself a prophetess, did then vent in the church, were called 'depths,' profound things, high attainments, but Christ tells what depths they were in his account; they spoke them depths, he calls them 'depths of Satan.'

To put a commendable name upon any sin or error, is a dangerous countenancing of it; to commend the wicked as righteous, whether they be so in respect of gross or of more refined and spiritual wickedness, is a countenancing of, and so a partaking with, that wickedness, Prov. xxi. 24. And well may the people curse, and the nations abhor him; because by thus countenancing the wicked, he encourages people and nations in wickedness, to their destruction. And he had need curse and abhor himself too, because as he involves others in guilt by countenancing, so himself in the guilt of all that he countenances.

(5.) By conniving at others' sin. Not declaring the danger and sinfulness of them as occasion is offered, not shewing our abhorrence and detestation of them, as becomes those who have tender consciences, who tender the honour of Christ and the souls of men. This is a tacit countenancing of such wickedness; silence in that case may be interpreted as approbation.

When we hear that Christ is blasphemed, his ordinances trampled under foot; when the prevailing delusions of Satan are related to us, the scandalous practices, the woful miscarriage, of those who bear the name of Christ; when we hear such things as should make our ears tingle and our hearts tremble, and are not accordingly affected therewith; when these are slighted, passed by as matters of small moment, especially when they are turned into matter of sport and merriment, which should not be heard or spoken of but with bleeding hearts and trembling spirits; they are hereby in some degree countenanced, when they are not, as they ought to be, detested.

When others see such carriage in those that pretend love to Christ and the things of Christ, and see them no more affected therewith, they have hereby occasion to think, Surely there is not so much evil in these opinions or practices, else they would be more laid to heart by those who seem conscientious otherwise; and by imagining them less (because they see them by us less detested), they may become more inclinable to them, more ready to close with the prevailing temptations of the times. So that this silent countenancing of such abominations, may occasion the fall of others thereinto; and so we may contract a double guilt of these abominations, by countenancing them where they are, and occasioning them where they are not. Oh what guilt is daily contracted by this silent countenancing of those horrid evils we daily hear of!

(6.) *By company.* You may countenance wickedness by too much associating yourselves with those that are guilty of it.

It is true there is some converse necessary, and we must do offices of love to all, and the good of their souls should be endeavoured as long as there is hope and opportunity of doing them good; and this may be done, if prudence and circumspection be used, without countenancing their sin; but there is an unnecessary society, a too much familiarity, which is dangerous. When we make those who are noted for wickedness, in judgment or practice, our companions, our familiars, this may be interpreted a countenancing of their wickedness.

If you would deal faithfully with them and your own souls, according to the rule of the gospel, you should seriously admonish them; if admonitions be rejected, or they not thereby reclaimed, then they are to be avoided, 2 Thes. iii. 14. Those Athenians are commended who would not wash in the same bath with the persecutors of Socrates; and it is reported of the apostle John, that when Cerinthus, a noted heretic in the apostle's time, came into the bath where John was, he presently left the place, would not be where Cerinthus was. And Polycarp, the apostle John's disciple, when Marcion saluted him, and asked if he knew him, Yes, says Polycarp, I know thee, thou first-born of the devil. And that was all the countenance he would give that impostor.

You know how the Lord resents it, that Jehoshaphat would associate himself with Ahab; and that expostulation which he puts into the mouth of the seer is very pathetical, 2 Chron. xix. 2. And he is afflicted also for joining with Ahaziah, chap. xx. 37. Why, but what danger was there in this familiarity? This; those that knew Jehoshaphat to be a good king, walking in the commandments of the Lord; and seeing him choose Ahab for his familiar, might thence conclude, Surely the ways of Ahab are not so abominable, else good Jehoshaphat could not be so intimate with him. And thus the bad opinion of Ahab being something taken off, they might be more inclinable to comply with him in his ways and worship; and thus might Jehoshaphat's familiarity with Ahab be a snare to others. *Noscitur ex socio.* We know we judge of a man by his companion, and men are apt to think we approve of those whom we choose for our familiars; and so by your company you may countenance wickedness, and thereby partake of it, though ye never act it.

(7.) *By rejoicing.* Those that take pleasure in the sins of others, do hereby make themselves partakers of their sins; so did they, of whom the apostle, Rom. i. 32.

So are they guilty of uncleanness, who, though they do not act it, yet take pleasure to hear or read of the uncleanness of others.

So they are guilty of participation, who are glad when others run with them to the same excess of riot; when others join with them in the same ways of error, superstition, or profaneness. Besides their personal guilt in acting those sins, they are guilty of the sins of their associates, by rejoicing in them.

So those that rejoice in the effects of others' sins, are glad that those whom they hate are oppressed, disgraced, undone by others. So the Edomites, insulting over the Jews in their sufferings and miseries, involved themselves thereby in the guilt of the Chaldeans' cruelties, which was the principal cause of those miseries, Obadiah, ver. 11, 12.

Thus you see how many ways we may be guilty of other men's sins, by countenancing them. You may countenance others' sin, and so partake of it, by defending, justifying, extenuating, commending, &c.

6. By *not hindering* sin. He that hinders not others from sinning, is in danger thereby to partake of their sins. It is a received rule, Qui non prohibet, facit. He that hinders not others from doing evil, does the evil himself; is guilty of, accessory to it. Only those two cautions must be added to limit the rule, cum potest et debet. He that hinders not sin when he can and should hinder it, is guilty of it. He that has both ability and authority, both power and a call to exercise it (as there are few men but have in one way, degree, or other), he is guilty of the sin he hinders not.

Indeed, if a man do all that in him lies to hinder sin, and yet it is committed, the guilt will lie upon the actor, thou art blameless, or if thou dost all that thou art called to, to hinder it; for every one is not called to act alike in all ways and degrees for hindering sin; some are called to more than others. Children and servants are not required to do that for the hindering of sin, which is the duty of parents and masters; nor are the people called to act against sin in the same way as ministers; nor are ministers called to act in the same way as magistrates. But it is the duty of all these to endeavour the hindering of others' sins, in ways which the Lord has assigned to them, and by means proper to their several degrees and places.

Now, those that do not, in their several spheres and stations, endeavour to hinder sin by all means proper to them and required of them, they thereby become accessory to, guilty of, the sins which they hinder not. And thus men may partake of the sins of others many ways.

(1.) By not punishing, censuring, correcting, in state, church, families. He that proceeds not against the sin of others according to the rules of the word, or laws agreeable thereto, makes himself guilty of it.

Thus magistrates are guilty when they execute not wholesome laws for the punishment of evil-doers. Thus Pilate involved himself in the guilt of Barabbas's murder, by acquitting him whom he should have executed, Mar. xv. 15. Thus the kings of Judah were accessory to the people's superstitions and idolatrous worship, though they be commended as upright in other things, because they tolerated and suffered the people to offer in the high places, 2 Kings. xii. 3.

Magistrates are appointed to be ministers of God, that they may be a terror to evil works, and revengers to execute, &c., Rom. xiii. 3, 4. That evil work which he is not a terror to he is guilty of. For this end he bears the sword, that those under him may be afraid to sin, and that the fear of suffering by him should be a restraint from sin. When he does not thus improve his power, the restraint is taken off, and sinners grow bold. 'Because sentence,' &c.

This is the end of that great ordinance, and of the execution of justice, Deut. xiii. 11. The Lord commands that seducers, though they seem prophets, pretend visions, and work wonders, ver. 1, shall be put to death, ver. 6, 9. And when justice is thus executed upon seducers, the Lord promises two happy issues and effects of such severity: all Israel shall hear and fear, ver. 11, and the evil shall be put away from them, ver. 5. It shall be put away, ye shall not be accessory to, charged with the guilt of it. Whereas by the rule of contraries it follows, where such evil is tolerated, such seducers suffered, evil continues in the midst of a people; and being not put away, is chargeable upon them who tolerate it, suffer it to continue.

The fear of thus partaking with others' sins made the ten tribes resolute to punish the supposed idolatry of their brethren with the sword, Josh. xxii. The children of Reuben, Gad, and Manasseh built an altar upon the borders of Jordan. The rest of the tribes, conceiving they had built it to offer sacrifice, contrary to the Lord's command, who had enjoined them to offer no sacrifice but in the place chosen and appointed by himself, hereupon, to free themselves from their guilt, they resolved to proceed against them in battle, ver. 12; and they declare the reason of it, ver. 18. Wrath will fall, not only upon you, but upon us, because, if we tolerate this, we shall be guilty of it, and so punished for it. Wrath will fall upon all; for, though you be principals, yet we, by suffering it, shall be accessories, and being hereby involved in the guilt, shall be involved in the punishment. And they prove it by an instance, ver. 20. And it is an argument from the less to the greater. If the whole congregation fall under the wrath of God for Achan's sin when they know not of it, much more shall we, if, knowing your sin, we tolerate it, and proceed not against it. The zeal of the Israelites, this jealousy over their brethren, is recorded to their praise, and if they had thus continued, they had not been overspread with guilt, nor overwhelmed with public calamities.

Men of place and office have much to answer for the sins of others. If all the excrements in a town should be laid at their doors, they would look on it as an high affront, a great displeasure. How much more grievous will it be to have the sins of towns and countries laid at their doors, charged upon their souls as guilty of them, by not hindering them, by not punishing and proceeding against them!

Thus churches may be guilty of the sin of a particular member, by not censuring the sin, and proceeding against the offender according to gospel rules.

Paul exhorts the church of Corinth to proceed against the incestuous Corinthian, to put away from among them that wicked person, to deliver him up unto Satan, 1 Cor. v. And he gives this reason, ver. 6. The leaven, which is but a little at present, being but in one person, it may diffuse its guilt through the whole church, may leaven the whole lump. If they tolerated this wickedness, they would be leavened by it, tainted with its guilt; therefore he urges, ver. 7, to purge it out.

Though Christ commend the church of Pergamos for many things, yet he has a controversy with her for tolerating those that taught false doctrine and loose practices, Rev. ii. 14, 15. And all the works, charity, service, faith, patience, of Thyatira, with her increase in these, could not exempt her from Christ's censure for tolerating false teachers and seducers, ver. 19, 20.

Thus masters are guilty of servants' sins, and parents partake of their children's sins, if they correct them not for sinning; if they suffer them to lie, swear, profane the Sabbath, neglect the ordinances, without correction. 'He that spareth,' &c., 'he hates his child;' for what greater sign of hatred, than to let him run on without let in that which will ruin both soul and body? He hates himself, too, by bringing his soul under the guilt of that sin, which he hinders not by correcting the sinner for it.

He that, according to his place and calling, does not punish, censure, correct sin, is accessory to it by not hindering of it.

(2.) By not complaining of sin. He that has not power to punish sin, may complain of it to those that have power; and he that complains not, is in danger to be accessory to the sin which he conceals.

I confess there are many temptations to keep men from the practice of this duty. It is counted odious to be an accuser; and so it is, when it proceeds from spite, malice, and revenge, and not from tenderness to the glory of God and thy brother's soul; but against the temptations which may hinder thee from complaining of other sins, set the danger of sin to him, to thee, and the command of God; see how strictly and punctually he enjoins it, without respect of persons and relations, how near and dear soever, Deut. xiii. 6, 8. And it is prophesied there shall be such zeal in the times of the gospel, as the Lord here requires under the law; see Zech. xiii. 3. And whereas it may be objected, If I should complain to magistrates, and cause open offenders to be punished, this is the way to be hated; it is answered, ver. 6, if the sinner be thereby reclaimed, he will be so far from hating thee as an enemy, as he will look on thee as a friend. What are these wounds? How comest thou to suffer at the hand of justice? Then he shall answer, &c., Those that occasioned them, inflicted them, were friends to me in so doing; they were friends to my soul, hindered me from that which would have ruined it.

There are many wholesome laws in force amongst us for the punishing of drunkenness, swearing, Sabbath-breaking, wizards, and other crying sins, for which the land mourns. The magistrate has discharged his duty in enacting these; justice cannot lay hold of them if they be not complained of. Where, then, will the guilt of this unrestrained wickedness lie, but upon those who conceal them; upon those who fear, or favour wicked men, more than they regard the favour or displeasure of the righteous God? Who will run the hazard of their own souls, and the souls of those sinners, rather than offend them, by bringing them to that shame or suffering, that might restrain them from sin. Oh what cause have we to be ashamed of, and humbled for our guilt in this particular! How heavy is it; how universal is it!

It is true, where private admonitions will prevail, and church censures may be had, these are first to be made use of; but where that is not regarded, or these cannot be exercised, if thou complainest not, thou art accessory to the sin which thou concealest, and mayest be involved in the same punishment. We read, 2 Sam. xxi., there was a famine in Canaan for three years; David inquires of the Lord what was the cause of it. He answers, it is because Saul slew the Gibeonites. The sin was Saul's, and his house; and it is not probable the Lord would make so many suffer for his sin, but that they were some way accessory to it; and how more likely than because they did not inform David of the Gibeonites' unjust sufferings, that so justice might be executed on the offenders? We see, when this was done, the famine ceased.

He that conceals sin from justice, when he is called to inform of it, is accessory to it; for he does not what in him lies to hinder it.

It may be thou art no blasphemer, nor seducer, no swearer, or drunkard, or open Sabbath-breaker; it is well. But dost thou not conceal these wickednesses? Dost thou not neglect to complain of them, that they may be discouraged, restrained, when thou art called to it? Why, this is enough to make thee accessory to these sins; thou dost not what thou canst to hinder them.

(3.) By not reproving or admonishing sinners. He that rebukes not, nor does not admonish, according to the quality of those who are guilty, makes himself guilty with them, Lev. xix. 17. To reprove another is a thankless office, and carnal men take it as an expression of hatred; but see how the Lord judges of it: 'He that rebukes not his brother does hate him in his heart.' The Lord knows how averse we are to this duty, and accordingly he proceeds; he begins with the answer of an objection, and concludes with an argument, And not suffer sin upon him; or, as the original may be as well translated, That thou bear not sin for sin;* so that he who reproves not the sin of his neighbour, bears his sin for him, burdens himself with the guilt.

Thus ministers become accessory to the people's sins when they reprove them not, are loath to displease them; sew pillows under them, and cry Peace, peace, &c., to those that continue in wickedness; tell them not wherein they sin, warn them not of the sinfulness and danger of their evil ways. And though those that are faithful in so doing be usually ill requited, yet better are the worst returns from men than the guilt of the blood of souls; see Ezek. iii. 17, 18. If he know they live in any sin, and warn, admonish them not of it, 'they shall die,' &c.; 'but their blood,' &c.

So parents are guilty of their children's sin, and accessory to their eternal damnation, if they rebuke them not sharply; if the sharpness of the reproof be not answerable to the heinousness of the sin. We have a dreadful instance of this in Eli, 1 Sam. ii. His sons were wicked, and he admonished them of it, but too mildly, with too much indulgence, not according to the nature of their offence; and for this the Lord threatens to ruin him, his sons, his family, and to judge it for ever, chap. iii. ver. 11–14. The Lord will judge his house for ever; not for the iniquity which he acteth, but which he knoweth; not for sins he committed, but for sins he restrained not; not because he joined with them, but because he frowned not on them. He was not severe enough in rebuking their sins; and so the Lord proceeds severely against the whole family, whereof he, being the head, was concerned as an accessory in the sin, and as a partaker of the suffering.

The Lord has appointed reproof as a means to hinder, to restrain sin; he that for fear, favour, or any sinister respects, forbears reproof, does not what he can to hinder it, and so is involved in the guilt of it.

(4.) By not mourning for it. He that mourns not for the sins of others, is in danger to partake of them. Mourning is a means to hinder the increase of sin; he that bewails not the sins of others, does not what he can to hinder them, and so may be accessory to them. The Lord, Ezek. ix., representing the destruction of Judah, he sends a man to mark those who mourned for the abominations of the city, that they might be preserved, while all the rest perished, ver. 4–6. Now we cannot suppose that all those who were destroyed were principals in those abominations, but accessories they might be, by not mourning for that which others committed; but those that sigh and cry for the abominations of Jerusalem, all of them escape, as being neither principals nor accessories to those desolating sins. Their grief and sorrow for them acquits them; and therefore the Lord takes such special care to secure them, that the public calamities might not touch them.

* Qu. 'him'?—ED.

The apostle, where he tells the Corinthians of their danger to be leavened, to be tainted with the guilt of that wicked person amongst them, in the same chapter he tells them the cause of it, they had not mourned for this wickedness, 1 Cor. v. 2. He calls them to repentance for another's sin; he would have them affected with grief and sorrow for it, that they might not be tainted with it. And when they had approved themselves herein, he commends their sorrow for that incestuous person's sin, by the effects which evidenced the sincerity of it, 2 Cor. vii. 11. Your sorrow for his sin appears to be after a godly manner, in that it wrought *carefulness* to correct the offence; *clearing of yourselves*, you hereby clear yourselves from the guilt of that wickedness, and the tolerating of it; *indignation*, you shew you are so far from approving, as you detest it publicly; *fear*, you shew yourselves afraid to partake of another man's sin; *vehement desire*, of removing scandal, and satisfying those that were offended; *zeal*, the intenseness of your desire to use all things for removing this evil; *revenge*, by censuring the offender, and casting him out, not suffering such wickedness to pass unpunished. By these effects the truth of their sorrow appeared, and by this sorrow they approved themselves to be clear in this matter, not accessory to his sin, not tainted with his guilt. Those, then, who do not thus mourn for the sins of others, cannot clear themselves from the guilt of others' sins.

It may be thou art not personally guilty of the blasphemies, apostasies, and scandalous evils of the times or places wherein thou livest; but dost thou not sigh and cry for these abominations, as those mourners in Ezra?* He that can be charged for not mourning for the sins of others, cannot plead not guilty to the sins of others as accessory, though not as principal; as not hindering, if not as acting their sins.

(5.) By not praying against the sins of others. Prayer is a sovereign means to hinder sin. He that prays not against it, is accessory to it, by not endeavouring to hinder it. Job knew the efficacy of this means; and, therefore, apprehending his children in danger of sin, he continually made use of it, Job i. 4, 5. It is the virtue of Christ's prayer that still preserves his people from destructive evils, destroying sins, Job xvii. 5. The apostle directs that prayers be made for kings and magistrates, though in those times the wicked persecutors, that their cruelty and wickedness might be restrained, so as the people might lead a quiet and peaceable life, 1 Tim. ii. 1, 2.

If ye pray not against the impostures of antichrist, that they may be detected and defeated; against the delusions of Satan as an angel of light, that he may be unmasked, his snares broken, and seduced souls, ensnared by him, reduced and delivered; against Satan's prevalency as a prince of darkness, that gross wickedness may not abound to the dishonour of the gospel and the profession of Christ; if ye pray not against the sins of the times, and those evils that appear in the places where ye live: ye do not what ye can to hinder sin, and so are accessory to it.

(6.) By not affording means whereby sin may be hindered. He that denies others the means requisite to the avoiding of sin, when it is his duty to afford them, is accessory to the sins of others by not hindering them; *e. g.* as we say, he that denies a man food, without which death cannot be prevented, is accessory to his death. So it is in spirituals; *e. g.* nothing is more destructive to the reign of sin and kingdom of Satan, than the preaching of the gospel. Therefore magistrates and others, that endeavour not (as it is their duty) to propagate the gospel, are accessory to the sins which reign in the absence of it.

* Qu. 'Ezekiel'?—ED.

So those that are careless of their children, servants, or other relations; provide not that they be taught to read, do not catechise, instruct them; allow them not time or means to get knowledge: they are hereby guilty of their ignorance, accessory to that soul-destroying sin.

(7.) By not applying severe providences for the hindering of sin. The Lord sometimes speaks from heaven against sin by remarkable acts of providence. These, if not applied by those that discern them, may involve such in the guilt of those sins, against which they are intended; *e.g.* when our brethren in America were in danger to be over-run with monstrous opinions, two women, the chief broachers thereof, brought forth such monsters instead of children, as might well be interpreted the voice of God against their monstrous errors. These were seasonably applied, and contributed much to the rooting of them out.

The applying of such providences tends much to the restraint of sin. And he that clearly discerns them, and does not apply them to this end, does not what he is bound to do for the hindering of other sins, and so is accessory to them.

Thus you see how many ways ye may partake of the sins of others, by imitating, concurring, occasioning, causing them, by countenancing, not hindering them.

Use. Learn hence your necessity of Christ. This is the end of law and gospel; this is the end of all our preaching, all your hearing: to learn your necessity of Christ.

And what more shews a necessity of Christ than the multitude of sins? And how does this truth shew the multitude of thy sins, since it hence appears thou mayest sin so many ways in the sins of others?

The multitude of thy personal sins are wonderful, even to astonishment; but add to the numberless multitude of thy own sins, the multitude also of thy other-men's-sins; and then consider what the weight of thy guilt is, and what necessity thou hast of a Saviour.

For thy personal sins, that before conversion, every act, word, thought is a sin, *tota vita*, &c. The character of an unconverted sinner is that of the old world, Gen. vi. 5. What cause to complain, as Ps. xxxviii. 4, 'Mine iniquities are gone over mine head; as an heavy burden they are too heavy for me.'

Then add to this incomprehensible number, the multitude of thy other-men's-sins, those which thou art accessory to. How many sins art thou guilty of by imitating others in sinning? How many by concurring? How many hast thou occasioned? How many hast thou been the cause of? How many hast thou countenanced? How many hast thou been guilty of by not hindering them? How many hast thou not corrected when it has been thy duty to do it? How many hast thou concealed, not complained of? How many hast thou heard and seen, and not reproved, rebuked? How many are there, which thou didst never mourn for, never pray against?

Oh what sums are here! Who can reckon them? What man or angel can take an account of them? Ps. xix. Who can stand under such a burden? Who can appear in the sight of justice with such guilt?

Men and angels cannot satisfy for any one sin, for the least sin. And who can satisfy for such numberless millions? Yet justice must be satisfied before any sinner find mercy.

Oh then, what need of Christ! What necessity of a Saviour! Flee to him who only has a righteousness sufficient to cover all these sins. Fly to him whose blood only can expiate all this guilt. Make haste to that fountain, that is set open for sin and uncleanness. There is not a drop in all the creatures, and nothing can cleanse thee but a fountain. Oh make haste to it, it is opened in Christ, and him only. Thy soul is pierced with millions of wounds, every sin wounds the soul. Oh look up to the brazen serpent, to Christ lifted up in the gospel. Without him thou art a dead man; all the world cannot save thee from eternal death. Give no rest to thy soul till thou be assured that, as thou art partaker of others' sins, so thou art partaker of Christ's righteousness.

UNCONVERTED SINNERS ARE DARKNESS.

Ye were sometimes darkness, but now are ye light in the Lord: walk as children of light.—EPH. V. 8.

HAVING given you a general account of these words before, I come to take a particular survey of them in the several parts.

You may look on them either as an argument, &c., the premises, conclusion; or as a description of the state of the Ephesians. He tells them what they were before conversion, *darkness;* what they are by the conversion, *light;* what they should be and do after conversion, *walk.*

These three parts offered us so many observations. From the first, their state before conversion, 'ye were darkness;' and what they were, that are we, and all men, till converted. This is not peculiar to the Ephesians, but common to all mankind since the fall; till conversion, all are darkness.

Obs. Those that are not converted are darkness. All and every one of the sons and daughters of men, till they be changed, converted, are darkness.

For explication, let me shew you what must be understood by conversion, what by darkness.

By conversion is meant that universal change which I described, &c. Let me only add this, that in Scripture, conversion, regeneration, vocation, renovation are the same thing, expressed by divers terms; the difference rather verbal than real, rather in word than reality. Conversion is the same thing with the new birth, with effectual calling, with renewing of the whole man, the planting of the principles of holiness.

So that, when I say, he that is not converted, &c., it is all one as if I said, He that is not born again, or born of God; he that has not the image of God repaired in him, that image which consists in holiness; he that has not Christ formed in him.

Not converted; *i. e.* he that is not effectually called, he that continues in unbelief and impenitency; he that answers not the call of Christ in the gospel; when he calls for faith, does not believe; when he calls for repentance, abides in the love and practice of sin; when he calls for obedience, lives as a child of disobedience.

Not converted; *i. e.* not renewed throughout in body, mind, and spirit, in heart and life; he that has not a new heart, a new spirit; he that is not a new creature, a new man, both inwardly and outwardly.

He that is not thus born again, thus called, thus renewed, is not converted; and he that is not converted is in darkness. But what is that?

You must not take it for outward darkness, the absence of that light which the eye, the outward sense, sees; you must not conceive so grossly of it. It is spiritual darkness which is here meant, and the Holy Ghost expresses an unconverted state frequently by this term, 1 John ii. 9, 11, *i.e.* not born of God, 1 Thes. v. 4, John xii. 46. You have descriptions of conversion, where darkness and light are made the terms of it, Acts xxvi. 18, 1 Peter ii. 9, Col. i. 13.

But what is it to be in darkness? What is this unconverted state that the Holy Ghost so often calls darkness? Take it in these four particulars.

To be in darkness is (1.) to be in sin, the work of darkness; (2.) to be under Satan, the prince of darkness; (3.) under wrath, the fruit of darkness; (4.) near to hell, the place of darkness. The Scripture by darkness ordinarily expresses some or all of these. When an unconverted state is called darkness, we are to understand by it a most sinful and miserable state.

(1.) In sin, the work of darkness. Sin is called in this chapter a 'work of darkness,' ver. 11. And he that lives in sin acts that work; he is said 'to walk in darkness,' 1 John i. 6. He that is not converted, he is wholly in sin, under the power, the pollution, the guilt of sin.

All the qualities and motions of his soul, all the acts of his life, are sinful, John iii. 5, 6. He that is but once born, not born again of the Spirit, owes his being to no other birth but that of the flesh; he is flesh, he is so wholly, only. By flesh is meant the corruption of sin: 'is flesh,' *i.e.* wholly corrupted by sin; his whole soul is full of sin, mind, conscience, will, affections; all are tainted with it, possessed by it, overspread with the pollution of it, Titus i. 15. There is nothing in his soul but what may be called flesh, *i.e.* sinful and corrupt, no principle of holiness.

Such a soul is sunk into sin; he is encompassed and quite covered over with sin. Hence that of the apostle, Rom. viii., 'in the flesh.' Nothing that they have, nothing that they do, can possibly please God, because all they have or can do is sinful, and so abominable to God. The state of Simon Magus is the condition of every unconverted sinner, Acts viii. 23. And why was he in this state? Because, though he was baptized and professed faith in Christ, yet he had neither part nor lot in regenerating, converting grace, ver. 21.

A sinner, till converted, is so held in the bond of iniquity as he can do nothing but sin. Baptism and the profession of faith cannot free him from this bondage to sin; nothing but converting grace can break this bond by which he is held in such slavery, as he can do nothing but sin: John xv. 5, 'Without me,' *i.e.* out of me; till ye be in me, united to me, ye can, &c. Now a sinner is never brought to union with Christ till conversion; till then he can do nothing that is spiritually good, and if so, he can do nothing but sin.

Even his sins are but a better sort, a more grossy* kind of sins, *splendida peccata.* 'The sacrifice of the wicked,' Prov. xv. 8, 9, xxvi. 9.

And further, though he can do nothing but sin; and so every thought, word, act, is put in the number of sins, by the Lord's account; yet not one of these sins can be pardoned till conversion. For there is no pardon till faith and repentance, and no repentance till conversion; till then he lies under the guilt of every sin. This is to be in darkness, to be in sin, the power, pollution, the guilt of it. He that is not converted is under sin, the work of darkness.

* Qu 'glossy'?—ED.

(2.) Under Satan, the prince of darkness. That is his title. The whole world is divided betwixt these two potentates, Christ the prince of light and life, and Satan the prince of darkness. Those that are converted, they are free subjects of Christ; those that are not converted, they are the vassals of Satan. He is their ruler, Eph. vi. 11, 12. These principalities and powers are the devils, and they are the rulers of the darkness, &c., *i. e.* of all those sinners that are yet in darkness, that are not yet converted and turned from darkness to light. The following words shew that those who are not thus turned are still under the power of Satan. He acts them, he commands them, he rules them, he possesses them, he challenges them as his own; till by conversion, they be ' translated from the power of darkness into,' &c., till then sinners are his children, John viii. 44; his instruments, Eph. ii. 2; his captives, 2 Tim. ii. 26. They wear his badge and livery, do his work, obey his commands. The image of Satan, the impressions of darkness, are on their souls; by this he challenges them as his own. If you pretend to Christ while unconverted, he may ask, Whose image and superscription is this? If prevailing lust, unsubdued corruption, speak it his, why, then, give unto Satan the things, the persons that are Satan's; he will not lose his due. If the image of Christ, the image of light and holiness, be not on your souls, you bear the image and superscription of Satan, and nothing can raze this out but converting grace. Till conversion, you are under Satan, the prince of darkness.

(3.) Under the wrath of God, the fruit of darkness. The day of God's wrath and indignation is called a day of darkness, Joel ii. 2. And this dismal day will never end until conversion, in respect of temporal or spiritual judgments. The favour of God is called light, ' the light of his countenance.' Till this light shine on a sinner, he cannot but be in darkness, and this light never shines until conversion.

To be in darkness, then, is to be under the Lord's indignation, under the curse of the law, under the threatenings of the word, under the sentence of condemnation, under the stroke of revenging justice. These are the expressions of wrath, which make the state of an unconverted sinner a state of darkness. All the calamities and miseries that are the effects of the Lord's wrath are called darkness in Scripture, Eccles. v. 17, vi. 4. To be in an unconverted state is to be exposed to all the expresssions of wrath.

(4.) Near to hell, the place of darkness. That is ' a land of darkness, as darkness itself.' It is called ' utter darkness,' Mat. viii. 12, 22; xii. 25, 30. So near is an unconverted state to hell, as it joins to it as an outer room; there is but a small, a weak partition betwixt them. If conversion do not bring the sinner out of this state, the partition will be broken, death will overthrow it, and then no passage, but into the outer room, into utter darkness. Hell is called the ' mist of darkness,' 2 Peter ii. 17. While a sinner is unconverted, he is in fetters, though not in chains; and his fetters will be turned into chains, if the power of converting grace break them not. He lies under the guilt of those offences for which the damned are adjudged to these chains. He is but under a reprieve; the sentence will be executed, if converting grace prevent not. Until thou be converted, thou art a child of darkness; this is thy portion, it is reserved for thee, thou art every moment in danger to fall into the woful possession of it. Thou canst lay claim to no other portion, canst hope for no other inheritance until conversion. To be in darkness is to be in danger of hell; it is a state bordering upon hell, it is in the confines, in the suburbs of it.

Use. Information. This shews the misery of an unconverted state. It concerns all sorts to take notice of it: those that are converted, that they may rejoice in their Redeemer, and be thankful for deliverance from this woful condition; those that are not converted, that they may bewail their misery, and thirst after deliverance.

The misery of an unconverted state is so great, as even this darkness will discover it. Let us follow the metaphor a little, the better to discern it.

1. Darkness is uncomfortable. So is the state of an unconverted sinner. How sad was the condition of Egypt, when the Lord plagued it with darkness that might be felt! Exod. x. 21. Alas! the darkness that overshadows thy soul is more lamentable. That might be felt; the misery of this is so great, it can scarce be understood. That was but for three days; this will be to the days of eternity, if conversion prevent not. How sad would the condition of the world be, if that which is metaphorically spoken were really effected; if the sun should be turned into darkness, and the moon into blood! Who would not be weary of his life upon earth, if the sentence of continual darkness should pass upon it? Alas! more miserable is thy condition if unconverted, because the want of spiritual light is a greater misery than the want of sensible light. The very light that is in thee is darkness. Oh how great then is that darkness!

This is one aggravation of the lamentable condition of Paul and his companions, in danger of shipwreck: Acts xxvii. 20, 'Neither sun nor stars in many days appeared.' Far worse is thy condition if unconverted; no sun, no star appears. The Sun of righteousness, the bright Morning Star, has never appeared in thy soul since thou wast born, nor ever will until born again. Thou livest in a woful region, thou sittest in a region of darkness, and in 'the valley of the shadow of death.' The sun shines not on thee; it is another world, another kind of men that enjoy it, those that are *antipodes* to thee.

It is true when the Lord is about the work of conversion, when a sinner is in the pangs of the new birth, or when a soul converted is deserted, he may be in such a condition as the prophet describes, Isa. l. 10, he may for a while 'walk in darkness, and see no light.' Ay, but such a one has some comfort, some support; he may 'trust in the name of the Lord, and stay himself,' &c.; as the mariners, 'though they saw neither sun nor stars,' Acts xxvii. 20, yet 'cast four anchors out of the stern, and wished for day.' They had anchors, though no light; and hopes of it, though it was not yet day. So has a soul in this condition, if converted or converting; he has anchor-hold, he may trust, &c.

Ay, but while thou art unconverted, thou hast neither light nor support; and though thou mayest strike some sparks out of worldly enjoyments, and compass thyself in them, yet 'for all this thou shalt lie down in sorrow.' Thy darkness is too great to be scattered with such sparks, ver. 11. How can they choose but lie down in sorrow, who must lie down in darkness, never to see the light!

2. Darkness is dangerous. He whose way lies near snares and pits, who is to pass over precipices, rocks, the brink of dangerous gulfs, and has no light to direct him, every step is the hazard of his life.

No less dangerous is the way of man ever since sin entered into the world. So many snares has Satan laid, so many pits has he digged, so near we walk to the brink of the bottomless pit, as without light we cannot make one step in safety. Even those that are converted have light little enough to secure them from ruin. Alas! then, what shall become of them who have no light at all, all whose paths are darkness? They are every foot in danger to be ensnared, to fall, to bruise and wound their souls, yea, to tumble into the bottomless pit before they be aware. Thus dangerous is an unconverted state, for it is darkness. The Lord Christ expresses this, John xii. 35. He knows not truth from error, good from evil, runs into dangerous mistakes; he knows not whether he be right or wrong, whether his way lead to heaven or hell, whether to the bosom of Christ or to the den of the devouring lion. He sleeps amongst serpents or murderers, and knows not where he is. He walks upon the very ridge of destruction; if he slips, he is ruined for ever; and yet he sees not where to set his foot. Alas! he is in darkness, Prov. iv. 19, John xi. 9. Though that stumbling-block be just before him which will ruin his soul and tumble him into hell, yet he knows not at what he stumbles, he sees it not, he is in darkness. Thus dangerous is thy unconverted state; it may sink thee into utter darkness before thou perceive. Oh that the misery of it might move to make haste out of it!

3. Darkness is fearful. We read of the 'horrors of darkness,' Gen. xv. 12. What more apt to engender fears than darkness, when dangers are on every side, and nothing visible that may afford confidence!

So the state of nature. The condition of a sinner unconverted is a fearful condition. He is encompassed with terrors on every side; such as, if he were sensible of them, would dash all his mirth and carnal jollity. An unconverted sinner, he is a *Magor-missabib*, like Pashur, Jer. xx. 3, he has fear round about him. Those whom the Lord has enlightened to see the dreadfulness of that state, they wonder that such can sleep quietly, or take comfort in any enjoyment, while they are not converted.

Is it not a fearful thing to stand guilty in the Lord's sight of millions of offences, every one of which deserves eternal death, and the Lord, in justice, is engaged to inflict it? To stand guilty, whenas the Lord will by no means clear the guilty? Yet this is the state of the unconverted.

Is it not a fearful thing to be delivered up to Satan, to be possessed by him, to be a slave unto him, to have no other guide but him, who will lead thee no other way but to ruin; to be disowned by Christ, as those who yield allegiance to the prince of darkness? Yet this is the state of such.

Is it not a fearful thing to 'fall into the hands of the living God;' to lie under the wrath of an unreconciled God; to lie open to the challenges of revenging justice; to find nothing belonging to thee in the world but the curse, and to have enjoyments mixed with the Lord's indignation? Yet this is the case; children of darkness are children of wrath.

Is it not a fearful thing to lodge the next room to hell; to find no other portion for thyself in the Lord's testament but everlasting fire, no other inheritance but the region of outer darkness? Yet this is the state of the unconverted.

Oh how dreadful is that state, where the terrors of sin, the terrors of Satan, the terrors of God, the terrors of hell, encompass a poor sinner, and he sees no way to avoid them! For he is in darkness, such as he sees nothing to support him under them, but some false rotten props, some broken reeds. The true grounds of confidence are hid from his eyes, cannot be discerned in this darkness.

Mercy is a support, but none find mercy but converted sinners. Christ is a support, but none shall find any saving benefit by Christ but converted sinners. The word is a support, but this speaks not a word of comfort to any but those that are converted.

Oh how fearful is that condition that shews no glimpse of hope, affords no ground of confidence! In the midst of such dangers, miseries, that can discover nothing that may cheer or support in those things that are the only grounds of comfort and support; nothing in mercy, nothing in Christ, his love, his blood, nothing in the word, nothing in the great and precious promises, to bear up thy soul in this woful condition. When the terrors of death, and sin, and hell encompass thee, where wilt thou go for comfort? What will be thy refuge? what will support thy sinking soul?

A converted soul, when he feels the wounds of sin, can look up to the brazen serpent for healing virtue; but what can he see, whither will he look, who is in darkness?

A converted soul, when the terrors of death or the greatest fears in this life assault him, he can cast up his eyes above the mountains, and discover salvation approaching. But what can he see, what can he discover, who is in darkness?

Wretched sinner, thou who goest on merrily in thy evil ways, no more minding conversion, &c., than if it were a fiction, be entreated to admit at last this one serious thought: time is coming, when fears and terrors, either in this life, or in death or judgment, will seize on thy soul, and shake thy heart, and overthrow all thy carnal supports, dash out all the sparks of worldly mirth. When thou wilt find what we speak of the fearfulness of an unconverted state are not words of course, thou wilt then find need of those spiritual comforts and supports which thou now neglectest. But whither wilt thou go for them? If thou fliest to mercy for comfort, being unconverted, mercy will say, It is not in me. If thou go to Christ, he will say, It is not in me; no comfort in me but for those that turn to me, for none but converted sinners. If thou goest to the word, it will say, It is not in me; I have no drop of comfort for any that turns not, for any that continues in impenitency and unbelief. Oh, sure that day which is making haste towards thee, however thou forget it, that day will be unto thee a day of darkness and of gloominess, a day of clouds and of thick darkness, a day of dread and terror, and like thy unconverted condition, most fearful. Darkness is fearful; that is the third misery of it.

Quest. But who are those that are in darkness? How shall we know whether we be in this unconverted state? Those that have any regard of their souls, hearing the misery of this condition, will be apt to make this inquiry. Those that are so wretchedly careless, as not to question it, not trouble themselves with inquiries about their conversion, may put it out of question they are not yet converted, they have neither part nor lot in this matter, they are not so much as in the way to it. As for those who are not thus desperate, but are doubtful of it, and desirous to search into the condition of their souls, it will be requisite in some few particulars to shew how it may be known who are in darkness, who are not; who are converted, who are not. And this will be useful, both for the conviction of those that are not, and the comfort of those that are; they are not converted, but in darkness;—

1. Who walk in the ways of darkness. The children of light do not walk in the paths of darkness. You may know your state by your way; ways of wickedness are ways of darkness: so Solomon, Prov. iv. 19, 'The way of the wicked is darkness.'

He that walks in any way of known wickedness, be it drunkenness, &c., neglect of ordinances, &c., he is in darkness. ' By their fruits ye may know them.' It is a sure rule, Christ himself lays it down; if you bring forth the fruits of darkness, you are in the state of darkness. Hereby he proves the unbelieving Jews to belong to the prince of darkness: John vii. 44, 'his works.' If ye do his works, you are under his jurisdiction, not yet delivered. Now, what are his works? Why, all wickedness, every sin. He that acts any sin wilfully, customarily, delightfully, makes it his practice, continues so, allows him so to continue. The apostle advises the converted Ephesians, as being both their property and duty, to 'have no fellowship,' &c., chap. v. 11. A convert may be surprised, overtaken with sin; but he has no fellowship, he is not familiar with sin, he delights not in it, it is not his companion, it is not his custom, nor his choice, nor his contentment, to converse with it. He looks upon every sin as a cheater, a murderer, a disgraceful, a dangerous associate, and therefore he will keep as far from it as he can; he is afraid, ashamed to have any fellowship with it. This is the temper of a convert, if you take him when he is himself.

Those, then, that are familiar with sin, in whose mouths and hands, in whose words and actions, you may ordinarily see it, who are no more afraid, ashamed of it, than of one whom they choose for a companion. Those who make any sin their interest, their delight, their practice, they have fellowship with it. You may know them by their companion, that with which they have fellowship. When oaths, profane, unclean discourse is familiar in their mouths; when they can lie, dissemble, revile, curse familiarly; when accustom themselves to any other way of wickedness, alas! darkness is here palpable. There is no conversion where no turning from sin. He is in darkness who allows himself to walk in any path of darkness, 1 John iii. 20.

2. Those that want spiritual discerning. He that has eyes and sees not, it is plain he is in darkness; what else should hinder his sight?

So they that have the same understanding, the same faculty of inward sight with others, and yet perceive not that in spiritual things, that those discern who are savingly enlightened, it is evident that spiritual darkness overshadows their souls.

He that sees not that beauty, that excellency in Christ, that necessity of him, as to be willing to part with all for him; to count that loss which he has taken for his greatest gain; to renounce his own righteousness, that he may be found in him; to renounce his own lusts, that he may be conformed to him; his own interests, that he may advance him; his own humours, that he may comply with him:

He that sees not that necessity of conversion, the new birth, as to trouble himself about it, to count himself miserable without it:

He that sees not such beauty in holiness as to prefer it before the choicest things on earth; to be in love with it, thirst after it; diligent in the use of all means to get it, increase it, strengthen, act it:

He that sees not that deformity, danger in sin, as to hate it above all things, to bewail it in himself and others, careful to avoid it, maintain a constant war with it, use all his strength to subdue it, rejoice in the crucifying of his dearest lusts, ver. 13:

He that has not this discerning of these and other spiritual things, it is evident he has eyes, but sees not; and what can be given as the reason hereof, but because he is in darkness? Such are in Egypt's condition; when converts, as the Israelites, have light in their dwellings.

3. Those that act not for God. The Egyptians, under the plague of darkness, are described by their unactiveness: Exod. x. 23, 'Neither arose any man from his place;' John ix. 4. A man in darkness may be in action about himself, but not in things at a distance; he sees not how to move towards them. The things of God are at a distance from every unconverted man; he sees not, he knows not how to go about it.

He is a stranger to acts of self-denial and mortification; a stranger to the life of faith, the exercise of grace, the vigorous acts of holiness, strict walking, constant dependence on Christ, a spiritual frame of heart in worldly business.

He cannot pray with enlargement, affection, fervency. He cannot meditate on Christ, and heaven, and spiritual things with delight; he cannot hear the word, so as to mix it with faith, to be affected with it, to run into the mould of it. Though he be employed sometimes in religious duties, though he be active in the things of God, yet he acts not at all for God. To act for God is to act out of love to him, with intentions to honour him, with respect to his glory. When men perform religious services out of custom, or to gain and keep their credit, or to stop the mouth of conscience, or to satisfy and make amends for some sin, he that acts for such ends, out of such principles, let him do as much as he will, even in a way of religion, yet he does nothing for God. And this is the condition of one not converted, he acts not out of love to God with respect to his glory, and therefore what he does is as though he did nothing He acts not for God who acts not from right principles, for sincere ends; and this bewrays an unconverted state. If the Lord incline you to be faithful to your souls, these things may be helpful to discover your condition, whether ye be light or darkness, whether converted or unconverted.

Use 3. Exhortation, to those that are converted, brought out of the woful state of darkness; let this stir you up to joy and thankfulness for your deliverance. 'You were sometimes darkness;' that is the state of every man by nature. Now, as it aggravates misery to have been once unhappy,* so the consideration of former miseries adds contentment to a happy condition. 'You were sometimes darkness.'

You have been formerly under the guilt of sin, enslaved to the tyranny of base lusts; you have been formerly vassals unto Satan, led captive by him at his will; you were 'by nature the children of wrath as well as others;' you were once in a condition as there was but a step between you and hell. Now, has the Lord delivered you out of this sad and woful condition? Can you say, we were 'sometimes darkness, but now light in the Lord'? Oh, love the Lord, praise him, rejoice in him, speak great things of his name.

Oh love that Redeemer, who sweat, and bled, and died to work this your redemption. Oh pity those, pray for them, mourn for them who are yet in darkness. Let your hearts be affected as David's, Ps. cxvi. 1, 3, 4, 5, 7, 8; xciii. 4.

But now are ye light. For explication. Light denotes several things in Scripture.

1. Spiritual knowledge. Light and knowledge are terms of the same import, 2 Cor. iv. 6. Light to discover God in Christ savingly, and to discern the things of God spiritually.

2. Purity and holiness. Sin and corruption is expressed by darkness, holiness and purity by light. In this sense the most holy God is called light, 1 John i. 5, spotless and perfect holiness, in whom there is not the least impurity. And in reference to us, ver. 7, such a light as is life, spiritual life, which consists in the principles of holiness and purity.

3. The favour of God, and the consequent of it, joy and comfort. The favour of God, the manifesting of his loving-kindness, is frequently expressed by the light of his countenance, Ps. iv. 6, the issue of which is joy and gladness, ver. 7. Light and joy explain one another, Ps. xcvii. 11. That which is light in the first clause is joy in the latter.

4. Glory and happiness. Heaven, the seat of it, is described by light, 1 Tim. vi. 16. It is called the inheritance, Col. i. 12.

* Qu. 'happy'?—Ed.

Light here may comprise all these. So that when we say, those that are converted are light, the meaning may be,

(1.) They are enlightened with saving knowledge.

(2.) They are enriched with the principles of holiness; the lustre thereof shines in their souls, and should appear in their lives; by virtue of this they should shine as lights.

(3.) They are in the state of favour and reconciliation with God. Though they have not always the sense of his loving-kindness, yet they are always the objects of his love. Though his face do not always actually shine on them, yet the sun is up, it is always day with them; joy is sown for them though they be not still reaping it, and every season be not harvest time.

(4.) They have title to glory. Heirs apparent to heaven, heirs of the inheritance, &c. Their title is certain, that they are said to sit with him in heavenly places.

Use 1. If those that are converted be light, &c., then those that are not converted are not light in the Lord. This necessarily follows by the rule of contraries. They may be light in appearance, or in respect of natural endowments, or moral accomplishments, or in the account of others, or in their own conceit and apprehensions, but they are not light in the Lord; and this shews the misery of an unconverted state, and it is useful to take notice of it more particularly. If they are not light in the Lord,—

1. They are not in the Lord. The phrase implies union; but such are without union to, without communion with, without participation of, without special relation to him; without his special protection, without his special favour, without his gracious covenant. It may be propounded to them that they have no actual interest in, or right to, the blessings, the mercies of the covenant. The tenor of it is, I will be thy God; they cannot apply nor challenge this: they may say, he is my Creator, he is my Judge; but not he is my God in Christ, my God by covenant; without God in their hearts, in their enjoyments, in their conversations. Thus the apostle describes the unconverted state of these Ephesians, chap. ii. 12, at that time, viz., when unconverted; without Christ, not united to him, not partakers of the benefits of his great undertakings; not pardoned by his blood, not acted by his Spirit, not crucified with him, not risen with him, not sitting with him in heavenly places, either in right hope, or first fruits of that blessed state, aliens from the church. An unconverted man, whatever he profess, or others account of him, is no more in God's sight a member of the church than a corpse is a man.

Strangers from the covenant. No more to do with the sure mercies of the covenants, the sweet contents of the great and precious promises, than a foreigner has to do with the privileges of one of our corporations, or a slave with the privileges of a child, or the legacies of his father's testament.

Without hope. So far from enjoying these, as he is, during that state, without hope of them, till he be enfranchised, till adopted, and no adoption till conversion.

Without God in the world. This is the saddest expression of all. If he had said without riches, or friends, or liberty, or health, or food, you would think it sad. Ay, but to be without God, that is infinitely more miserable than to be without all these; yet this is the state of every unconverted sinner, not born again; he is not light in the Lord, and so not in the Lord, and so without God in the world.

If a converted soul want riches, the Lord can supply that want. 'The earth is the Lord's,' &c.; or friends, the Lord can supply, 'when father and mother forsake.' 'All men forsake me,' 2 Tim. iv. 16. 'I will never leave thee, nor forsake thee,' Heb. xiii. 5; or liberty, Ps. xviii. 19; or food, 'The Lord is my Shepherd, I shall not want,' Ps. xxiii. 1. Ay, but if a man want the Lord, if he be without God in the world, what can make up that want? Let him have all the world, and want God in the world, and all that he enjoys will but add to his miseries. Without God, without all that is truly comfortable and desirable. Yet this is the state of an unconverted sinner.

2. They want the saving knowledge of God in Christ, they are not light in this respect. The darkness of ignorance and misapprehensions is upon the face of their souls; the prince of darkness, the god of this world, has blinded their minds, 2 Cor. iv. 3, 4. Though they may be knowing men in other respects, yet as to spiritual, saving, experimental, effectual knowledge of Christ, and the things of Christ, they are in darkness. They may have much knowledge of the Scripture and divine things, as to the letter, clear, notional, and speculative apprehensions of gospel truths; but as to spiritual discerning of any of these, they are in darkness, 1 Cor. ii. 14. The things of the Spirit of God he may apprehend literally, notionally, speculatively; but not spiritually, experimentally, practically. They hear, and read, and apprehend much of Christ, but not effectually, not so as to renounce all for him. They know him not, so as to find the power of his resurrection, the fellowship of his sufferings; not so as to be made conformable to his death; not with such a knowledge as the apostle there describes, Philip. iii. 8-10. They read, hear of holiness, but are so far from knowing what it is by experience, as they are apt to think no such thing now to be attained in this world, as the holiness which the Scripture describes; and finding no such thing in themselves, judge those who pretend to it hypocrites and dissemblers; know not how to worship God in spirit, how to subdue a lust, how to resist a temptation, how to improve an affliction, how to escape a snare, how to avoid a stumbling-block, how to improve ordinances for growth in grace, how to improve Christ for spiritual strength, life, influence, so as by his strength to do all things; know not what the state of their soul is, where they are, whither they are going, darkness having blinded them, as the Assyrians, 2 Kings vi. 20, thought they were in Dothan, whenas they found themselves in the midst of Samaria, in the midst of their enemies; think themselves in the way to heaven all their life, till in the end, alas! they find themselves in hell.

Tell them of the new birth, sanctification, self-denial, the power of godliness; produce Scriptures, which expressly shew that without these there is no salvation; bring characters by which these may be discerned: yet they see them not, they believe not; for they know not these effectually, they are in darkness. They are no more apprehensive of these things, than if you were discoursing to a blind man of colours, or if you were describing the sun to a man that never saw the light. And why? They are not light in the Lord.

3. They want the favour of God. They are not under the beams of divine love, the light of God's countenance does not shine on them, and so they are not light in the Lord. They may conclude this from success, prosperity, plenty, and outward comforts; but this is but a fallacy, a delusion. The Lord's greatest enemies may abound with corn, and wine, and oil, &c., but the light of God's countenance is not lift up but upon converted souls. There is a veil of darkness before the Lord's face; this is never rent, removed, till conversion. Those that are unconverted, want that which is the life and joy of the converted soul; that which sweetens all his afflictions, and

makes all his enjoyments comfortable. This is it which is better than life; those on whom it shines not may well be said to sit in darkness, and in the valley of the shadow of death. This dismal shadow never vanishes till the Lord's face shine, and this never clears up till conversion. You may discern the state of a returning and an unconverted sinner, expressed in the state of the church and the rest of the world, Isa. lx. 2. Behold darkness covers impenitent souls, and gross darkness unconverted sinners; but if thou be converted, the Lord shall rise upon thee. Alas! They know not what it is to walk in the light of God's countenance all the day; not one glimpse of that light of life appears unto them; for they are not light in the Lord.

4. They want the lustre of holiness. This is one thing which concurs to make converts light in the Lord. This light shines nowhere on earth but in the hearts and lives of such; those that are unconverted shew themselves either strangers or enemies to it. They are carnal, sold under sin, know not what belongs to an holy frame of heart; think heaven may be attained without strictness, holiness, as the Scripture requires, and the lives of the saints there recorded hold forth; jeer, deride, abuse it, under odious names; place all their holiness in some outward performances or observances; holy discourse and employments are wearisomeness to them.

Here is a misery indeed; want that, without which no man can see God; and this they want, because not light in the Lord.

5. They want discoveries of future glory, they are not light in the Lord; they have not so much light as will discover it at a distance; there is no dawnings, no approaches, no appearances of that blessed light. It is midnight with a sinner while unconverted. No crevice to let in the least light, the least hope of glory, while he continues in that dismal state. The morning star, that ushers in that happy day, first appears in conversion, Acts xxvi. 18. Till a sinner be turned from darkness to light, till he be converted, there is no hopes of obtaining an inheritance among those that are sanctified; no appearance of this till then, because till then not light in the Lord.

Put all these together, and then view the sad and lamentable condition of every unconverted sinner. If not born again, thou art without God, Christ, the Spirit of Christ, the saving knowledge of Christ, the least glimpse of God's love, the least sparkle of holiness, the least hope of glory; and all this, because not light in the Lord.

But how shall we know, who are in this state, whether or no we be light in the Lord? To direct you herein, let us come to a

Use 2, by way of examination. Hereby ye may know whether ye be converted. Every convert is light in the Lord; those, therefore, that are not light in the Lord are not converted; these are so conjoined, as he that knows the one may conclude the other. Examine, then, whether ye be light in the Lord, if ye would know whether ye be converted. In order hereto observe these particulars:

1. Light is delightful. *Totus mundus luce nihil habet jucundius*, a greater and wiser than he, Eccles. xi. 7. The light of the word is delightful to one that is light in the Lord. There is a great affinity between these lights, both proceeding from the same Father, 'the Father of lights:' Hence the discoveries of the word are sweet, acceptable, delightful, to one that is savingly enlightened.

Not only the discoveries of Christ and mercy, privileges and promises, pardon and glory, but that light of the word which discovers to him the corruption of his heart, the sinfulness of any practice, the danger of sin; that word which searches his conscience, and discovers the condition of his soul, detects his failings and sinful miscarriages, not only a word of promise and consolation, but a word of reproof and conviction. This is sweet and acceptable to one that is light; he can bless God for, and rejoice in, that word that condemns and discovers his secret sin.

He therefore that cannot endure the word that discovers his misery and sinfulness, that searches his conscience and reproves his sin, cannot endure searching sermons nor those that preach them, such as tend to awaken his conscience, and rouse him out of security, and condemn his sinful practices, cries out that he hears nothing from such but hell and damnation, and that which may make him despair; he hereby shews clearly he is so far from being light in the Lord, as this is a plain evidence he hates the light. I speak not this for nor of myself; it is the word of Christ; if you will take Christ's word, such a man hates the light, John iii. 19, 20. He that is so in love with his sin, be it what it will, as he would not have it reproved, condemned, hell and wrath denounced against it, Christ pronounces, he hates the light, loves darkness, &c. It is plain darkness is his element, he is not yet converted, nor yet turned from darkness to light; he that is light in the Lord is of another temper, as you may see, ver. 21. He is so far from declining, being impatient of a searching, discovering truth, as he comes to it of his own accord.

2. While there is light there is heat. שמש *à* שם *et* אש.* Heat, as philosophers tell us, is an inseparable property of celestial light. We see a concurrence of these in fire; indeed, there may be an appearance of light where there is no heat, as in glow-worms, but where there is any real light, there is some degree of heat more or less.

Answerably, they that are light in the Lord are zealous for the Lord, eager in following him, ardent in love to him and desires after him, fervent in spirit in serving him. They will not content themselves to offer up lukewarm, heartless services unto God. When they find the danger of such a temper, they bewail it, judge themselves for it, it is their affliction; there is a spiritual heat for the Lord in those that are light.

Therefore, where there is a customary indifferency, and carelessness in religious duties, those that ordinarily serve him, as though they served him not, give him but the lip, or knee, or outward man, not heated and enlivened with the vigorous motions of the soul towards God.

Where there wants ardency of affection in spiritual duties, eagerness of soul after growth in grace, communion with God, and enjoyment of Christ in the use of ordinances, no such longing, thirsting, panting, breathing after Christ, conformity to him, participation of him, fellowship with him, serviceableness to him, ability to please, honour, advance him, as after those things that men's hearts are set upon, and hotly pursue in the world; this argues clearly an absence of spiritual heat, and if thou wantest this heat, thou art not light in the Lord.

3. Light is progressive. We see, after the day-break, the light grows clearer and clearer, till it come to its full brightness; Scripture expressions lead us to this observation, as well as experience; in the morning light is in its youth. Hence שחרות, the word which the Hebrews express the morning, is used for youth, Eccles. xi. 10. At noon the light is in its manhood, its full strength; we have that expression, Judges v. 31. The light from its birth grows and increases, till it comes to its full strength, when the sun is in the meridian.

Thus it is with those that are light in the Lord, as Solomon expresses it,

---

* That is, שמש, *the sun*, is from שם, *the heavens*, and אש, *fire*.—ED.

EPH. V. 8.] UNCONVERTED SINNERS ARE DARKNESS. 367

Prov. iv. 18. This light is but a spark at first, and often accompanied with much smoke, but by degrees it breaks forth into a flame.

Such grow in grace and in the knowledge of Christ; they go from strength to strength, and from one degree of holiness and spiritual knowledge to another; this light daily prevailing against the darkness of ignorance and corruption, till at last it be brought forth to victory.

There is a growth of knowledge in the extent of it; it discovers one truth after another, unlocks one mystery after another, and daily scatters the clouds of misapprehensions.

In the clearness of it, sees gospel truths with more and more evidence, as that blind man's sight was restored by degrees, Mat. viii. 23, 24. At first he saw men, as trees walking; after, ver. 25, he saw every man clearly. Those truths of Christ, those gospel mysteries, which at first he sees but confusedly and obscurely, he by degrees discerns evidently and distinctly, in their proper complexions, proportions, connections, so as to discern betwixt things that differ, so as not to take one thing for another, nor to be easily imposed on, deluded or mistaken with shows and appearances, to take a show for a reality, to exchange a real truth for one in appearance.

In the firmness of it. At first the light makes but a weak impression; he has not fast hold of it, not firmly grounded in it, is but a child in understanding, apt to be tossed to and fro; but by degrees he comes to be established in the truth to a full assurance, carried with full sail into the embracement of truths revealed in the gospel, he is 'rooted and grounded.' Those winds of doctrine and error which overthrow others, and toss them out of all sound principles, though they shake him, do but root him faster by shaking of him, as well grown trees are by a tempest.

There is a growth in the spiritualness, the efficacy, the experimentalness, the practicalness of his knowledge. This light has daily a more spiritual and powerful influence upon his heart, to spiritualize it in his motions, intentions, inclinations; upon his conscience, to make it tender; upon his affections, to kindle them to God, and dead them to the world; upon his conversation, to reform and beautify it with more holy and exemplary actings.

There is a growth in grace, too, in every one that is light in the Lord. This light of holiness shines more and more, prevails against inward distempers and outward miscarriages, bears down the interest of darkness, *i. e.* of the flesh and of the world. He that is light in the Lord, when he is himself not under the darker clouds of temptation, desertion, grows daily more holy, humble, self-denying, heavenly, zealous, out of love with sin, estranged from the world, more in the exercise of faith and the actings of love, more jealous over his own heart and watchful over his ways. This light, where it is in truth and reality, will shine more and more, and such as these fore-mentioned are the beams of it.

That light which puffs up and defiles, makes men proud or loose in their principles or practice, it is not from the Father of lights, nor does it evidence that thou art light in the Lord; nay, rather it is from him who transforms himself into an angel of light, and argues that thou art yet darkness, under the jurisdiction of the prince of darkness.

If thy growth be in the principles of darkness, and thy improvement no other than in the works of darkness, knowest not by experience what it is to grow in holiness, heavenliness, &c.; art a stranger to ardent desires, serious endeavours after it; thou dost but delude thy soul against clear evidence of Scripture if thou conclude thyself light in the Lord.

Or suppose there be some improvement of light, if this make thee decline from the strict and holy ways of Christ, more loose in thy walking, more negligent of spiritual duties, more careless of thy heart, more indifferent as to the truths, ways, worship of Christ, this light, how much soever it be imagined, is not light in the Lord, but rather in Satan. Light in the Lord would not lead thee from the Lord, but nearer to him, in more holy walking, and a more humble, spiritual, heavenly frame of heart, for light in the Lord is an increasing light, it shines more and more, &c. It daily brings thee nearer to him, and the nearer to the sun, to the fountain of light, the more lightsome; as in joy and hopes of glory, so in the lustre of spiritual knowledge and holiness.

Oh that the Lord would make you faithful in examining the state of your souls hereby, that you may be able to pass a right judgment of it, whether you be converted or no, whether you be darkness or light!

Use 3. Consolation to those that are converted. If thou art a convert, thou art light in the Lord, and this light discovers thy condition to be safe, comfortable, glorious, durable.

1. *Safe.* If thou canst conclude by Scripture evidence, I was sometimes darkness, &c. The Lord has brought thee into a safe condition; thou art freed from those fears and dangers that thy former darkness exposed thee to. Neither the horror nor the dangers of darkness need disquiet thee; the Lord has 'delivered thy soul from death, thine eyes from tears, and thy feet from falling.' Before conversion, whilst thou walked in darkness, thou wast every foot in danger of the snares of death, every step in danger of falling into hell, and thy condition more fearful, because thou hadst not light to discover thy danger. But now the darkness is past, the Lord has shined on thee, and thou mayest walk cheerfully, confidently, safely before the Lord in the land of the living.

O happy change! before in the shadow of death, of eternal death, but now in the land of the living; before in the most dismal darkness, next to hell, but now in the light of the Lord; before on the brink of destruction, without a light, without a guide, but now in the path of life. He has set thy feet upon a rock, and the Lord himself is thy light and safety. Thou mayest triumph with David, Ps. xxvii. 1; the reason, he shall set me upon a rock, ver. 5.

Thou seest multitudes playing upon the very brink of hell, but a step between them and eternal death, and no light to guide a step, and so they are every moment in danger to tumble into the bottomless pit; and yet in such darkness as they will neither see their danger, nor believe those that shew it them. This was thy condition once, thou wast darkness as well as others; but now thou art light, &c. The Lord has by conversion set thy feet upon a rock; there thou art safe, whilst thou seest multitudes wrecked in the gulf of destruction, sinking into utter darkness, round about thee. Oh the wonder of distinguishing mercy! thou mayest now say, 'Return to thy rest,' &c.

2. *Comfortable.* Light and joy in Scripture are put one for the other; and Solomon tells us, Prov. xiii. 9, 'The light of the righteous rejoiceth.' What cause have they to rejoice who are light in the Lord; who are in him, united to him, in covenant with him, under the beams of his love, under the sweet influences of his loving-kindness! This is the state of the converted. Those who have been under the sad apprehensions of God's wrath, under the anguish of a wounded conscience, encompassed with the terrors of the Almighty, when they see nothing in his face but clouds and frowns, hear nothing from his mouth but threatenings, see nothing in his hand but revenging justice,—and this often is the condition of those that walk in darkness,—such will need no arguments to prove that it is a comfortable

condition to be light in the Lord, to see his frowns turned into smiles, his threatenings into promises; to see mercy take place of justice, and instead of the bitterness of death, to taste the 'loving-kindness which is better than life.'

It is true, the days of darkness are not always so dreadful to every unconverted sinner; we see them spend their days in mirth and jollity, but this is because they are past feeling. This is one sad effect of this darkness, it hinders a sinner from seeing his misery; if he did apprehend it, his life would be as death unto him. There is always cause of dread and horror, though in the dark it is not seen. What can be comfortable to him who spends his days in darkness? This was once thy condition; but if thou beest light in the Lord, let me speak to thee in the apostle's words: 'Rejoice in the Lord always; and again I say, rejoice.' The horror of darkness is past, the shadow of death is vanished, the darkness of an unconverted state, the sad emblem of hell, is scattered; the light of life now shines round about thee, and oh what sweet discoveries does it make! Look where thou wilt, the beams of joy and light break in upon thee. Look upward, there is light in God's countenance shines on thee; look inwards, there the day-spring from on high has visited thee, the fountain of light and joy is seated in thy soul; look backward, the night is far spent, the day is at hand, thou art not of night nor of darkness; look forwards, thou art not far from possession of the inheritance of the saints in light; look any way, light is sown for thee, and joy, &c. Oh that is precious seed, and will be more and more fruitful, till thou reap the full harvest in eternal light! 'Happy is the people that is in such a case; yea, happy is that people whose God is the Lord;' or, which comes all to one, who are 'light in the Lord.'

3. *Durable.* Not safe, comfortable, happy for a moment, but for ever; for it is light in the Lord. If thy light were in thyself, death, or other calamities, might extinguish it; if thy light were in the world, and outward enjoyments, it might go out of itself, for the light hereof is but as the crackling of thorns; if thy light were in wickedness, it would certainly be put out, Job xviii. 5, 6. But what can put out that light that is in the Lord? Light in other things is like them, vain and fading; but light in the Lord is as he is, everlasting. Everlasting knowledge, joy, holiness, happiness is the portion of converted souls; because they have all these in the Lord. It is the honour and security of Christ's ministers that he styles them stars, there is their light and stars in his right hand, so they are light in the Lord, held in his right hand, and so held for ever; for what can pluck them thence? Rev. i. 16, 20.

The security of Christ's people, lesser lights, is no less; they are in his hand, and in his Father's hand, and shall shine there for ever, John x. 28, 29. Here is the happiness of thy condition. If once thou be light in the Lord, thou shalt never be darkness; for thou art light in him in whom is no darkness, nor can there be any. He is in himself everlasting light, and will be so to them that are in him, Isa. lx. 19, 20. Once light in the Lord, and so for ever. It may be clouded and obscured, but this light can never be put out. This is not the least happiness of this condition, that whatever happiness is essential to it is everlasting.

4. *Glorious.* Nothing visible on earth more glorious than light; and these are put one for the other in Scripture, 1 Cor. xv. 41. What is their glory but their light? Those who are converted have hereby a double glory, one as they are light, the other as they are light in the Lord, light in the Lord of glory. He is a glory to them, even as a robe of light would be to our body; such, and much more, is the Lord to a converted soul, Isa. lx. 19.

Though their outside may be vile and contemptible in the eyes of men, yet they are 'glorious within,' Ps. xlv. 13. Every soul espoused to Christ is styled the daughter of a King, the daughter of the King of glory. A garment of wrought gold seems glorious, but there is a garment which far exceeds this in glory. What would you think of one clothed with the sun? Would not this seem a glorious object? Why, so is the church described; and that upon earth, though the vision was in heaven, Rev. xii. 1. This woman is the spouse of Christ, the church; she is clothed with the sun, the Sun of righteousness: a glorious garment indeed; and being a garment, must reach every member. Here is thy glory if converted: though thou be hated, despised, reviled, vilified; though thou be in a forsaken, a persecuted condition, as the woman was now in the wilderness, ver. 6; yet thou art light in the Lord, light indeed, being clothed with the Sun. Christ himself is thy glory.

Thus you see how sweet and happy their condition is who are converted, who are light in the Lord.

Here is support against fears and dangers. Men and devils, death and hell, cannot prevail against thee; thou art safe.

Here is support under crosses and afflictions, pain and sickness. No condition can befall thee but here is enough to make it comfortable. Thou art light in the Lord; whatever thou mayest meet with in the world, thou mayest find light and joy in him.

Here is comfort against temptations, against backslidings, apostasy in these apostatizing times, thy condition is durable, it is founded in the Lord.

Here is comfort against the contempt, the scorn, the reproaches, the slanders, the dirt which the profane world casts on thee. Whatever they say or think of thee, thy condition is glorious, thy glory is from and in the Lord; thou art light in the Lord.

In the Lord. This phrase may denote that he is the author of this light, and all included in it, and that it is effected by union with himself; they have it all by being in him. Ἐν in the New Testament often is of the same import with διά, light in him, *i.e.* by him, 2 Cor. v. 19. It is he that gives the light of this knowledge, 2 Cor. iv.; it is the Lord that sanctifies us throughout, 1 Thes. v. 23; it is he that is the God of all consolation, Rom. xv. 5, 2 Thes. ii. 16; and causeth comfort to spring in the heart, by causing his own face to shine. It is he that gives us title to glory, making us partakers of the adoption. The converted are heirs of God; and all this they have by being in him, united and made one with him; by being joined to him who is the fountain of knowledge, and holiness, and comfort, and glory.

Walk as children of light. Here he shews what they should do after conversion: walk answerable to their state; being light in the Lord, should walk as children of light.

Obs. Those that are converted should walk as children of light. Before they walked as children of darkness, for they were darkness; now as children of light, for they are light in the Lord.

Two things must be explained: 1, what it is to be children of light; 2, what it is to walk as children of light. These expressions being opened, the truth will be clear.

For the first, it is a Hebrew phrase, and the apostle being a Hebrew of the Hebrews, though he writ in Greek, yet mixes therewith some phrases of his mother tongue, as is usual with the rest of the apostles. So that the knowledge of the Hebrew (the original of the Old Testament) tends much to the understanding of the New Testament, though writ in another language.

And they have the best advantage of interpreting this, who have some skill in that. Now, that we may understand this phrase, which is very pregnant, let us observe how it is used in other places. It denotes several things.

1. *Descent.* That is the natural and proper signification of it, a child is from his father; so they are called children of light, who are of the Father of lights. Children of darkness are of their father the prince of darkness; but children of light are born of God; they owe, they derive their second, their new birth from him. Christ, the light of the world, is formed in them, they take this name from their Father; he is light, and those that are born of him are children of light.

2. *Propriety.* So Mat. viii. 12, υἱοὶ τῆς βασιλείας; those that challenge a title to the kingdom, a propriety in it as their inheritance. Those did but groundlessly challenge the kingdom, but these have a full title to all those blessed things that the Scripture expresses by light, these belong to them only peculiarly. They only have spiritual knowledge, holiness is their peculiar. The joys of the Spirit, the light of God's countenance shines on them, and a stranger does not enter into their joy; they are heirs of the promise, the only heirs of the inheritance of the saints.

3. *Destination.* 1 Sam. xx. 31, בן מות, one who is near to, worthy of, destined to death; so children of light, because they are ordained to it. They are predestinated to be conformed to the image of Christ in knowledge and holiness; chosen vessels, whom the Lord has set apart in his eternal counsel, to be filled with joy and glory. Whatever their portion seem to be on earth, in this vale of misery, it is but a valley they are to pass, and they will be in eternal light; there is but a valley, a step between them and glory.

4. *Residence.* Isa. xxi. 10, corn is בן גרני, ' the son of my floor,' because that is the place where it is laid up and abides. Children of light, because they abide in the light. Those that are unconverted, their element is darkness, sin, wrath, misery; here they walk, here they abide. But when a sinner is converted, his element is light. Such are not of the night, nor of darkness; the Day-spring from on high has visited them; the Sun of righteousness is risen upon them, and in his light they see light. In this they walk, in this they abide, and shall never see darkness, spiritual darkness, hell, wrath, misery; they are translated from thence into another kingdom, a region of light. The light may be clouded, but never quite extinguished.

5. *Constitution.* The Hebrew doctors call the name Jehovah, בן ארבע אותיות, ' the son of four letters,' because it is made up of four letters. So those that are converted may be called the children of light, because spiritual light is the constitution of their souls. Their minds, hearts, affections, are of a lightsome, *i. e.* a spiritual and heavenly temper; spiritual light in their minds, holiness in their wills, joy, delight, hopes of glory in their hearts.

6. *Obligation,* 2 Kings xiv. 14, בני התערבות. It is rendered hostages, but it is the ' sons of the contracts ' or covenants; those that were given to insure the engagement whereby Amariah had bound himself to the king of Israel. Those that are converted are in this sense children of light, because they are obliged to walk as those that are enlightened from above; to walk holily, to be followers of God as dear children. There are strong engagements laid upon them, they are bound by covenant thus to walk. This leads to the

Second question, What is it to walk as children of light? It is in this we shall have the substance of the text, and the scope which the apostle aims at in this chapter, indeed in the whole epistle, yea, in all his epistles; and therefore it calls for special enquiry and attention. Take it in this.

1. To walk at a distance from darkness, ver. 11 ; from sin, which is the work, which is the cause of all those woful things which the Holy Ghost expresses by darkness. 'What communion has light with darkness?' 2 Cor. vi. 14. He speaks of it as a most absurd incongruous thing, that those that are light should mingle with darkness. This is it which the Lord expects, this is it which this relation calls for. Those that are children of light, should have nothing to do with sin, with any sin whatsoever. Every degree of darkness is contrary to light; so every sin, small or great, open or secret, is opposite, contrary, altogether unbeseeming the blessed relation of a child of light. They may be ashamed to challenge this title who dare make bold with any sin, much more with gross sins.

Light is beautiful; a child of light is a pleasant child in the Lord's eye, as he calls Ephraim. Oh, but sin is the loathsomest defilement, the most odious deformity in that pure eye that cannot behold iniquity! Those that labour not to avoid every sin, wallow in it, besmear, pollute themselves with it, are they children of light? Are they not rather bastards, unworthy pretenders to this relation?

It is the very nature, the new nature of a child of light to avoid sin; as it is the nature of every man and woman to shun that which will make him ugly, loathsome, and deformed.

A child of light should avoid 'the very appearance of evil,' 1 Thes. v. 22; not only gross, open, scandalous evils, nor only secret, refined sins, which he knows to be evil and sinful, but even that which has the appearance of it; at such a distance should he walk from spiritual darkness, as not to come near the appearance of it. He hates the garments spotted with the flesh, Jude 23; not only sinful filthiness itself, but the appearance of it, though it be but in a garment. How charily will one keep a costly robe, a rich garment, from spots and stains! Children of light are covered with a robe of light; it behoves them to be fearful of it; this is that alone which spots and stains it. And these spots are not easily got out, it will cost more than the garment is worth to cleanse it from the stain of sin; nothing will do it but the precious blood of him who is God blessed for ever.

Light is comfortable. Oh but sin is the saddest, the most uncomfortable evil in earth, nay, in hell; children of light had need walk at a distance from this.

Light is glorious; so is the state of a child of light. Oh, but sin is the most shameful thing that ever appeared in the world : it turned the glory of the fallen angels into shame; it turned the glory of innocent man into shame. It is as shameful spewing upon the glory of a child of light; shameful spewing indeed, even as if a dog should vomit in thy face (it is the Holy Ghost's expression), this could not be such a shame to thee as every sin is in the eye of God. Oh what reason to avoid it!

If you would walk as children of light, you must be afraid of sin, hate it, grieve for it, labour to expel it.

Be afraid of it. Fear sin as hell; fear the darkness of sin as that utter darkness; indeed, it is more to be feared, for it is sin that made hell a place of darkness, *quod efficit tale, est magis tale*. If it made hell to be so, it is more so itself. Fear it as death, as the king of terrors; for it alone makes death terrible, it is the sting of it.

Hate it as thou wouldst hate for ever to live in darkness; as a poor freed prisoner hates his dungeon, as he hates to return to those fetters and vermin that were formerly his misery.

Grieve for it; for the remainders of it in thyself, for its over-spreading others. Grieve at it as thou wouldst do to see a gross, noisome, unwholesome fog deprive thee of the sight of sun and heaven. Such is the sad issue and woful nature of sin.

Labour to expel it; to expel the remainders of darkness out of thy soul. It is not enough for children of light to escape gross darkness, the pollutions of the world; nor is it enough to avoid the outward acts of sin. But this is the great work of a child of light, to maintain a constant combat with the remaining powers of darkness in his soul; make it his business to mortify those lusts and corruptions which, it may be, no eye sees, to stop up the fountain of darkness. As Christ is the fountain of spiritual light, so the heart is the fountain of spiritual darkness. 'Out of the heart,' &c., Mat. xv. 18, 19.

The great work of a child of light is about his heart. He is careful of his life, too, but he finds it an easier matter to avoid the outward acts of sin, to cut off the branches, than to kill it in the root; to subdue and mortify it in his heart, this is to stop up the fountain.

He should look upon it as a great part of the work he has to do in the world, not only to free his conversation from darkness, but to scatter it where it is most firmly seated, to scatter the remainders of it in his mind, will, affections. He fasts, mourns, prays, believes, and is diligent in the use of all means, that his inward and secret corruptions may be crucified, this soul-darkness more and more expelled. Thus must they walk, who walk as children of light.

2. To walk boldly; to be herein followers of God as dear children. How followers of God? The apostle tells us, 1 Pet. i. 15, 16, the light of holiness should shine in the lives of those that are Christ's; holiness both exercised and diffused.

Children of light must live in the exercise of holiness. It is not enough to be habitually sanctified, to have the habits and principles of spiritual life and holiness. Walking denotes motion and activeness. Holiness is spiritual light, wherever it be; but if it lie in the heart inactive, unexercised, it is but as a candle under a bushel. It should shine forth in the exercises of holiness. This precious talent is not given to be buried, or hid in a napkin; it should be improved and drawn forth in lively and vigorous actings. There should be the exercise of patience, humility, self-denial, heavenliness; the actings of faith, love, fear, hope; the motions of zeal, desire, delight. The armour of God, the whole armour of light must be put on, so as to be in readiness to act for God upon all occasions, Rom. xiii. 12. Grace unexercised is like armour laid aside; the apostle likes not this posture, he bids put it on. We must be always on our guard. We must be always ready for action.

Holiness diffused. Holiness must be extended to the whole conversation of a child of light. It is not enough to manifest a holy temper now and then by fits, under afflictions, or in good company, or in religious duties. A hypocrite may make a show of this upon such occasions; but he must walk holily, his whole course must be holy; he must be heavenly in worldly employments; holy in common affairs, even his recreations and earthly business. This is to walk as children of light.

3. Exemplarily. Children of light must walk so as to be light unto others, and this in divers particulars.

(1.) Unblameably. So as to give no cause of offence to the weak, nor no cause of reproach to the wicked. Carnal and perverse men will seek and take occasion to reproach those that belong to God, nor can the best many times avoid this; but though they will be apt to take occasion, yet should they be careful to give none, that they may be blameless in the sight of God, however carnal men censure them; and so the Lord will justify them, however the world charge and accuse them. Christ himself could not walk so, but those that bore ill will to him would take occasion to charge and reproach him; but though they took occasion, he gave none. 'The disciple is not better than his Master, nor the servant than his Lord,' John xv. 20. If our dear Lord could not escape the censures of wicked men, his servants must not expect it. If they run not with others to the same excess of riot, they will be charged with pride, singularity, covetousness, hypocrisy. This cannot be avoided so long as the evil spirit, the accuser of the brethren, rules in the children of disobedience. But this must be with all care avoided, that though they will take occasion, yet no just occasion may be given to these charges and censures. The children of light must use all diligence to walk in all good conscience towards men. Or if men will be so perverse as to mistake, and misconstrue their carriage, yet must they so walk as they may approve their hearts and ways to God, and so they may appeal to him in the midst of all censures and reproaches, 1 Pet. iii. 16.

Labour to walk, as Zacharias and Elizabeth, 'in all the commandments and ordinances of the Lord blameless,' Luke i. 6; that if the wicked will have a quarrel, they must pick one, no just occasion may be offered. To this the apostle exhorts, upon the same ground which is in the Philip. ii. 15. If you give just cause to others to blame and censure, this is a cloud to the light, this becomes not those that are light in the Lord. They should walk so as they may be 'found of him in peace, without spot and blameless,' 2 Peter iii. 14.

(2.) Their walking should be convictive. It should discover and manifest the sinfulness of those who walk in the ways of darkness. One contrary sets off another. It is the property of light to discover the hidden things of darkness; the conversion* of a child of light should be a real reproof to the men of the world. It is true, this is the way to incur their hatred; for those that walk in darkness hate the light, because thereby their deeds are reproved. But, however, this is it which your relation calls for; your strictness should reprove their looseness, your zeal their indifferency, your faith their unbelief, your conscientiousness in holy duties, their negligence of them. Though it sometimes incur their hatred, yet it may, it has, through the blessing of God, occasioned their conviction, their conversion. The light of your holy, heavenly walking should discover their darkness; this may leave a prick in the conscience of an unconverted man, and thy life may prove a real sermon, to bring him to God, 1 Peter iii. 1. There wants not experiments of this kind. Thy walking should be convictive, if thou walkest as a child of light.

(3.) Their walking should be imitable, *i.e.* worthy of imitation; so order their ways, as they may be a pattern unto others; so shine, as others may follow the light, not in affectation of pre-eminence, or singularity, in unwarranted opinions or practices; but in close following of Christ, and walking exactly according to the rule of holiness. Follow me as I follow Christ. Walk so as to be examples, so as to provoke others to love and good works, so as to shame the lukewarmness, formality, carnalness of others.

(4.) Their walking should be an ornament to their profession. There should be such a light in it as to beautify their profession, adorn the gospel, and make the ways of Christ lovely in the eyes of others; such a light as should not only put wickedness out of countenance, but gain credit to the professors and profession of Christ; such a lustre in your conversation as may reflect glory upon God. Let your light so shine, Mat. v. 16, so as to render the power of grace, and the excellency of religion, conspicuous, admired.

* Qu. 'conversation'?—ED.

4. *Cheerfully.* Being children of light, they are children of joy. That is their portion, they are all *Barnabases,* sons of consolation, and should walk accordingly.

Walk cheerfully, as in the light of God's countenance, as in that light that discovers to them the fountain of joy, the true grounds of all solid comfort, the great and precious promises, the high and glorious privileges, the sweet and honourable relations they have interest in.

Whatever tribulation they have in the world, in Christ they have peace. None in the world have true cause of joy but children of light. It is true they should be shy of carnal mirth; this is below them, the spring-head of their joys is higher, and the streams purer, and the taste sweeter, and more durable.

It is a disparagement to them and their relation, to be dejected with those things which sink the spirits of worldly men.

In the greatest outward calamities, though they are not to put off natural affections, yet they are never so to mourn, but as those that have hope, as those that have cause to rejoice in the Lord. When they hear and see such things as may occasion trembling, yet they may rejoice in trembling, as the prophet sweetly, Hab. iii. 16–18. When the children of darkness have fear in their greatest joy, these may have joy in their greatest fear. Though they be sometimes called to mourning, yet is there a blessed seed of joy in their mourning, Mat. v. 4, John xvi. 20. They are called to humiliation, and brokenness of heart; and as it consisteth in humble, self-denying, and mean thoughts of themselves, it should be their constant frame; but as it consisteth in anguish of mind, and dejection of heart, and disquietment of spirit, it becomes not their condition: their life should be a life of heavenly delights; they should get above doubtings, fears, soul-disquietments. Thanks, praise, joyful obedience, delight in God, cheerfulness in his presence, in his service, in doing, in suffering, is that which this relation calls for; and those who would walk like children of light must thus walk.

If it be inquired how we may walk as children of light? Besides what is said already in the explication, which may serve for this purpose, I shall lay down some rules which may help you both as directions to guide you in this way of walking, and as characters whereby you may thus discern whether you thus walk or no.

1. *Walk not according to opinion.* Groundless and false opinions, that is the rule by which most walk; not only the men of the world, but professors, seduced by their example, or by the darkness and corruption of their own minds and hearts. They judge of things, not as they are in truth and reality, nor as the Scripture or right reason represents them, but as others think of them, though groundlessly and erroneously, and regulate their walking by such a judgment. This is in Seneca's style, *secundum opinionem vivere,* to live according to vulgar opinion, and is a rule below those, who would live in the use of common reason, much more below those who are the disciples of Christ, and ' have learned of him, and been taught by him as the truth is in Jesus ;' the children of light should be far above this, and leave it to such as are in darkness. With them, *omnia ex opinione suspensa sunt,* the worth or value, the good or evil, of things is measured by false opinion, not by true measures.

For instance, how came riches, great estates, abundance of superfluities, to be so highly valued, above all by many, and too much by those who profess themselves crucified to the world, and the things of it? How came we by this great esteem of that which is much and great in the world? We are no led to it by the Spirit of God; the Scripture hath scarce a good word for riches, Heb. ii. 6, Mat. xiii., 1 Tim. vi. And reason and experience tell us that so much of the world hath more of care, and trouble, and vexation, and more danger of temptation, cumber, and hazard to ourselves than a competency. Whence is it, then, but from vain opinion, without Scripture, without reason? These things are of high esteem in the opinion of the world; this carries it against all, even those that are redeemed from the earth are swayed down by it. They are seduced by the common opinion, though it be a vulgar error. Men commonly think exceeding highly of these things, though no good reason can be given why they do so. Persons are valued for what they have, not for what they are. And he is a singular, a rare person, that does not more or less follow the common opinion.

So for curious fare, and fine apparel, and sumptuous accommodations, what is it that sets a value on them but vain opinion, when in reality that which is less, or meaner, would be as much or more for health, and strength, and comeliness, and all the ends for which these things are afforded us? All these it would satisfy, only it will not satisfy common repute, and the vain conceit of the generality concerning these things.

Now the children of light should be far from following this rule, else they walk not like themselves. It is for those that are blind, or in the dark, to judge of things, or value them by their vain opinion, and order themselves accordingly. This should not sway your judgments, nor order your designs, nor regulate your practices as to these outward things. It is a blind guide, and leads those that follow it fully into the ditch, and those that follow it but in part into by-paths, and such wherein the children of light should be afraid and ashamed to be found. Let not this guide you in your particular callings, nor measure your estates, or order your fare or habit, or accommodations; you have another rule, the Scripture and enlightened reason. The light of the word is the rule for the children of light. Observe what this discovers concerning these things, not what the world vainly thinks. There you have the judgment of the Spirit, the mind of Christ; this you should follow, not the opinion of the world, which lies in wickedness and in darkness, Rom. xii. 2. The children of light are 'transformed by the renewing of their mind,' so as they may discern 'what is that good, that acceptable, that perfect will of God,' to which the will and opinion of the world is opposite, and therefore they must not be conformed to it.

I might give you other instances as concerning sin. How is it that some sins pass for small, which the word of God declares to be great and dreadful; and some things which the Scripture represents as sins are counted no sins; and sin in general, which the Lord pronounces to be the greatest evil, is counted a less, a more tolerable evil than many outward grievances? Why, vain and common opinion carries it in these cases against the verdict of the Holy Ghost.

So for holiness. How comes it to be so little valued and regarded, when the Lord hath said so much concerning the absolute necessity and transcendent excellency of it? How is it, that a show of it will serve some, a little of it (so much as will barely be sufficient to bring one to heaven) will serve others? How is it, that many things are more esteemed, more passionately affected, more eagerly pursued? Why, vain opinion prevails here also, to the disparagement of that which is most valuable, and to the advancement of that which is but loss and dung in comparison.

To add no more. How is it that a low, afflicted, suffering condition is feared and shunned, as if it were the greatest evil on earth, whenas, being sanctified and improved, it may be more for the honour of Christ, and more for the advantage and prosperity of the soul, than the prosperous and flourishing condition in the world, and may more promote the main design and interest, both of Christ and his people? This can have no better ground than vain opinion, which Moses followed not, when he 'chose rather to suffer,' &c., and 'accounted the reproach of Christ,' &c., Heb. xi. 25, 26. He had not respect to common opinion, but to something else; nor did the apostle regard it, but something of another nature, 2 Cor. iv. 16–18.

2. Follow the light of the word fully. Make use of it to discover the whole will of God, concerning the duty of his children, that you may comply with it, and order heart and life by it. Study not only the promises and privileges which belong to your state (though this must be part of your study and inquiry); but also your duty in the full latitude of it (for it is of large extent, Ps. cxix. 96); what you owe to God, to yourselves, families, relations, brethren, enemies, all men, and inquire with a design to conform your souls and conversations to the whole will of God. Decline no part of it, whatever it be. Those that are in darkness may stumble upon some duties, but they are partial in the law, Mal. ii. 9. They accept faces (as in the Hebrew). Some duties please, some disquiet them; they pick and choose, some are taken, others are left, as their humour, interest, inclination serves them; some parts of their conversation is lightsome, but darkness is upon other parts thereof.

It must not be thus with those who would walk as children of light. The light of holiness must shine in every part of their souls, in every part of their lives; so as to be 'holy in all manner of conversation,' in an impartial, universal observance of the will of God, Ps. cxix. 6. Then may they be confident that they walk answerable to their state and relation, when they respect all; then need they not be ashamed, as those that live in contradiction. They walk not as children of light, who walk not in all, as Luke i. 6. All must be regarded and observed, but there is occasion to mind you more especially of some, of which you should have a particular care.

(1.) Those that are too much neglected by professors. Those to whom God hath made known his will have been subject, in several ages, to some neglects, which, prevailing, have proved fatal to them in the issue. You may see what neglects the Israelites of old were guilty of; their not worshipping God after his appointment, did principally bring the captivity. Afterwards, in Christ's time, there were some great pretenders to a more than ordinary holiness, were strict and severe in many duties, but declined others, of which they are admonished by Christ: 'These things ye ought to have done, but' &c. They were much for outward holiness, but neglected inward purity; very punctual in divers rites and observances, but overlooked the $βαρύτερα τοῦ νόμου$; seemed strict in the duties of the first table, which respect the worship of God, but omitted those of the second, little regarding righteousness and mercy. In the ancient church after Christ, the fatal neglect seems to have been their not keeping close to the rule of the word, in administration of worship, ordinances, and discipline, taking liberty to add or diminish, or vary herein, as they pleased. The consequence whereof was the letting in an inundation of corruption, which in fine settled in popery in the west, and a woful degeneracy in other parts of the world. In other places which have been reforming and cleansing themselves from these corruptions, there has been much care about doctrinals, and zeal and industry about the points controverted in religion, but too much. In general, I fear there is much guilt upon professors for not bringing forth fruits worthy of the gospel; those fruits of the Spirit, for which the Spirit of Christ was many years striving with us in the ministry of the gospel, not being filled with those fruits of righteousness; also for not improving those means and advantages we sometimes had for the carrying on of Christ's work amongst us, and the promoting of his interest in our own hearts and lives, and in others; and since the Lord's hand hath been stretched out against us for not learning righteousness by his judgments, not inquiring duly what design he had upon us in thus judging and chastening us, not complying with his design. So that it is a common complaint, that generally we are no better for our sufferings, still as proud, and vain, and selfish, and worldly; still as unmortified, as little refined as if we had not been in the furnace.

Children of light should better discern what God aims at in afflicting, and more readily follow him whither his correcting hand leads them.

Particularly, while we advance faith, let us not depress good works, but be careful to maintain them, Titus iii. 14, and to walk in them, Eph. ii. 10.

While we profess and magnify love to God, let not brotherly love be lost amongst us; that impartial universal love, which is called for everywhere in the New Testament; let not our love be confined to parties.

While we would have forbearance from others, let us not refuse to forbear one another in tolerable differences.

While we lay great stress upon hearing the word, let not other duties and ordinances be slighted or slightly attended.

While we oppose religious rites and ceremonies of human invention, let us neglect nothing which the Scripture shews to be of the substance of religion.

While we are for spiritual worship, let us not tolerate in ourselves an unspiritual, a carnal temper of heart in worshipping God.

While we are zealous for pure ordinances, let us not neglect the end and due improvement of them.

While we like not the gaudy and pompous dress of worship under the gospel, let us not be proud, and vain, and gaudy, in our own dress and garb.

While we seem tender and scrupulous in worshipping God, and what worship we offer to him, let us not overlook love and peace, righteousness, and mercy towards men: of which more anon.

Not to be tedious: let me commend some scriptures to your serious consideration, wherein some of the duties of Christ's disciples are laid down; and observe if divers of them be not too much neglected by those who profess subjection to Christ: Mat. v. 39, *ad fin.*, and Mat. vi. 19, 20; Mat. vii. 12; Rom. xii. 9, *ad fin.*; Gal. v. 22, *ad fin.*; Eph. iv. 25, &c.; Philip. ii. 1-5; Col. iii. 12-14; 1 Thes. v. 12-16; 1 Tim. vi. 17, 18; James i. 22-27; 1 Pet. iii. 8, &c.

To explain these passages is not my business, and many of them are plain. They are part of the rule by which a child of light should walk; and some of the duties herein specified have their observance amongst us; but whether many of them be not too much neglected and overlooked by those who profess an universal subjection to Christ, as their Lord and lawgiver, when you have duly perused, and seriously considered them, and compared the lives and deportment of professors therewith, you may be able to judge. If you would walk as children of light, be careful, especially, of those duties, those acts of holiness, the exercise of those graces, those parts of gospel obedience, which you see professors too apt to neglect; your great concernment in this may excuse me for staying so long upon it. Too much neglect of practical godliness, and the power of it; and we in these nations have our neglects too; the Lord hath not been scourging us all this while for nothing. These have had some hand at least in preparing the furnace, and heating of it.

(2.) Those for the neglect of which we are reproached. The Lord sometimes instructs his people by the mouths of enemies, and minds them of their duty, by such as little regard their own. We are charged at this day with the neglect of moral virtues, and the duties of the second table;

ministers for not pressing of them, and hearers for not making conscience to practise them : such as these, meekness, lowliness, peaceableness, mercifulness, liberty, charity, truth, faithfulness, candour, righteousness, temperance, patience, &c. Now this is a heavy charge, and great guilt is upon us if we deserve it, for those are things of great necessity and excellency. When they are from a right principle, and directed to a right end, they are not moral virtues only, but Christian graces, part of the divine nature and of the image of God; half of our religion consists in the exercise thereof, and those that are to seek here are but almost Christians. These are so far from being the children of light, that they who are destitute of them are below some of them who are in darkness. You find them even in the New Testament frequently and importunately called for: 2 Pet. i. 5, 6, 'Add to faith, virtue,' *i. e.* all moral virtues, say some; however, divers of them are here specified, ver. 8. Much of the fruitfulness of a Christian lies in these things, and he that lacketh them, whatever he have, whatever attainment he pretends to besides, is barren, ver. 9. He is blind, he is in darkness, he doth not, he cannot walk as a child. Godliness is not in its power, where it commands not the exercise of these. Those who take themselves to be in a higher form, and slight these things as below them, and pretend to be wholly taken up with spiritualness, heavenliness, living by faith and intimate communion with God, so as to neglect what should order their conversation towards men, are less absurd and preposterous than one who will needs be in his grammar when he hath not learned his primer, and thinks he can read well enough when he is not able to spell, or does not know his letters.

(3.) Such as the providence of God, and your present condition more particularly calls you to. Children of light should make use of the light, to discern in all circumstances that part of God's will, wherein they are more especially concerned, and apply themselves to special observance of that which is most seasonable, as *ex. gr.*

When you are under affliction, and the hand of God is upon you, if you walk under the cross as children of light, you should see (though such as are in darkness cannot, or will not) when his hand is stretched out, and humble yourselves under it, 1 Peter v. 6. You should observe what his hand points at, and take notice what he is correcting in you; what he would have you to reform, to leave, to do, to suffer; what his design is in thus exercising you with sad dispensations, and how you may serve it, and fully comply with it.

When your outward condition is prosperous and successful, you should be thankful, you may rejoice; but rejoice with trembling, as considering that outward prosperity is usually more hazardous to your souls than afflictions and sufferings; and a fair gleam often ushers in a storm, Ps. xxx. 6.

When you have abundance of this world, and outward comforts are still flowing in, use what you have faithfully for God, and employ, lay it out for those ends for which he hath entrusted you, as becomes those who are but stewards, and expect shortly to give an account of their stewardship; and as those who make account at present, that the tide may turn, as you see it daily doth, and that it may be low water with you ere long. Employ what you have, so as you will wish it had been employed when it is gone (for shortly it will be gone from you, or you from it), and then the comfort and advantage (which is more valuable than the things themselves) will remain, whatever be lost.

If you be cut short in these enjoyments already, learn now to count the all-sufficiency of God your riches, to value more, and be more diligent for that treasure which is above the reach of danger, and so may grow truly rich, rich unto God with a little, when others are poor, very poor in abundance.

When you have provisions for your souls, be careful that your souls thrive. If your souls be lean in a year of plenty, what will they be in a famine? If they be like the heath in the wilderness, when they have been watered with the first and latter rain; take heed lest the Lord command the heavens, &c. Learn of the ant, who provides her meat in summer, Prov. vi. 6–8; she knows by instinct winter will come; we have had some touches of a winter already, and sharper weather may come. When you are abridged of soul advantages, you have special warnings from heaven to be faithful in a little, lest the Lord take from you even that which you have. Children of light should above others be wise in their generation, to know their seasons and the duties of them, their light otherwise may add to their guilt, and make it greater, more conspicuous, and lead the Lord to more severity. You are upon trial, upon your good behaviour, one year more you are forborne after apparent hazards of being cut down; if more fruitfulness appear not, you know what follows, 'cut it down.'

(4.) Those that have a special tendency to endear religion and the ways of Christ to others, to acquaint those who are strangers to it with the excellency thereof; to convince those who are prejudiced against it, to win those and conquer them who are enemies to it.

There are many acts required of us which are of this nature and quality, and might through the blessing of God produce these happy effects. And the children of light are greatly concerned to make these their constant walk, to be very much in them if they will walk like themselves. But these acts are not those wherein secret converse and walking with God consists; not the inward actings and motions of their hearts towards God; not the more retired exercise of their graces betwixt God and their souls, for these others are not acquainted with, nor will they believe or regard them, unless there be some visible demonstration thereof. That which has this effect upon them must be something that they may see or be sensible of; something which they or the world may have advantage by; something which is lovely and commendable amongst the sons of men, for which they commonly have some reverence and esteem; in which there is some light and lustre which strikes their senses, and through them reaches their minds and consciences.

And this is it which Christ calls for in general from all the children of light, Mat. v. 16. We must do nothing to be seen of men, that we may have praise and applause, but many things we are bound to do which men must see, so as to be thereby provoked, obliged to glorify God in speaking and thinking well of his laws and ways. There is a light shines in good works, those works whereby we do good in the world, or do good to the place where we live, and to the persons with whom we deal and converse, which reflects glory upon God, when it makes them believe there is a singular goodness and excellency in that religion which produces so good effects. When they find by experience in those that profess it, such uprightness and candour, such bounty and mercy, such tenderness over others in all their concernments, such readiness to supply them, to relieve them, to be helpful to them every way, both for heaven and for the world, the children of light should not spare purse nor pains to effect this. And that is wretched and miserable sparing indeed, which opens the mouths of sinners against professors, and hardens their hearts against Christ's ways. Oh, let none that pretend to be light in the Lord, bring such a cloud of darkness upon their profession; 'better a millstone,' &c., and they and their estates sunk in the sea than give scandal.

The apostle Peter seconds the advice of Christ in words to the same effect, 1 Peter ii. 12. Such good works should be visible in the walking of children of light, that their persecutors (for *the day of visitation* there is probably a day of persecution), beholding them, may not only be silenced, and speak no more of them as evil-doers when they see and hear of so much good done by them, but may be won to a good opinion of their way (rendered by their good works so lovely), and so persuaded to embrace it and enter into it as the best way in the world. Oh that professors would fill their conversation with such acts and works, that those without may have a real convincing demonstration that their way is the best way in the world.

See how importunately the apostle Paul calls the children of light to the practice of those things which might commend and endear their profession to others, Philip. iv. 8. Whatsoever things are σεμνὰ, venerable, high in their esteem; whatever are προσφιλῆ, amiable, obliging to their affections; whatever are εὔφημα, commended in their discourse; if you have any regard of virtue, or to anything that is praiseworthy, make these your designs, propose these to yourselves as principally to be aimed at in your practice. There is no way so advantageous for the children of light to shine as lights in their stations, and to appear in the world like themselves, as this.

(5.) Those to which you have most averseness, to which your inclinations do least lead you; as there are some evils to which we are naturally more inclined than to others, so are there some parts of our duty, some acts of holiness to which we are more backward than to others. And as we are in most danger to fall into that evil to which we are naturally most addicted, so are we most subject to decline those acts and duties to which we have the least inclination; and as we are concerned to observe most what sin our corrupt nature is most prone to, and [to be] most watchful against it, so we are obliged to take notice especially what part of our duty we are most apt to decline, and to strive most with our own hearts to bring them to a compliance with the will of God in that particular. And herein the children of light will approve themselves to be children indeed, most obedient, and most dutiful, and most affectionate children, when they cross their own inclinations to comply with his will. Hereby you will have the comfort and evidence that you follow the Father of lights fully, when you follow him in those steps which you are naturally most averse to tread in, and most prone to skip over them, or turn aside from them.

And the same may be said of those parts of the divine will which cross our interest, the interest of self, of the world, or of the flesh, those which are inconsistent with our ease, our pleasure, our gain, and worldly advantage, or our safety, or our credit. Those who would walk as children of light, must follow their Father and observe his will, in those acts and duties that are unpleasing to the flesh, in those that are most difficult, in those that are very chargeable and expensive, in those that are reproached and disgraced; in those that are hazardous, and expose them to danger in their estates, or liberty, or lives, in all that is dear to them in the world. No fear, no hazard, no difficulty must stop them in their course, in the race set before them by their heavenly Father, nor turn them aside from it, who would walk and have the comfort of walking as children of light; and thus walking they will be indeed followers of God as dear children.

(6.) Those which you are under temptation to neglect. Many times we are more tempted to neglect some than others, and in more danger to neglect them then when under temptation. The children of light should walk so as to see their danger and avoid it. Those whose necks are under oppression or persecution, when the yoke is heavy and pinches sore, are in danger to neglect that special duty of the gospel, to love their enemies, and pray for them, and do good to them, which yet is the proper character of Christians, and their excellency above all others, *amicos diligere omnium est*, &c. So brethren, when they are of different ways and persuasions, those differences are apt to alienate their affections, and they are in danger to lose brotherly love, and to neglect the acts and offices of it one to another, which yet is a duty on which the gospel, next to faith, lays the greatest stress, and calls for most frequently, and with greatest importunity. They walk not as children of light, who walk not in love with one another. The apostle tells us they are in darkness, and walk in it, and are blinded by it, 1 John ii. 8–11.

So those that engage themselves much in the world, are in danger to neglect their families, and the duties they owe to God, and the souls of their relations, if they neglect not their own too.

Children of light should be wary where they are in most danger, and that is where they are under temptation. If you would walk as children of light, you must follow the light of the world fully, especially in the particulars specified.

3. Walk above the world and earthly things. Children of light are clothed with the sun; the moon, the world is under their feet, Rev. xii. 1. It has no high place in their minds or hearts; riches, pleasures, honours, and respect are thrown down in their thoughts, and cast out of their affections, they are not the design of their lives; the world is their footstool everywhere, and serves, does not command them.

They have no high esteem of the world, nor of those things that are of most value in dark minds; condemn riches and greatness, which others adore or admire. The light hath discovered to them something of another world, which outshines and disparages all that this world can tempt them with. They are ranked amongst the worst of children of darkness, who 'mind earthly things,' Philip. iii. 18, 19.

Their hearts and affections are estranged. They are to the world's breasts, which promise pleasure and plenty, as a weaned child; the world is crucified to them. It is now (whatever it was while they were darkness) as a lifeless untempting object, has no more beauty nor comeliness to draw out their affections to it, than a dead carcase, a crucified thing. They are in gross darkness that are in love with the world; 'the love of the Father is not in them;' it would not be so if the true light had shined in them. The apostle is positive, 1 John ii. 15; and more sharply, James iv. 4.

They seek it not. It is not pursued as their design; they follow it not to embrace it, but to crucify it; they seek it otherwise as though they sought it not, with some indifferency whether they have it or not, so they may have those better things. Other seekers of it are in palpable darkness, Mat. vi. 31, 32. They would be loath to leave no difference betwixt the children of light and the children of this world, betwixt the disciples of Christ and the Gentiles. Let the Gentiles that are in darkness, and see nothing better, seek these things; children of light 'seek those things that are above.' If a way be opened for them by the providence of God, to get more of the world, they proceed therein moderately, and very cautiously, lest the world should encroach upon their heavenly interest, lest the world should steal away those thoughts and affections, that care and time, and those endeavours which are due to God and to their souls; and lest, having more in trust they should not be faithful. They seek not the world for worldly ends, that they may rise higher and fare better, more deliciously, or that they may have more esteem and reputation (these are the low unworthy ends of sensualists and worldlings for themselves and their posterity); but that they may do more good, and be more serviceable, and more honour their profession, and shew the sincerity of their aims by really and freely employing what they get for those noble and generous purposes.

But I have formerly spoken to you more of this on another subject; and the Lord has since spoken to you concerning this in another language. Your guilt will be great, your condition very lamentable, if nothing prevail with you to walk as children of light in this particular; when the Lord has thundered from heaven, by one dreadful judgment after another, which seem directly levelled against worldliness.

4. *Walk in the sight of heaven.* Children of the light are the 'children of the kingdom,' heirs of heaven and glory, begotten again to an inheritance, &c. And that is one reason why they are called children of light, because they are heirs of the inheritance of the saints in light. If they walk like themselves, they walk as travelling towards their own country, and going to take possession of their inheritance and portion in another land, another world, and to look upon this world as a strange country, and upon themselves in it as strangers and pilgrims; upon their habitations, as inns and lodgings in a journey; upon their enjoyments, as the accommodations of an inn, in which they are to rest as it were but for a night, and to leave all as it were the next morning; and upon what they meet with in their way, whether pleasing or displeasing, as things wherein they are little concerned, being in a journey, passing from them, and hastening homewards: all the occurrences of this life being but as the passages of one day, compared with that eternity which is in their eye.

Under such apprehensions should children of light continually walk in the world, while their minds and hearts are at home, their conversation in heaven; their eye not upon the trifles of this life, but upon their portion and inheritance, their longings for possession of that happiness, those riches, those joys, that glory which shall be revealed. The view of this at a distance, their thoughts of it, does quicken, comfort, encourage them, put spirits and life into them, in all their actings for God, and motions towards him, or sufferings for his name's sake. This fortifies them against all the terrors and all the allurements of the world. They should make use of this to disgrace all that the world can tempt them with, to brush down, as a cobweb, whatever is a snare to a worldly heart.

What are the riches and treasures of the world but loss and dung, compared with those riches of glory, the treasures of our Father's kingdom?

What are the delights of sense, and pleasures of the world, but drops of mud? Drops, compared with those rivers of pleasures which are at God's right hand; and mud, compared with the pure river of the water of life, those pure, sinless, satisfying, enhappying, everlasting delights.

What is all the honour and splendour of the world, but as the glittering of a glow-worm to the glory of the sun in its full brightness, when compared with the glorious inheritance of the saints above?

What are the things on earth, which earthly hearts most affect and admire, but as trifles and children's playthings, compared with things above? A sight of that country which they seek, that place they are walking to, will help them to look upon all the glory of the world with contempt and disregard; and when they walk as children of light, they walk in such a sight of it.

Such a sight of it, as will also encourage them against all the sad things they may meet with in their walk. What though there be darkness here, days of blackness and thick darkness; there is everlasting light, without approach of night or spark* of darkness. What though there be troubles and afflictions, sufferings and tribulation, yet there is peace that shall never be disturbed, rest that can never be disquieted. After all that this world can do to disturb and disquiet us here below, there remains a rest for the people of God, an eternal rest.

What though we be tossed to and fro here, without any certain dwelling-place, and must think of removing as soon as one would think we were settled; yet there is a city that has foundations, where shortly we shall be settled to full contentment, so as no malice of men or devils shall ever remove us.

What though we be poor and mean, have little, and are in no way to compass more on earth; yet 'God has chosen the poor of the world, rich in faith, and heirs of a kingdom,' of such a kingdom, as all the kingdoms of earth are but toys and baubles to it.

What though all our earthly enjoyments be utterly uncertain, they may be consumed, or lost, or forced from us on a sudden, we can no way secure them a year, a week, a day to an end. Oh, but we have an inheritance; we have enjoyments and treasures above, which lie at no such uncertainties. They are reserved for us in the heavens, above the reach of rust, and moth, and water, and fire, and injustice, and violence. We look for a kingdom that cannot be shaken, 'though the earth be removed, and the mountains,' &c., which cannot be consumed, though the earth should be turned to ashes, and elements melt with fervent heat.

We are passing through a valley of tears to the joy of our Lord; through the malice and rage of men, to the enjoyment of that God who is love itself; through menaces and threatenings, to inherit the promises; through men's reproaches and hard measures, to the blessed welcomes of Christ, and his everlasting embraces. The sight, the thoughts of this, arms the children of light against all temptations, encourages them against all hardships and sufferings. So it did the apostles and primitive Christians, 2 Cor. iv. 16-18. This is to walk as children of light, 'not looking at things that are seen,' &c.

Motives. 1. Otherwise you live undutifully, as disobedient children. It is your Father, the Father of lights, that enjoins you to walk as children of light; if you walk otherwise, you are unlike your Father, you cannot please him, you disobey him, you are so far children of disobedience.

2. You cross God's design in honouring you with this title and relation; for this end you are begotten again, born of God; for this end he 'called you out of darkness into his marvellous light,' and made you 'light in the Lord.' If you walk not as children of light, you walk cross to God, and will be found a resister of him in a high degree, as those that would frustrate his design, and make him fall short of his end in thus honouring you.

3. You walk in a contradiction to your state and relation. So far as you walk not as children of light, you walk as children of darkness; and that is as if one that is advanced to be a prince should live as a shark or a beggar; or as if one that has the soul of a man should live like the beasts of the field.

4. You undermine your hopes, and weaken your title to the inheritance of the saints in light; you cannot plead your title to that inheritance further than you live like heirs of it; you live not like heirs if you walk not as children of light.

* Qu. 'speck'?—ED.

OF CHRIST SEEKING FRUIT, AND FINDING NONE.

He came and sought fruit thereon, and found none.—LUKE XIII. 6.

THESE words are part of a parable, the occasion of which we may find in the former verses. Some there present told Jesus what had befallen those Galileans, whom Pilate had slain at the altar, and sacrificed them while they were sacrificing; and so mingled their blood with the blood of the beasts that they were killing for sacrifice.

He, willing they should make good use hereof, would have them to apprehend the danger themselves were in, and thereupon to break off their sins by repentance, lest some such sudden stroke falling upon them, they should perish in impenitency.

And because he foresaw they might evade this, by imagining they were in no such danger, upon a supposition they were in no such guilt as those Galileans, he shews them the vanity of these imaginations, and tells them plainly, they had guilt enough upon them to ruin them, unless they did repent, ver. 2, 3. And, that he might make the deeper impression on them, he repeats it under another instance of like nature, ver. 4, 5, as if he had said, Do not think yourselves secure, upon a conceit that your sins are less than theirs, who were thus surprised by death and judgment; you have sin enough to destroy you, unless you prevent it by repentance.

And having told them that, unless they repented, they should also perish, it might be inquired, how they should perish? To which he seems to answer by this parable: they would perish, as this fig-tree did, which being planted in a commodious place (a vineyard), and having all advantages to render it fruitful, yet continued barren; whereupon the owner of it, after all means used to improve it, and the exercise of patience year after year, in expectation of some fruit, meeting with nothing but disappointments, resolves it shall cumber the ground no longer, but gives order to have it cut down.

This is the sum of the parable; and the ἀπόδοσις, the meaning of it, is this: those persons who are planted under the means of grace, and have all helps and advantages requisite to make them spiritually fruitful, they ought to bring forth the fruits of the Spirit. The Lord, who has so planted and privileged them, expects it of them; and if they answer not his expectation, he may bear with them for some years, while his servants, those who labour in his vineyard, the ministers of the gospel, are taking pains with them, and using all means proper for their improvement; but if, after all this, they continue still barren, he will have them cut down; they shall have a standing no longer in his vineyard; no more care and pains shall be lost upon them; they shall not encumber the ground any longer, nor possess the place, on which others being planted, would bring forth fruit; in fine, they shall be destroyed.

The words I have pitched on are the beginning of the parable, which affords us this

Observation; Those who enjoy the means of fruitfulness should bring forth fruit; those who are planted in the Lord's vineyard, and have a standing under the means of grace, should be fruitful.

This is clear in the words, and indeed in every part of this parable.

1. They are planted in the vineyard for this purpose. That is the proper place for fruit-trees; another place than the vineyard would serve them, if they were not set there for fruit.

2. The Lord, who gives them place here, expects it. He is said to come and *seek* fruit, ver. 6, 7. It is that which he has just cause to look for.

3. He heinously resents it when he finds no fruit, and expresses his resentment to the dresser of his vineyard. It is an abuse of his patience; the longer he bears with such barrenness, the more it is abused. It is a provocation that he will not bear long with. After three years' forbearance, he passes that severe sentence, *cut it down.*

4. It is an injury to the place where they stand. They cumber the ground, that is the reason of the sentence, ver. 7. It takes up that room which might be better employed; it sucks away that moisture which would make others fruitful; it overdrops the plants that are under it, hinders the spreading and fruitfulness of others. A better improvement might be made of the ground; it is a loss to the owner of the vineyard, when such a plant is suffered, καταργεῖ; which may signify the spending the heart of the ground to no purpose, ver. 7.

5. Those who have most tenderness for such, can have no ground to seek a long forbearance of this barrenness. The dresser of the vineyard will venture to beg no more forbearance than one year, after that he yields it up to excision, vers. 8, 9.

6. All labour and pains, all care and culture, in digging about and dunging it, is lost upon it. Those whom the Lord employs to use all means for their improvement, have nothing left them in the issue, but occasion of sad complaint, that they have laboured in vain, spent their strength for nought, Isa. xlix. 4.

7. Such will certainly be ruined. Where fruit is not found, nothing can be expected but cutting down. The lord of the vineyard will not spare them, and the dressers of the vineyard will not longer intercede for them. All in a little while agree in that fatal conclusion, *cut it down.*

All these, and each of them, make it evident, that those who are planted under the means of grace, are highly concerned to bring forth fruit.

The most pertinent and profitable inquiry, for further clearing of this truth, will be, what fruits it is they should bring forth? What we are to understand by *fruit,* and that *fruitfulness* which is so much our duty? And of this I shall give you an account by the quality, quantity, and continuance of it. To these heads we may reduce those severals, whereby the Scriptures express to us what this fruit is.

I. For quality. It must be *good* fruit. Grapes, not 'wild grapes' (as the prophet expresseth in a parable very like to this, Isa. v. 2, 4). Wild grapes are for the wilderness, not for the Lord's vineyard, Mat. iii. 10, and vii. 19. Good fruits are acts of goodness; taking acts largely, as comprising words, thoughts, actions, motions inward and outward. Acts of goodness opposed to sinful acts; as Basil, ἔργα δικαιοσύνης ἀντικείμενα τῇ ἁμαρτίᾳ: good acts, opposite to what is evil and sinful. Now *bonum est ex integris causis*, that acts may be good, there must be a concurrence of all the causes requisite to make them good, and constitute their goodness. And these causes we have specified in Scripture, which I shall briefly touch.

1. As to the efficient. Good fruits are called 'fruits of the Spirit,' Gal. v. 22, Eph. v. 9; such fruits as the Spirit of grace helps us to bring forth, by sanctifying the heart, which else is no soil fit to bring forth good fruit, and influencing, moving in it, and acting it when it is sanctified. The fruits of the flesh, the fruits of our own spirit, as they are carnal, selfish, and earthly, are no good fruits. The fruits of the Spirit are good fruits, and those only.

2. As to their matter and form. Good fruits are such as are called 'fruits of holiness and righteousness.' They are acts of holiness, Rom. vi. 22, taken in that latitude, as comprising godliness, sobriety, and righteousness, according to the apostle's distribution, Titus ii. 12. Then we bring forth good fruits, when we 'live soberly, righteously, and godly.' Acts of piety towards God, and acts of justice towards men, and acts of sobriety towards ourselves, are the good fruits we should bring forth.

These are called 'fruits of righteousness;' that word being also taken largely, as containing all that we owe to God, to others, to ourselves, 2 Cor. ix. 10, Heb. xii. 11, James iii. 18.

And as to the form. Then they are good fruits, when produced in a way and manner conformable to the rule of holiness; when thoughts, and inclinations, and designs, and affections, and words, and actions, are ordered by that rule, then we bring forth 'fruit unto holiness.' When we think, and intend, and affect, and speak, and act in such a manner as the rule of righteousness requires, then we bring forth the fruits of righteousness, the good fruits which we ought to bring forth.

3. As to the end. Good fruit is such as is brought forth unto God, Rom. vii. 4; then we bring forth fruit to God, when what we think, and speak, and act, is in reference to him, out of obedience to his will, with an intent to serve him, out of a desire to please him, with a design to honour him. When the serving, and pleasing, and glorifying, and enjoying of God is the end of all; a special goodness is hereby derived upon all our fruit, it is then brought forth unto God. When we bring forth fruit unto sin, unto the flesh, unto the world, that is cursed fruit. When we bring forth fruit to ourselves, that is no fruit in God's account. Accordingly Israel is called an empty vine, because she brought forth fruit to herself, Hosea x. 1. They are empty trees that have no other fruit; it is none, or as good as none, no good fruit that is brought forth to ourselves; that is only good which is brought forth to God.

More particularly, that it may be good fruit, it must be.

(1.) Real. A show, an appearance of fruit will not suffice. If it be not real, it has not a metaphysical goodness, much less a moral or spiritual. The fig-tree in the gospel made some show of fruit; but Christ finding none upon it really, he cursed it, and it withered, Mat. xxi. 19. It must not be like the apples of Sodom, which has nothing to commend it, but only a fair outside. Fair appearances may delude men, and pass for better fruit with them than that which is good indeed. But God is not, cannot be mocked;

it is he that comes to seek fruit, and it is not the fairest shows will satisfy him, it must be real.

(2.) It must be such as imports a change of the soul, that brings it forth, Mat. iii. 8; ἄξιον τῆς μετανοίας, fruit worthy of another mind, another soul than he had before. Athanasius explains the word by μετατίθεσθαι τὸν νοῦν ἀπὸ τοῦ κακοῦ πρὸς τὸ ἀγαθόν, a change of the mind from evil to good, Mat. vii. 17, 18, Luke vi. 43. The tree, *i. e.* the heart, must be good before it can bring forth good fruit; but naturally it is an evil and corrupt tree, and grows wild, it must be transplanted into another soil, or engraffed into another stock, that the nature and quality of it may be changed, that its fruit may be good, else that which it brings forth will be wild grapes, corrupt fruits, not such as the lord of the vineyard comes to look for. Your natures must be changed, your hearts must be renewed, your souls must be taken off from the old stock wherein ye were born, and have continued, and engraffed into Christ ere your fruit can be good, John xv. 4, 5. The old soil of nature brings forth nothing but briars and thorns, such as is near unto cursing, ' whose end will be burning ' (as the apostle, Heb. vi.); or at best, it brings forth nothing but fine weeds. The best thoughts and actions of an unregenerate person, how goodly or specious soever they may seem to himself or others, are but *splendida peccata*, gilded evils, or sins of a better gloss. The soil of your natures must be quite altered by renewing grace, before it can produce anything good in the account of God. Regeneration is as necessary before good fruit indeed, as natural life is before action. You must be born again before you can bear good fruit.

(3.) It must be distinguishing fruit; such as no trees can bring forth but those that are good, and such as will make their goodness apparent, Mat. vii. 16, 20; such as may approve ye to God and your own consciences, to be trees of righteousness, the planted of the Lord, and such as may make this known to men too, so far as by visible acts it may be known; such as may carry a conviction with them to the consciences of others, that you are indeed what you profess yourselves to be, such as will leave them no just exception against it, 1 Peter iii. 16.

Such fruits as no formalist, no hypocrite, no mere moralist can shew; something singular, that you may not be nonplussed with that question, What singular thing do ye?

Something more, something above and beyond, not only what the men of the world do, but what common professors can reach.

Such, by which you may be known to be not only new creatures, but of some proficiency in the knowledge of Christ, and the course of practical godliness, according to your standing. Such as will demonstrate to the world, that you are holy, humble, mortified, self-denying, public-spirited, heavenly-minded, truly crucified to the world; and have not only a form, but the power of godliness, that you do not only profess this, but are thus.

(4.) Seasonable. That it may be good fruit, it must be brought forth ' in due season,' Ps. i., Mat. xxi. 41. The lord of the vineyard looks for fruit in his season, Mark xii. 2, Luke xx. 10. There is a season for everything, Eccles. iii. 1, and then, if ever, it is good; good words are good fruit, when in season, Isa. l. 4, Prov. xxv. 11. But there is a time when they are not good fruit, and that is the time the apostle speaks of, James ii. 15, 16. Good words alone are not at this time good fruits; in such a case they are not in season, for this is the season for good works. So good thoughts are good fruit, when in season, when we are called to meditation, but not when we are called to prayer; then they are not good, because that is not their season.

That is most acceptable fruit, which is in due season, Num. xxviii. 2. The best offerings, if unseasonable, would be unacceptable. Even the actings and exercise of grace, if it be not in season, will not be good fruit. Patience, when we are provoked, is good; but not when we hear God blasphemed. Spiritual rejoicing is excellent fruit, but not while we are called to mourning.

The actings of grace have a more particular goodness in their proper seasons. Faith in hard trials, patience in tribulation, meekness in provocations, contentment in wants, courage in dangers, humility in the midst of applause, crucifiedness to the world, in abundance of it, in a confluence of riches and delights: here they are excellent fruit; this is their season.

(5.) Sound. A fair skin is not enough to commend fruit for good, if it be rotten within. And so is our fruit, if the inward temper and motions of the heart be not correspondent to the outward actions and expressions. If we use the words of a prayer, but the heart prays not, the soul is not in motion towards God, the affections go not along with our confessions or petitions. Or if we praise God, but make not melody in our hearts, the soul exalts him not, the mind has no high apprehensions of him, no inward motions of love and delight, while our lips speak his praise. This is to 'draw near unto God with our mouths only,' Isa. xxix. 13. The fruit is not sound, if the heart be not in it. You offer to God but the parings or the picture of fruit, without this; which is to mock God, not to offer the fruit he desires.

So when we speak of heavenly or spiritual things, without a spiritual sense of what we speak; when we relieve our brethren, but without inward affection or compassions to them; when we put the outward conversation in some handsome order, but neglect the temper and posture of the inward man: this is but such fruit as the Pharisees did bear, Mat. xxiii. 25-28. Whatsoever appear in your words and actions, if the heart tolerate unruly passions, or harbour unmortified lusts, or give free way to selfish, carnal, earthly inclinations, your fruit cannot be sound at heart; you may please yourselves or others with it, but God will never count it good; if it have the outward shape of fruit, yet there is worms and vermin in it, which make it good for nought.

II. For the quantity. It ought to be *much*, John xv. 5, 8. There should be,

1. A fulness of fruit. Those that enjoy the means, must not only bring forth fruit, but be fruitful; should bear abundance. Heart and life should be filled with it, Philip. i. 11. You count not that a fruitful tree, when one or two branches only bear fruit, and the rest have nothing but leaves, or when each branch has a fig or two; but when all the boughs are full. It is not fruitfulness when there are 'two or three berries in the top of the uppermost bough, or four or five in the outmost branches,' as the expression is, Isa. xvii. 6. Every branch should have fruit, and should bear some plenty of it. Both heart and life should bear fruit, and every branch of both; every power of the soul, and every part of the life, must bring forth plenty, abundance of it: Philip. iv. 17, 'fruit that may abound.' The mind should be filled with knowledge, and taken up with good thoughts. The heart should bring forth good inclinations, holy intentions, spiritual affections, all the graces of the Spirit, and should abound therein. Love, upon which the other affections depend, should abound, Philip. i. 9, 1 Thes. iii. 12. And we must abound in every grace, if we would be fruitful, 2 Pet. i. 5-8. Unless we will be barren and unfruitful, these graces, all of them, must not only be in us, but abound.

And there must be fruit in the outmost branches too, in the conversation;

this should be full of fruits, ready to bring forth every good word and work, James iii. 17.

Scriptural knowledge and good thoughts are but some fruit in the uppermost branch. If the other boughs be bare, the tree is far from being fruitful. Good inclinations, purposes, desires, are but as some berries in the middle boughs. A tree may be barren for all these. And good words or works are but fruit in the outmost branches. A tree is not full of fruit, and so not fruitful, if all the main branches do not bear and bring forth plenty. Mind, and heart, and life, must bring forth fruit in some abundance. Knowledge should abound in the mind; holy affections and spiritual graces should abound in the heart; and ' out of the abundance of the heart' should ' the mouth speak,' and all other parts act for God, so as to be ' always abounding in the work of the Lord.'

2. A proportionableness to the means of fruitfulness, to the plenty and power of them. So much as will answer the care and pains is taken with them. If a man take more pains, and be at more charge in opening the roots of a tree, and dunging it, and pruning it, in fencing and watering it, and it bring forth less or no more fruit than another that has no such care and pains taken with it, it will scarce pass for a good, a fruitful tree. That is barren ground, which brings forth less, after all care and culture, than that which has less tillage.

Those who enjoy the gospel in great light, power; who have the mysteries of it clearly discovered, practically enforced, and brought home to mind, conscience, will, affections, so as the light, force, and influence of it may reach the whole man, the whole life, and have this continued many years; if they bring not forth more fruit than such as have the gospel, but not with such advantages, under a less powerful and advantageous ministry of it, they are wofully defective in fruit-bearing; for we are told, Luke xii. 48, ' men expect more from those to whom they have committed much.' And so does the Lord; and those that answer not his expectation, in a case where reason and equity amongst men do justify it, are sinfully defective in the quantity of what they bring forth.

It cannot be well resented, if the Lord reap sparingly where he sows bountifully. When the Jews sowed much, and brought in little, Hag. i. 6, there was a judgment, a curse in it, and so some guilt and provocation. So may the Lord's husbandmen judge, those that labour in his vineyard; when they improve all their skin, run all hazards, take all pains, spare no cost, are ready to spend and be spent for the improvement of souls, and yet it comes to little, here is some curse upon the ground, or such barrenness as deserves a curse. If he who (as I have told you on another occasion) received five talents, had but gained three, or made no more improvement thereof than he that received but one, he would scarce have been counted a profitable servant. The improvement should be answerable to what is received.

It is true, all that are good ground bring not forth fruit alike, some thirty fold, some sixty, some an hundred. If thirty be answerable to the means of fruitfulness, it may be an argument of good ground; but if sixty be but brought forth, where means are used sufficient to improve it for bearing an hundredfold, the ground may be under the censure of barren.

3. An increase. Those who enjoy the means of fruitfulness, must grow more and more fruitful. The longer they stand in the vineyard, and continue under the means of grace, the more fruit they should bear. You expect not much of a tree the first year; but after it is of standing to bear, you expect it should every year increase in fruitfulness, and bring forth more and more.

So the Lord expects from us. Our proficiency and fruitfulness should be according to our standing. The longer we continue under the means of grace, the more fruitful should we be; there should be an advance and increase of fruit every year, John xv. 2.

There must be a growth in knowledge, in grace, 2 Pet. iii. 18; a growth in faith, in charity, 2 Thes. i. 3. There must be more acts of grace; it should be more in exercise; and the actings of it should be more and more strong and vigorous.

There must be a growth in good works too, a walking on therein, Eph. ii. The longer standing, the more good we should do; we should do good to more, and do them more good; the branches should spread, and the fruits extend to the refreshing of more.

That which is little at first, must grow much; and that which is now much will not be enough, unless it grow more. It will not be sufficient, that we abound in knowledge, in holiness, in good works, or any fruits of righteousness, unless we abound more and more, 1 Thes. iv. 1. We must abound more and more in all things wherein we ought to walk, and whereby we may please God, *i. e.* in all pleasing fruit. A tree that bears no more in after years than it did the first, you will not esteem a good or a fruitful tree, Ps. xcii. 13, 14, still עוֹד, yet more.

4. Variety. Their fruit must not only be much of some sort, but of every sort. They must not only abound in some kind of fruit, but must bring forth fruits of all kinds. It is enough to make another tree fruitful, that it bears much fruit of one sort, but a tree of righteousness is not fruitful unless it bring forth all the fruits of righteousness, of what sort and kind soever. It must be so far like that tree of life, Rev. xxii. 2, which bears twelve manner of fruits. It must bring forth all manner of fruits which become the gospel; not light and knowledge only, but heat and affection; not some only, but all holy affections; not some acts of holiness only, but the exercise of every grace in all its variety of actings, so that all grace may abound; not inward thoughts and motions only, but outward acts of goodness, and all sorts thereof; not some good works, but 'every good work,' Col. i. 10, 11. He that is fruitful indeed is fruitful in every good thought, in every holy affection, every heavenly grace, and in every good work, and labours to abound therein, 2 Cor. ix. 8. Not only in every good work, but every good thing, 2 Cor. viii. 7.

III. For continuance. It must be *lasting* fruit. Of which in three particulars.

1. The fruit they bear must continue. It must not wither and come to nothing before the Lord of the vineyard come to reap it. The apostle Jude speaks of some trees 'whose fruit withereth,' and in the next words says, they are 'trees without fruit,' Jude, ver. 12. So that withering fruit is no fruit in the language and account of the Spirit of God; and trees that bear no other fruit are barren, *i. e.* trees without fruit. Such was that fruit brought forth in the thorny ground, Mat. xiii. 7, and that in the stony ground, ver. 5, 6. Such fruit are good thoughts when they are not realised upon the heart or in the life. Thoughts of good things that never come to good, and convictions that vanish too soon, fall short of conversion in the unregenerate, and of reformation in others. Such are good inclinations, purposes, desires, that are not pursued into action; and good affections and resolutions, that never come into execution. As when a person has some thoughts and intentions of leaving an evil way, a course of worldliness, or lukewarmness, or slothfulness, or intemperance, or Sabbath breaking, but the pleasure, ease, or advantage which Satan or his own deceitful heart promises him in such a way, stifles them in the birth, so that they never see

the light; or when one inclines or purposes to betake himself to that strict way of godliness which the gospel calls him to, but persecution, or fear of sufferings, nips those resolutions in the bud; or when some good motions and affections are raised by the word, but when the sermon is ended, the cares of the world, riches, pleasures, Luke viii., of this life, or some such quench-coal, extinguishes them; or when sickness, affliction, or apprehensions of death and judgment, brings them to serious reflections upon the evil of former ways, and some intentions to abandon them and take a new course, but upon recovery of health, and the removal of God's hand, fear vanishes, and those impressions wear off, and all good motions prove but *ægri somnia*, as a dream, which he forgets when he awakes, and minds no more, however it affected him when it was working in his fancy.

Whatsoever it is that thus springs up, but continues not till it be ripened, how good soever it seem, what hopes soever it gives, it is not such fruit as the Lord expects. Thus vanishing, it leaves those who bear it unfruitful, Mat. xiii. 22. They are not fruitful who bring not fruit to perfection, Luke viii. 14, τελεσφορεῖν, a word used of women that go their full time, do not miscarry nor bring forth abortives. She that still miscarries, and brings not forth live children, will be a childless woman, how often soever she conceive. And so will he that brings not forth lasting fruit be a barren and fruitless person, how fair soever he bud.

2. They must continue bearing fruit. The good ground did approve itself to be good, because it brought forth fruit 'with patience,' Luke viii. 15; ἐν ὑπομονῇ, which may as well be rendered according to the import of the word, and more congruously as to the sense of the expression, 'with perseverance.' They only are good and fruitful ground, who persevere and hold out in bearing fruit. A tree that bears the first year, but afterwards brings forth little or nothing, may be cut down amongst those that do but cumber the ground. The Galatians, who made a fair show of fruit at first, but afterwards intermitted, are bewailed by the apostle as barren, and such on whom he had lost his labour, Gal. iv. 11.

3. They must be bearing it always; not only *semper*, as a tree that fails not of fruit once a year, but *ad semper*, as if a tree should bear fruit all the year long. Some tell us of a fig-tree in Palestine that never was without leaves or without fruit on it, and that it was such a tree which is mentioned, Mark xi. 13, though that degenerated, and was then fruitless. Those of the Lord's planting should be like the best of those fig-trees, on whom fruit might be found all the year round. Their season for fruit is not only autumn or summer, but every quarter, every month, every day, every hour; whenever they are found without fruit they are culpably barren. All time whatsoever, every moment, is their season for fruit-bearing; and the Lord looks for it not only once a year, but every part of the year, and may proceed against them whenever he finds it not, though he come and look for it every hour. Every part of a Christian's life, when he is in a capacity to think, or speak, or act, is a fruit season; and every thought, word, and action should be fruit unto God in one respect or other, else he cannot answer it, 1 Cor. x. 31. It is good fruit that glorifies God, and nothing else. Whatsoever we do, not only in religious, but civil and natural actions, it should glorify God; and therefore whatever we do should be good fruit. God is most glorified when we bring forth much fruit, John xv. And when whatever we do is fruit unto God, then we bring forth much fruit, and bring it forth always.

Use 1. This leads us to take up a lamentation for the barrenness of the place, the unfruitfulness of the people of this land. No people under heaven that have the gospel, and the means of fruitfulness, with more advantages than we; no people from whom the Lord might expect more and better fruits than from us. But when he comes year after year seeking fruit, what does he find amongst us? How few are there in comparison that brings forth good fruit; how much fewer that bring forth much fruit; how many that bring forth little or nothing but leaves! Nay, well were it with us if the generality of this people did not, instead of good fruit, bring forth cursed fruit; instead of that which should please the Lord, bear that which is a high provocation to him.

How may the Lord take up that complaint against us which he did of old by the prophet, Isa. v., he 'planted us in a very fruitful hill,' and we have turned into a Sodom. He 'fenced' us to keep out cattle and wild beasts; and those that are fenced in are turned wild beasts, beasts of prey. He gathered out the stones thereof;' and yet it is almost all become stony ground. He 'planted it with the choicest vine;' and it is become a degenerate plant, and brings forth grapes of gall. He 'built a tower in the midst thereof,' a place for the keepers of it, most convenient for oversight; and it is turned into a Babel. He 'made a wine-press therein,' sent priests and prophets to press the people to obedience; and instead of pressing out that pleasant liquor, grateful to God and man, it is made use of to press the souls and consciences of those that are obedient. He 'looked for grapes, and behold, wild grapes.' He looked for good, for choice fruit, and behold, corrupt, rotten, and poisonous fruit. He looked for such fruit as the choicest plants bring forth; but 'our vine is the vine of Sodom,' &c. Deut. xxxii. 32, 33, he 'looked for judgment,' as ver. 7. He looked for the fruits of holiness, and behold, the most horrid profaneness, contempt of God, rejecting of his gospel, perverting of his ordinances, corrupting of his worship, profaning of his name, of his day; superstition, atheism, infidelity, blasphemy, and overflowing perjury.

He looked for the fruits of righteousness, and behold, injustice, violence, blood-guiltiness, outrageous intemperance, brutish, impudent uncleanness. Behold, all those abominations, and more, and worse than all those for which the Lord had a controversy with degenerate Israel of old: Hosea iv. 1-3, 'Therefore does the land mourn,' because the people of it do not mourn for these rebellions; therefore do those that dwell therein languish, and complain of a general consumption.

We declare our sin as Sodom; and we that should have been the best people in the world have made ourselves worse generally, and more vile than many of the heathen. Some dim, weak principles of morality prevailed more with many of them than the gospel in all its evidence and power has prevailed with thousands and thousands amongst us.

We justify those nations whom God has destroyed, those churches which he has laid desolate for their provocation. We seem to out-vie them all in wickedness. And is there not something that aggravates our rebellions against God, and heightens the provocation of them above what can be found amongst others? Clearer light, and greater mercies, and mighty strivings with us in the ministry of the gospel.

And besides this, the impudence, incorrigibleness, and universalness—of our unfruitfulness, shall I say? that is too mild a word—of our gross, abhorred wickedness, does testify against us.

We have got a whore's forehead; we despise shame, we glory in our shame; we boast of that at which the sun may blush; we harden our faces as a rock; and he that would bring us to shame shall but dash himself against it. It is a shame not to bring forth good fruit, and he that speaks but of the fruits of the Spirit will be derided.

We are incorrigible. The Lord has been pruning us to prevent the bearing of this cursed fruit, and he has done it with a severe hand, has made us bleed again and again; and after all we grow wilder and wilder, and our luxuriances sprout out in greater length and number. He has 'laid the axe to the root of the tree,' year after year; yea, given some terrible strokes, and threatened that he will not suffer us still to be a growing reproach to him and to his gospel; but all to no purpose; nay, he has cast many thousand fruitless branches into the fire before our eyes, and hereby shewed what the rest may expect. But what effect has all this had upon us? We seem not only past shame, but past fear. We out-dare heaven, and sin in the face of God, when he appears most terrible, when he is revealing his wrath from heaven against our sin; we set at nought his dreadfullest judgments, but rush through plague, and sword, and fire in our course of rebellion; and say, in effect, Tush! we regard not what the Almighty has done or can do to us.

And this is growing universal. All flesh, all sorts corrupting themselves. Wickedness is mounted aloft, and is subduing the nation, and having all advantages, finds little resistance; it goes on in triumph; it has been too hard for that which should make the greatest opposition; the sword of justice is turned another way; the sword of the Spirit is hid too much in corners. What can stop it? What weapon is there formed against it? Who can check its successful progress? It comes in like a mighty flood, has borne down all its banks; its roarings are as the noise of many waters; it is a deluge, and as to these nations like to prove universal.

And what will be the issue of this, what heart does not tremble that considers it? If we brought forth no fruit, none that is good, that is enough to provoke God to cut us down, as you see in this parable. But when we bring forth gall and wormwood, Deut. xxix. 18; when, instead of good fruit, our branches are full of caterpillars and vermin; when we are so far from bringing forth pleasant fruits, as we bear in abundance that which God abhors: how shall we escape? How dreadfully shall we fall! By what a terrible stroke may we expect to be cut down; and what shall secure us from it? Who shall intercede for us? The vine-dresser did plead and prevail here with the lord of the vineyard for some forbearance of the fruitless fig-tree; but our vine-dressers, where are they? Are not thousands driven out of the vineyard? They may not dig about it, not dung it; they must* use the means to prevent its ruin; and those that remain, too many of them mind something else, and content themselves with other fruits than the Lord looks for.

Oh, what, how much have we done to render our condition hopeless, and past remedy! What need is there of mourning and great lamentation! What necessity of strong cries, and great wrestlings, to prevent the woful consequences of our unfruitfulness in all that is good and desirable; our fruitfulness in all that is provoking, and in that which is most so. How highly are they concerned who bear any good fruit to bring forth still more and better, that so when the tree, the nation, is an eye-sore to God, and the very sight of it provokes him to cut it down by some astonishing strokes, yet seeing some branches well replenished with fruit that he takes pleasure in, he may yet spare the whole a little longer.

Use 2. For exhortation. If those that enjoy the means of fruitfulness ought to bring forth, then are you highly concerned to take notice of it as your duty, to be fruitful, and to comply with the Lord herein. The Lord has vouchsafed you the gospel, and the means of grace; he has planted you by the rivers of waters, in a very fruitful place; he has been a dew unto you,

* Qu. 'must not'?—ED.

and has watered you with the first and latter rain; he has sent his labourers amongst you, one after another, and has employed them to dig about you, and dung and water you; to take all pains, use all means; to spend their time, their parts, their strength, themselves for this purpose ; he has been pruning you by judgments and afflictions, and thereby been lopping off whatever might hinder you from being fruitful ; he has warned you, by what has befallen others for their barrenness ; he calls upon you by his word, by his providence ; he has declared it to be your duty, indeed the sum of all that he requires of you, that upon which hang all the law and the prophets. The whole duty of man, the whole duty of Christ's disciples, is fruitfulness. And indeed, if he had never commanded it, never required it in the Scripture, never spoke one word for it, yet what he has done to you has made it your duty, a duty of greatest moment, and indispensably so. The means of fruitfulness you have enjoyed obliges you strongly to bring forth fruit, and to bring forth good fruit ; the plenty of them engages you to bring forth much fruit; the continuance of them calls upon you to continue fruitful. If you answer not this call, and these engagements, you will be inexcusable ; for there is nothing more equal than this which the Lord requires of you. You will involve yourselves in dreadful guilt ; for there is nothing more sinful than barrenness in these circumstances. You expose yourselves, and all that is dear to you, to the greatest hazards; for there is nothing more dangerous than unfruitfulness in this case. You bereave yourselves of the blessed advantages which attend fruitfulness, or are the happy consequences of it. Let me enforce this duty on you a little more largely by these considerations now pointed at.

(1.) Consider the equity of it. It is a duty grounded upon the greatest equity, that those who enjoy the means of fruitfulness should be fruitful. It is so equal, that the Lord appeals to the judgment of those from whom he requires it ; the case being so clear that their own consciences cannot but give sentence in favour of it, Isa. v. 3, 4. And these inhabitants of Jerusalem to whom he refers it were parties, ver. 7. When the Lord has done all that is requisite to render a people fruitful, there needs no other judge, no other witnesses against them but their own consciences, if they be found barren. The case is so plain, a party may be trusted to give sentence in it. And is not this your case ? May not the Lord say of you as he did of his vineyard of old, ' What could have been done more to make you fruitful, that I have not done ?' If after this you bring not forth such fruit as he expects, you will be self-condemned ; there will need no more evidence to cast you than what your own consciences will bring in against you; if there were no other judge to pass sentence against you, your own consciences will do it. It may be now conscience is asleep, or you are too busy to attend to its sentence ; but affliction, or death, or judgment will awake it, and force you to hearken to it. And these are not far off, though you may dream so. The time is at hand, when your consciences will justify the Lord in his severest proceedings against you for barrenness. Set thyself before the judgment-seat of Christ, where thou must shortly stand ; and suppose he should demand of thee, Where could I expect fruit, if not in the place where thou wast planted ? Where should I look for fruit, but in my vineyard ? Should I look for it in the wilderness ? From whom should I expect more and better fruit than from thee, to whom I vouchsafed the means of fruitfulness with greatest advantages ? ' Wherefore, then, when I looked for grapes, didst thou bring forth wild grapes ?' Wherefore, when I expected fruit, did I find nothing but leaves ? a specious and barren profession, instead of heart and life full of the fruits of the Spirit ? What wilt thou answer in this case ? Thou wilt either be speechless, or else speak nothing but the sentence of thy own condemnation. A heathen, a wild Indian, a rude Mahomedan, a blindfold papist, or any that wanted the means, may have something to plead for himself in this case; but thy conscience will stop thy mouth, and leave thee self-confounded; the iniquity of thy barrenness will be so great, so evident, as thou wilt find nothing to cover it. An unfruitful soul will not have so much to say as the unprofitable servant, though what he said signified nothing: Mat. xxv. 24, thou canst not say, 'Lord, I know thee that thou art a hard man, reaping where thou hast not sown, and gathering where thou hast not strawed.' The Lord has been no such hard master to thee, if he be so to any. When he calls for fruit, after all means of improvement afforded, he looks but to gather where he has strawed, and reap where he has sown. And, 'Who plants a vineyard,' says the apostle, arguing from equity, 'and eats not of the fruit thereof? or who feedeth a flock, and eateth not of the milk of the flock?' 1 Cor. ix. 7. The common sense of mankind declares the equity of God's expecting fruit, where he vouchsafes means for that end; and that barrenness in that case is so unequal and unreasonable, that all who are guilty of it must needs be inexcusable.

(2.) Consider the sinfulness of being barren: how much, how great guilt it involves you in; how heinously guilty unfruitfulness will make you.

[1.] It is a complex sin. It is many sins; it is in a manner all sins in one. Its name is legion; it has whole troops of sins under its conduct. It is not a breach of one commandment only, not a transgression of one precept or part of law or gospel, but a violation of all. It is good fruit that every command of the law, every precept of the gospel, calls for; and he that brings not forth good fruit, makes nothing of law or gospel, tramples upon both, lives in disobedience to all. He not only disobeys the whole 'word spoken by angels,' 'every transgression and disobedience whereof receives a just recompence of reward,' Heb. ii. 2, but the word spoken by the Lord of angels. He disobeys the gospel in every part of it, and the doom of that see 2 Thes. i. 7, 8.

[2.] If you bring not forth fruit, you bring forth weeds. If you bear not good fruit, you will be fertile in that which is naught. The ground will be covered with something; if it produce not corn, or grass, or useful herbs, it will bring forth briars, or thorns, or weeds. You will be always bringing forth something; if it be not fruit unto God, it will be fruit to the flesh, or the world, or yourselves.

If God reap nothing of you, the devil will. The soul is a most active being, and will be still in motion one way or other, upward or downward. If it move not towards heaven, it moves towards hell; if it be not in motion after God, it will be moving towards the world or sin; if it act not for God, it will be in action against him; if your thoughts, designs, affections, be not employed upon good objects, they will employ themselves upon those that are vain, or worse. It is against their nature to stay long unemployed; or if they should stand idle, even idleness is bad fruit, if that which is sinful be so; it is worse than an useless weed.

If you be not fruitful in good works, you will be fruitful in works that are naught, unless when you do nothing; and that is naught too, as he found it, who hid his talent, though he employed it not to any wicked use, as you may see by his doom, Mat. xxv. 30.

Simple barrenness is not all you are guilty of, when you are unfruitful (though there is heinous guilt in that alone), but the necessary and unavoidable consequent of it, is something else which is as bad or worse. There are, and will be, cursed fruits, of one kind or other, where there is not good fruit.

[3.] Unfruitfulness renders you burdens of the earth. A fruitless soul is good for nothing; like the vine, which, as the prophet describes it, Ezek. xv., is not of use for timber or work, no, not so much as to make a pin of, fit for nothing but the fire, and of little use there. When it is not good for fruit, it is good for nothing, it only 'cumbers the ground,' is but an injury, an incumbrance to the place where it grows, spends the heart of the earth to no purpose, and takes up a place unprofitably, where others being planted might bring forth fruit. If some heathens or Americans had enjoyed the means of grace and the powerful ministry of the gospel, that many souls amongst us have continued fruitless under, in all probability they would have made a better improvement thereof, and brought forth more and better fruit. Upon this account does the Lord Jesus upbraid those cities in his time, with whom the gospel prevailed not to repentance and unfruitfulness, Mat. xi. 20, 21, 23.

[4.] It is a reproach to the gospel of Christ, and the religion there taught us; disparages its power and efficacy, when it prevails not with those who profess it, for the effects and fruits which are pleasant and acceptable to God and men, when yet it is professed to be most effectual for this purpose. It is the glory of the gospel, that it is a doctrine far transcending all that the sons of men have been acquainted with; that it is most powerful to heal the corrupt and degenerate soul of man, and advance it to the highest improvement; to make it partaker of a divine nature, and engender in it holy and divine qualities; to lead men to a divine life, in all acts of holiness and righteousness, which may render them conformable to God, useful and serviceable to others, and happy in themselves.

But now in those who enjoy the gospel, profess the knowlege, belief, and embracement of it, and yet continue unfruitful, none of all this appears. The world may make use of such barren souls, as arguments that the gospel is no such excellent doctrine, has no such divine power or efficacy, produces no such desirable effects. For why? No such thing is visible in the temper or deportment of multitudes who profess that they believe and embrace it. They are but like other men, and exceed not many who were never acquainted with the gospel; no more humble, no more holy, no more self-denying, no more public-spirited, no more heavenly-minded, no more mortified, as to many lusts and passions, no more crucified to the world, as to the riches, delights, and splendour of it, no more candid and sincere in dealings, no more merciful, no more serviceable, no more active to do good in the world, no more fruitful in good works; and where is then the singular excellency and power of the gospel? The light of nature has been effectual in some, to restrain them from those enormities, from which many that enjoy the gospel abstain not. The doctrine of the heathen philosophers has led many to the practice of moral virtues, whenas many professors of the gospel are lamentably defective in points of morality. Oh, what dishonourable reflections does this cast upon the glorious gospel of Christ! How does this tend to lay its honour in the dust, and turn its glory into shame; and what disparages the gospel, reflects upon Christ himself, the author of it, and the divine Spirit by which it was inspired, and on whom its efficacy depends. It is well the gospel has better evidences of its power and excellency, than unfruitful professors, otherwise the divine original of it might be questioned, and the transcendent virtue and efficacy of it would be decried. However, this is the tendency of your barrenness, to make Christ and his gospel be blasphemed. If you would not be accessory to so horrid a crime as such blasphemy, you must bring forth good fruit, and much of it, and continue to bear it, that when either God or man comes to seek fruit on you, it may not be to seek, there may be no disappointments.

[5.] It is a grievous affliction to those whom the Lord employs as his labourers, and makes them sad, whom the Lord, of all others, would not have made sad. Those whom the Lord has sent into his vineyard, and fitted for that great work, they cannot be satisfied with their wages; no, not that great 'recompence of reward' which he has promised them, unless they see the success of their labours. If their hearts be upright before God, and of a temper answerable to their calling, they value nothing like the fruits of their ministry, how much approbation, how much love soever they have, how free and liberal encouragements and supports soever they meet with. They have not the desire of their hearts, unless they see the fruits and effects of their labours upon the souls and lives of their people, unless they be brought to a fruitful profession of Christ, and grow up therein, Philip. iv. 16, 17. They were careful to supply his necessities; but this, though he took it well, was not that which he desired in comparison; nor was it acceptable, but upon that account, as it was fruit, and signified that his ministry had such effect upon them as would be abundant joy to them at the great account. He had a great, a passionate, love for souls, and an exceeding joy when he perceived they prospered, 2 Cor. vii. 3-5. He took all pains, run all hazards, to make them fruitful; he could freely spend and be spent for this, 2 Cor. xii. 15. Nor was his life dear to him in comparison of it, Acts xx. 22-24, Philip. ii. 17. Those that are faithful and duly qualified for the great work of the ministry, are in some measure like-minded, though not in the same degree. They have a great love for souls, an earnest desire to make and to see them fruitful; they travail in birth with them till Christ be formed in them, till they be born again, and till they bear fruit answerable to their new birth. And when they are disappointed, it is grievous to them as miscarrying is to a woman that passionately desires children; the frustration has in it some pain and anguish, like that of a miscarriage. Have they prayed, and wept, and studied so long, so much, to so little purpose? Have they sacrificed their worldly interest in his service, and deprived themselves of all advantages of thriving in the world, and left their dear relatives and posterity to want and contempt after them? Have they spent their time, their strength, their parts, their spirits, consumed themselves in wasting studies, and all their labours in the issue in a manner fruitless? Shall little or nothing be left them at the last but that sad complaint, 'I have laboured in vain, and spent my strength for nought;' I have lost so much, hazarded so much, done so much, and all in vain; this people will not be gathered, or those that seem to be gathered will not be fruitful; only 'two or three berries in the upmost branches, or four or five in the outmost boughs.' Oh, where are the children that I hoped would have been given me, and that I have been so long in travail for? Alas! is the curse of a barren or of a miscarrying womb upon me? Have I been in pain, and cried out in my pangs, and brought forth nothing but wind? Shall those who for all holy fruitfulness should have been my joy and my crown, be my shame and reproach; leave themselves and me under the reproach of barrenness; barren souls, and a barren ministry? Oh how does these thoughts cut and sting those who have occasion to entertain them! Oh what tears do they wring out in secret! Oh if you were conscious to the inward wounds and heart-bleedings hereby occasioned; to the fears and jealousy, lest they have not been upright with God, lest they have run before they were sent, because they seem to have run in vain; lest they have been unfaithful, because to unsuccessful in the work of God! It is true those that are fearful and jealous this way have ordinarily least cause to be so, but that frees them not from the trouble and afflictions of such fears; nor does it excuse those whose barrenness occasions it. And though they have this ground of comfort, that 'though Israel be not gathered,' yet their 'judgment is with the Lord, and their work,' their reward, 'with their God,' Isa. xlix. 14; notwithstanding, all this will fall heavy somewhere; those who continue unfruitful must answer for all this; their lost labour, their fruitless hazards, the consumption of strength and spirits, their torturing fears and jealousies, their grievous disappointments and afflicting miscarriages, will all be charged on your account if you continue barren. All these will the Lord require at your hands, if you will not believe the report of Christ, or not believe it effectually and fruitfully; all these, and more than I can reckon, will add to the burden of your guilt, and make your condemnation more intolerable; all these will rise up in judgment and bear witness against you. But even the thought of this is grievous to ministers tender of the souls of sinners; that when they expected joy in their fruitfulness here and happiness hereafter, instead thereof they must be produced as witnesses against them at the great day, and make heavier the condemnation of such whose salvation they had been so great a part of their days labouring for and thirsting after. Oh, if you would not cause so grievous an affliction to those whose joy and crown you should be, if you would not be involved in so great guilt, and so dreadful condemnation, bring forth such fruits now as may prevent it!

[6.] It is a disappointment to the Lord. He looks for fruit; he comes, he sends to you for it. So in the text, and verse 7, and Isaiah v. 2, 4; he sends, Mat. xxi. 34, Mark xii. 2, Luke xx. 9, 10. Wherever the Lord vouchsafes means of fruitfulness, he expects fruit; and it is an expectation which the common sense of mankind declares to be highly just and reasonable, and so a disappointment herein will be more intolerable. If a husbandman bestow so much cost and pains upon a piece of ground, as is sufficient to make a part of the wilderness fruitful; and when harvest comes, and he expects a rich crop, he finds no more on it than if he had done nothing to it, or nothing answerable to the tillage, how will it trouble him! Such ground will undo the tenant, and make a landlord repent that ever he purchased it. So it is here, such frustrations will afflict men. But how can the great God endure it in those that are so much below him, and are more concerned, in reference to their own advantage, to bear fruit than the Lord to reap it? He has but the honour of it; you have the comfort, the profit, the happiness. Will you frustrate his expectation, when your own interest obliges you to answer it? A disappointment here is such a provocation as the Lord will not long endure. What an iniquity this is, and how the Lord resents it, is evident by what he expresseth, Jer. ii. 21, 22. The Lord had taken as much care in planting this people, viz. under his ordinances, as a man could have of the most choice plant, and expected fruit answerable; but they, as if they had been degenerate plants or wild slips, bare not such fruit as he looked for; and the blur of this iniquity was such, as all the ways or means they could devise should never either cleanse or cover it, never free them from the guilt or pollution of it; but the Lord would always have it in his sight, as a provocation of special remark. Oh if you would not be guilty of such a sin as the Lord will mark out, so as never to overlook it, never to pardon or cleanse you from it, beware of unfruitfulness! The Lord has branded this for such a sin.

[7.] It hardens the world. It tends to root religion out of the earth, at least out of the place we dwell in, and to plant atheism and infidelity in the room of it. Those amonst us upon whom the power of religion has not yet seized, they easily discern the vanity and imposture of other religions professed in the world. If there be any worthy to be embraced, it must be the religion of Christ. Oh, but what can commend this to them, or to any, but the fruits of it? And where should they expect the fruits of it, but in those who profess they believe, embrace, and find the power of it? If such as these bring not forth more and better fruits than others, they will be ready to conclude, that their religion (even that of Christ) is no better than others, and so no religion at all worthy of entertainment. And is it not much from hence that multitudes amongst us, to comply with the custom of the country, outwardly profess the religion of it, but inwardly are atheists, and have no religion at all in their hearts? Does it not strengthen and encourage this atheism and irreligion which so lamentably abounds amongst us, when they see so little of the fruits thereof in those that profess it? Who will trouble himself much about that which is useless and worthless? And what is religion better, of what worth or use is it, if it be fruitless? If it take not them who profess it off from the world; if it mortify not their lusts and passions; if it raise not their souls above earth and self; if it ennoble not their spirits, and make them not public and active to do good, abounding in good works; if it be not full of mercy and good fruits; if it make them not better in their families, towards their relations, to all with whom they converse; it will be concluded good for little or nothing. Nothing will appear in it to attract their affections, to command reverence or esteem, or to persuade them to entertain it in their souls; nay, they will be apt to think that professors who are not fruitful are but atheists like themselves, and that they do not really believe what they profess; and so that there is nothing indeed of religion but in pretence and profession, and so they need not trouble themselves about more. Oh, 'Woe be to those by whom offences come! It were better a mill-stone were tied about their necks, and they cast into the sea.' But such offences will come, and such you will give; they will not only be offences taken, but given, if you continue barren and unfruitful in the knowledge and profession of Christ. Your unfruitfulness is an engine to exclude or banish religion out of the hearts of men, and to leave atheism and infidelity in full possession. And will you do such disservice to Christ, and to the souls of men? What can you do worse to either; or, what is there that you should more tremble at that this, which is of such a horrid and dreadful tendency?

[8.] It is a sin most highly aggravated. It has two ingredients, to instance in no more, that make a sin exceedingly sinful. It is against clear, much light, and distinguishing mercy.

First, It is a sin against all light. The light of nature discovers much of that wherein our fruitfulness consists to be our duty. The light of the law clears up that of nature, wherein it is obscured by corruption, and adds more evidence and force to it. The whole light of the gospel does still more illustrate and enforce it. The common reason of mankind shews fruitfulness to be a duty, where there are means of fruitfulness vouchsafed. There is no conscience but must come under the power of this evidence, and acknowledge it not only just, but equal.

So that to continue unfruitful is to live in disobedience to all light, to run counter to nature, law, gospel, reason, equity, and conscience. It is to offer violence to the light and dictates of all. It is forcibly to hold a truth in confinement, and violently to imprison it, when all these struggle and contend for its liberty. And what a high provocation it is to detain a truth in unrighteousness against the dictates but of one of these, against natural light, you may see, Rom. i. 18. The wrath of God is revealed from heaven against those who unjustly smother a truth which natural light would have to act freely. What wrath will be revealed against those who fetter and enslave a truth, that it cannot move and act freely in heart and life, when all light requires and strives for its liberty! The severity wherewith it is threatened shews its heinousness, Luke xii. 47.

Sins against knowledge are voluntary. There is more of the will in them, and wilful sins are presumptions, and these are 'the great transgressions,' Ps. xix. 13; such a sin is unfruitfulness. When a man knows fruitfulness to be his duty, and has means sufficient to make him fruitful, why is he barren but because he will be so? You cannot say, you know it not to be your duty; you cannot say, though you know it, ye have not means to enable you to bring forth fruit; why, then, are you not more fruitful but because you will not? Oh, take heed of sinning wilfully after ye have received the knowledge of the truth; there was no sacrifice for such sins under the law, Num. xv. 30, 31.

Secondly, It is against distinguishing mercy; it is against the gospel and the means of grace; against the end for which they are vouchsafed and continued; and these are favours which he vouchsafes not to many others, Ps. cxlvii. 19, 20.

To sin against common favours is a great provocation; it argues an intolerable perverseness and disingenuousness in him that will do it. And you will better digest an injury from a stranger, or any to whom you never shewed kindness, than one whom you have continually obliged, Ps. lv. 12.

But there is a peculiar provocation in sins against peculiar mercies; these give an accent to the sin, and make it remarkably sinful. The Lord hereby frequently aggravates the sin of his people, as being thus rendered more heinous and provoking than the sins of others, Isa. i. 2. This is it that may astonish heaven and earth, that when I have treated them, and them alone, as children, yet their demeanour should be so unanswerable to such kindness, care, and tenderness. The creatures without sense may have some resentment of such a provocation, Jer. ii. 31. If the Lord had been a wilderness to us, it had been more tolerable to have found us barren; but when he has been a Sharon, a Sorek to us, our unfruitfulness has no pretence to cover its shame. Christ may say to us, as he said to his disciples, Luke x. 24, 'Many prophets and kings have desired,' &c. And we have seen and heard such things as others had not the happiness to see nor hear; shall they be to us as vain things? Vain things they will be, and unprofitable, if they produce no fruits in us. Do we thus requite the Lord? Shall we make such unworthy returns for peculiar favours, and such as the rest of the world are strangers to? When he has made such a gracious distinction betwixt us and others, shall we bring forth no better fruits than the common? If we go not beyond all others in fruitfulness, after peculiar means afforded us for that purpose, our sin will exceed that of all others in sinfulness. You see by these particulars how heinous a crime barrenness is in those who have means sufficient to make them fruitful. And by this you may discern how dangerous it is, how much severity it will meet with, what wrath it kindles, what judgments will follow it, for these will be answerable to the greatness and heinousness of the provocation.

But to move you the more effectually to a duty of so great consequence, let me set before you the dreadful danger of neglecting it in some particulars,

(1.) Barrenness exposes to the curse of God. It is a cursed evil, Heb. vi. 8. It is so 'nigh unto cursing' as there is no escaping it without better fruit. Christ warned not only his disciples, or the Jews, but us, when he cursed the fig-tree on which he found no fruit. That barrenness must expect nothing but a curse, even from him ' in whom all the nations of the earth are blessed, Mark xi. 13, 14, 20, 21. It seems strange that Christ should curse it for want of figs, when it was not the season for that fruit. The meaning may be, it was not a seasonable or a good year for figs. Fig-trees did not bear well that year (for *yet* in the translation is not in the original). But even so it shews severity, and teaches us that in such places where persons are generally and ordinarily unfruitful, and good fruits are rare, much out of request, yet this will be no plea to secure any from the curse, if they be found without fruit. Christ himself, from and through whom alone we expect blessings, will curse barren souls, whatever show they make, whatever excuse they have. He works a miracle to warn us of this, and impress it the deeper on those whom it concerns. Immediately the curse takes effect, and the tree withers, and is dried up from the roots, ver. 20, and Mat. xxi. 19.

And how dreadful is it to be under the curse of God, that will cause all to dry up by the roots, estate, relations, body and soul to wither! When man curses, God may bless; or when God curses, Christ may turn it into a blessing; but when Christ curses, who then may bless? And even Christ will curse those that are unfruitful. The king of Moab thought that if Israel were but under Balaam's curse, he should smite them or drive them out, Num. xxii. 6. But what shall become of those whom God, whom Christ curses? For assuredly those whom he blesses are blessed, and those whom he curses are cursed.

Oh, if the curse of God be dreadful to you, let unfruitfulness be so too, for the curse of God is entailed upon unfruitfulness, a curse that will certainly take effect, and may do it suddenly, and can never be turned into a blessing but upon your turning from this sin.

(2.) This will put you out of God's protection, and provoke him to pull down the fences by which he secures you from the rage of Satan and his instruments, and the fury of those who would devour you or lay you waste. So much is expressly threatened for this sin, Isa. v. 4–6. And this was executed upon that people afterwards, as the psalmist expresses it, either by way of prediction, as a misery approaching, or of lamentation, as of a calamity already inflicted, Ps. lxxx. 12, 13. The psalmist's question is answered by the prophet, ' Why hast thou broken down our hedge?' &c. It was because ' instead of grapes, they brought,' &c.

This will provoke the Lord to withdraw his protection, which is your only defence, and then you lie open to all miseries, and are exposed to the will of those that hate you; then they may have their will of you, upon your estates, liberties, soul-concernments, upon all your pleasant things; then may you be eaten up and trodden down, and laid quite open to spoil and ruin. What man will be at the charge and trouble to keep up a fence about a piece of ground, of which he reaps no more than of the common, and that which lies unfenced? You may judge by what yourselves would do, that it cannot be expected that the Lord should continue to fence those in as his vineyard, who, when he looks for fruit, prove but like the heath in the wilderness.

(3.) Barrenness will deprive you of the gospel and the means of grace, Isa. v. 6. The Lord will deny the means of improvement when he finds they are afforded in vain; he will have no more labour and pains lost upon them; he will not always employ and spend his labourers to no purpose; he will either send no more labourers into such a fruitless vineyard, or call them away whom he has sent, or suffer them to be thrust out, in judgment to those who are not improved by them, and leave them like the heath in the desert, which knows not when good comes, Jer. xvii. 6, shall have no benefit by that which is the greatest advantage to others, Mat. xxi. 43. Those who bring not forth the fruits of the kingdom, such as beseem it, such as are required by it, the kingdom shall be taken from them, and given to those who will bring forth such fruit. The kingdom of God, *i. e.* of the Messiah, that blessed state and administration brought into the world by Christ, and begun at his coming; that which was of old promised as the greatest happiness that the world should ever see; that which was so ardently desired by kings, prophets, and righteous men, and for the discovery of which the angels longed; that fulness of Spirit, of light, of grace, of hope, of comfort, of happiness, of redemption, of salvation, which the kingdom of Christ holds forth, and accompanies the happy administration of it by the gospel then preached and published, and the ordinances and officers by his regal power instituted, and his Spirit in both then more largely poured out and more powerfully working: those that bring not forth good fruits are in danger to be deprived of all this, as though they were left out of this gracious administration. They shall be cut off from all the blessings, all the privileges, all the advantages of the kingdom of Messiah. They shall be left in such a state as though Christ had never come, nor had erected a kingdom in the world; as though the acceptable year of the Lord had never been published; as though the day of salvation, the day of greatest joy to all nations, had never dawned.

Oh dreadful condition! Christ shall profit them nothing; nor shall his kingdom and government anything avail them.

'The kingdom,' *i. e.* the gospel of the kingdom, ' shall be taken from those who bring not forth the fruits of it,' (that is in effect the same.) The unfruitful shall be deprived of all the privileges and advantages of a gospel-state; this sin will bereave a people of the gospel, upon which their glory, life, peace, comfort, and hopes depend. So that unfruitfulness will deprive a people,

[1.] Of their glory. When the gospel is gone, the glory is departed, the crown is fallen from their heads.

[2.] It hazards the life of the barren, the life of their souls; for the gospel is the word of life; for it conveys life, and preserves it. By this they are ' quickened, who are dead in sins and trespasses;' it is the immortal seed by which they are begotten, and born again, 1 Peter i. 23, and it is that by which those who are born again are nourished, 1 Peter ii. 2. It is the bread of life; and when it is taken away, the staff of bread is broken, that which upholds and keeps the soul in life; the loss, the want of it is a famine, Amos viii. 11, 13, not a famine which starves the body, but which destroys the soul. No such evil arrows of famine, as those that stick in the soul; none so dreadfully destructive: and unfruitfulness prepares such arrows, and sharpens them, and provokes God to shoot them.

[3.] It cuts you off from peace with God. The gospel is styled the ' gospel of peace,' Rom. x. 15. It is 'the word of reconciliation,' 2 Cor. v. 18, 19. Herein he offers terms of peace, upon which accepted he will be reconciled to sinners. And while the gospel is continued, he is treating with them about this happy peace; his ministers are ambassadors for this purpose. But when the gospel is gone, the treaty is broke off; his agents that managed the treaty are recalled; the Lord will no more offer peace to such; they shall no more hear of it, nor of any inclinations in the Lord to it. God of hosts hereby declares that he is an enemy, and will be so. This is like to be the dreadful issue of this sin.

[4. It robs them of all true comfort. The gospel is the ground of all our comforts; the sum of it is 'comfortable words,' Zech. i. 13. It contains that which alone can make every relation, every enjoyment, every condition comfortable. Without this, the pleasantest place or state in the world is but as a dry and thirsty wilderness, wherein there is no water; the best enjoyments of this world are but miserable comforters. Take away the gospel, and the sun is, as it were, turned into darkness, and the moon into blood; and all the lower springs, from whence you fetch your comforts, send forth nothing but waters of Marah, waters of bitterness, or, which is worse, and more dangerous, streams of sweetened poison. Such are sensual delights, such are worldly comforts, when not healed and corrected by the sovereign virtue of the gospel. You may bid adieu to all that is truly comfortable when the gospel leaves you, for all the sparks which you can strike out of the world, or its enjoyments, you will lie down in sorrow and darkness— in such a dismal and comfortless condition will this sin leave you. This is the woful tendency of it, since it tends to deprive you of the gospel.

[5.] It blasts all hopes. It is through the grace of the gospel that we have, as everlasting consolation, so good hope, 2 Thes. ii. 16. There is the foundation of all our hopes; and when the gospel is removed, their foundation is gone, they all fall and vanish. 'If in this life only we have hope in Christ' (says the apostle, 1 Cor. xv. 19), 'we are of all men most miserable.' And where have we any ground for hopes beyond this life, but in the gospel? What but this can let in any glimmerings of hope for life everlasting? Nay, even for this life we have no hopes in Christ, but through the gospel. Take away the gospel, and you take away from sinners all hopes, both for this life and for the life to come. When left without this, they are left without Christ, without God in the world, and without hope either for this world or the world to come. There remains nothing for them, but a fearful expectation of judgment, and fiery indignation. Into such a hopeless and desperate condition does unfruitfulness plunge barren souls; it provokes God to take away the gospel, and he has threatened he will for this cause do it. They are in apparent danger to have the gospel of the kingdom taken from them, and therewith their glory, life, peace, comfort, and hopes. If this do not make unfruitfulness dreadful to you, what will, what can do it?

(4.) This will suspend heavenly influences, without which the gospel itself can do you no good. This the Lord threatens for the unfruitfulness of his vineyard, Isa. v. 6. The rain and other influences of the heavenly bodies are not more necessary to the plants below, for their life and growth, than the concurrence, and operation, and influences of the Spirit are necessary for the life and growth of our souls. The gospel and ordinances cannot be effectual upon us without these, but these may be, and are, in some cases, effectual without them; let the ground be never so well planted, or tilled, or manured, yet without rain, and heavenly influx, nothing will grow, or thrive, or come to maturity; all will languish and wither away. So will our souls consume and pine away, whatever ordinances we enjoy, if the Spirit of Christ concur not, if we be not influenced from above. The ministry of the apostles, of the greatest of them, of persons extraordinarily qualified and assisted, will not take effect, will prevail for no increase without this, 1 Cor. iii. 5-7. Their planting and watering had come to nothing, if God had not concurred, if it had not been for the divine influence; it was this that gave the increase. And if there had been no Paul nor Apollos to plant or water, no such instruments, or none at all, this could have given an increase, as we see in Cornelius.

Now these influences, without which the gospel and ordinances, in what power and plenty soever you enjoy them, will not be effectual; which are so necessary, that without them, what means soever you have, what pains soever be taken with you, your souls will certainly wither and pine away; your unfruitfulness provokes God to withhold them; he threatens it, and his truth and justice requires the execution; his Spirit will not always strive, when his strivings are still resisted; he will not always move when he finds his motions still stifled and smothered; he will not always suffer his influences to be lost upon you. The Spirit will withdraw, and then spiritual judgments (the first-born of his wrath) do follow. Then has the word and ordinances such a woful operation upon them, as hinders them from being converted and healed; quite opposite to those gracious ends for which they were first appointed, Isa. vi. 9, 10. And this befell the Jews afterwards, for their unfruitfulness, and non-improvement of what they enjoyed, as is evident by the application made thereof by our Lord Jesus, Mat. xiii. 12–15.

(5.) Unfruitfulness brings temporal judgments and calamities. It brings them suddenly, and in a short time; and such as are desolating, laying them waste; and such as are transcendent, and speak greater severity than those which befall such as enjoy not the means of unfruitfulness.

[1.] It exposes to sudden calamities. They come swiftly upon such as are barren under the means of fruitfulness. The Lord is not wont to forbear them so long as others; he has not so much patience, no such long-suffering for them. It is such a provocation as he will not bear long with. This is plain in this parable: three years the fruitless fig-tree is suffered to stand in the vineyard; it might have grown many years longer, if its barrenness had not exposed it to a violent stroke, and brought it to an untimely end; but within that time, such trees usually bear, if they be good for aught. So long he bears with it, but after three years he passes the sentence of excision, and orders it to be cut down. And though the importunity of the vine-dresser prevails for one year's longer forbearance, yet that is all that could be obtained. No longer reprieve than for one year; if that year produce nothing, the vine-dresser also will have it cut down. A tree in the forest or the highway, though it bear no fruit, will be suffered to stand longer than in an orchard, a place of choice plants and fruit-trees; it is a greater eye-sore there. A man will bear with weeds in the highway, or a common, well and long enough, but he cannot so long endure them in his garden. The Lord can bear with the heathen, or any that enjoy not the means of grace, their barrenness is not so great a provocation; but those who have a standing in his orchard, and are planted under the means of fruitfulness, he cannot so well forbear, he will not so long endure, Acts xvii. 30. While they had not the light of the gospel and his ordinances, ὑπεριδών, he overlooked them, took no severe notice of them; their unfruitfulness was passed by: 'But now he commands,' &c. He resolves to take another course; he will be quicker with them, unless they repent, and 'bring forth fruits meet for repentance,' πᾶσι πανταχοῦ, 'all, everywhere.' And, Acts xiv. 16, he suffered that in the wilderness which he will not suffer in his vineyard; he will not suffer so long now as he did then; he will cut down those speedily now under the means of grace, who might have stood long, though barren, without them. Those whom the heat and influences of the gospel does not ripen for fruit, it makes them sooner ripe for wrath and judgment.

[2.] It brings desolating judgments, such as lay a place and people utterly waste: this is threatened for this sin, Isa. v. 6. In the original it is wasteness, the Hebrew using the abstract to express a superlative. As Isa. i. 7, desolation, *i.e.* most desolate, so here, the fruitless vineyard shall be made wasteness, *i.e.* utterly, extremely waste; so that it shall not differ at all from the common; nothing shall be left in it, to signify that it was before a vineyard, that it was ever planted or enclosed, or any cost bestowed on it, or any special care taken of it.

This is a desolating sin; it will turn Sharon into a desert, and make that place which was like the garden of God to become a wilderness. It will ruin a valley of vision, and turn it into the valley of the shadow of death. It will make such a place as mount Zion like to ruined Babylon, as it is described Rev. xviii. 2, 'when it was become,' &c., or as by the prophet, Isa. xiii. 21, 22, and xxxiv. 13, 14.

And it is utter ruin that is denoted here in this parable, by cutting down. It is not stripping off the leaves, or cutting off all the branches, or cleaving the body of the tree, that unfruitfulness exposes to; but a greater severity, such as will quite ruin it, a hewing it down by the roots, Mat. iii. It is to be hewn down where the axe is laid, and that is, by the root, so as to leave no hope that ever it shall grow again. If you would not be utterly ruined; if you would not bring desolation upon the place of your abode, nor have a hand in bringing the axe to the very root of it, oh take heed of continuing unfruitful!

[3.] Judgment shall be more terribly executed upon such, who, having the means of fruitfulness, do not improve them, than upon those who never had them. They shall be ruined in a more dreadful manner than any other. This sin fills more vials of wrath, and fills them fuller; and they will be poured upon those who are guilty of it, and continue so, with more fury. The Lord will empty all his vials upon them; even the dregs thereof will be their portion. There is abundant evidence for this, in his proceedings against his ancient people. Israel had the privilege of enjoying the means of fruitfulness above others, Ps. cxlvii., and they not improving them, are threatened more severely: Amos iii. 2, I have done more for you than for others, 'therefore I will punish you more than any.' The execution of the threatening was answerable, Dan. ix. 10; there is their unfruitfulness, ver. 11; there is the threatening executed, ver. 12; there is the exceeding terribleness of the execution. Under the whole heavens none had enjoyed such means of grace; and under the whole heavens none met with such wrath. Tribulation and anguish will seize upon every people, 'every soul,' that brings not forth fruit; but most of all, upon those who enjoy most means: Rom. ii. 9, 'to the Jew first.' On them shall it seize most terribly, because they first, and most, enjoyed the gospel and means of grace. No other that are barren shall escape the wrath of God; but upon them the wrath came 'to the uttermost,' 1 Thes. ii. 16, εἰς τέλος, to the uttermost, both for extremity and continuance: wrath in the highest degree, in its perfection; and wrath of largest extent, for its duration. It drew tears from Christ, to consider the dreadful issue of their unfruitfulness, though they were his enemies, Luke xix. 41–44. All this, because they did not fruitfully improve the day of grace. This brought upon them so great tribulation, as never was known in the world before that time, nor should be ever after, Mat. xxiv. 21. The world never saw such instances of dreadful severity in any people, as in those who have been barren under the means of fruitfulness. The day of a gracious visitation, the time wherein the means of grace are vouchsafed, when it is not improved, will make way for such a visitation, as will make the ears of all that hear thereof to tingle; a 'day of blackness, and thick darkness;' but blacker and darker upon those to whom the day of grace has been most lightsome.

The Lord has visited you more graciously than others. But if you bring not forth fruit answerable hereto, if you 'neglect this great salvation, how shall ye escape?' How? Why, any people in the world shall escape better than you, when another day of visitation comes. 'It shall be more tolerable' for heathens, for Turks, for papists, for the darker parts of the Protestant world, for any people on earth, than for those that are barren in this nation; nay, for many people in this nation, 'than for you.' There is more wrath treasured up, there will be more indignation poured out on you, than any, if you continue unfruitful. You have had more means; the Lord expects more fruits of you. If you bear not more, you must certainly bear more wrath. The Lord has rods for others, but he has scorpions for you. His little finger will be heavier upon you, in the day when he judges unfruitfulness, than his loins upon others.

[6.] This brings eternal wrath; the fire that never goes out was kindled for unfruitful trees. They are good for nothing else but the fire, John xv. 2. He takes it away; he cuts it off. But that is not all; it is cut off, in order to burning, ver. 6. Fruitless branches shall not be endured on the tree; such trees shall have no standing in the vineyard, they shall be cut down. To be cut down in God's wrath is dreadful. But that is not all which unfruitfulness will bring upon you; there is something more terrible follows: cutting down is in order to casting into the fire, Mat. iii. 10; so John Baptist told the Pharisees and Sadducees; so our Lord Jesus tells us all, Mat. vii. 19. Mercy itself has no more favour for the fruitless. Jesus, who alone 'delivers from the wrath to come,' will deliver none who continue unfruitful from this wrath. He it is that passes this doom upon them, 'the lake that burns with fire and brimstone' is the place for barren souls. That fire which 'the wrath of God, like a river of brimstone, kindles' and keeps flaming everlastingly, that which will burn and torment for ever and ever, is the portion of the unfruitful. Nothing less; nothing more tolerable than exquisite tortures, such as fire is to our bodies; nothing short of everlasting burnings. This will be the issue of your unfruitfulness. If you continue therein, it will be so certainly. Delude not yourselves with vain hopes; Think not the leaves of a specious profession will secure you. This will but provoke the flame, and make it rage the more.

Think not to escape, because you bring not forth so bad fruits as some others, because you wallow not in gross wickedness and open profaneness. Nothing will secure you but good fruits, such as I have before described. Those whom our Lord Jesus, at the last day, will send into everlasting fire, are not described to be gross sinners, but barren professors, Mat. xxv. 41–43. Those on his left hand are pronounced by the Judge of heaven and earth accursed, and turned into hell; not for outrageous wickedness, but for want of good fruits. Neglects, omissions, and mere want of fruit, though you abound not with vermin, is enough to damn you, and to send you from Christ's presence with a curse, amongst the devil and his angels. This shall not only be the doom of those who know not God, and are not acquainted with the gospel, but of those especially who are the 'children of the kingdom,' in respect of profession and privileges, and bring not forth the fruits of it, Mat. viii. 12. Those that know not God shall not escape. No more shall those that obey not the gospel; though they profess it, though they know it, though they believe it, yet if they obey it not, *i.e.* if they bring not forth the fruits which it enjoins and requires them to bear, if they deny not ungodliness and worldly lusts, Christ himself will be revealed from heaven, to take vengeance on them in a most terrible manner, 2 Thes. i. 7–9.

They that are barren under the means of fruitfulness, shall not only be turned into hell, but they shall suffer more in hell than others; their torment shall be more grievous than of those who never had the means of fruitfulness. The righteous Judge will double their sufferings in the place of torment. It will be more tolerable for the worst of sinners, who perished without the means of grace, than for such, Mat. xxv. 20-22.

The ancient inhabitants of Tyre and Sidon were some of those cursed Canaanites, against whom the Lord will have greater severity used in this world than any other, give charge they should be utterly rooted out, and not suffered to breathe upon the face of the earth; yet the condition of these cursed Canaanites should be more tolerable in hell, their torments more easy than those of Chorazin and Bethsaida, who enjoyed the gospel and means of grace in power and plenty, but made no fruitful improvement thereof, vers. 23, 24. Capernaum, the city where Christ much resided and preached, was exalted above others in respect of gospel enjoyments, and as it were lifted up to heaven; but by her unfruitfulness was cast down lower into hell, and sunk under a heavier burden of wrath. The inhabitants of that city, for the wretched non-improvement of the means of fruitfulness vouchsafed them, were to suffer more in hell than the inhabitants of Sodom and Gomorrah, the most abominable of sinners, upon whom God rained a hell upon earth. Oh then, if ye will be forewarned to flee from the wrath to come; if you would escape the damnation of hell; if you would not sink lower, and suffer more than others; if you would not have that dreadful furnace made hotter, more tormenting, more intolerable to you than to those of Sodom: bring forth fruits worthy of the gospel; there is no other way to escape so great damnation.

(7.) This has actually ruined and laid desolate the first and ancient churches. This has buried in ruins the most famous and flourishing churches that ever were in the world; it has brought desolation upon a world of them, so many for number as it may astonish us. This has rooted out the Christian name from a great part of that vast empire which is called the world in the New Testament, and has left little but the name in other parts where the gospel first and most prevailed. Come see what desolation this sin has made in the earth, and tremble at the sight thereof, and learn to look on it as a sin which is followed with ruin and destruction, wherever it prevails. Its name may be Abaddon and Apollyon, Rev. ix. 11, the destroyer. It is the 'abomination that makes desolate.'

There were multitudes of churches and Christians in Africa, for the space of two thousand miles, such as were eminent for their profession and sufferings too, where now there is not one to be found that professes Christ.

There were once many hundred thousand Christians in Egypt, many flourishing churches in the provinces of it, which are now vanished, and almost come to nothing.

There was a glorious church at Jerusalem, very many churches in Judea and Palestine, the foundation thereof laid by Christ himself, the structure raised by the apostles. But now where are they? The structure laid in the dust, and the foundation razed. This sin has plucked up, even by the roots, that which was planted by Christ himself, and extraordinary officers divinely inspired, and miraculously empowered; and what then can stand before it?

There was a church at Antioch in which the Christian name first began; many churches in Syria, Mesopotamia, and the regions round about. But where are they now? The eye that saw them can see them no more.

There were most flourishing churches in the lesser Asia, in Pontus, Galatia, Cappadocia, and other regions of that once happy country, where the gospel rode in triumph in the ministry of Paul and other apostolical men. But now they are subdued by a barbarous hand, the seven golden candlesticks quite overturned, and more than seventy times seven besides them laid in the dust.

There were multitudes of churches in Thrace, Macedonia, in Greece and Achaia, Philippi, Thessalonica, Berea, Athens, Corinth, and others in great numbers, and through all those countries. But what small, what woful relics of churches or Christians can there now be found!

Then for Italy, and other parts nearer us, where the gospel was once effectual, and religion in its power and purity in former times flourished, are now over-run with popery. It was this sin that broke down the banks, and made way for that deluge of Mahomedanism which has drowned the primitive churches, and overwhelmed the eastern and southern parts of the once Christian world, and let in that inundation of popery, which has prevailed so far and so long in the west. The apostle speaks of 'all the world,' which then brought forth fruit through the gospel, the word of truth, Col. i. 6. And it spread further, and prevailed more and more in that world, after the apostles' time. But how little of all that world has that sin left in Christ's possession! This has divided it almost all betwixt Turk and pope; it is but a little, in comparison, that is left to Christ's share. It was once a vine, to which that the psalmist speaks of could not be compared, Ps. lxxx. The Lord prepared room before it, and did cause it to take deep root, and it filled not only a land but a world: 'the hills were covered,' &c., vers. 10, 11. But for unfruitfulness were 'her hedges broken down, so that all they that passed by the way did pluck her. The boar out of the wood has wasted it, and the wild beast of the field has devoured it.' This is the foundation of that apostasy under which the world, which once owned Christ, now groans. God gave so many churches a bill of divorce; God 'gave them over to strong delusions,' because they 'received not the truth in love,' *i. e.* because of their unfruitfulness, according to the apostle's prophecy, 2 Thes. ii. 10, 11. If they had received the love of the truth, they would have obeyed it; if they had obeyed it, they had been fruitful. (For what is fruitfulness, but obedience to the gospel?) Because they were unfruitful, God gave them up to those delusions and impostures which now prevail in the world, and have done for many ages, supplanting and smothering the doctrine of Christ, which once triumphed everywhere. So that it is unfruitfulness that has ruined all, and has given Satan possession of those large countries and many kingdoms which were once the kingdoms of the Lord, and of his Christ. This sin has ruin and desolation following it, wherever it comes. What people, what church, can be secured against such a destructive engine, which has ruined a world, and amongst the rest, laid desolate those churches which were once the glory of Christ, and the joy and crown of the apostles! This has wasted, this has consumed them. Look upon the ghastly face of them everywhere, and learn to fear, learn to abhor unfruitfulness, which has made such fearful havoc in the world, and has turned the most glorious and flourishing churches that ever the world had into ruinous heaps.

(8.) This is the main ground of the Lord's controversy with us at this day. That the Lord has a controversy with us in this nation, is so evident, as scarce any amongst us can question it. The Lord has declared it from heaven with a loud voice, the voice of terrible judgments, and such as one way or other have reached every one amongst us. He has pleaded it so, as we have not only heard, but felt it.

All will agree in this, that God is and has been contending with us; and also, that it is our great concernment to inquire after the ground of it. And when we descend to particulars in this inquiry, there may be some difference; men's apprehensions may be various, according as their interests, their principles, their prejudices are various; yet must all agree in this, that nothing can be pitched on with more certainty, than our unfruitfulness. Herein we cannot be mistaken, we may resolve on this, upon such grounds as cannot deceive us. For this we may observe all along in Scripture, that unfruitfulness (the means being vouchsafed), wherever it be found, is always a ground of God's controversy. And the Scripture, that is the rule by which we must now judge and discern. And so sufficient it is for this purpose, that we have no need of a discovery by special revelation.

If we have been barren under the means of fruitfulness, there needs be no doubt to any who will be directed by the Scripture, but that the Lord contends with us for this. And it is too apparent that we have not brought forth fruit worthy of the gospel; we have been far from fruitfulness, answerable to the means of grace we have enjoyed. Now if the Lord have always contended with a people, when he has found them barren, under the means sufficient to make them fruitful, and this be our case, this our guilt, we need not be to seek why the Lord has been and is contending with us. If this be the cursed thing which has always troubled those with whom it was found, and it be found in our tents, we may conclude this is the Achan, this is it which has troubled us. And indeed, whatever particular can be justly fixed on, as the cause of the Lord's displeasure, it is comprised in this, either we have not brought forth grapes, or we have brought forth wild grapes. So that all, in the issue, may be resolved into unfruitfulness; and therefore, if you would not have the Lord to contend with us still, if you would have the Lord's controversy cease, with a people that are as stubble before him, take away the ground of it; bring forth more and better fruit; cast out this Jonah, if you would have the storm laid that threatens to wreck us. This will lay it, and nothing else. Take what course you will, if you continue unfruitful, the Lord's anger will not be turned away, but his hand will be stretched out still.

(9.) This is it which has bereaved us of all we have lost. To instance only in the concernments of our souls, which should be, of all other things, most precious to us. This is it which has restrained the liberty of the gospel, and retrenched us as to that plenty of the means of grace we might have enjoyed. For we find not, in all the Scripture, that ever the Lord straitened a people in these respects, but because they did not fruitfully improve them. It is our unfruitfulness that has cut us short, and brought our souls to 'a morsel of bread.' This is it which has broken our assemblies, and removed our teachers into corners. This is it that has smitten the shepherds, and scattered the flocks, and laid the heritage of God almost desolate. To this we owe our breaches, our dispersions, our fears, our hazards. There had been no laws of any such tendency, if our unfruitfulness had not concurred to make them; no instruments to attempt any such thing, if our barrenness had not raised them.

We should overlook other things, and cast our eye upon that which has set them a-work, and without which they had never moved. That which has disturbed us, that which has abridged us, is not so far off as we are apt to look. It is in our own hearts and lives; it is the unfruitfulness of both. We need look no further upon any cause or instrument, but as that may help us to a more severe reflection upon our barrenness. Let us never be so unjust as to accuse others; let us blame ourselves as most blameworthy, and turn our anger upon that which most deserves it, our non-improvement of what we enjoyed; and if the condition of others be more lamentable than ours, and their hazards greater; if any be in danger to have their souls poisoned or starved for want of spiritual food, or want of that which is wholesome, let this engage us to bewail unfruitfulness, and to fear it, and to abhor it. No souls amongst us had ever known want, or suffered by spiritual famine, had it not been for their barrenness under plenty; and if we would have our wants supplied, our breaches repaired, and the stroke of our wound healed, the way is plain before us; let us bring forth more and better fruit, and it will quickly be done.

(10.) This endangers the loss of what is left us. All that is come upon us will not excuse us, if we continue under this guilt: Mat. xxv. 29, [From] 'him that hath not,' *i. e.* who fruitfully improves not what he is entrusted with, 'shall be taken that which he hath,' though he have but a little. Whatever we have lost, which our souls once enjoyed, we have something left. The Lord, notwithstanding all forfeitures, does still entrust us with a little; he is trying us somewhile longer how we will improve it. We are now upon our good behaviour in this respect: if we improve it not to more fruitfulness, what can we expect but that he should take from us 'even that which we have'? The sun is now clouded and somewhat darkened; but then it will set, though it seem noon-day. The staff of bread (that by which our souls live) is cracked now, but this will quite break it; we are cut off from a full harvest, but this will not leave us so much as the gleanings; our teachers are removed into corners, but this will pluck them thence, so that our eyes may not so much as see them there. The scarcity will end in a famine, and that famine may not only reach us, but our posterity, and hazard the souls of this generation, and that which is coming. Our candlestick may be quite removed, and we left like those dismal places which were once eminent churches, but are now synagogues of Satan, or ruinous heaps. If this sin have done that in the green tree, what shall be done to the dry? And if those ancient churches escaped not, where shall we appear? Oh, there are horrid and prodigious miseries and devastations in the bowels of this sin. If it should but bring forth what we have feared, we may think it bad enough. Oh, but it may be delivered of miseries and calamities greater than ever entered into our hearts to fear.

When I consider what this sin has done in the southern and eastern parts of the world; how it has stripped them of gospel enjoyments; stripped them naked, as in the day when they were born, and made them as a wilderness, which were once like the paradise of God; I cannot keep my heart from trembling at what may befall these western parts for the same sin. I know no way, I see no hopes we have to fare better than those who groan under Turkish slavery, or perish in popish darkness, if we bring not forth better fruit.

Our barrenness is our danger; we are afraid of other things, but then we fear, where no fear is, in comparison. We fear the malice and violence of those who bear ill-will to us, and grudge us what liberty is left us; we fear their counsels, designs, suggestions, practices; but none of these can prosper or succeed, unless our barrenness make them prosperous: none of these can move us, can prejudice us, unless our unfruitfulness arm God against us. The foot of pride cannot come near us, the hand of the wicked cannot remove us, if this do not open their way; but if we continue barren, we can neither expect the return of what is gone, nor the continuance of what is left. We shall be so far from being entrusted with more, as even that which we have shall be taken from us.

Thus I have shewed you the equity of this duty. There is, there can be nothing, more reasonable, more equal, than that you should be fruitful; you will be utterly inexcusable, self-condemned, if you are not. How heinously sinful barrenness is! it will involve you in the greatest guilt. How extremely dangerous it is! it will expose you to all that is dreadful.

Let me, as a further inducement to fruitfulness, touch some of the great and blessed advantages which attend and follow it.

1. Hereby you glorify God. This is the best, the only way you have to give him glory, John xv. 8, Philip. i. 11. We glorify God, not by adding anything to his essential glory, for that is infinite, not capable of any addition; but declaratively, by declaring that he is glorious, by giving a testimony to his glorious perfections, by making it appear that he is glorious. And there is a voice in good fruits that declares this; a light in them that discovers it, makes it apparent to others; and so engages them to acknowledge it, and thereby to glorify him, Mat. v. 16.

By bearing good fruits, and bringing them forth to God, we declare and acknowledge his greatness and goodness, to which his other glorious excellencies are reduced. His *greatness;* for good fruits are acts of obedience to him, and thereby his sovereignty, dominion, and authority over us, is really acknowledged. His *goodness* too: for, by bringing forth fruit to God, and not ourselves, we seek him, and not ourselves; we please him, we serve him, we aim at him; we live to him, and not to ourselves, and so shew we have resigned up ourselves to him as our last end; and so declare him to be our chief good, and that which we count absolutely best of all. And this gives God the glory that is due to him as God, as the greatest and best, *Maximus Optimus.*

And we have no other way to glorify God but by bearing good fruits. *No fruit* disparages him: *bad fruits* are an affront to him. There is in both a contempt of his greatness; an abuse, a denial of his goodness. If you be unfruitful, God has no honour by you; you do nothing but dishonour him; you deny him to be glorious, or worthy to be so acknowledged; you live in opposition to that great end of God, which he aimed at in all that he has done for you, or for the whole creation. You do your part to leave God without honour in the world; for from whom on earth should the Lord expect glory, if not from you? The inferior creatures will rise up in judgment against you, and condemn you; for they all honour God, by bringing forth such fruits as they are capable of. You, from whom most fruits are expected, are only barren, and most a dishonour to God, from whom, in all reason, he might look for most glory.

But then, bringing forth fruit being the way, the best way, to glorify God, it is your greatest perfection, your highest excellency. The angels themselves can do nothing better, nothing higher; they do, it is true, glorify him more; but they cannot do more than glorify him. There is nothing higher, nothing more excellent than this, for it is the highest end of the great God himself; you pursue the same design, which the Lord himself has been pursuing, from the foundation of the world to this day, and will be for ever; you act in a conformity to the great God, and in a subserviency to his chief end, than which there is nothing more noble and excellent, nothing more desirable to God, or men, or angels; you can do nothing that will more please God, or will more advance him, or will render you more like him. On this account he will glory in you, Isa. lxi. 3.

2. This is the way to have much of God's presence, much communion with him. It is the presence of God that makes heaven glorious, and it is communion with him that is the happiness of heaven. The more fruit you bring forth, the more of heaven will you have upon earth; the more of that

presence and communion which makes heaven a place of glory and happiness. The Lord will be much with those in whom he delights and takes pleasure; and he takes pleasure in those who bear good fruit, for that is pleasant to him; he calls it 'pleasant fruit,' Cant. iv. 13; hereupon the spouse sues for Christ's presence, ver. 16. And he needs not much entreaty where there are such attractives: he comes immediately, chap. v. 1. Christ comes, and entertains himself with this fruit, which is so pleasant to him, as he expresses it by what is most delicious to us.

We cannot entertain Christ with anything so acceptable to him as the fruits of the Spirit, and he will not be a stranger where his welcome and entertainment so pleases him. If your souls be as gardens, as orchards replenished with pleasant fruit, Christ himself will frequently be with you, he will delight to walk there. It is the way to have your daily course a walking with God. None can expect such clear discoveries of Christ, such gracious visits, such blessed interviews, so constant intercourse with him, as those that are fruitful. If you have little of Christ's presence, if he be seldom with you, if you have cause to complain of distance and strangeness, examine whether he find not little in you that he likes, little good fruit. He is not wont to deal so with those whose fruits please him, Isa. lxiv. 5, 'worketh righteousness;' *i. e.* who brings forth the fruits of righteousness. If you would have the Lord to meet you in your worldly affairs, so that you may converse with God while you are conversing with men, if this be desirable to you, see that you be then working righteousness. If you would have the Lord meet you in his ordinances, make fruitfulness your end and design in the use of them, then will your assemblies be, as the tabernacle is called, Lev. i. 1, 'a place of meeting;' not of meeting one another, but of meeting with God. There will you see his face, and hear his voice, and spy his goings, and feel his workings, and taste the refreshments which attend his presence, and flow from communion with him.

3. This is the way to have more of the means of grace, to have them in more plenty, power, liberty: Mat. xiii. 12, 'To him that hath,' *i. e.* who fruitfully improves what he hath. If he have little, he shall have more; if he have much, he shall have abundance. This we are further assured of by the Lord's proceeding with those who faithfully improved their talents, Mat. xxv. 21–23. Would you have more advantages for your souls than former unfruitfulness has left you? Would you have the gospel and ordinances without restraint? Would you have his worship in public without sinful or suspected mixtures? Would you be brought out of corners, set in a large place, to praise the Lord in the great congregation? Would you have your lights no longer under a bushel, but set upon their candlesticks, and made burning and shining lights indeed? Do ye long, mourn, pray for this, that the gospel might have a free passage, that it may run and be glorified, none might obstruct or obscure it? Why, here is a plain and open way for the procuring of all this: be faithful in the little you now have, make a more fruitful improvement of it, and the Lord, in due time, will entrust you with more.

This is the way to have more means for your soul's improvement, and more of those heavenly influences which are necessary to make them effectual. Isa. xxvii. 2, 3, 'Red wine' was the best, the most generous wine that country afforded. The vineyard which produced this, which brought forth the best fruit, the Lord undertakes to water it every moment. Endeavour to bring forth better fruit, satisfy yourselves with no other than the best, and the Lord will take special care of you; he himself will water you, and do it every moment. You shall never want any assistance, any refreshment, which may make your souls grow and flourish.

4. This will be your safety, whatever your dangers be; your security against all attempts, whether subtle or violent. Whoever threaten or design upon you, whoever would bereave you of what is precious to you, this is the way to defeat all their attempts, to turn all their counsels into foolishness. Take this course, and it will confute all your own fears, and establish you when all things totter and shake about you. The 'vineyard of red wine,' that which brings forth good fruit, the Lord undertakes for its security, Isa. xxvii. 2, 3. If they prevail, it must be against God; for he it is that keeps it. If they find it without defence, it must be some time that can neither be referred to night nor day; for by night or day none shall hurt it, every moment of both the Lord himself will keep it. They may attempt, but at their peril, as ver. 4; it will be with no other success than if briars and thorns should make an attempt upon a consuming fire. Those that will be like pricking briars and thorns to the people under God's protection, instead of burning them, shall burn themselves; for the Lord will keep and secure those that are fruitful as with a 'wall of fire,' that which will not only fence them, but destroy their opposers, Zech. ii. 5.

When the Lord has 'purged his people,' Isa. iv. 4, and made them fruitful, so that their fruit shall be excellent, ver. 2, and every one in Jerusalem shall be called holy, ver. 3, then does the Lord undertake to secure them and their assemblies, so that they might meet together for the worship of God without fear of danger or disturbance, ver. 5. The Lord himself will be unto them, both at home and in the places where they meet to serve him, what the pillar of fire and cloud was to the Israelites in their way to Canaan, both their conduct and a wonderful protection. As that interposed betwixt them and the Egyptians, Exod. xiv. 19, 20, 24, so will the Lord interpose betwixt his people and those that endanger them, and will as effectually secure them and their soul-concernments as if that miraculous pillar were again commanded to attend them; and upon all their glory there shall be a defence. He will cover them when assembled for his service as that cloud covered the tabernacle when it was within filled with his glory, Exod. xl. 34, &c. Neither heat when it is fair, nor storm when it rains, shall annoy them. You see the way to be secured from the dangers of every season; the way to have what you think in danger, and for which your hearts sometimes tremble, kept safe and secret, as though you were overshadowed by the Almighty; the way to be kept from disturbance, and fear of it.

5. Thus you may preserve others also, and save them from ruin, who are in great danger of it. A whole tree may be spared for some fruitful branches when it is very near cutting down, Isa. lxv. 8. As a man offended with a vine that is not fruitful, according to what he expects, gives order to have it stubbed up, yet before the order is executed, spying some grapes or clusters on it which may afford good wine, is moved thereby to spare the whole tree; so may the Lord, when he is ready to execute judgment, forbear a multitude for his servants' sake, for some few amongst them who are fruitful. When a family, a town, a country, is too generally barren, and the Lord thereby provoked to cut it down by some destroying judgment, yet if he find some branches (though not comparable in number to the whole) replenished with such fruits as he delights in, the whole may fare better for those few, and be spared for their sakes.

The holy seed, those that bring forth the fruits of holiness, may be the support of a place when it is falling into ruins, according to that, Isa. vi. 13.

The Lord would proceed in a way tending to the utter desolation of city and country, ver. 11, 12, yet there being a remnant, a small part of them, like a tenth, which were a holy seed, holy in heart and life, these should be such a security to those who had escaped, as trees are planted on the sides of a bank, which keep it from mouldering away. The holy seed, those few which were fruitful in holiness, should be the substance, *i. e.* the support of the rest, so that all should not run to ruin. You see this is the way, not only to be safe yourselves in a day of judgment and common calamity, but to preserve others from perishing, whose barrenness is bringing swift destruction upon them; you may hereby secure your families, though there be too many fruitless branches therein; you may preserve the places where you live, though under the sentence of excision, and in great danger to be cut down; you may be common saviours, so far as this title is communicable to men; yea, who knows but if the people of God would improve the means of grace, and the prunings by judgments and afflictions, to more fruitfulness, this land, under the curse of barrenness, and in danger to be cut down by desolating judgments, and whose cursed fruits provoke the Lord to make its plagues wonderful, might yet be spared and preserved from utter desolation, yea, and entrusted further with more means of improvement. The tree is not quite dead while there is fruit seen in any of the branches; and if after the danger of cutting down more fruit appear, there would be hopes that by some more improvements it might be made yet more fruitful; and so more encouragement, not only to give it time, but to bestow more cost and labour on it. So it is amongst men, and the Lord declares himself willing to proceed accordingly. If the old branches did but bring forth more and better fruit, and there were some hopes of new buds also, the condition of this people, though extreme dangerous, would not be utterly desperate. You see upon what the hopes of it depend. Oh, do not blast them! Bring not all into a hopeless state by continuing fruitless.

6. This is the most safe and certain way to get assurance. Good fruits will be an evidence that you are in a good state, that you are engraffed into Christ, John xv. 15. If you be fruitful, it will signify that Christ abideth in you, and you in him, Rom. vi. 22. Those who bring forth the fruits of holiness may conclude that they are the servants of God, and that they shall receive the reward of faithful servants, everlasting life: Mat. vii. 16-18, we may conclude what the tree is by the fruit it bears; we may conclude this probably of others, but more certainly of ourselves; we may see what others act, and are obliged in charity to think it good when it seems so; but we cannot discern from what principle, or for what ends they act, and so cannot be sure that what seems good in others is really so, 1 Cor. ii. 11. But we may discern our own principles and ends, and so may pass a judgment upon our own acts with more certainty, and consequently upon our state.

If we bring forth good fruits, this will be a surer evidence to us that our spiritual condition is good; and the better our fruit is, *i. e.* the more free from carnal, worldly, or selfish mixtures, the clearer will our evidence be; the character wherein it is writ will not be so blotted and blurred; we shall not be so puzzled to read it, and to discern the sense and signification of it. And the more our fruit is, the fuller will our evidence be; the characters will be larger, and more legible; we may discern them better, even in an hour of temptation, when others, who have them writ in a smaller hand, will be at a loss.

Fruits of the Spirit will be an argument to prove the Spirit is in us; and fruits of holiness will signify that we are sanctified; and fruits of righteousness that we are in the state of the righteous. But the better, the more these fruits are, the better, the firmer grounds of assurance will they be to us. A fulness of fruit will beget a plerophory, a fulness of assurance. The richer we are in the fruits of holiness and good works, the more riches of assurance may we expect.

Those that complain for want of assurance, and are afflicted with fears and doubts as to their spiritual state, can take no more effectual course for their relief than by bringing forth more and better fruit. The less fruit, the less and dimmer light you will have for the discovery of a saving state; more and better fruit will be as the setting up of greater and clearer lights for the discerning of it.

Whether assurance is ordinarily had, by the immediate testimony of the Spirit, is a question with some. But this is unquestionable, the Spirit never testifies the state is good, but where there are good fruits. So that where they are not, it is a foolish and vain presumption to expect any such testimony of the Spirit. And to believe we have such a testimony, without such fruits, is to delude ourselves, and belie the Spirit of God.

And this is unquestionable, that the Spirit helps us to discern the sincerity and goodness of the fruit we bear, 1 Cor. ii. 12 ; and so testifying to our spirits that the fruits we bring forth are good, and such as are proper and peculiar to the children of God. Hereby 'the Spirit itself beareth witness with our spirits, that we are the children of God,' Rom. viii. 16.

So that if assurance be by the immediate testimony of the Spirit, it never testifies a good condition where good fruits are not. If it be by the immediate testimony of the Spirit, good fruits are the *medium* by which it helps us to conclude it. Therefore no assurance can be had, no testimony of the Spirit will be given of a saving state, where there are not good fruits. All persuasions of a good condition, without good fruit, are but vain, groundless presumptions; all hopes of heaven are but dangerous delusions. These will be grounds of hope, and nothing without them ; and the more, the better they are, the firmer and clearer will the grounds of your hopes be, and the more will they advance towards confidence and full assurance.

7. This is the way to comfort, when it is most needful, and when it will be most comfortable. In reproaches, temptations, afflictions, yea, in death, and at judgment, when the vain comforts of fruitless souls will vanish, and end in remorse and terrors, and be as the giving up of the ghost, Job xi. 20.

In reproaches. When men speak against you as evil-doers, and your conscience bears you witness that your lives have been and are full of good fruits, either you may convince them that they wrong you and their own souls, and have the comfort of bringing them to glorify God by an acknowledgment thereof, 1 Peter ii. 12. Or if they be hardened in their prejudice, and resolute not to be convinced by any evidence sufficient for that purpose, you may appeal to God, and comfort yourselves with that blessedness which Christ makes the portion of those who have all manner of evil spoken against them falsely, Mat. v. 11. And reproach will not leave any such sting in your conscience, as in theirs who are conscious that their unfruitfulness, and not walking worthy of the gospel, has opened the mouth of reproachers.

In temptation. Satan will not so easily fix any fiery dart on you as on others, if you have been fruitful indeed ; you have a better shield to secure you from the wounding impressions of them. You will have more to confute the false accusations wherewith he would disturb you, and call in question your integrity ; you will have more to allege for yourselves, and that which will be harder for him to answer or gainsay ; you may repel him with more confidence, and more advantage when there is little or nothing in your conscience to take part with him.

In afflictions. It is a great comfort to know that we are not afflicted for our barrenness; and who can know that but those that are fruitful? Good fruits yield the most sweetness in pressures, and such as are able to sweeten the bitterest afflictions, and to cause the bitterness of them to pass away: Heb. xii. 11, the 'fruits of righteousness' are 'peaceable,' because they bring peace and joy, instead of that grief which the chastenings are accompanied with. This turns the storm and tempest wherewith an afflicted soul is tossed, disturbed, discomposed, into a sweet calm and serenity. This brings that 'peace of God, which' not only surpasses all that is afflictive, and is sufficient to drown the sense thereof, but 'passes all understanding, and keeps the heart and mind' in a quiet, composed, comfortable posture, when all is stormy and ruffled round about. The apostle had experience of it, when, having given an account of his great troubles and hazards, 2 Cor. i. 8–10, he adds, ver. 12, he could rejoice, notwithstanding these troubles that threatened him with present death, when his conscience bore him witness, that his conversation had abounded with good fruit (that which was sincerely good) in the world, and towards those to whom he was more particularly related.

And at death, when there is most need of comfort, and when all outward enjoyments will give out, and prove miserable comforters, what joy will it be to reflect upon the days of lives past as fruitful seasons, which have brought forth fruits pleasant to God, and advantageous to the world; to look upon our time, parts, and enjoyments as employed for Christ, in ways of fruitfulness and serviceableness to God and men; to have the testimony from our consciences, that it has been the design and business of our lives to live to God, and bring forth fruit to him, and not to ourselves; to please him, and not to gratify our own, or the humours of others; to advance him, though it laid us under reproach; to lay out what we had for him, though we and ours have suffered by it; to be able to say, as he, Acts xxiii. 1, and xxiv. 16. But their life will look upon them with as pale, and ghastly, and frightful face, as death itself, who can spy little in their days past but cyphers, and must reflect on them as unfruitful, unserviceable, insignificant days: days rather consumed than lived and fruitfully employed; days spent in the pursuit of the world, for the profits or pleasures of it, or the external advantages of themselves or their posterity; days wasted in the service of their lusts, or the service of their great idol mammon, or in the service of themselves; melted away either in idleness, or in that which God had not made their works; days so consumed, not improved for God in ways of fruitfulness. When death is approaching, what comfort can there be in such review! This is the way to make the day of death a day of blackness and thick darkness indeed. Oh, if you would have comfort in death, lay up a good foundation for the time to come; abound in the acts of holiness, and the fruits of righteousness: that is the way to do it, if you will believe the apostle, 1 Tim. vi. 18, 19.

And then at judgment, if you, in the sense of the worthlessness of what fruits you have brought forth, should not venture to fetch any comfort from thence, Christ himself will bring it you, and thence derive it, as he has plainly declared beforehand, Mat. xxv. 34–36. Good fruits are not the cause of the reward; they do not deserve it, they did not purchase it; that is the honour of Christ, of Christ alone. But he alleges them as the reason of this comfortable sentence. And Christ himself will be no ground of comfort to you without these There is no true comfort, either in life, or in death, or at judgment, without good fruits; and the more, the better they are, the greater, the sweeter comforts both now and then, both here and hereafter.

8. This is your beauty, your ornament, your glory, in the sight of God and men. What is the excellency of a fruit-tree but fruitfulness? What leaves soever it have, what blossoms soever it shew, yet if in the season it bear no fruit, all its flourishes are blasted, and he that owns it will make no account of it. The excellency of the trees of righteousness, the planted of the Lord, is to abound in the fruits of righteousness; and as these are a glory to God, of which before, so they are an honour to the gospel, an ornament to your profession, that which renders it lovely and beautiful in the eyes of all men, and a special glory to the fruitful themselves. God himself does seem to glory in such, Isa. lxi. 3. Those of the same profession may glory in them, and those that hate and malign them will either be convinced, or silenced, or condemned, in the judgment and conscience of the world, for condemning them. 'There is one glory of the sun, another of the moon, another glory of the stars, one star differing from another star in glory;' for all the difference in degrees, all are glorious, for all are luminaries. And such is the glory of the fruitful, they are all luminaries, though some greater and some less. By holding forth the word of life in a conversation full of the fruits thereof, they shine as lights in the world, Philip. ii. 15, 16, Prov. iv. 18. 'The path of the just,' of him that bears fruits of righteousness, 'is as the shining light,' and the more fruits he bears, the more and more does he shine. Clouds of reproaches are hereby scattered; such a light will break through them, it cannot be hid; the splendour of it will be apparent and conspicuous to the world, in despite of malice and detraction, Mat. v. 16. There is a light in good fruits, which attracts the eyes of the world to it, and stays not there, but reflects glory upon the Most High.

9. Christ will own the fruitful here and hereafter, John xv. 8; so shall ye declare yourselves to be 'my disciples indeed, if ye bring forth much fruit.' Upon this account Christ will own you for his disciples, as those that have so learned Christ as he would have them, as those that have 'heard him and been taught by him, as the truth is in Jesus,' Eph. iv. 16, &c.; as those that imitate him, as disciples should their master; as those that follow him, and tread in his steps, and would be conformed to that great pattern. When they make it their business in the world to do good, as he 'went about doing good,' Acts x. 38; when they strive to 'be holy, as he was holy, in all manner of conversation,' 1 Peter i. 14, 15; when it is their design to 'fulfil all righteousness,' and their 'meat and drink [is] to do his will': he will not be ashamed to own such for his disciples. But barren professors he will be ashamed of, as being a real shame and reproach to him; and he will declare it, he will disown them, and thrust them from him, as we do that which is shameful to us, Mat. vii. 20–23. The most specious profession, the fairest pretences, the most splendid performances, such as prophesying, and casting out devils, and working miracles in the name of Christ, without real fruits in universal obedience, will be no plea that Christ will regard. Whatever they profess, whatever they do, though what they have done amount to wonderful works, if they have not done the will of the Father in bringing forth good fruits, Christ will disown them; they must depart from him, as those he is ashamed of, pretenders, not true disciples.

But the fruitful he will own, as here, so in the last day, and expresses it in terms so transcendently affectionate and comfortable as will leave no sense of any trouble, loss, hazard, or suffering that they have met with in the way of fruitfulness, Mat. xxv. 34. Compare this peerless sentence with the dreadful doom of the unfruitful, ver. 41. The fruitful must 'come,' the barren 'depart;' those pronounced 'blessed,' these 'accursed;' those called to a 'kingdom,' these sent into 'everlasting fire;' those to inherit and reign with the Father and Christ for ever, these to remain with the devil and his angels. Oh, what words can be invented by men or angels apt to make so deep an impression upon the mind and heart of man as these words of Christ? If you have any sense, any regard or belief of Christ when he speaks words, each of which have the joys or terrors of an eternal state in them, there needs no more be said to engage you to fruitfulness, or to render barrenness dreadful to you. I will only add this,

10. Good fruits, good seed; whatever you do or suffer for God, you sow, and shall assuredly reap what you sow with abundant advantage. This is frequently expressed in Scripture, Hosea x. 12. The saddest act of seed-time has assurance of a joyful harvest, Ps. cxxvi. 5. And the harvest shall not fail to answer the seed, 2 Cor. ix. 6, and Gal. vi. 7–9. And he makes use of this as a motive to fruitfulness, ver. 10. It is seed that cannot possibly miscarry; it is under the Lord's husbandry: not the least grain of it shall be lost, no, not that which seems to be quite thrown away, Eccles. xi. 1. That which seems as utterly cast away, as what seed is thrown into the water, shall return with plentiful increase. It is the Lord that looks after it; he is engaged to take care that it grow, and it is he that gives the increase. It depends not upon the temper of the soil, nor the seasonableness of a year, nor the heavenly influence, which may occasion a miscarriage in other husbandmen's seed after all care and pains. Your expectation will not be frustrated; yea, it will spring up beyond, above all you can expect or imagine, when your expectation is most enlarged, and your apprehensions raised to the highest. It will bring forth not only thirty or sixty fold, but what Israel's seed produced, an hundredfold, Gen. xxvi. 12. You have the best assurance for it that heaven can give, the word of Christ, Mat. xix. 29, 'an hundred fold here in this life' (as it is expressed by the other evangelist, Mark x, 29, 30), the largest increase that any seed ever yields on earth; but hereafter it will produce so many hundred, so many thousand fold, as is past all account; it will nonplus all art, all artists to cast it up, for 'eye hath not seen,' &c.

It is expressed in a gross sum, 'life everlasting.' But how much that comprises no man nor angel can understand; so much joy, glory, happiness, as passes all understanding.

Oh, if a husbandman were ascertained of this, that how much soever be sowed, it would all yield him at last an hundredfold, he would sow all the ground he had, and labour to get more, and spare no pains, no cost; the hope of so rich a crop would let him think nothing too much. Oh, if we did believe God, and what he so clearly expresses, that all good fruit is seed, and that it will yield so much, 'the increase of God,' an exceeding great increase, we should think it our concernment not to sow sparingly, we should think we were highly injurious to ourselves not to 'abound more and more in all fruitfulness.'

And thus, if you will be moved by reason or equity, by fear or hope, I have offered something that may put you upon motion toward more fruitfulness. If this have made any impression on you, it will be seasonable to give you some directions for the promoting of your fruitfulness, and to discover what it is that keeps many so barren, notwithstanding all the means of improvement they enjoy. And to begin with this latter;—

1. Unmortifiedness is one main impediment of fruitfulness. The less

mortified we are, the less fruit we shall bear; and that little will be the worse for it, it will neither suffer it to be much nor good. And so we may observe that the method wherein the Holy Ghost in Scripture leads us to fruitfulness is answerable: there we are directed, first, to 'put off the old man, with its deceitful lusts,' and then the new man will act in holiness and righteousness, bringing forth the fruits of both. So the apostle Paul, Eph. iv. 22–24. And the same apostle first describes 'the works of the flesh,' and will have them destroyed, and then proceeds to the 'fruits of the Spirit,' insinuating that these cannot grow unless the other be first rooted out, Gal. v. 19, 20, &c.

Unmortified lusts and affections render all the means of fruitfulness ineffectual. The word, which is the seed that produces good fruit, cannot take root, cannot be fruitful, till these be stubbed up, and therefore the Spirit of God leads us first to this, James i. 21, 22. You will be hearers only, and not doers of the word; the word will not be an engrafted word, bringing forth saving fruit, unless these be laid aside. So, 1 Peter ii. 12, if those evils be not mortified, thrown away with indignation, purged out as bad humours, that both take away the stomach and hinder digestion, and turn what is received into the same noxious quality, you will not grow strong nor fruitful by the word; it will not be λόγος καρποφορούμενος, Col. i. 6, a 'fruitful word.' So, Jer. iv. 3, 4, rid your hearts of inordinate lusts and affections, or else nothing will thrive or grow that can be accounted good fruit; all means of improvement will be as seed cast upon ground which is overgrown with thorns and weeds, it will come to little or nothing. Carnal, selfish, worldly lusts, while they are tolerated or not subdued, they are as weeds or vermin to the seed or to the fruit; they hinder it from being either much or good; either they hinder it from springing up, as brambles or thorns do; when these grow thick, the crop will be thin; or they spoil or destroy it after it appears. Either as locusts or caterpillars, they destroy it in the blossom; or as worms and other vermin, they eat into it and corrupt it when it should come to maturity.

Begin with the work of mortification if you would be fruitful; make use of all means afforded you for this purpose; be diligent and unwearied in the use of them. Improve judgments and afflictions for this purpose, as I have lately directed you. There is no expectation your fruit should be much or good, unless you pluck up these weeds and brambles which pester your hearts and lives, and leave little or no room for good fruit; unless you destroy these vermin which devour the seed, so that little comes up, or corrupt the fruit when it is come up, so that it is become good for little or nothing. Unmortified lusts will let little take root or grow, and afterwards they corrupt or rot that little, hinder it from being pleasant fruit to God, as that is not pleasant to you which is rotted or worm-eaten.

An unmortified Christian cannot be fruitful; his lusts take up much of the ground where good fruit should grow; his time, his parts, his enjoyments, yea, his soul, is otherwise employed than to bring forth good fruits, so far as it is under the power and command of these lusts; and that little which he bears is full of vermin, the tolerated corruption of his heart corrupts and spoils it. It cannot be so much nor so good as in those who have 'crucified the flesh with the affections and lusts.'

2. Worldliness. That is a principal impediment to fruitfulness. Carefulness either to get or keep much of the world, eagerness either after the plenty or the pleasures of this life, is assigned by Christ himself as the main cause of unfruitfulness: Mat. xiii. 20–22, 'The cares of the world, and deceitfulness of riches,' συμπνίγει τον λόγον, do as it were take it by the throat and strangle it; or as thorns and brambles, with rank roots, suck away the fat-

ness of the earth which should nourish the corn, and so destroys it. Thus does the world engross the strength and vigour of the soul, which should be put forth in good fruits, and converts it to its own use; it stifles good motions, inclinations, affections, resolutions raised by the word, and never suffers them to come to maturity. The other evangelist is more particular in the account he gives of the world's mischievousness this way, Luke viii. 14. Here are three engines, by which the world does this mischief in worldly hearts: The cares of the world; when men are too careful, too busy about it. The riches; when they too highly value them, and too much affect them, and too forwardly pursue them; when the deceitfulness of riches seduces them to a high opinion of riches, a great affection to them, an eager following after them; when they believe what they deceitfully promise, and expect great advantage and great pleasure in outward abundance. The pleasures of this life; when they please themselves too much in the getting or enjoying much of the things of this life. This chokes the word, makes the best means of improvement ineffectual; all good conceptions hereby prove abortive. Whatsoever the word does towards fruitfulness, the world undoes it. Even when the soul is big with good motions begotten by the word, the world makes it miscarry; they become like the untimely birth of a woman, that never sees the sun, Ps. lviii. 8; such do not τελεσφορεῖν. When the heart of the ground is eaten out, and the moisture and fatness of it sucked away by thorns and brambles, sow what you will in it, you will find it barren. When the world takes up the thoughts, the heart, the affections, the time, the strength, the endeavours which is necessary for the producing and nourishing of good fruit, what can be expected, even under the best means for improvement, but barrenness? Indeed, if the design in seeking riches were to be 'rich in good works,' and they were accordingly so employed, the world might be helpful to us. But it is a rare thing to have it so sought, and so used, for God, and not for ourselves and relatives only or principally. And while this is so rare, worldliness, so much branded in Scripture, is common, and barrenness general. A worldly spirit, whatever it profess or pretend, what zeal soever it shew in some little things, is and will be unfruitful. 'You cannot serve God and Mammon:' you cannot bring forth fruit to God, and fruit to the world. What the world will spare for God, will neither be much nor very good. There is little time for it, there is little heart for it; the world takes it up. God must have none but the world's leavings, some crumbs that fall from its table; this will not amount to much. Nor can it be very good; it will have a tang of the world, an earthish taste; it will savour of the temper from whence it proceeds, and have some worldly mixtures that will taint it. And though others, or yourselves, do not discern it, the Lord can and will; and less like it, the more it tastes of a worldly spirit.

If ever you would be fruitful indeed, get the world crucified, get it laid low in your thoughts, get it cast out of your hearts. Demean yourselves towards it, in your daily course, as a weaned child. Get your hearts, which have been set upon the world, set upon your work, that which the Lord has sent you to do. Let it not engross your time, which is necessary for your souls, for your families, or for others whom you ought to improve and help on towards fruitfulness; that time which is necessary for prayer, for examining your spiritual state, for meditation, and working the word which you hear or read upon your hearts.

You must be more indifferent towards the world, if you would be 'zealous of good works,' of good fruits; as Christ's peculiar people should be, those whom he has purchased and redeemed from the earth; and you will not be fruitful unless there be some zeal and fervour for more and better fruits.

3. *Privateness of spirit.* When a person is confined to himself, himself single or multiplied, he and his relatives, thinks himself little concerned to look further; shuts up himself, in a manner, wholly in the narrow circle of his own concernments or that of his family and relations; seldom draws any lines beyond it, rarely acts further; or what he does of larger extent, is little and extraordinary: such a one cannot bring forth much fruit, for the sphere of fruitfulness is very large, and reaches far beyond ourselves and ours; and the Lord expects we should walk and act to the full extent and latitude of it, or else he has little fruit of us. Several graces which respect others will be unexercised, several talents will be hid and buried. Such as would be advantageous to others at a greater distance will not be employed, the improvement of which the Lord calls for. Much of that we are entrusted with, and must give an account of, will lie waste, which would yield fruit desirable to God and men. And so far we shall be accounted barren, as we do not bear fruit where we might and ought, by the employment of our graces, gifts, accomplishments, estates, and outward enjoyments. He that brings but forth fruit to himself, how much soever it be for bulk and quantity, is barren, and no better than an empty tree in the Lord's account, Hosea x. 1. He that will be fruitful indeed, must have fruits reaching as far as the apostle will have them extended, Gal. vi. 10. The household of faith is far larger than our own household and relations; but the *all* he mentions is far larger than the household of faith. Now, he that would bring forth fruits worthy of the gospel, such as it requires, must extend them beyond himself and relatives, to the household of faith; and further much than that also (though that be of large extent), even to all. He must do good to all, to some more especially, but to all in some measure. Without any limitation, but that of opportunity; nothing but want of this will excuse our neglect of any of these *all* from barrenness. Get public spirits, get larger souls; privateness and littleness of spirit, narrow and contracted souls shrunk up into themselves, seldom moving, like the snail, out of its own shell, will leave you under the guilt of much barrenness. A selfish person will be an unfruitful tree, though planted in the Lord's vineyard.

4. *Indulgence to carnal ease and slothfulness.* The calling of the husbandman is laborious; he that will improve his land in fruitfulness, especially if it be naturally barren, must be no sluggard. We must 'give all diligence' if we would not be 'barren and unfruitful in the knowledge,' &c., 2 Peter i.; otherwise heart and life will be overrun with weeds instead of good fruit, Prov. xxiv. 30–32. It is 'the diligent hand that makes rich,' Prov. x. 4. Men are easily convinced that they must be diligent in their particular callings if they will thrive; but either they think it no duty to be rich unto God, rich in good fruits, or else they think there needs not such diligence for this; both which are pernicious delusions. 'The men of this world are wiser in their generation than' those who profess themselves to be 'children of light;' they rise early, &c., to improve their estates, whereas these use little or no diligence to improve the means of grace for fruitfulness. Where is that diligence which the Scripture calls for, under the notions of striving, running, wrestling? phrases which import the putting forth of all our strength, and continuance therein.

5. *Mistaking that for good fruit which is not so.* Now, because it is necessary, and very useful for all sorts to have this mistake more fully discovered, I shall be a little more large and particular herein, and endeavour to shew how many ways we are apt to be mistaken about the goodness of our fruits; and to be satisfied with that as good which is not so in the account of God.

(1.) Some take that to be good, which is indeed bad fruit; and to be pleasing to God, when, indeed, it is a provocation to him; think they do him service, when they are serving themselves, gratifying their own corruption, and sacrificing to their own lusts. Christ tells his disciples of some who would think they did God service when they were persecuting his faithfullest servants, John xvi. 2; and this was the fruit of error and ignorance, ver. 3. Through such ignorance and error, persons and things may be so disguised and misrepresented, as that may be taken for a crime which is a duty, and that for heresy which is a necessary truth; and those for flagitious persons who are not only innocent, not guilty, but eminently holy; and so these may be persecuted with a heat, which is taken for holy or heroical zeal, when it is devilish enmity against God, his truths, servants, and ways. And herewith may they be transported, who are in the common account the most knowing and the most holy; for such were the scribes and pharisees in Christ's time, such was their esteem amongst the vulgar. They persecuted the apostles, yea, Christ himself, to the death, and thought they did therein good service to God; and it passed for good fruit, when it was the poison of asps and the cruel venom of dragons. Herein they are followed by the papists, and by those who disclaim this name, but walk in their steps; who, out of a zeal to a church which their own interest has framed, and against schism, contempt, and disobedience, which have as little ground as their other chimera, are all in thunder and lightning. And some of their judgments and consciences may be so deluded and infatuated, as to think it good service to God, and good fruit in the church, to ruin those who conform not to them; and having no hopes of fire from heaven, to gratify their blind, selfish zeal, make wildfire of their own to do it. Yea, those who are neither papists nor formalists, being under the power of error or ignorance, in particulars which they suspect not, are in the like danger. To censure those things as sins, which are innocent; and to make conscience of those as duties, which are crimes forbidden, or at least things not commanded; and to embrace those as lovely truths, which are foul mistakes: and the more zealously they act in reference to such things, the better fruit they may think it; whereas, quite contrary, the more it acts, and the higher it rises, it is still worse and worse. You have lamentable instances hereof, both concerning a mistaken church and a mistaken kingdom, and also in other less observed particulars, which I cannot insist on.

So you may see the zeal of some run out against the opinions and practices of others, under pretence they are dangerous and of bad consequence, when the bottom of all is envy or revenge speciously dignified; and the design is, the disparaging or depressing of those who are thought to outshine them. Ill-will to those whom they affect not, is the root; and evil-speaking, or detraction, the fruit of it. And yet it passes for good fruit, because it is supposed to be a good cause that is so managed, and that supposed evil to which it is opposed; but God will not account this good fruit, whatever men do.

(2.) Some take that to be good fruit which is only negatively good, in comparison of what is stark naught: conclude it good, because it is not the worst of all, or not so bad as that which some others bring forth. Such was the fruit of the pharisee, which he thought to be very good, when he is represented as boasting of it, Luke xviii. 11. The pharisee is not alone in his mistake, or his confidence; others amongst us are ready to presume their fruit is good, and they not much concerned to look after that which is better; because it is not quite so bad as is visible in many, or the most about them; they are not so profane, or so superstitious; they neither blaspheme nor persecute; they swear not, nor forswear; they neither scorn nor hate that which is good; they are neither drunkards, adulterers, or oppressors, nor sordidly covetous; they wallow in no such ungodliness and wickedness as they see others do; they bring forth better fruit than many, and so conclude it is good enough, they need not trouble themselves further. But what a deceit is this! as though it were enough to prove a tree fruitful, because it has no vermin or caterpillars on it. There is no more fruit in mere negatives, than a tree has in winter, when it has not so much as leaves to cover it. This is but one half of what the pharisee had to allege for himself; and the end of your fruit will never be acceptance with God here, nor eternal life hereafter, unless it be more and better than that of the pharisees, Mat. v. 20.

(3.) Some take that to be good, which, though it be not bad in itself, yet has no goodness in it. Such are they who are great zealots for things which they count indifferent (*i. e.* such as are neither good nor bad in themselves), yet urge them with more eagerness, and are more severe in exacting that which they acknowledge to have no goodness in it, than any of the fruits of holiness or righteousness; these are neglected, and the neglect of them excused, if those be but observed. There needs no other mouth to condemn such than their own. God calls for good fruit; that which they most mind is what they declare to be not good. The best they can say of such fruit is, that it is neither bad nor good. But it will be bad enough in consequence, when it hinders them, and makes them hinder others, from bringing forth better.

Let us be warned by the follies and excesses of others not to be much taken with anything whose goodness is not manifest. This will dangerously divert us from that which is good fruit indeed. The life, and heart, and strength, and vigour of religion, which should put forth itself in fruits of holiness and righteousness, will be sacrificed to trifles and shadows, or will run out in some worthless grain or fruitless excrescency. Be sure that person or church will not be fruitful in God's account, whose excellency is the bringing forth of that which is not confessedly good.

(4.) Others think their fruit is good, when the goodness of it is but imaginary and fancy: such as those whose religion is notional, who are most pleased with their notions, when they are most thin and airy, and spun into a fineness which makes them of no use; admire them most, when they are least intelligible; and think them the highest attainments when they are out of the common road, above ordinary capacities, if not without common sense; make most of them, and hug them with most passion, when they do them least good, and neither heart nor life is better for them. Sure, whatever excellency persons may fancy in such notions, they are plainly flourishes, not fruits. Those that love to spin religion into such cobwebs, take the course to starve their souls, and keep themselves fruitless; cobwebs will neither keep them warm, nor nourish. These are not good fruit in themselves; but that is not the worst; they will hinder those who doat on them from being otherwise fruitful. Those that are troubled with the rickets are not thriving children, though their heads be bigger than others. When religion is run up into the head in notions, heart and life being left destitute of the virtue and power of it, must needs be barren: a notional professor will have little fruit but in fancy; and the like danger there is when religion is turned into matter of quarrel and controversy. This turns the soul, which should be as the fruitful vine, into a thorn or a briar, where you may find many prickles, but little desirable fruit. The contentious ages of the church were barren, in comparison of the more ancient and primitive, when religion was a plain and easy thing, and not so perplexed with contentions and controversies: *ut magnæ cujusdam artis fuerit orthodoxum esse;* that it was a matter of great art to be orthodox (as Erasmus speaks of the fourth age). Godliness as practical, was then declining; but it was even expiring, grown decrepit, and past fruit-bearing, when the chief supports of it were the schoolmen, who, instead of practical truths, and what would have nourished souls unto fruitfulness, threw amongst them some bare bones to pick; hard, abstruse, intricate questions, which exercised the brain, but drew up the heat and spirits from the heart, and left that languishing: to which that may be applied, Heb. xiii. 9.

When divines and other Christians affect to be controversial, they grow less practical; and it is in practice that fruitfulness appears. Satan would bring all religion into question, and employ all in controversy. He knows what advantage he has thereby, to divert them from that which is most fruitful and edifying. Quarrelsome and contentious spirits are no soil for the peaceable fruits of righteousness. There may be some fruit of controversy, which the corruption and perversion of degenerate minds has made necessary; but as it is ordinarily managed, it is sour and crabbed fruit, and such as will need many correctives to render it good and wholesome.

(5.) Others think they bear good fruit, because they have something that makes a goodly show, a fair appearance. They make a great profession, they are furnished with excellent guests; their parts and accomplishments are not contemptible; they have a form of knowledge, a sound judgment in matters of religion, some understanding of the Scripture, abilities to pray, and to discourse of the things of God, and are apprehensive of the mysteries of the gospel. Some such fruits they had whom the apostle describes, Rom. ii. 17–20. If these had been good fruit, it had been a good foundation for the time to come; whereas the apostle tells us, they 'treasured up wrath,' ver. 5. Indeed, these are not fruit, but leaves; and though the fair show they make may give hopes of fruit at a distance, as the fig-tree did to our Saviour, yet you know the issue of that goodly appearance, when he found no fruit thereon, according to expectation, nothing better than leaves, he cursed it, and it withered, and was suddenly dried up by the roots. If you think such shows, such leaves, fruit good enough, and this conceit hinder you from care to bring forth something better, they will not shelter you from the curse of Christ, and the execution of it, nor keep the axe from the very root. If 'every tree which brings not forth good fruit, shall be hewn down,' &c., how can they escape who bring forth nothing but leaves?

(6.) Others think their fruit is good enough when it is but partially good; they do things that are good, but they do them not well; the matter of what they do is good, but they neglect the manner, or the end, or the proportion, something integral or essential to its goodness, without which, if it be good at all, or may be so accounted, yet it is far from being completely good. It is hereby utterly maimed and crippled, or no better than a dead work. So some, they will hear the word, and hear it frequently and attentively, but not effectually, so as to obey it; or, if they will obey, as Herod did in many things, Mark vi. 20, yet they obey it but where it pleases them, and suits their humours and tempers, but not where it crosses their inclinations or interests. And through this defect their hearing is no good fruit, nor their obeying neither; and if they think otherwise, they deceive themselves, in the apostle's judgment, James i. 22.

They will yield to Christ in many things, but not in all. They are but almost persuaded to be fully his disciples; they stick at some of the terms on which he offers himself; though they can digest many, there is something too much, themselves to be denied, something too valuable to be forsaken and relinquished, some part of the cross too heavy to take up; and being but 'almost persuaded' to be his, the fruit they bear, how much soever it be, is but almost good.

They will leave many sins, but not all; or if they abstain from the outward acts, yet they do not mortify them; or if they be in some course of mortification, they halt, and make stands in it, and will not go through.

They will be charitable, and relieve those that are in want and distress; but then, either this must excuse them from other good works; or else they are defective in this, not rich in distributing, though this be the end why they are entrusted with riches, and the best improvement they can make thereof. They do it not proportionably to others' necessities, no, nor to their own superfluities. They can expend more upon their own unnecessary excesses than upon the pressing wants of the members or messengers of Christ; can spare it more freely when it ministers but to pride and vanity, and the excesses of their garb, furniture, or entertainment, than for the feeding, clothing, and refreshing of Christ mystical.

(7.) Others take that which is but questionably good, to be best of all, and accordingly mind it and pursue it as though there were not only some unquestionable, but some eminent goodness in it, and, consequently, overlook, or too much neglect, those things which are really and undoubtedly better. And this we may observe, both in matters of opinion and practice; both in positive duties, and opposition of sin. So you may see some persons grown fond of an opinion to such a degree as to lay the greatest stress on it; to lay out themselves almost wholly for the advancing and propagating of it; to contend for it as for life and death; to disparage all that are not, as they think, friends enough to it, and blast those that oppose it; to shew more heat and passion for it than those truths that are vital and fundamental, and have the most sovereign influence upon heart and life for fruitfulness; and yet, when it is duly and impartially examined, it may prove a question whether it be truth or no; and a matter of great difficulty to clear it from error, if it can be vindicated at all from such a censure.

You may see others, to whom some particular practice is very much endeared; they look upon it as a duty of greatest moment; they are ready to censure all that concur not with them in it. Those duties that are evidently and indispensably so must give way to it, and be neglected or little regarded in comparison; and yet, after all, to those who are without passions and pre-engagements, it may be a question whether it be indeed a duty.

You may see others have a great zeal against some things which they count unlawful; they fly out against them, as though there were no other, or no greater wickedness; they judge those who do not avoid them unfit for society with Christians; they are ready to censure those who cannot see reason to be so rigid and severe against them as themselves. And those things which are plainly and unquestionably evil in themselves or others are overlooked by this means, or little taken notice of in comparison. And yet, when those who are fearful of sin, and think themselves highly concerned to suffer none to lie under guilt, whom they can convince of it, do examine the things so condemned without prejudice, they find it questionable whether they be so sinful, or else exceeding difficult, if feasible, to find good grounds for the conviction of others, and not at all advisable to condemn so peremptorily, without good ground, and such as they may hope will be convincing.

Satan, the enemy of our souls, and of their fruitfulness, makes use of diversion as one of his main stratagems. If he can but make us neglect truths or duties that are unquestionable, he cares not how much we doat upon those that are questionable. If he can but make us indulgent to ourselves in real evils, he will allow us to be as severe as we will against others for things doubtful. He can make use of our zeal when it is misguided; of our heat let out groundlessly; to the rendering of it ineffectual, contemned and disregarded, when it is duly employed. He can set up a blind, and if we spend all our shot upon that which should be directed against real enemies, he has his design; he hereby makes that run waste which would otherwise render us fruitful. As if the heart of the ground should be spent in nourishing such plants and herbs that are of uncertain use, and of whose virtue, what it is, and whether it be any or none, we are doubtful; it must needs be to the prejudice of those fruits which are unquestionably good and useful.

(8.) Others take those for good fruits which are only artificial, and of their own devising, and commend to us a fiction of mortification, and holiness, and divine worship, not of God's prescribing, but of man's invention. Such are they who place mortification in some outward severities, and harsh usages of the body, chastening, afflicting, and pinching it, as though this were the crucifying of the flesh, which the Scripture calls for; as though they could mortify the body of sin, by curbing the outward man with a ' touch not, taste not, handle not;' and by neglecting the body, not shewing it respect due to it, in gratifying it with what is needful, according to that of the apostle, Col. ii. 23, where you may discern of what account it is with God. Being after the commandments and doctrines of men, it may have a show of wisdom, humility, and mortification, but is no such thing really.

And such is their sanctity, who, neglecting holiness of heart and life, will have a holiness in garments, utensils, and the very walls. Real holiness was at a low ebb when this counterfeit came in request; it is a weed that throve most when the church was growing a wilderness, and is but a slip of a degenerate plant where it grows rankest.

And such is that worship which the art and fancy of man devises for God; this can be no good fruit, with what colours soever it be set off; this is so far from pleasing God, as it highly provokes him. How can it do less, when it is a preferring of human contrivances before the divine wisdom? And what the fruit of it will be, we may learn by the threatenings denounced against it, Isa. xxvii., and by the censure of it: Mat. xv. 7, 'In vain they worship me,' when the doctrine by which their worship is regulated and ordered is the traditions of men; in places and times devised of their own heart, 1 Kings xii. 33. It is vain worship at the best, and that which is vain is fruitless. It supplants that which would yield most fruit, and draws with it a neglect of the commands and institutions of God, as the other evangelist shews, Mark vii. 7–9. That which is of this nature and tendency is cursed fruit, whoever bless themselves with it.

(9.) Others take that for good fruit which is no more than buds, the mere embryos and rudiments of it. Such are good motions, raised by the word or by afflictions, or apprehensions of death or judgment, but vanishing before they have taken effect. Some good inclinations, some purposes and resolutions to be better, but not pursued to execution; the heart starting from them like a deceitful bow, which returns to its unbent posture before it have delivered the arrow. Some transient impressions, which promise well, but pass away like the morning cloud; some stirring affections, which melt away as snow before the sun, and influence not the life with any lasting efficacy; some joy in the word, such as was in those hearers represented by the bad ground, Mat. xiii. 20; some delight in the ordinances, such as was in Ezekiel's hearers, Ezek. xxxiii. 32; some remorse and sorrow for sin, such as was in Ahab, 1 Kings xxi., and the Israelites, Ps. lxxviii. 47; some desires of spiritual things, as in the Jews, John vi. 34, who yet believed not, ver. 36; some wishes for heavenly enjoyments, as in Balaam, Num. xxiii. 10; some convictions also of sin and misery, and desires of freedom, but being not followed with sincere endeavours, prove abortive, and reach not the new birth. These are hopeful in their first appearance, but resting in them is the way to fall short of fruitfulness; for they are but blossoms, not fruit, and being nipped or blasted by the world, or prevailing corruption, or the powers of darkness, and not suffered to knit, or at least to come to consistence and maturity, they prove no good fruit. Those only are fruitful indeed which bring forth fruit to perfection; when the blossoms miscarry not, but knit and come to some ripeness; when there is a patient continuance under such good impressions, and under the means appointed for the ripening of them, Rom. ii. 7; but though there be no such continuance therein, yet these, making a specious show, are apt to be taken for good fruit, and so take men off from endeavouring after that which is good indeed.

(10.) Others take that for good fruit which is good only morally, not spiritually. They are prudent, and modest, and sober, chaste and temperate, meek and patient, candid and ingenuous, true and faithful in their words, just and righteous in their dealings, and have their conversation honest in the world. Now these would be good fruits indeed (and none can be justly counted fruitful without them), if they proceeded from a right principle, and were acted for a due end; if they sprung from a new nature, and were brought forth unto God, out of obedience to him, and with an intent to please and honour him; if the Spirit of grace were the author of them, and the end why they are exercised were answerable, they would be fruits of the Spirit, good fruits indeed. But when they are the issues only of a better natural temper, of moral principles, and selfish considerations, when they have no other rise than nature somewhat refined, but not thoroughly changed, and rise no higher in their design than self, and have no other end but what is common or sinister, they are not fruits proper to the garden of God; they may be found in the wilderness, even amongst the heathen. There is a fineness, a loveliness in them; they are but finer weeds, and such as may grow in the common of the world. When they are destitute of a spiritual principle and end, they make up but an ethnical and natural, not a Christian and spiritual, morality. It is a pity that things so amiable and desirable should do any hurt; but they are apt, when rested on as fruits good enough, to hinder the growth of what is truly and spiritually good, yea, and to take them off from so much as looking after that which is better. It will be harder to convince such than others that they are unfruitful, and, till such conviction, they are not so much as in the way towards fruitfulness.

(11.) Others take that for good fruit which is good only externally. Such are they who are much in the external exercises of religion, perform the outward acts of godliness and holiness in public and private, attend the ordinances of worship, and submit to those of discipline, and would have holy administrations according to divine prescription; like them best when visibly conformed to the pattern in the mount, the rule of the word; spend the Sabbath in these holy employments, attend the word diligently, repeat it to others, employ some thoughts in meditating on it; read and search the Scriptures, as hoping therein for eternal life; express a firm belief of the whole as truly divine and infallibly true; reverence the name of God, so as not to endure any gross open profanation of it in themselves, or it may be in others; pray everywhere, in public, in their families, and in secret too; discourse of heavenly and spiritual things currently, as occasion is offered; sing the praises of God, to outward appearance, devoutly; seek the knowledge of God and of their soul-concernments themselves, and take some pains, have some care to instruct others.

And are not these good fruits? Indeed they make such a goodly show, that those who bear them may be apt to think they are not obliged to bring forth any better. Here are the external lineaments of holiness well drawn, and to the life, so as the piece may be taken for that very thing, of which it is but a picture, and a mere artificial representation. But, you know, the draught of the best artist is not indeed the fruit of the womb, though it may be exactly like a child; there wants a soul to inform and enliven it. There is the colour and proportion of the several parts, but they are not living members. And so it is here. If the soul concur not in these exercises of religion, if that do not enliven them, and be stirring and active therein; if the heart be not in motion towards God, while the outward man is employed in holy duties; if the heart pray not, while the lips pronounce the words of a prayer, or the ear attends them; if the affections keep not time with the expressions in praises, or petitions, or confessions; if the soul comply not with the word, and run not into the mould of it, so as to admit the impressions of it intimately and effectually; if God be not worshipped in the spirit, and the heart kneel not, or lie not prostrate before him when there are outward postures of reverence; if the soul outmove not the lips in our addresses to him, and the inward man, the powers of the soul, be not thoroughly engaged in these holy services; why, then, all these religious employments are but bodily exercise, which profits nothing, is altogether fruitless. Here is but in all this a form of godliness, without the power and life of it. This makes but the picture, the mere skeleton of a fruitful Christian; the proportions and bare resemblance of him, but without life and soul. Here is the colour and the figure of good fruit, and such as may deceive the eye, but all is only the effect of art, which can represent that to the life that has no life in it, and can make that seem good fruit which is really no such thing. Yet because these are so like good fruit, they are taken to be the same, and those that bear them presume they are good enough, and are thereby hindered from minding or endeavouring to bring forth better.

This, and the other mistakes mentioned, are dangerous impediments to the fruitfulness the Lord expects from those that enjoy the means; and therefore I have the longer stayed in the discovery and removal of them.

6. Let me add another, but more briefly; and that is, looking more at comfort than at duty, studying the privileges to which we are advanced more than the service to which we are called, labouring more to get assurance than to do our work. All excesses in some things occasion defects in others. While we are too much in any one thing, we shall be too little in others, and it may be, such as are more necessary. Assurance and comforts are desirable, but fruitfulness is absolutely necessary. If we do not diligently and faithfully mind our duty in the latitude of it, and apply not ourselves wholly to the work the Lord has set us to do, we shall be found unfruitful. And then what place, what ground will there be for comfort or assurance? What claim can we lay to the privileges we are so much taken with? The end why the Lord offers us comfort and assurance of his love, is to make us cheerful in his service, and to encourage us in his work, and engage our hearts in it thoroughly. Now, if we mind the means more than the end, we act irregularly and irrationally.

What will you think of a servant who minds his refreshments more than his work? who takes more care, and spends more time about his meals than in his labour and employment? Will you think him a profitable servant, or expect much fruit of his labour? You are too like such servants when you are eager for comforts and spiritual refreshments, but less active for God in a way of serviceableness, and more backward to do or suffer what he calls you to. This is to be more for yourselves than for him; and while you are so disposed, he is not like to find much fruit on you. It is no commendation of Ephraim when he is compared to a 'heifer that loves to tread out the corn,' Hosea x. 11. It was the way of thrashing in those times to tread out the full sheaves with the feet of their cattle; and while they were so treading, their mouths were not to be muzzled, Deut. xxv. 4, so that they were eating while they were at this work, therefore they liked this work, but were averse to the toil of the yoke and the labour of the plough, where they had not such liberty and encouragement. Ephraim was like one of these heifers; he loved the service that was sweetened with a present reward, and would pay itself while it was a-doing, but declined that which was laborious, and was not attended with such refreshments. Those of this temper will be less serviceable, and so less fruitful.

The way to get comfort and assurance, and the sweet sense and improvement of your relations to God, and the privileges wherewith he honours and enhappies his servants, is to be 'constant and unmoveable, always abounding in the work of the Lord, for then your labour shall not be in vain in the Lord.' The issue of it will be, the testimonies of his love and acceptance. But to be earnest for joy and comfort, and remiss in the Lord's work, is the way to fall short both of assurance and fruitfulness.

Be not then so solicitous about *receiving* good, as in *doing* good. It is a more blessed thing to do than to receive. It is a directer way to abound in those fruits which the Lord will crown with rich blessings. Be not more careful to know that the Lord is your God than to shew yourselves to be his servants, by faithfulness, diligence, and activeness in the work of God. He that will mind his duty, and make it his business to be every way serviceable, and proceed in that way, though he walk in darkness, and see no light in God's countenance, is in the most probable way to comfort, but in a most certain way to fruitfulness.

7. Beware you be not much taken up with little things. These will take you off from the greater, wherein your chief and most valuable fruits consist. Let truths and duties have that proportion of your thoughts and endeavours which their weight and moment require. The 'tithing of mint, anise, and cummin,' will occasion the neglect of things which are βαρύτερα τοῦ νόμου, 'the weightier things of the law.' There are some matters of opinion and practice that are but in the skirts of religion and godliness, far from the heart of it, *e. g.* the less considerable questions about rites, order, discipline, &c. If these take us up as much or more than the vitals of godliness, we are like but to make an inconsiderable improvement in the main. And then whatever our proficiency be in minute things, and such as are not material, it will turn to no great account when God comes to seek for fruit. If we be more busy about the fringe and the lace than the body and soul of religion, or if that which is but as the hair be of more regard with us than the head of it, we may be fruitful in trifles, but barren in what is of greatest value and consequence. This is as if a gardener should take much pains in watering and pruning one small branch or sprig, but should do nothing at all to the main arms, or the body, or the root of the tree. That is not the way to make it bear well.

Having discovered the impediments which hinder your fruitfulness, and therewith shewed you the necessity of removing of them, and the way to do it, I proceed to some positive directions, such as, being duly observed, may promote your fruitfulness more directly.

1. Labour to be sensible of your barrenness. The sense of an evil is the first step towards its removal. He that observes not his distemper, and has no sense of it, will not look after cure, nor so much as think of it; it is like to grow upon him, and continue so till it prove mortal and incurable. He that is past sense is often past cure, and he that is without sense is so far without hope of relief that he is not in the way to it, nor will so much as seek it. Ephraim's condition was dangerous indeed, when there was cause to complain of him, as Hosea. vii. 9. If you would be fruitful, get true and effectual apprehensions of your unfruitfulness, such as may impress a lively and stirring sense of it upon your souls and consciences; endeavour to understand what the nature of it is, how much, how far it prevails, wherein it consists, and in what particulars you are chargeable, what are the causes of it, and what the danger; labour to see these severals, so as your eye may affect your heart, and so affect it, as it may set all in motion towards cure and redress.

(1.) Labour to know what is the nature and extent of your unfruitfulness, whether it be total or partial only; whether you be wholly barren, and bear no good fruit at all, or only bring not forth so much and so good as the Lord may expect from you. Get acquainted with the state of your souls; if there be not an universal change wrought therein, if the fallow-ground of your hearts be not ploughed up, no good fruit at all can grow there. If this be your condition, and you are not sensible of it, you will never look after that great change, without which you cannot be in any capacity for fruitfulness.

(2.) If you be not wholly fruitless, but only defective in part, labour to understand where the defect is, in quantity or quality. Be apprehensive of both, and how far it reaches, and the severals wherein it appears. Get a particular sense hereof; that is the best way to an universal redress. While you have only confused apprehensions of your unfruitfulness in general, and are not sensible of the particulars wherein distinctly you are guilty, you will do little or nothing towards a cure, or nothing to purpose; neither can others do it for you. A person that complains he is ill, but minds not where or how, nor gives any account of it so as the particular distemper may be discerned, is not in the way either to help himself or to have help from a physician. Resting in confused apprehensions and general complaints of barrenness, without searching in what parts of heart and life it lies, is the way to continue still unfruitful. Neither yourselves, nor others for you, can apply themselves particularly, and so not effectually, to remove it.

Search then every part of your souls, and every part of your conversations where fruit should appear, and observe what branch of either is too bare; how far your fruit is too little, how far it is not good; where it grows not thick enough, or where it is spoiled and corrupted.

Look into your minds. What is the good fruit that should grow there? High apprehensions of God; frequent meditation of his attributes, word, works, holy thoughts, minding of heaven and things above, and minding other things in a subserviency thereto; making use of the world, the objects and occurrences therein, to make it self-pregnant with spiritual thoughts and motions heavenward. Take notice how fruitless your minds are herein, how little they are so employed, how seldom such thoughts have admission, how short their stay is, how cold their welcome, how inconsiderable their efficacy, how easily they are diverted, how often stifled, how much your minds and thoughts run waste; what vanity, impertinency, curiosity or carnalness corrupts them, so that the fruits of your minds are neither much nor good. How near, how like you are to those who delight not to retain God in their thoughts, and the things of God. Get such a sense of this as the nature and consequence of it calls for.

Look into your hearts. The good fruits which these should bring forth are the acts and exercise of graces and holy affections to God and others. Observe if the exercise of some be not almost wholly neglected, if others be not seldom acted, though there be frequent occasions for it. If, when they do act, it be not very weakly, feebly, with much mixtures of corruption; and so, if your best fruits be not, as it were, very much worm-eaten, if not half rotten; take such notice hereof, as may strike your hearts with a due sense of it, and of the consequence of it.

Look into your lives. Observe what fruits these should bring forth unto God, yourselves, your families, those to whom you are specially related, what and how much unto the household of faith, unto strangers, unto enemies, what their several conditions and circumstances call for, what your several talents oblige you to, what variety of occasions and opportunities require, what you owe to their souls, what to their other concernments, what acts of godliness, of sobriety, of righteousness, of mercy, of charity, you should abound in. Observe how many of these are omitted, how many slightly performed, how many sorely corrupted in respect of their principle, or their matter, or their manner, or their end. These diligently observed, if either multitude or weight would make you sensible, will help you to a great and a particular sense of your unfruitfulness.

(3.) Be sensible of the causes of your barrenness. Make diligent inquiry after them, and engage yourselves to a careful observance of them. It is here, as in other cases, to know the cause is half the cure.

Take notice what weeds they are which choke the seed, what vermin it is that corrupts the fruit. You will not take pains to pluck up those or destroy these, unless you be sensible what mischief they do you. Search out those inward distempers which hinder your souls from thriving and growing fruitful. Be sensible of them, as of such a judgment as locusts, and canker-worms, and caterpillars, and palmer-worms were counted of old, when they destroyed the fruits of the earth, and made the land barren and desolate, as it is expressed, Joel ii.; such desolation will tolerated lusts make in your souls. Observe whether it be spiritual sloth or too much business; whether negligence of your souls, or too much eagerness after earthly things, or little things in religion; whether it be mistakes or prejudice. The former account given you of the impediments of fruitfulness, may be helpful to you herein. If you discover the true cause of your barrenness, and be sensible how pernicious it is, that will make you resolute against it, and so contribute much towards more fruitfulness.

(4.) Be sensible of the sinfulness and danger of barrenness, how much guilt it will involve you in, what dreadful calamities of all sorts it will expose you to. Those many particulars which I made use of as motives before, will serve also as means for this purpose. And let them be remembered and so improved to make you more and more apprehensive how exceeding sinful, how extremely dangerous it is to continue barren under the means of fruitfulness. The more sensible you are of this, the more careful, the more active will you be to produce more and better fruits; and that is the next way to more improvement. It is want of sense that hinders action, and it is through want of activeness that nothing goes forward in our spiritual course. A barren womb was counted a shame, a reproach, a curse. How impatient was Rachel of it! Gen. xxx. 1. And what an affliction was it to Hannah! 1 Sam. i. 8, 10, 11.

Spiritual barrenness is a greater grievance in itself, and should be so to us, and no less resented by us. And if we were duly convinced of our unfruitfulness in the severals wherein we are guilty, and truly sensible of it as our sin, our shame, our reproach, our burden, one of our greatest afflictions; if we had such a sense of it as would make it fearful, and shameful, and grievous, and afflictive, and burdensome to us : this would lead us (as it did them of old) to take such courses as would not suffer us to continue long unfruitful. But we are so, and we continue so, because we make little or nothing of it, we go lightly under it, we are too well content it should be so. There is no such longing for deliverance from this affliction, as from outward petty grievances; none of Hannah's sore weeping for this barrenness; we are in no such bitterness of soul on this account. And why is it thus, but either because we are not apprehensive that we are unfruitful, nor how far, nor wherefore, nor wherein; or else because we have no such sense of the evil of it as our souls should be possessed with. A due sense of it, as of a dangerous and burdensome grievance, would bid fair for an effectual redress; this would set all in a quick motion towards it ; this would beget such longings, such wrestlings, such diligence and activeness for it, as would not fall short of abundant fruitfulness.

2. Get new natures. There must be that great and universal change made in your souls, by renewing grace and the Spirit of regeneration, before you can bring forth good fruit. You must be born again before you can bear much, nay, before you can bring forth any fruit at all that is truly good. Nothing more evident in Scripture than this. You must be 'renewed in the spirit of your minds,' and 'put on the new man,' Eph. iv. 23, 24. That new man, that new nature, must be created in you, which consists in holiness and true righteousness, before you can bring forth the fruits of holiness and righteousness. Holiness and righteousness planted in the soul at our new birth is the root of all good fruit. You may as well expect that herbs or corn will grow without a root, as that any good fruit should grow where holiness and righteousness is not first rooted in the heart.

Therefore that is the method of the Spirit of God in Scripture ; when he calls for good fruit, he first advises to look to the root, Col. iii. 10. 'After the image of God,' which consists in holiness and righteousness, there is the root; and these being planted, he proceeds to call for good fruit, ver. 12–14, and afterwards requires relative duties, which are the fruits proper to wives, husbands, children, fathers, servants, masters, in the rest of the chapter and the beginning of the next. These fruits will not be brought forth till the new man be put on, *i. e.* till renewing grace be planted in the soul. So the Lord requiring better fruit of the Jews, that his fury might not consume them, in order thereto calls upon them to get their hearts circumcised, Jer. iv. 8. That which is called *circumcision of the heart* in the Old Testament, is *renewing and quickening by the Spirit of regeneration* in the New Testament, Col. ii. 11, 13.

The soil must be good, that the fruit may be good. The old soil of nature unrenewed bears but such fruit as that Heb. vi. 8. The fruit cannot be good unless the tree be good, Mat. vii. 16–18. So Luke vi. 43–45. He that brings forth good fruit must be first a good tree ; and he is a good tree, as the metaphor is explained, who is good at heart, *i. e.* in whose heart there is a treasury of grace. No good thing, no good fruit, can be expected where there is not such a treasure within. You may as reasonably look for figs of thorns, or grapes of brambles, as good fruits from those whose hearts are not sincerely good, whose souls are not enriched with this heavenly treasure, the treasure of grace and holiness. Nay, those who are not born again and quickened by regenerating grace, are not only bad trees, in Scripture phrase, but such as are dead. That is the state of every unregenerate soul, he is 'dead in trespasses and sins,' and some 'twice dead, and plucked up by the roots,' Jude 12. And what fruit can you expect from a dead tree? Till you be 'quickened by the Spirit' of Christ, and made 'alive unto God,' all the fruits you bear will be no better than 'dead works.'

Oh then, if ever you would bear any fruit that is good, any fruits that God can take pleasure in, if you would 'flee from the wrath to come,' that dreadful wrath which is coming upon all who are barren, mind the new birth, make sure that you are born again; mind this as that 'one thing needful,' that one thing upon which all fruitfulness, and consequently all happiness, depends. Beg this of God, above all things in the world, that he would give you new hearts and make you new creatures; that he would raze out the image and superscription of Satan, which naturally every soul bears, and impress on you his own image, created in holiness and righteousness. Give no rest to your souls till you have some evidence that you are renewed in the spirit of your minds, and in the frame and temper of your hearts; till you can say upon some good ground, 'Old things are passed away, and all things become new.'

Till then the best of your fruits will but have a show of goodness, such as may delude you and deceive others, but will never procure you comfort here or reward hereafter. 'Be not deceived, God will not be mocked,' Gal. vi. 7–9. 'He that is in the flesh' can do no other than 'sow to the flesh;' and he is in the flesh who is acquainted with no other birth but his first, his carnal and natural birth, who never knew what it was to be born of the Spirit,' John iii. 5, 6. 'Marvel not that I say unto you, Ye must be born again;' I say no more than Christ, than the apostle says; till then, you will never bear fruit of which you can reap anything but corruption, *i. e.* the temporal and eternal ruin of body and soul. If you expect anything better, you will find yourselves miserably deceived.

And take heed you be not deluded by others. There are some teachers admirably wise in their own conceit, who, having no experience of the new birth in themselves, or following Pelagius, who flattered nature and denied the necessity of renewing grace, they waive the doctrine of regeneration, and call upon their hearers for morality, as though that were all in all: wherein they proceed as wisely, and are [as] like to prove successful, as if they were pruning a dead tree to make it fruitful, or taking pains with a bramble to make it bear grapes, or looking for fruits where there is no root. That no fruit truly good can be expected where the new birth is not the foundation, and renewing grace the root of it, is a truth so clear in Scripture, that if an angel from heaven should preach any other doctrine, we might upon good ground count him a deluder.

3. Get the inward principles of holiness strengthened and enlarged if you would be fruitful. The first thing you are to mind is to get grace planted in the heart; without this, as I now told you, there can be no good fruit at all. The next thing is to get it fortified and increased; without this there cannot be much fruit, and without much you cannot be fruitful. The Lord expects not only *some* good fruit, but *much* of it, proportionably to the means of improvement vouchsafed. He looks for much, of those to whom much is committed. And indeed it is not good enough, though it may have some goodness in it, unless it answer his expectation. And on this account it will not be good unless it be much, and much it cannot be when the principle it produces is weak and little. For good fruits are the acts of holiness

in heart and life, and everything acts as it is; *operari sequitur esse*. That which is but small and feeble cannot ordinarily do much nor do it so well. Where grace is weak, it will but act feebly; the acts of it will neither be so many nor so vigorous, and so our fruit will neither be so much nor so good as when grace in the heart is much and strong. When it is such, the virtue of it will reach farther, and be able to fill a larger sphere of fruitfulness, and there will not be such mixtures of corruption to vitiate or rot it. When a tree is well and firmly rooted, it will grow higher, the body of it stronger and more bulky, and the branches more and also more spreading, and so it will be capable of bearing much more fruit than another. Holiness in the heart is the root of all good fruits (as I shewed before). That the trees of righteousness may be strong and spreading, and so very fruitful, you must look well to the root; you must dig about it, and open it, and water it; I mean you must be diligent, by all means, to have holiness thrive in your hearts, to make it strong and keep it active, to remove whatever may hinder its spreading, or obstruct the diffusing of its virtue into the several branches of your souls and lives. 'Give all diligence,' that every grace may increase and abound, 2 Peter i. 5–8. 'If these be in you and abound, you will not be barren,' &c. To be rich in inward holiness is the way to be full of good fruits, rich in good works, for out of the good treasury of the heart those good things proceed; and when this treasure abounds there, out of the abundance of the heart will they flow freely and plentifully. It is not enough that the soil be good, unless it be kept in heart; it is not enough that your souls are sanctified, unless they be kept up in a gracious temper, always ready and disposed to exercise grace upon all occasions. That is the way to be ready to every good work, Titus iii. 1. And so whenever the Lord comes seeking fruit he may find some.

4. Be much in the use of ordinances. They are the means appointed by God for the improvement of his people's souls to fruitfulness; and being duly used, they will not fail to attain their end, they will certainly produce good fruits. You may be as confident of it as that meat and drink will nourish you, or that rain in season will make the earth fruitful. For the means of grace are, by the Lord's appointment, that to your souls which meat is to your bodies, or rain is to the ground. That of the prophet seems spoken of a promise for deliverance, but it holds true of the word in general, and we may conclude the same in proportion of the other ordinances, Isa. lv. 10, 11. And it follows, ver. 13, those who were before unfruitful as the briar and thorn, shall be like fair and goodly trees, they shall abound in graces and good fruits. The Lord would never have appointed those means for this end, but that they are apt to effect it, and it would be a disparagement to him who so appointed them if they should not attain it. But then they must be duly used; let me tell you how, briefly, in three or four particulars.

(1.) Your hearts must be employed in them. The soul should be thoroughly engaged therein, Jer. xxx. 21. We should strongly oblige our hearts, and make a covenant with our souls to approach unto God, when we go about holy duties, otherwise we shall but do the work of the Lord negligently; and so, when the blessing of the ordinances is to make us fruitful, they may leave us under the curse of barrenness; for, Jer. xlviii. 10, negligence in worship is less tolerable than in the work there spoken of. You must hear, as for life, Deut. xxxii. 46, 47. You should pray, as if you were in a conflict; put out the strength of your souls, as if you were wrestling; συναγω-νίσασθαι, is the apostle's word, Rom. xv. 30. So use the ordinances, and they will not fall short of their end; the blessing of them will come down upon your souls, like rain upon the mown grass, to refresh and make you fruitful.

(2.) Come with an appetite, longing for the blessings of them; come with souls pinched with their spiritual wants, sensible that you need them; as your bodies, when faint or hungry, are sensible that they need refreshment, 1 Peter ii. 2. If you would grow strong and fruitful by the word, come to it as the hungry infant comes to the breast, so as nothing else will satisfy it. If you come as you do to a meal with a full stomach, no wonder if you be 'sent empty away,' Luke i. 53. He will fill with the good things of his ordinances those that come hungering after them, but the full he sends empty away, full of nothing but the soul-distempers they came clogged with. Why do so many continue unfruitful under the means of grace, but because they come out of custom, are too well content to go as they come, are too indifferent whether they reap any spiritual advantage thereby or no? Alas! when so exceeding much might be gained hereby, we get no more, because we no more desire it. 'The Lord's hand is not shortened,' &c., but we are 'straitened in our own bowels;' our desires are contracted, and shrunk up into nothing; our mouths are shut, when the Lord's hand is open. Nothing can get into our souls till desires open them; these would make us drink in those heavenly showers, as the dry chapped earth drinks in the rain, and fruitfulness would be the issue of it in our souls, as it is in the ground, Heb. vi. If we came to the ordinances with earnest and sincere desires after the blessings thereof, a blessed fruitfulness would be our portion, we should then be under the influence of that sweet promise, Mat. v.

(3.) Content not yourselves with the ordinances without the presence of God in them. He is present everywhere, by common acts of providence, but more in some places than others, according as he more or less appears and shews himself in his power and glory. He is said to be most in heaven, because he is there most gloriously manifested; but next to heaven, most in his ordinances: there he gives us ground to expect a more special presence than elsewhere ordinarily on earth. And then is he so present when he concurs with his ordinances, makes them powerful and effectual; when he shews his goings, discovers his glory, exerts his power, distils his influences. Then is he present with them, when in the use of them he shines into the mind, stirs in the conscience, opens the heart, moves the will, excites the affections. So that there is no fructifying virtue in the ordinances unless the Lord be present there. So that to be contented with the use of ordinances, without the divine presence, is to be satisfied with an empty dish, instead of that which should nourish and refresh you. Heaven would not be heaven without that glorious presence; and the means of grace will not be the means of grace, cannot be the means of fruitfulness, without this special presence. There is no healing virtue in these waters, nothing to heal those distempers which keep you barren, unless the angel of his presence descend and trouble them, or move upon them.

And therefore, whatever other circumstances commend or endear the ordinances to you, be satisfied with nothing without this special and efficacious presence. Beg this importunately before you go, as Moses, Exod. xxxiii. 13–15. The Lord had assured him, ver. 2, that he would send an angel before him; but the conduct of an angel, without the presence of God, would not avail them, nor satisfy him. If the ordinances were administered to you by angels, yet would not they be effectual, nor you fruitful, without the Lord's presence. If Paul should preach to you, if Apollos were your minister, yet would not the word be fruitful, unless God gave the increase; that so depends upon his presence and concurrence, as nothing, no act, that which is extraordinary and miraculous, can yield an increase without it, 1 Cor. iii. 6, and so he applies himself to God for it, 2 Cor. ix. 10.

Be importunate for this presence of God before you come, and come with such longings for it as David expresses, Ps. lxiii. 1, 2; whatsoever he saw in the sanctuary (and there were glorious things to be seen), nothing would satisfy his longings and thirstings, but the sight of the glory and power of God there; nothing but that presence which he was wont to have: 'As I have seen thee,' &c.

And when you find the Lord withdraws, when at any time you enjoy not his presence; when your hearts are hard and dead under the ordinances, not touched from above, not warmed, not affected, not in motion; when, by the ineffectualness of your attendance on them, you find reason to conclude that he is absent, that you see not his goings, feel not his working, find no footsteps nor impress of the divine presence on your hearts: let the Lord know that you count this a grievous affliction, that you cannot tell how to live without his presence; that the ordinances, however otherwise the special solace of your souls, are no joy to you without him. Give him no rest till he return, and impregnate the ordinances with his influences, and make them fruitful, and you by them, with his presence, Cant. iv. 16. By refreshing gales, and fruitful inspirations of his presence and Spirit, graces are quickened, strengthened, increased, acted; they flow forth, and abound in pleasant fruits.

(4.) Use not the ordinances for themselves. Account them not your end, but the means to attain it. Look not upon your use of them as the fruit which God expects, but as the way to that fruitfulness. Do not think your fruitfulness consists in hearing, reading, praying, meditating, conference, or communicating; this is as if the husbandman should think his harvest lay in tilling, and ploughing, and sowing his ground: if he mind nothing more, and look no further, his barn will be empty at the year's end, and he undone in the conclusion. These are not the fruits of the earth, but the way and means to make the earth yield them. So are the ordinances; if you use them, and look at no other fruit, you will reap little but your labour for your pains. Their end is something further than their use; if you rest in the use of them as the end, you will fall short of fruitfulness, which is their end indeed, and continue barren.

God will not count you fruitful, because you are much and often in the use of ordinances, no more than a vine-dresser will count a vine fruitful, because it is much dunged, and often watered; if he have no other fruit of it, his labour is lost, and the tree in danger to be cut down as fruitless. That is your case, that is your danger, if your fruit be but your being employed in holy duties. This perishes in the using, and you may perish for all this, as those that are barren. He that useth the means, as though it were his end, both abuseth the means and loseth the end. Rest not in your performance of holy duties, how much, how well soever you seem to perform them, unless you find some good effect thereof upon your hearts and in your lives. For all your diligence and exactness herein, if nothing more, nothing better come of it, let it be as grievous to you as it would be to a gardener, if, after much pains in digging, and planting, and watering, he should see nothing spring up, or grow, he would look upon himself as in danger to be undone. And so may you; nor will the use of ordinances help or secure you, unless they help you to be fruitful; and if you would have them helpful to you this way, you must use them for this end, and not as if they were the end of their own use.

(5.) Make fruitfulness your business. Look upon it as your greatest concernment in this world, and accordingly mind and pursue it. Let it not be a *πάρεργον*, something that you mind on the by, when other things you are more taken up with will give you leave; but make it the main work, and great design of your lives, to be fruitful and live fruitfully. It is for want of this usually that we remain barren. There is such a concurrence of all other things requisite to make us fruitful, that our great defectiveness herein cannot rationally be charged upon anything so much as this, that we do not make it our business to abound with good fruits. The Lord has declared himself willing, yea, desirous, that we should be filled with the fruits of the Spirit. He calls for this importunately, by his word, by his providences, by our own consciences; he threatens and afflicts us for want of them; he affords us means abundantly sufficient for this purpose; he promises his concurrence and assistance, to make them effectual; he furnishes us with abilities, opportunities, and advantages for the improvement of them. We have much more to secure our success herein than in other affairs, wherein we ordinarily succeed well enough, using but common prudence and industry. What, then, can be the reason that we are not more successful in this, that so many who are planted in the Lord's vineyard bear so little fruit? So far as I can discern, in ordinary cases, the true cause of this is, because we do not make fruitfulness our business. When we have pursued this in our thoughts so far as we can, it must at last be resolved into this as the main reason of it, we make it not our chief work and design to be full of good fruits; something else is more our business, more minded, more designed, more pursued. We have something else more in chase which diverts us; our hearts are more upon some other business; the main streams which should carry us to this run some other way. We mind this as though we did not mind, and seek it as though we sought it not. We seem to seek this, but we strive not for it; we move towards it, but we run not; we offer at it, but we wrestle not; and it is running, striving, wrestling by which effectual endeavours for fruitfulness are expressed in Scripture. We act not [at] such a rate as becomes those who make it their grand design, nor as we see others act for that which they make their business. We follow not this as a man whose heart is on the world pursues some promising worldly design; and manage not this affair as careful, industrious men manage their business. We do not take such care and pains about it. This seems to me to be the principal cause why many, who, in respect of the means they enjoy, might be filled with the fruits of righteousness and holiness, are very much to seek in many of them.

Since, then, there is a concurrence of all other things, all that is requisite on God's part, to render you fruitful, and this is the chief *remora* that stops it on your parts, resolve for the future to be no more wanting to yourselves in that which infinitely concerns you. Make it but your business, bestow but on it that care and pains which you allow to that which you make your business in the world, and you may be certain of more success than any can insure to you in earthly undertakings. It is a sure way to be fruitful, to be rich in all good fruits.

(6.) *Make use of afflictions to promote fruitfulness.* Pruning is a means to make a tree fruitful, Lev. xxv. 3. So the Lord, when provoked to deny the means of fruitfulness, because they were not improved, threatens the barren vineyard shall be no more pruned, Isa. v. 6. Afflictions are that to the soul which pruning is to a fruit-tree; as necessary, as advantageous, to render it fruitful. Hence those plants which the Lord will have improved he will purge or prune them, John xv. 2. Those branches he has no hopes of, *αἴρει*, he cuts them off for the fire; but those which he intends to make more fruitful, καθαίρει, he purges, he prunes them. As a vine-dresser cuts off the suckers, lops off the twigs and superfluous branches, which are good for nothing, but spend the sap which should make the better boughs fruitful, so does the Lord, as by other means, so by afflictions, cut off those luxuriances which suck away the strength of the heart that should run out into good fruits. If, then, you would be more and more fruitful, make use of afflictions and outward calamities, which the Lord exercises you with for this end. Submit to pruning, and see that it be improved for this purpose. But how may afflictions be so improved, for the rendering of us more fruitful? Briefly,

[1.] Observe what excesses you are apt to run into; what useless excrescences or luxuriances sprout out anywhere in your souls or lives; what suckers there are which spend the strength of your hearts, in any degree unprofitably. Take notice what it is that takes up more of your thoughts, affections, endeavours than is due to it; what relation, what enjoyment, what design or business, what recreation or refreshment, is wont to hurry you into excesses, and to take up more of your hearts, or time, or talents that it ought to have. Make use of afflictions, to wean you from these, and to keep you within your bounds, which they tempt you to transgress. Apply them as wormwood and gall, as offered on purpose by the Lord to embitter those things, the lusciousness of which has endangered and ensnared your souls, and drawn you into too great neglects of God and your heavenly interests, upon the due minding of which depends your fruitfulness. Those excesses and inordinacies spend the sap, and strength, and vigour of your souls unprofitably, which, if it ran the right way, would turn into good fruits. Make use of afflictions to lop these off, though it go to the quick to do it; sharper chastenings must do it if others will not serve the turn, unless the Lord will leave you under barrenness. When afflictions are sharp and bitter, say, These are the issue of my excesses and inordinacies, and I am like to suffer more by them if they continue. And so make use of sufferings in any kind, to dead the heart to them; then they are lopped off and wither when the heart dies to them. And these suckers being cut off, the other branches will better thrive, and be more fruitful.

[2.] Exercise faith for this purpose. Depend on God for such an issue and effect of afflictions, that he will so order and manage them that they shall tend to make you more fruitful, that he will help you to such an improvement of them. Dependence on the Lord for it doth engage him to do it. Those that trust him 'shall not be ashamed;' *i.e.* shall not be disappointed, Rom. x. 11. It is disappointment that makes ashamed, when he falls short of what he confidently expected. Those that in faith expect this of the Lord, shall not find their expectation frustrated, shall not meet with any disappointment that will make them ashamed of their confidence, Ps. ix. 18. The expectation of the afflicted shall not come to nothing; the Lord will not forget to answer his expectation. Do but trust God, and he will not herein fail you. And there are two strong supports of faith, great encouragements to believe that he will sanctify afflictions, so as to make you fruitful: his design, and his promise.

First, It is his end and design in afflicting his children. It is not to satisfy his justice, nor to give vent to his anger, when he is full of it, nor to please himself in the smart of those who have provoked him; but, as he graciously expresses it, Heb. xii. 10, that is his end in chastening his children, to make them more 'partakers of his holiness' than they were before, and without chastening, and so more capable of bringing forth the fruits of holiness. So John xv. 2, when the vine-dresser makes use of the pruning-hook, and cuts the vine, and makes it bleed, his design is not to kill it, but to make it more fruitful. And such is the Lord's end in pruning his people by afflictions; and this being his design, we may be sure he is not willing to lose it or to fall short of his end; that would be a dishonour to him, such a one as the sons of men cannot digest. And upon this ground faith may raise itself into confidence, that he will promote fruitfulness by afflictions, since that is the end he proposes to himself in afflicting, and these are the means he uses for the effecting of that end. And it is not for his honour to lose his end, or to use means which are not effectual for the accomplishing of it.

Secondly, You have his promise for it. He has passed his word, and engaged his truth and faithfulness, that afflictions shall have this effect, Heb. xii. 11; it will bring forth these fruits. This, when God's method is observed, is so certainly future, that he expresses it as present: 'It bringeth forth.' It is confirmed by experience too: *Solidissima pars est corporis, quam frequens usus agitavit* (Seneca). Rom. v. 3–5, affliction puts these graces upon trial and exercise, and exercise strengthens and increases them; and hence the fruit of affliction is more 'precious than gold,' 1 Peter i. 7. It is hereby tried, and often trials put upon frequent exercise; and the more it is acted, the more it is strengthened, and consequently the fruit of it is more and better; more both in quantity and value, precious fruit.

Now, the Lord having promised, and given experiments too, of his faithfulness in performing his promise, what can be more desired for the encouragement of our faith? Act it accordingly, believe the Lord, so shall your souls prosper. It will not only purify the heart itself, and purge out those distempers that keep you barren, but engage the Lord to make afflictions effectual to promote your fruitfulness.

[3.] Seek him for this purpose. He intends this by afflictions, and has promised it; but for this he will be sought unto. After the Lord had declared his intention, and given his word that he would plant what was desolate, yet he adds, Ezek. xxxvi. 37, Be importunate with the Lord, that he would make you fruitful by afflictions; pray, and that your prayers may be prevalent, pray in faith; and that faith may be strong, let the design and promise of God be its support. This is the way to put life and spirits both into your faith and prayer. The apostle James, having given an account of the fruits which afflictions are apt to produce, James i. 2, 3, adds, ver. 5, 'If any want wisdom,' to make such a fruitful improvement of afflictions, 'let him pray for it.' But how must he pray? Every mode of praying will not serve the turn. He tells you, ver. 6, this is the way, in brief, to make use of afflictions for fruitfulness; I have given a large account of it.

(7.) Labour to make all things subservient unto fruitfulness. Improve all that you are entrusted with, all that you can make any such advantage of, for this purpose. Make use of parts, and gifts, and other enjoyments, for this end; manage them all so as the product of them may be good fruits. It is true, holiness in the heart is the root and stock upon which, and upon nothing else without it, that which is truly and spiritually good doth grow. But other scions, though otherwise incapable of bearing good fruit, being grafted into this stock, may bring forth excellent fruit; the sap and juice of grace conveyed into them, changes their nature and quality; and instead of that which is wild and degenerate (which is their natural issue), makes them capable of bearing fruit pleasant to God and man.

And as by the influence of grace they may be improved for such fruitfulness, so the Lord expects we should actually so improve them. They are talents which are committed to us for this end; and the Lord, that has entrusted us with them, and made us stewards of them, looks that such advantage should be made thereof, and will call us to an account for it. We must shortly give an account of our stewardship; and if we cannot shew good fruit, as to the improvement of these talents, we shall be found unfaithful stewards, unprofitable servants, and in danger to have a process formed against us accordingly.

Those who have more advantages than others, should be careful to bring forth more and better fruits than others; or else they will not be able, when the great day of reckoning comes, to give a good account of it.

[1.] Those that have a better natural temper, have this way an advantage thereby above others. Grace in such a temper is like apples of gold in pictures of silver; it is as a diamond better set, the lustre and beauty of it more appears; but then, if we would improve it for fruitfulness, the use of it must not be to please others, or to set off ourselves, or to gain love and reputation to ourselves, but to insinuate ourselves the more advantageously into others, to do them good, to sweeten spiritual advice and reproofs, which, though for the health and recovery of their souls, yet, as bitter pills, and unpleasant receipts, would not otherwise go down; to commend the grace of Christ to those that are without, which appears more commendable thus set off, than in a crabbed, and sour, and severe temper; to render the ways of Christ more pleasant and lovely, so as to overcome prejudice, and melt obstinacy into a compliance. You know the sun is more powerful when it shines in a clear heaven, than when it was clouded, and the weather stormy; and so has grace the more advantage for a fruitful efficacy upon others, when it is not encumbered with a cloudy or stormy temper. And when it is not so improved, the advantage is so far lost, and the fruits not brought forth, to which they are hereby more than others obliged.

[2.] Natural parts should be improved to fruitfulness. Any clearness of judgment, or quickness of apprehension, or strength of memory, when it is receptive or retentive; any degree of these should be made use of for our Lord's advantage, and the benefit of others, else we let ground, which is improveable, lie fallow, and so far we shall be found barren. Those that have least of these owe something on this account; those that have more, ought herewith to be more serviceable, and so more fruitful. They are accountable according to the proportion of what is committed to them. Our faculties are not given us for nothing, or for our own use only, or to exercise them as we please; the end even of these is fruitfulness, the producing of that whereby we may please and honour God, and do good to others. Our Master gives us not tools for no purpose; he expects work, and that we should use them in his service; and the better the tools are, the better work does he look for. When we have more than others, we should be helpful thereby not only to ourselves, but also to those who have less. A good understanding should be a guide to others in the ways of God, so far as there is a call and opportunity to give them light. A quick apprehension should be a relief to the slowness and dulness of others in spiritual things; as it grasps more and more easily, so it should communicate more freely, and offer it more clearly, according as several capacities require. A good memory should be a good treasury, for the enriching both of himself and others with the precious things laid up there. Both things new and old, things taken in for daily use or laid up for constant store, as an householder, in a free entertainment, brings forth, according to that, Mat. xiii. 51, 52; and so a good man, Mat. xii. 35. The more good to ourselves and others is the issue of natural accomplishments, the more fruitful we are.

[3.] So spiritual gifts, though but common, should be improved for the bearing of good fruit; and those who would be fruitful indeed, must so use them. A gift of prayer and utterance; a faculty of expressing ourselves to God or to man, as occasion requires; ability to discourse of the things of God, or to make use of other common things in subserviency thereto: the chief fruit of such gifts is edifying; and the apostle directs to this as that which was principally to be aimed at in the use of gifts, when they were extraordinary, 1 Cor. xiv. 12. The gift of prayer should be improved in praying for and with others, as our place requires. Those that restrain it are enemies to the fruit of it, whatever is pretended or offered instead of it. You may carve the bark of a tree, and cut it into forms and figures of grapes, or other fruit; but that is the effect of art, it is forced upon the tree; it is not genuine fruit, nor that which is expected of a fruit-tree. The gift of discourse should be improved, as there is occasion, for reproof, admonition, instruction, comfort, exhortation; for provoking one another to love and good works. This is good fruit, and tends to make others fruitful.

[4.] So power and interest may be improved for fruitfulness. Interest in the esteem or affections of others, should be made use of to draw them into ways wherein they may bring forth fruit unto God, and to lead them on to more and more fruitful walking. Interest in those that are great, to engage them to be a refuge from the storm, and a shadow from the heat; such storms and heats are as injurious to good fruits, or those who bear them. So power or authority over others should be improved by superiors of all sorts, for the weeding out of sin, which chokes good fruit, for the bringing of those under them into fruitful ways, under fruitful influences, and for the keeping of them there; which was the Lord's confidence of Abraham, Gen. xviii. 19, and the endeavour of Moses and Joshua, in reference to their people.

[5.] Outward enjoyments, they afford advantages for fruitfulnes. And the apostle calls for their improvement this way, and shews withal what fruits they may be helpful to bring forth, 1 Tim. vi. 17, 18. That is the best that can be said of riches, they give those who have them a capacity to do good; they give them the advantage to be rich in good works, which are more precious and valuable riches by far than outward abundance; and they are richest this way who are most 'ready to distribute,' most 'willing to communicate;' as ready to use for God what he gives them as to receive more; as forward to be rich in good works as to be rich in the world. It is a great degeneracy, and most unworthy a Christian, to be otherwise disposed; to be eager after much, but backward to employ much in ways of fruitfulness. Then only are we faithful stewards; then only do we employ plenty for the ends for which it is given; then only is it a complete blessing, when it runs out freely in good fruits for the advantage of God's interest in the world, for the promoting of knowledge, holiness, and righteousness, and the means that tend to promote them; for maintaining the gospel and ministry of Christ, and upholding his worship and institutions; for the repressing of his enemies, for the relief of his members; and, in the apostle's words, for doing good to all.

When they help you to rich expressions both of love to Christ, brotherly love and charity to all; then do they make you rich indeed, rich and full of good fruits. And so must you endeavour to use them, if ever you would have true comfort in them, or ever expect to give a tolerable account of them. He will never be found a faithful steward who improves them not for such fruitfulness.

[6.] The world, not only as it is an enjoyment, but as it is an object, may help you to good fruits. You may see that in the creatures, in the occurrences, in the course and administration of the world, which may acquaint you with God, and bring him to your thoughts, and raise your apprehensions of him, and engage your affections to him, your love, delight, fear, desire. You may see that in it that is sufficient to embitter sin; a world of motives to set your hearts against it. You may see many things in it which may help you to the exercise of holiness; much to encourage faith, to teach you wisdom, to engage you to thankfulness, to lead you to self-denial, and make you humble and vile in your own eyes; much to wean you from things below, endear heaven to you, and make ye in love with the appearing of Christ. These are good fruits; yet even this world will help us to them, if it were duly improved for this purpose. And if you would be fruitful indeed, the world, and all you have and are, must be made use of to promote your fruitfulness.

(8.) Aim at universal fruitfulness. Make it your design and endeavour to be fruitful in all things which the Lord requires of you, or commends to you as good fruit, and towards all objects and persons who ought to taste the goodness of it, and should reap any fruit of you. Be fruitful in all things which the Holy Ghost calls good fruit. Satisfy not yourselves with some small things; a little shrivelled fruit will not answer the Lord's expectation. Content not yourselves with some great things so as to neglect others, though small in your account. The want of that which you count small may be a great neglect, and things little in themselves are often great in their consequence, and the want of them may render things great in project little or nothing in the issue. And so it is certainly when nothing will be effectual or acceptable, unless all be designed and endeavoured, which is the case here, Ps. cxix. 6. Let him do what he will, he that minds not the doing of all that is required, of bearing all the fruit that is expected, will be ashamed in the issue, can have no confidence that he will fare better.

Be not contented with a few things, whatever they be, small or great, no, nor with many things neither. When *all* is a duty, neither few nor many will be a discharge. Where all is expected, even in many things (while short of all) there will be a disappointment, and that is the case here; not a few, not many fruits only, but all is our duty and our Lord's expectation. The apostle's prayer for the Hebrews shews it, Heb. xiii. 20, 21. He prays the Lord would accomplish in them whatever is wanting, so καταρτίσαι signifies. And something is wanting where there is not every good work, every good act, wherein mind, or heart, or life should be fruitful. For if we endeavour not to do all and every good work, inward or outward, we do not his will nor that which is εὐάρεστον, well-pleasing in his sight. He is not well pleased unless we design to do all that pleases him, to bear all pleasant fruit. Labour then to be fruitful in all.

In *holy thoughts*. Let them be frequent, Ps. cxxxix. 17, 18. Let them be pleasing and delightful, else they will not be frequent, and so the mind not fruitful, Ps. civ. 34, and cxix. 97. Let them be fixed, else they will not be effectual; let them have good entertainment till they have done their business, till they have left some impression upon the soul, whose influence may reach the life. If they vanish before, they prove untimely fruit.

Be fruitful in *good inclinations*, that the tendency of your souls may be upwards, and the constant bent of it towards God; that you may be still in motion either towards him or for him; towards him even through the crowd of earthly business, and for him in those things wherein others are for themselves.

In *good designs and intentions*, that all of them, in all undertakings, may be the pleasing, and honouring, and enjoying of God, that none may be tolerated that cross these, none entertained or pursued but in a subserviency unto these. And a due observance of, and inquiry into them, whether they be of this nature and tendency, that according as you find them, so or otherwise they may be suppressed or promoted.

In *good purposes and resolutions*, for God, and all that pleases him; against sin, and the world, and self, and all that offends him. And look that they be firm and effectual, followed into execution, that they may not prove, as they do in too many, only buds and blossoms, blasted and perishing without any effect, but a short flourish; so they will not be complete fruit, but only vain shows of it. Let them be like those of David, Ps. cxix. 116, as firm as what is ratified by an oath, and such as will not fall short of performance; so they will not fail to prove good fruit.

In *heavenly graces*. In the acts and exercise of faith, hope, repentance, self-denial, contempt of the world, heavenliness, mortification, &c. The acts of these are the fruits of the Spirit. And that you may be herein fruitful indeed, the exercise hereof should be so frequent as that such acts may make up your life. That the life which you live may be a life of faith, of repentance, of self-denial, a life above the world, a living in heaven while you are on earth, a walking with God while you converse with men, and advance above the things of time and sense while you are in the midst of them, and a dying to self and the world while you live in it. Such fruits reach heaven itself, while their root is here below, and they will distinguish you from every degenerate plant, yea, and from such as are the planted of the Lord, but prove shrubs, and thrive not.

In *holy affections*. In love to God, his image, his people, his truths, his ways, all that he commends as lovely; delight in him, and all that pleases him; desires of him, and all that he declares to be desirable; zeal for him, his whole interest, and all his concernments; fear of sin, and hatred of every evil way and motion, above all things that are dreadful; rejoicing in God more than all things which you are apt to make your joy; and mourning for that which dishonours and displeases him as the greatest grievance; jealousy of whatever may tempt you from him, or render you disloyal to him, less regardful to him, or less affectionate to him. The acts of these affections are choice fruits, and the more you abound therein, the more will you abound in fruits which the Lord himself takes special delight in; these signify the heart is set upon God, and that is a posture which not only pleases him, but yields an advantage to derive virtue from him, which will make you more and more fruitful, even to the utmost extent of what you can desire, Ps. xxxvii. 4.

In *spiritual discourse*. Such as is the fruit of a gracious heart, and may produce the like fruit in others, Eph. iv. 29; such as is good, $εἰς\ οἰκοδομὴν\ τῆς\ χρείας$, for the edifying of others in things that are useful, and may promote grace, or minister spiritual advantage to them. Such fruit the same apostle calls for, Col. iv. 6; let it be such as ought to proceed from a gracious soul; let it be savoury and wholesome to the souls that bear* it, seasoned with such prudence as may accommodate it to every one's capacity, condition, and necessity, that so they may relish its gust, and turn it into spiritual nourishment.

In all good actions, Col. i. 10. Not in some few, or some small, or some eminent works that are good, but in 'every good work;' and to persist stedfast and constant in every of them, 2 Thes. ii. 17; prepared for all, 2 Tim. ii. 21; furnished for all, 2 Tim. iii. 17; ready for every one, Titus iii. 1; following them, and not staying for occasions, but seeking occasions,

* Qu. 'hear'?—ED.

1 Tim. v. 10, and following them zealously, Titus ii. 14, as those that would be patterns unto others, Titus ii. 7; and all to be well reported of on that account, 1 Tim. v. 10; and as careful to maintain them as themselves or families, Titus iii. 8; so as to account abundance of them their riches, 1 Tim. vi. 18. Not confining yourselves either to some acts of religion, or some acts of charity, as though these were all, or these were enough; not satisfying yourselves with those of the first table, as the pharisee, or those of the second, as the moralists; but ' walking in all the commandments,' Luke i. 6; making good works your daily course, your constant walk, as God has made it, Eph. ii. 10; not baulking a step, but passing quite through it, going constantly from one end to the other of the whole walk. Let this be the design and business of your lives, to be fruitful.

2. In all things. And fruitful also towards all who should reap any fruit of you, or to whom you are obliged to bring forth good fruits.

(1.) Towards God. All good fruit must respect him one way or other, as the end and motive, though others be the object of it, else it cannot be good. But the fruit I here intend must respect him more directly and immediately; God must be the object of it, and not the end only. And that you may bear fruit, get more and more acquainted with God. A clear, and full, and effectual knowledge of God, is not only good fruit itself, but also the seed of all other good fruits, towards God, or ourselves, or others. Without some degree of it none that is truly good can either spring or grow; and the clearer, and fuller, and more efficacious it is, the more will it contribute to make all your fruit both better and more abundant. The want of it, or defect in it, is an error in the first concoction, which, according to the degrees of it, is of dangerous consequence, and hardly to be prevented; and being not redressed (as it cannot be easily if neglected at first), will run into spiritual distempers instead of good fruits.

Oh then, whatever you are ignorant of, get acquainted with God! Study his perfections and excellencies, order all other studies and inquiries, so as they may serve and promote this. You may move towards other knowledge as the way, but this you must follow as the end, and then you will not fail of it, Hosea vi. 3. Let his majesty, and greatness, and power, and presence, and wisdom, and goodness, and transcendent glory and excellency every way, be often in your thoughts, always in your eye, as that which you must mind, and are most taken with. That is the way to have his greatness and his goodness pass before you; to see him, as far as mortal eye can see him, so far as he can be seen on earth. The more you desire and endeavour this, the more full and clear sight you will have of him; and the more fully and clearly you discern him, the more effectual will your sight of God be; and the more effectual it is, the more fruitful will it be in those fruits which respect God more particularly, which we may reduce to acts of admiration, submission, and complacency.

[1.] Acts of *admiration*. Get high adoring apprehensions of God, and by the sight and contemplation of his glorious excellencies, endeavour still to raise and advance them more and more. When they are highest, they are infinitely below him; that is the unavoidable weakness of our natures and capacities. We can never give him the glory that is due to his majesty, that is better fruit than human nature can bear; but something we are capable of, and the least that can look for acceptance is to advance him in our esteem above anything, above all things that are counted worthy of esteem, so that he may have the highest place in our minds. Nothing may take place of him, nothing may come near him; all that finds entertainment in our minds and thoughts must stoop and lower to him, and be made his footstool, while he alone has the throne in our judgments, and is exalted above every other object, even those we count of greatest value. He ought to be adored and admired, so as other things must be contemptible to us in comparison. The higher our apprehensions of him are raised, with the more force they will fall upon the lower faculties, and put them into more vigorous motions towards more and better fruit.

[2.] Acts of *subjection*. Get your wills into a posture submissive to God, and observant of him in all things. Keep it in a readiness to submit to him, and every signification of his will and pleasure, without opposition or resistance, without exceptions or reservation, without any backwardness or lingering, that this may always be the voice and language of it, 'Behold, I come,' Ps. xl. 8, and Ps. xxxvii. 31. 'Thy law is within my heart,' transcribed and drawn upon it, so that the act and motions of it within answer the severals of the law without, as a fair copy answers the original; so that the will of God may be found and discerned in the heart, as it may be seen and read in the word; as if the words and characters of it were impressed on the soul in a lively manner, begetting real motions within, in a conformity to the word without. Urge the promise and covenant for this, 2 Cor. iii. 3, Jer. xxxi. 33, Heb. viii. 10, that the Lord would make the bent, temper, dispositions, motions, and acts of the heart and will, conformable to the divine will, as it is expressed in his law, so that there may be no clashing, no differing, no varying betwixt his law in the heart and his law in the word, but a likeness, an answerableness, an agreement, a compliance, a readiness to do whatsoever he requires, to forsake and abandon whatsoever he forbids, to lose and part with whatsoever he would not have you keep and possess, to suffer and undergo whatsoever he will inflict, or may be inflicted for his sake. Such a submission of the heart to God is excellent fruit; it is the heart of godliness, and fills all the veins and arteries, all the other parts with good blood, with that good fruit wherein godliness consists. When the will is subdued to the will of God, this being the commanding faculty, all the rest depending on it, submit with it. And the power of godliness, though it may seem a paradox, consists much in submission; and then it is most powerful when it prevails most with the will, to a lowly and entire submission unto the divine will. The bearing of this fruit brings with it all the fruits of godliness. The attendant of it is an observance of God, expressed in all acts of worship, inward and outward; in the acts and exercise of graces and affections, which are the soul of worship; and in performance of those duties, and waiting on him in those ordinances of his appointing, which are, as it were, the body of worship. When soul and body are united, and we offer them up together frequently, sincerely, conscientiously, worshipping him both outwardly and in the spirit, adoring him with the whole man, honouring him both with soul and body, then we offer unto him holocausts, sacrifices acceptable to him, and not corrupt or curtailed offerings; then we bring forth the fruits of godliness, fruits unto God, such as respect him directly and immediately, and such as he expects to reap of us.

[3.] Acts of *complacency*. The glory, and power, and goodness of God are the heads to which our weakness reduces all his perfections and attributes, the fruits which we bring forth unto God, should answer all these, and be a real and honourable acknowledgment of them. Acts of admiration acknowledge his glory and excellency, acts of subjection do acknowledge his power and sovereignty, and acts of complacency acknowledge his goodness and graciousness. The acts whereby we testify that we believe he is infinitely, transcendently good and gracious, that we have tasted him to be so, are some of the chief of those good fruits which we should bring forth unto God. And so we act, and such fruit we bear, when we move towards him as the object most desirable, and can truly say, as Ps. lxiii. 25; when our hearts embrace him, cling to him, clasp about him, as that which is most amiable and lovely; when the heart can sincerely say, 'I love the Lord,' Ps. cxvi. 1; I love him more than all the persons and objects that ever I had affection for, above all that ever I saw, or enjoyed, or counted lovely.

When we rest in him as that which is most delightful; are more taken with him, and satisfied with him, than that which has most pleased us. When he terminates the motion of the soul, and the heart, restless and unsatisfied with all other things, stays here, and desires to go no farther, as having found that in God which contents and satisfies it, that with which it is so pleased as it is at rest, Ps. cxvi. 7, and says of the Lord as the Lord doth of Zion, Ps. cxxxii. 14, and as David, Ps. xvi. 5–9; when God is as to him, ראש שמחתו, Ps. cxxxvii. 6, the head, the top of his joy, the crown of his rejoicing, and that which he can really prefer before his chief joy on earth. such acts as these are sweet fruits indeed, most pleasant to God himself. It is not sorrow, and mourning, and heart-trouble, and inward dejection, and soul-affliction, that the Lord is so much pleased with; these are fruits good in their place and season, but of an inferior quality, and not desirable, but as lower steps to help us up to this higher pitch of complacency in God. A life of delights in God is a life fruitful of that which most pleases him, which most honours him. It is nearest and likest the life of heaven, and the fruit of it is very much like that which grows there; only that is fully ripe, here it is but growing. If you would be fruitful indeed, aim at all fruitfulness towards God, you see partly hereby in what acts it consists. Let it be your design and endeavour to abound more and more therein, and most in those which he counts best.

(2.) There are fruits which respect yourselves which you must mind if you would be universally fruitful. The apostle gives us all these in one word, Titus ii. 11, 12. To 'live soberly' comprises many things; it is to live temperately, and chastely, and humbly, and modestly, and contentedly. The fruits which respect our personal and private capacities are the acts and exercise of temperance, chastity, &c.

Temperance as to meat and drink. Affecting neither too much, nor that which is delicate; avoiding all excess in quantity or quality. A moderate use of these refreshments, so as may best consist with health, and render the body most serviceable to the soul, Luke xxi. 34.

Chastity. Keeping body and soul pure in every state, married or unmarried, 1 Thes. iv. 4, 5.

Humility. A lowliness of mind, esteeming others better than themselves, as the apostle defines it, Phil. ii. 3. A peculiar excellency of the religion of Christ, in the neglect of which the wisdom of the world befooled itself, their wise men not teaching it. But Christ made himself a pattern of it, his whole life being a continued example of humility, John xiii. 15.

Modesty. Repressing curiosity, boldness, uncomeliness.

Contentedness in all estates and occurrences, Philip. iv. 11, 12, 1 Tim. vi. 8, Heb. xiii. 5. These are fruits (however overlooked by any) of great value and consequence. And though something like them may be found amongst those that are strangers to God, yet those who neglect them are certainly strangers to God. And being graffed upon a new nature, and ordered by spiritual motives, and directed to spiritual ends, they are not mere moral qualities, but supernatural graces, and special fruits of the Spirit. The more we abound in them and exercise them, the more fruitful we shall be in the account of God. And if we be careless and negligent of the acts thereof, we shall be barren and destitute of good fruits even towards ourselves. And what fruits can be looked for, towards God or others, from such who are barren towards themselves?

(3.) Be fruitful towards others. There are many branches of heart and life that must be full of fruit to others. For direction herein take these three rules:

[1.] Be much in relative duties. Very much of our fruitfulness does consist in the duties we owe to our relations. And they are the most fruitful souls who bear most of these fruits; and whatever show they make, they are barren who neglect these. Where the Spirit of Christ is operative and efficacious for the bringing forth good fruit in any, he not only makes the persons good in themselves, but makes them good towards all their relatives, good parents and good children, good husbands and good wives, good masters and good servants; makes them endeavour to be good one to another in all their concernments, but especially good to their souls, careful of their spiritual interest, that these miscarry not, that this may be promoted. They are scarce good absolutely who are not good relatively. If there be any good fruit on such it is but little, and many branches must needs be bare. And this relative fruit is of so great consequence, that the apostle insists largely thereon, even in short epistles. That is the subject of a great part of Ephesians, chapter v., and of many verses of the 6th chapter. It is almost half of the 3d chapter to the Colossians, and part of the 4th. He counted such fruit of great importance, else, when he designed to be brief, he would not have stayed so long in pressing these.

[2.] Accommodate yourselves to the several conditions, capacities, and necessities of others. That is the way to do them most good, and so they will reap the best fruit of you. The apostle gives particular direction herein, 1 Thes. v. 12, to ver. 16. We find elsewhere what fruit we owe to the household of faith, viz. brotherly love, $\varphi\iota\lambda\alpha\delta\epsilon\lambda\varphi\iota\alpha$, a particular affection, and special expressions of it. And what to others, viz., charity, and readiness to do them good, 2 Peter i. 7, Gal. vi. 10. To those that fall, Gal. vi. 1, 2; to the scandalous, 2 Thes. iii. 14, 15; to those that are weak, Rom. xiv. 1, and xv. 1, 2; to those that prosper, Rom. xii. 15; to the afflicted, ibid., and Heb. xiii. 3; to strangers, Heb. xiii. 2; to enemies, Mat. v. 44, Luke vi. 27, 35. Rom. xii. 20, 'Heap coals,' not to consume them, that is revengeful, and condemned by Christ, but to melt them, and dissolve their enmity and obstinacy; as refiners heap more coals upon those metals that are hard to be dissolved, not to waste them, but melt them, and make them more useful. And the apostle not only enforceth this way of fruitfulness by precepts, but commends it by his own example, 1 Cor. ix. 20–22. That which is thus suited to the several circumstances of others is fruit in season, and that is the best; and what is not so is scarce good.

[3.] Labour to make all acts of converse and intercourse with men acts of grace and virtue, and so even your common affairs and dealings in the world may yield good fruit. When you make use of your word to others, use none but words of candour, and Christian simplicity, such as may plainly signify your meaning, that your mind may be understood by your words, and nothing concealed, or reserved, or formed so ambiguously and subtilely, as to delude, or prejudice, or any way abuse those you deal with. Also to be strict and severe with yourselves as to truth and faithfulness, that your word may carry with it the security of a bond or an oath; that you may give no occasion to that scandalous rule, which those who are a shame and reproach to the Christian profession, have given occasion for, that every one must be dealt with as though he were a knave or a cheat. Oh what have we been fruitful in, while such a maxim is any way necessary amongst those that profess the religion of Christ?

Be just and righteous in all, and towards all, whatever you may lose or suffer by it. Whatever you may gain by swerving in the least from the rules of justice and righteousness, overreach not those who seek to overreach you. And when you have to deal with such whose weakness offers you some advantage, use equity; and when you might gain by the necessities of others, be merciful and compassionate; be meek and patient to those who provoke you, humble to those who despise you, and ready to forgive those that wrong you, Col. iii. 12, 13. You will have still occasion, in your common affairs, for the exercise of some or other of these gracious qualities; and if you would act them as you have occasion, you might make the acts of your ordinary converse gracious acts; and so your whole life would be full of good fruits, such as would be pleasant to God and man, and sweet and comfortable to your own souls. Order but your intercourse with men, according to that admirable rule of Christ in all those instances which give occasion for its observance, Mat. vii. 12, and your whole conversation in the world would be made up of gracious acts, and consequently would abound with good fruits.

And thus I have shewed you how you may be fruitful in all things, and towards all persons, and so how you may arrive at that which should be your chief aim, universal fruitfulness.

9. Though universal fruitfulness should be our aim, and the increase of all good fruit should be carefully promoted, no part of our souls or conversation should be unimproved, no branch of either should be bare or not well replenished with fruits of holiness or righteousness; yet there are some of these fruits that we are to regard more especially, and bestow more care and pains, that they may be multiplied, and grow, and ripen. The want or neglect of any good fruit is not to be tolerated, but there are some which require more care and industry, and we are obliged to concern ourselves more about them, lest they be wanting, or dwindle and thrive not, or rise not to their due proportions, or come not on, as the seasons of grace require, towards ripeness and maturity. Let me instance in some particulars, of which you should be more careful that they be not wanting.

(1.) Those to which you are more averse, and find or should observe yourselves less inclined. Such fruits you will be in most danger to neglect; and where there is most danger, there should be most care and industry to avoid it. There are some good fruits we are less disposed to, either because of the unhappiness of our temper, or because they are more out of our way, or because they consist not so well with the employments we are most taken with, or because they comply not with our worldly interest, or because opposite to some corruption not subdued, or some evils that we are more addicted to than others; or from some other cause which may be discovered by observance of, or inquiry into, your hearts and ways, or the use of other means proper for this purpose. So there are some more averse to meditation, a frequent and due entertainment of holy thoughts, find it hard to employ their minds upon God, and heaven, and their spiritual state; upon the word, or works, or attributes of God; though such thoughts be both good fruits themselves, and much tend to the nourishing of other good fruits, so that many cannot thrive without them.

Others who, it may be, can more easily employ their thoughts to good purpose, are more barren in good discourse; find it harder to raise it, or continue it, through slowness of speech, or too much modesty; or fear, it may be, to express themselves much in that with which their hearts are not much affected, as thinking it some kind of hypocrisy; or because the spring in the heart is low as to spiritual things, and it is 'out of the abundance of the heart that the mouth speaks.'

Others, it may be, are swift and forward enough to *speak* of good things, but too slow to *do* them; backward to act for God, or may be active for themselves, but not active for the good of others.

Some may be well inclined to acts of worship, and will not omit them, but too much decline acts of charity and mercy; or will relieve the outward wants of others, but shew little compassion to their souls, in such acts as should minister to the relief of their spiritual condition.

Others may be much in holy duties, and in outward acts of righteousness and mercy too, but too little in the inward exercise of grace and holy affections, wherein the spiritual worship of God, and communion with him, consists.

Now, it is your great concernment to observe what you are backward to; what fruits of mind, or heart, or life, which respect God, yourselves, or others, you are most apt to neglect or be defective in; to take care that it may be discovered, and to be willing to be convinced of it, and to be apprehensive of the sinfulness and danger of it; and to apply yourselves more to that which you are more subject to neglect; to be most careful and watchful where you are most in danger; to take more pains to bend the bough the other way, when you see it growing crooked. Your neglects of defectiveness, wherever it lies, may be of greater consequence to you than you are aware of. It may be this is the ground of God's controversy with you, though you have not taken notice of it. It may be this is the rise of your afflictions, and you may expect harder measures if this be not reformed. It may be this which you overlook is the way wherein you might be most serviceable, and the Lord lets you not succeed in other ways because you will not walk in this. It may be, this hinders the prosperity of your souls, and keeps you from being so fruitful as otherwise you might be in other respects. It may be, this encourages others to continue barren when they see you so, and thus diffuse the guilt of it farther than yourselves. And no doubt you gratify Satan in this, and serve him in promoting that particular design which he has herein upon you, and grieve the Spirit of Christ, striving against him within you for it. If you would be delivered from the consequences of this evil, so sinful and so dangerous, yield not to your temper, or inclination, or whatsoever makes you backward and indisposed to that fruitfulness, in any kind or degree, which the Lord calls you to and expects from you. Set yourselves against that averseness and the causes of it, so far as you can discover them, and strive to overcome it; seek strength from above to prevail against it.

(2.) Those fruits which are too much out of fashion, such as are too much neglected by the generality of professors, in which the country or age wherein we live is too barren. It has been the unhappiness of every age to run itself into some great neglects, and to continue therein, and when an evil grows common, and those that are of reputation for wisdom and holiness are tainted with it, it gains credit, or at least connivance, it loses its name, and passes for a better and more tolerable thing than it is; it is not accounted a sin, how sinful soever it be; it will hardly be discovered when it has the countenance of many that are good, and some of the best; there is little hopes of conviction in such circumstances, and so little or no probability of reformation. But where there is the greatest difficulty, there should be the most vigorous endeavours to master it; and where the tide runs strongest, we are concerned to take the most pains to stem it. We should not suffer ourselves lazily to be carried down with the stream, but the stronger it is, strive more against it. We must not make custom, nor common opinion or practice, no, not of professors otherwise strict and conscientious, our rule to judge of all the fruits we should bring forth, or what fruitfulness we should labour for, but go to the law and to the testimony, and what fruits Christ, and those infallibly directed by him, call for from the disciples of Christ, and in what degree and extent they require them, and order yourselves according to that rule, and follow none but as they follow Christ, and walk according to what he prescribes. And after the light of the word, other means may be useful for the discovery of barrenness, in any particulars where the sight of it is too much lost in common practice. And particularly we may make use of the charges and reproaches of enemies for this purpose. *Fas est et ab hoste doceri.* An enemy may sometimes teach us that which a friend may suffer us to be ignorant of. It is known that the papists charge us to be Solifidians, all for faith and nothing for the fruits of it, not minding good works. We are here concerned to give the world a real confutation of this charge, and to shew that the genuine principles of the gospel which we profess, our faith in Christ and love to him, is more effectual, and makes us more fruitful in all good works, than their corrupt principles of justification or salvation by the merit of works is or can be in them. Others charge us with the neglect of moral righteousness, greediness of riches, and the want of those fruits which the contempt of the world brings forth. Our course in this case is not to recriminate, though we may have ground enough, but impartially to examine how far the charge is just, and to reform whatever less or more we are guilty of, and to roll away the reproach by endeavouring to remove all occasion and suspicion of guilt in the severals of the charge, and to make it appear that a new nature and regenerating grace is more powerful to produce all fruits of righteousness than their moral principles, and that we are crucified to the world, and desire not much of it, but to enable us to do more good, and to be more serviceable to God and men. And while others accuse us, we have too much cause to accuse ourselves for want of brotherly love, and the many and precious fruits of it; which divisions and difference in way or opinion has involved almost the whole generation of good men in the guilt of, which has been so common, and so the due sense of it so far lost, that it is well if the hand of God, stretched out against us for it, will make us effectually sensible of it. Let us examine whether we be not much to seek in those fruits of the Spirit which the apostle commends to us, Gal. v. 22, the first and principal whereof is love, and the rest dependents on it. Are not these fruits too much out of fashion?

And since it has been a day of judgment with us, a long day, even for several years, let us observe whether we be not to seek in those fruits which the righteous judgments of God should have produced; and particularly, since they seem to have been directed so as to strike most at our worldly interest, have we learnt hereby more fruitfully to improve the world? neither to hug it too close, and confine the fruits and advantages of what we have to ourselves and ours, nor to let it run out in pride, and vanity, and excess in habit, accommodations, entertainments, or otherwise? Are not the bad fruits which the world is apt to bring forth more in request than the good? Let us take care that we be not involved in the guilt of common barrenness; our danger is the greater here, and therefore we should have a more particular regard we be not wanting in those fruits which are too commonly neglected.

(3.) Those which you are more engaged to bring forth, either by inward abilities or outward enjoyments, or particular convictions. Great care should be taken to answer great and special engagements, especially when they are laid on us by the great God. Now these, amongst others, are the ways whereby the Lord does oblige us to some special fruitfulness, when he enables particularly for it, or gives means and encouragements to that end more than others have, or has convinced any that he expects of them, and that their neglects, in this or that particular, is sinful, and such as he will visit for and proceed against.

Those that are furnished with grace, and gifts, and accomplishments, which enable them to instruct, convince, quicken, encourage others in the way to heaven, must be careful to abound herein more than such who are not so well qualified for such purposes. Those that have much of the world are highly concerned to do more good with it than those that have less. It is the special charge of those who are rich in this world to be 'rich in good works,' 1 Tim. vi. 18. It will be a shame to such if those that have less do more, and a sin, too, which those that are faithful in a little will rise up in judgment and condemn. For those who are rich in the world to be poor in good works is intolerable barrenness.

And those that have convictions, drawing them to such and such ways of fruitfulness, should be exceeding careful to walk in such ways more especially, otherwise their own consciences will be their torturer and executioner, if they should escape other sufferings. The unprofitable servant knew what his Lord expected; this made his sin the greater, and his sentence the more severe, Mat. xxv. 24, 26. He knew and was convinced what would be required of him, and therefore should have been more careful to improve what he had fruitfully; and because he was not, ver. 30, he was cast into outer darkness.

(4.) Those fruits, whose goodness and advantage is most extensive. There is a special excellency in such fruits, which calls for a special care, that they may be cherished and increased. *Bonum, quo communius, eo melius.* That is the best fruit which does most good, which does good to most, whose goodness reaches farthest. The apostle gives those extraordinary gifts the pre-eminence whose advantage was most common and communicative, and would have preferred an ordinary gift which tended to the promoting of common and general fruitfulness before those extraordinary and miraculous gifts which were but for personal or more private advantage, as appears by his discourse, 1 Cor. xiv. 1–4. He prefers prophesying before the gift of tongues, because in the use of this he that had it did but edify himself, but the use of the other edified many, ver. 12. This is the way to excel in fruitfulness, when our fruits become a common harvest, where all that come may reap. Such fruits we should take more care and pains for, which may reach not only ourselves but others; not only their bodies, but their souls too; not only few of them, but many; and do good, not only to this or that person, but to a community. A particular person this way fruitful becomes a common good, a general blessing, and is so much more rich and valuable as a common treasury is more than a private purse.

(5.) Those which you may be tempted to neglect, either because they are difficult, or reproached, or costly, or hazardous. Your ease, your credit, your safety, your worldly interest, will be ready to interpose here, and endanger your barrenness herein, unless you be careful and resolute for them.

[1.] Those that are difficult and cannot be brought forth without pains and industry. It is enough to sweeten all, and make it easy, to consider it is for God. For whom will you take pains if not for him? Should not what you bring forth for him be the fruit of some labour? That which can be done with ease you may do for any one, and shall the Lord have no more from you than any may challenge? None ever repented of any pains they took for God, but that ease which makes you decline such fruits must be repented of, or else it will have a dreadful issue.

[2.] Those that are reproached. Such as may expose you to scorn or derision, or hazard the reputation of your wisdom or moderation. Be sure they be good fruits, and then resolve, with David, 'I will yet be more vile than thus,' 2 Sam. vi. 22. To sacrifice our reputation with men in bringing forth fruit to God is the way to greatest honour with him, before whom the noblest and greatest reproachers are vile persons.

[3.] Those that are costly. You may be tempted to think (though nothing but a worldly unbelieving heart will think it) that it impairs your estates, or lessens the provisions you intend for posterity. Check such temptations with that of David, 2 Sam. xxiv. 4. Those that cost you most will prove best cheap; you have the Lord engaged to make it prove so. And it is for the Lord, whose stewards you are but in all you have, and should you grudge to serve him with his own? And the Lord in such cases is trying you, whether the world be dearer to you than himself. And remember how the Lord resented such offerings as were cheap, and mean, and little worth, Mal. i. 8. The blind, and the lame, and the sick, cost them little or nothing, and such they could offer freely. But what is the issue of such thriftiness? ver. 14. They are deceivers in God's account, and cursed by him, who, when they should offer to him that which is best and of most value, put him off with something that is worthless and costs them little. You see what need there is to be careful you decline not those fruits that are costly.

[4.] Those that are hazardous, and expose you to sufferings. Flesh and blood will be apt to decline these. Corrupt self, and carnal reason, and worldly spirit will call upon you, when called hereto, to spare yourselves. But such fruits most glorify God, and will most honour those who bear them. They evidence the greatest love to Christ, and will yield the most comfort, and will be crowned with the greatest reward. And therefore, as there is necessity to be careful that they be not declined, so greatest encouragement to be fruitful herein.

THE LORD RULES OVER ALL.

His kingdom ruleth over all.—Ps. CIII. 19.

This is a psalm of praise, wherein the Lord is magnified for his mercy especially. This mercy is the more to be praised and admired, because the object of it is so unworthy and contemptible, man, who is so sinful, ver. 3, 10; so weak, ver. 14; so frail, ver. 15, 16. Man, in his greatest flourish, is but like the grass, which is soon cut down, or withereth; or like a flower, which fades of itself, or is blasted with a puff of wind. Oh, but the Lord's mercy is more durable than life. The shortness of our lives would be a sad consideration indeed, if the mercy of God did end with our life. Oh, but this follows us when we leave the world, beyond death and the grave; and can reach those that we leave behind us too: ver. 17, ' His mercy is from everlasting to everlasting, and his righteousness to children's children.' Here mercy that will survive us, that will never die; that we may meet with in another world, when our place in this shall know us no more; and faithfulness, that will continue from generation to generation, and will be mindful of children's children when we are dead and gone. And the comfort of this, ver. 18, belongs to those that believe in him, and shew the truth of their faith by sincere obedience, by care and mindfulness to do his will. To shew everlasting mercy to such is part of his covenant; and if we deal not unfaithfully with him, as to our part, we need not doubt but he is willing to perform his part. And as he is willing, so he is able too; for he has all power in heaven and earth; he has all things under his dominion, and rules over all, ver. 19. His throne is in heaven; he rules and reigns there. But though the glory of his kingdom do most appear in heaven, yet is not his kingdom and dominion confined to heaven, it reaches every where, thing, place; it rules over all. The whole world is his kingdom; his dominion extends over all. The words need not more explaining, but what we shall offer afterwards.

Obs. The Lord rules over all. All things belong to his kingdom, and are under his dominion. He reigns everywhere, and rules all and everything.

Nothing is more plain and express in Scripture than both his reign and the extent of it. For the first, Ps. xciii. 1, 2, Ps. xcvii. 1, 2, where we have his royalty, and his throne, and the basis of it; so מכון signifies; and Ps. xcix. 1. His throne is not only in heaven, but between the cherubims, amongst his people, ver. 2; and not only in Zion, but above all people. For the extent of it, add but 1 Chron. xxix. 11, 12, 'Thine, O Lord, is the greatness, and the power, and the glory, and the victory, and the majesty: for all that is in the heaven and in the earth is thine; thine is the kingdom, O Lord, and thou art exalted as head above all,' &c.

For the explication of the universal dominion of God, so necessary, so useful to be understood, and that we may lay a groundwork for the application, which may be exceeding profitable and comfortable to us at all times, especially in the worst, I shall endeavour to give you a clear and particular account of the act, the object, and the mode of it.

For the first, *to Rule*, includes these three things:

1. Authority. Rule, without authority, is but usurpation. God is the fountain of all just authority: Rom. xiii. 1, 'There is no power but of God.' All such authority, whether economical in a family, or civil in the state, or ecclesiastical in the church, is from God; and he, from whom all is derived, has incomparably more himself. His authority is sovereign; all else in the world (how sovereign soever called and accounted), it is subordinate to his; under it, subject to it, depending on it; and so far as it is not subject, it is usurpation and rebellion. He is the 'King of kings,' &c., Rev. i. 5; and the authority of the greatest monarch is not so much, compared with his, as that of a constable, or the meanest officer, compared with that of a prince.

2. Power. To keep those who are to be ruled in subjection; to make them yield and submit to the authority of the ruler. Without this he will be but a ruler at courtesy, and rather have the name than the reality of a governor. Now the Lord has all power; he is $\pi\alpha\nu\tau o\kappa\rho\acute{\alpha}\tau\omega\rho$, the Almighty ruler; he can make the powers of earth or hell to stoop to him, or crush them; and usually in Scripture, where his rule and government is mentioned, his power is annexed: Ps. lxvi. 7, 'He ruleth by his power for ever,' משׁל עולם. He ruleth by his power over the world: Rev. xix. 6, 'The Lord God omnipotent reigneth;' Rev. xi. 17, 'Thou hast taken thy great power, and hast reigned.'

3. The actual ordering and disposing of what is under him, for the ends of government—the actual exercise of power and authority for this purpose. And so, when the Lord is said to rule, the meaning is, he shews his authority, and uses his power, in the ordering and disposing of all things as seems good to him. He makes them all serve his end and design; he works all things according to the counsel of his will; he orders all things in a subserviency to those purposes he had from eternity; he actually so disposes of all things so as to serve the ends for which they were appointed. And in this respect it is said, John v. 17, 'My Father worketh hitherto, and I work.' He is still at work, still ordering all by his providence. He is not like an artificer, who, when he has made a clock, and set it in order, and hanged weights upon it, leaves it to go of itself; but (as one says) more like a musician, who, knowing his instrument will make no music of itself, does not only tune it, but actually touch the strings, for the making of that harmony which pleases him.

This, for the first, what it is to rule; and what we are to understand thereby, when God is said to rule. Let us now see what he rules—what is the object or subject of his government; and that is no less than all things, 'He ruleth over all.' Now, that we may more distinctly view this, let us look upon it in the several parcels which make up this *all*.

1. He rules both heaven and earth: Isa. lxvi. 1, 'The heaven is my throne, the earth is my footstool.' Both heaven and earth are under him,

both are subject to him. The glory of his kingdom appears most in heaven, but the power of it reaches the earth, yea, and hell too. That is the proper place of rebels indeed ; but he has them in chains ; they will not yield obedience, but he keeps them in subjection, and shews that he is their ruler by executing justice upon them, and making them feel the power of his wrath. They would not obey the laws of his government, and therefore the penalty is inflicted on them ; and this is an act of government, as well as enacting laws and propounding or giving rewards.

2. He rules not only heaven and earth, but all the parts thereof; the whole world, and every part of it, Ps. cxiii. 5. In heaven, the angels, whether they be thrones, or dominions, or principalities, or powers, Col. i. 16, are subject to him, and ordered by him as he pleases ; for he has put them in subjection unto Christ also, as he is Mediator, 1 Peter iii. 22. And he orders them as his servants, as 'ministering Spirits,' Heb. i. 14 ; he says to one, Go, and he goeth, Mat. viii. 9. As a servant stands in the presence of his lord, waiting for his orders, ready to receive his commands, and to do his pleasure, in such an humble and observant posture do the angels stand in the presence of their sovereign.

And as the thrones and principalities in heaven are under his rule, so are the kingdoms of the earth, 2 Chron. xx. 6. Nebuchadnezzar, one of the proudest and mightiest tyrants on earth, was forced by the hand of God (to whom the greatest kings on earth are less than worms) to acknowledge this, Daniel v. 20, 21, and iv. 32, 34, 35. He acted as one who had none above him, none to control him ; but the Lord made him know he was a subject, and that whoever possess the kingdoms of the earth, yet the Lord is indeed the ruler of them.

Yea, his dominion reaches unto the sea, Job xxxviii. 8–11. The sea, in his greatest rage, submits and obeys as under his rule and government, Ps. lxxxix. 8, 9, and xciii. 2–4. He can as easily still the rage of the furious, when it is like the swelling waves in a stormy sea ; or if they will storm against their great sovereign, can make them know subjection as he did Pharaoh, Ps. lxxxix. 19 ; Behemoth and Leviathan, the king over all the children of pride, are ruled by him, and he will rule over those that are prouder than he, and make them stoop or break them.

3. He rules not only great things, but small. The least things in the world are ruled and ordered by him as well as the greatest. *Dii magna curant, parva negligunt ;* that God regards great things, but concerns not himself with small matters, was the speech of those that knew not God ; nothing at all is exempted from his government, the least things are under his disposal. The conception of Laban's cattle may seem a small thing; yet the Lord concerned himself in this, and admonished Jacob in a dream how he disposed thereof, Gen. xxxi. 11, 12. He takes care of the meanest creature, Ps. cxlvii. 9, Mat. vi. 26 ; the lilies, the grass of the field are under the influence of his government, vers. 28–30 ; he clothes them, they are his subjects, wear his livery; nay, there is not the least sparrow falls without his order, Mat. x. 29 ; there is not so much as a hair, but is under his notice and disposal, ver. 30 ; he orders and overrules the very least things as well as the greater. Things so mean and inconsiderable as we mind them not, judge them not worthy of our thoughts, care, or regard, they are all under the government of God, and he actually orders and disposes of them.

4. He rules not only all beings, but all motions, Acts xvii. 28. As those things that live, have their life from him, and those things that have not life, have their being from him ; so both have their motion from him, he

gives it, and he orders it. All the motions in the world are governed and overruled by him; all the wheels of this great engine, as they are of his framing, so, whether they be greater or less they move not without him; he sets them on motion, he quickens it, he stops it when he will; he directs it how and whither he pleases. If a sparrow move not without him (as before), what motion can we imagine exempted from his government and disposal? How could Paul be so confident of the safety of his company, that not a hair should fall from the head of any of them, Acts xxvii. 34, but that God who has the ordering of all things and motions, even to that of a hair, had assured him of it! vers. 23, 24. When a man, in the battle mentioned 1 Kings xxii., drew a bow at a venture, who was it that guided the motion of the arrow, so as to smite the king of Israel rather than any about him? who was it that directed it, so as to enter between the joints of his harness, rather than to hit some other part of his armour, ver. 34, but that God who had designed and foretold his death? ver. 17.

5. He rules not only actions, but events, so that acts and undertakings have not such an issue as they promise or threaten, but such as the Lord pleases to order. That which is unlikely to succeed has the desired issue, and that which is likely to prosper, succeeds not at all; because all events are in God's hands, and he disposes of them, not as we think probable or improbable, but as he thinks fit: 1 Kings xx. 11, 'Let not him that girdeth on his harness boast himself as he that putteth it off.' Why so? Because the event is in the hands of God, and he can dispose of it against those that are most confident, and for those who see little cause to expect it, Eccles. ix. 11. 'Time and chance happeneth to them all,' *i. e.* their endeavours have such success as the hand of God will guide them to; yet this, though it order all things, being invisible, things seem many times to fall out rather at adventure, than according to the regular endeavours that have been used in order to them. Herein the people of God, whatever advantages they have had for the carrying on of their affairs to a good issue, yet still ascribe it unto God, and owe him so much as though they had done nothing, being sensible that whatever they did, it would have come to nothing, if he had not given a good event, Ps. xviii. 39, 40, and Ps. xliv., from the 3d to the 8th verse. And he is their king, their ruler upon this account, because their deliverances and successes were from him; he overruled all to issue in good events.

6. He rules and orders not only the substance, but the circumstances of things and actions. To instance in time and place. How was it that Abigail came to meet David just at that time, which if she had slipped, he had massacred Nabal's family? Why, God sent her, which is the account David gives of it, 1 Sam. xxv. 32, 34. How was it that the decree of Augustus, for taxing of the world, came forth just at the time when Mary was ready to be delivered? Why, the Lord so ordered it, that what he had so decreed and foretold concerning the birth of Christ in Bethlehem might be fulfilled, Mat. ii. 5. When Nebuchadnezzar went to war, and was in doubt whether to fall upon Rabbah of the Ammonites or upon Jerusalem, Ezek. xxi. 20, 21, how came he to a determination? Why, the Lord over-ruled all the means he used for his direction, so that he resolves to bend his force against Jerusalem, because God had determined to have it destroyed.

7. He rules and disposes both end and means. God had an intention to make his people, who were before *Jezreel*, the *scattered* of the Lord, to become *Jezreel*, the *seed* of the Lord, to bless them with plenty; and hereupon so orders the means, as they might see his hand herein bringing about this end, Hosea ii. 21, 22. Here is the Lord, in the first place—I will hear—

influencing all the means, from first to last, so as Jezreel has the end of all the blessing promised.

The Lord stands in no need of means to accomplish the end he aims at. But when he will make use of means, he shews his all-governing and over-ruling power, not only in blessing means that are good, and proper, and usual, but in making any kind of means to serve his turn; so he can dispose of bad instruments to promote a good end. Thus he made use of the Assyrian to accomplish his whole work upon mount Zion, Isa. x. 12, though he had no such thought nor intention, but a quite other design, ver. 7. And he can make strange and unusual means accomplish his pleasure, as well as usual and ordinary. So he orders the ravens to feed one prophet, 1 Kings xvii., and two bears to destroy those who mocked another, 2 Kings ii. 24.

8. He rules and disposes not only things orderly, but such as seem most confused. Not only such affairs as are so well ordered that we may easily be persuaded some divine influence does dispose of them; but those that have such a face of confusion and disorder, that it will be hard to believe that the Lord has any hand therein; even such does he rule and order, though we see him not acting therein, till the darkness and disturbance be over. What horrid disorder was there in the actings of Jacob's sons, conspiring against their brother, throwing him into a pit, selling him to the Ishmaelites, Gen. xxxvii. Who could suspect that the Lord had a hand in any of this ? Yet his hand was in it all. The confusion and disorder of it was indeed from the visible actors ; but the Lord was all this while working this chaos into a beautiful form, and when he had done, then it appears with a lovely face, and is so represented by Joseph himself, Gen. l. 20, and xlv. 4, 5, 7, 8. Who could have expected that such a dismal cloud would have thus cleared up ? But this is the Lord's doing, and such things he is wont to do, while he is ruling over all, and all are over-ruled by him.

If you should see such a black and dismal face of things as may tempt you to conclude that God has forsaken the earth or the place where you are, that he can never mingle with such confusions, or intermeddle in such horrid disorders, stay a little before you yield to such conclusions. The Lord once, out of chaos, brought a well-ordered world. He rules still; and can, when he pleases, out of mere confusion and darkness, bring forth a new heaven and a new earth, wherein righteousness may dwell.

9. He rules and orders things, both necessary and contingent or casual. Things necessary, such as proceed from necessary causes, which act in one certain uniform way, and cannot of themselves vary nor proceed otherwise; such are the course of the heavens, the eclipses of the luminaries, the seasons of the year, the ebbings and flowings of the sea. The Lord gave law to all these, and keeps them to the observance of it, yet overrules them, and gives them other orders when he pleases. The heavens declare the glory of God this way, Ps. xix. 1; not only by their fabric and influences, but by their course and motion, which he instanceth in verses 4–6, Ps. lxxiv. 16, 17. He has settled all the climes of the earth, and the seasons of the year, Jer. xxxi. 35, 36. The Lord has fixed the course of these things, they cannot vary therein of themselves; but he himself can change it when he thinks fit, and has given instances of his overruling power herein. He has changed the course of the sun, and made it stand still, as in Joshua's time; or go back, as in Hezekiah's time. And the course of the sea too, how uncontrollable the motion thereof seems to be! The Red Sea and Jordan are evidences that he who rules all can overrule anything.

So things contingent and casual, which fall out uncertainly or accidentally, which those who know not God ascribe to chance and fortune, the Lord orders them, they fall out as he pleases. He disposes of them certainly, how uncertain soever they be in respect of other causes, Prov. xvi. 33. The lot is so ruled and directed by the Lord, that it falls just so as he would have it, and can do no otherwise; so when a man is slain casually, the Lord is said to 'give him up to death,' Exod. xxi. 13. There is an instance which will clear it, Deut. xix. 4, 5; in this case, which is so every way accidental, the Lord is said to deliver the man into the hands of him that slays him.

10. He rules and orders not only that which is good, but that which is evil and sinful. God is no way the cause, no way the author, of sin. It is the work of the devil, he brought it into the world; but being there, and the Lord permitting it to be there, Acts xiv. 19, Ps. cxviii. 12, he takes such order about it that it may appear he rules over all, and that there is not anything in the world but is subjected to his government and under his disposal. Accordingly,

(1.) He limits and bounds it, so that it proceeds not so far as Satan and the depraved will of man would have it; otherwise it would overwhelm the world, and no flesh would be saved. He restrains it in many by common grace, and breaks the power of it in his people by effectual grace. He withheld Abimelech from sinning when he had a mind to it, Gen. xx. 6.

(2.) He overrules it to good ends, and disposes it to excellent purposes. So the horridest sin that was ever acted in the world was ordered by him, to promote the most blessed and glorious ends; and so he had disposed of it in his eternal counsel, before the actors were in motion or in being, Acts iv. 27, 28 and ii. 23. They designed therein the satisfying of their own malice and cruelty; but he disposed of it to the getting himself the greatest glory, in the redemption and salvation of lost sinners.

So the wickedness of men, in afflicting and persecuting his people, is overruled by God to the destroying of wickedness, the promoting of holiness, and the preparing of greater glory for them. He orders sin, so as it tends to destroy sin; the sin of oppressors, so as to purge sin out of his people, Isa. xxvii. 9. Isa. i. 25, he turns his hand upon them, in letting loose the hands of oppressors and persecutors against them. So that there is a double hand in their sufferings: the hand of wicked men, and that would destroy the oppressed; the hand of God, and that would destroy their sin. And the hand of God prevails, and thereby shews that he rules over all. He orders sin, so as it tends to promote holiness, to advance its opposite, Rom. v. 3, 4, Heb. xii.; he orders it so as to make way for greater glory, 2 Cor. iv. 17. Thus he brings the greatest light out of the blackness of darkness, and 'turns the shadow of death into the morning,' thereby making it evident that he rules over all; makes the greatest evil advance the greatest good; and that which is the worst of all, to serve the best and most glorious purposes.

11. He rules things natural and voluntary. Natural, such as have their next causes in nature, the hand of God rules therein, as in thunder and lightning, Job xxxvii. 2, 3; wind and rain, Jer. x. 13, Ps. cxlviii. 7. Not to stay upon other particulars, read Psalms civ. and cvii., and you will see plentiful evidence hereof in these and many other instances.

But more particularly, he rules things voluntary; such are intelligent and rational beings. Man in special is the subject of his government. Those amongst the sons of men that are his he disposes and takes care of, yet in a more peculiar manner. The Scripture is full and clear in expressing how man is governed by him in birth, and life, and death. He takes order about his conception, formation, and birth, Job x. 9–11, Ps. cxxxix. 14–16. He fixeth the period of his life, and determines how many his days shall be upon earth, Job xiv. 5. He orders what his state and condition shall be while he lives, Ps. lxxv. 6, 7, 1 Sam. ii. 7, 8, Ps. cxiii. 7, 8. He rules the mind and heart, Prov. xxi. 2, Ps. cxix. 36, and cv. 25. No heart so obstinate but he can bend it; none so fast closed but he can open it, Acts xvi. 4; none so refractory but he can turn it whithersoever he will; none so frozen and congealed but he can melt and dissolve, and make it ductile as water. He alone has the sovereignty over the hearts of men: 'he opens, and no man shuts,' &c. The will, that impious faculty that will stand out when the whole man besides is conquered, he can subdue at his pleasure, and make it run into a ready compliance with his own will. He rules the tongue and words, Prov. xvi. 1. Man without him can neither prepare his heart to speak, nor speak what he has prepared; both is from him, who has the command both of heart and tongue; and he can guide the tongue to speak what shall be more effectual than what it was prepared to utter. Augustine is a remarkable instance hereof, who, beginning his sermon, was led to another subject than what he designed, and was prepared to speak of; and found afterwards that he was overruled thereto by the hand of God for the conversion of a seduced soul, which the discourse he had intended, it is like, would not have touched.

He rules and orders his feet and paths. If we were left to take our own course, whither would we run? Jer. x. 23. Who then shall direct him? Ps. xxxvii. 23. When we have found out a way which our own judgment thinks best, and our own inclination leads us to, the Lord often leads us out of it, and directs us better, Prov. xvi. 9. He rules hands and actions, Ps. xviii. 34. It is he that holds and guides the hand, or else it would make nothing but blots; his guidance is the sufficiency and strength of it for every service, for any work he calls us to. And so Nehemiah seeks it: Neh. vi. 9, 'Now therefore, O God, strengthen my hands.'

Thus the Lord rules over man, and over every part, and every act. Indeed, of all the creatures on earth, man only is capable of that which is properly government; he is the only subject that can be ruled by laws. Accordingly, he has enacted laws for us, and enforced them with penalties, and encouraged obedience to them, by promises of reward. And according to our observance of his laws he will judge what subjects we are, and will answerably proceed in the execution of them; by enhappying those with the reward promised who shew themselves faithful subjects, or by inflicting the penalty on those who prove refractory and disobedient. And thus doth the Lord most properly rule over men; though, in a larger sense, he rules over all things.

I might shew how he rules over his people in a more peculiar manner than over other creatures or other men, how he orders and overrules all things to secure them from evil and to do them good, how he commands all things to serve them for these purposes, Ps. lix. 13. His government reaches unto the ends of the earth; but he makes it known he rules in Jacob in a more special manner, he having a particular respect to them in his whole government, Deut. xi. 12. But the enlargement of this I reserve to the application.

I should proceed to the third general proposed, and give an account of the mode of this government, shewing what kind of rule it is, by some properties of it, whereby its excellency and transcendency above all other will be manifest.

1. It is a supreme sovereignty. He that rules over all has none above him, none co-ordinate with him, none but such as are below him, indefinitely

below him, none but what are subjected to him, and under him at an infinite distance.

The powers of heaven, those that are called thrones and principalities there, are not only subjects to him, but his servants. They attend in his presence, and while they wait on him they adore him; the splendour and lustre of his majesty is greater than they can well behold, Isa. vi. 1, 2. 'With twain they covered their faces,' as not able to endure the infinite splendour of his glory and majesty, no more than our weak eyes are able to behold the sun shining in his full strength. 'And with twain they covered their feet,' as abashed in sense of their own vileness and imperfection, in comparison of the incomprehensible perfections of their glorious sovereign. 'And with twain they did fly,' to shew their readiness to execute his commands, their swiftness in doing him service. They do not only serve but worship him, Heb. i. And as to be a servant is simply something less than to be a subject, so worship denotes greater subjection than any other service. Thus are the powers of heaven subject to him.

The powers of hell tremble before him, James ii. 19. Though they be called the 'rulers of the darkness of this world,' and the chief of them the 'god of the world,' yet before the Supreme Majesty of heaven they have not the confidence of free subjects, but tremble as slaves. Those that have led all men captive are the Lord's prisoners; they are in a lower and worse capacity than other of his subjects, they are rebels under punishment for their disobedience. He is ruling them, and will rule them for ever, in wrath. He has them in chains, they cannot stir without his leave; they could not so much as enter into a herd of swine till they had begged leave. Thus are the powers of hell subject to him.

As for the powers on earth, the highest and greatest of them are but his under-officers, and more under him incomparably than the lowest and meanest of their subjects are under them. They have their power and commission from him; he has limited them as he saw fit; and if they will not keep their bounds, and really acknowledge their subjection to their Great Sovereign, he will 'rule them with a rod of iron, and break them in pieces like a potter's vessel,' Ps. ii. 9, 10. A mighty Cham, a great Mogul, a grand Signior, the highest prince and potentate, is no more to him than a worm, or a fly, or a grasshopper is to us, no more than a potter's vessel, which is of less worth than any living creature is to us. They are but a small part of their dominion, that which is under their government, but their whole dominion is as nothing to the Great King, Dan. iv. 35. So that to him they are not the thousandth part of that which seems to be nothing, so much inferior are they to the Supreme Majesty of the world, and so much should they be subject to him; and if they will not, he will be 'terrible to the kings of the earth,' Ps. lxxvi. 12. He will cut off the proud, and cruel, and presumptuous spirits of oppressing Nimrods, and that in a terrible manner. He will make them know (though they be apt to forget it) that they are subjects, and that the Lord reigns and is their Sovereign, and that the kingdom is his alone who rules over all; that he is 'the blessed and only potentate, the King of kings, and Lord of lords,' 1 Tim. vi. 15, the only Supreme and Sovereign ruler, and Lord of all.

2. He rules absolutely; his government is unlimited, for who can bound him who rules over all? Other rulers are limited by laws or contracts, but none give law to God, nor lay obligation on him but himself; he has no other bounds but his own wise and holy will, and his will is law to heaven and earth, and all creatures therein, Dan. iv. 35, Ps. cxv. 3, and cxxxv. 16. It is too great a power for any mortal man to be trusted with, to make his

will a law and rule to others. The Lord has subjected all to his laws, and if others will entrust their rulers with a freedom to do whatever they will, they do it at their peril. The corrupt and depraved will of man may prove a pernicious law; but as it is the prerogative of God, so it is the advantage of the world that the will of God should be its law, and that all things should be ordered according to his pleasure, because his will is infinitely and perfectly wise, and holy, and good.

3. He rules irresistibly. His government is uncontrollable. None can give check to his orders, nor hinder him from accomplishing his pleasure, Isa. xlvi. 10, 11. Whatever he pleases shall be done, and woe to those that attempt to hinder him, Isa. xlv. 9, Jer. xviii. 3, 4, 6. No powers in the world can any more hinder the Lord from ordering all in heaven and earth as he pleases, than the clay can hinder the potter from forming it into what shape he list. So Dan. iv. 35, Job ix. 12, 13. As none should question his proceedings, so none can stop them. Those who presume they are strong enough to help others, shall not be able to help themselves when he falls upon them; they must stoop, yea, fall irrecoverably, Job xi. 10. Whatever the Lord undertakes, whether to save or destroy, whether to do good to those that please him, or hurt those that offend him, he will do it unavoidably; there is none can hinder him, Rom. xi. 9, 2 Chron. xx. 6. All the resistance that any created power can make to the Lord in his course of governing the world will be but like that which a snail can make to the foot that treads on it, and will crush it. All the impediment they can give him is no more than a fly can give a wheel that is whirled about with a strong hand. All attempts of the powers of hell or earth to hinder the Lord from ordering all as he pleases will be as ridiculous, Ps. ii. 1–5.

4. He rules perfectly. There is not the least weakness or imperfection in his government, as there is in that of other rulers; nothing of error or mistake; nothing that the most excellent prudence would order otherwise; nothing defective, for want of judgment as to things present, or want of experience as to things past, or want of foresight as to things to come; for he has all things, past, present, and to come, clearly before his eyes, in every act of government, and in his ordering of every particular, Ps. cxlvii. 5. The Lord is great, as he is the ruler of the world; and as he rules all things with great power, so with infinite wisdom. It is an infinite understanding that governs the world, Prov. iii. 19, 20. And as there is perfection of wisdom, so also of righteousness, in his government, Ps. xcvii. 1. 2, the basis of his throne (as before) Ps. xxxvi. 5, 6. All these perfections, so infinitely great in all dimensions that none can give an account of their height, and depth, and length, and breadth, do shine forth in preserving man and beast, in the Lord's disposing of all things in the world, from the highest to the lowest.

5. He rules all at once. Orders all things, in heaven, and earth, and under the earth, together. Men cannot do two things at once, but first dispose of one business and then of another; order the affairs of one place now, and when that is done, despatch the concernments of another. But the Lord orders all the affairs of all parts of the world at once; he can mind them all together, how infinitely various they seem; the multiplicity of them is no more distraction to him than if he had but one thing in hand. He has a governing hand over all things, in all their actions and motions, throughout the whole world, and his hand is in them all at once; and in those affairs which he manages by instruments, while they are acting under him they are acted by him, and he acts immediately in them all; how far soever they may be asunder, he influences them all together.

And though this be hard to conceive, yet must there be no doubt of it, if we believe that God rules over all. For since there are many millions of things in being and motion at once, if the Lord did but order one or few things at once, the greatest number of them would be and move without him. Since he rules over all, and none subsist or move without him, he must be conceived to put forth millions of governing acts at once, as many together as there are things and motions in the world.

6. He rules easily. The government of the whole world, and all things in it, gives him not the least trouble. He takes care of all without any solicitousness; he orders all, without any toil; he acts all, without any labour; he does it continually, without any weariness. Οὐ γὰρ κάμνει ὁ Θεὸς προσάτων, οὐδὲ ἀσθενεῖ πρὸς τὴν πάντων ἐργασίαν, *Athanas. contra Arian. Orat.* 3. God is not weary with ordering the universe, nor is all the work of the world too much for him; he does it all with as much ease as we do that which may be done with a word, or a look, or a beck; he rules the world as easily as he made it. 'God said, Let there be light, and there was light,' Ps. xxxiii. 6, 9. He does not properly speak; he did not so much for the making of the world; it was enough that he willed it. Μόνον ἐθέλησε καὶ ἐποίησε τα πάντα, *id. ibid*; he only willed it, and all things started out of nothing; and with as much ease, with such a word he upholds and governs the world, Heb. i. 3; by his word he upholds all things in their being, and order, and motion; his word is enough for all. It is sufficient that he wills it: Τὸ βούλημα μόνον ἱκανόν ἐστιν αὐτοῦ πρός τὴν τῶν πάντων δημιουργίαν; his word or will was enough to make all, it is enough to govern all; it costs him no more toil or trouble, than a word of our mouth, or an act of our will costs us, Ps. cxlvii. 15–18; he rules and orders all things as easily as if he had but one thing to order; all are not so much to sovereign power and all-sufficiency, as any one, the least, the easiest is to us; he rules the world, as if an artist could make a clock go with his eye, and keep it in true and constant motion only by looking on it; the most miraculous acts of his government are done as easily as we breathe, Exod. xv. 8, 10.

7. He ruleth continually. His government is indefectible, he is always ruling over all, without ever ceasing, without the least intermission. If the Lord should but withdraw his governing hand a moment, all the wheels of the great fabric of the world would stand still or fall to pieces. When those whom we call the rulers of the world are asleep, or idle, or worse, God is still at work; his over-seeing eye is ὀφθαλμός ἀκοίμητος, an eye that 'neither slumbers nor sleeps,' Ps. cxxi. 3, 4, Zech. iv. 10, 2 Chron. xvi. 9. They run, they are always in motion, never shut, never diverted, ever beholding the whole earth, to shew himself strong in the government of it, Exod. xv. 18, Ps. cxlvi. 10. 'The Lord shall reign for ever,' for ever; not only because of the continuance of this sovereign dignity, but because of the ever continued exercise of his regal power.

Thus much for the explication of this grand truth.

For the proof of it, there is little need of reasons and arguments, when there is so much evidence from Scripture, as I have already given an account of. Only take notice of these three particulars:

1. The Lord has right and title to rule over all.
2. He is able to rule all. And,
3. He is concerned, and so willing to exercise such an universal government.

Each of these alone will be a sufficient confirmation of this truth, but taken all together, they make up abundant evidence. He that has right to rule, may rule if he be able; and he that is able, will rule actually if he be concerned. But the Lord *may* rule over all, he has right to do it; and he *can* rule over all, he is able to do it; and he is *willing* too, being highly concerned to do it; and therefore he actually governs all.

1. The Lord has right and title to rule over all. No creature has so much right to rule over any one thing as he has to rule over all; for all things are his own, Ps. lxxxix. 11; heaven and earth, the world, and the fulness of it, *i. e.* whatever is in it, all things wherewith the world is replenished, Ps. lxxiv. 16. So particularly man is his own, Ps. c. 3, and all that men enjoy are his, 1 Chron. xxix. 14, 16; all are his own, because he made them all. And so you may observe in the texts before quoted, where the Lord is spoken of as proprietor; his making of them is mentioned, that being the foundation and ground of his propriety. Indeed, nothing can be so much our own as that is God's which is created by him; by virtue of this, everything created is his own in the fullest sense; absolutely, without any limitation; totally, without any co-partner; principally, without any subordination; primarily, without any derivation of title from others; independently, without any dependence upon any other for his title; so that what we count most our own, is not near so much ours, as everything is his.

Now, an absolute owner or proprietor has right to possess, or make use, or dispose of, or order what is his own as he sees fit, Mat. xx. 15, Esther i. 22. The world is more the Lord's than any man's house is his own, and so has all right to rule it. The same word, *dominus*, signifies both a lord and an owner; and *dominium*, both rule and property; so far as any one hath property, so far he is a ruler, and may dispose of what is his own. And we have them joined together in Scripture, 1 Chron. xxix. 12, where you have the kingdom or dominion, and the right or title to it (all are thine). The Lord's kingdom rules over all, because all his own.

2. He is able to rule over all; he, and he alone is in a capacity to do it. And this is evident by those infinite perfections of his, which I have given you an account of heretofore.

(1.) He is *almighty*. He can do all things, and therefore he can order and rule everything; he can keep all in subjection, and make them serve the ends he has appointed them, Rev. xix. 6. Omnipotency is sufficient for the government of all things. An universal power is more able to rule all, than our limited particular power to govern any one thing.

(2) He is *omnipresent*. Everywhere present, and so can observe and take order about everything wherever it is. He fills heaven and earth, Jer. xxiii. 24; no part of the world, but he is fully in it; he more than fills it, 2 Chron. ii. 6. There is not any part of the world which is at the least distance from him; and therefore he is in a capacity to order and govern all.

(3.) He is *omniscient*. His knowledge is infinite, and reaches all things, and therefore he knows how to order all things, and how to extend his rule over all. He understands the nature, and temper, and power, and motions of all creatures, and accordingly discerns how they may be ruled, how they are to be ordered, Heb. iv. 13. The minds and hearts of men which are not subject to the government of any creatures, because they are not known to any, are open to the eye, and under the inspection of God, and so under his rule and government. And thus it is evident that the Lord is able to rule over all, and all-sufficient for the government of all things.

3. He is willing to rule over all. He has not only right and power, but a will to govern the world; and so nothing is left to make us doubt but that he actually rules it. That he is willing is evident, because he is highly concerned. The end for which he made all would not otherwise be attained if he did not order and dispose of all in a tendency thereto, Prov. xvi. 4. He

made all things for his own glory; but they cannot promote this end, they will not glorify him, unless he concur, and order, and rule, and overrule them. He made all things, *ad responsum ipsius*, to answer him, so some; *ut obtemperent ipsi*, so others to the same sense, that they may obey him. But that they may obey him he must keep them under his rule and government, otherwise his end in making them may be lost. Now the Lord is not willing to be frustrated in his great design, and therefore willing to rule all for the promoting of it. And hence we may certainly conclude that he actually rules over all.

I will but endeavour to remove one objection out of the way, and then proceed to application.

If God rule over all, then all things would be excellently ordered. But there seems to be one thing remarkable in the government of the world, which men are apt to think would be otherwise ordered if the Lord did concern himself in the governing of all things. And it is this: in all ages good men have ordinarily fared worst, and those that are bad have fared best in the world. These have ruled, while those were under hatches; these have prospered and flourished, while those have been oppressed or afflicted; these have had power, and plenty, and successes, while those have been under wants, sufferings, persecutions. This has not only occasioned the heathen who knew not God to question his providence and universal government, διὰ τοῦ ὁρᾶν, ποτὲ μὲν ἀγαθοὺς δυστυχοῦντας, when they see the misery of good men, ποτὲ δὲ κακοὺς ἐν ἑαυτοῖς εὐποροῦντας, and the prosperities of bad men; but it has been a stumbling-block to the best of God's people, which some of them could hardly get over: Ps. lxxiii. 2, 3, 4, 5, 12, 'My feet were almost gone; my steps had well nigh slipped. For I was envious at the foolish, when I saw the prosperity of the wicked. For there is no bands in their death; but their strength is firm,' &c.; whereas he himself, and the generation of the righteous, met with other measures: ver. 14, 'All the day long have I been plagued, and chastened every morning.' So Job, when himself was under so grievous afflictions, observed the wicked were in great flourish, Job xxi. 7; and Jeremiah expostulates with the Lord about it, as a strange dispensation, of which an account could not be easily given, Jer. xii. 1, 2.

But in answer to this, 1, There would be no reason to question the universal government of God upon this account, if the nature and tendency of prosperity and afflictions were but rightly apprehended.

It is thought a disparagement to the government of the world that wicked men fare well therein. But if outward prosperity do not make them fare well, the show will vanish. Now, prosperity is so far from being good to evil men, that there is scarce anything worse in this world than to prosper in ways of wickedness. It is as if a physician should leave a wilful patient to please himself with such a diet as will heighten his distemper, and tends to make it incurable. Would you think this a favour, or that the sick person is well dealt with, how much soever his fare pleases him? No better, no more favourably does the Lord deal with wicked men when he suffers them to prosper in their evil ways. Alas! this prosperity tends to harden them in wickedness, and to fasten them irrecoverably in the ways that lead to destruction: Prov. i. 32, 'The turning away of the simple shall slay them, and the prosperity of fools shall destroy them.' 'The ease' (for so we may render that which we read the *turning away*) 'of the simple,' their freedom from afflictions, tends to ruin them, though they are so simple as not to understand it. 'And the prosperity of wicked men' (for these are fools in Solomon's language) 'will destroy them.' And is it any great favour for the Lord to give them that which will prove destructive to them?

Their prosperous state is but a fattening them for the day of slaughter. And thus the prophet resolves this difficulty, Jer. xii. 3. And so some understand that of the apostle: James v. 5, 'Ye have lived in pleasure on the earth, and been wanton ; ye have nourished your hearts as in a day of slaughter.' A beast that is intended to be killed is put into fat pasture, and seems to fare better than another that is left to shift for itself on a bare common. But a fat pasture is no sign of favour unless it be a favour to be killed sooner. Look upon prosperous sinners as fattening for slaughter, as preparing for a sudden, terrible fall, and their prosperity will be no exception against the divine government of the world. Says Isidore, We ought not to lament those who smart when they offend, Ἀλλὰ τοὺς ἀτιμωρητί ποιοῦντας, but those that go on in sin unpunished. As it is not so grievous to be sick as to have no cure, those that suffer here are in the way to be healed, but those that go on unpunished, εἰς ἀναλγησίαν ὁδεύουσιν, lose all sense of their disease, their case is next to desperate. If their path were hedged up with thorns, or met with some rubs in the way, it is like they might take up; but when their way in wickedness is plain and pleasant, they are never like to stop till they run themselves into eternal ruin. Nothing makes the case of a sinner more dangerous and desperate than a continued prospering in sin.

And as wicked men cannot be reasonably accounted to fare well for all their flourish and outward prosperity, this being so dangerous, so destructive, so much a curse, so dreadful a judgment, so on the other hand, those that are good cannot be thought to fare ill because of their afflictions and sufferings in this life; for afflictions are necessary for them, considering the sickly complexion of the best souls in this life, even as physic is for a diseased body. If the Lord did not use this method, it would signify he cared not for them, regarded not whether they were well or ill, whether they lived or died; ὁ τεμνόμενος καὶ καιόμενος πρὸς θεραπείαν ὁδεύει, when they are lanced and seared, they are under cure; ἀπὸ τῆς ἀλγηδόνος θεραπείαν καρπωσάμενος, though it be grievous, it is the way to their recovery. This helps them to more health, and strength, and life, in the inner man, 2 Cor. iv. 16 ; this makes them more fit for service, more fit for communion with God, and capable of greater glory, ver. 17. And does God deal ill with them in thus doing, in dispensing that which is so necessary, so highly advantageous to them ? Is there anything in this dispensation thus truly represented that can impeach God's government of the world ? Is there anything that does not become him, that does not speak the ordering of a divine hand ?

2. If these things were of another nature ; if prosperity did signify some favour to those that are bad, and afflictions did speak more severity to those that are better; yet the small continuance of them makes them inconsiderable. Their 'light afflictions are but for a moment,' no more is the prosperity of the other. Compare it with eternity, and it is nothing. Θεοῖς πᾶν ἀνθρωπίνου βίου διάστημα τὸ μηδέν ἐστιν, to God, the whole space of a man's life is as nothing. What if the Lord were severe to his children for this moment, it is nothing to that everlasting kindness which they shall shortly meet with, but never be deprived of. He loves them here, but it is not fondness, or feminine tenderness, to let them have that which pleases them though it be hurtful. *Illos fortius amat*, it is a strong, a masculine love, which is to do them good, and keep them under sharp discipline, if nothing else will do it. But this will be needful but for a while, it is but for a moment.

The wicked, on the other side, they are under the sentence of condemnation. And what if he give them a little respite, and let them take some refreshment betwixt the sentence of death passed on them and the terrible execution? Alas! in a few moments they are to die, to die eternally. And is this such a forbearance, is this so great a favour, as to make it a question whether the proceeding do become the Ruler of the world, the Judge of heaven and earth!

3. This exception will have no force, can take no place, in those who believe a future judgment. The great Ruler of the world has several acts of government, which have their appointed times, and to which he proceeds gradually and regularly. Here in this life he gives his laws, and expects what observance they will meet with. He has reserved judgment and execution in distributing rewards and punishments till this life be ended; they are principally for another world. The Lord, in great wisdom, passes from one to another distinctly; but vain men would have these confounded and run into one another. They would see judgment before trial, and execution before the assizes; and crowns and rewards before the combat be ended, before the race be finished, before those who are to be judged have given full proof of themselves, Heb. ix. 27; Acts xvii. 31, 'Because he hath appointed a day, in the which he will judge the world,' &c. If he had not appointed such a day, and given assurance of it; if all things should proceed with good and bad to eternity, as they do for a little time: then there might be some more colour for this exception. But we would have all done here, and appoint the day presently, and so leave no work for the great day of his appointing. If the Lord should proceed with all here according as they are and do, περιττος ἦν ὁ τῆς κρίσεως λόγος, Isid. lib. v. epist. 215, the appointment of a future judgment would be in vain.

Stay but a while till things be ripe for judgment, or do but believe what God has given assurance of, that the Judge is at the door, and will speedily reward all according to their works, and then all will be clear. The day is at hand when God will fully vindicate his government, not only to the reason of men (as he does now), but to their senses, and then there will be no occasion to complain that those that are bad fare well, and those that are good fare worse. Then you will see the righteous ruler of the world making a vast and everlasting difference betwixt good and bad; and in the mean time you have as much reason to believe it as if you saw it now.

Use 1. For information. This serves to inform us in several things which much concern as in point of belief and practice. Particularly,

1. In reference to superiors, whether civil magistrates or church governors, or heads of families, or rulers of others in any capacity. Hereby we learn,

(1.) That all are subjects in respect of God. He rules over all, and therefore all are to acknowledge him as their sovereign, and themselves as subjected to him. The highest on earth are as much subjects to the great God as the meanest of their vassals are to them; and those, whoever they are, who consent not to this subjection, and demean not themselves accordingly, they are rebels to God, whatever they are amongst men. So he accounts them, and they may expect he will proceed answerably against them. So Saul, though a king, his not observing of God's command, is branded as rebellion, and aggravated as a crime equal to witchcraft and idolatry, 1 Sam. xv. 22, 23. They are to subject themselves to the sovereign of the world with trembling, and to serve him with fear, Ps. ii. 10, 11.

(2.) They are but officers in subordination to him; the highest of men, no more than under-officers. For he rules over all, and therefore is above all, and so there are none but who are under him. He alone is supreme, and the greatest are below him at an infinite distance; he is higher than the kings of the earth, Ps. lxxxix. 27, Eccles. v. 8. The higher powers are all under him, whose being ruler over all speaks him the Most High. It is no disparagement to the highest on earth, no, nor to the principalities and powers in heaven, to be counted his underlings.

(3.) All their authority is derived from him. If he rule over all, none have power to rule but what he gives and allows. None have any authority but whom he authorises. All subordinate officers derive their authority from the supreme magistrate; if they challenge or use any more, they usurp. He is the fountain of all authority; there is none in channel or cistern but what comes from the fountain, Rom. xiii. They have their commission from him; they have no more, no other power, than is contained in the commission which they have from the supreme governor of the world; what they act beyond it, against it, is no act of authority, but of presumption and usurpation.

(4.) All authority should be exercised for him; and that has no authority, whatever it be, which is not for him. He that is the original of all power in church, state, and families, must needs be the end of all, Rom. xi. 36, Heb. ii. 10. All is from him, and all is for him, who rules over all. That which is not for him is so far by no authority from him, for he gives no authority but for himself. What, then, is that which is against him? Any law, or order, or command, of powers higher or lower, which is against the will and interest of God, is no act of authority, for there is no authority but what the Lord gives; and to be sure he gives no authority against himself, Deut. i. 16, 17, 2 Chron. xix. 5–7.

(5.) Hence we may learn how we are to obey our superiors. He that rules over all must be first obeyed, and all others as they stand in relation to him. They are under him, and subordinate to him, and so must be obeyed in subordination to him, and no otherwise; never above him, never against him. When their wills not agreeing with his come in competition, then he who rules over all must have the pre-eminence in this case. The equity of it is so clear, we may appeal to the consciences of any who acknowledge the sovereignty of God, as the apostles did: Acts v. 29, 'We ought to obey God rather than men.' The case is more clear than if we should put it so, whether it be better to obey the prince or a constable, judge ye; for he that rules over all is infinitely more above the highest on earth, than the greatest monarch is above the meanest officer.

When any of the sons of men, whether magistrates, or pastors, or parents, or masters, enjoin us to neglect anything which is our duty, or do anything which is a sin; not to obey them is no disobedience to any authority, for none has the least authority to enjoin any such thing. God, who is the rise of all authority, never authorised them to require any such thing. Such injunctions, though they be the acts of such who are otherwise in authority, yet they are not authoritative acts, but private, or worse. And not to comply with them is not to disobey authority, but to disown usurpation upon and rebellion against him who rules over all; and none will question these but those that neither understand what God is nor man.

2. We may learn much hereby concerning the nature of sin; that which may lead us to hate it and fear it, and not only avoid, but mortify it; this will shew us how great a crime it is, how dangerous, how unreasonable.

(1.) How great a crime it is. It affronts the greatest authority in the world; it provokes the supreme Majesty of heaven and earth; it dishonours him who rules over all. That is a rule obvious to and acknowledged by all, the greater the person is whom we offend, the greater and more heinous is the offence: Τῇ ποιότητι τῶν προσώπων τὰ ἁμαρτήματα κρίνονται (says Chrysostom). We judge of offences by the quality of the persons offended. It is a crime (as he goes on) to injure a private person, but more criminal to offer an injury to a ruler. And still the greater the ruler is, the more heinous is the crime. How then does that crime rise, which strikes at the sovereign Majesty of the world; which offers injury to him who rules over all, in comparison of whom the greatest potentates on earth are but as grasshoppers! The greatness and heinousness of sin is unmeasurable, even as the greatness of that God whom it offends is incomprehensible. An offence against a king (says Isidore, lib. iv. epist. 179), κἂν μικρὰ γὰρ, though it be small, μεγάλα τῇ ἀξίᾳ τοῦ πεπονθότος κρίνεται, yet is judged great because of the dignity of him that suffers by it. What sin then can be small, which is directed against the great Ruler of all things? No sin can be little, being against such a Majesty, in comparison of whom all things, the greatest of all, are as nothing.

(2.) How dangerous it is. The violation of God's law must needs deserve a greater penalty than the violation of any laws of men; for what are all other lawgivers to him who gives laws to heaven and earth? or what is their authority to his who rules over all? To neglect the charge of a constable, is nothing to the crossing the edict of a mighty prince. What, then, is it to break the law of God, betwixt whom and the greatest prince the distance is incomparably greater than between the mightiest monarch on earth and the meanest officer!

And as the penalty is more grievous, so the inflicting of it is more certain and unavoidable, for he that rules all can order anything to do execution upon a sinner; and whither will ye fly from him who rules everywhere? or who can deliver you out of his hands who rules over all? Do ye provoke the Lord to jealousy? Are you stronger than he? What powers will you muster up to secure you from him who overpowers all? Will you 'call to the mountains and rocks to fall upon you, and hide you from the face of him that sitteth on the throne'? Oh, but he can cleave the rocks, and cause the mountains to melt like wax before him; for he rules over all, and rules irresistibly.

(3.) How unreasonable it is. He that ventures on sin, must do it without reason. Since God rules over all, there is nothing can be reasonably hoped for to draw to sin, there is nothing can rationally be feared to fright him to sin.

[1.] For fear. It is most unreasonable and absurd to fear where no fear is, and not to be afraid where there is most occasion of fear; but sin is most irrational both these ways. You are not afraid of God when you sin against him, when you do that which most provokes him; yet he is most to be feared, since he rules over all; for, upon this account,

First, He can make anything a suffering, even that which you most value, which you most affect, and that from which you have the greatest expectations, from which you look for the most comfort, the greatest security. He can order your greatest friends, your most endeared relations, your sweetest and most valued enjoyments, to be your sufferings and punishments, and can make you feel his indignation against sin, in and by any of them, or all of them. If he do but speak the word, that will be enough to turn them into quite other things than you account them; to make them your dangers, when you look they should succour you; to make them your grievances, when you look they should be the refreshments of your lives; to make them your tormentors, when you expect them to be your comforters. For everything must and will be, not what you think it is, but what he will order it to be; for he rules over all, and can overrule everything to be and do what he will, and to prove such to you as he pleases.

Secondly, As he can make anything to be a suffering, so he can make any suffering to be most grievous. He can make anything prove an affliction, and he can make any affliction, even that which you make lightest of, to be intolerable. He can put a hell into anything, and can make that which you count but a spark to give you the tortures of the most dreadful flames, and can order that which you think you can go lightly under to sink and crush you; for he rules all, and everything obeys the order that he gives it. That which seems little will prove great, a greater affliction and calamity than you imagine; and that which seems light will be too heavy to be borne, if he who rules over all will so dispose of it.

Thirdly, He can make all things to be his executioners. He can employ any of them in heaven, or earth, or hell—those that can do you most mischief, or that you are most in danger of, most obnoxious to, most afraid of —and can give any of them commission to inflict his wrath for sin; yea, or if need were, he could employ them all together to make the sinner miserable. There is not any of them would decline the employment if he laid a command upon them, they would all concur together to pour out his indignation, if he did but give them order; for he rules over all, and can overpower all to do his pleasure.

Oh, what madness is it to sin against such a God; to provoke him who rules over all! If sin did not bewitch men, if it did not deprive them even of the ordinary use of reason, they would never venture to sin upon any consideration; since there is that in sin, which, if considered, is so dreadful, as to outweigh whatever may be put in the balance against it, as if it were nothing. Particularly, how little or nothing is there in the fear of man, if weighed, to sway any to sin against this great Ruler of the world? To fear man, in this case, is to be afraid, where there is no cause to fear. For,

First, What need he fear man, or any creature, or all of them together, who is under the protection of him who rules over all? What is it to be under the protection of him, who can dispose of all things in the world for your safety, who can order anything to secure you against the rage and violence of all? What need he fear, who stands for him, who has all things that may endanger or secure him at his beck and command? While you refuse to sin, you stand for God; and while you are for him, he is for you. And what stands he for, who rules over all? If you know him, you will make account, that all other things, if they should be all set against you, stand but for cyphers. They are no more, when set against him who overrules and overpowers all. For,

Secondly, They can do nothing, more or less, against you, without him; nothing without his permission, without his power, without his concurrence. Balaam had as great a mind to do Israel a mischief as any, being under the power of such temptations to do it, as most suited his corrupt temper; but for all that, he professes he could do nothing at all, Num. xxii. 17, 18, beyond the word of the Lord. What if those whom you displease, by refusing to sin against God, be as fierce as lions, yet the Lord is the keeper, he has them fast; they cannot come near you, unless he let them loose. If you provoke him to let them loose upon you, there is danger; but the danger is in offending him, not them. It is he, therefore, that is to be feared, not they. If they should break loose, he can break their teeth, or maim their paws, or disarm them of their strength, and make them as weak or as tame as you would have them; or can call them in with a word when they are running upon you with open teeth. If he do but say, *Down, sirrah!* the fiercest of them cannot so much as wag, will not dare to move in the least against you. One word of the great Ruler of the world will make them crouch and lie at your feet, and fawn upon you, instead of tearing and devouring you. And is it reasonable then to offend God, who has such command over them, for fear of them, who can no way stir or move without him?

Thirdly, If they should be permitted to do all they can against you, yet that is little or nothing, in comparison of what he can do, whom you incense by sin. They can but only touch your bodies or outward concernments; but he is Ruler over all. He has dominion, not only over your bodies and estates, but over your souls; and he can order and dispose of them unto everlasting miseries or happiness as he pleases. It is but a little that you hazard, a very inconsiderable thing, for an inconsiderable time, by offending men; but you hazard all, and all to eternity, by sinning against God; and that is so great and dreadful a hazard, so much in all reason to be feared, as should swallow up all fear and respect of the other, Luke xii. 5. To sin against God to avoid any danger from men, is to fear him who can do no more than 'kill the body,' and not to fear him who can 'destroy both body and soul in hell;' which is, as if a man, to escape a shower of rain, should throw himself into the sea. Is that the way not to be wet? Or, as if one, to save the scorching of his clothes, should throw himself headlong into the fire. You would think the fear which put a man upon such a course were absurd indeed, and such as became none but a distracted person: no more reasonable, no more void of madness, is any fear that drives a man to provoke him who is Ruler over all.

[2.] Nor are the hopes more reasonable which may be made use of, to allure us to sin against this great God. In that he is ruler over all, it appears that all such hopes are vain and delusive, and such as grossly abuse the souls of men.

Particularly, *first*, can ye hope for secrecy? Oh, but how or where can ye be secret in respect of God? He that rules over all rules everywhere; and so, not only his presence, but his ruling power, is in every place. It is in every quarter, in every corner of the whole world. It reaches from the highest heaven to the centre of the earth, yea, to the bottom of hell, Ps. cxxxix. 7, 8, &c. Nothing, no place, is out of the eye, or in the least distance from the ruling hand of God. If you will presume to be anywhere secret, or to act, or speak, or think, anything secretly in respect of God, you must find out a place where he rules not. If you dig into the bowels of the earth for a retirement, or dive into the bottom of the sea, or withdraw as far from all company as heaven is from earth, or cover yourselves with as thick darkness as any is in hell, all will be in vain: not only his over-seeing eye will be upon you, but his all-ruling hand will be with you, wherever you are, or whithersoever you go. The darkest, the closest, the remotest retirement, is no more out of his presence, no more out of the reach and stroke of his all-ruling power, than the most open or public place in heaven or earth.

Or, *secondly*, do ye hope for pleasure in sinning against God? Oh that word, *against God*, is enough to dash all hopes. Will he suffer you to have any true pleasure in displeasing him, who can and does order all things as he will? He rules over all, and so rules all the concernments of pleasure or pain, of grief and delight, and can dispose of them as he pleases. He can make that which you fancy to be the greatest pleasure in the world, to prove the bitterest thing that ever you meddled with, and can not only embitter the act or object which you count delightful, but can so order it, as it shall turn all you have besides into bitterness, and make all your other enjoyments as gall and wormwood. No art can prepare so bitter infusions as that hand that rules all. Ask Cain what that pleasure proved which he took in satisfying his malice. It was such a delight as made his life a burden to him ever after, Gen. iv. 13. Ask Amnon what that pleasure proved which he had in defiling Tamar; or Zimri, in the Moabitish woman; they would tell you the bitterness of death was in it. Ask David what pleasure his lust afforded him; he will tell you, such as a man takes in having his bones broken, Ps. li. 8. If you fancy such pleasure as this, you may have it in sin here, and that which is more intolerable hereafter; but if you look for better, you are like to be deceived, so long as God rules over all.

Or, *thirdly*, do you hope to gain by sin, or to get any advantage in unlawful ways? This hope is as vain and unreasonable as the other. If God rule over all, and all actions and events be ordered by him, you can get no gain without him. If he order it, it will be either in mercy or in wrath. To hope that he will order anything in mercy, which is got by dishonouring him, is a madness; and if you have it in wrath, it is such an advantage as you may wish the worst of your enemies, if you might wish them that which will prove the greatest mischief. What gained Achan, by his wedge of gold? or Judas, by his pieces of silver? or Ananias, by his sinful saving? No more will you gain really by sin, whatever show of advantage there may be. It will prove no better than the coal which the eagle stole, which though she thought a booty, yet it served only to fire her nest. If God rule over all, and order everything as he pleases, what can be the matter of your hope? To look that he should order that to answer your expectation, which lies directly cross to his will, is as unreasonable as what is most so. And thus you see how absurd and irrational an evil sin is, since it can be promoted by no fears, by no hopes, but what are without or against all reason.

Use 2. For exhortation. If the Lord rule over all, let us give up ourselves to be ruled by him. His ruling power and dignity calls for this subjection; and let us be ruled by him, and subject to him, in all things. The extent of his dominion calls for this. He not only rules, but rules over all. Let me insist upon this a little distinctly.

1. The Lord rules, therefore we ought to be ruled by him, and to resign up ourselves to the government of God. He stands in relation to us as our ruler; this obliges us to subject ourselves to him. Let us give our consent to be his subjects, and shew our subjection by all obedience; and for the manner of it, our subjection should be answerable to his dominion. We must submit to him, not only as a ruler, but as to such a ruler as the Lord is.

(1.) We must be subject to him as supreme. The higher the authority, the greater must the subjection be. Now, God is the sovereign Lord of the world; all other governors rule but under him, and for him, in his name, and by his authority. Those whom the apostle calls ἐξουσίαι ὑπερέχουσαι, transcendent powers, they are, in reference to the supreme Ruler of the world, but διάκονοι and λειτουργοί, Rom. xiii. 4, 6, 'ministers of God,' such as officiate under him. We are to be subject to them for his sake, but subject to him for himself, ver. 7. The greatest tribute, fear, honour, to the greatest and most supreme Ruler. The highest power should have the most submissive subjection.

(2.) We must be subject to him absolutely. For his government is absolute, and has no bounds nor limits, but his own will. Our subjection must be answerable, without reserve, without limitation; extending as far as the will of God, yielding to every part of it, not excepting any particular, great or small; whatsoever he would have us do, or suffer, or part with. We must yield to his will, whenever he signifies it, without questioning the reason or equity of it, or excepting against it for any seeming difficulty or danger, however it cross our humours, or carnal inclination, or worldly interest. It must be in all things correspondent to what they profess in one particular, Jer. xlii. 5, 6. 'Whether it be good, or whether it be evil, we will obey the voice of the Lord our God.' We must not say, I will submit to his will in this or that; but as for such and such, which are so hard, or hazardous, or reproachful, or expensive, I must be excused. This is not the voice of one that is truly subject to God, but of a man that would rule himself, and be no further in subjection than he list.

(3.) We must subject ourselves to him freely and cheerfully. He that rules all irresistibly should meet with no resistance, no opposition from us. He that rules all easily should find us easily yielding to his whole will, without any backwardness or reluctancy. We should shew that we will be ruled with a word, with a beck, with a look from God; for so he rules the rest of the world. We should not put the Lord to use force, to take the rod, or bring us to it, as we do those that are stubborn, by foul means. None of his commandments should seem grievous to us, for they are not so in themselves, 1 John v. 3. We should not need to be drawn or haled to it, but run of our own accord, Ps. cxix. We have a great example for it: Heb. x. 7, 'Lo, I come to do thy will, O God.' Ps. xl. 8, 'I delight to do thy will; thy law is in my heart.' It is in my heart to observe thy whole law. Thy will is not only in the written laws, but in my heart; there is that *within* which freely answers all thy laws *without*.

(4.) We must be in subjection continually. Not submit to him only by fits, and in a good mood, but live, as constantly under his government, his state and relation. As a ruler [he] abides for ever, and therefore so does our relation as subjects. We are not obliged only to some acts of obedience, but are continued in a state of subjection to him; his laws are always in force, and therefore should have observance every moment. He ever rules, and therefore we should be ever obeying. Our whole life should be an uninterrupted course of obedience, and a continued testimony of our subjection to him who reigns for ever and ever. The Lord will own no other as loyal subjects, but those whose subjection and obedience is continued, John viii. 31. If you continue in subjection to my word and will, then are ye my subjects indeed, not otherwise. He will reward no other subjects, Gal. iii. 10, James i. 25. So much for the first, 'He rules;' therefore we must be subject, and our subjection should be correspondent to his dominion.

2. *He rules over all*, therefore we should be ruled by him in all. We should resign up all to be governed by him; we should give up all that is within us, all that belongs to us, to be ordered and disposed of as he would have it. Not any faculty, not any motion, not any part, not any act, not any enjoyment, not any affair should be by us exempted from his government, but all given up to be ruled by him, whose prerogative it is to rule over all.

1. Let him rule our minds, and all the powers thereof.

(1.) Our understanding. Let them be ready to learn of him, and be taught by him, and shew their subjection by being teachable and tractable in all matters of divine revelation. Whatever he declares to be true, let the understanding yield to it, close with it, embrace it as a divine truth, though we cannot penetrate the depth of it, nor discern the mode of it, nor reach the reason of it. Let it be captivated to the authority of God, declaring his mind and truth, so as to make no question of it, nor yield to any arguings against it, but to take his word for the truth of it, without further dispute, admitting no wisdom nor understanding against the Lord.

(2.) Our judgment. Let them be ruled by his judgment. Let us judge those things to be contemptible which he has declared to be so, whoever have high esteem of them, as the things of the world, riches, pleasures, honour, greatness; let us judge those things to be excellent, and worthy of all esteem, which he has commended to us, whoever despise them, as mortifiedness, holiness in its strength, life, exercise, and the gospel and means which tend to promote it; let us rather count those dogs and swine who trample upon these than question the judgment which the Lord has passed upon them; let us judge that to be most hateful and dreadful, which he has so represented to us: sin, more hateful, more dreadful than poverty, or slavery, or any affliction, or the greatest suffering whatsoever; and shew that our judgments are ruled by God, in demeaning ourselves towards these accordingly, as Moses did, Heb. xi. 24, 25. Let us judge those things more worthy to be our design and business which the Lord has commended to us as most worthy to be so, than those to which the generality of the world do give the pre-eminence. Heaven, and the things above, and the concernments of eternity, should be our design and business, if we will submit to the judgment of God. If we will rather follow the judgment of the carnal and sensual world, in preferring the things of time and sense, and the concernments of this present life, as fittest to be made our great work and business, we shew we are not those who will be ruled by God in our judgment of things.

(3.) Our thoughts. If we will have him rule over all, we must endeavour to bring every thought into captivity and subjection to him, 2 Cor. x. 5. Let those thoughts be stifled which the Lord will have suppressed; those rejected, which he would have excluded, Jer. iv. 14. Let those be entertained, which he would have admitted; and those cherished, which he would have abide in us, Ps. cxxxix. 17, 18. Everything, even to a thought, should be ordered as he would have it, if we will observe him as he ought to be observed, who rules over all.

2. Let him rule our wills. Here especially should the throne of God be erected and established, as rulers choose their royal seats in the places which are most advantageous for the government of the rest. If the will be in subjection to God, all will submit to his government; but if this be not subdued to him, nothing will be subjected to him to any purpose, Prov. xxiii. 26. This, above all, is that upon which all the rest depend. He that must have his own will is no subject of God's; they that are truly subjected to him, his will is theirs. 'Not my will, but thine be done,' said our great pattern. When the will lies prostrate before God, and wholly applies itself to his will, then does all yield to his dominion. 'Lord, what wilt thou have me to do?' was the first act of subjection which Saul paid to the universal sovereign. It must be enough to sway you in any case whatsoever, to know that it is the will of God.

Particularly (1.) the will should be ruled by him in its inclinations. We should be careful that the heart incline to those objects, and no other; in that way, and no otherwise than the Lord would have them. What objects he has set before us, and commended to us as fit objects for our wills; to these they should incline, shewing averseness to any other; his will should be the line in which they move, and by which they are regulated. They must stop or advance at every signification of his pleasure; and beware of any bias from self, or the world, which may make them turn aside from the right way, or from their due objects.

(2.) In elections or refusals. When we are deliberating what means must be used for the accomplishing of any end before us, the will of God must still preponderate, and always cast the scale. The means must be pitched on which the Lord offers, and which have warrant from his will; not those which eagerness after the desired end, or hastiness to be eased of some present grievance, or carnal wisdom or example, or the seeming success of others, or our own commends to us.

(3.) In our ends and intentions. These must be so under his government, as no ends must be aimed at, but what the Lord propounds to us. The serving, and pleasing, and enjoying, and honouring of God must be our last and chief ends; none but in subordination to these, none but what will serve and promote these.

Not the pleasing, or advancing, or securing of ourselves or others, or anything else, must be our end; but in the second place, and in subserviency to those which the Lord has made supreme; of which we have frequent mention, Col. i. 10, 1 Thes. ii. 4, 1 John iii. 22, 1 Cor. x. 31, 1 Pet. iv. 11. To aim at this as the principal, and at none at all which will not serve this, nor at any that may serve it but in a subserviency to it, is the best character of a loyal subject to the King of kings, and a clear evidence that the will is in due subjection to the great Sovereign of the world.

3. The conscience must be ruled by him. This must be subjected to him, and to him alone; for he alone is the Lord of the conscience. It is the will of God that obliges conscience; and this should suffer itself to be bound up by it, as nothing else should oblige or disoblige it but the will of him who rules over all. Though it be the freest faculty, and the most exempted from the control of any other authority, yet in all its acts and offices it must be in full subjection to God. Whether it oblige or impel, it must do it by virtue of his authority and will; whether it discern or direct, it must do it by his light and direction; whether it accuse or acquit, it must do it according to his order and sentence. It must demean itself in all as his vicegerent. Βροτὸς ἡ συνείδησις Θεός. Conscience is God's deputy, and must in the exercise of this office confine itself to the orders and instructions of its sovereign Lord, he who rules all.

4. The affections must be ruled and ordered by him, and must receive law from him, as to their objects, and degree, and order.

(1.) The affections must have no other object, but what he proposes and directs them to. We should love nothing, but what he would have us love, 1 John ii. 15. We should fear nothing, but what he would have us to fear, no, not those things which we are naturally afraid of, Rev. ii. 10, Mat. x. 26, 28, Isa. viii. 12, 13. So we must desire nothing which he would have us to avoid; nor mourn for anything, but what he has made the matter of our grief; nor let anything be our hope or expectation, but what he has made so, Ps. lxii. 5.

(2.) For the degree. He has assigned it, and the assignment must be observed. The affections are the waves, the motions of the heart, and he has said to them, as to those of the sea, 'Hitherto shalt thou come, but no farther.' And we should labour to keep them within the prescribed bounds. The Lord himself should be loved above all, in the highest degree, Mat. xxii. 37. To other things he has assigned a far lower degree of affection: Mat. x. 37, 'He that loveth them more;' *i. e.* he that loveth them anything near so much; he that loveth them not much less. In the other evangelist it is, 'He that hateth them not,' Luke xiv. 26. We are to love God, *in toto valde*, Deut. vi. 5, בכל מאדך, 'with all thy vehemency;' but other things must be affected with some indifferency, 1 Cor. vii. 29, 30.

(3.) For the order of our affections, that must be such as the Lord has disposed it. He must be loved for himself; all other things must be no otherwise affected, but for his sake; either because they come from him, or lead to him, or are some way like him, or help us the better to serve him; always for some respect to him, so that he must be the end and the rise of our affection in all things which we affect. To love anything, or desire it, or delight in it for itself, is to advance it into the place of God; and this is quite opposite to that subjection which is due to the Lord, and an open perverting of that order which he has set for our affections, and which must be carefully observed by those that will be subject to him.

I shall but briefly touch the rest, having stayed longer on these particulars than I intended.

The *fancy* must be ruled by him, the vanity of it corrected, and the vagaries of it restrained by the awe of his authority.

The *appetite* must be kept under his government. It must not be indulged in anything that may prove an occasion of sin or disservice to God. A straiter hand should be kept over it, that it bring in no provisions to the flesh. Those that feed themselves without fear, Jude 13, are unmindful of the subjection they owe to God; nay, the appetite should not be pleased, but for the better pleasing of our sovereign Lord; not for the sensual delight itself, but to make us more cheerful in his service, and better disposed for our work, and more affected to the spring of all that pleases us.

The *senses* also must be kept under his rule and order, who rules over all. We should not touch, nor taste, nor handle, nor look, but as he would have us. Such a covenant as Job made with his eyes, Job iii. 1, should be made with all our senses, to oblige them to that subjection and observance which everything and part of us owes to the universal sovereign.

The whole *body* should be wholly ruled by him, Rom. xii. 1. Service is the greatest subjection, and the body should be offered up in such service. It is λογικὴ λατρεία, reasonable, most agreeable to reason, that it should be given up in such subjection; or it is that which the word requires, so λογικὴ may signify. It is *secundum os verbi*, as the Syriac renders it, according to the mouth of the word; it is (as all acceptable service and worship must be) prescribed by the word. The Lord, in his word, does require, that not only the soul, but the body, should be in such subjection to him, as to be wholly at his service.

The *body*, and every part of it. To instance only in the principal; the tongue should not move, but as he would have it, and that it may not, the like course should be taken with it, as David took. He knew 'the tongue is an unruly member,' so he puts it under the government of God, Ps. cxli. 3. He would have it so watched and guarded as nothing might issue out but what pleased the Lord. The hands, Ps. cxix. 48, the employment of our hands should be that which he commands.

Finally, all our *ways*; every step should be ordered according to that rule which he has enjoined us to walk by: Ps. cxix. 133, 'Order my steps in thy word.' In the disposing of our affairs, in the improving of our talents, in the employing of our estates, we should consult with him how he would have all ordered; and when we know his will, that should be a law to us, a law worthy in our account of so much more observance than any other, as he is superior to all.

And so I have shewed you how we are to subject ourselves to God, and to give up all to be ruled by him, since he rules over all. Now, to persuade you to resign yourselves and your all to be governed by him, let me add something by way of motive.

1. Take notice of the necessity of it. He is the ruler of the world, and will be; he will not lose his right, nor can any deprive him of it, nor hinder him from exercising his universal authority; he has power enough to make

it good against the opposition of ten thousand worlds ; he would cease to be God, if he should cease to be the ruler of all things. And, therefore, as sure as he is God, he will rule you one way or other. If you will not consent that he should be your ruler, you shall find him rule you whether you will or no. Even those that are so much addicted to sin, as to be enemies to his government, maugre all they can do to decline it, shall feel the power of it ; for he will rule even in the midst of his enemies, Ps. cx. 2. If you will not stoop to his gracious sceptre, he will crush you with a rod of iron, Ps. ii., Rev. xii. 5 ; if you will not submit to his ruling power, he will bring you under his feet, 1 Cor. xv. 15 ; if you will not consent to be ordered by his laws in all things, he will exercise his dominion and authority over you, by inflicting the dreadful penalty of his disobeyed laws, Isa. i. 19, 20. You may be under such a government as to be subject to it is more desirable than the greatest dominion in the world ; but if you refuse this, he will rule you in a terrible manner, and threatens it with an oath that you may be sure of it, Ezek. xx. 33.

2. Consider the equity of it. The Lord is in all right the ruler of all things ; he has all right to rule over you. You are his creatures, you are the work of his hands, he made you of nothing ; you are more his own than anything is yours that your hands ever made, than anything is yours that you count most your own. And shall not the Lord have the ordering and disposing of that which is his own, so much his own ? When you are so absolutely, so wholly his, will you not be ordered and ruled by him ? This is such iniquity to God, such injurious dealing with the Most High, as the whole frame of the world may be astonished at ; and accordingly the Lord seems to appeal to heaven and earth against it, Isa. i. 2, 3. The ox knows his owner, will be ordered and ruled by him, but those over whom the Lord has much more dominion, and who are far more his own, and whom he has much more obliged, they will not be subject to him, nor ruled by him, they rebel. This is such unequal, such injurious carriage towards God, as the very lifeless and senseless creatures may well abhor it—heaven and earth may be astonished at it.

3. Consider the advantages you may be sure of by subjecting yourselves to God ; they are great and many. I shall but instance in two or three.

(1.) You will be under the protection of God. And the advantage of this is answerable to the greatness of him who obliges himself to vouchsafe it. It is above all other, because the Lord rules over all. A prince owes protection to his subjects, and is obliged to secure them, both from private injustice and open violence ; while they submit to his government they ought to be secured by it, he is the minister of God for that end, Rom. xiii. And will not the Lord protect those who submit to his government ? He is infinitely more able to do it, because he rules over all, and he is no less willing ; his relation to them as their ruler gives assurance of this. He is concerned in point of honour that those who will live under his government should live there safely ; that those who will be ruled by him should not suffer for it. It is the glory of his kingdom that, as it rules over all, so the true subjects of it should be safe above all, Isa. xxxiii. 15, 16. Those who shew themselves the subjects of God by observing his laws in such dangers as threatened Judea, in Sennacherib's invasion, he will take care they shall be secured. Though they dwell in the plain, most exposed, they shall be as safe as if their habitation were on high, above the reach of danger. He will be to them as a munition of rocks, an impregnable fort, such as can neither be battered nor undermined, such as need neither fear forcing nor starving. Hezekiah could secure one of his subjects from the violence of another, but he knew not how to secure them against the Assyrians. Oh, but the Lord can secure his subjects against all the powers of the world, against all the powers of darkness. He who rules over all can overpower all. He has the whole *posse* of the universe, and can raise it when and for whatever purpose he will; the whole militia of heaven and earth is at his beck and command.

He has provided such a guard for each of his faithful subjects as will secure them not only against all the force on earth, but all the power of hell, Ps. xxxiv. 7. There is an host of angels encamp about those that fear him. All the guards that princes have are nothing to this. Any one of this host is more than a whole army, can destroy the greatest army of men in a moment, Isa. xxxvii. 36. Such attendance, such security will the Lord afford his subjects, wherever they are, in all their ways, Ps. xci. 9–12.

(2.) He will take care of all your concernments. He that rules over all, can and will order and dispose of all your affairs for you. You need not be careful and solicitous about them. He that rules over all, if you be willing to have all ordered by him, is willing to take the care of all your concerns upon himself, Philip. iv. 6, 7. When you are apt to be perplexed about the public, or your private affairs, or those of your posterity, address yourselves to him by a petition, take but the course which he has prescribed you, and so leave all to him who rules all, who has provided that hereby you have such tranquillity and quietness of mind and heart as will free you from all anxiety and trouble.

Oh what a privilege, what an advantage is it to be a subject to such a ruler! Those that will be ruled by him may not only be freed from danger, but from all care and trouble; he will have this lie upon himself, not upon his subjects, 1 Peter v. 5, 7. Do but humble, do but submit yourselves to him, as becomes the subjects of so great a Lord, and then you need care no more, he will take all the care for you, and so takes it all off from you, Ps. lv. 22. Is anything too heavy for thee? Such is the indulgence of thy sovereign Lord, he would in no wise have thee burdened, he would rather have thee cast it upon him. He who rules all with ease can as easily bear all, and he is willing to bear all, rather than any of his subjects should be burdened with anything.

Who would not be subject to such a Lord? Who would not resign up himself to such a government, where the ruler is ready to bear all himself, and will lay nothing that is heavy, leave nothing that is grievous, upon any subject of his? And that you may not doubt but the Lord is willing to ease you of all care and trouble, know further, that he counts it a disparagement to his government to have you solicitous and troubled about the things which he undertakes to rule and order, for what does it signify but that the Lord either is not able or not willing to order them for the best, and as they should be ordered? And by doubting of this you impeach the excellency of his government, or entrench upon it; as if you said, if you were able you would order things otherwise, as though you knew how to govern better. Hence, when Melancthon was extremely solicitous about the affairs of the church in his days, Luther would have him admonished in these terms, *Monendus est Philippus ut desinat esse rector mundi*, Let not Philip make himself any longer governor of the world. When we ease ourselves of cares and fears by casting them upon God, we acknowledge his government, and acquiesce in it, rest pleased and satisfied with it; and this being much for his honour, there is no doubt but he is willing thus to ease us of our burdens, by rolling all upon him who rules over all.

The government is upon his shoulders, he is sufficient for it; let him alone with it. Trouble not yourselves about either public or personal concernments; if you be his subjects indeed, you will find him disposing of all for the best; he will order them better for you than you can do for yourselves, he will order them better than you can think. When you or others have run affairs into such disorder as you cannot expect that anything but evil and mischief will be the issue thereof, yet he can retrieve all, and either prevent the evil or turn it into good. Yea, he not only can, but will, so overrule it, for those that are willing to be ruled by him: Rom. viii. 28, 'All things shall work together for good to them that love God.' Who can make all things thus to work but he that rules over all? It is he that can set all on work, and make them work together, concur jointly (though the severals be of quite other tendencies) for the good of his subjects. And he will do it, for his government is not domination or tyranny, which respects only the interest of the ruler, without regard of the subject's good, for that is the difference between tyrannical and regular government; Ἡ μὲν τύραννις πρὸς τὸ οἰκεῖον, a tyrant minds his own pleasure, profit, and greatness, (Isid. lib. iii., Ep. 194). Ἡ δὲ βασιλεία πρὸς τὸ τῶν ἀρχομένων συμφέρον βλέπει, but lawful government minds the good of the subject. Though the Lord be absolute, and infinitely above those whom he rules, and expects no advantage by them, yet so far he condescends as to order all things for the good of those who are truly subject to him. He has made such a connection betwixt his glory and their happiness, as whatsoever advances his honour tends to promote their happiness. And in his government of the world he disposes of all things accordingly. Do but subject yourselves to him, and give up yourselves to be wholly ruled by him, and you will find that he takes such care of all your concernments as to order them far better for you than you can or would dispose of them by your own prudence or the assistance of others, if they were left to be ordered by yourselves, or ruled as you would have them.

(3.) He makes all his subjects to be kings. Every one that will be ruled by him shall have the honour and power of a king, Exod. xix. 5, 6. If you will be subject to me, and shew it by obeying my voice and observing my laws, ye shall be 'a kingdom of priests,' *i.e.* ye shall be both 'kings and priests,' as it is expressed, Rev. i. 6. The same thing expressed in another phrase, 1 Peter ii. 9, βασίλειον ἱεράτευμα, 'a kingly priesthood,' *i.e.* not only priests, but kings. Amongst all nations the greatest dignity and honour was that of kings and priests. And this honour have all that will be subjects to God; they are not only priests to offer up spiritual sacrifice to God, but kings, and kings not only hereafter in heaven, but here on earth, Rev. v. 10, 'Hast made us unto our God kings and priests, and we shall reign on the earth.' Kings, you may say! Alas, they seem far from any such thing on earth! Where, or how, or over what do they reign? Why, they reign over that to which the greatest kings (that will not be subject to God) are miserably enslaved. They reign over sin, over their lusts and passions, which are the rulers and commanders of the princes of the earth. While they seem to rule all, they are in bondage and slavery to the corruptions of their hearts, they reign no otherwise but as serving divers lusts; and this is a more woeful bondage and servitude than that of a galley slave. While they take upon them the government of others, they cannot so much as govern themselves, but are at the command and under the power of their own passions and lusts. But he that will be subject to God, sin shall not have dominion over him; he shall subdue it, and be above the power of it, which is a royalty which few princes can glory in. He shall have power to govern himself, and to rule his passions, and corrupt inclinations, which are too unruly for the greatest on earth.

He shall reign over the world too; he shall overcome it, 1 John v. 4; he shall be above the pleasures, and profits, and greatness, and honours of it, by which it tyranniseth over the mightiest potentates; he shall have those under his feet which rule in the very hearts of others, Rev. xii. 1. This is a royal power indeed, and peculiar to those who resign up themselves to be governed by God. Here is power, and honour, and royalty in the greatest reality: Βασιλεία, πλοῦτος καὶ δόξα, ὀνόματα μὲν παρὰ τοῖς ἔξωθεν. Kingdom, and riches, and glory are but names amongst those that are without, πράγματα δὲ παρὰ Χριστιανοῖς, but the realities are theirs who are subject to Christ.

Oh what a temptation is a kingdom to the heart of man! What will he not do, or hazard, or suffer? What blood will he not shed, what ruins will he not make, to get or keep an earthly kingdom? Why, here you may have one upon easier and better terms, and such an one as is the greatest reality. Those of the world are but nominal kingdoms in comparison of it. Give but up yourselves to the government of God, and you shall reign indeed; he makes all his subjects kings; you shall reign here in the excellent way expressed, and you shall reign for ever and ever in immortal glory.

4. Consider the excellency of it in some particulars.

(1.) The excellency of the ruler derives some dignity upon the subject. The greater and more eminent a prince is, the more honour it is to be related to him, even as a subject. What honour is it then to be so related to him, whose glory is above the heavens! It is really a greater excellency for kings to be his subjects, than it is otherwise that they are kings. The angels would not exchange their subjection to God for a dominion over the world. Ἡγούμενος ἀρχὴν εἶναι μεγίστην τὸ ἀρχεῖν ἑαυτοῦ δύνασθαι τό τον λογισμὸν τῷ θυμῷ καὶ ταῖς ἡδοναῖς ἐπιστῆσαι, (Isidor. Ep. 223, lib. 3). The Queen of Sheba counted it a happiness to be a servant to such a prince as Solomon, 1 Kings x. 8; what is it then to be subjected to him, in comparison of whom Solomon, in all his glory, and wisdom, and magnificence, was but as a worm? She adds, ver. 9, 'Because the Lord loved Israel for ever, therefore made he thee king.' It is for none but those whom the Lord loves, and has a particular favour for, to be in special subjection to such a sovereign as rules over all. Μέγα γὰρ ὄντως ἀξίωμα (says Chrysostom), δοῦλον εἶναι τοῦ Χριστοῦ καὶ μὴ φαίνεσθαι: it is a great dignity indeed to be a servant of Christ; a subject of God really, and not in appearance only.

(2.) This will make way for Christ's reign upon earth; so that all the kingdoms of the world might become the kingdoms of the Lord, and of his Christ. If all would consent to be his subjects, there would be nothing to hinder him from reigning. There has been a great debate whether Christ shall personally appear and reign on earth in the latter days; I will determine nothing concerning that question, *pro* or *con*, only what my subject leads me to. If Christ should appear on earth in person; yet if the inhabitants of the world would no more subject themselves unto God than they do now, it cannot be expected that they should treat him better than when he was on earth before. Holiness, we see, is persecuted everywhere, the image of Christ is generally hated and scorned. And if he be thus used in effigy, in that which is but like him; if his resemblance cannot escape scorn and violence, how would he be used in person by those who are so far from affectionate subjection to him, as they shew a high antipathy to anything that is like him? The beast that has such antipathy to man, as to fly upon his picture wherever he sees it, would much more tear the man himself. Oh, but those who hate holiness are his professed enemies. He has many that profess themselves to be his friends, and they sure would give him better entertainment; no, even from these he would have no good entertainment, further than they have before subjected themselves unto God. For some there were, when he appeared on earth formerly, who passionately longed for his appearance, professed themselves to be his people, his subjects, his own peculiarly; and yet when he came, they would not own him, John i. 11.

Nay, those who are his own indeed, and not only seem and profess to be so, and such as bear his image, and partake in some degree of his Spirit, unless they be yet further subjected unto God than now they appear to be, are in danger not to give Christ due entertainment. The most probable way that I can find, to judge how they would receive Christ, is to observe how they receive one another, Mat. x. 40. Those who agree in all essentials of Christ's doctrine, and walk by the same rules in practicals, and discern the image of Christ in one another, yet if they differ from one another in matters of less amount, this we see is enough to take down their esteem of them, to abate their affection. This is enough to cause contention and division, to occasion distances and estrangements, and to draw them to evil surmising, and evil speaking, and ill treatments of one another. And why will not these differences have the like effect on them towards Christ, as towards one another, if he be found to differ as much or more from them, as they do amongst themselves? And it is most certain that he will differ from them all, since he is the truth, and they every of them err in some, yea, in many things. So that unless there be more subjection of mind and heart unto God than is yet effected, if Christ should appear, he is like to be no better entertained by his own people than a dissenter, than one that differs from them in such things too for which their minds and hearts are much engaged; and what entertainment such a dissenter is like to have, you may judge by what you see amongst yourselves.

But some may say, Christ's appearing will be in such a way and manner as all will be ready to receive him. I answer, so did the Jews think of old concerning his first coming, and were confident of it upon the same grounds, viz., the ancient prophecies upon which others now do raise this confidence, and yet they being not duly subjected to God, that event proved quite contrary to their confident expectations; they, instead of receiving him, did oppose him to the death, and those who had the greatest expectations of him proved his greatest enemies.

Indeed, if Christ should appear in such a way as to bring all into a full and voluntary subjection to him, then he would have a due reception in the world; but the foundation of such an entertainment would be that subjection which I am calling for; this is that upon which his glorious reign so much depends. The more you subject yourselves in mind, heart, and life, to the government of God, the more you prevail with in the world to give up themselves to it, the more you promote the kingdom of Christ, and the clearer and the more open do you make the way for its coming; but without this you do nothing towards it, no, nor they who in other ways fancy they do most, without this, they rather hinder than advance it. If Christ should appear on earth, yet without this subjection to him, his kingdom would not be advanced in the world; and if he should not appear personally, yet if the inhabitants of the earth did but thus subject themselves to him, he would reign gloriously.

(3.) This tends to rectify all the disorders of the world, whereby it is become a place of affliction and calamity, of confusion and misery to the sons of men. So far as we can prevail for this subjection unto God, so far will all grievances be redressed, and all things reduced from the miserable posture wherein they now are, to that lovely order and happy constitution which at first they had. The Lord at first created all things in admirable order, and in a direct tendency to the use, and comfort, and happiness of man. How did they fall into such woful disorders, as they now rather tend to be his afflictions, and grievances, and calamities? Why, all this fell out by man's departing from his subjection to God; that was the first disorder, upon which all things else fell into these woful confusions; and so far as man returns to that subjection, so far will all be reduced towards their primitive serviceableness to his comfort and happiness.

The world is now like a body, all whose parts and members are broken and out of joint; the parts which served it before being disjointed, do now afflict it, and what was helpful and comfortable before, is now painful and grievous. Now, all was broken and put out of joint, as to man, by his fall from his submission to him who rules over all; and the woful issues of this misplacing and unjointing of things will continue, uselessness and painfulness will remain till they be set in joint again; and there is no setting of them further than man is brought back to his proper place, and set in due subjection to God. If this were once fully done, the world would have a new face, and those things in it which ensnare and endanger you would be your security; and those which trouble, and pain, and afflict you, would be helpful and comfortable to you; and those which are your vexation and misery would ease and relieve you, and tend to make you happy. Such would be the excellent effects of a due subjection to God and all the world.

5. Consider the danger of not resigning up yourselves to the government of God, so as to be ruled by him in all things.

Particularly, (1.) You can have no comfortable relation to God till you consent to be his subjects, and give up yourselves to be ruled by him, for this is the foundation of all that is honourable to him, and comfortable to you. You are not his servants, you are not his friends, you cannot be his children, till you be sincerely and voluntarily his subjects; till then he will never own you in any such relation as will afford you comfort in life or death. You are his creatures indeed, but some of the worst that ever he made, worse than the beasts that perish; none worse in the world, unless it be the devils. And why are they devils, but because they would not be ruled by the Lord? You are the work of his hand, but such a work as even a man may be ashamed of, such a work as throws itself out of the maker's hand, and will not be ordered by that wisdom and power that gives it a being.

You are not his servants, you can expect no comfort or advantage from any such relation. Indeed, you can lay no claim to it, for, saith the apostle, Rom. vi. 16, 'Know ye not, that to whom ye yield yourselves servants to obey, his servants ye are to whom ye obey; whether of sin unto death, or of obedience unto righteousness.'

You are not his friends, nor will he ever so account you, or so deal with you; for what prince will count those his friends, who live under his dominion, and yet will not be subject to him? If you submit not to his government, you are enemies to it; and those that are enemies to his government, how can they pretend to be in any respect his friends? Job v. 14, 'Ye are my friends, if you do whatsoever I command you.' He admits none to be his friends upon other terms.

You are far from being his children, if you will not be subject to him.

He who enjoins children to obey their parents, Eph. vi. 1, will own none as children who would not obey him: Mal. i. 6, 'If I be a Father, where is mine honour? If I be a Master, where is my fear?' He has neither fear nor honour from those who will not subject themselves to him; they own him neither as Lord nor Father, and he will own them neither as children nor servants.

(2.) You are rebels and traitors to the sovereign Majesty of the world, if you will not give up yourselves to be ruled by him. He that is under the obligation of a subject, and will not consent and subject himself to him who is of right his ruler, is a rebel. Now, all persons whatsoever belong to the universal kingdom of God, that kingdom which rules over all. All are under the greatest obligations to be wholly ruled by him; he has all right to govern them in all things; and therefore those who hold out, and will not submit to his government, are rebels against God. Those who are stiff-necked, and will not stoop to his yoke, will not be ruled by his laws, they are rebellious, Deut. xxxi. 27; yea, he that would not submit himself to God, would not have him to rule over him; he that would not be ruled by God in all things, would not have him rule over all; and he that would not have him rule, is a traitor to him whose throne is in the heavens. He would dethrone God, and have him deprived of his universal dominion. The language of his heart and actions is, 'We will not have this God to rule over us;' or that which Pharaoh spoke out, 'Who is the Lord, that I should obey him?' or that of those traitorous conspirators against the Lord and his Christ, Ps. ii. 3, 'Let us break his bands in sunder, and cast away his cords from us.' Contrivances to sin are rebellious conspiracies against the universal Sovereign; and their acts of sin are acts of hostility, a bearing arms against him who rules the world; and, according to the apostle's style, they are 'weapons,' Rom. vi. 13, $ὅπλα\ ἀδικίας$. You take up weapons, you bear arms against the great God, with a design to depose him, or cast off his government, while you stand out and will not submit to it. If you would not be guilty of such horrid treason and rebellion against the Most High, you must subject yourselves to him in all things.

(3.) If you will not be subject to God, you subject yourselves to the devil, for it is he that seduced men at first from their allegiance and subjection to the God of heaven. He prevailed with men to fall off from their rightful Sovereign, and he is ever since the head of that faction which he seduced; and hence he is called 'the god of the world,' 2 Cor. iv. 4, and their 'prince,' Eph. ii. 2. So far as any are 'children of disobedience' in respect of God, so far they are under the 'prince of the power of the air;' so far as you will not be subject to God, so far you are Satan's slaves, 'led captive by him at his will,' 2 Tim. ii. 26. And there is no hope of recovering yourselves out of the snare of the devil, no freedom from that woful slavery and captivity to that hellish tyrant, but by resigning up yourselves to be ruled by God. Christ invites you to come under his sweet and gracious government, Mat. xi. 29. If you will not be persuaded, you leave yourselves irrecoverably under the tyranny of Satan, who will continually harass you in the basest drudgery, and keep you in servitude to divers lusts. The viler any person is to whom one is enslaved, the more intolerable is the slavery. What is it then to be in bondage unto the devil? nay, that which is worse, that which has made him a devil, unto sin? This will be your state; nor can it be better, till you give up yourselves to be wholly ruled by him who rules over all, Rom. vi. 16, 17, 19.

(4.) The Lord can arm all creatures against you. He that rules over all has every thing in the world at his beck, and under his command; and can order all, or any of them, to do what execution he pleases on any that affront his government. He could arm the angels against Sennacherib and his host; he could arm the stars against Sisera, Judges v. 20; he could arm the clouds against the old world, the winds against Jonah; he could arm the sea against Pharaoh and the Egyptians, and the fire against Sodom, Gen. xix. 21; and against King Ahaziah's soldiers, sent to apprehend the prophet, 2 Kings i. 10, 12; and the air with infection against David and his people; and the earth against Korah and his accomplices; and many creatures on earth, as the locust, the canker-worm, the palmer-worm, which he armed against Israel, Joel ii. 25.

Yea, he can arm a man against himself, and make any part of him to do execution upon the whole. It is grievous to have friends and children armed against him, as they were against David. What is it, then, for a man to be armed against himself, and to be made his own tormentor? But he who rules over all can give a commission to any part of man's soul or body to do execution upon himself. So he armed Judas's conscience against him, and you know what execution that did. He armed Pharaoh's will against himself, hardening his heart to his destruction; and the spirit and heart of Sihon, Deut. ii. 30. He armed the memories of the Jews against them, Lam. i. 7, and ii. 19, 20, and made the thoughts of himself afflictive to David, Ps. lxxvii. 3. The fancies of the Moabites, 2 Kings iii. 22, 23, they imagined the waters to be blood, and drew such a conclusion from that fancy as ruined them; and that wonderful change which befell Nebuchadnezzar is ascribed to the power of fancy, the Lord so over-ruling it, that he imagined himself to be a beast, and demeaned himself accordingly for so many years, Dan. iv. 33; so Asa's feet, 1 Kings xv. 23; Saul's hands, 1 Sam. xxxi. 4; and Adonijah's tongue, 1 Kings ii. 23; and the Bethshemites' eyes, 1 Sam. vi. 19; and the humors in the Egyptians' bodies, Exod. ix. 10.

Oh how dangerous is it not to subject yourselves to him who so rules over all, that he can arm all things, or any thing, against you! even yourselves against yourselves, your bodies against your souls, your souls against your bodies, or any part of either against both!

(5.) If you will not give up yourselves in subjection unto God, all creatures in heaven and earth may rise up in judgment against you, and condemn you. Your guilt will have as many aggravations as there are or have been creatures in the whole world. And how heavy will that guilt be, which has so many, so innumerably many, to burden and aggravate it! You have no associates herein through the whole world, but only the devils; all other creatures, from the highest angel to the meanest worm, to the least particle of air or earth, are in continual and absolute subjection and obedience unto God, Ps. cxlviii. 1–6. All these, as they were made at first by his command, so have they been ordered ever since by his statute. They never have, never will, transgress it in the least; but perform a perfect, a continued obedience to his orders, doing all that he would have them do, and nothing else. Thus is the superior part of the world in subjection to him; for the lower part, see vers. 7–10. All these are ever fulfilling his word, performing his pleasure, shewing themselves wholly at his command: He says to one, Go, and he goes, &c. And shall man only, of all creatures in heaven and earth, stand out against God and refuse to be at his command? There is not a hill, nor a tree, nor a beast, nor a fowl, nor a creeping thing, not a spark of fire, nor a drop of rain, nor a puff of wind, but may bear witness against your non-subjection to God, and declare against it as intolerable, and most worthy of the fiercest wrath of the great God. We (may they say) never had such endowments, such encouragements as the children of men; we were not capable of such obligations as the Lord laid upon them; we had no fears of everlasting sufferings, nor were ever quickened with hopes of eternal rewards, and yet we never transgress his will and pleasure in the least, all our motions were conformed exactly to his orders; whenas refractory men will do what they list; let the Lord order what he pleases, they will do what is good in their own eyes, not what seems good to him. There is not any of those creatures but may bring in such a charge against you, nay, all together may form such a plea against disobedient man, and appear at God's tribunal as his accusers, and swell his charge, and burden his guilt, with the weight of the whole creation, and call for the greatest severity, and justify the heaviest sentence that can be passed against him.

When you are tempted to cross the will of God in any particular, say thus to yourselves, What am I about to do? There is not any other creatures else in the world, but the devils, would do thus. The irrational, the senseless, the lifeless creatures, do all fulfil his word; and shall *I*, whom the Lord has infinitely more obliged, be a transgressor of it? Shall I make myself worse than the beasts that perish, when the Lord had made me but a little lower than the angels? Shall I make myself worse than fowl, or plant, or any creeping thing? Have I no pattern to follow but that of the devils? Shall I make myself so liable to the condemnation of hell, as the whole creation may pass the sentence of such a condemnation upon me, and bear witness that nothing heavy enough can be inflicted on me? Shall I run into such guilt, against which every creature in heaven and earth will be both a witness and a condemner? Oh then, what will plead for me, when all things in the world appear against me? Who will justify what every creature condemns? What will hide me, what will secure me from the wrath of him that sits upon the throne, when the whole creation will offer me to his vengeance, and declare me most worthy of it for ever?

6. If you will not subject yourselves to him, he will ruin you. He that rules over all, will, and must have his will on you; there is no resisting, no avoiding it; all hopes of escaping, or faring better, are mere delusions: Job ix. 4, 'He is wise in heart, and mighty in strength: who hath hardened himself against him, and hath prospered?' If you can deal with such a God, as, ver. 5–8, which 'removeth the mountains, and they know not: which overturneth them in his anger; which shaketh the earth out of her place, and the pillars thereof tremble; which commandeth the sun, and it riseth not, and sealeth up the stars,' &c., then, though you be stiff against him, you may hope to prosper. But if this great God who rules over all, will be too hard for you, then there is no way, but either submit or perish: Ps. ii. 12, 'Kiss the Son, lest he be angry, and ye perish,' &c. Kissing hand or feet is a token of subjection and homage, 1 Sam x. 1, Gen. xli. 40, ישק כל עמי, shall obey thee, and receive law from thee. Those who will not give up themselves in such subjection are exposed to his wrath, and so in danger to perish from the way, in danger to be trodden under foot. It is a dreadful doom which remains for those who will not have the Lord to rule over them, Luke xix. 27. If you will not have the Lord to reign over you, he will have you executed as his enemies, and he will see execution done himself.

Thus much to persuade you to be ruled by God, and to give up yourselves to be ruled by him in all things. If the Lord have made it effectual to bring you to such a happy resolution, it will be seasonable to shew how you should demean yourselves as his subjects. Particularly,

1. Know your distance from the universal Sovereign, and be sensible of

it. How far is he above you who rules over all! Earthly princes will have their subjects know their distance, and shew it by a reverence answerable thereto. Why, those that are upon thrones, in comparison of men, are but as it were upon the dunghill, in respect of him whose throne is in heaven; and the greatest empire on earth is but as a molehill, compared with that kingdom which rules over all. What high and awful apprehensions should we have of the great Majesty of heaven and earth! Jer. x. 6, 7, 'Forasmuch as there is none like unto thee, O Lord; thou art great, and thy name is great in might. Who would not fear thee, O King of nations?' Superiority challenges reverence, Mal. i. 6. Fear and honour is due even to masters of families, much more to the rulers of kingdoms and empires. What, then, do we owe to him, in comparison of whose dominion, such an empire as that of Ahasuerus, Esther i. 1, 'An hundred twenty and seven provinces,' are not so much as one family? Heb. xii. 9, 'We have had fathers of our flesh which corrected us, and we gave them reverence.' And so we have kings and governors, and we give them reverence. 'Should we not much more be in subjection' to the King of kings? The highest angels are but mean subjects to him who rules over all, and the most glorious amongst them are but to his glorious majesty what glow-worms are to us; and the greatest princes in the world are but to him as crowned grasshoppers; their power, and greatness, and majesty is so little or nothing, compared with his, as they deserve not the name of potentates in comparison. He who rules over all is 'the only potentate,' 1 Tim. vi. 15. And if we should look upon ourselves as far below them, and be sensible of our distance, what sense should we have of the distance betwixt God and us! How infinitely is he above us! How inconceivably are we below him who rules over all! Let the sense hereof rest upon us, and influence heart and life, and the acts of both continually, Ps. xcvi. 9, 10.

2. Let him have the pre-eminence above all, in your thoughts, and affections, and designs. He that rules over all ought to be exalted above all, and in all, and by all. Let him have the highest place in your minds; let your thoughts advance him above that which is highest there; let him have the chief place in your hearts; let his sceptre be advanced there, and make everything stoop to it; let the Lord alone reign there; let him have the throne, and other things be made his footstool. Though his throne of glory be in heaven, yet he disdains not to own an humble heart as his throne here below, Isa. lvii. 15. That is an humble heart that stoops to God, that lies low before him, and would have everything else to do so, that he who rules over all may have the pre-eminence in all things. As he is exalted above all, in respect of his kingdom and dominion, the greatness, and power, and glory of it, so should he be answerably exalted in our souls. Those that are true and faithful to the supreme ruler of the universe will be careful to have him so exalted, 2 Sam. xxii. 47, Neh. ix. 5, 6, Ps. lvii. 5, 11, and xcvii. 9, Isa. ii. 10, 11, and v. 15.

3. Be tender of his honour. He is counted no good subject who maintains not the honour of a righteous ruler. He that will venture to dishonour God himself, or is not troubled when he is dishonoured by others, shews no such respect as is due from a subject to the universal sovereign, Ps. lxix. 9. You should resent that which dishonours God, as if yourselves were struck at. The relation betwixt God and you requires this; he that is honoured or dishonoured is your ruler, and therefore you are concerned in it, and should be affected with it as your own concern. The more glory is due to him, the more should it be laid to heart when he is dishonoured. It is a super-eminent glory, an honour above all, which is due to him who rules over

all, therefore any dishonourable reflections upon him are and should be counted more intolerable.

To see the King in his glory is the ardent desire of every soul that is loyal to God. It will then be the affliction of such a soul to hear him reproached, to see him disregarded, and his authority slighted, Ps. cxix. 136. It is necessary, in order to the end of government, that the ruler should be in honour, otherwise he will not be in a capacity to promote the common good, to which civil government is subservient. Oh, but the common good itself must be measured by the honour of God, the supreme ruler; and that must be counted best for us, and for all, which most honours him. All things must lower to this, even that which is *suprema lex*, and has the supremacy in other well-ordered governments. That which glorifies him must be judged our happiness, and that which dishonours him our misery.

4. Be very observant of his laws, and every part thereof, commands, promises, threatenings. What subjection can we shew to the great ruler of the world, if we will not live in an observance of his laws, which are not only most righteous in themselves, but most advantageous to his subjects? Acquaint yourselves with them; let them be your study and meditation, that you may know in all particulars, upon all occasions and emergencies, 'what is the good, and perfect, and acceptable will of God.' His laws declare this to us, and we should have them always in our eye, always at hand, that they may be as light to us by day, and a lantern by night, Ps. cxix. 105; that these may give us light in all our ways, and may direct all our steps; that we may never be at a loss, never to seek concerning his will, and what he has enjoined us. Those that are careful to *obey*, will be careful to *know* the law, the rule of their obedience, in its true sense, and utmost extent, in its power and spirituality; not only in the body, but in the several branches of it, great and small. We are as much concerned as the Israelites, in that command, Deut. vi. 6-9, 'These words which I command thee this day shall be in thine heart; and thou shalt teach them diligently unto thy children,' &c. Joshua, the great ruler of Israel, was thus to shew himself under a higher government: Joshua i. 8, 9, 'This book of the law shall not depart out of thy mouth; but thou shalt meditate therein day and night, that thou mayest observe to do according to all that is written therein,' &c. And kings are this way to declare themselves subject to the sovereign of the world: Deut. xvii. 18-20, 'When he sitteth upon the throne of his kingdom, he shall write him a copy of this law in a book: and it shall be with him, and he shall read therein all the days of his life,' &c. And being acquainted with his laws, we must not dispute any of his commands. This is counted malapertness in other subjects, when there is no suspicion of unrighteousness in the injunctions of their superiors. How intolerable will it be in reference to the laws of God, which are the issues of infinite wisdom, goodness, and righteousness! We should pay a free, cheerful, unreserved, and present observance to all his commands, Ps. cxix. 60.

We should fear his threatenings too. These contain the penalties wherewith his laws are enforced. To make light of them is to slight him who rules over all. When he enjoins a thing under pain of his displeasure, that is as much as if it were enjoined under pain of death, for 'in his favour is life;' and therefore his displeasure should be as dreadful to us as death. It is the property of those that are his best subjects, and such in whom he most delights, to tremble at his word. Isa. lxvi. 1, 2.

His promises also should have a great influence on us in all ways of obedience, both because they are so great and wonderful. What prince would ever promise his subjects that if they should observe his laws they should reign with him. Yet this the Lord promises those that are subject to him, Mat. xiii. 43, 2 Tim. ii. 12, Rev. iii. 21. As also because they are so free and gracious. The Lord was not in the least obliged to promise or bestow any reward for our obedience; we owe him all we do, and much more. And who will expect a reward for paying his debt, especially when he pays but a small part of what he owes? He promises all that we can desire, and all that he promises are acts of grace. He had more right to make laws, as others do, without annexing anything to them but penalties. Oh how should we value and admire the riches and freeness of his grace in those great and precious promises! What an influence should they have upon us in all acts of obedience! How free, and hearty, and affectionate, and entire should our subjection be to such a Ruler, who, when he was not in the least obliged to give us anything, hath graciously promised to give us all, and not to let the least act of subjection pass, without a recompence of reward! Mat. x. 42.

5. *Promote his interest.* You cannot be faithful subjects unless you be true to the interest of your sovereign Lord. This you must prefer before all particular interests of yourselves or others. This you must maintain against all, and venture all you have in the defence and for the advancement of it. He is no true friend to the government under which he lives, who will prefer his private interest before the public: this is both disloyalty and folly. As if one would let the ship sink and think to save his cabin. God's interest is the public interest; your own, and the interest of the world, is involved in it, and must swim or sink with it. Nothing should take place of it, nothing should be admitted to come in competition with it. If you will not shew yourselves true subjects to it, you are both foolish and unfaithful. Selfishness and privateness of spirit, neglecting his interest, who rules over all, for some little things of your own, will make you guilty of both.

Now the interest of God, as he is King of nations, consists in the number and quality of his subjects. It is his interest that more should be subject to him, and that they should be more subjected to him; that his kingdom should be populous, and that the people of it should be such as may prove the strength and ornament of it. You have both, Ps. cx. 3. The Psalmist gives an account here of the kingdom of the Messiah: his throne, ver. 1; his sceptre, ver. 2; his subjects, ver. 3; both the number and quality of them. They are numerous: 'From the womb of the morning thou hast the dew of thy youth; *i. e.* thy subjects shall be for number answerable to the drops of dew which the morning brings forth (as it were out of its womb) so plentifully as to cover the face of the whole earth. Then for the quality of them, they shall be 'a willing people,' not subdued and brought into subjection by force of arms, but resigning themselves voluntarily unto his government. עַם נְדָבֹת; a people of free will offering, such as freely offer up themselves, and all they have, in and for his service, and that 'in the beauties of holiness;' holiness shining forth in its lustre, and appearing in them in all its beauties. Herein lies the interest of God in the world; if you will be true to it, faithful to your sovereign Lord, make it your business to enlarge his kingdom by bringing more under his government, and making yourselves and others such as may be an honour to his government; growing in grace more and more, and holding forth the power and beauty of holiness in a daily course, and to that end, striving to uphold and promote the gospel, that is the sceptre, the rod of his power. That is it whereby the world must be prevailed with to come under his government. When the gospel is suppressed, his sceptre is thrown to the ground. Those that oppose it and stop its course are the greatest enemies to his interest, and those to whom the gospel in its power and liberty is not dearer than liberty or estate, or any other outward concern, they are not faithful to him who rules over all, nor true to his interest.

And take heed of anything which may tempt any to fall off from this government, or may hinder any from coming into it. Those who by passionate, or selfish, or froward, or rigorous, or unrighteous carriage, beget in others an ill opinion of this government, they are not friends to it, they do great disservice to the interest of God; 'it were better a mill-stone were hanged about their neck,' &c., Mat. xviii. 6. Walk so as you may win and oblige others to come in and submit to this government; let your conversation be such as may convince the world that subjection to God in all things is that which tends to the happiness of families, of kingdoms, and of the whole earth. That is the way to make them 'a willing people,' to enlarge the kingdom of our great Sovereign, and so to promote his interest. If those who profess themselves subjects of God would order themselves according to the rules of his government, there would be little need of miracles to convert infidels.

6. You must have the same friends, and the same enemies. Those that are friends to God and his government, you must not count them nor treat them as your enemies for any little differences; their relation to God must drown the sense of personal feuds and particular provocations. And those that are enemies to God and his government must not be the persons of your intimacy and delight, though you may have pity and compassion for them: Ps. cxxxix. 20-22, 'They speak evil against thee wickedly, and thine enemies take thy name in vain. Do not I hate them, O Lord, that hate thee? and am not I grieved with those that rise up against thee? I hate them with perfect hatred; I count them mine enemies.' Though they pretended to piety, yet when their talking of God was with a design to act wickedness, their enmity to the Lord herein was hateful and grievous to him. He resented it as if it had been enmity against, injury offered to, himself.

And those who submit to the government of God, and thereby shew themselves his friends, must be embraced by them as such, though they may differ from us, and disoblige us in other particulars. We must be wary how we judge or censure them for such differences, lest we entrench upon the prerogative of him who is the Lord and Ruler of us both, Rom. xiv. 3, 4. In things that are indifferent really, and not in pretence, we are not to judge another, we have no right to do it. He is the judge of him and us, who is Lord and Ruler of both. Our common relation to our sovereign Lord, and their subjection to him, must keep up love and friendship amongst all that are the friends of God, in the midst of such differences as may tempt us to be unfriendly.

7. Submit to God in all his dispensations. In those especially which may tempt you to impatience or discontent, in wants, in losses, in disappointments, in hard measures from men, in sufferings and afflictions of all sorts. For why? The Lord rules over all; all that befalls you is ordered and disposed by him. Others are but instruments and under-causes, whom he makes use of in the administration of worldly affairs; and rules and over-rules them as he pleases. Look upon him as the sovereign ruler, and upon these dispensations as acts of his government. I know not what can be more prevalent with you, to submit and be satisfied. Not to submit, is to rise up against him who rules over all. To murmur and repine, is to quarrel with God's ruling your affairs. Not to be quiet and contented, is to shew yourselves unsatisfied with his government. And is this to demean yourselves as becomes the subjects of such a ruler? It may be you have not so well con-

sidered the heinousness of this misdemeanour, neither against whom, nor against what it is directed. Is it not against him who rules over all ? and against him as ruling, against his government ? As though your affairs might have been ruled and ordered with more wisdom, or more goodness, than the Lord exercises in his administrations towards you. As though you would not have the Lord to rule over all, but had rather order your affairs yourselves, than have them ruled at such a rate, and ordered in such a manner, as the great God sees fit. How does this strike at the glorious sovereignty of God ! What reflections does it cast upon the Lord of heaven and earth ! Those who were subject to God indeed, have expressed another temper : the sense of God's ruling hand, in the sad things that befell them, has made them silent, patient, submissive, and well satisfied with and under severe dispensations. What more grievous things have befallen you, than Eli was threatened with, 1 Sam. iii. 11-14. And what says he ? How did he entertain this sad message ? Ver. 18, ' It is the Lord.' It is he who has dominion over me ; it is He who has all right to dispose of me and mine, as he thinks fit. And Aaron expressed as much by his silence, when his two sons were consumed by fire from God, Lev. x. 2, 3 ; and so did David, when he was near consumed by the stroke of God's hand, Ps. xxxix. 9.

What can you lose more than Job, who lost estate and children at once ? Yet how submissively does he demean himself upon this consideration : Job i. 21, ' The Lord gave, and the Lord hath taken away,' &c. He is the Lord of what I had, and gave it me ; and the Lord of what I have lost, and took it. I had but the use of it, he had the right, as being Lord of all, and so might well dispose of it as he thought fit ; and therefore blessed be his name, adored and admired be his government and dominion, both in giving and taking away !

What more dreadful can come upon you than Hezekiah was threatened with, 2 Kings xx. 17, 18, yet he expresses himself not only as patient, but satisfied : ver. 19, ' Good is the word of the Lord.' It is the Lord, and it is his word, his act. He is not only *maximus*, the sovereign Lord, the ruler of all, but *optimus*, the best of governors, and therefore his acts of rule must needs be good : δύναται πάντα, βούλεται ἄριστα, Isidor. lib. ii.

The Lord ruling over all makes it not only our duty to be patient under, contented with, submissive to, all his administrations, but the consideration of it is a means to help us, and a motive to oblige us thereto. He is the universal ruler ; he has all right to dispose and order us and ours, and all things, as he sees good. It is his due, and shall we not allow him what is due to him ? Shall we not be contented that he should use his right ? Must he forbear that at our pleasure ? Shall he not make use of it but when and how we think fit ? Does this become his subjects ? Or rather, is not this to take upon us to rule, instead of God ?

Those dispensations which we are apt to be unsatisfied with, they are acts of God's government ; and what will we be satisfied with, if his governing will not please us ? Is not his government most wise, and most gracious, and most righteous ? Can anything be more prudently ordered than the wisdom of God does order it ? or anything better disposed of than goodness itself does manage it ? or anything less liable to exception than that which is most righteous ? If we will not be satisfied with those acts of government, which are the issues of infallible wisdom, and infinite goodness, and most perfect righteousness, what will content us ? If there be impatience under these, where will patience have its work ? If we will not submit here, how can we, when, or wherein will we, ever shew ourselves subject ?

8. Address yourselves unto God upon all occasions, and look to him for redress; hereby you will honour him as the universal governor. This will be an honourable acknowledgment, that he rules over all; when you have recourse to him in all, and apply yourselves to him for all, and rely upon him accordingly. Whatever you want, whatever you fear, whatever you feel that is grievous or afflictive to you, apply yourselves to him, who is able and willing to supply and relieve you, whatever your case be, and gives you assurance of it in that he rules over all.

He is able. For he who rules over all is the all-sufficient governor. He wants no wisdom, he wants no power, who is sufficient for the government of the whole world. He that can rule all can do all for you himself; or he can order anything else to do it, if he will make use of others; for he has all at his beck, and under his power and dominion.

And he is ready too. He is always at hand; you need not travel many miles to make your case known, you may find him everywhere; for he that rules over all is a ruler in all places, in all things. And you may have immediate access to him; you need make no friends, or bribe any courtiers, to get you audience; you may have as free and ready access to him as to any other.

Nor will it be, or will he count it any trouble to him to hear or relieve you, though millions with you should apply themselves to him at once. He that can so easily rule all can in a moment despatch the affairs of millions together, and can more easily give you and all redress, than you can seek it.

Nor need you fear to meet with a repulse. It belongs to him, as he is ruler over all, to order all your affairs for you, and dispose of all your concernments. That is his prerogative, as he is the sovereign of the world; and your privilege, as you are his subjects in a special manner; and both may make you confident that he is willing you should have access to him for these purposes at any time. You can never come unseasonably, as you may do to other rulers, for he is always actually governing all and everything, and is no more hindered by his administering of all than if he had but one thing, one person, to look after; you have a general warrant, and special encouragement to come to him at any time, and so you need not fear to come before you are called. No such danger, no such penalty, as upon Ahasuerus's subjects, to whom it was death to approach him, when they were not called, except the golden sceptre was held out to them, Esth. iv. 11. His sceptre is continually held out to you, to every subject of his. And though he have כסא הדין, a throne of judgment, yet you may always find him upon כסא רחמים, a throne of grace, as he was represented in the temple, always upon the mercy-seat, ever ready for acts of grace and mercy. He will have his throne denominated from grace. It is the special glory of his reign and government to shew himself gracious, freely merciful, to every faithful subject, how mean soever. Grace is enthroned in his government, and reigns there; and therefore we may come to him with all freedom, and the greatest confidence, that we shall obtain mercy, and find grace, whenever we come, Heb. iv. 16. Let us come, and that $\mu\varepsilon\tau\grave{\alpha}\ \pi\alpha\dot{\rho}\dot{\rho}\eta\sigma\acute{\iota}\alpha\varsigma$, 'with all freeness,' declare to him all our wants, and all our griefs. For the Lord our Sovereign offers himself to us upon a throne of grace, that so we may always obtain mercy, and find grace $\pi\rho\grave{o}\varsigma\ \varepsilon\ddot{u}\varkappa\alpha\iota\rho o\nu\ \beta o\acute{\eta}\theta\varepsilon\iota\alpha\nu$, 'for seasonable relief,' for supply and redress whenever we need it, when it will be best and most seasonable for us to have it. Thus to address ourselves to him is both our duty and our privilege, we honour him hereby, and acknowledge that he rules us in all things; and having such encouragement for it, let us not neglect it.

9. Commit your affairs unto him; devolve all your concernments on him; entrust him with the ordering of them; leave all to be ruled by him who rules over all: Ps. xxxvii. 5, 'Commit thy way unto him.' The word is, גּוֹל, 'Roll thy way,' any, every particular wherein thou art concerned, upon God; trust him with the managing of it, and set thy heart at rest. There is no fear that anything committed to him will miscarry; trust him but with it, and he will bring it to pass, he will give it a good issue. Leave events in his hands, in whose they are; he can order them best, who admirably rules and orders all things. Thy weightiest concerns are not too heavy for him, and he thinks not the least of them below him; he takes care of all, even to a hair, Mat. x. 30. Those who thought that God did προνοεῖν τῶν οὐρανίων μόνον, take care only of celestial things; or if of earthly, yet οὐ πάντων δέ, ἀλλὰ τῶν ἐξόχων, not of all, but only the greatest, the affairs of eminent persons, and princes: those who entertained such conceits did err, not knowing the Scriptures, nor the universal and unlimited dominion of God. In what potentate did he more concern himself than in Lazarus? He resents the concernments of the least and meanest of his subjects, as though they were his own, Mat. xxv. Oxen and sparrows, their provisions, their motions, are ordered by his government; much more does the care of it reach his people, 1 Cor. ix. 9.

Therefore, live in a continual dependence on him, in all, and for all; in whose hands all things are, and through whose hands all things do pass. Though he rule all, yet he has not so much business on him as to neglect any, or suffer the least to miscarry; he is as sufficient for all, as if he had but one to mind. *Sic gressus meos considerans, veluti me solum consideret;* he so looks after me, as if he had none but me to look after, says Augustine. Trust him, therefore, with all, and quiet your hearts in believing that he who rules over all knows best how to rule and order all that is yours, Ps. cxviii. 8, 9. If a prince should bid you trust him with some affair of yours, and assure you, on the word of a king, he would take care of it, you would think this a great security; and yet it might miscarry, and you, for all this, might be disappointed; that is too ordinary. Oh, but you have a king to trust with your concernments, and he requires you to do it, who never disappointed any that relied on him (though he have the government of the whole world upon him), to this day, nor ever will do; he that trusts in him shall not be ashamed, Rom. x. 11. If a relation of yours that is rich, should bid you leave your child to him, he will take care of it, you would be apt to think it well provided for. May not your children be better provided for by committing them to God, when he assures you he will take care of them? Is he not infinitely richer, and wiser, and better, who has all under him, and rules all as he will, and will order all for the best? A rich friend may leave your child an estate; but whether it will be good or bad for him, it is not in his power to determine: an estate may prove his ruin, and he that gives it him cannot help it. But he who rules over all, as he knows what will be best for you and yours, so he can order all for the best. He can secure *much* from being a snare, and he can order a *little* to prove better than much. Therefore leave yourselves and yours, and all, to him who rules all.

10. Observe the Lord ruling all. Take notice of his ruling hand; acknowledge it in all, and ascribe all to it. Let not second causes and instruments be so in your eye, as to overlook him who rules them, and all they do. Look through these, upon him who is all in all. They have not only their life, their being, but their motion from him. All in the world seem on wheels, and are still in motion; but who is it that moves them? If the

hand of him who rules over all did not touch them, they would all stand still. What can the clay do to form itself into any shape, or to serve its owner for any use, if it were not ordered by his hand? What could the rod or the axe do, if there were not a hand to move them? Your enjoyments are but as such clay; your afflictions are but as such a rod. Why is your eye so much upon them, who move not of themselves to do you good or hurt? Why look you not at the hand which moves and orders them, and all things, as he pleases? Isa. x. 5, 'The staff in their hand,' *i.e.* all the power they have to smite and afflict, ' is mine indignation,' which arms them, and sets them a-work. It is as unreasonable for us to look so much at them, as for them to ascribe so much to themselves, ver. 15. Shimei seems set a-work by his own malice, or a revengeful resentment of what the house of Saul had suffered by David; but David looks farther, 2 Sam. xvi. 10–12. There was in Job's losses and calamities, a concurrence of all sorts of causes and instruments, Job i., both natural, the fire, ver. 16, and the wind, ver. 19; and voluntary, the Sabeans, ver. 15, and Chaldeans, ver. 17; yet Job overlooks them, and takes notice of God only: ver. 21, ' The Lord gave, and the Lord hath taken away.'

Observe the perfections which shine forth in his governing all things, and give him the glory thereof. Observe the power of his government, overruling all things to do, not what they would, but what he will; the wisdom of it, ordering all to serve his purposes, even such as seem mere casualties, and the issues of no contrivance at all: ' This is of the Lord,' Isa. xxviii. 29, the goodness and excellency of it, in turning evil unto good. Which Joseph was so taken with, as the evil of the instruments is not taken notice of, Gen. xlv. 5, 7, 8. The universality of it is observable, not only in great, but the smallest things. The increase of the cattle, which were to fall to Jacob's share, was none of the greatest of his concernments; and he had a natural cause managed by his own prudence, to ascribe it to; but he ascribes it wholly to God, Gen. xxxi. 7–9. Not to the white-straked rods which he laid before the cattle when they conceived, nor to the operation which those had upon their fancies, but all to the Lord. Thus should we give the Lord the glory that is due to him, as ruling and governing all things, Ps. xcvi. 6–9, and xxix. 1, 2. And why so? Because his government is powerful, majestic, irresistible, universal, as from ver. 3 to the 10th.

11. What you offer to the Lord, be sure it be the best; the best you have, the best you can offer him. If you be to bring a present to a great ruler, you will not (unless you despise him, and have a mind to affront him), bring him the refuse of what you have, but the best and choicest of all. All your services are presents to the great God who rules over all; will you offer that to him, which you would not dare to offer to your governor? Mal. i. 8. When you tender to God dead, heartless, unaffectionate, distracted, lukewarm prayers or praises; when you draw near him carelessly, irreverently, hear as though you heard not, or do any of his works negligently; it is as if you should pick out the blind, and the lame, and the sick, for a present to your prince and governor; it is so much worse, and more provoking, as he is above all other princes and rulers, who rules over all. You would not offer a corrupt thing to an earthly prince; and shall such a thing be tendered as a present to the King of kings, whose greatness and majesty is dreadful to the whole world? ver. 14. So much as he is greater and more dreadful than other kings, so much the more careful should you be to offer nothing to him that is corrupt, nothing but the best of all you have or can offer, Ps. xlvii. 7. Praise him with all your art and skill. Let his praise be the work of your souls. Let your understandings engage heart and affections therein; for so it becomes

you, since he is King of all the earth. So consider him, when you draw near him; the best of all is due to him, and too mean for him who rules over all.

12. Prepare to be judged by him. Judgment is a principal part of his government of intelligent creatures. Here he gives us laws, and expects an observance of them; hereafter he will judge us according to them, else his laws were in vain, Eccles. xii. 13, 14. So observe what he commands, as those who are sure to be called to account, Rom. xiv. 10, 12. Here he entrusts you with many talents, gifts, parts, time, opportunities, estates, all enjoyments, encouragements, advantages; he declares how they must be employed, and will call you to an account for them. See that you improve them so, as those who expect to give an account, that you may be able to do it with joy, and not with grief. He who rules over all, is ready to judge both quick and dead, 1 Peter iv. 5. See that your account be ready, Philip. ii. 12, 1 Peter i. 17. You live not as under his government, unless you live under some effectual apprehensions of approaching judgment.

13. Rejoice in him, and in his government. Let it be your triumph that the Lord reigns. This is matter of rejoicing to the whole world, Ps. xcvi. 10–13, but more especially to his faithful subjects, Ps. cxlix. 2. If he reign, if he rule over all, he will avenge your wrongs, he will redress your grievances, he will ease you of your burdens, he will secure you from your fears, he will regard your necessities, he will be tender of your concernments, he will receive your petitions, he will break your oppressors, he will subdue your enemies, for they are his. He will order all for your advantage; he will make his government your happiness, and your subjection perfect freedom. Subjection, in other cases, is some abridgment of liberty, but he is such a ruler that the more you are subject to him, the more liberty you will enjoy. Not a liberty of free subjects only, but of sons; not a common, but a glorious liberty, Rom. viii. 21. If you have given up yourselves to be wholly ruled by the Lord, he is your friend, your father, your husband. And oh, what honour, what happiness is it! What cause of joy and triumph, to be so nearly related to so great a king; to have such interest in him who rules over all, as these most endearing and obliging relations give you!

He is your friend. If you subject yourselves to him, he is in covenant, in a league of friendship with you; he is your ally, obliged to look upon your enemies as his. Oh, if those who bear ill-will to Zion, and to you, did but well understand who it is that is allied to you, who it is that is engaged to stand by you, what a potent friend and ally you have and are sure of; they would never venture to move a hand, or a tongue, or secretly to contrive any evil against you. He that toucheth you toucheth the apple of his eye, strikes at his eye who rules over all.

He is your husband. Your subjection to him is the condition of the marriage-covenant. And what happiness is it to have the King of kings, and Lord of lords for your husband; one so potent, so glorious! Oh how contemptible are the most noble and honourable relations on earth to this. 'Αἱ γαμεταὶ συνεκλάμπουσι τοῖς τῶν συνοικούντων ἀκτίσι (Justin. Novel. 105, c. 2), Wives shine with the beams of their husbands. The splendour and nobility of the husband is derived upon his wife. To be married to a king is one of the greatest honours in a kingdom. Oh, what is it to be in so near a relation to him to whom the greatest kings in the world are subjects and underlings, at an infinite distance below him!

He is your father. If you honour him, by subjecting yourselves to him as children should to their parents, he will own you as his children, and you may have all from him that can be expected from such a father. And what may you not expect from such a father, who has all the powers, all the riches of the earth, all the world at his will? What will become of those who hate, and wrong, and oppress the children of such a father? What need they fear, what can they want, who have the King of nations, the great Lord of heaven and earth for their father? Oh, what cause of joy is here! Oh, how stupid and senseless must we be, if all the joys, the honours, the riches, the happiness of this world be counted comparable to what this relation affords! Rejoice in the Lord, rejoice in your King always; and shout for joy, all ye upright in heart.

Use 3. If the Lord rule over all, then here is great encouragement to his people, those who have truly subjected themselves unto him, and whom he owns as his subjects. The people of God heretofore, in the saddest circumstances wherewith they have been surrounded, have found this to be the strength of their hearts, that 'the Lord reigneth.' This has been a reviving cordial to them, even when both flesh and heart has been ready to fail. This has borne them up when the rage and violence of men has been ready to bear them down, This has been their support under sinking pressures. And it may be it should be so to us. Whatsoever our fears and dangers be, whatever our wants and necessities, whatever confusions we see about us, how low soever the interest of Christ and his people appear; whatever sufferings, troubles, calamities, are upon us, or threaten us; how violent and powerful soever our enemies be; yet, since the Lord reigns, since our God rules over all, hence we may take heart, this may refresh and revive us, this may support and encourage us. This is a ground of hope when all seems desperate, and may afford us strong consolations when everything seems to look upon us with a sad and dismal countenance.

Particularly, 1. In fears and dangers. When our dear concernments are in apparent hazard; when liberty, or estate, or life; when our religion, when the gospel, when our glory, and all our pleasant things are in danger; and when it seems unavoidable, by anything that we or others concerned with us can do, to prevent or remove it; yet here is our encouragement, he that rules over all is sufficient to do it, and can, if he please, make anything or all things concur with him to that purpose. He can secure us and our concerns from dangers, or in them, or by, or after them. For what cannot he do, to whom all things in heaven and earth are subject, and must and shall do whatever he pleases?

(1.) He can secure us *from* dangers. In this David was confident, Ps. xxxii. 7. He who rules over all has all that endangers any, all that are endangered, absolutely at his dispose; and so can secure his servants, either by keeping and removing danger from them, or them from it.

[1.] By keeping or removing danger from them : ' In the floods of great waters they shall not come nigh him,' Ps. xxxii. 6. He can either turn them back, or interpose a bank betwixt them, and those who are in danger to be overwhelmed by them. There is a gracious promise for this, grounded upon this very relation : Isa. xxxiii. 20–22, ' Thine eyes shall see Jerusalem a quiet habitation, a tabernacle that shall not be taken down; nor one of the stakes thereof shall ever be removed, neither shall any of the cords thereof be broken : But there the glorious Lord will be unto us a place of broad rivers and streams. For the Lord is our judge, the Lord is our lawgiver, the Lord is our king, he will save us.' A large and deep moat or ditch is a security to a city. But the Lord would be round about his people, not only as a moat, but as a large river. Horse or foot could not approach them, thus secured; nothing could endanger them but ship or galley, but neither should these do it, either with help of wind or oars; the stream of his protection should be of so stiff and strong a current, that no vessel of any force to annoy them should be able to stem it. This the people of God may be confident of, because he is their ruler, ver. 22. Thus the Lord promises to remove from Hezekiah and his people the danger which the rage of the Assyrian threatened them with, Isa. xxxvii. 28, 29. Thus he secured the Israelites from Pharaoh and his host; he interposed betwixt them and the danger, and kept it off, Exod. xiv. 19, 20. And in the like manner he promises to secure his people and their assemblies for worship, and to interpose as effectually between them and danger, as if they had the pillar of fire and cloud betwixt them and their enemies' violence, Isa. iv. 5. God will be the same to them, and their places of meeting for his worship; which that pillar was to the Israelites; he will be amongst them, and above, and round about them, to keep off danger from them.

[2.] By keeping or removing them from danger. So was Lot secured; the Lord made more haste to remove him from the danger than he himself, Gen. xix. 16. So when Moses was exposed to danger of perishing, the Lord so ordered as he was rescued from it by Pharaoh's daughter, Exod. ii. Yea, he sometimes makes use of death itself to convey his servants from danger, Isa. lvii. 1. ' The righteous is taken away from the evil to come.'

(2.) He can secure us *in* dangers. He who rules over all can so order it, as danger itself, that which seems most so, shall not prove dangerous: Isa. xliii. 2, ' When thou passest through the waters, I will be with thee; and through the rivers, they shall not overflow thee; when thou walkest through the fire, thou shalt not be burnt, neither shall the flame kindle upon thee.'

Fire and water we count the most unmerciful elements, and such as threaten most danger; yet they are so much at the command of God, that the fire will not burn, the rivers will not drown, when he gives them such order. He preserved Noah in the midst of the deluge which drowned the world, and made the whale prove an ark unto Jonah. Fire, in its greatest rage, could not so much as scorch the three faithful Jews, though cast into the midst of its flame, Dan. iii. 27. The fire had no power upon them, because He who rules over all over-ruled it. Moses counted it (as he might well) a wonder, to see a bush burning, and not consumed, Exod. iii. 2, 3. Hereby the Lord signified, that he can keep his people safe in such circumstances, as threaten no less their ruin, than the fire endangers the consuming of a bush, when it is all on a flame. We need not go far for instances of something like this wonder; multitudes kept unscorched, untouched, when in the midst of those who are set on fire of hell.

And as the fiercest elements, so the fiercest creatures become tame and harmless, when He who rules over all will have it so. The hungry lions durst not touch Daniel, when God had given them order not to do it: they could not open a mouth, when God will have it shut; nor stir a paw to hurt him whom the Lord would save harmless, Dan. vi. 22. 2 Tim. iv. 17, He was in the mouth of a lion, and yet safe there; in the power of a wild and cruel beast, in the shape of a man, and yet there, as good as out of danger. And so was David, when his soul was amongst lions. And so you have known many more, for many years, amongst such who have had rage and power enough to have devoured them, and yet (through the restraint of him who rules over all) have not touched them, Psa. xlvii. 9. When all the males amongst the Israelites went up, from all parts of the land, to Jerusalem, as they were enjoined thrice every year, all their concernments at home were exposed, as an easy prey, to their enemies, who did encompass them on every side; none were left at their dwellings able to make any defence. In such apparent danger, what was their security? Why, the shields of the earth belong to the Lord; he would be instead of all shields to them, when they were left destitute of anything to guard them. And one way was, that He who rules over all would so over-rule the minds and hearts of their enemies, that they should have no inclination at such a time to attempt anything upon them, Exod. xxxiv. 24. If we have had experience of the Lord's thus working in the minds and hearts of them that might endanger us when we are about his worship, let him have the glory of it, who rules over all, and can dispose of all, so as to keep us safe in the midst of disturbances and dangers.

[3.] He can secure *by* dangers. Everything is not what it seems, but what he who rules over all will have it. That which seems our safety, shall prove our danger; and that which seems our danger, shall prove our safety, when he will so order it. Joseph, by being in Egypt, a place in all reason more dangerous than his father's house, was preserved from the malice of his brethren. And Paul was secured from the rage of his own countrymen, by appealing to Nero, by running into the mouth of that lion.

[4.] *After* dangers. When those that endanger you have done execution in inflicting what they threatened, or bereaving you of what you enjoyed, the Lord can retrieve all, and can restore you into the same or a better condition, than that which they have disturbed or spoiled. Thus when Chedorlaomer and his confederates had seized upon Lot and his goods, and carried him away captive, the Lord made use of Abraham, with a small company, to rescue him, and recover all, Gen. xiv. 16. And Melchizedek ascribes it to him whose throne is in heaven, under the notion of the 'most high God,' ver. 19, 20. So when the Amalekites had burnt Ziklag, and bereaved David and his associates of all their relations, their substance, their habitation, and reduced him to so great distress, as there was no glimpse of encouragement for him but only in the Lord, he found *that* all-sufficient; the Lord enabled him to recover all, besides the spoils of the enemy, 1 Sam. xxx. 18, 19; and he gives God the honour of it, ver. 23. Joel ii. 25, he promises, by succeeding plenty, to make up the loss they sustained by the years of famine which the locust, &c., had occasioned.

When a spoiled people return unto him, he will convince them, that they have been no losers by their losses. He can as easily restore the years which the spiritual locusts and caterpillars have eaten, and can bring a plenty which will more than countervail the scarcity, wherewith the worst of vermin have afflicted souls, Psa. lxviii. 9–11, Isa. xli. 17, 18. When the work of God, and all that he has been graciously doing for a people many years, is quite overwhelmed, and seems as water spilt on the ground, which cannot be gathered up, he that rules over all, who 'says to the north, Give up, and to the south, Keep not back,' Isa. xliii. 6, can gather it up all when he pleases, and restore every drop, when it seems all dried up and lost; yea, instead of drops, can give floods, Isa. xliv. 3.

You see what an encouragement this affords against dangers, whatever they be. He that rules over all can prevent them from doing any hurt, or repair all the hurt they do with greater advantage; can make them to be no dangers, or make them to prove your safety; for all things must be and do what he would have them, who rules over all, and over-rules all at his pleasure.

In all wants and necessities, which concern inward or outward man, it is a great encouragement to consider that the Lord rules over all; for this assures us, he is both able and willing to afford supplies, so far as they are needful to us, or good for us.

(1.) There is an all-sufficiency in the Lord, infinitely larger than all your wants and necessities. He that rules all, can order you what supplies and provisions, for soul or body, he pleases. All the treasure in the world is at his disposing, Hag. ii. 8, 9. The people complaining of the want of gold and silver to adorn the temple, and make it answerable to that of Solomon, the Lord declares, that ought to be no discouragement. If he thought fit to have it so sumptuous, he could easily furnish them; for silver and gold was all his, and all at his disposing. The woman, reduced, in the siege of Samaria, to so great extremity, as she was forced to eat her child, applies herself to the king for help, but in vain, as to the obtaining of any supply, if she had sought that, 2 Kings vi. 26, 27. Kings, who should relieve their subjects, may be at such a loss, as they can neither relieve these nor themselves. Oh, but the King of kings, he that rules over all, is never at a loss; no true subject of his ever sought to him in vain, Isa. xlv. 19. Let me shew how he is able to satisfy your wants, in some particulars.

[1.] He can make want to be in effect no want, for he so rules all as everything must be what he orders it to be. If he will have plenty to be as bad as want, it will be no better; and if he will have want to be as good as plenty, it will be no worse, it will be as good to all effects and purposes. He can make you not to need what you have not; he can serve the uses of what you cannot have another way, and can make you as contented and well satisfied without it as those that have it, and better too; and so can order it that you shall neither need it nor think you need it, and so can take away all need, both real and in opinion also, which is often the more troublesome need of the two. He can make a little to be as good or better than much; better for the soul, and as good for all exigencies of the body: Ps. xxxvii. 16, 'A little that the righteous hath is better than the riches of many wicked.' His smallest pittance is better than all the rich and great possessions of all wicked worldlings; so he can make up the defects of grace in its weakness, in its infancy, by his own actual influence, so that holiness, when it is weak, shall do more by virtue of this than holiness in greater strength without it, so that even in this sense that paradox of the apostle holds true, 2 Cor. xii. 10, 'When I am weak, then I am strong.'

[2.] He can make your expenses increase your estate. When you lay out what you have as he would have you, he can make it, like the widow's oil, to multiply and increase as you pour it out, 2 Kings iv. You have his word for it, 2 Cor. ix. 9, 10. The apostle is exhorting them to be free and bountiful, for the relief of those in want. And whereas it might be objected that such liberalness might bring themselves to straits and necessities, he tells them the Lord can make them the richer for and by relieving the poor. That is the way to have all-sufficiency in all things, both for themselves and others; so as to abound in every act of bounty is the way to be enriched in everything, so as to be able to express all bountifulness, the way to increase, not to prejudice, their estates. And so in spirituals: the more is communicated to others, the more is the stock increased, whether of grace or knowledge.

[3.] He can order all creatures (if need be) to bring you in provisions; for he who rules over all has all things subject to him, at his command, ready to fulfil his word and observe his orders: Hosea ii. 18, 'I will make a covenant for them with the beasts of the field,' &c. A covenant with them, not only not to hurt his people, but to help, relieve, supply them. And this is founded in the Lord's dominion over them, 'I will make.' By virtue of this they are as sure of all this from the creatures as if there were an express covenant for that purpose, ver. 21, 22. Heaven and earth and all creatures shall be so forward to supply the wants of Israel (now returned unto her subjection unto God) that they shall, as it were, seek the Lord to be employed for that end, seek him to enable them to supply her needs; and he will hear them, and employ and empower them, from the highest to the lowest, to furnish her with what she wants.

So he can order all things to relieve spiritual wants and weaknesses. Not only his ordinances but their outward enjoyments, their afflictions, yea, their falls and miscarriages, he can make all these work, singly or together, for the increase of holiness, the embittering of sin, the crucifying of them to the world, the advancing of mind and heart towards heaven. He can raise them higher by their falls, as he did Peter, and teach them to profit by worldly objects and enjoyments, and cause the rod to bud and bring forth the peaceable fruits of righteousness, Heb. xii.

[4.] He can single out any of the creatures, and give them effectual order to supply you. Such, from whom you expect no such thing, those that are never wont to do it, those that are most unlikely to serve you herein, yea, or those that are most opposite to it.

First, He can supply you by unexpected means or instruments. He can order those to do it from whom you could not look for it. So the Lord moved the barbarous people in Melita to shew great kindness to Paul and his company, after they had suffered shipwreck, Acts xxviii. 2, 10, and the wise men to supply Joseph and Mary.

Those who want supplies expect them from relations, friends, acquaintance, but the Lord can stir up strangers to do it. A remarkable instance hereof I have had from a credible author. A faithful woman being brought, in a strange place, to great extremities by the extravagancy of her husband, her children crying for bread, and she having nothing to satisfy them, gets out of doors, as not able longer to bear the cries of her little ones, whom she could not relieve; and while she was lifting up an afflicted heart to God, she spies a horse laden with provisions, the sight whereof makes her say within herself, 'Oh, what a mercy would it be if this were brought to my distressed family'! And even so the Lord had ordered it, stirring up the heart of a stranger, who had some notice of her necessities, to send that provision to her house. And some of you have heard of a godly minister who sent his maid to the market, but could not furnish her with money to buy necessaries. She meets with one she knew not, who unexpectedly gives her money for her master, enough for her occasions. And others have had experience of provisions made for their souls in a way wherein they could never have expected it. He that rules over all can do exceeding abundantly, both for soul and body, above all that we can think or look for.

Secondly, He can supply you by unusual means and ways. Our eyes are upon the means which usually help us to supplies; when these are out of sight, our hearts fail us, we sink into discouragement and despondency. But this becomes not those who believe and acknowledge that the Lord rules over all. He is not confined to usual and ordinary ways; he has all subject to him; both ordinary and extraordinary are at his command; and he can supply us, or do whatever he pleases, by whatsoever he will: Mat. iv. 4, 'Man shall not live by bread alone, but by every word that proceedeth out of the mouth of God.'

Bread, or ordinary nourishment, is not of necessity to the life of man; God can sustain or nourish him by any other means; whatsoever he pleases to order for that purpose will do it. His word is sufficient of itself to sustain him, or sufficient to provide for him in an unusual way, or sufficient to empower anything to feed him, even that which is not used for such a purpose. The text to which this refers is Deut. viii. 3, 'He fed thee with manna, that he might make thee to know that man doth not live by bread alone.' He fed them so many years by a means so unusual, that neither they nor their fathers knew it, that they might understand what dominion the Lord has over all things for our sustentation; that his word is enough for us, able to procure us anything, able to sustain and nourish us by anything whatsoever.

And the Lord has not left these latter times destitute of some experiments that he can provide for his people in unusual ways. When the protestants in Rochelle were greatly distressed by a long and close siege, multitudes of small fishes were daily brought up to them by the tide, such as had not been seen in that haven before, nor continued after the siege was raised.

Thirdly, He can supply you by improbable instruments, and such as are most unlikely to do it. It was improbable that the prophet Elijah should be sustained by a widow woman who had not enough to sustain herself and her child, 1 Kings xvii. 12, and she was a heathen too, and so might have an averseness to shew any kindness to a Hebrew. But the Lord so ordered it, and there was no resistance to his order, ver. 9. But it was more unlikely, which we meet with in the same chapter, that the ravens should feed him; for the raven is a voracious creature, and more like to devour what was brought him, than to bring him anything. And, which is more, it is $\mu\iota\sigma\acute{o}\tau\varepsilon\kappa\nu o\varsigma$, an unnatural creature, unmerciful to her own brood; is so far from feeding any other, that she will not so much as feed her own young ones: for that is her character, $\tau\acute{\iota}\kappa\tau o\nu\tau o\varsigma\ \mu\grave{\varepsilon}\nu\ o\grave{\upsilon}\ \tau\rho\acute{\varepsilon}\varphi o\nu\tau o\varsigma\ \delta\grave{\varepsilon}$, she brings them forth, but forsakes them, and will not feed them. The Lord hereby shewed his absolute dominion over the creatures: he can overrule them to do whatsoever he will; he can make them act for the relief of his people even against their own natures; he could make the ravens kind to and diligent for the prophet, though they have no care, no kindness for the fruit of their own womb; he did but command it, and it was done, vers. 4-6. They provided him his dinner and supper daily and constantly while he stayed there. Though all probable means for the sustaining of soul or body should fail, yet is there enough in the Lord to encourage us. He who rules over all can provide for both, any way he pleases, even by the most improbable means, as well as any; in the most unlikely ways, as well as the best.

Fourthly. He can supply you by the most opposite instruments, such as would far rather starve soul or body, than afford the least relief to either. Thus he enriched the Israelites by the Egyptians when they had enslaved them, and designed nothing better for them than to keep them poor and miserable in hard bondage, Ps. lxviii. 30, and lxxii. 6. When Samaria, besieged by the Assyians, was reduced to such extremity, as, 2 Kings vii. 25, an ass's head was sold for eighty pieces of silver, ten pounds, when the whole ass at other times was but counted worth a tenth part of it; and a fourth part of a pint, a cab of doves' dung at five shekels (a cab was as much of that dung as would serve a man for a day) went at above twelve shillings and sixpence; the Lord takes order that they should be plentifully supplied out of the stores of their enemies, who had designed to starve them, chap. vii. 16. Ps. lxviii. 30, 'Rebuke the multitude of spearmen, the company of bulls,' &c. The bulls, *i. e.* such proud and powerful men as demean themselves towards those under them, as bulls do towards the lesser and weaker cattle. The Lord can bring them under, and make them glad to buy their peace, and to enrich those with their own stores, whom they had exhausted and impoverished, Ps. lxxii. 8-10. He that commands his servants, when their enemy is hungry, to feed him, can command their enemies to feed them, and can make them do it, whether they will or no. When they are bereaved of refreshments for soul or body, he can make the hands which spoiled them to repair them, and to restore what they violently took away.

Thus, when the Philistines looked upon their taking away the ark, as the greatest advantage that ever they had over Israel, and most matter of triumph, that being the pledge of God's presence with the Israelites, and so their strength, their glory, their happiness above all people on earth, one would have thought they would as soon have given them their country as restored this, yet the Lord forces them to do it, and so orders it, that the Philistines, of their own accord, send back the ark to the Israelites.

What cannot he do for the restoring of the gospel, and making provision for souls, even by the enemies of it, who could bring back the ark to his people by such means, in such desperate circumstances?

2. *Obj.* I do not doubt but he is able to afford me all supplies for soul and body, but is he willing to do it?

Ans. There is no more occasion to doubt of that, so far as it will be good for you, and that is all you can desire, Ps. xxxiv. 10, and lxxxiv. 11, and lxxxv. 12. He will supply you in all your wants with whatever is good: Philip. iv. 19, 'My God shall supply all your need, according to his riches in glory by Christ Jesus.' There are glorious riches treasured up in Christ for this purpose, and out of that treasury he will supply all your needs, even as [to] the things of this life: Mat. vi. 33, 'Seek first the kingdom of God, and all other things shall be added unto you.' Seek to get into the kingdom of God, subject yourselves to him in all righteousness, and then he that rules this kingdom will provide all these things for you, so that you need be no further careful or solicitous about it. And you have sufficient assurance of it, in that he rules over all, and over you in special, having given up yourselves to be ruled by him.

[1.] Consider, a ruler who is mindful of his office will not suffer those who are ruled by him to want what is needful if he can easily help it. Even Pharaoh took care that his subjects should have necessaries in the years of famine, Exod. xli. Good rulers mind that as the end of government, that those who are under them *sint beatissimi*, as the orator expresses it, may live happily. And he is justly counted a tyrant, who, regarding only his own pleasure or profit, minds not the necessary concernments of his subjects. How far is the Lord of heaven and earth from this, whose goodness and mercy is as large as his dominion, even over all his works? Ps. cxlv. 9.

[2.] He makes provision for those whom he less regards; he is ready to supply all creatures; and can we think him unwilling to do it for those who are peculiarly his subjects, to whom he is more specially related, and for whom he has a more particular affection? Ps. cxlvii. 5, 8, 9. It is one of the glories of his kingdom, that he provides for all that belongs to it, Ps. cxlv. 10–16. It is an argument of very little faith to doubt, that he who is willing to provide for all, is not much more willing to supply his own. Our Lord Jesus himself tells us so, Mat. vi. 26, 28–30.

[3.] The greater any ruler is, the more may reasonably be expected from him, unless where greatness is but a large cypher, or an empty flourish. What then may be expected from him who rules over all, to whom the greatest on earth are as nothing, less than nothing and vanity; from him 'who only does great wonders, Ps. cxxxvi. 4, and is still willing to do them, as what follows shews, 'For his mercy endures for ever'?

It is a great dishonour to the glorious Majesty of heaven and earth to doubt that he is not willing to act like himself, and to supply you, so much more, so much better than any, as he is incomparably above all: 2 Sam.

xxiv. 23, 'All these things did Araunah as a king give unto the king.' He acted magnificently, more like a king than a private person.

The Lord shews his magnificence, by providing continually for those who depend on him; it is his glory, and therefore there can be no question of his willingness, no more than of his power, to relieve his people in all their necessities, outward or inward; he that rules over all, is ready and able to do it above all.

3. Against the power and violence of enemies. How great soever it be, how terrible soever it seem, how much soever heightened with successes, however enforced with malice and rage, how little soever you see to resist or oppose it, yet need you not be discouraged, you will see no cause for it, if you do but duly consider that the Lord rules over all. This power and rage, whatever it be, is subject to him; he can manage, and order it, and dispose of it as he pleases; he can make it less, or make it useless, or make use of it far otherwise than they intend, or make it nothing, when or however he will.

(1.) He can make it less. He can abate the power and assuage the wrath of man, and bring it down to what degree he pleases; for it is wholly under his dominion and power who rules over all. He can with greatest ease prick the bladder, and make the tumour fall, how much soever it swell. When the wicked are like the raging sea in a storm, foaming out wrath and rage, threatening wrecks and ruin to this or that person or party, he that 'ruleth the raging of the sea,' Ps. lxxxix. 9, let him but speak the word, and that will be enough to hush the storm, and still the waves, and make all as calm as you can wish. It is the greatness of their power that makes it formidable; but how great soever it seem, it is nothing to his who rules over all, and has the ruling of it. It is little or nothing to him, and he can easily and suddenly make it so to you.

(2.) He can make it useless. And be it never so great, if it be rendered useless, it is as good as none. He that rules over all can effectually forbid and hinder the use of any power. Let the arm of flesh be never so big, and strong, and sinewy, if the Lord lay hold on it, it cannot stir, nor move in the least, no more than the arm of a dead man. If the mastiff be never so fierce, yet if he be muzzled, there is no fear of him. Thus can the Lord deal with the fiercest of those you fear: Ps. cxxxviii. 7, עַל אַף. He can put a muzzle upon their nose, or put a hook into it, so that they cannot bite, nor be able to stir, but as he pleases. When the Philistines dreaded Samson's strength, to render it useless, and not to be feared, they put out his eyes; so can the Lord render the greatest power useless, by binding those that have it, so as they shall not see that they have it, or see how to use it, or see how to take or improve any advantage by it. How useless was the power of the Sodomites when blinded! The whole city could do nothing against one family. The Lord can as easily, and does more ordinarily, blind the mind, and take away a spirit of discerning, Job xii. 24, 25 and v. 12; how, see verse 14, Isa. lix. 10. Or if they have their eyes, he can take order they shall not find their hands; and what can they do, how useless is their power, who cannot find their hands! Ps. lxxvi. 5. When they come to do their work, they have their hands to seek; the Lord can take them away when he pleases, and so render their designs and undertakings ridiculous, and all their force and power useless.

(3.) He can make them use it otherwise than they intend. If it be not rendered useless, yet shall they not be able to use it as they will, but as he pleases who rules over them and all. He can overrule them, so as it shall no way hurt you, and then you need not fear it; or so as it shall be for your advantage, and then you may rejoice in it.

He can turn it upon others whom you are little concerned in, or think not of. He can find them other work than their power is prepared for; he can interpose another object betwixt you and their fury, and make that a screen to you; he can raise them another enemy, where their power and rage shall spend itself, and never reach you. When Sennacherib had struck a great terror into Hezekiah and his people, by this does the Lord encourage them: Isa. xxxvii. 7, 'He shall hear a rumour,' that shall divert them; and what that was, see verse 9, 'He heard say concerning Tirhakah king of Ethiopia, He is come forth to make war with thee.'

He can turn it against a common enemy. Such were the Philistines to David; and the Lord turns the force of Saul, which had encompassed David, against them, against David's enemies, 1 Sam. xxiii. 27, 28. You think the power and rage you fear will fall upon you, but the Lord can order it to fall upon those whom you are concerned should fall by it. And so the greatness of it, which is formidable to you, will be your advantage; the greater it is, the better it will be for you.

He can turn it against themselves. They bend their bow, and make ready their arrows, and are going to shoot with all their might; but where the arrows will fall they know not. He has the ordering of that who rules all things, and he can order them to fall upon their own heads instead of yours, Ezek. ix. 10, Ps. vii. 16. Little did the children of Ammon, and Moab, and mount Seir, think that the great force they raised for the ruin of Jehoshaphat should be made use of to destroy themselves; but so he ordered it who rules over all, and so it came to pass, 2 Chron. iv. 23.

He can turn it for you, and make it serve you and your interest, though it was raised and levelled directly against you. Saul's power and preparations made use of against David, when Saul was taken away, came into David's hands; the greater the power of his enemy was, the more was it for his advantage. The Lord, by turning the hearts of your enemies, can engage all the power which you now dread for you; and that is as easy a turn to him as any other, who rules the heart of man as easily as anything else, Prov. xxi. 1. Those who get power, and increase it, to become thereby dreadful unto others, know not for whom they get it, or for whom it shall be used; that must be as he who rules over all will order; and he can, and often does, dispose of it against those who have it, and for those against whom it is designed and levelled. He ordinarily will have it used quite otherwise than those who are in power would have it.

(4.) He can break it, and can easily and suddenly (how great and formidable soever it is) bring it to nothing, and that many ways.

[1.] He can break them himself. He that can rule all things needs no help, no power of men to do it: Ps. lxxxix. 10, 'Thou hast broken Rahab in pieces: thou hast scattered thine enemies.' He can deal with all that oppose him and his people, as he did with Pharaoh, called Rahab. It is no more to him to crush the mightiest of them all, than it is for you to crush the snail that is under your foot. He shews how he will deal with those who combine against him and his interest, Ps. ii. They look big now, like rocks or mountains, and seem to threaten heaven with their lofty aspiring tops; but when he takes them in hand, they will prove but like potter's vessels, and shiver all in pieces, like an earthen pot under the weighty stroke of an iron mace: 'Whosoever shall fall on him shall be broken; but on whomsoever he shall fall, he will grind them to powder,' Mat. xxi. 44. All their force against him, as that of the waves against a rock, shall serve only to dash themselves in pieces.

[2.] He can raise the whole power of the world against them, for he who rules over all can muster up all the forces of heaven and earth with a word; and what is that which disturbs you to all this? How many did he arm against Pharaoh, when he would not let his people go to serve him? Yet those which plagued Pharaoh were but as it were a few stragglers in comparison of what the great Ruler of the world can raise in a moment. How many does he threaten to array against Israel, in case they would not be ruled by him! Lev. xxvi. 21, 'Seven times more, and yet seven times more.' But indeed they are past all numbering, beyond all computation; the greatest volumes in the world would not be a sufficient muster-roll for the forces of him who rules over all. The angels are but a small part of his army, as it were his own company or regiment; they are spoken of but as making up one chariot, Ps. lxviii. 17; yet they are myriads and thousands, infinite numbers. And these, with all the rest, fully under command; let him but give the word, and all would be ready together to what execution he pleases. Oh what are all the oppressing powers on earth to the Lord and his hosts! How soon, how easily, can he break them!

[3.] He can break them and their power by the least and weakest thing. He need not raise his whole force to do it; any one thing will serve, if he give it a commission. Such is his power and dominion over all, that anything will be able to do whatever he would have it. A tile, a gnat, a fly, a worm, any disease, will lay the most potent in the dust when he gives order for that purpose. It will fall without hand when he pleases, as that great oppressor did, Dan. viii. 23–25. The little vermin could soon make an end of Herod's power, when he put it forth to vex certain of the church, Acts xii. 1, 23.

[4.] He can break them by themselves; make them tumble with their own weight, crush them with their own force; and employ themselves, or those whom they count their own, to hew down the bough they stand upon, or cut off the arm wherein their strength and power lies. He that rules over all, can overrule everything to act as he would have it, though it be against itself. He can break them,

First, By their own relations; can bring their destruction out of their own bowels. Thus fell the great terror and oppressor of Judea, Sennacherib, when Hezekiah and his people had no strength against him, 2 Kings xix. 37. When the child is come so near the birth, there is the greatest and sharpest pain, and when the woman's strength is quite spent, and the child so feeble it cannot help itself, there is the greatest danger. And this was their condition; though the blasphemy, cruelty, insolency of the enemy had made him ripe for ruin, yet the people distressed by him had no power to effect it. What, then, shall the oppressor escape? No; what they could not do against him, the Lord employs his own sons to do. After he had seen the deliverance of God's people, and the destruction of his own, they bereaved him of life who had received life from him, ver. 37.

Secondly, By their own party; by those which raised them and were their support. He can make one leg strike up another, and that which slipped first to break the other in the fall. Thus, when the men of Shechem conspired with Abimelech in a tyrannical design, the Lord so orders it that he first breaks them; and those of them which were left brake him, according to the imprecation of Jotham, Judges ix. 20. He that rules over all, thus disposed of it, vers. 56, 57.

Thirdly, By their own attempts. He can make the blows of the violent to rebound upon themselves, and push them into the pit which they had prepared to bury others in. Thus Haman's attempts upon Mordecai and the Jews proved his ruin, and the instrument of death he had erected does execution upon himself. And Pharaoh's violence against Israel, which would pursue them even into the sea, overwhelmed him and his people, and made an end of them at once. He who rules over all, can cause any engines of violence to recoil upon those who manage them, and hit themselves instead of those they aim at.

Fourthly, By their own hands. He needs no hand at all to break them; but if he will employ any, he can make their own hands as well as any other serve to ruin them, Ps. ix. 6. There was no need that David should lay hands upon Saul, the Lord could take order that he should lay violent hands upon himself. He can overrule their hand to work them into such entanglements, as they shall find no easier way out, than by letting out their own souls, and opening the passage by their own hands.

Fifthly, Their own counsels. When they say, Come, let us work wisely, the Lord can order it to prove no wiser, than the contrivement of a subtle head against itself, Job v. 13. He makes their craftiness become a snare to themselves, and gives such wheels to their counsels as carry them headlong as from a precipice; and the more violent they are, the more fiercely they drive, with the more force do they fall to the breaking of themselves: Ps. x. 2, 'Let them be taken in the devices that they have imagined.' The event will answer the prayer, for the prayer of faith is in such a person a prediction. The web that he weaves to catch the poor fly, the Lord can make use of to entangle the spider, whose fine and subtle device it is.

Sixthly, By their own fears: Prov. xxviii. 1, 'The wicked flee when no man pursueth.' There needs no other to rout them, but their own fears. The Lord can order this, both to pursue and do execution, Lev. xxvi. 36, 37. Their fear shall put them to flight, and pursue them when there is none to follow them, and make them do execution upon themselves, when there is none else to do it. The Lord promises Israel, by these means, to discomfit and destroy the Canaanites, Exod. xxiii. 27. He who has the command of all, and so can raise what passion he pleases in the heart, will raise and arm their own fears against them, and thereby put them to flight, and bring destruction upon them, 2 Chron. xiv. 14. Their own fears made those who had aided the Ethiopians and their cities, and all they had, an easy prey to Asa and his people.

Seventhly, By their own fancy. The Lord needs no other force to rout and break the greatest powers on earth, than the power of their imagination. Thus were the Syrians broken, when there was not a hand lift up against them, 2 Kings vii. 6, 7. The Lord made such impression upon their imagination, that they fancied they heard such a terrible noise (if it had been really audible, the besieged might have heard it as well as they), and upon this fancy they are all in confusion, run away as for life, and leave all they had to their enemies. Let but the Lord arm the fancy of the mightiest on earth against them, and that will be enough to ruin them.

Eighthly, By their own mistakes. When they think they are in Dothan, he can set them in the midst of Samaria, and so leave them in the power, and at the mercy of those whom they have most injured, as he did the Syrians, 2 Kings vi. So the Moabites' mistake of the waters for blood, drew them out of their strength, engaged them on a great disadvantage, and so was the occasion of their ruin, 2 Kings iii. 22, &c.

You see what encouragement we have from the Lord's ruling over all, against all opposite power and violence. He can assuage it or render it useless; he can divert it, or break it, and that by anything, even by themselves, by anything of them, either by their power or their weakness.

Here is encouragement as to the lowness of the interest of God and his people in the world, and in these parts of it that we are acquainted with.

The interest of God seems to be at a very low ebb amongst the inhabitants of the earth. The kingdoms of the world seem to be the kingdoms of Satan; he rules them and keeps them in subjection to him, and his will and laws have more observance than the will and laws of God. The rod of his strength doth not reach the greatest part of the earth; the gospel, which is his sceptre, has little or no place left in many regions where it once prevailed; and where it yet has any entertainment, it meets with great opposition, is under much restraint, and in danger to be suppressed. Many there are that rise up against it, few in comparison that own it by any due subjection to it; and these hated, oppressed, persecuted, kept under hatches, and in danger to be rooted out; and the special interest of God, which lies in his true and real subjects, like to suffer in and with them.

This is matter of great discouragement to those who truly honour the great sovereign of the world, and tender his interest; but for all this the Lord reigns, and will do; he still rules over all; and this duly considered, is enough to strengthen the weak hands and the feeble knees, to inspire the dejected with courage and spirit, and make them bear up cheerfully under the sad apprehensions of the declining or sinking of that interest which is due to them. For,

1. The greatest part of the world does still continue in subjection to God, and gives him the honour due to the universal sovereign; all creatures do it but apostate men and devils, and these are but a very small part of the whole creation, and little or nothing compared with the whole fabric of heaven and earth, which continues absolutely subject to their sovereign.

2. He rules as much over wicked men and spirits, as over those who voluntarily subject themselves to him, though not in the same manner. The power, and wisdom, and justice of his government, is as much honoured upon them, though not the mercy of it. And how far it is his interest to extend the mercy of his government, we must leave it to him to judge, who is the only competent judge of it; it is above our capacity, and beyond our measures.

3. As to his interest which is concerned in his peculiar people, it shall never be quite suppressed, never extinguished in the world. So long as God rules, he will maintain it, he will uphold it; but in what places, in what degree and manner, and by what means, must be left to him, the *arcana* of whose empire, and the mysteries of his governing are incomprehensible.

This is plain. (1.) When it is weak, he can strengthen it; when it seems falling, he can uphold it. It was weak, indeed, amongst the Israelites when the prophet complains, 1 Kings xix. 10, 'I, even I, only am left.' But the Lord better upheld it, and kept it up in more strength than he apprehended, ver. 18, 'I have left me seven thousand in Israel which have not bowed the knee to Baal.' The interest of God may be many thousand times stronger than it visibly appears or we see ground to conceive it. It was weak in Zerubbabel's time, lying in a few contemptible restored captives, and these in the midst of raging enemies, ready and resolved to crush them; and yet when they had no strength of themselves, nor any arm of flesh, nor any worldly prop to support them, he who rules over all was their strength and upheld them, and his interest in and by them, Zech. iv. 9, 10. How weak and despicable soever they and their undertakings for God might seem, the Lord would make it appear they were not to be despised; his work should prosper in their hands, they should effectually carry on his interest in building his temple. For these seven, the eyes of the Lord, *i. e.* his governing providence reaching over the whole earth, was engaged with them.

(2.) When it is straitened and pent up in a narrow compass, he can enlarge it; when it is but as a cloud like a man's hand, he can extend it so as to cover the face of the heavens, and make it spread far and wide. Time was when it seemed confined to Abraham's family, but the Lord promised it should reach all the families of the earth, and be diffused through many nations; and he that rules all those families and nations made it good. And this our Lord Jesus holds forth to us in divers parables or resemblances, Mat. xiii. 31–33. The Lord can make his kingdom, when it is but like a 'little leaven,' to diffuse its virtue to every part of the world; when it is but like 'a grain of mustard-seed,' to grow up into a vast tree; he hath done it, and can do it again.

(3.) When it is sinking, he can bring it up again. Let the enemies of God fall never so heavy upon his interest, they will never be able quite to sink it; it will up again one where or other, either in the same place, where it seems at some desperate plunge, or in some other, where before it appeared not, or in both. When that great persecution was raised at Jerusalem, at that time the centre of Christ's interest in the world, where the great concerns of the gospel then lay principally, and in a manner only there, Acts viii. 13, the enemies thereof made account to sink it quite. But how were they disappointed! While they had it under water there it gets up, and gets head in the cities and countries round about, far and near, yea, in that place, a little after, where it had the greatest plunge. They bear it down in one town, and it breaks out almost everywhere else, and by that means, too, which they used to suppress it. So when the woman, by the violence of the great red dragon, was forced from her former state and place, and when he would have left her no place nor being on earth, the Lord prepared a place for her in the wilderness, where she should have subsistence and nourishment, Rev. xii. 6. When he poured forth a flood after her, with a design to have washed her away from the face of the earth, to have overwhelmed her utterly, ver. 15, the Lord disappoints him, ver. 16. The divisions in the empire diverted the torrent of persecution, and swallowed it up; as some.

(4.) When it seems dead, he can revive it, and give it a resurrection and life, Hosea vi. 1, 2. Much of the interest of God was involved in the people, yet how low were they brought, even to the grave; not only torn, and smitten, and wounded, but, as it were, dead and buried! Yet, though they were dead, the Lord undertakes to revive them, and so his interest with them; though they were buried, he would bring them out of the grave (the desperate condition, which seemed like their sepulchre), he would raise them from the dead, and make them live in his sight. He that rules over all is the Lord both of death and life; both civil and natural is at his disposing, he can give or restore it to whom and when he will. And death, in every sense, will resign up any under his power when the Lord gives order.

After the captivity of the ten tribes, the two remaining were the only people in the world which visibly owned God and his interest; when they were carried away captive also, and their temple burnt, and no place left for the solemn worship of God, of his institution, this might well seem a deadly blow to the interest of God on earth. Answerably, their state, in these desperate circumstances, is expressed by dry bones, when the body is not only deprived of soul and life, but buried and in the grave, quite consumed, neither skin, nor flesh, nor sinews left, nothing but the dry bones, and these not set together, but scattered here and there in the valley, not so much as the form of an anatomy left, Ezek. xxxvii. 1, 2. Well might it be made a question, as it is, ver. 3, 'Can these dry bones live?' Is there any hope, any possibility of it? What could be more hopeless than the recovery of this people, and God's interest embarked with them in such a condition, which the Lord himself thus represents? Yet he who rules over all, who has all things absolutely at his command, and can do what he will with a word, could, with a word, cause these scattered and disordered bones to come together, bone to his bone, in that admirable order as they are placed in the body of man, and lay sinews, and bring flesh upon them, and cause breath and life to enter into them, so that they 'stood upon their feet, an exceeding great army,' as ver. 6–9, &c. Thus could the Lord revive his slain interest and the destroyed people which had owned it; and that with a breath, when all hopes of any such thing was lost, and all seemed to be cut off for ever.

The meaning of this encouraging vision is expressed, ver. 12–14, 'I will open your graves, and cause you to come out of your graves, and bring you into the land of Israel,' &c. So Rev. xi., when the witnesses, those who gave their testimony for the interest of God against antichristianism, are slain, *i. e.* (as is probably conceived) by persecution and violence brought into such a condition as they could scarce be numbered amongst the living, when they are, in a civil sense at least, quite dead, the Lord shews he can revive them, and raise his fallen interest with them, ver. 11, 12. He will not only restore them to their former place and station, but advance them higher than ever.

That he who rules over all is sufficient for all this, will be more evident if we consider particularly,

1. He wants no *wisdom*. He that is wise enough to rule and order all and everything in the whole world, wants no wisdom for the upholding or restoring his own interest. Those who are wisest for the managing of their interest are but fools to him. The apostle, where he styles him King, calls him also 'the only wise God,' 1 Tim. i. 17. The profoundest and most improved wisdom deserves not the name of wisdom compared with his. He is only wise, he alone. None so well understand their interest, none so apprehensive of what may endanger it, none so knowing what may promote it, or for the ordering of all things in a subserviency to it. The wisdom of angels is but folly to him.

2. He wants no *power*. He that rules over all has power to keep all in subjection, to make all things obey him, to force all to move or stand still at his beck. It is the Lord God almighty that reigns, Rev. xi. 7. It is the God 'which quickeneth the dead, and calleth those things which be not as though they were,' and makes them to be what he calls them by so calling them. It is he who has power to rule and order all things in heaven and earth as he will. If some wise men had the power to order all things as they pleased, they would never question the securing of their interest. What fear is there, then, that the Lord will let his interest miscarry, when he has power at will, no less than infiniteness of power, as well as wisdom?

3. He wants no *instruments* to serve his interest, nor can want any, if the whole world will afford enough, for all in heaven and earth are in his hand and ready for his use, who is κύριος καὶ παμβασιλεὺς τῶν πάντων (as Athanasius), Lord and absolute Sovereign of all things. The highest angels think it their chief honour to serve his interest, and to serve it in any capacity, and so, we find, are called sometimes his chariot, sometimes his warriors, sometimes the conduct of his people, sometimes their purveyors, always his ministers. And he can make the most untoward instruments to serve his

turn, whether they will or no. The crookedest tool will become straight in his hand, who overrules all things to be and do what he will have them, Isa. xlvi. 11.

4. He wants no *opportunities*, through want of which many a man's interest miscarries; for times and seasons are in his hand, he has reserved them in his own power, Acts i. 7. He rules them as he does all things else. That must be a season which he will have so. He can make any part of time to be a fit season, and what we count unseasonable he can render it the fittest opportunity. He can remove when he pleases whatever in us or in others renders that unseasonable which would promote his interest. The unfitness of the subject, the incapacity of the matter, the unpreparedness of his people, cannot nonplus him who rules over all, or make him to seek or leave him at a loss for a season; he can overrule these, or anything else, into a seasonable compliance and subserviency to him in any moment.

5. He wants no *will*. For who can doubt that the great ruler of the world is not willing to secure and advance his own interest? Sure this must be pleasing to him, and ' He will do all his pleasure,' Isa. xlvi. 10.

Obj. But if he be so willing and all-sufficient to maintain his own interest, why does he suffer it to decline and be borne down, and his people who only own it, and sincerely design the promoting of it, to be oppressed and kept under hatches, to be deprived of power, kept low and weak, and for the most part in an afflicted condition, and their necks under persecution? By this he seems not willing to uphold or advance his own interest in the world.

Ans. 1. We may mistake his interest, and are apt to judge that to be for it which is not. We are apt to think that if the Lord would put his people in a prosperous and plentiful condition, and give them power and greatness, and free them from the cross, and advance them in a worldly station above others, and enable them to shake off the yoke, and to keep those under who oppress and persecute them, this would be more for his interest than the low and distressed state which is commonly their portion. But it is otherwise, and the Lord, who rules and disposes of all with infinite wisdom, knows it, and he has not only said but done enough to make his people understand it. He has given experiments thereof in several ages sufficient to convince us, though we be slow to understand or believe that which does not please us. He has tried his people with outward prosperity, and sometimes with power and greatness, and this has proved more prejudicial to his interest than that low afflicted condition which we are more impatient of. There are instances enough of this; it is well if we ourselves in these nations be not an instance of it.

We have ground enough, both from Scripture and experience, to believe that his interest lies not so much in the outward prosperity of his people, as in exercising them with afflictions and sufferings, and appearing for them therein. This seems to be most for his honour, and best for them too, if they judge like themselves, and count that best which prove so to their souls. That which is most for his honour is most for his interest. Did he not get more glory, by keeping his servants untouched, unscorched, in the midst of the raging flames, than if he had kept them from being cast into the furnace? Does it not honour him more to let the world see that he can keep the bush, when it is burning, from being consumed, than if he should keep the fire from coming near it? Is it not more to keep a spark alive in the midst of the waves, than to make it flame in a chimney, and more for his honour that can do it? Why, thus does the Lord do, and thus does he honour himself, by keeping up a people for himself in the midst of the rage and fury of the world. They are like a combustible body in a fiery furnace, or like a bush flaming, or like a spark in the midst of the sea, and yet kept alive, secured, preserved. Who can do such a thing but he who rules over all? How much is this for his honour! A thousand preservations from trouble, danger, and extremities keeping these from coming near them would not be so much, if at all taken notice of, would be in a manner lost upon them, would not be observed with any such honourable reflection upon the great God, as his upholding, maintaining, and delivering them when they find themselves in the mouth of dangers, and in the midst of extremities.

It is better for his people too; better for their souls than that condition which is more pleasing to flesh and blood. And that which is better for their souls is more for his interest. It makes more for peace and holiness. They have ordinarily more peace with God, when they meet with tribulation in the world; more peace within, when more trouble without. When affliction lies heavy, sin lies light, was the observation of a wise and holy man. And then holiness thrives more under afflictions, and corruption has less advantage against us than in a prosperous condition: 2 Cor. iv. 16, 'Though our outward man perish, yet the inward man is renewed day by day.' Though he was harassed by affliction, and brought low as to his outward state, yet his soul had great advantage by it; he lost nothing, but what the eagle loseth by moulting her old feathers; she gets fresh and more beautiful plumes, and is renewed into a better state. His inward man is hereby renewed, and refined, and holiness more revived and reinforced. He was freed more from the incumbrance of the old man, and that corruption which brings and keeps the soul in a crazy and decrepit condition. And thus it is ordinarily with the people of God. Hence Isidore, writing to one of Pelusium, from his own experience, gives him this advice, Pray earnestly (says he) that the Pelussets, μήποτε δυνηθῆναι ἃ βούλονται, may never be in such a condition as they desire; for they are better when they are low and oppressed, ἢ μικρὰ ἀνανεύοντες, than when they get up, though but a little.

2. We may be mistaken about the ways and means which the Lord uses to secure and advance his interest. We may think that tends to ruin it, which he makes use of to promote it. The cutting of the vine, and making it bleed, to those who have no skill, may seem the way to kill it, whereas it tends to make it grow and flourish more, and render it more fruitful. The Lord can make his interest flourish by such ways and means as seem to threaten the destruction of it. Never did it prevail more in the world, never did it rise and spread itself with so great advantage, as in the apostles' times, and some ages after, when it met with the greatest opposition, and was destitute of all worldly advantages, and was assaulted with such violence, as did in all appearance threaten its utter overthrow. But after it got the countenance and power of Christian emperors (though that, we would think, should have a quite contrary effect) it declined and dwindled away, and all sunk in a little time into woful degeneracy, as appears by the complaints of those ancients in the fifth age, who were sensible hereof, and bitterly lamented it.

So unfit are our understandings to be the measure of these things, that what we apprehend to be best for it proves worst, and what we think destructive to it, proves its advancement, as it is ordered by him who rules over all.

3. Though his interest should decline for a time, yet would that be no argument that he is unmindful of it, or unwilling to look after it. No, though it should seem a long time to us. For that time which we think exceeding long is little or nothing to him. The woman's being in the wilderness for twelve hundred and sixty days, Rev. xii. 6, her continuance in an obscure ejected state, as it were an exile, and excluded from common

society for so many years, seems a very long time to us, but to him it is not so much as so many hours; for 'a thousand years to the Lord is but as one day;' nay, not so much, Ps. xc. 4, but as a 'watch in the night.' A watch in the night is but the eighth part of a natural day, a very little while; but yesterday, when it is past, is nothing.

5. Here is encouragement against all troubles, afflictions, and sufferings whatsoever. He who rules over all, has the ruling and ordering of these, of whatever of this nature befalls you; and being under his command, and at his disposing wholly, they must be and do what he would have them, nothing else, nothing worse than he thinks good; neither more nor less than he sees fit. They can do you no hurt, if he forbid them; they will do you good if he command them; and if they would lie heavy or long, he can relieve you when he will, or effectually order any other thing to do it.

(1.) He can hinder them from hurting you; for he has the ruling of them, as of all things, and they must be what he would have them. If he will have them to befall you without hurt, they will be no ways hurtful to you, they can do you no harm, there will be nothing in them to dismay or discourage you. He can make trouble to be as no trouble; sufferings, such as you shall not suffer by; so the apostle found it, 2 Cor. iv. 8, they were in trouble, but it did not trouble them. That befell them which would have distressed others; but the Lord ordered it so as it was no distress to them. He can make want to be as good as no want, 2 Cor. vi. 9, 10; they were poor, but as good as not poor, they could enrich others; they were in want, and yet as good as if they wanted nothing, as if they had possessed all; sorrowful, but as good as not sorrowful, always rejoicing. So he can make pain to be as easy as no pain, and heavy pressures to be as light as that which weighs nothing. If there be any snare in them, he can keep it from entangling you; if there be any malignity therein, he can expel it, so as it shall not endanger you; if there be any sting in them, he can pull it, so that it shall not touch you, you shall not smart by it. There is enough in him to encourage us, whatever troubles we may meet with. Since he who rules over all can render them altogether harmless, what is then left in them to discourage us? It is folly and weakness to be dejected at that which can do us no hurt.

(2.) He can make them an advantage to us; for he rules them as he does all things, and they must and will do what he would have them. He can make troubles do us more good than freedom from troubles will do us. He can make them heal us; for he can heal by stripes, and turn that into a sovereign antidote which we shun as poison. He can make us wise by them: Ps. xciv. 12, 'Blessed is the man whom thou chastenest, O Lord, and teachest him out of thy law.' He can enrich us by them: Heb xii. 10, 'They chastened us for their own pleasure; he for our profit.' He can make them comforts to us: Ps. xxiii; 2 Cor. vii. 4, 'I am filled with comfort in all our tribulations.' He can prefer us by them: 2 Cor. iv. 17, 'Our light affliction, which is but for a moment, worketh for us a far more exceeding weight of glory.' He can enhappy us by them: Mat. v. 10, 'Blessed are they which are persecuted for righteousness' sake: for theirs is the kingdom of heaven.' He can make us safe by them, secure us from greater: Ps. xciv. 13, 'That thou mayest give him rest from the days of adversity.' He can make them every way expressive of his love and delight, Heb. xii. 5, 6, Prov. iii. 11, 12. What, can the best condition you can choose do more for you than the Lord can order your troubles to do? And whatever occasion of discouragement you see in them, it will vanish if you do but duly look upon him who rules over all.

(3.) If they lie too heavy, or stay too long; if they be ready to do you hurt, or not like to do you good: he can relieve you, or can command anything else to bring you relief and deliverance. To instance in some particulars:

[1.] He can relieve you from heaven or from earth; for he is the Ruler of both, and has all things in either wholly at his command. He can order the angels to do it; we have many examples in Scripture, and warrant there to expect it now. The angels relieved Lot, Gen. xix. 9, 10; an angel stopped the mouths of the lions, Dan. vi. 22; so an angel delivered Peter, Acts xii. 7–11; so an angel relieved Hezekiah and his country by destroying the host of the Assyrians, which I instance in (passing by others) to clear that obscure text, where it is promised, Isa. xxxi. 8, 'They shall fall by the sword,' neither of the strong nor of the weak. Should they fall by neither, why then by no sword at all. It seems a contradiction; by a sword, and yet by no sword. But all is clear if we understand it of the sword of an angel; for that was no sword of man, either strong or weak.

Nor ought we to confine this relief by angels to Scripture times; they may and do relieve and deliver the people of God now, and have done in all ages. The ministry of angels for our relief is held forth in general expressions, without limitation to special times or extraordinary persons: Ps. xci. 11, 12, 'He shall give his angels charge over thee to keep thee in all thy ways,' &c.; and Ps. xxxiv. 7, 'The angel of the Lord encampeth round about them that fear him, and delivereth them.' (And he prays not for a miracle: Ps. xxxv. 5, 6, 'Let the angel of the Lord chase them. Let their way be dark and slippery, and let the angel of the Lord prosecute them.') Mat. xviii. 10, 'Their angels do always behold the face of my Father which is in heaven.' Heb. i. 14, 'Are they not all ministering spirits, sent forth to minister for them who shall be heirs of salvation?' They continue still ministering for the relief of the heirs of salvation, only we take not notice of them, because they appear not in a visible shape, as they did some time heretofore, and we have no such way to know what is done by angels for us as they had. There is no Scripture now to declare and record what is done by them, since the canon of the Scripture was finished. And if the Scripture had not ascribed something there mentioned unto angels, they might have been (as they are now) referred to other causes. *Ex. gr.*, if the Holy Ghost, Acts xii., had not told us that an angel smote Herod, and so put an end to his persecution, we might have looked no further for his death than such a disease as Josephus ascribes it to, and calls διακάρδιον ὀδύνην, and ἄθρον τῆς κοιλίας ἄλγημα (Ant. lib. xix. c. 8); and the owl which he says Herod saw sitting over his head would scarce have been taken for an angel.

So the mortality in David's time might have been ascribed to the pestilence without looking farther, if the Scripture had not mentioned an angel as the instrument, 2 Sam. xxiv. We need not sink into discouragement when we see no relief to be had on earth, we may lift up our eyes above the mountains; he whose throne is in heaven can from thence bring salvation.

And he is not a God of the hills only, and not of the valleys. He can raise relief out of the earth when he pleases: Rev. xii. 16, 'The earth helped the woman,' &c. So Paul and Silas were delivered by an earthquake, Acts xvi. 26; so Ps. xviii. 6, for David's relief, you may see a concurrence of heaven and earth, angels and clouds, thunder and hail, wind and rain, fire and water, darkness and lightnings. He who is the Ruler of all these, and all things, interposed as effectually for the deliverance of his servant as if he had made all these conspire to effect it.

[2.] He can do it by things great or small. Sometimes the Lord is reprasented as acting for a distressed people 'with a high hand and a stretched-out arm,' Exod. vi. 6; sometimes as bringing relief with a word, Ps. xliv. 4, '*Command* deliverance for Jacob.' He that rules over all is a King of such power, has all things so much at his command, that he can bring deliverance with a word; he can with one word bring יְשׁוּעוֹת, many deliverances. With a breath, Ps. xviii. 15, 'the channels of waters were seen, and the foundations of the world were discovered; at thy rebuke, O Lord, at the blast of the breath of thy nostrils.' This was one way whereby he relieved David against his enemies overpowering him, ver. 17. With a smile: Dan. ix. 17, the shine of his face, his smile, was enough to restore his desolate sanctuary into a flourish. He can make the highest and strongest stoop to the meanest offices for his people: Ps. lxviii., 'Moab is my wash-pot, over Edom will I cast out my shoe.' The washing-pot is the vilest part of household stuff, for the washing of the feet, the lowest part of the body; and the shoe is held forth to be untied or taken off by the meanest servant. The Lord made Moab and Edom, those stout nations, subject themselves to Israel, in such a way, for the meanest services. So Rev. iii. 8, 9, 'I will make them come and worship before thy feet.' And he can order the least things to make way for their deliverance. So the frogs, and the lice, and the swarms of flies, Exod. viii., and the hail, Exod. ix., and the locusts, Exod. x., are made use of by the Lord to make his people's way out of the house of bondage. Small and great are at his command, who rules over all; strong or weak are all one to him. The strongest shall do the meanest work, and the weakest shall do the work of the strong, if he order it.

[3.] He can relieve you by motion or rest, either by action or sitting still. He can make his people active, or any others active for them, if that be the way he likes to bring relief; if not, he can order it to be done though they act not at all, contribute nothing toward it, stir neither hand, nor foot, nor tongue for it: Exod. xiv. 13, 'Stand still, and see the salvation of the Lord.' One would have thought, if ever there was need to bestir themselves it was now, when Pharaoh and all his host was at their heels, ready to fall upon them, and cut them off utterly if they did not make a stout resistance.

Was this a time to stand still? Yes; this is the best way, when the Lord so will order it. He can bring salvation when they move not at all, act nothing towards it, when they both hold their hands, and hold their peace. So 2 Chron. xx. 17, 'Ye shall not need to fight in this battle: set yourselves, stand ye still, and see the salvation of the Lord.' Isa. xxx. 7, 'The Egyptians shall help in vain: therefore have I cried concerning this, Their strength is to sit still;' your strength, Heb. *Rahab* (as the Egyptians are called for their power), is not to busy yourselves, to get assistance from the Egyptians or others; this course which he prescribes will be a greater strength, a better security to them than any Egyptian could afford them.

[4.] He can do it either by friends or enemies; either by those who would, but cannot, by making them able. So he enabled Abraham, with a small inconsiderable company, to rescue Lot from the joint forces of many kings, in the height of their successes and triumphs, Gen. xiv. 14; or by those who can, but will not, by making them willing: Prov. xvi. 7, 'When a man's ways please the Lord, he maketh even his enemies to be at peace with him.' He can overrule those whose designs and intentions are nothing but wrath and ruin, to entertain thoughts of peace and amity.

When the great council amongst the Jews were engaged against the apostles, and intended to slay them; when they were, as the word διεπρίοντο signifies, Acts v. 33, furious like wild beasts, ready to tear and devour what is next them : Gamaliel, a leading man amongst the Pharisees (and so one that had enmity enough against Christ and his followers), is stirred up to give moderate counsels, and the hearts of the rest are on a sudden inclined to agree with him; so the storm is laid, and the apostles escape, vers. 40, 41.

So Paul, being in extreme danger, takes occasion to declare that the doctrine of the resurrection, for which he was questioned, was that which the Pharisees embraced in opposition to the Sadducees; and hereupon the Pharisees, instead of seeking his death on a sudden strove for him, Acts xxiii. 9, whereas he might have expected, and at other times found, that they were his fiercest enemies. As the Jesuits, they hate all protestants, but if one fall off to them, who was before a Jesuit, him they abhor above all; he shall not live, if they can any ways compass his death. Of such a temper were the Pharisees, enemies to all Christians, but more enraged against Paul, because he was once of their way; yet the Lord so overrules them, that when he was in their hands, instead of seeking his death they strive for his life, declare him innocent, and insinuate that his persecutors are 'fighters against God,' ver. 9.

[5.] He can do it either by good or evil. That which is good is of itself of such a tendency, and he can overrule and dispose of that which is evil to serve the same purpose. What the midwives told Pharaoh is suspected for untruth; yet thereby the Lord preserved the children of the Israelites, Exod. i. 19, 20. It is a horrible thing for a people to arrive at the full measure of their wickedness; yet this, in the Amorites, made way for the deliverance of Israel out of Egypt, and their possession of the land of Canaan, Gen. xv. 16.

It was a malicious suggestion of the princes of the Philistines against David, 1 Sam. xxix. 4, 5. But the Lord so ordered it, as hereby David was freed from great distress, and his way made out of such a strait as his own wisdom could otherwise have never discovered; for hereupon he was dismissed the army, where, if he had stayed, he must either have been treacherous to the Philistines who had obliged him, or a traitor to his own country and people, in fighting against them; but by this means he comes off untainted either way, and very seasonably too, for the rescue of all that he had, then seized on by the Amalekites. If they had not thus and then impeached him, and called in question his loyalty, he was like to lose both a good conscience, and all that he had besides. So can the Lord dispose of the malice of enemies, as it shall serve his servants for the greatest advantages.

It was very grievous to Hezekiah, if not his sin, to part with not only so much of his own treasure, and that of the house of God, but to spoil the temple also of so much gold, as was forced from him for the satisfying of Sennacherib, 2 Kings xviii. 13–16. But hereby he got one advantage which countervailed all, and made him capable of the great and wonderful deliverance which the Lord afterward wrought for him and his people; for his father having made an agreement with the Assyrian to pay tribute, if he had not paid it, the breach had been on his part; but having given what was demanded, and the Assyrians after this invading them, the breach and unfaithfulness was on their part, and so his cause was good, and the Lord accordingly owned it, appearing wonderfully for his relief.

[6.] He can do it by things natural, or supernatural, or artificial. So he delivered Jonah from the destruction wherewith the sea threatened him by a whale. The means that relieved him was natural; but that he should be relieved by such a creature was supernatural, being otherwise such as was more likely to destroy than preserve him. But he who rules over all can order the most unruly things in nature to act as he will, even against or above what is natural to them. The whale was absolutely subject to the command of this great ruler: he 'prepared' it, Jonah i. 17; it was ready at his order to follow his instructions; received him into his mouth without any hurt to him from its teeth; swallowed him down, though the throat of the whale is said by naturalists to be so narrow, as it cannot let down anything of such a bulk. He was, as the word is, in the bowels of the fish, and there kept safe three days, neither choked for want of breath, nor digested into the substance of the fish; and then, at his word, delivers him safe on shore, Jonah ii. 10.

Noah and his family were delivered by the ark, an artificial expedient of God's own contriving, the Lord both of nature and art. This might seem as strange as the former to those who had never seen any such thing on the waters before. That a vessel of such a form and bulk, with so vast a lading, so many creatures, and provisions for a year sufficient for them all, should live so long on the waters, was a signal instance that the Lord hath nature and art at his command for the relief of his people. Thus was Paul delivered from death by a basket, Acts ix. 23. Those trumpets, pitchers, and lamps were by the Lord made effectual to relieve Israel and ruin their enemies, Judges vii.

[7.] He can do it by that which is real or imaginary. He can work real impressions by that which is merely imaginary. Accordingly some understand that in Isaiah xxxi. 9, 'afraid of the ensign,' if they spied but an ensign on some watch-tower, though in their own country, they should fancy it to be some banner of their enemies, and so fly, as though their enemy were at hand, though there was none near them. Such a course did the Lord take to deliver his people from the Assyrians. And so were the fancies of the Philistines disturbed, that they imagined their friends to be enemies; and so saved the Israelites a labour of doing execution upon them, they themselves destroying one another, 1 Sam. xiv. 16. The Lord can make a fancy do as much for his people as the greatest reality.

[8.] He can do it by things necessary or contingent. That the sea should keep its channel, and the clouds their place, and the years their seasons, is according to the course of nature, necessary; yet all was so overruled in the flood, that the earth became a sea, and the clouds met the lower waters, and the seasons of that year lost in the deluge; yet all contributed to Noah's deliverance, and made it more wonderful, he was saved by water, 1 Peter iii. 20.

How contingent was it that Ahasuerus could not sleep one night, that he should have a mind to read when he could not sleep, that he who read to him should light upon that place which mentioned the good service of Mordecai! Yet so the Lord disposed of these contingencies, in order to the Jews' deliverance, Esther vi. 1, 2. How contingent was it that the Jews' conspiracy against Paul's life should come to the knowledge of Paul's kinsman; that the chief captain should admit him, hearken to him, believe him, that he should take such order to secure him; but that the Lord overruled all for the deliverance of his servant, Acts xxiii.

[9.] He can do it by that which is deliberate or casual. Esther asked deliberately, and upon advice, for the preservation of her people; but the casualty of the *purim*, or lots, in order hereto, was purely of his disposing who rules and overrules all, Esther iii. 6, 7. Haman designed to massacre all the Jews; but, according to the superstition of the heathen, he would have a lucky day to execute his bloody project; and to find such a day he makes use of lots, and this he did some time the first month. But the Lord so ordered the lots, as the day they directed him to fell not out till the twelvemonth after; so that the Jews, and their friends at court, had a year's time to counterwork this cruel project. And in that time, all was so overruled by him who rules over all, that the plot was quite defeated, the mine discovered, and fired upon those that laid it, Esther ix. 1. Their supposed lucky day proved a dismal day to them; and they found the Lord had so ordered the lot, as it led them to the day of their ruin instead of the day of destruction to the Jews.

[10.] He can do it by well-grounded actings or mistakes. Not only by such actings as are undertaken and pursued upon right grounds and true apprehensions, but by such as proceed upon mistakes and misapprehensions. So was Jehoshaphat delivered, and all in confederacy against him ruined, 2 Chron. xx. 22. He set ambushes against them; he employed his angels invisibly to destroy some of them; and the rest seeing them slain, but not seeing by whom, supposed it done by some of their own troops; and so concluding them treacherous, upon this mistake fall one upon another, till all were destroyed, and so Jehoshaphat and his people delivered from their fears and great distress.

Sometimes he works deliverance for them by their own mistake. That which Possidonius relates, in the Life of Augustine, is remarkable for this purpose. He being to preach at a town some miles off, as he was going missed his way; and, as he understood afterwards, that mistake was ordered for the securing of his life, his enemies lying in wait for him in the way which he should have gone (if his guide had not misled him) with a design to have killed him—*atque per hunc, quem postea cognovit, errorem, manus impias evasit*—and so by this mistake he escaped their wicked hands.

[11.] He can do it not only *by* means, but *without* or *against* means. *Without* means, Deut. xxxii. When there are no means left within or without, none to be had at home or abroad, then will the Lord compassionately resent their distresses and relieve them. *Against* means, Acts xxvii. When Paul and his companions were in great extremity, the mariners are ready to betake themselves to the boat as the only means to escape, but the apostle tells them unless they stayed in the ship they could not be saved; and following his advice they were delivered, in a way repugnant to that which the seamen judged their only safety.

So was Jacob's family preserved and relieved by that means which many of the chief in it thought it their interest to destroy. Gen. xlv. 5, 7, 'Be not grieved, nor angry with yourselves, that ye sold me hither; for God did send me before you to preserve life. God sent me before you to preserve you a posterity in the earth, and to save your lives by a great deliverance.'

SINNERS UNDER THE CURSE.

Cursed is every one that continueth not in all things which are written in the book of the law to do them.—GAL. III. 10.

THE way to Christ lies through the sense of misery. The foundation of our misery is sin, sin original and actual; of original sin, the corruption of our natures before. The words hold forth a sinner's misery by reason of actual sin.

The coherence stands thus: the apostle is endeavouring to bring the Galatians into the way of truth and life, out of which they were bewitched. He endeavours to persuade them that justification is by faith in Christ, not by the works of the law. He brings many arguments to prove this; one of them abundantly demonstrative you have in this verse. It lies thus: our present observance of the law leaves us under the curse, *Ergo*, it cannot justify. The consequent is evident. The antecedent he proves by an artificial argument, the testimony of God: 'It is written.' Every imperfect performance of the law is cursed; but all our observance of the law is now imperfect. No man continues in all, &c., and therefore every man, without some other provision than the law affords, is cursed.

The words are a categorical proposition; the parts of it are the subject and the attribute, which, that we may explain, we will briefly consider them apart. And,

1. The attribute, 'cursed.' This curse is the penalty of God's violated law, and so an evil of punishment. This evil of punishment being assigned by divine justice, must be proportionable to the evil of sin. If it be proportionable to the evil of sin, it can be no less than the everlasting wrath of God. The product of this everlasting wrath is the sinner's eternal death, begun here and consummated in hell. This death was the penalty of the first covenant, 'Do this, and live;' fail of performing this, and thou shalt die; die every way, spiritually, temporally, eternally. The expression in the text is according to the tenor of that covenant, so that the curse here is death, especially eternal death, and they are cursed who are under the sentence or execution of it. Now, who these are the other part of the proposition discovers, 'Every one who continues not,' &c.

2. There is the subject expressed as fully and pregnantly as anything in Scripture. Here is no less than a threefold universality; it extends to all persons, times, things.

(1.) It is extended to all persons, every one. It is not *some;* for so, many might escape. It is not *many;* for so, some might escape. It is not the *greatest part;* for so, a considerable part of mankind might be excepted. It is not *all;* for that might be taken *de generibus singulorum,* for some of all sorts; for so, some of every sort might be exempted. But it is *every one,* simply and absolutely; universal, without restriction, without exception; every one, Jew and Gentile.

Adam himself not excepted; the curse seized upon the root, and so diffused itself into every of the branches.

Nay, the second Adam, Christ himself, is not exempted; he taking upon him our sins, came under our curse.

Sin and the curse are inseparable. Wherever sin is, the curse will be, even there where sin is but by imputation. Conclude but all, every one, under sin, and this conclusion will prove an argument to conclude all under the curse.

(2.) It is extended to all times. 'That continues not.' It is not enough to begin well, it is not enough to persist long, if at length there be any desisting from a practical observance. There must be a continuance, without the least moment's interruption. Wherever there is a breach, the curse enters. If a man should punctually observe the law an hundred years, and at last fail but a moment. A moment's intermission in a life of Methuselah's continuance exposes to the curse; the last* moment's discontinuance of a perfect observance lets in the curse; for so it runs, 'that continues not.'

(3.) It is extended to all things: 'In all things that are,' &c. If a man should avoid all things forbidden, yet if he do not all things commanded. Suppose a man should commit no sin, if he should omit any duty; suppose a man should do many things, as Herod, yet if he do not all; suppose he should do the more important things enjoined, the $βαρύτερα\ τοῦ\ νόμου$, the weightier things of the law, if he neglect but the least, he is nevertheless cursed.

The neglect of performing duty, as well as of avoiding sin; neglect of some, as well as neglect of all; neglect of anything, as well as the neglect of everything; the neglect of the least things, as well as of the greatest, exposes to the curse. Not only neglect of sections and paragraphs, the great momentous things of the law, but neglect of iotas and tittles, things which seem of smallest concernment, brings under the curse. How small soever they seem, if they be but written, it is enough. The largeness of the expression brings in all; cursed is all and every person that continues not in all and every moment, to do all and every thing, great and small, written in the law. Hence take this,

Obs. The sin brings the sinner under the curse. Any sin whatsoever, the least sin that can be committed, exposes the sinner to the everlasting wrath of God, and makes him liable to eternal death.

1. The least sin deserves everlasting wrath. Eternal death is due for the least sin, and that by the determination of divine justice.

2. The least sin is under the sentence of eternal death, is condemned already by the sentence of the judge of heaven and earth.

3. And the least sin will, if not prevented by the course prescribed in the gospel, bring the sentence into execution, and actually plunge the sinner into everlasting burnings. To be under the curse includes all this, either expressly or by implication. The desert of the least sin is eternal death; sentence according to desert, and execution according to the sentence. There needs no more for explication. In the process, I shall observe this

* Qu. 'least'?—ED.

order: I. Premise something by way of caution ; II. Bring some arguments to confirm it ; and, III. Apply it.

I. That the expression may not be mistaken (when I say *the least sin*) observe, there is no sin absolutely little. Every sin is big with guilt and provocation. Ποῖον ἁμάρτημα μικρὸν τολμήσει τις εἰπεῖν; who dare call any sin little, since it is committed against the great God ? If we speak absolutely, every sin is great; but if we speak comparatively, some sins are greater than others. And so those that are not the greatest, we call them less, not because they are small in themselves, but because they are not the greatest. Astronomy teaches us that the earth, compared with the heavens, is of no sensible magnitude, it is but like a point; yet considered in itself, we know it is a vast body, of a huge bulk. Compare an idle word with blasphemy, it will seem small ; or a vain thought with murder. Ay, but consider these in themselves, and they are great sins. There needs no other proof of this than what I am to undertake in the next place. They make liable to eternal death.

I shall insist the more upon the proof of this truth, because its usefulness depends upon the belief of it; and if we regard the practice of men rather than their profession, there is little faith as to this point in the earth, there are too few that effectually believe it.

II. The arguments I shall draw : 1. from general testimonies of Scripture ; 2. from instances in some particular sins which pass for small in the world ; 3. from the object against which sin is directed ; 4. from the continuance of that law, which at first made eternal death the penalty of the least sin.

1. Argument. We have the Lord's testimony to this truth, which is more to faith than any demonstration to reason : Rom. vi. 23, ' The wages of sin is death.' Of sin in general, and therefore of every kind of sin ; for that which belongs to the *genus* belongs to every *species*. The least sin as to essence and formality is as truly sin as the greatest ; for degrees do not vary the species. If death, then, be the wages of sin in general, it is the wages of the least sin. Death, that is, eternal death, as appears by the antithesis in the latter clause of the verse. It is that death that is opposed to eternal life. Eternal death is the wages of the least sin, as due to it as wages are to a hireling, as due as a penny was to him who had wrought all day in the vineyard. The Lord, in point of justice, is engaged to repay the least sin with eternal death.

But that which is but indefinitely delivered here, is universally expressed, Rom. i. 18, ἐπὶ πᾶσαν ἀσέβειαν καὶ ἀδικίαν; against all, without exception, without distinction ; and where the law does not except and distinguish, we are not to do it. Against all ; every deviation, the least declining from the rule of righteousness is unrighteousness. And therefore since it is declared against all, it is declared against the least sin ; since the least is unrighteousness as truly as the greatest, in respect of its formality, though not equal in respect of degree.

But that which we do but collect from this text is express, Mat. v. 19, ' He shall be the least,' *i. e.* he shall not be there at all. The following verse justifies this exposition ; he shall have no more place in heaven than the scribes and pharisees, who shall in no case enter into it ; if he receive according to the demerit of the least sin, no place will receive him but hell.

2. *Arg.* I prove it by some instances of those sins which the world count least. Those sins which men make light of are burdened by the Lord with threatenings of everlasting wrath. I will shew this in five particulars, which will be sufficient to make an induction.

(1.) Omissions of good. These pass for venials, for *peccadilloes*, with many. If they escape the gross pollutions of the world, they promise themselves exemption from the curse, though they omit or neglect the duties of holiness, the exercise of godliness in their families or in secret. Whereas we see in the text the curse is expressly directed against omissions, against those who do not and continue not to do what is written. The wrath of God will be poured out upon those families, not only who blaspheme and profane his name, but those who call not upon his name, those who set not up the worship of God in their families, Jer. x. 25.

Men are apt to think they shall escape well enough, if they misspend not their time in gaming and lewd practices, though they do not lay it out for the great concernments of eternity;

If they employ not their parts against God and his people, though they employ them not principally for him;

If they spend not their estates in drunkenness, uncleanness, and like excess of riot, though they lay not them out for God, the support of his truth, the maintenance and propagating of his gospel, and comfort of his members;

If they grossly abuse not their talents, though they bury them, or improve them only for themselves, not for their Master's advantage.

But oh, ask the unprofitable servant what a delusion this is! Why was he cast into outer darkness? Mat. xxv. 30; why, not because he did wickedly abuse his talent, but because he did not employ it for God, he hid it in the earth, ver. 25.

Who are they who must depart into everlasting fire? Mat. xxv. Not only who persecuted, reviled, abused, the people of Christ, but those who did not clothe, and feed, and visit them, and entertain them, ver. 42, 43. For mere omissions they are cursed, and turned with the devil and his angels into hell.

(2.) Secret evils, those that are confined to the heart, and break not out into visible acts. Men are apt to think that the Lord is such a one as themselves, that he will take little notice of those things which men cannot take notice of, and therefore are secure if no pollutions taint their lives, whatever evils lodge secretly in their hearts. But this is a delusion too, Eccles. xii. 14. Why will he bring them into judgment, but that justice may have its course against them? Time will come when you shall be arraigned before the Lord's tribunal for the most secret and retired motions of your hearts, arraigned in order to condemnation. If a man would so live as the world could never take notice of any sin in his whole life, yet if he gave liberty to the motions and secret acts of an evil heart, here will be matter enough at judgment to condemn him for ever. It may be thou wast never guilty, as to outward act, of murder, atheism, blasphemy, adultery; ay, but if there be any motions, any secret tendency to these in thy heart, this is enough to make thee liable to the curse, to the condemnation of murderers, &c., Mat. v. 28. A wanton glance, though none perceive it, a lascivious motion, though it pass no further than the secret of thy heart, is enough to render thee an adulterer in the sight of God, and to involve thee in the condemnation of adulterers. And it is as true of the other abominations.

So specious was the outward deportment of the pharisees, as their conversation, by the testimony of Christ, did appear to be really beautiful; but because they tolerated many secret corruptions in their hearts, see with what indignation he falls upon them: Mat. xxiii. 33, 'Ye serpents,' &c. That interrogation is a vehement negation. Though there be no scandalous act in your lives, the very secret corruptions of your hearts, if cherished, if tolerated, will make it impossible you should escape the condemnation of hell.

(3.) Idle words, how fearless or careless soever ye are of them, are suffi cient to bring you under the curse, Mat. xii. 36, 37. You must not only give an account before the tribunal of Christ of corrupt, lascivious, blasphemous, profane, revengeful, injurious, spurious, but even of idle words, of 'every idle word,' of such discourse as is unnecessary, unprofitable, unedifying, though not otherwise offensive. Why must we give an account of these, but because they are debts; such debts as, if they be not forgiven, if satisfaction be not tendered, thou shalt be delivered to the judge, and the Judge will cast thee into that prison, out of which thou shalt never come till thou hast paid, that which thou canst never pay, the utmost farthing?

(4.) Vain thoughts, the unaccountable vagaries of the cogitative faculty, the mere impertinencies of the mind, are of no less concernment to the soul than everlasting condemnation, Acts viii. 22. What need he pray so doubtfully for pardon, but that these thoughts had brought him under the sentence of condemnation? Isa. lv. 7, those thoughts which denominated their subject אִישׁ אָוֶן a man of iniquity, must be forsaken, at least as to resolution and endeavour, or else there is no pardon, no mercy. Evil thoughts, while not forsaken, are unpardonable, they are such as infinite mercy will not pardon; and what then remains for these but a fearful expectation of judgment and fiery indignation? But, it may be, the thoughts in these two instances were more than vain. See, then, Jer. iv. 14; Jerusalem's heart must be washed from wickedness, else she cannot be saved. This wickedness (if the latter part of the verse expound the former, as is usual in Scripture) is made up of her vain thoughts; whilst these have free entertainment, there can be no admission into heaven, no salvation. 'Wash thy heart from these,' &c.

(5.) Motions to sin without consent. Such motions as, arising from our corrupt natures, are suppressed, stifled in the birth, these expose to the curse. For the law requires a conformity to itself, both in qualities, motions, and actions, but such motions to sin are a nonconformity to the law, therefore sinful, and consequently cursed; for the penalty annexed to the law is due to every violation of it.

Besides, that which pollutes and defiles the soul makes it incapable of heaven, but such motions pollute and defile the soul. The corruption of our nature is as an ulcer, these motions to sin are as the putrefaction issuing out of that ulcer. Such corrupt matter defiles the man, however he be offended at it; consent is not necessary to make it a defilement; and, being a defilement, till it be removed it leaves the soul in an incapacity for heaven and glory; Rev. xxi. 27, there shall in no wise enter into it anything that defiles; and there is no place for those who are excluded heaven but the bottomless pit. This is the second argument, which, if we gather up its parcels, runs in this form. If omissions of good, secret evils, &c., then the least sins expose to the curse, for amongst these are the least sins we can discover. But omission, &c., expose to the curse, *ergo* the least sins expose to the curse.

3. *Arg.* The least sin is infinitely evil. And we usually ascribe infiniteness to these two: God the greatest good, and sin the greatest evil. God is infinite essentially, sin is infinite objectively; infinitely evil because against him who is infinitely good, because injurious to an infinite God; an offence of infinite majesty, a contempt of infinite authority, an affront to infinite sovereignty, an abuse of infinite mercy, a dishonour to infinite excellency, a provocation of infinite justice, a contrariety to infinite holiness, a reproach of infinite glory, an enemy to infinite love. It is infinitely evil, and therefore deserves to be infinitely punished, for justice requires that the punishment should be proportionable to the offence. A punishment intensively in-

finite cannot be inflicted, because a finite creature is not capable of it, therefore it must be infinite extensively, and what it wants in degrees must be made up in duration. Because the infinite treasures of wrath cannot be laid out at once upon a finite creature by reason of its incapacity, therefore justice will be expending thereof by degrees to all eternity. The least sin, being infinitely evil, deserves infinite sufferings, infinite in respect of duration, *i. e.* everlasting sufferings.

4. *Arg.* From the continuance of the law. The law which was first given to mankind, obliged to perfect obedience, and consequently prohibited the least sin, the least imperfection, and the penalty was eternal death. When this law continues in force, eternal death is due to the least sin. But this law is still in force, for neither did Christ repeal it, neither is the gospel an abrogation of it. Christ did not repeal it; he professes the contrary, Mat. v. 17, 18. The gospel does not abrogate it; the apostle testifies the contrary, Rom. iii. 31.

The preceptive part, whereby it obliges to perfect obedience, and the avoiding of the least sin, this continues inviolable. [Only the sanction whereby it engages hereto under the pain of eternal death, this is not so peremptory. The tenor of the law is still the same, and to this day runs: 'He that continues not in all things to do them' is cursed, shall die eternally; but the gospel brings an exception, he shall die except he believe and repent.

But as for those who continue in impenitency and unbelief, the law is in full force against them, neither the obligation is removed, nor the rigour of it mitigated.

Those that do repent and believe, they have the advantage of the gospel exception; but it is upon this ground that the law is first satisfied, both as to the obligation and penalty, though not by themselves, yet by their surety.

So that the law is abrogated to none at all, mitigated but to few, and the mitigations as to them respects not the demerit, but the event of their sin; it makes not their least sin not to deserve death, but prevents the execution, so as they receive not what sin deserves, their surety having suffered according to their demerits.

So far was Christ from altering the constitution of the law which makes death due for the least sin, as he would not so much as hinder the execution of it; nay, rather than the penalty denounced should not be suffered, he would suffer it himself.

To conclude. Since the law is not abolished but established by Christ, and since this law, thus established, makes eternal death the penalty of the least sin, it necessarily follows that the least sin exposes the sinner to eternal death.

III. *Use* 1. For conviction; 1, To gross sinners; 2, To formal professors.

1. To gross sinners, in whose lives the characters of wickedness are so large and visible, as he that runs may read them. These words should be to you as the handwriting on the wall to Belshazzar, Dan. v. 6. They should make your countenance change, your thoughts troubled, your joints loosed, and your knees smite one against another. Is he cursed who continues not in all things to do them? How will the curse fall upon him who continues in all things to transgress them?

Does the least sin expose to the curse of God? Oh then how heavily will the curse of God fall on you for your great enormities!

Is the wrath of God due for the omissions of good? Oh what wrath will be revealed from heaven against your abominable practices!

Is everlasting death the wages of secret evils? Oh what shall be the wages of your open wickedness! your drunkenness, uncleanness, injustice, profaneness! How shall these escape the damnation of hell?

Must ye be accountable for idle words in order to condemnation? Oh, what account will ye give of your oaths and imprecations, of your scoffs, slanders, and reproaches, of your lascivious and corrupt communication?

Do vain thoughts hazard salvation? How just then will be your condemnation for your contemplative wickedness, your covetous, lustful, revengeful thoughts?

Are the motions to sin, without consent, enough to damn the sinner? How shall you escape with your beloved sins, your plotted mischief, your contrived wickedness?

Will the least sins, which ye count but as atoms, sink the sinner into hell? How then can you stand under gross evils, which are as mountains in comparison?

If hell be kindled for small sins, sure it will be made seven times hotter for them. 'If the righteous scarcely be saved, where shall they appear?' Why, where they shall 'call to the mountains,' &c., that they may have neither appearance nor being.

You that persist in gross sins, you discern here the state of your souls. If God be true, if there be any truth in the word of truth, this is your condition, you are under the curse, you are condemned already; for anything you know, the execution may be the next day, the next moment; there is but a step betwixt you and death, your souls and eternal death.

2. To formal professors; those who think their condition good because they are not so bad as others; think they shall escape the curse merely because they have escaped the visible pollutions of the world, who are apt to say with the pharisee, Luke xviii. 12, 'I am not as other men are, extortioners, unjust, adulterers, or even as this publican.' As if this were sufficient to justify them, to exempt them from the curse! Oh remember the Lord often condemns those who justify themselves, and denounces a curse against those who are ready to engross to themselves the blessing.

It may be thou dost not act that wickedness which is frequently perpetrated by the sons of Belial amongst us. Oh, but let thy conscience answer, Dost thou not omit the exercise of holiness and mortification? Dost thou not omit, in whole or in part, the duty of religion and godliness? Or when thou performest them, is it not negligently, as though thou performed them not? Oh consider, there is a curse denounced against those who perform the work of the Lord negligently. How can they then escape the curse who neglect to perform it? It may be thou performest those duties but by fits unconstantly; oh remember, the curse reaches those, not only who do them not at all, but continue not to do them.

It may be thou wholly abstainest from open wickedness. Thy conversation may be as unblameable as the apostle's was while a pharisee, Philip. iii. 7. It may be, $ἄμωμος$, $ἄμεμπτος$, such as a captious censorious man cannot justly challenge, either for visible commission or omissions. Ay, but dost thou not freely entertain or peaceably tolerate some secret corruptions in thy heart? Are there not some secret invisible lusts which thou dost not constantly bewail and endeavour to mortify? Why, then, though thy conversation be as a whited sepulchre, as a gilded monument, and appear beautiful indeed outward, yet if there be any dead bones, any rottenness, any tolerated corruptions within, thou canst no more escape the curse than the pharisees, upon whom the Lord Christ showers down curses. If thou art indifferent, so thy outside be clean, whatever fill thy heart, be sure the curse will be one ingredient. Open wickedness makes a large breach for the curse to enter; ay, but any secret allowed lust will open a door to let it in. *All things* include both externals and internals, and the words run so, ' Cursed is every one,' &c.

It may be thou tremblest at blasphemy, and fearest a profane oath, and art offended at unclean, lascivious speeches, and abhorrest injurious slanders and false accusers; ay, but dost thou make no conscience of idle words? Dost thou not, as to these, set a watch before thy mouth and keep the door of thy lips? Why, then, thou leavest it open for the curse to enter, for that reaches all, even every irregular word.

It may be thou entertainest no atheistical, adulterous, or bloody thoughts; ay, but dost thou endeavour to wash thy heart from the wickedness of vain thoughts? If these quietly lodge in thee, the curse will rest on thee, for *all things* include all acts, words, thoughts, that are not exactly conformable to the law: and ' cursed is every one,' &c.

It may be thou dost not plot wickedness upon thy bed, nor study how to make provision for the flesh; ay, but dost thou bewail the unvoluntary motions of thy soul unto evil? Do not these lead thee to the spring-head, the corruption of thy nature? Does not this deep call effectually for deep sorrow and humiliation, for the pollution and woful degeneracy of thy nature? Why, then, though thou wash thee with nitre, and take thee much soap, yet thine iniquity is marked out before God (though no eye see it), and thou art marked out for the curse; it will cleave to thee as the leprosy of Naaman to Gehazi, which will continue on you while you continue in this state.

Use. 2. Exhortation; 1, To those that are under the curse; make haste for deliverance. You that live in gross sins, you that have gone no further than to an outward conformity to the letter of the law, hearken to this word as that which infinitely concerns you. Either you have continued in all things written in the law to do them, or have not. If you say you have continued, &c., you grossly, you wofully deceive your souls, and the truth is not in you. If you have not continued in all things, then either the word of God is false, or you are cursed; either you must give the lie to the Spirit of truth, or believe that the curse, the everlasting wrath of God, hangs over you.

Since you are under the curse, either you must bear it yourselves or some else must bear it for you; the justice of God can admit no *medium*. Bear it yourselves you cannot; alas, it will sink you into the bottom of hell, and there oppress you to all eternity. No creature can bear it for you; the heavens mourn for it, the earth groans under it, a great part of the angels are pressed down by it into the bottomless pit; and for men, every one must bear his own burden. What, then; is there no relief for a woful cursed sinner? No deliverance from the wrath of God? No redemption from the curse of the law?

Here comes in the glad tidings of the gospel: ' The Lord has laid help upon one that is mighty,' upon Christ, who was only able, who was only willing to bear man's curse, who is both able and willing to deliver sinners from it; but then you must come to him for deliverance, in a way honourable to him, prescribed by him. You must believe his word, the word of the curse; you must apply it, you must be affected with your misery by reason of it; you must be willing to accept of him upon his own terms. As he is willing to bear your curse, you must be willing to take his yoke. You must shake off security, self-confidence; renounce your sin, your dearest lusts; those which have brought the curse upon you, abandon them as cursed things. You must resign up yourselves wholly unto Christ, as your king, your redeemer.

This is the way. Why linger you? Why do ye not make haste to get into it? Is this a condition to be rested in? Can you live at ease while you are every moment in danger of everlasting death? Can you take comfort in any enjoyment while the curse of God is mixed with it? Can you sleep securely while your damnation sleeps not? Oh give no rest to your souls, no rest to your eyes, till you find rest from Christ. The fiery serpent, the curse of God, has stung you, death is seizing on you; oh look up unto the brazen serpent, look up to Christ, else there is no hope of life! The avenger of blood, revenging justice, pursues you; oh make haste, fly for your life unto the city of refuge, unto Christ the only refuge from the curse! Make haste, escape for your life, lest justice overtake you, and you perish without remedy.

2. To those that are delivered from the curse. You whom Christ has redeemed from everlasting wrath, you whom he has saved from going down into the pit, you whom he has rescued from these everlasting burnings, oh praise, admire, adore, rejoice in your Redeemer. If the curse of the law have stung your consciences, how sweet, how endearing, will these two expressions be! How will they draw out your affections to Christ! Gal. iii. 13; 'And Jesus, who delivered us from the wrath to come,' 1 Thes. i. 10. Oh, was he content to bear the curse rather than I should bear it, to be cursed that I might inherit the blessing, to lie under the wrath of God rather than it should sink me into hell! Was he content to die that he might save my life, and to drink up the dregs of divine vengeance that I might not taste of the second death? Oh, love the Lord! Bless the Lord, O my soul!

Oh how wretched had I been if Christ had not been so wonderfully gracious! How cursed and miserable, if Christ's love had not been so infinite! Every act, every word, every thought of mine had been cursed; every ordinance, every enjoyment, every relation of mine had been cursed. I had been cursed in my going out and coming in, in life and at death, cursed here and cursed for ever hereafter. Had it not been for Christ, I had been of all creatures most miserable. Say, Oh why am I not under the same curse, in the same condemnation with others? Why am I not in their woful condition, who continue under the curse, and continue senseless under it; who dance upon the edge of eternal ruin, and sleep upon the brink of the bottomless pit, every moment in danger to drop into the lake of fire? Oh the wonderful love of Christ! Oh the wonders of that distinguishing love, which has set my feet upon a rock, when others are split upon the curse, and wreck their souls in the gulf of eternal wrath! Oh, what shall I render unto Christ for this love? This should be your constant inquiry, and the answer to it is the work of eternity.

3. To all. If the least sin bring under the curse, then look upon the least sin as a cursed evil. Let your apprehensions, affections, actings, be answerable. Say not of any as of Zoar, 'Is it not a little one?' &c. Hate the least sins as you hate that which is destructive, that which will destroy the whole man. Fear them as you fear the curse of God, everlasting death; resist them as you would resist a mortal enemy, the wounds of a cruel one; avoid them as you would avoid the wrath, the indignation of the Most High; bewail the pollution wherewith they stain the soul, as that which the Lord is of purer eyes than to endure: 'Avoid all appearance of evil,' 1 Thes. v. 22. As we shun not only the possession of Satan, but the appearance of the devil; as you not only shun the embracements of a serpent, of a toad, but startle at the approach, at the appearance of them; Jude 23, 'Hate the garments spotted with the flesh.' Not only the flesh, or the spots thereof,

but the garments spotted. As you are afraid not only of a plague-sore, or of a person infected with the plague, but of garments of an infected person; anything, the least thing, that may convey infection. Marcus, bishop of Arethusa, he would not in the leastwise countenance sin, not to save his life. The terrors of death could not move him to give *ne obolum quidem;* not a halfpenny to re-edify an idolatrous temple.

The Christians, in their contests with the Arians, would not countenance their error by yielding to them the least letter, so much as an iota; they would not change their ὁμοούσιος into the Arian ὁμοιούσιος, no, not to avoid the fury of a persecution. They were so far from quitting the thing, as they would not so much as quit the word. I might bring a cloud of like examples, but I will not be prevented.

This is the way to shew you love Christ entirely. That love to Christ is great indeed that will not offend him in the least.

This is the way to evidence your sincerity. Hypocrites and formalists may avoid gross sins, open wickedness; but that is an upright heart indeed that will not decline in the least. That is a heart after God's own heart that will fulfil πάντα τὰ θελήματα, all his wills, every part of it. Hypocrites and formalists shall be clothed with shame and confusion, but then shall not you be ashamed when you have respect to all God's commandments. Then has Christ, then has grace, an absolute sovereignty in the soul, when not only the arch-traitors, but the petty *Boutefeus*, are quelled; when both great and small are brought into subjection unto Christ.

But to enforce this more distinctly, let me represent to you the heinousness of the least sins in some particulars. Nor will I digress; the considerations will be such as have a near affinity with the truth, and such as do tend to confirm and illustrate it.

1. There is something of atheism in these small sins. It is atheism to deny there is a God, to deny the Lord to be God. Now, these less sins are a denial of God; if not expressly, yet by interpretation; if not directly, yet by consequence; for he that denies any excellency to be in God which is essential to him, denies him to be God. If that rule be true, which is received without contradiction, *quicquid in Deo est Deus;* if every perfection be God which is essentially in him, then he that denies any perfection which is in him, denies him to be God. Even as he that denies a man to have a reasonable soul, to have a will and intellect, denies that he is a man; or he that denies that the sun is a luminary, denies that it is a sun; or he that denies a piece of metal to be gold or silver, thereby denies that it is current money, when nothing else is current money amongst us.

But these less sins deny many perfections, which are essentially in God. His omniscience, truth, holiness, justice; nay, they deny all in one, denying him to be the chief good.

Why do men venture more freely upon secret sins than upon open wickedness, but that they say in their hearts, God sees not? Is not this to deny his omniscience?

Why are men so bold with these smaller sins, but that they believe the least of them do not bring under the curse of the law, will not expose them to the everlasting wrath of God, though he expressly affirm this? And is not this to deny the truth of God?

Why do men so little regard these lesser sins, but that they think the Lord does not much regard them, is not much offended with them? And is not this to deny his purity and holiness?

Why do men think it harsh to be restrained from these lesser evils by such dreadful menaces and penalties, but that they in their thoughts represent it as *summum jus*, extremely rigorous. And is not this to question the justice and righteousness of God?

I might shew you how the least sin denies several other perfections, but it will suffice to instance in one, which denied divests him of all at once.

The least sin denies God to be the chief good. To clear this, observe that the chief good and the last end are convertible. He that denies God to be the last end, denies him to be the chief good. Then further, every human act has an ultimate end, this is clear and granted; then the least sin being an human act, must have some ultimate end; so that if the Lord be not the last end of that sinful act, he is thereby divested of this prerogative; he is denied herein to be the last end, the chief good. But the Lord cannot be the end of any sin whatsoever; it can in no wise, in no respect, be referred to him as its end; therefore the least sin can be no other than a denial that the Lord is the chief good; and if it deny this, it denies him to be God. See here the desperate tendency of the least sin, and tremble at it: 'The fool has said in his heart, There is no God,' Ps. xiv. 1. This folly is bound up in every heart. It is bound, but it is not tongue-tied; it speaks blasphemous things against God, it says there is no God. There is a difference indeed in the language: gross sins speak this louder, there are crying sins; but though less sins speak it not so loud, they whisper it. But the Lord can hear the language of the heart, the whisperings of its motions, as plainly as we hear one another in our ordinary discourse. Oh how heinous is the least sin, which is so injurious to the very being of the great God!

2. There is something of idolatry in these small sins. For idolatry, Rom. i. 25, μετάθεσις τῆς προσκυνήσεως ἀπὸ τοῦ πεποιηκότος ἐπὶ τα κτίσματα, Naz. Orat. 33. Now, the acts of the soul are the principal acts of worship; those of the body are but inferior and subservient thereto. Then is the Lord honoured with the highest act of worship, when he has the pre-eminence above all in our minds and hearts; and therefore when any other thing has the pre-eminence of God, we make an idol of it, and give it that worship which is due only to the Most High, which is flat idolatry.

But now, in admitting these small sins, we prefer other things before God, and so give that worship to others which is due only to God, and hereby become in effect idolaters.

He that will offend God, to please himself in the least sinful indulgence, he prefers his pleasure before God.

He that will do that which deserves the loss of God's favour, to gain any temporal advantage,—the less the worse,—prefers his profit, advantage before God.

He that will hearken to Satan suggesting the least sin, rather than to the Lord forbidding, threatening, dissuading from it, prefers the devil before God.

He that will hazard the loss of communion with God (as the least sin does, considering its demerit), rather than abandon his sin, he prefers his sin before God. He prefers these before God, they have the pre-eminence of him; he gives that worship to pleasure, profit, Satan, sin, which is due only to God. Now, I beseech you, should we not tremble at this apprehension? What idolatry is it to worship the devil; to worship sin, which is worse than the devil! And yet, the premises considered, it will evidently appear that such idolatry there is, virtually and interpretatively, in the least sin that is deliberately acted.

3. There is something of murder in admitting the least sin. The least is a deadly evil, of a bloody tendency, as to the life of the soul, Ezek.

xviii. 20. He says not, 'that sinneth thus and thus, that sinneth in this or that degree,' &c., Rom. vi. 21. No matter how small the seed be, the fruit is death. The least is a deadly evil, and that should be enough to make it formidable. A spider may kill, as well as a lion; a needle run into the heart or bowels may let in death, as well as a rapier or cannon bullet; a small breach neglected may let in the enemy, and so prove as destructive as if all the walls and fortifications were thrown down.

Sin is compared to poison, the poison of asps, Ps. cxl. 3, and the venom of dragons, Rom. iii. 8, Deut. xxxii. Now a drop of such strong poison may kill as well as a full draught. The tongue is but a little member, says the apostle, James iii. 5, yet he calls it a world of iniquity, ver. 6. This little member he calls a fire, ver. 6, and yet 'behold how great a matter a little fire kindleth,' it 'sets on fire the whole course of nature.' You know what a spark will do, when it falls into gunpowder; it often fires it as effectually as a brand. What less than the sting of a adder? Yet what more deadly? Such, so destructive is the least sin. Sin is expressed hereby, 1 Cor. xv. 56. An error, a sin in opinion (counted by some in these times a small sin), is compared to a gangrene, 2 Tim. ii. 17. Now what is more dangerous, what more destructive than a gangrene? Yet this you have occasioned by the prick of a pin.

Look upon the least sin as the Scripture represents it, as full of deadly poison, as a spark in powder, as the sting of a serpent, as tending to a gangrene, and you will see more reason to dread it, because it is deadly, destructive, than to slight it, because it seems small.

4. The least sin is a violation of the whole law, and therefore more heinous, of more dangerous consequence than we are apt to imagine: James ii. 10, he that offends in the least, offends in one; and by offending in the least, becomes guilty of all. You may think it strange, that an idle word, &c., should make one guilty of blasphemy, idolatry, murder, adultery, and all other abomination, but the apostle affirms it, and so it is unquestionably true.

The law, with its several precepts, is like a copulative proposition; though it consist of ten or twenty several parts, yet if one fail, the whole becomes invalid; he that denies one, denies all. The reason is, because the truth and validity of such a proposition depends upon the copulation or connection, which by the default of one part is dissolved. There is a concatenation of duties in the law, they are linked one to another; break but one link, and the whole chain is broken.

The reason why one violates all is drawn, ver. 11, from the authority of the lawgiver; the precepts of the law, they are as a string of pearls, they are strung upon the authority of God; break but the string in any part, and they all fall. The authority of God is as a pillar that supports the tables of the law; pluck but this from them, by the least tassel, and the tables fall, the whole law is broken.

Or the least breach is a violation of all *dispositivè*, because the least sin may dispose the sinner to every sin. (The authority of God is as a bank to secure the law from sin's encroachments; make a break in this bank, though you intend it but for a little water; yet the whole river may find the passage, and overflow all.) A sip of pleasing tempting liquor may tempt a a man to drink, and that may incline him by degrees to large draughts, till at length he come to wallow in that which at first he did but desire to taste of. So it is in sin; the least degree leaves a disposition to a further, a higher degree, and so, if it be not quashed betimes, is apt to carry on the sinner to height, and breadth, and depth of excess.

There is in the least sin, as in plants (and other creatures) a seminal virtue, whereby it multiplies itself. The seed at first is a small inconsiderable thing, but let it lie quietly on the ground, it will take root, grow into a bulky stock, and diffuse itself into variety of branches. Sin is like that grain of mustard seed (a comparison used by Christ in another case), Mat. xiii. 31, 32, which indeed is the least of all seeds, &c. It grows till at length it becomes a receptacle for Satan to nestle in, where he may hatch all manner of wickedness in the branches of it.

A sinful motion (if not stifled in the conception) will procure consent, and consent will bring forth into act; and one act will dispose to others, till custom have begot a habit, and a habit will dull and stupefy the conscience. And when the modesty and purity of the conscience is violated, it is in the highway to prostitute itself at every solicitation, and to entertain all comers, lies open to all wickedness.

Oh the danger, the prodigious fruitfulness of the least sin, which can multiply itself by degrees into all the wickedness that the law forbids! The least is, in this respect, a violation of the whole law. Oh take heed of admitting any, though it seem small. Stand upon your guard; if you open the wicket to one, you may have a whole army rush in upon you; the guilt of the least may involve you in the guilt of all.

5. The least part of the law is more valuable in God's account than heaven and earth; a tittle of the law of more account than the whole fabric of the world. He had rather heaven and earth should perish, than one iota of the law, Mat. v. 18. First, heaven and earth shall vanish, rather than the least letter, one $ἰῶτα$, rather than the least apex, the least point, one $κεραία$ of the law shall pass away. So much more valuable is the law, &c., as he seems more tender of the least point of this, than of that whole fabric. But lest this should seem a paradox, let us a little inquire into the ground of it.

The end has the pre-eminence in point of value and dignity; it is more valuable than all the means; and of all the means those are most valuable which contribute most to the attainment of the end. Now the supreme and sovereign end of all is the glory of God; that therefore is most valuable, wherein he appears most glorious, wherein most of his glorious perfections are displayed.

In the fabric of heaven and earth the power and wisdom of God appears; in this respect they declare his glory, by shewing his mighty power and wisdom, Ps. xix.

But now in the law of God there is a more ample and glorious appearance, there is an effulgency of more divine excellencies. This not only declares his wisdom in proportioning rewards and punishments to obedience and disobedience, and his power in giving law to the creatures, and to execute and accomplish what he has threatened and promised; but herein also is displayed his sovereignty and authority, his mercy and justice, his holiness and righteousness. His holiness and righteousness in the preceptive part, his mercy in the promissory, his justice in the minatory, his authority and sovereignty in all. Behold, here shines forth, not a single star or two, but a constellation of divine excellencies, and this of the first magnitude. Well may the Lord be so tender of the law, when it so much concerns his glory.

Besides, that is more valuable which comes nearer to the highest excellency, which most resembles the idea. That is the best, the fairest copy, which comest nearest to the original. But the law has in this respect the pre-eminence of heaven and earth. In earth there are some dark shadows of God; in heaven (the visible heaven) there are some plainer, some more visible footsteps of God. Ay, but the law is his image. Why was man said to be made according to the image of God, but because he was made according to the pattern in the mount? The law was writ in his heart. The Lord did, as it were, stamp the law, wherein was engraven his own likeness, upon the soul of man, and so left thereon the impressions of holiness and righteousness, the lineaments of the divine nature. The conformity of man to God, both in the first creation and second, consists in his conformity to the law of God.

Moreover, consider the great things of God, τὰ μεγαλεῖα τοῦ Θεοῦ, the great things, both of creation and redemption, were ordered in a subserviency to the law of God, and this does exceedingly enhance the value of it. Earth, that was made for man as a convenient place for the observance of the law; heaven (the third heaven), as a reward of obedience to the law; hell, that was created as a punishment of disobeying the law; the gospel, that was published to establish the law, Rom. iii. 31. Nay, Christ himself, he was sent, he came to fulfil the law. This was the end of his glorious undertaking, the end of his obeying, of his suffering, ver. 17. This is assigned as the ground why the law is preferred before heaven, &c., ver. 18. Christ, his spotless holiness was to fulfil the precept of the law; his death and sufferings were to satisfy the threatening of the law; both life and death were that the promise of the law might be accomplished. The Son of God must live as a man, and die as a slave, rather than one iota of the law should not be fulfilled.

No wonder, if heaven and earth must perish, rather than one tittle of the law fail, since the Son of God must become man and die, rather than the least part of the law shall not be accomplished; sure the Son of God is of more value than heaven and earth.

Now, since upon clear grounds the least part of the law is more valuable than heaven and earth, consider what ye do when you sin, when you offend in the least. It is better, more tolerable to do that which tends to the destruction of heaven and earth, the ruin of the fabric of the world, than to violate the least command, than to offer violence to the law by the least sin.

Oh what weight does this lay upon the smallest sin! In the respect forementioned, God has more dishonour by the least violation of the law, than if heaven and earth were turned into nothing.

6. The least sin is the object of infinite hatred. The Lord infinitely hates the least sin; he hates it, is not only angry for it, offended with it, grieved at it, but he hates it; he hates it perfectly; there is not the least mixture of love, liking, or approbation, nothing but pure hatred. The will of God as to sin is pure hatred in the abstract; he hates it eternally; possibly he may be reconciled to the sinner, but never to the sin. Whilst he is himself, whilst he is God, he hates it, *i. e.* from everlasting to everlasting; he hates it infinitely, for the hatred of an evil object is proportionable to the goodness of the subject where this affection is seated. Now God is infinitely good, and therefore his hatred of evil must be proportionable; he must hate it infinitely. When I say infinitely, I say he hates it more than tongue can express, than heart can conceive, more than men or angels can either express or imagine. 'Who knows the power of his wrath?'

The largest apprehension cannot measure the dimensions of it, the height and depth, length and breadth of it are, like God himself, incomprehensible.

Yet to help your apprehension a little, collect all the hatred that, since the foundation of the world, has had place in all the creatures, suppose all this were compacted in one soul; conceive further an object offered to it made up of all hateful ingredients in earth or hell; suppose this hatred hereby sublimated to the height, drawn out and extended to the utmost: the imagination of such a hatred, such an affection, may astonish us; oh, but all this would be nothing, not so much as a drop to the ocean compared with that hatred, wherewith the Lord hates the least sin. This is infinite, this is an ocean without banks or bottom.

Now consider this seriously; will ye do that which the Lord infinitely hates? I will not do this, will a child say, my father hates it; I dare not do this, will a servant say, my master hates it. Oh, but their hatred is nothing to God's, and shall this be less regarded? Oh, tremble to do that which the Lord hates with an infinite, with an everlasting hatred. Count not that small or light, which is burdened with the infinite hatred of the most high God.

7. There is more provocation in the least sin against God, than in the greatest injuries against men. Let all the injuries imaginable be put together, the total sum of them will not amount to so much as a single unit against God. For that rule is unquestionable, *quò persona in quem peccatur nobilior est, eo peccatum gravius est*, the greater the person is whom you offend, the greater, the more grievous is the offence; the dignity of the person puts an accent upon the injury. The law makes it not so heinous to smite an inferior, as to affront a magistrate; it is more heinous to clip the prince's coin, than to kill a private person. Every degree of dignity in the person injured raises the injury a degree higher; but now the highest dignity amongst men is but finite, the majesty of God is infinite; and therefore the least sin against God is so much more heinous, than the greatest injury you can do to the greatest of men, as that which is infinite exceeds what is but finite; there is incomparably, unproportionably, infinitely more provocation in it; for *finiti ad infinitum nulla proportio*, betwixt that which is finite, and that which is infinite, there is no comparison, no proportion. It would be counted intolerable to spurn at a prince, or throw dirt in the face of majesty. Oh, but this is infinitely less than the least offence directed against the majesty of heaven. For the distance is greater betwixt God and the greatest monarch on earth, than betwixt the greatest prince and the meanest subject, nay, than the most contemptible fly or vilest worm. You would count it intolerable, if your servant should kick you, or your child should spit in your face. Oh, but you do more, that which is infinitely more provoking, in the least sin you commit against God, because your obligements to him are more, and the distance infinitely greater. The least sin is an infinite injury in respect to its object, and that is more than all the greatest, the most provoking injuries that can be offered to the sons of men. Oh that ye would consider this seriously, and look upon the least sin as infinitely injurious to the great God.

8. The least sin requires infinite satisfaction. Such an injury is the least sin, as nothing can compensate it, but that which is of infinite value; this is grounded upon the former. The least sin is an infinite injury; now the rules of reason and justice require, that what is given for satisfaction should be proportionable to the injury; nothing therefore can be a compensation for an infinite injury, but that which is of infinite value.

And since it is so, where shall the sinner find such a compensation? 'Wherewith shall we come before the Lord,' to satisfy for the least sin? (to make use of the prophet's words, Micah vi. 6, 7). Can these satisfy the Lord, for the injury the least sin has done him? Oh no! Ps. xlix. 8. The redemption of the soul from the guilt of any sin is far more precious; if something infinitely more valuable be not offered for it, it ceases for ever, we may desist from it everlastingly as altogether unfeasible.

If the blood of all the men on earth was sacrificed to satisfy for the least sin, if all the angels in heaven would offer themselves to be annihilated for the expiation of the least sin, this would not be effectual.

If heaven and earth, and all the treasures thereof, and all the creatures therein, were put into one sum, and offered as a recompence for the injury of the least sin, this would fall infinitely short of the value of a just compensation; these would not be so much as a mite, when more than a hundred thousand talents are due and in justice required; for the value of these is finite and limited, but that which compensates the injury of the least sin must be of infinite value.

Consider what ye do when ye venture upon the least sin: you do such an injury to God as heaven and earth, men and angels, can never make amends for; you do that which may undo you for ever, which may ruin your souls eternally, though all the saints and angels in heaven should interpose to their utmost to prevent your ruin. 'Without blood there is no remission,' Heb. ix. 22. This supposes that by blood remission may be obtained; but what blood? It is not the blood of bulls and goats, nor of the cattle on a thousand hills; these are too low priced for such a purpose. It must be blood of infinite value; it must be the blood of God, Acts xx. 28; the blood of Christ, who was God as well as man—man that he might have blood to shed, and God that he might derive an infinite value upon that blood. Such is the stain of the least sin, as nothing can fetch it out but the blood of Christ.

Consider then, when thou art under temptation, when thou art solicited to a sin which thou countest small, say thus to thy soul, Either this sin will be expiated with the blood of Christ, or it will not. If it be not expiated with the blood of Christ, then it will ruin me, soul and body, for ever, without remedy, without redemption. If it be expiated, satisfied for by the blood of Christ, oh then resolve concerning it, as David of the water of the well of Bethlehem, 2 Sam. xxiii. He longed for it, his mighty men broke through the host of the Philistines to procure it for him; but when they brought it, he would not so much as taste; his reason, see verse 17. So say thou, so resolve: Far be it from me, O Lord, that I should do this! Is not this the blood of Christ, who not only hazarded but lost his life for me, that I should have a hand in that which shed the blood of Christ, and put to death the Lord of life.

9. The least sin is now punished in hell with those torments that will last for ever. Hell is the reward of the least sin, not only in respect of its demerit, but in regard of the event. The damned do now feel the weight of God's eternal wrath for those sins which they made light of, Mat. v. 25. The moral of the expression is this: those that will not be reconciled to God here shall be tormented in hell for ever hereafter; they shall be cast into hell, and not come out till they have paid the utmost farthing, *i. e.* till they have satisfied for the least sin, for every sin. Sins are debts run upon the score of justice; of these debts some are greater, some are smaller; there is the debt of talents and the debt of farthings; divine justice must be satisfied for all. He does not say he shall not come out till he have paid every talent, but till he have paid the utmost farthing. The sinner can never satisfy for the least, and therefore for the least must everlastingly suffer.

The least sin is enough to kindle that fire that never goes out. Those sins which ye count but as wind, idle words, are enough to blow this into a flame that will never be quenched, Mat. xii.

The least corruption is enough to breed that worm that never dies. We have experiments enough on earth to persuade the belief of this. We have diverse dreadful representations here of what the least sin can do in hell hereafter. Have ye not known such a sin as we count small kindle a hell in the conscience of the sinner, and make him feel the tortures of hell upon earth? Hell is enclosed in the least sin. If the Lord do but unfold it, do but lay it open to the conscience, there needs no other devil, no other tormentors, to make the guilty sinner conceive he can scarce be worse in hell. There is the materials of hell in the least sin; let but the Lord speak the word, let him but breathe on it, it will kindle in an instant, and scorch, as though it were set on fire of hell. And if the least sin be matter apt enough to kindle such flames now when it is but green, oh how will they kindle on it in hell when it is dry, when the sinner is cut down by the last stroke of justice! Look upon the least sin as thus represented, as burdened with the weight of everlasting wrath, as kindling those everlasting burnings. Judge of them not by the suggestions of Satan, not by the cries of despairing, tormented souls, and then you will see reason to fear them as hell, rather than to slight them as small.

10. *The least sin is worse than the greatest punishment.* The least sin is worse than hell, worse both than the tormentors and the torments. Sin is worse than the devil, for it was sin that made him a devil; it turned the angels of light into spirits of darkness. Nay, if the least sin had place in the most glorious angel now in heaven, the malignity of it would be still as powerful, as mischievous; for aught we know, it would in an instant transform the highest seraphim into an ugly fiend. The least sin is worse, too, than the greatest punishment, the greatest torments; for the least is contrary to God, opposite to his nature, will, holiness, nay, his very being, reflects dishonour upon all; whereas punishment is an act of divine justice, the proper issue of an infinite excellency, and that which, in its sphere, tends to make the Lord as glorious as the act of any other attribute.

Sin is the act of degenerate creatures, fallen men and devils as such; but punishment is the act of the holy and righteous God, and that as he is such. And is there here any comparison? Can the unrighteousness of men come in competition with the justice of God? Is there any room to question which is better, justice or injustice, light or darkness?

Punishment is but *malum creaturæ;* sin is *malum* both *Deo et creaturæ.* Sin is evil both to God and the creatures, punishment is only evil to the sinner. Now the rule, *malum quo communius eo pejus,* evil, the more extensive it is the worse it is, is true here with infinite advantage. Evil of sin is so much the worse by how much an infinite good, to which it is opposed, is better.

Punishment is evil to the creature, but it is only a physical evil; but sin is both morally and physically, in every respect, evil, therefore worse than any punishment. Punishment is for repairing of what breach sin has made; now which is better, the restorer or the destroyer?

If reason were perfectly rectified, and the will of man exactly conformed to the divine nature, he would choose *horrorem inferni,* rather than *turpitudinem peccati,* the torments of hell (abstracted from all sinful mixtures) rather than the least sin.

Consider, then, what ye do, when ye venture upon the least sin; you choose that which, upon a true, a rational account, is worse than hell.

Use 3. Information.

1. See here an impossibility for a sinner to be justified by his observance

of the law, or according to the tenor of the first covenant. The law requires to justification a righteousness exactly perfect; but the best righteousness of fallen man is as a menstruous rag. It is not only torn and ragged, but spotted and defiled. The law curses every one that continues not in all things; whereas in many things, in everything, we offend all. If man could, by the utmost improvement of his remaining abilities, spin up a garment of righteousness that would cover him, yet if there were but one hole to be found in it, the curse would there enter; whereas now, alas! it is nothing but holes and rags. If the Lord had not made other provision for the justifying and saving of man than the law holds forth, then no flesh would be saved. Oh what cause have we to admire the rich grace of the gospel!

2. See here the dangerous error of those who make account to be justified and saved by works; by their conformity to the law, or observance of it. The apostle is express, ver. 10. An imperfect observance of the law leaves the observer under the curse, but all observance of the law by fallen man is imperfect; no observance of all, no continuing in the observance of all, imperfection in both.

True, say they, it is imperfect as to the avoiding of small venial sins, but perfect as to the avoiding of gross and mortal. Ay, but the law makes no such distinction, and *ubi lex non distinguit*, &c. The law curses all without exception; the least sin exposes to the curse, wrath, death. Oh enter not into the secret of these men! They are Babel-builders; think with their own hands to raise a structure, whose top shall reach to heaven. Ay, but these words confound them and their language; this text is as a thunderbolt, overthrows them and their structure, and tumbles both into the dust.

They have got a ladder indeed, by which they think to mount up to heaven, but the rounds of it, being the works of their own hands, are all rotten. And this text snaps them all in pieces; they that have no other footing must fall unavoidably, and fall as far as the curse will sink them, and that is weighty enough to press them into the lower hell. 'By the works of the law no flesh living can be justified.'

3. See here our necessity of Christ. All that continue not in all things are liable to the curse, and this is the condition of all. Either we must be delivered from the curse, or else we perish. Now who is there that can deliver us? Why, none but Christ, Gal. iii., Ps. cx.

The necessity of Christ to redeem from the curse due to gross sins, that is obvious, that will be easily acknowledged. Ay, but there is as great a necessity of Christ in reference to small sins. You see a necessity of Christ in respect of the sins of your unconverted state; oh, but there is as much need of him as to the sins you are guilty of since conversion. You see a necessity of Christ in reference to gross sins, blasphemy, intemperance, &c. Oh, but you have need of him in respect of the sins and failings of your best thoughts, actions, designs, prayers, &c., your holy duties, when performed in the best, the most holy, affectionate, heavenly manner. For the curse reaches the least failing; and if Christ redeem you not from the curse due thereto, the least will certainly damn you.

We should be apprehensive of our necessity of Christ, his blood, his redemption, his mediation, and our application of it, in every thought, every act, every step, every motion in the world. If Christ interpose not, the curse will meet us everywhere; in every employment, in every enjoyment, nay, in every ordinance. The curse falls upon every offence, and in everything we all offend.

There is a necessity of Christ in reference to the least failing, though it be but one. Suppose that Christ had redeemed a sinner from the curse due to all his sins, one only excepted, and suppose that one sin were but a vain thought, or an idle word, or some dulness under an ordinance, or some wandering in a holy duty, yet this one sin, though so small, would be such a handle for the curse to fasten on, as men and angels, all the creatures in heaven and earth, could not remove it; the curse would drag that soul to hell without recovery. Oh, then, what need have we of a Saviour! Get lively apprehensions of your necessity of Christ. Walk continually under the sense and power of these apprehensions, and be often making applications of the blood and mediation of Christ to your souls.

So hath the Lord ordered the way to salvation, as that every one should see a necessity of Christ; a continual necessity of him, and a necessity of him in all things. And it is evident upon this account, because 'cursed is every one that continueth not in all things to do them.'